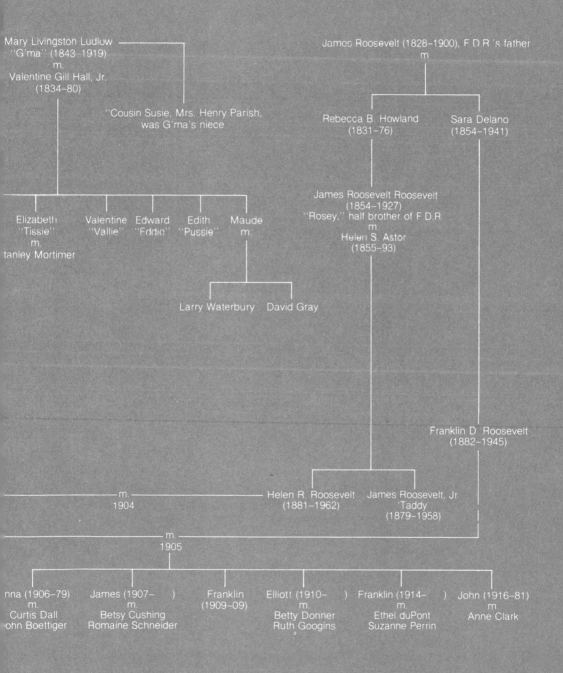

Mary Livingston Ludlow
"G'ma" (1843–1919)
m.
Valentine Gill Hall, Jr.
(1834–80)

James Roosevelt (1828–1900), F.D.R.'s father
m.

"Cousin Susie, Mrs. Henry Parish,
was G'ma's niece

Rebecca B. Howland
(1831–76)

Sara Delano
(1854–1941)

Elizabeth
"Tissie"
m.
tanley Mortimer

Valentine
"Vallie"

Edward
"Eddie"

Edith
"Pussie"

Maude
m.

James Roosevelt Roosevelt
(1854–1927)
"Rosey," half brother of F.D.R.
m.
Helen S. Astor
(1855–93)

Larry Waterbury   David Gray

Franklin D. Roosevelt
(1882–1945)

m.
1904

Helen R. Roosevelt
(1881–1962)

James Roosevelt, Jr
'Taddy'
(1879–1958)

m.
1905

nna (1906–79)
m.
Curtis Dall
ohn Boettiger

James (1907–   )
m.
Betsy Cushing
Romaine Schneider

Franklin
(1909–09)

Elliott (1910–   )
m.
Betty Donner
Ruth Googins

Franklin (1914–   )
m.
Ethel duPont
Suzanne Perrin

John (1916–81)
m
Anne Clark

Love,
Eleanor

Love, Eleanor

Eleanor Roosevelt and Her Friends

Joseph P. Lash

Foreword by Franklin D. Roosevelt, Jr.

DOUBLEDAY & COMPANY, INC.
GARDEN CITY, NEW YORK
1982

Library of Congress Cataloging in Publication Data

Lash, Joseph P., 1909–
    Love, Eleanor.

    Includes index.
        1. Roosevelt, Eleanor, 1884–1962. 2. Roosevelt,
Franklin D. (Franklin Delano), 1882–1945–Family.
3. Presidents–United States–Wives–Correspondence.
I. Roosevelt, Eleanor, 1884–1962. II. Title.
E807.1.R48L37   973.917′092′4   [B]
ISBN: 0-385-17053-X   AACR2

No copyright is claimed on U.S. Government material found in Chapter XXII.

Library of Congress Catalog Card Number: 81-43383

Design by M Franklin-Plympton

Contents

Foreword

IN 1979, when the Franklin D. Roosevelt Library, without notice to the Roosevelt family, opened to the press and scholars the correspondence between my mother and Lorena Hickok, I urged that my mother's letters be read in the context of those written to other close friends and that her style of writing be judged in the framework of what was considered customary and conventional when she was growing up.

As my mother's literary executor, I undertook to publish her letters, holding nothing back from publication that might enable the public to judge for itself my mother's activities and character and the nature of her relationships to those closest to her.

As far as letters were concerned, she may have been "the writingest lady" of our time, and it will take a shelf of books to print a correspondence that numbers in the thousands. I therefore asked Joseph P. Lash, the author of *Eleanor and Franklin,* to edit them for publication, withholding nothing that might bear on my mother's relationship with those closest to her. *Love, Eleanor* is the first of two volumes. The second will cover the end of World War II and her highly productive years on her own.

In the course of Lash's research he obtained under the Freedom of Information and Privacy Act (FOIPA) an astonishing set of FBI-Counterintelligence documents. These not only assert that there was an "affair" between my mother and him, but portray my father as peremptorily summoning my mother to the Oval Study at the White House, where in the presence of others the two engaged in a family tiff that ended in Lash's being sent at my father's direction to a dangerous combat post overseas.

At the time I was on duty as Executive Officer of the destroyer *Mayrant* off Sicily, so I cannot testify from personal knowledge. I would note, however, that these allegations were based on the account of an aggrieved Counterintelligence officer. I find the episode unbelievable. It would have been out of character for my father and mother to have acted the way they are reported to have acted. There were of course shadows in their relationship, but both were large-minded, self-disciplined people who kept their tensions to themselves. The notion that they might have engaged in marital recriminations in front of staff and aides is totally inconsistent with their semi-Victorian upbringing and their personal reticences. We children well knew that side of their characters. Such gossip should not have found its way into the records of G-2 and the Federal Bureau of Investigation. If any refutation were needed of the FBI-Counterintelligence allegation of an affair between my mother and Joe Lash, it will be found in the letters between them that are published here.

Important as is a refutation of this allegation by Counterintelligence, I hope the more compelling story told in this book of my mother's love will not be overshadowed. She had an extraordinary capacity for affection as her children can testify. She was always there when we needed her. That was one kind of love. Another was her attachment to a few close friends. Her letters speak for themselves, but to me they represent a rare example of sublimation—a word it is well to remember that is related to "sublime."

Franklin D. Roosevelt, Jr.

By Way of
Introduction

WHEN I WAS WORKING on *Eleanor and Franklin* and
spent day after day at the Franklin D. Roosevelt Library in
Hyde Park, New York, I recall vividly the afternoon I came
upon some letters of E.R.'s that she wrote during World War I that
were clearly anti-Semitic. I was so taken aback, found it so difficult for
the moment to reconcile these racist sentiments with the sympathetic
woman I had come to know two decades later, that it was with relief
that I saw the clock approach five when the library closed. I took the
offending letters and placed them carefully at the corner of the table,
hoping somehow that overnight they might vanish. But by the next
morning as I set out from Wildercliffe, where I was living in Rhine-
beck, New York, to do my daily research stint at the library, I knew I
would have to deal with those letters.

It has been my experience that it is precisely the unsettling document
of this kind, the material or interview that does not fit into the established canon, the letter or remark that upsets preconceptions, that is
most productive. It prods the biographer away from shallowness and
conventionality. It gives his portrait depth and density and enables him
to invest it with some of the complexities and ambiguities which, if we
look at ourselves, we see present in our own natures. I purposely say
"some" of the perplexities, because there are truths about ourselves that
we find it too painful to admit, even to ourselves, and that we try to
conceal and in the end destroy.

When I was writing *Eleanor and Franklin,* I did not have access to
the correspondence between Eleanor Roosevelt and Lorena Hickok.
The latter's deed of gift stipulated that these 3,500 letters were to be
kept closed until ten years after her death, which was 1978, and opened
then except for those that might embarrass living persons.

The letters created a stir when they were discovered, for they revealed a friendship of intense intimacy, an intimacy expressed by Eleanor in an effusion of terms of such tenderness as to suggest physical as well as emotional intimacy.

There is nothing in this correspondence that detracts from the picture of Eleanor Roosevelt as a woman of mercy right out of First Corinthians, one who achieved her greatest charge of happiness out of service to others, who made an indispensable contribution to the Roosevelt presidency and the New Deal, a woman who had painfully fought her way through to the very radical concept of the equality and brotherhood of all men and women, and, acting on that principle, inside the White House and out, became, as Arthur Schlesinger has said, the most liberated woman of the century. One might well stop there. Biographers are fond of quoting Tennyson's remarks about Byron. "What business has the public to know of Byron's wildnesses?" he asked. "He has given them fine work and they ought to be satisfied."

But of course we are not, and I personally find it difficult to argue that a great woman's inner drives, her life-style, her relationships insofar as they can be disentangled, do not shed light on her achievements. In any case, the letters are there and what are we to make of them?

It is no wonder Sigmund Freud considered biography an impossible enterprise. How can the historical observer purport to portray, let alone explain, what was hidden in his subject's soul? Are we to recount only what was done and said and written, or may we guess at what was thought and felt? When does discussion of unexplained anomalies in the subject's behavior become gossip instead of analysis? What is the authority of the biographer to exercise his intuition? Biography may be an impossible enterprise, but history is bloodless without it. Indeed, Ralph Waldo Emerson said, ". . . there is properly no history; only biography." His observation reflects the belief that what is critical in the study of human events is the question "why?" The answer to that question can only be sought in the minds of the participants in the historical event we study.

Eleanor Roosevelt had that same sense about the events of which she was a part. Her relationship to causes and movements was through people. The relationship was reciprocal. Without people whom she cared about in a movement, she did not feel she understood it in its detail and complexity. And their genuine affection for her gratified her need to be of use, one of the governing principles in her life. Her approach to race, for example, was neither intellectual nor sociological, a matter neither of statistics nor syllogisms, but of individual people whom she had made it a point to know in all their flawed humanity. Mary McLeod Bethune was the fifteenth of seventeen children, some of whom had been sold to slavery. "She's real black," a Negro policeman said admiringly of her. Eleanor worked with her closely, but her reluctance to peck her on the cheek, as she did other friends, showed her the residue of racial feeling in herself, what the Negro resented and the white had to overcome. Not until she kissed Mrs. Bethune without thinking of it, she told her daughter Anna, did she feel she had at last overcome the racial prejudice within herself.

When I began to write biography, I appealed for pointers to Leon Edel, the Henry James biographer who also was a neighbor on Martha's Vineyard. His advice was invaluable. "Set the scene, Joe," he advised. That may seem obvious. It was not for a man whose background was essentially political. While Eleanor Roosevelt was alive, I kept diaries. Through her friendship I was privileged to be present at dinners at the White House at which President Roosevelt was often present. The give and take of the political discussions fascinated me; what I did not note was the setting, the clothes people wore, the motion of the arm and fingers, the pitch of the voice, the glint or glow of the eye, those thousand and one details that enable one to draw a portrait rather than a cartoon.

But I learned to choose the scene and select the details that characterize it. When I began *Eleanor and Franklin*, I rushed down to Sarasota, where David Gray, Mrs. Roosevelt's uncle-by-marriage, lived. He was ninety-six and failing. At the beginning of the century he wrote fox-hunting stories which were quite the fashion. During World War II he had served as our Minister to Ireland. The first sentence of his reply to a question often made sense. Then he trailed off into mystic incoherence. What should a writer read to give him a sense of New York Society at the turn of the century? I asked him. Without hesitation he replied Edith Wharton's *The House of Mirth*, the tale of Lily Bart, the doomed beauty who was disinherited when she refused to conform to Society's mores. It is still possible to get up a lively argument among the present members of the Livingston, Delano, Astor, and Chanler clans, the members of the Knickerbocker enclave on the Hudson in which Eleanor grew up, as to which of Eleanor's Hall aunts was the model for Lily Bart.

The first scene in which Eleanor Roosevelt's life was set was New York Society's version of the Victorian Age, a period remarkable for the contrasts between its starchy exterior and the turbulent sentiments that seethed within it. Henry James, whose portraits of the Victorian Age, like the Age itself, are full of allusion and implication and the throbbing awareness of what is not seen or said, wrote a book called *The Bostonians*. The title was meant to suggest both the proper Bostonian reformers of the late nineteenth century and what was once referred to as a "Boston marriage," a relationship between two women that was more intimate than friendship yet was not necessarily sexual and that was common in New England. The novel was first published in 1886.

"I wanted to write a very American tale very characteristic of our social conditions," Henry James said of its origin. "I asked myself what was the most salient and peculiar point in our social life. The answer was the situation of women, the decline of the sentiment of sex, the agitation on their behalf." In the end, James deliberately leaves in doubt the nature of the central relationship of this "Boston marriage." He leaves an unchallenged ambiguity typical of the age. The crucial issue was not what was, but what was known, and what was acknowledged.

As the private papers of respectable Victorians—Americans as well as British—become available, it is often a shock to discover the gap between obeisance to public mores and private lives. Mary Woolley, president of Mount Holyoke College, appointed by Herbert Hoover as the feminine member of the U.S. delegation to the disarmament conference, turns out to have had an almost lifelong love affair with the head of her English Department, a woman with whom she shared a house. The early journals and letters of M. Carey Thomas, the second president of Bryn Mawr, were used by her editor, Marjorie Housepian Dobkin, for a sparkling portrait of *The Making of a Feminist*. Her niece, Millicent Carey McIntosh, herself the president of Barnard, wrote in her foreword: "She tried to break our feminine bonds to our parents, to the idea of marriage, to domesticity."

A few years ago all previous conceptions of Edith Wharton were radically deepened by Professor R.W.B. Lewis's portrait of the novelist. His account of the passionate love affair between Edith Wharton and the journalist Morton Fullerton showed a woman of powerful sexual drives. "Edith Wharton in love," said Fullerton, "displayed the reckless ardor of a George Sand." Even more startling was Professor Lewis's discovery of the outline of a Wharton story about incest, "Beatrice Palmatto." The outline included a fragment that Professor Lewis rightly labels, despite its literary quality, as pornography "which no respectable magazine would have published."

Carroll Smith-Rosenberg, in a pioneering article "The Female World of Love and Ritual: Relations Between Women in Nineteenth Century America," showed that ardent "same-sex" emotional ties were by no means confined to Boston and were "casually accepted in American society." Her analysis supported the suggestion in Henry James that whether these nineteenth-century women "had genital contact" was not the essential question. Rather the letters and diaries of the thirty-five families she studied showed an intense physical and social intimacy that seemed to parallel and be bolstered by the taboos and "severe social restrictions in intimacy between young men and women" that characterized Victorian America. "Girls routinely slept together, kissed and hugged each other. . . . Yet these eighteenth and nineteenth century friendships lasted with undiminished, indeed often increased intensity throughout the women's lives." Smith-Rosenberg's original views, which substituted "a cultural or psychosocial for a psychosexual interpretation of women's emotional bonding," demonstrate that only a beginning has been made in the understanding of "same-sex relationships."

Mrs. Roosevelt had a small circle of friends to whom she wrote in longhand—as she did to Hickok, or, as she called her, "Hick." Her energy was extraordinary and these letters were usually written at the end of a long, crowded day. This form of communion with those she cared about recharged her emotional strength. She needed these relationships to keep from engulfment by public duties. With this small group of friends—and they included men as well as women—she used expressions of endearment as passionate as those to be found in the Hickok correspondence, equally open to many interpretations, equally suggestive in some cases of a physical relationship. Those friends included Nancy Cook and Marion Dickerman, Elinor Morgenthau, Earl Miller, Mayris Chancy, Trude and Joseph P. Lash, David Gurewitsch. The key letters to these people which are here reprinted allow a better perspective on the Hickok correspondence. Through these letters we can see Eleanor Roosevelt's emergence as a world leader.

Eleanor Roosevelt was a woman of great vitality whose affectionate nature overflowed and which constantly sought opportunities to lavish love upon those she cared about and those who needed her love. Hers was a temperament that craved response. But that response within her family, given her husband's nature and vocation and her children's preoccupations, as well as her own hesitations, tended to be meager. Franklin did not offer her the love for which she yearned. In the 1920s as she learned to adjust to that fact she jotted down in a diary that she kept briefly some pregnant words that she found in a book, "No form of love is to be despised."

In addition, the Lucy Mercer affair represented for her a failure as a woman, a rejection of herself as a woman. She came away from it with the conviction that she had first developed when her mother had called her "Granny" of her own plainness and unworthiness. She did not wholly shake that feeling until her triumphant years alone at the United Nations. She was drawn to people similarly maimed. A scion of the WASP aristocracy, she had been humbled. She never tired of hearing Marian Anderson sing the aria from Handel's *Messiah* "He was despised, and rejected of men/A man of sorrows/And acquainted with grief." Louis Howe helped her in her time of humiliation to find a role and a vocation. Anna, her daughter, once came into her mother's room in the house on East Sixty-fifth Street and saw Mrs. Roosevelt sitting at Louis's feet while he stroked her hair. It upset Anna. Eleanor loved Louis. He had helped her. He had thought about her, her needs, her development, when everyone tended to trample over her to get to F.D.R.

Louis was as misshapen-looking a man as they came, and Eleanor would say they were the two homeliest people in New York politics. But that gave her a sense of security in the relationship. No one was going to take him away. Moreover, he needed her. But was there a physical relationship? Anna discounted it. So does the author of this book.

Louis Howe helped Eleanor to find a vocation after the shattering events of the Lucy Mercer affair. Hickok aided her in another of her life's crises when Franklin's election to the presidency threatened to undermine the life she had so painfully constructed for herself independently of Franklin yet supportive of him. In the White House she feared she would be a bird in a gilded cage, a creature of routine, pomp, and ceremony. As an Associated Press reporter assigned to cover the First Lady, Hickok sensed that here was a woman who did not want to go into the White House. That startled the reporter. To Eleanor it was a revelation to find a journalist who thought about her, who did not see her simply as an appendage of the President-Elect. Hickok helped her to think through how to hold onto her individuality while still doing the job that was required of the First Lady.

Everyone has a vital center, the seat of their emotional lives, of the thrusting feelings that direct growth and sustain life. It can be snuffed out by the indifference or selfishness of family, colleagues, friends, or by the obligations and routines that stupefy. That emotional life is kept alive by ministering and responding to the needs and affections of others, particularly those who by some mysterious alchemy lodge their arrows in our heart. The people to whom she wrote and who are represented in this book played that role at various moments in Eleanor's life. Hickok did so in 1933.

Was their relationship then a lesbian one? That is to be doubted, but the time is past when "lesbianism" is to be considered a term of reproach rather than a style of fulfillment. Moreover, who is to say what "lesbianism" is?

An old friend of Eleanor's, Esther Lape, together with Elizabeth Read, with whom she shared a Greenwich Village apartment, gave one night a week in the early Twenties to reading French literature with Eleanor. On a trip to Paris she sent Eleanor a copy of André Gide's *Les Faux-Monnayeurs*. The homosexual theme shocked Eleanor. "I read the book as the story of sensitive relationship sensitively told," said Esther. "She read it in terms of forbidden subject. She couldn't bring herself even to consider homosexuality. Generally her reaction was not so final, but in this case it was."

Mrs. Roosevelt has been called the most liberated woman of the century. She is constantly surprising the historian, but he cannot forget that she was also the woman who wrote to her husband in the midst of one of the first conventions of the League of Women Voters, after it had changed its name from the National American Woman Suffrage Association, "I prefer doing my politics with you." Like many other great women—George Eliot, Beatrice Webb, Virginia Woolf—she is solicitous rather than hostile to men, including her husband.

Many of the letters in this book are published for the first time. In addition, the Eleanor Roosevelt story is reviewed in light of the new material that has appeared since the publication of *Eleanor and Franklin,* including some rather startling material relating to the author's relationship to Mrs. Roosevelt made available under the Freedom of Information Act.

This book is an effort to understand some fragments of biographical reality. The fragments raise questions to which there cannot be complete answers. I do not hope to paint a definitive reality. Mark Twain turned a phrase that more aptly describes what may be achieved. When Helen Keller, deaf, blind, and largely mute from age nineteen months on, became a militant socialist and a Wobbly after her graduation from Radcliffe, the conservative journals for which she could do no wrong, as long as she limited herself to appeals for help to the deaf and blind, objected to her political and economic pronouncements. What does she know of those complex subjects? they challenged her. Her friend Mark Twain remarked, "A well put together unreality will serve." Perhaps all that biographers can claim for their portraits is that they are well put together unrealities.

A Few Acknowledgments

Many people have helped with this book, beginning with Ken McCormick, who, after Franklin D. Roosevelt, Jr., his mother's literary executor, called him, immediately sensed the rareness of the story that Eleanor Roosevelt's letters to her "friends" might show, and obtained Doubleday's consent to its publication. He has been helpful, too, with sage editorial comments drawn from a lifetime's experience with getting books out of people like Helen Keller, who had something to say, and Dwight Eisenhower, about whom opinions differ.

In addition, I have to register my debt to two remarkable women, both of whom read the manuscript as carefully as if the book was theirs, as indeed it might have been. My wife Trude, who knew Eleanor Roosevelt every bit as well as I did and who had a better sense of how women reacted than I did, went over every chapter in detail and made many suggestions that were more than stylistic.

I am equally grateful to Merloyd Lawrence. She had edited my *Helen and Teacher* and in the course of that disclosed a profound sense of the psychology of women as well as an artist's feeling for form and character. Her offer to read the manuscript of *Love, Eleanor*, although it was being published by another house, was, as it has proved to be, a stroke of good fortune. Each chapter came back with its pages dog-eared and its margins scribbled with notes.

In some cases I was unable to accept Merloyd's suggestions. I found it impossible as a historian, or perhaps it might be said I did not have the courage or resourcefulness to follow her advice, to prune away the nuggets that were of historical value. Merloyd conceded their value, but felt they should be excluded because they did not shed light on the book's central thesis of Eleanor's nurturing relationship and the growth and energies it released. I suspect that Merloyd may have been right from the point of view of aesthetic form, but as a Roosevelt historian I could not resist new and illuminating items about the Roosevelt years gleaned from Eleanor's letters.

A few sections, especially in the early chapters, may sound reminiscent of *Eleanor and Franklin*. Familiar as that story is, readers want their minds refreshed. Without an understanding of Eleanor's relationship to her father and mother, to Mlle. Souvestre, Franklin, Lucy Mercer, Eleanor's behavior after World War I cannot be satisfactorily explained. Moreover additional material has turned up since *Eleanor and Franklin* about Eleanor's youth that lends an added freshness to those chapters. The Franklin D. Roosevelt Library, under Dr. William Emerson, and the National Park Service were unfailingly helpful in the location of letters and photographs.

The manuscript of this book, like some of my previous ones, was typed by Freda Weiner.

I want, too, to record my joy at having my son Jonathan, a law-loving lawyer, take several chapters in hand and make them read more coherently.

The reader may ask in the light of these last paragraphs: What was Joe Lash's contribution? It is a question I have asked myself. Perhaps I have managed to add to the present generation's understanding of the way it was during a rare moment in American history. For me the opportunity to relive the experiences in parts of this book has caused an extraordinary emotion.

Love,
Eleanor

I

Two Brothers

"SOMETHING LOCKED ME UP," Eleanor Roosevelt wrote Lorena Hickok in 1934. She was then almost fifty and sought to explain to Hickok, who was her closest confidante in the 1930s, her inability to let herself go. Not only did she feel herself to be subject to constraint, but it upset her to see people she loved relax self-control. She considered the supreme good of human feeling to be "a quiet heart & a sense of security," which is what she wished Hick at Christmastime 1938. In a further effort to explain herself to Hick she suggested that it was her bereaved childhood that had spoiled her for spontaneous surrender to her feelings.* "I think it was when I was a child & is now a habit, but there is much peace & calm about it."

So it is to the greatest bereavement in her childhood—the death of her mother and the loss of her father—that this book turns, and to the scene she always carried in her heart. She wrote about it hauntingly in the first volume of her autobiography *This Is My Story*. She was eight when her mother died, her father exiled, and she and her two smaller brothers had been left by her mother in the care of Grandmother Hall.

> After we were installed, my father came to see me, and I remember going down into the high-ceilinged, dim library on the first floor of the house in west 37th Street. He sat in a big chair. He was dressed all in black, looking very sad. He held out his arms and gathered me to him. In a little while he began to talk, to explain to me that my mother was gone, that she had been all the world to him, and now he had only my brothers and myself, that my brothers were very young, and that he

* E.R. to L.H., July 21, 1938.

and I must keep close together. Some day I would make a home for him again, we would travel together and do many things which he painted as interesting and pleasant, to be looked forward to in the future together.

Somehow it was always he and I. I did not understand whether my brothers were to be our children or whether he felt that they would be at school and college and later independent.

There started that day a feeling which never left me—that he and I were very close together, and some day would have a life of our own together. He told me to write him often, to be a good girl, not to give any trouble, to study hard, to grow up into a woman he could be proud of, and he would come to see me whenever it was possible.

When he left, I was all alone to keep our secret of mutual understanding and to adjust myself to my new existence.*

There were events that she kept in her heart, Eleanor wrote Hickok in 1935, and that made "certain things look pretty odd in the future." She disliked psychoanalysis but she might have written her recollection for Sigmund Freud as a portrayal of the childhood trauma which forever conditioned the way she loved. Her love for her father strengthened her to meet many of life's challenges, but it also dammed up sexual response and diverted desire from acquisitiveness to benevolence. And even if the origins of her temperament were much more obscure and she was the born nurturer who from early childhood on wished other people's good, the episode with her father shaped and illustrated her general disposition, so the story of *Love, Eleanor* should begin with that ill-starred man.

"In our family group," Henry James wrote in partial explanation of his sister's invalidism, "girls never seem to have had a chance . . . her tragic health was, in a manner, the only solution for her of the practical problem of life." Elliott Roosevelt, the father of Eleanor, was a handsome, mustachioed sportsman whose life gradually was overwhelmed by a combination of inexplicable ailments, accidents, and his own addiction to drugs and alcohol. Eleanor attributed her father's headaches, blackouts, depressions to a constitutional weakness that may have been caused by a tumor of the brain and that explained the use of alcohol and drugs. Alice Roosevelt Longworth, Theodore's first child, put it differently: "The great argument in the family was whether he was an epileptic." However, the biographer reviewing Elliott's life is struck by curious incidents in that life and strange anomalies in his character as

* *This Is My Story*, by Eleanor Roosevelt (New York: Harper & Bros., 1937), pages 20, 21.

perceived by his family that suggest he may have foundered upon "the practical problem of life."

Elliott was the younger brother of the future President Theodore Roosevelt. He died when Eleanor was only ten, but he had adored his tiny daughter, and she him. Although he was virtually banished from his family for the last three years of his life, in Eleanor's memory of him he could do no wrong. Throughout Eleanor's life he filled her thoughts and feelings and did much to shape them.

Elliott was the third child of the first Theodore Roosevelt, a powerful bearded figure, to whom his children were devoted, and who championed New York City's earliest ventures into social services. The second Theodore Roosevelt, born in 1858, went on to become an outstanding American president, the personification of the "strenuous life," but in their early years Elliott was the leader, and Theodore's jealousy of this most companionable younger brother, although rigorously repressed, was strong. Their mother, Mittie, wrote her husband in 1861 when Theodore was not yet four and Elliott not quite two:

> Elliott came into my bed and fell asleep while I was stroking his ears. Teedie was miserably jealous about his sleeping by me.

Theodore was allowed to join Elliott in their mother's bed:

> Teedie was in the most *lambent* frame of mind. He would say, "Ellie, shall I stroke your little ears?" Ellie would assent and lie perfectly quiet, then Teedie would say to me [in] the almost hysterical manner, "Oh, do look Mamma, how he do obey me."

As they grew up, the two brothers were very close and extremely competitive. Asthmatic in his boyhood so that Elliott had more than once to protect him from bullies, Theodore struggled to prove himself against his brother. His diaries are studded with ratings of himself against his brother:

> Went on all day hunting trip in the wagon: I never shot worse, while Elliott hit about everything he fired at.
> Nellie [Elliott] stayed up from town, and so I spent the day with him; we rowed around Lloyd's–15 miles, and virtually racing the whole way. As athletes we are about equal; he rows best; I run best; he can beat me sailing or swimming, I can beat him wrestling or boxing. I am best with the rifle, he with the shot gun, etc., etc., etc.

During 1873, the first Theodore deposited them in Dresden with a repectable German family while their new house was being built at 7 West Fifty-seventh Street. Elliott wrote home, ". . . last night in a round of one minute and a half with Teedie, he got a bloody nose and I got a bloody mouth." Theodore was then fifteen and Elliott, although thirteen, was the leader. "We three measured ourselves yesterday," Elliott wrote his father, "and these are the results (of course in our stockings). Teedie 5 ft ½ inch, Ellie 5 foot 4 inches, Conie [their sister] 5 feet . . ."

Elliott excelled with natural ease in physical and social pursuits. "Elliott was really the sailor of the family, an expert sailor, too," wrote Corinne in her book *My Brother Theodore*. A few years earlier, 1869, speaking of romps on the Pincian Hills in Rome, Corinne reported, "In their contests of running and racing and leaping my brother Elliott was always the leader, although Teedie always did his part whenever his health permitted." Arrestingly, she testified, "My brother, Elliott, more naturally a *social* leader, influenced the young naturalist to a greater interest in *humankind*. . . ."

Elliott's charm equally affected John Sargent Wise, a fiery Virginia Whig congressman, who spent a day with the Roosevelt boys, "elite young sportsmen," he called them. He was in New York together with the former Confederate General Sorrel, and he later wrote that Elliott was "the most lovable Roosevelt I ever knew . . . he was nothing like so aggressive or so forceful a man as Theodore, but if personal popularity could have bestowed public honours on any man there was nothing beyond the reach of Elliott Roosevelt."

Elliott's manly qualities were combined with traits regarded as feminine—gentleness, sympathy, and expressiveness. When the first Theodore, at forty-eight, fell ill of intestinal cancer, the young Theodore, then at Harvard, was kept in ignorance of his father's condition so that his studies should not be interrupted, but Elliott was at home, and his younger sister Corinne wrote, "Elliott gave unstintedly a devotion which was so tender that it was more like that of a woman, and his young strength was poured out to help his father's condition."

Corinne's reference to womanly tenderness was not casual. She was a poet, careful in her use of words. She shared Elliott's affectionate, ardent temperament and remained close to him even in the terrible years at the end as his life fell apart. This devotion to Elliott especially endeared Corinne to her niece, Eleanor. Thirty years after her father's death, Eleanor wrote to Corinne:

> . . . and I think it is so lovely of you to give a bed in Father's name at the Soldiers and Sailors Club. I have never done anything in his memory but I always do some little thing on his birthday which I think he would have liked to do. I remember so many things he did when I was little, not only for me, & they were always a little different from the way other people did them!

Elliott, although a robust and athletic youth, was already afflicted by sudden seizures. He wrote a postscript that he labeled "private" to a letter to his father from St. Paul's School in New Hampshire:

Yesterday during my latin lesson without the slightest warning I had a bad rush of blood to my head, it hurt me so that I don't remember what happened. I believe I screamed out. Anyway the Doctor brought me over to his house and I lay down for a couple of hours; it [*sic*] had by that time recovered and after laying down all the afternoon I was able to go on with my afternoon studies. I lost nothing but one Greek lesson by it. It had left me rather nervous and therefore homesick and unhappy. But I am all well now so don't worry about me. I took some of my anti-nervous medicine, and I would like the receipt of more. You told me to write you everything or I would not bother you with this— but you want to know all about me, don't you?

Love from Ellie

P.S. II Don't forget *me* please and write often.

The prescribed remedy in those days for ailments such as the blackout suffered by Elliott at St. Paul's was travel and out-of-doors life. Elliott went to Texas frontier country where he was a guest at Fort McKavett. It was then garrisoned by a regiment whose officers were friends of the first Theodore. Men still went armed against the Indians. "Our life during the days in camp," he wrote his "Dear Little Motherling," whose Southern "melts" were famous in the family, "was of course but one continual hunt and I am sorry to say very little shoot . . ." Although he was only sixteen, he was "chums" with the post commander. He was "free from all troubles with my head except on my return from the turkey hunt which the General got up for me last week," another letter informed his father—and he did seem to function better away from home and family, especially his brother Theodore.

In January 1877 he returned to Texas with some friends to hunt buffalo. The young adventurers published a paper, V*ox Buffalorum,* a copy of which Eleanor Roosevelt treasured. Elliott's companions are identified as "Gymnast," "Mogul," "Kangaroo," and "High End." It is full of teenage high jinks and jests, pen and ink drawings, and there are repeated references to "Nell" and "Nellie." These were nicknames for him used by his family, although he signed his letters "Ellie." "Nell" may have been an allusion to Dickens' *The Old Curiosity Shop.* In any case, it was a name he was to use lovingly to address his daughter Eleanor. The feminine characterization of Nell by the journal's editor is startling. It is not written disparagingly. The emphasis is rather on an attractive kind of femininity. Elliott is even referred to as "she." The journal for February 4, 1877, reported:

. . . Nell's spirits rose as she reflected that she had four parcels of Tobacco stored away in New York but her beaming smile failed when it was hinted by some envious Buff that she could not get it down by telegraph.

An entry for January 14, 1877, declared: "Wanted: Somebody to help Nell keep her attire in order." There are constant references to "Nellie." "Nell's legs are growing longer or her pants shorter or one t'other." Nell was also the camp's ladies' man. "Nell again," an entry read. "We acknowledge ourselves to be devoted admirers of the fair sex and love them all from sheer inability to do otherwise. . . . Nell we want you to go to extremes." On January 28, Nell's gender is used indiscriminately: "Nell has killed his first buffalo. We are afraid that she will fall over backwards she holds her head so high up."

Vox *Buffalorum*'s mixture of genders is astonishing, especially in view of the admiration and affection in which Elliott was held by his campmates. All the boys came from a society characterized by rigid differentiation of gender roles. Male and female spheres were separate, distinct, and well defined. And woe to him or her who challenged what was thought to be the natural order of things. Old New York was composed of people, wrote Mrs. Winthrop Chanler in *Roman Holiday*, "who dreaded scandal more than decision, who placed decency above courage. . . ."

New York Society modeled itself consciously on British aristocracy and Victorianism. It stamped its character on all its adherents. The elder Theodore Roosevelts, whose founding ancestor had arrived in New Amsterdam in 1647, belonged to the oldest of old New York. Their name and station earned them privilege and imposed strict duties.

Young Theodore occupied his place with sure determination and enthusiasm. He was a self-starter. He was a boy naturalist, filling his, and Elliott's, room with reptiles, insects, and small creatures. Later, while still at Harvard, he began the studies that led to his writing of *The Naval War of 1812* and that won plaudits in England as well as America. Not long after he finished Harvard, he went into politics on the State Assembly level. "Uncle Jim, Em and Al bitterly opposed to my candidacy of course," he noted in his diary. But he persisted and won, beginning a notable public career.

He placed high value on duty, patriotism, and courage. The future Rough Rider, for example, was even unhappy about the role of his father, whom he adored, in the Civil War. The first Theodore, although only twenty-nine, had bought a substitute. Not out of cowardice. As Anna* wrote, "My father felt terribly about [not] enlisting, but Mother was very frail, and felt it would kill her for him to fight against her brothers [they lost their citizenship because of their work for the Confederacy]."

Mittie's sister, Anna Bulloch, lived with them on East Twentieth

---

* Theodore's older sister, also called and referred to in this text as "Bammie," "Bamie," and "Bye." She was often called all these names even by the same member of her family.

Street during the Civil War. She heard Teedie pray for the Lord of Hosts to "grind the Southern troops into powder." Theodore was, in fact, the archetypal Victorian male, upright, self-righteous, touting strength of mind and body, and apparently free from doubt. Elliott was more feminine both in his perceptions and in his expression. His private papers, especially his letters as a young man, are full of vivid images and sensitive observation.

He used some of the money left him by his father to underwrite a round-the-world trip that included a hunting expedition after the markhor and ibex in the Himalayas. Writing to his mother from the Himalayas, he regrets that "this entire sheet is filled in with nothing but that everlasting I," a familiar sensation among many writers. He invites his "dear Little Motherling," to whom, along with his sister Corinne, he felt especially close, to "spend six months wandering around Europe if you felt like it next summer." He is sympathetic to Indian aspirations for self-rule, and, in an introspective moment en route to Kashmir, exclaims, "Oh! these people, what a puzzle to me this world becomes when we find out how many of us are in it, and how easy for the smallest portion to sit down in quiet luxury of mind and body—to say to the other far larger part—lo, the poor savages. Is what we call right, right all over the world and for all time?"

The relativity of moral standards expressed by Elliott hardly would have commended itself to Theodore. But Elliott in Gilgit, surrounded by his "Hindoo" bearers and the vast mountains, finds it "horrible to contemplate the way so many of our friends at home and abroad, we Christians!! do eat and drink. Gluttons and Drunkards most in comparison to what is necessary as proved by those we despise as Heathen, these Hindoo."

Yet Elliott did find pleasure in the life of the outdoorsman-traveler.

> I am very fond of this life Bammie. No doubt of it. I thought to rather put a slight stop to my inclination by a large dose of it but for the great drawback that none of you are with me to enjoy it. It would be very nearly perfect in its way. Not, I think. "Our way" for that means life for an *end*. But this for the mere pleasure of living is the only life. There is something in becoming such a friend of nature's that you know her every look and change. . . .

This letter, however, ended on a plaintive note: "Oh, Bammie," he writes wistfully, "how I do crave after knowledge, book learning (only those who read most say it is not entire found there) education and a well balanced mind." He had not the energy and self-discipline to seek what he said he desired. A long letter to Bammie from Gilgit, India, revealed a temperament prey to self-doubt. There was little for him to do in New York, he wrote: "that any of you my own people could be proud of me for, and naturally I am an awfully lazy fellow. I know Sister Anna will keep her eyes open and about her for chances for the boy. If some of the wise and strong among you don't make a *good* chance for me on my coming home I'll make but a poor one for myself I fear." Theodore, while he welcomed Bammie's counsel, never would have left such a decision up to his sisters.

Returning home, Elliott courted and married Anna Hall, nineteen, a belle and a scion of the landed Livingstons and Ludlows. She and her three sisters were all beauties. The letters that Anna received on the announcement of her engagement from those in his family closest to Elliott emphasized his tenderness. Although she was older, Bammie wrote to Anna, she wanted to say that "he is such a tender, sympathetic, manly man that I have ever turned toward him in many sad moments for help and strength and feeling. . . ." Corinne, although suffering from a "quincy sore throat," penciled a note of delight: "He loves you with so tender and respectful a devotion, that I who love my darling brother so dearly, cannot but feel that you as well as he have much to be thankful for. . . ." From Liverpool his Aunt Ella wrote her "darling Nell" that "your nature is so loving and tender that you will not fail in love—I feel sure. . . ."

Theodore, who later dedicated his second book, *Hunting Trips of a Ranchman*, "to that keenest of sportsmen and truest of Friends, my Brother Elliott Roosevelt," could not refrain from moralizing in his congratulations:

> Nell, you are indeed to be thought happy: and so I think is sweet Mistress Anna, for I know you, who have been such a good son, will surely make a true, tender and loving husband. It is no light thing to take the irrevocable step you have just taken, but I feel sure that you have done wisely and well, and we are all more than thankful to have so lovely a member added to our household circle.

Ten years later, after the "Nell" whom he loved had turned into an addict of drugs and alcohol, Theodore's private judgment of "Mistress Anna" was more severe. He wrote to Bye in 1890:*

> Anna, sweet though she is, is an impossible person to deal with. Her utterly frivolous life has, as was inevitable, eaten into her character like an acid. She does not realize and feel as other women would in her place. San Moritz would be in my opinion madness; he must get away from clubs and social life. . . .

* This and many other Theodore Roosevelt letters to Bye, including those that dealt with Elliott's afflictions, turned up in the vault of Theodore's birthplace. Some believe they were deliberately sequestered from the bulk of his papers in order to shield Elliott's daughter Eleanor from knowledge of their contents. They were not made available to this writer when he worked on *Eleanor and Franklin*.

Theodore's rectitude was such that some saw him as somewhat prudish. In his Harvard diaries he wrote "Thank Heaven I am absolutely pure. I can tell Alice [Lee] everything." When a kinsman married a French actress, Theodore banished him from his thoughts! "He is a disgrace to the family—the vulgar brute." Sexual conduct was prescribed in the tablets of the Medes and Persians. Tolstoy was not exempt. Although he conceded Tolstoy was a great writer, he disapproved of Anna's and Stiva's conduct in *Anna Karenina*. He had questions about second marriages including his own, even when the husband or wife had died.

Elliott was more open-minded. He wrote to his father from Fort McKavett an amused description of the rooms of Lieutenant Colonel Prime, the officer who had taken the young Elliott under his wing. The letter had none of Theodore's prudery:

> He is the only church member besides General Clitz in the Regiment and the abrupt changes in some of the ornaments in his rooms are very queer, for instance, under a good copy of one of the old master's religious works are two fancy french pictures of ballet dancers and a sporting peice [*sic*] under another. He is a very nice gentleman and I like him extremely.

Theodore settled at Oyster Bay, thirty miles east of Manhattan; Elliott began to build a house at Hempstead, much closer to the city but still green and wooded. He and Anna were members of a young patrician set that dictated the pace and style for old New York. Helped by his family, he sought to make a career in the financial district, but his real interest lay in his horses and dogs, in the polo matches and the hunt. Yet he was shadowed by accidents and his disabling fevers and headaches. He was a reckless member of the Meadow Brook foursome and Theodore, no slouch himself in the saddle, thought the pace too much for his brother. "I do hate his Hempstead life," confided Theodore to Bye. "I don't know whether he [Elliott] could get along without the excitement now, but it is certainly very unhealthy, and it leads to nothing." Elliott had confessed to Anna during their courtship that his "old Indian trouble" had hit him at Tivoli, the Hall house on the Hudson. The trip down had been "pretty bad," but "Herm Livingston and Frank Appleton were on board and very kind so I pulled along very well." "You will have to hurry up and marry me," another letter after an accident in a polo match at Meadow Brook warned her, "if you expect to have anything left to marry. It seems to me that I get from one bad scrape into another."

"Elliott has had a really hard illness during this last week," Theodore informed Bammie. "He has had two abscesses in his neck; they prevented him from swallowing, and drove him nearly mad with pain—to complicate matters he got a severe attack of rheumatism. He looks ghastly, cannot even sit up in bed, and has been kept much under the influence of anodynes, but the doctor now says he is improving rapidly."

Elliott's letters were a litany of ailments and accidents. The worst came in 1889 during rehearsals for an amateur circus at the Waterbury place in Pelham, New York, where he fractured his ankle. Incorrectly diagnosed as a sprain, the ankle break was so painful that he was unable to eat and at night sobbed for hours, until at last the leg was rebroken and reset. "I wish he would come to me for a little while," Theodore wrote from Oyster Bay, "but I guess Oyster Bay would prove unsufferably dull, not only for Elliott but for Anna." Elliott insisted on riding again when he was scarcely able to sit on a pony, but the very frenzy with which he performed such feats suggested a man who needed to prove himself.

The relief that Elliott found from his miseries was in alcohol and drugs. By the end of the 1880s, Theodore was urging him and Anna to take drastic action to halt the surrender to his addictions. He should either go into a "retreat" of some sort, meaning an asylum, or go on a long trip attended by a doctor.

After a southern sea journey in 1889 without his family failed to help Elliott, as was inevitable, and the birth of Elliott, Jr., in October, the whole family took off to Europe in search of a cure.

Before doing so, Elliott made pregnant a pretty domestic to whom he gave a locket. "K.M.," as she is referred to in family letters, now threatened Theodore, one of the three Public Service Commissioners and the acknowledged head of the Roosevelt family, to reveal the scandal to the world unless she were paid off. Elliott was inclined at first to deny everything. Theodore wanted to believe him, at least in part. "Of course he was insane when he did it," Theodore insisted. Elliott's tone altered, however, when Theodore described the persuasiveness of K.M.'s evidence. Instead Elliott argued via transatlantic mail about the amount of money she should be paid to disappear from sight. "I fear K.M. may be on the warpath," Anna alerted Bye. She appears to have been paid off and fades from history, possibly to Latin America. Not before, however, she was visited by an agent of Theodore. He "has seen the baby; he went over to Brooklyn believing the case one of mere blackmail; he came back convinced from the likeness that K.M.'s story is true. It is his business to be an expert in likenesses."*

* In the summer of 1981, Edmund Morris, the first Theodore Roosevelt biographer to tell the story of Katy Mann and the illegitimate child fathered on her by Elliott, sent the author a copy of a letter from a woman who signed herself as Mrs. Eleanor Mann Biles. She described herself as the granddaughter of Katy Mann. "[M]y father was Elliott Roosevelt Mann, the baby with the 'Rooseveltian features.'" Katy Mann had received "no money or settlement of any kind," the letter continued. "What had been left in trust for my father was stolen by the 'honorable' lawyer. . . ." In

Theodore, once his brother had admitted he had seduced the girl, was unappeasable. He advised Bammie, who on Anna's urgent plea had gone over to Europe to stand by, that Elliott's action was "little short of criminal. She [Anna] ought not to have any more children, and those she has should be brought up away from him." Anna must be made to understand, Theodore followed up in a letter to Bammie in Paris, "that it is both maudlin and criminal—I am choosing my words with scientific exactness—to continue living with Elliott . . . Do everything to persuade her to come home at once, unless Elliott will put himself in an asylum for a term of years, or unless better still he will come home too. Once here I'll guarantee to see that he is shut up."

Anna's letters from Europe portrayed an Elliott who was prey to nervousness, melancholy, sobbings, and angers. He may have been driven to alcohol, drugs, and recklessness by the agonies of a brain tumor, but his overwhelming feelings of guilt also showed a deep-rooted personality conflict.

She was deeply worried about him, Anna wrote to Bye from Innsbruck in October 1890:

> He is settled into a melancholy from which nothing moves him . . . he tortures himself with questions night and day. He believes himself everlastingly lost & ashamed to meet anyone. . . . He says you & Uncle

---

today's world of single parenthood, Mrs. Biles went on, it no longer was a stigma to acknowledge "illegitimacy" in one's origins. She asked Mr. Morris for additional information and leads. Morris forwarded her letter to Harvard, the Franklin D. Roosevelt Library at Hyde Park, the T.R. Association at Oyster Bay, suggesting that the recipients help her if they had information. The author of this book could find no evidence that Eleanor Roosevelt knew of "Elliott Roosevelt Mann." He wrote to Eleanor Biles. Her reply because of illness was unfortunately delayed. She sent me copies of letters that her father, Elliott Roosevelt Mann, sent to Mrs. Roosevelt at the end of 1932. The first, on behalf of his mother and himself [11/26/32], congratulated her on becoming "First Lady," adding that his mother possessed a photograph of Eleanor made when she visited Bad Reichenhall, Germany, "and which you so kindly sent her as a gift of remembrance. Also mother informs me that she was known as 'Katie' in your parents household in Westbury, L. I." To this Mrs. Roosevelt replied [12/3/32]. She used a "49 East 65th Street" letterhead, but the postmark was "Hyde Park":

> I was very interested to receive your letter and to learn that you were named after my father.
> It was nice of you and your mother to congratulate us and both my husband and I deeply appreciate your good wishes. I shall hope sometime to see both you and your mother.

Whether this was one more formal and routine acknowledgment of the thousands of letters that poured in to the Roosevelts after election, or whether Eleanor knew the Katy Mann story and preferred not to show awareness of it, is unclear. Elliott Roosevelt Mann wrote her immediately [12/16/32], thanking her for her graciousness and knowing that important matters pressed for her attention, "happy to await your wishes" in regard to seeing him and his mother. To this letter Eleanor never responded, Mrs. Biles wrote to me.

Jimmie have told him he has irretrievably disgraced himself, which he knows now was true, so he says he cannot go home. . . .

He is the saddest object I have ever seen & so good & so patient. Ask Theodore to write him praising him for keeping straight & pulling himself together.

The family, led by Theodore, applied to the courts to have Elliott adjudged insane and his property, which Theodore estimated at $175,000, placed in trust for his wife and children (in 1891 a second son Hall had been born). But Elliott contested the proceedings and finally, in January 1892, Theodore went to Paris to bring his brother home. The outcome is reported in the diary that a cultivated woman who had become Elliott's mistress kept and that ended up in later years in the possession of Eleanor.* The woman did not spare Anna and Theodore:

This morning with his silk hat, his overcoat, gloves and cigar, E. came to my room to say goodbye. It is all over, only my little black dog, who cries at the door of the empty room and howls in the park, he is all that is left to me. So ends the final and great emotion of my life. "The memory of what has been and never shall be" is all that the future holds. Even my loss was swallowed up in pity—for he looks so bruised so beaten down by the past week with his brother. How could they treat so generous and noble a man as they have. He is more noble a figure in my eyes with all his confessed faults, than either his wife or brother. She is more to be despised, in her virtuous pride, her absolutely selfish position than the most miserable woman I know, but she is the result of our unintelligent, petty, conventional social life. And why is it that the gentle, strong men always marry women who are so weak & selfish. Perhaps the feeling of protection and care given to a feebler nature is part of the charm. If she were only large-souled enough to appreciate him.

Theodore, who saw moral situations in black and white, described his encounter with Elliott differently:

Won! Thank Heavens I came over. . . .

Today I went out with Cachard, having the amended deed, to Suresnes, found E. absolutely changed. I had been perfectly quiet, but absolutely unwavering and resolute with him, and he now surrendered completely, and utterly broken, submissive and repentant. He signed the deed for two-thirds of all his property (including the $60,000 trust); and agreed to the probation. I then instantly changed my whole manner, and treated him with the utmost love and tenderness. I told him we would do all we legitimately could to help him get through his two years (or thereabouts) of probation; that our one object now would be to see him entirely restored to himself, and so to his wife and

---

* A poem by Corinne (Mrs. Douglas Robinson), "One Woman to Another," was inspired by this woman.

children. He today attempted no justification whatsoever; he acknowledged how grievously he had sinned, and failed in his duties; and said he would do all in his power to prove himself really reformed. He was in a mood that was terribly touching, how long it will last of course no one can say. . . .

In agreement with his brother, Elliott returned to this country and went to Dwight, Illinois, to spend six weeks undergoing the "Keeley cure" for alcoholism, because, he explained, that was his wife's wish. He then settled in Abingdon, a small town of some fifteen hundred inhabitants in southwestern Virginia, where he served as representative of his brother-in-law Douglas Robinson, who had inherited large holdings of mountain land. "He was the life of every party," the local newspaper recalled in later years. "The girls and young ladies were in their height of glory when invited to drive with him behind his fast-stepping trotters in his two-seated yellow jersey, or his high-seated trap. The fellows about town, old or young, found him a congenial and delightful addition to any of their masculine conclaves."

This account, written when Eleanor became First Lady and visited the area, was only partly true. As Theodore wrote to Bye at the time:

> Elliott has been giving the Abingdon people a taste of his mettle. Recently, while sitting "reading" (?) stark naked, he upset a lamp and burned himself badly. The good Abingdon people at once wrote to me that this would be a good opportunity for me to come down and "influence" him; but I declined with bland thanks. Seriously, I explained to them that it was absolutely useless. As they have invited the experience they must go through it by themselves.

Elliott had promised to respect the separation agreement with Anna: "Do you think she realizes that all her so often expressed in letters, fears as to what I would do were groundless?" he complained to Bammie. "Nothing is further from my thoughts than her fear of running back to see her whenever I feel lonely or trying to see the children. Do you think she knows and feels that I am exercising the strongest, most manly courageous self control in this matter?" Mrs. Hall kept him away even when Anna entered the hospital in 1892 for what proved to be a fatal illness. He raced to New York, but arrived too late. Afterwards he saw his daughter Eleanor, aged eight, in Grandma Hall's parlor and the doomed man spoke of their future together.*

She treasured the letters he sent her, and impatiently awaited the times when he came to New York and took her for a drive. She blocked out from memory the unhappier aspects of such visits—her fear of his reckless driving, his forgetting her when he left her with the doorman of his club, the promises to see her that were not kept. In 1894 he rented

* See Chapter I, pp. 1–2.

an apartment on West 102nd Street in New York. He did not let his children or those in his family, Theodore, even Bammie, who disapproved of his style of life, know of his comings and goings.

"I do wish Corinne could get a little of my hard heart about Elliott," Theodore firmly counseled Bammie. "She can do, and ought to do nothing for him. He can't be helped, and he simply must be let go his own gait. He is now laid up from a serious fall; while drunk he drove into a lamp post and went out on his head. Poor fellow! if only he could have died instead of Anna!" A few days later Theodore wrote to his "darling Bye" that Elliott was "up and about again; and I hear is already drinking heavily; if so he must break down soon. It has been as hideous a tragedy all through as one often sees. . . ."

That same day Theodore wrote to Corinne and the letter reverberated with intimations of what Elliott might have become. "Poor Elliott," Theodore wrote to his "Darling Pussie,"

I wrote him, and in response he asked me about his diary in India, and when I would have the piece ready for him; in response I wrote him that it would be ready in a couple of weeks. He answered by a note that was very painful because it was so incoherent and so grateful. I do not know how he is, and his constitution is so marvellous that I suppose he will continue indefinitely as he is. . . .

Finally on August 14, 1894, he died.

Theodore, notified by Corinne, left Washington precipitately to view his brother's body. "Theodore was more overcome than I have ever seen him," reported Corinne, "and cried like a little child for a long time." But he vetoed "the hideous plan" to bury Elliott at Tivoli next to Anna. He was buried instead in the Roosevelt family plot in Brooklyn's Greenwood Cemetery "beside those who are associated only with his sweet innocent youth."

Theodore's grief-laden description of the dead Elliott underlined the psychological confusion and conflict that attended his poor brother:

It was his fall, aggravated by frightful drinking, that was the immediate cause; he had been drinking whole bottles of anisette and green mint, besides whole bottles of raw brandy and of champagne, sometimes half a dozen a morning. But when dead the poor fellow looked very peaceful, and so like his old generous gallant self of fifteen years ago. The horror, and the terrible mixture of sadness and grotesque, grim evil continued to the very end; and the dreadful flashes of his old sweetness, which made it all even more hopeless, I suppose he has been doomed from the beginning. The absolute contradiction of all his actions, and of all his moral even more than his mental qualities, is utterly impossible to explain. For the last few days he had dumbly felt the awful night closing on him; he would not let us come to his house, nor part with the woman, nor cease drinking for a moment, but he wandered

ceaselessly everywhere, never still, and he wrote again and again
to us all, sending to me two telegrams and three notes. He was
like some stricken, hunted creature; and indeed he was hunted by the
most terrible demons that ever entered into man's body and soul. . . .

At the funeral Theodore noted that "the woman and two of her
friends behaved perfectly well, and their grief seemed entirely sincere."
This presumably was the woman who had been his mistress in Paris.
Evidently she was not with Elliott at the time of his death. He had
spent a few weeks that summer at her house on the New England
shore. He had often spoken to her of his sister, Corinne Robinson. She
now wrote to Corinne:

> Will you not tell me how he died? He seemed so much stronger when
> he left, that even the physician was astonished at his vitality, and I
> hoped for his children, he would try to take care of himself. He was so
> strong, and had such a gay, sweet nature, that I could not realize seeing
> him with my own children, so interested in their work and play, that
> he was mentally and physically so worn out.
>
> I do beg of you to have his children's memory of him—a beautiful
> one; his tender courtesy, his big—generous heart and his wonderfully
> charming sweet nature, ought to be kept before them. If in saying this,
> I am overstepping the line of discretion or courtesy, I beg you to for-
> give me.
>
> Believe me, dear Mrs. Robinson, your brother suffered greatly, only
> as a big tender man like him could suffer . . .
>
> . . . One thing you can do for him—see to it that he does not lose
> the place he deserves in his children's lives. He loved them and ought
> to have been with them.

Corinne sent her letter to Theodore and Bammie. Even the straitlaced Theodore was impressed. The letter seemed to him "unusually
good." She was a woman of remarkable tact, he felt. A year later she
again wrote Corinne. Elliott's death had been "wrong," as an old boat-
man who had taken them both sailing had said. "It was wrong—and
when I think of him, and contrast his life with his brother's, it seems a
cruel mockery of whatever power does guide affairs to have let his life
end as it did." She did not fail in appreciation of Theodore: "I am so
glad your brother is gaining the applause his virile splendid manliness
deserves, and what a compensation to you he must be."

The contrast of Theodore's "virility" and Elliott's "tenderness" was
the crucial point and this woman saw it clearly. A few years later
Theodore's adored son, eleven-year-old Ted, came down with what
Edith Roosevelt's biographer calls "nervous prostration."* Theodore,
who was then Assistant Secretary of the Navy, sent him to be treated

---

* *Edith Kermit Roosevelt*, by Sylvia Jukes Morris (New York: Coward-McCann &
Geoghegan, 1980), pages 170–71. She was Theodore's second wife.

by a physician in New York. "The unexpected diagnosis was that Theodore had long been driving him too hard both physically and mentally. Theodore, chastened, promised never again to press Ted, who had 'bidden fair to be all the things I would like to have been and wasn't.' "

Elliott was not as fortunate as young Ted. The final episodes of his life—the cycle of frantic defiance of family and social convention, tormented regret and penitent surrender, and the self-destructive acts that accompanied this behavior were but the ultimate outward manifestations of a conflict that had consumed him from within. The critic Van Wyck Brooks said of Mark Twain's self-accusations and sense of guilt:

> It is an established fact, if I am not mistaken, that these morbid feelings of sin, which have no evident cause, are the result of having transgressed some undeniable life-demand peculiar to one's nature. It is as old as Milton that there are talents which are "death to hide."

Elliott was raised amidst a society governed by a morality full of absolutes and rigidly defined sexual roles, a society stern in its judgment of deviance. Yet he was a man full of traits regarded as feminine. He was soft, tender, and compassionate, gentle in his own judgments and spontaneous in his ways.

The confusion and ambivalence in Elliott emerged starkly from Theodore's account in 1894 after Elliott's death:

> His house was so neat and well kept, with his bible and religious books, and Anna's pictures everywhere, even in the room of himself and his mistress. Poor woman, she had taken the utmost care of him, and was broken down at his death. Her relations with him have been just as strange as everything else. . . .

Elliott was the "tender, manly man." He nursed his father with womanly solicitude. Yet the women found his guardsman's masculinity fatal and forgave him his eye for the pretty ladies. Even Fanny Parsons, the friend of Corinne's who was dedicated to Theodore, acknowledged Elliott's charm:

> If he noted me at all I had received an accolade, and if on occasion he turned on all his charm, he seemed to me quite irresistible. But all the time I knew that his real worship was at the shrine of some mature and recognized belle of the day.

There were great love and fellowship between Elliott and Theodore as they went through their youth, but as they grew to adulthood the differences between them became more pronounced. Theodore the asthmatic weakling overcame his ailments. Elliott became a captive of his. Theodore sought to conquer, Elliott merely to find a way in which to enjoy his life and survive. There was no place in Theodore's world for a man characterized by ambivalence, gentleness, or spontaneity. Yet there was no way that Elliott could live up to the image of a man that society demanded and his brother epitomized. With a brother as judgmental and aggressive as Theodore, who was also the acknowledged leader of the family, Elliott must have felt compelled to repress and fight his effeminate characteristics. But he paid a dreadful price in a restlessness of spirit that pressed against the world of sport, society, sex, and moneymaking. None of them quite contented him, and this may have been the root of his nervousness, the explanation of his illnesses, his susceptibility to accident, his failure in business, his self-destructive alcoholism and addiction to drugs. But in Eleanor's memory of him, he was the father whose letters she treasured and ultimately published, and who called her his "little golden hair." She danced for him and he hoisted her in the air and swung her about. He called her "little Nell."

Theodore's competitiveness, belligerence, aggressiveness responded to what America, at the turn of the century, wanted in its president. While Elliott's niece, Alice, called him "a weakling," his tenderness, solicitude, his intellectual tentativeness were traits that better reflect a later America, the time of his daughter, and afterwards.

II

Mlle. Souvestre

THE MOST IMPORTANT person in Eleanor's youth, she later wrote, in addition to her father, was Mlle. Souvestre, the headmistress of Allenswood, a finishing school outside of London that Eleanor attended at the turn of the century. She was a woman of sparkling intelligence who took the fifteen-year-old Eleanor in hand and for three years gave her the love that a cultivated older woman can bestow upon a younger.

In 1948, "Bennett" (Mrs. Philip Vaughn, née Marjorie Bennett), Eleanor's roommate at Allenswood, wrote that she was sending her a book about the school and its remarkable headmistress:

> I have ordered a little book to be sent to you which I think may be of interest. It is written by Miss [Dorothy] Strachey who used to give literature classes at Allenswood, and is an account of the impression made upon her as a young girl at Les Ruches, by Mademoiselle Souvestre, just before the quarrel with her partner there. Mme. Bussy wrote "Olivia" about 15 years ago but has only just recently had it published. Leonie [Gifford, another Allenswood classmate] and I have both liked it very much, and thought you might. It is quite short and so would not take up much of your valuable time!

Eleanor's reply has disappeared. Its contents may be surmised from Bennett's next letter. "I had your nice little note yesterday. Many thanks. I am glad you liked 'Olivia.' It seemed to take me back so far! . . ." That was all, yet after Eleanor's father Mlle. Souvestre was the most important formative influence on her early life. One might have expected a reference to the book, to Mlle. Souvestre. There was none. Her silence related perhaps to the book's theme. *Olivia* is a thinly veiled account of the ruptured romance between Souvestre and the woman who assisted her in the management of Les Ruches.* Written with distinction and passion, it has taken its place in lesbian literature.

In a diary that Mrs. Roosevelt kept at the first United Nations General Assembly in London in 1946 where she was one of five members of the United States delegation, she noted, "At 5 old Mme. Bussy [Strachey] came for tea. She has moved here from Nice and having endured starvation thinks the British are sissies. She left at 5:30 and I did a little on tomorrow's column. . . ."

Although an indefatigable writer of letters, Eleanor did not write to *Olivia*'s author in 1948, yet when she had been First Lady there had been a poignant exchange between the two.

Eleanor had studied Shakespeare with Dorothy Strachey at Allenswood. The latter in the early 1900s had married a well-known but destitute French painter, Simon Bussy, and had settled with him in Nice. Before she wrote *Olivia* she had translated many books of "her friend, André Gide," a gifted artist and well-known homosexual. The Bussys made their home in Nice into a cultural center and had a daughter, Jane. Mother and daughter, according to Professor Charles R. Sanders, an authority on the Stracheys, did "highly important work in the French underground" during World War II.

When Eleanor was First Lady, out of the blue a letter came to her in July 1942 from Keeler Faus, an American consular officer who was stationed in Vichy under Admiral Leahy. He had been introduced to Dorothy Strachey Bussy by André Gide. That "very lovely old lady" had said to him, "If you happen to see Mrs. Roosevelt while you are in Washington, you might give her my kind greetings. I feel sure she will remember me. She was one of my students. . . ." Faus had sent Mme. Bussy some tea after his visit to her in Nice. She had thanked him. Her letter interestingly underscored the changing role of woman.

So much did I love English literature that when I was quite young—very long ago—I took to teaching it. In those days before the emancipation of women, it was a rather bold thing to do, for I was a 'young lady in society' and had no need to earn my living. A great many of my acquaintances, both among my contemporaries and my elders, disapproved of me for a variety of odd reasons, but my parents always understood and encouraged . . .

Mrs. Roosevelt scratched a note on the corner of this letter for Tommy [Malvina Thompson] her secretary, to transcribe: "Send her some tea if he will take it. I am delighted to hear about her. Ask to

* Souvestre's school at Fontainebleau, near Paris, had been called Les Ruches.

lunch—to stay. Has he a wife?" Keeler Faus did lunch at the White House and Mrs. Roosevelt gave him some tea and her card to deliver to Mrs. Strachey-Bussy. Faus subsequently informed Mrs. Roosevelt of Mrs. Bussy's reception of the gift. "She held the package in her hands, read aloud 'The White House' on the little envelope containing your card, and carefully laid the box on the table as though it were a priceless treasure—as indeed it is in France at present."

He enclosed a note that Dorothy Bussy had given him for Mrs. Roosevelt. It gives some picture of Eleanor at Allenswood:

Dear Tottie,

(I hope this old familiar name won't sound disrespectful to you, but really it's the only one I know you by!) When my young friend Keeler Faus brought me yesterday your kind message and lovely box of tea, what visions rose up in my mind of our beloved Mademoiselle Souvestre, of Allenswood, of a tall, slim, elegant young girl who was so much more intelligent than all the others! Since then how many things have happened! You have become the greatest lady of your great land. I have adopted France for my country in addition to my own England. There is no need to speak of England but France's voice is less easily heard, and it is a joy to me to say that *all* the France I know, and I think I know the best of it, looks to that great country of yours with the deepest admiration, gratitude and hope. . . .

Dorothy Strachey was not unknown to Eleanor, therefore, when Bennett sent her *Olivia.* Her failure to write to her was eloquent even if one is unsure of what it meant. Perhaps Mrs. Roosevelt did not know or did not admit to consciousness the meaning of the tender, ardent, and loving relationship that existed between the young Souvestre and her associate at Les Ruches and that is described in *Olivia.* Perhaps she knew and understood that society demanded a high price from those who showed too much familiarity with a lesbian relationship.

Dorothy Strachey was sent to Mlle. Souvestre at Les Ruches when she was sixteen, a year when "I first became conscious of myself, of love and pleasure. . . . Yes, people used to make joking allusions to schoolgirl crushes. But I knew well enough that my 'crush' was not a joke." The student body of Les Ruches numbered thirty and it had a sizable staff, which included a music mistress. Mlle. Souvestre, who is called Mlle. Julie in the book, is described: "a rather broad face, a low forehead, dark hair . . . parted in the middle, gently waving on the temples," delicately formed features, chin "fine and firm . . . the eyes were grey, impenetrable, burning." Mlle. Julie gave literature lessons. Mlle. Cara, her associate, gave no lessons. Mlle. Julie was the lovelier; Mlle. Cara the kindlier. "It was Julie who had the capital, the influential friends, the energy, the intellect, the commanding personality. It was

Cara who had the charm that gained fond mothers' hearts and the qualifications that made the enterprise possible. She had passed all the necessary examinations, and Julie none."

Souvestre's attractions, those that persuaded distinguished families of Europe and America to send their daughters to her, are implicit in Dorothy's portrait: ". . . Mlle. Julie was witty. Her brilliant speech darted here and there with the agility and grace of a hummingbird. Sharp and pointed, it would sometimes transfix a victim cruelly. No one was safe, and if one laughed with her, one was likely the next minute to be pierced with the shaft of irony. But she tossed her epigrams about with such evident enjoyment that if one had the smallest sense of fun, one enjoyed them too . . . But her talk was not all epigrams. One felt it informed by that infectious ardour, that enlivening spirit which were the secret of her success as a schoolmistress . . . . having contacts with the eminent men and women in many countries, she had too a spontaneous and open mind. . . . To sit at table at her right hand was an education in itself."

Until Julie and Cara had their falling out "they were a model couple, deeply attached, tenderly devoted . . . They were happy." But egged on by a new German instructress, Cara became jealous of Julie, especially of her hold over the girls. Cara's defense was to affect invalidism. When she found Olivia asleep on the threshold of Julie's apartment, fury seized her and she cried out, "Oh, yes, you go to their rooms at night—Cecile's, Barretta's, and now hers! You do! You do!" Julie decided the school had to be broken up. Lawyers were called in, and Julie, shrugging her shoulders, although she had "put every penny of capital into the school," was generous to Cara. But then Cara under mysterious circumstances took an overdose of chloral and died before the doctor's arrival.

Julie would not let anyone stay with her, even Signorina, the tiny mistress who danced attendance upon her. "'She was my friend, she said,' Signorina later told Olivia. 'She was the only person I ever loved, and am I not to spend the first night alone with her. Tomorrow you and Frau Riesener can do as you please but tonight I'm going to be alone.'"

Although *Olivia* is fiction, others besides Dorothy Strachey attested to the truthfulness of its account, not only of why Souvestre broke up the school at Fontainebleau but of her winning personality and remarkable educational philosophy. Pastor Charles Wagner, an evangelist and widely known author whose book *The Simple Life* had such enthusiasts as Theodore Roosevelt and Felix Adler, described the school at Fontainebleau as the place where Souvestre was able "at the same time to satisfy her great need for affection and her great need to teach." Another close friend, Alexandre Ribot, a former French premier, said that "she founded at Fontainebleau, with a friend, who had the best of her heart, a house of education, 'Les Ruches.'" Although a good Frenchwoman, she broke up the school and, he added, "After times of cruel sadness, she created a new school near London—and her originality pleased English society where she counted illustrious friends."

Another pupil of Souvestre's at Les Ruches had been Eleanor's Auntie Bye, Anna, her father's older sister. Like Dorothy Strachey she had been sent there when she was sixteen. Bye's father, the first Theodore Roosevelt, had enrolled her there in 1870. "When Bamie came home from Fontainebleau," wrote Lillian Rixey in her book about Mrs. Sheffield Cowles, which she called *Bamie*, "she seemed to all the family to have become, almost overnight, a very sophisticated young lady indeed."

In Eleanor's autobiography, *This Is My Story*, she says only that the siege of Paris at the time of the Franco-Prussian War had been such an "ordeal" for Mlle. Souvestre that she had left France. The siege may have been a factor, but not the central one and *Olivia* would have told Mrs. Roosevelt otherwise except that she did not choose to notice it. Neither had Auntie Bye, who was always an ardent advocate of Souvestre and whose presence at Les Ruches weighed heavily in the family decision to send Eleanor there as well as her cousin, the young Corinne Robinson.* Bye's looks were among her special bonds with Eleanor. They conveyed strength of character. People remarked on her thoughtful blue eyes, but Bye was not a beauty like her mother, Mittie. She remembered ruefully the four young Harvard men who had traveled down the Nile at the same time and who had been dazzled by Mittie, who was much more the object of their attention "than I was, for I do not think I ever let myself be young." The remark might have been made by Eleanor, who never forgave her mother for calling her "Granny." Bye's gracefulness, like Eleanor's, was self-taught and self-willed. A nurse had dropped her when she was a baby and injured her spine. She learned to ride and dance only because of the diligent exercises that their doctor had suggested. But like her brother Theodore, and her niece Eleanor, she had the stamina and will to follow a prescribed course. And in a convention-ruled society, she quietly went her own way, and did so with approval of that society. That, too, must be credited to Mlle. Souvestre, as much as to anyone. Bye's niece, Alice Longworth, said of her, "If Auntie Bye had been a man, she would have been president." Her commanding personality expressed itself early: within the family the other children turned to her for counsel. When the Georgia-born Mittie Bulloch Roosevelt, the mother of the Roosevelt flock, found the strenuous life of her family too much for her

* Daughter of Corinne Roosevelt Robinson, Eleanor's aunt.

after the Civil War, she retreated to her own sitting room, and the first Theodore turned over the reins of the household to Bye.

She had a wide circle of acquaintances, and when Aunt Gracie, Mittie's sister, looked in on Bye's first reception, her startled comment, according to Bye, was that "she had never expected to come to my house and meet people whom she only knew by their caricatures, which showed the attitude people took at that period of history to those in public life." Edith Wharton, a contemporary of the Roosevelt children, wrote that in old New York authorship, public service, politics, even the acquiring of wealth, seemed vulgar to its "men of leisure," to whom sports, travel, the development of lavish country estates were the staples of conversation and interest. Bye was an exception. Because of her gaiety, sympathy, and wit, she was always "the center of any gathering," wrote her niece, young Corinne. Bye was dazzlingly blue-eyed and cast a spell on everyone, but she also had "a tongue like a flail," did not suffer fools gladly, and was "a far harsher, firmer character than Mother." Later when she settled in Farmington Village near Hartford, Connecticut, she held court even there.

In 1884, Theodore's first wife, Alice Lee, had died of Bright's disease shortly after Alice's birth. Bye had become little Alice's foster-mother, sharing a house with Theodore and his daughter. Bye's arrangement with him measured her discretion and sense of the appropriate: "Theodore lived with me at 422 Madison Avenue after his wife Alice's death —but I always insisted we were visiting one another for that would be an easier relationship to break than had we made a mutual home. And this proved the case," she added in the history of the Roosevelt family that she wrote out for her son, Sheffield Cowles, Jr., "when he married his second wife, your Aunt Edith. Alice was hardly four years old, and it almost broke my heart to give her up."

Edith was jealous of Bye's influence over Theodore and Bye knew when she was beaten. She retreated. She accepted the invitation of a widower, James Roosevelt, "Rosey" Roosevelt, Franklin's half brother, who was First Secretary in London, to join him there and serve as hostess as well as foster-mother of his tiny daughter, Helen. Rosey had squired Bye around before he married Helen Schermerhorn Astor. The latter had died only recently. Bye went over at Rosey's invitation. Little scandal touched her presence at the embassy. Such was her competence —"Oh, Energy! Thy name is Bamie!" Theodore had once written—that she soon served as the Ambassador's hostess as well as Rosey's. She was presented at court even though it was against the rules. Then in her fortieth year, in 1895, beginning to be stout, she married William Sheffield Cowles, the embassy's naval attaché. Was he "Captain" or "Commander?" a dumbfounded Theodore cabled. "For many years," wrote Bye later,

> my career was that of an odd-job man. There were always children arriving in the world or ill, and I was always at one house or the other; very busy with their families, with no time to even remotely think of getting married, so that I always said it took the solitude of a London season to give me time to become engaged.

"Dear Auntie Bye," eleven-year-old Eleanor wrote her in one of her letters that have survived from that period:

> It was very good of you to write to me, all about it, it seems so funny to think that you are engaged. Thank you very much for the check you sent Brudie and me.
>
> Please come home as soon as you can for I am sure that Helen had you long enough now.
>
> I am still in the country but we are going down next Tuesday. I am so glad Alice is going to be in town this winter. I wish she went to school with me then I would see her every morning. I have got to stop now and I must go to my german lesson.
>
> Goodby with a great deal of love from your little girl
>
> Eleanor

Although Theodore had to consult family lawyers who insisted that Bye should wait because of obscurities in Cowles's divorce, she went ahead, and Senator Henry Cabot Lodge, an old friend, assured Theodore "with much glee, that Captain Cowles was 'all right, a Republican and a jingo!'"

Bye's only child, a son, W. Sheffield Cowles, Jr., was born at the end of the Spanish-American War (1898) just as his mother neared forty-four. Commander Cowles, freed from embassy duties, was given command of a ship. That happened just as Theodore was appointed Assistant Secretary of the Navy and Bye's return to the States facilitated her renewed ability to consult and advise her brother. In 1899, while Theodore still was Governor of New York, Commander and Mrs. Cowles purchased a four-story brick house on N Street in a fashionable part of Washington. Bye turned her house into a social mecca, "The town now boasted a social leader in the tradition of Mme. Roland and Mme. Du Deffand and their famous French salons, for politics and society were one and the same to Bye and both were equally fascinating." So wrote her biographer, Lillian Rixey, and quoted a letter to Mrs. Cowles from a British friend:

> You talk of being quietly in politics. That is the only part of your letter one cannot quite understand. 'Quiet' has no connection with the content! You have seen everyone & some more. . . .

The N Street house was within walking distance of the White House, and after Theodore became president he was often there. It was well known in the family, Eleanor Roosevelt told Lillian Rixey, "that Uncle Theodore made no major decision in foreign or domestic policy without first discussing it with Auntie Bye."

Bye's sister, Corinne (Mrs. Douglas Robinson), although completely devoted to her, occasionally was not wholly charmed, at least within the confines of her own family. "Auntie Bye is still pretty official," Corinne observed tartly to young Corinne, "but not as much so I think as usual." Bye came up from Washington to see her sister, who was bedridden. "Auntie Bye thinks that she has come just to see me," she wrote her daughter, but then after an enumeration of the plays Bye had secured tickets for and the engagements she had made, she added, "but I really enjoyed seeing her yesterday—" There would be similar laments over Eleanor's hectic schedules.

After the death of Eleanor's parents, she and her brother Hall, nicknamed "Brudie" lived with Grandma Hall. This meant a brownstone in New York City in the winter, which although remembered by Eleanor's classmates as dingy, was at a fashionable address, and the Hall house at Tivoli overlooking the Hudson, part of the Livingston enclave, the rest of the year. Grandma Hall was widowed and had her hands full with her spirited, beautiful daughters, Tissie, Pussie, and Maude, and two sons, Vallie and Eddie, who incidentally were known as outstanding tennis players. There were problems. Grandfather Hall, although a man of wealth, had died intestate. The aunts and uncles were an unruly lot. Grandma Hall loved Eleanor and Brudie. She did everything for them that Society demanded, but does not appear to have been a woman of force or overflowing affection. Nor did she encourage Eleanor and Brudie to see much of their boisterous Oyster Bay kin. That was to Edith Roosevelt's (Mrs. Theodore Roosevelt's) satisfaction, who wrote not long after Elliott died:

Anna's children are with Mrs. Hall, still at Tivoli. I believe they are very well but as you know I never wished Alice to associate with Eleanor so shall not try to keep up any friendship between them.

Eleanor continued to go to the private classes of Frederic Roser after her father's death. These were conducted in the schoolrooms of elegant Fifth Avenue mansions. A composition that young Eleanor wrote for her Roser class, *Antoine Lemaire*, reflected her intense feeling of isolation and yearning to be loved. The hero, an orphaned boy who is taught to play the violin, dies during a recital after he has learned that his childhood love had married another. "I thought you would be faithful," he reproaches her despairingly, "but I might have known better. No one ever gave me love." Eleanor underscored the moral. The boy was a "born genius" but "the thing which the boy yearned for most was love." Another composition that she wrote a few years later when she was fourteen or fifteen shows the weight she attached to truth and loyalty.

> It may seem strange but no matter how plain a woman may be if truth and loyalty are stamped upon her face all will be attracted to her & she will do good to all who come near her & those who know her well will always love her for they will feel her loyal spirit & have confidence in her. . . . It is often said that friendship and loyalty are the petty illusions & dreams of youth & that as one grows older one gives them up & forgets them but to me this seems wrong for the greatest men (&) women are those who have been loyal & honest & have believed in friendship to the end.

She was also passionately romantic, as shown in a fondness for Peter Ibbetson in the Du Maurier novel. Orphaned at twelve (like Eleanor) Peter Ibbetson withdrew to an "inner world" where he learned to "dream true"—that is, to evoke at will the people he loved and to carry on a fantasy life with them in his "private oasis."

At Oak Terrace at Tivoli, Eleanor "dreamed true." She was tall, blue-eyed, with the creamy complexion of her Georgia ancestors, long-fingered, tireless, and born under the mark of gravity. Her mother had not called her "Granny" for nothing. Her Auntie Bye had a comparable sense of responsibility. Thoughtful Bye was the exception to Grandma Hall's ban. She was the link between the Oyster Bay Roosevelts and Eleanor and Brudie at Grandma Hall's. "Eleanor wrote me the dearest letter," she wrote to Mrs. Hall from London. "I do so long to see her and Brudie once more and I am indeed glad if she seems more and more like precious Anna [Eleanor's mother]. . . . I will write Eleanor soon again."

Eleanor's mother had wanted her to benefit from Mlle. Souvestre as Bye had, and Bye bolstered Grandma Hall's decision to have Eleanor go to Allenswood, just as she urged that Eleanor's cousin, little Corinne, go there too. If Bye knew why Souvestre had closed the school at Les Ruches, it did not affect her attitude towards the headmistress.

Eleanor arrived at Allenswood when she was fifteen. She became Marie Souvestre's favorite, as much as Joseph Chamberlain's daughter Beatrice, the sister of Austen, the half sister of Neville, had been. Souvestre was almost seventy when Eleanor entered Allenswood. But her passion and commitment had in no way abated from the days at Les Ruches. "Another old friend passed away," Beatrice Webb noted in her journal in 1905, "Marie Souvestre, a brilliant woman, handsome, warm-hearted, the very soul of veracity and keen-witted." Beatrice Webb placed Marie Souvestre's portrait near those of Herbert Spencer, Haldane, George Bernard Shaw. "She must have counted for much in the lives of many women coming from the lists of the governing class in England, France, America and Germany," Mrs. Webb further wrote, and summed her up as a "brilliant and irreligious Frenchwoman" who had "the charm of past beauty and present attractiveness. . . ."

Beatrice Chamberlain was one of the women who came from England's governing class and had attended Les Ruches. Her traits remind one of Eleanor. Neville Chamberlain's biographer, Keith Feiling, describes Beatrice as "the most selfless of beings, blazing with intellectual ardour and public spirit." She appears in Dorothy Strachey's *Olivia*, where she is called Laura,* whose portrait was on Mlle. Julie's table. "I had never seen such a face, I thought, so frank, so candid, so glad and so intelligent," said Olivia. She asked Laura, who had returned to Fontainebleau for a visit, whether she had loved Mlle. Julie. " 'Oh,' said Laura, 'you know I do. She has been the best part of my life. My father's too busy to talk to me much. She has opened my eyes to all I like best in the world, showered me with immemorable treasures.' " But when Olivia pressed on with questions that suggested a love affair with Mlle. Julie, Laura looked at her "with her clear, untroubled eyes which had a kind of wonder and a kind of recoil in them, 'there's nothing else. I just love her.' "

Pastor Wagner said of Mlle. Souvestre, "The first great passion and the first great affection of her life was her father. She lost him young." That was a tie between headmistress and Eleanor. There were others. One of Eleanor's classmates, Helen Gifford, told the London *Daily Mail* in 1942, during Mrs. Roosevelt's visit to England at the time of the Blitz, of the impression Eleanor made when she appeared at Allenswood.

> I remember the day she arrived at the school, she was so very much more grown up than we were, and at her first meal, when we hardly dared open our mouths, she sat opposite Mlle. Souvestre, chatting away in French. . . . She took a serious view of life, and once confided to me that all she wished for was to do something useful: that was her main object.

Souvestre sent Mrs. Hall her own acute reaction to the fifteen-year-old:

> All what you said when she came here of the purity of her heart, the nobleness of her thought has been verified by her conduct among people who were at first perfect strangers to her. I have not found her easily influenced in anything that was not perfectly straightforward and honest but I often found that she influenced others in the right direction. She is full of sympathy for all those who live with her and shows an intelligent interest in everything she comes in contact with.

* Some feminists insist that Laura is modeled on Eleanor Roosevelt.

As a pupil she is very satisfactory, but even that is of small account when you compare it with the perfect quality of her soul.

Eleanor was at Allenswood from 1899 to 1902. Souvestre obtained Grandma Hall's permission to have Eleanor accompany her during her holidays through Western Europe. We do not have Eleanor's letters at the time either to Souvestre or to her grandmother to document her capacity for an affectionate and mature friendship with a much older woman. But we do have some of Souvestre's letters. Writing to Grandma Hall, she speaks of Totty's (the nickname her aunts had given her) intelligence and eagerness to learn, and she adds:

. . . it is impossible to wish for oneself a more delightful companion in travelling. She is never tired, never out of sorts, never without a keen interest in all that she sees; the more I know her, the more I see what a helpful and devoted grandchild she will be to you. Ah! to me! What a blank her going away must leave in my life!

Eleanor made a place for herself at the school, and Mlle. Souvestre, who did not suffer fools easily, had promoted her to the place opposite her at table. In Paris, Souvestre took her in hand and, learning that most of her dresses were hand-me-downs from her Hall aunts, had her assistant, Mlle. Samaia, take her to the leading dressmaker in Paris for some new gowns. Eleanor's handwriting ceased to be a child's insecure scrawl, and now, in the emphatic script of later years, she wrote to Auntie Bye:

. . . I am so glad that you like Washington & that dear baby is so well. Thanks many times for sending me the letters from Alice, Corinne & Teddy. I enjoyed them so much but they made me quite envious for I wanted to be with them so much. I am sending the letters back to you. I would love to have a photograph of Admiral Dewey & it would be too lovely to have his autograph, too. You were too sweet to think of it.

School does not open till to-morrow but I came back yesterday with Mlle. Samaia who brought me over from Paris. Hilda Burkinshaw is here too & I like being back soon for it gives you lots of time to get settled & this term I am sleeping with two other girls—the room will be in a mess & I shall be glad to be out of it. I had such a nice time at Mrs. Whitmore's* & they were all so nice to me. Their dance was great fun & Gladys & Hilda are dears. They went back to their school in Paris on the 11th & as I didn't leave till the 20th I took them to Ruy Blas & we had a grand time together. Mlle. Souvestre does not arrive until to-night, but I will give her your love then. She has sprained her ankle, poor thing, & I am afraid she is going to have a rather painful trip over. I am so sorry.

* Eleanor called them her "Woolryche-Whittemore cousins." They lived in a handsome parsonage in the North of England.

Goodbye now dear Auntie Bye, many kisses to baby & best love to you & Uncle Will

from your always loving Eleanor

During Eleanor's final semester at Allenswood, she was joined by young Corinne Robinson, who was brought there by her mother. Both Mrs. Robinson and Mrs. Cowles were in London for King Edward's coronation, and after Bye returned to the United States, Mrs. Robinson stayed on, joined during several weekends by Eleanor and young Corinne. "I found Eleanor's prayer book and a pair of black garters, however!" she advised her daughter after one such stay. While Mrs. Robinson's symbolism might have been exquisite had Eleanor shown any Jezebel-like charms, the prayer book was a constant, well-thumbed companion and would be at her bedside at her death some sixty years later. Little Corinne, to distinguish her from her mother, was two years Eleanor's junior, "bubbly," as she described herself, irreverent, and a good student. How strongly she contrasted in temperament with Eleanor, who was grave and sympathetic and provoked such comments as purity of heart. If one accepts the view, as this author does, that "the faculty for happiness like a good French accent is usually learned early in life or never at all,"* Eleanor's fatalistic attitude towards the achievement of happiness, an attitude that she later asserted, can already be seen. Mlle. presented herself to Corinne a little differently than to Eleanor. "The classes with Mlle. Souvestre are very interesting, but sometimes she gets terribly mad, and then I do pity the poor girl she is mad with. She pushes her round and screams and yells. . . . I like her much better when not at lessons. It's very interesting to hear her talk. I sit nearly opposite her at table. . . ." She noted another example of Souvestre's tempestuousness:

> To-day Mlle. S. has been in a rage as Signorina went out. She always seems restless and ragey when the latter is not here. She sat on the stairs for an hour and a half by a certain door and every one that opened the door she yelled not to let it bang. I was so frightened at the yell it of course slipped & banged with the most terrible noise. She was so mad that she could hardly say anything so I hurried away!

Together with Eleanor she talked with "Sou," as they called her, about Negroes and religion and the Boer War. The last ended with the defeat of the Boers while Eleanor and Corinne were at Allenswood. The English girls celebrated with an impromptu dance and a Thanksgiving service, but Sou was "so furious about peace and on Monday got so excited talking about it . . . that I thought she was going to fall off the bench. . . ." Corinne found Sou's ideas about religion "very peculiar. . . . In our French class we had a very violent discussion in which

* *Tennyson: The Unquiet Heart*, by Robert B. Martin (Oxford, 1980), page 85.

she asked us all our opinions as to why it was any good to pray. Everything we said she contradicted till I asked her, 'What do you think Mlle.?' at which she announced that she never told anyone her opinions and only liked to hear those of us children to amuse her and that she only went to church to amuse herself often in that way."

The more understanding, compassionate picture of Souvestre drawn by Eleanor in *This Is My Story,* which was written in the 1930s, may only have represented the difference between young Corinne's sixteen years of age when she was making her diary entries and Eleanor's fifty-one when she wrote her book, but there also was a depth to the relationship between Souvestre and Eleanor that Corinne's lacked if for no other reason than that Corinne found with her mother the concern and intimacy that the motherless Eleanor achieved with the schoolmistress.

"My Elijah mantle did not compare with Eleanor's," Corinne said in 1967. "I wasn't pure and good and fine and all those things but Mlle. Souvestre enjoyed me all the same. Often at the end of our talks she would say, 'Totty—so intelligent, so charming, so good.' Then she would throw up her hands and add, 'mais elle n'est pas gaie!'" She recalled how the girls at Allenswood expressed their attachments for each other. It might almost have been a paragraph out of Carroll Smith-Rosenberg's, "The Female World of Love and Ritual," published in 1974. "When I arrived she [Eleanor] was 'everything' at the school. She was beloved by everybody. Saturdays we were allowed a sortie into Putney which had stores where you could buy books, flowers. Young girls had crushes and you left them in the room of the girl you were idolizing. Eleanor's room every Saturday would be full of flowers because she was so admired."

Souvestre's mixture of forcefulness and grace served Eleanor as a model, just as it had Bye, just as it excited the Stracheys. In an exercise book that Eleanor kept at Allenswood she wrote: "I have spent three years here which have certainly been the happiest years of my life."

"They miss Totty awfully here," young Corinne wrote to her mother after Eleanor returned to the United States in mid-1902. "It is awfully funny there does seem to [be] something gone and you don't know exactly what it is." Corinne thought about it a good deal and when she came to write her memoirs [unpublished], she was more illuminating:

> I found that Eleanor, called Tottie by Mlle. Souvestre was the most important person at the school and was loved by Mlle. Souvestre with a deep devotion and appreciation of her remarkable qualities. Eleanor was a much finer influence than I, but because I was her cousin, I was accorded a place in Mlle. Souvestre's affection, which I might not have had otherwise.

Souvestre's letters to Eleanor reflect the tenderness and wisdom that bound the two. They also show Souvestre's scorn for the amenities and frivolities that Society prescribed for Eleanor's coming out as she returned to the United States.

Geneva, July 7, 1902

My dear little girl:

I am happy in the thought that these three years of such sustained and productive work on your part have also been a period of joy and rest for you and that they will, at the end of your adolescence and at the beginning of your youth, be a period you will look back to for a long time with satisfaction and serenity. But now all of this is going to disappear quickly into the mist of the past. From this very minute, when I am writing to you, life, your life, which is entirely new and entirely different, and, in several respects entirely contradictory, is going to take you and drag you into its turmoil. Protect yourself to some extent against it, my dear child, protect yourself above all from the standpoint of your health which is not strong enough, in these next years, to sustain the strain of this worldly rush. Give some of your energy, but not all, to worldly pleasures which are going to beckon to you. And even when success comes, as I am sure it will, bear in mind that there are more quiet and enviable joys than to be among the most sought-after-women at a ball or the woman best liked by your neighbor at the table, at luncheons and the various fashionable affairs. Tell me how you have found your grandmother and your little brother.

The latter does not yet know the value of your warm sisterly tenderness; but he will learn that gradually, and you will become for him what you desire to be.

A thousand and a thousand tendernesses to my Totty whom I shall always love.

M. Souvestre

No one at the time knew Eleanor as well as Souvestre did. When the latter wrote of the "contradictory" currents in Eleanor's makeup, she did so on the basis of solicitous observation. The conflict that Souvestre foresaw on one side ranged "duty," which prescribed conformity with Grandma Hall's and Society's wish that she "come out" and behave as a daughter of old New York. That meant to find a husband, raise children, attend dinners and balls. But there was also the side of her nature that made Souvestre her model in the use of her energy for purposes of education, commitment, accomplishment, and quiet elegance.

Souvestre's next letter, in the delicate way it distinguishes between vanity and affection, showed why Lytton Strachey called her *"cette grande femme,"* but also the affectionate closeness that characterized all Eleanor's important relationships. Souvestre well understood the importance of "duty" to her "dear little Totty," who presumably had advised her of clashes with her Aunt Pussie, particularly over her aunt's efforts to usurp Eleanor's relationship with Brudie.

17 VIII 02 [August 17, 1902]

My dear little one,

First, regarding your request for my portrait. I would have given it to you before, and with what pleasure, but as far as offering it on my own —never. It is one of my principles. Peoples' impressions are many-sided. There are those who prefer a changing and diverse image presented to them by memories of a familiar face instead of the frozen expression of a photograph or portrait. One often requests a photo not because one wants a keepsake, but to please the person represented. Among my friends and myself it is understood that I am insensible to this sort of minor flattery. But as I know that it is for yourself that you wish a photo, you shall receive it.

. . . .

So, my poor little one, you are already in the grip of a moral problem, and obliged not to exhort yourself to do your duty, generally a simple task for most people, but reduced in your case to asking: Where is the duty? I always knew that this moment would come. What I wish is that it had not come so quickly, and that before entering into this inner struggle you would have been to some extent bolstered to meet those complications of life created by circumstance. I hope it is not a problem concerning your brother. I know that it is something that touches you in the most intimate fibers of your being, and I would not wish that the conflict, even an interior one, would place you under such a burden.

In any case, do set aside, and for as long as you can, these very grave decisions, so that, at a later time, observation and reflection may give you the capacity to see all sides of the question. . . .

I am in Switzerland at Pully. When the weather is good I live in the sky, when the weather is bad I live in the clouds. I would very much like to have you with me. I miss you every day of my life, but it is a selfish regret for which I blame only myself. You are more in your element where you are than you would be with me. Mlle. Samaia is at Chexbres with her sister, at 4 or 5 [one word illegible] from me. Au revoir my dear child, I love and embrace you.

M. Souvestre

Mlle. Samaia was "the bustling little figure," as Dorothy Strachey put it, who danced a lifelong attendance on Souvestre. She was housemother and dean, always, complained young Corinne to her mother, trying to stuff her with suet pudding, which she hated, or seeing to it that the thirty girls at the school were properly attired or did their reading. She ended up as the head of the school, which she inherited from Souvestre.

Eleanor wanted to return to Allenswood. The life of a schoolmistress, in the style of Souvestre, appealed to her. She did not manage to return despite Allenswood's blandishments, as is evident in another letter.

My dear little Totty,

Your affectionate letter has given me great pleasure, and I thank you for it most sincerely. At the risk of reawakening your regrets, I cannot keep from once more telling you what an immense emptiness you will leave behind at Allenswood for all those who knew and loved you. It will be a veritable celebration if you can come and spend a few days with us next year, and I truly hope that you will not forget us: even in the midst of your mundane activities I am convinced that you are too sensible to not grant more than a wistful memory to your schoolgirl years.

I am curious to know what impression you will derive from your first season. I hope that "society" will stimulate you. I am certain that meanwhile you have spent a delightful vacation. . . .

The next letter (October 5, 1902) is the last that seems to have survived. We learn that Eleanor, at Mlle. Souvestre's initiative, had intervened with a President, her Uncle Theodore. She was unsuccessful, but it would not be the last time she intervened with a President. Souvestre wanted Eleanor to defend herself against evenings out, pleasures, flirtations. She feared Eleanor's estrangement from "all" that she knew her to be. With delicious irony, she spoke of "the big season of social dissipations," a sentiment that Totty reciprocated:

Dear Child:

I have just given to your aunt Mrs. Robinson, the picture you requested. If by chance she should forget to give it to you, ask her for it, for she will surely have it among her belongings.

Yesterday, quantities of letters from you arrived at Allenswood. There were none for me among the ones I distributed, but I hope I shall be luckier next week. Leonie's letter to Mlle. Samaia, written from your home, was of much interest to me also, since it portrays you, in your surroundings, as you wouldn't present yourself.

I am happy to see that your brother is becoming more and more attached to you. I can understand how your aunt's regrets, seeing the preferences of such a dearly loved nephew pass from herself to you, are a source of sorrow to you. But as it is, after all, the direction his affection should take, your aunt will finally accept what is legitimate. Moreover, it seems to me your aunts are carried away in a whirl of exciting social activities which protects them against lasting regret of a sentimental nature. Dear child, my mind is so divided in respect to you. I should like to know that you are happy, and yet how I fear to hear you have been unable to defend yourself against all the temptations which surround you; evenings out, pleasure, flirtations. How all this will estrange you from all that I knew you to be!

. . . .

Please tell me when the big season of social dissipation starts in New York? When does it end? Is it immediately after the carnival season, and is it true that we shall see you here in the spring?

Thank you for going to your uncle on behalf of Mr. Scott. I meant to write and dissuade you from attempting it, for after what I heard of Mr. Carneggie [*sic*], it seemed impossible that Mr. Scott should obtain what he hoped for. Have you seen your uncle since your return? If the newspapers are to be believed, the car accident he suffered lately, an accident so fatal to others and which had seemed so trifling for him has had unexpected and serious consequences. Is he really recovered now?

Ah! how we miss you here, my dear child. There are many new girls and, as is their habit, the English girls do not know how to welcome them, and leave them in the corner. You would have known how to make them feel rapidly at ease, and happy in circumstances so different from their usual lives; for some are German, others French, another one, coming from Algeria and born of English parents, is neither English nor French, but looks a pure Algerian. There is a new English girl, very bright and lively, and another one, quite stupid. Finally, your fellow Americans are going to present quite a respectable front, 4, and if another one whose coming your aunt Mrs. Robinson announces, eventually does arrive, they will be 5. Bennett came for the opening of school. I wish she were here much more often, for she has the best influence on the girls, and they love her. However, I don't believe that her mother feels much pleasure at seeing her take such an absorbing interest in her former school, and I do not call on her as frequently as I would wish.

. . . .

You never told me how your money problems were resolved. Have you the control of a definite sum given you as long as you are a minor, or does someone simply pay your expenses, without your having to worry about balancing your expenses against a definite sum given you?

Till soon, my good child. Winter is coming, the flowers are dying in the garden, the horizon is hidden behind a heavy, motionless curtain of gray mists, the sad days are beginning in this country where they are sadder than anywhere else. I wish you what we lack: light and sun.

Tenderly yours,
M. Souvestre

This is the last letter in Eleanor's files from Mlle. Souvestre. Nor has history yet been able to locate the letters, if any, that Eleanor wrote to the headmistress. The words "if any" are used advisedly. Eleanor's silence may not have been accidental. She knew and in some measure shared Souvestre's hopes for her and the expectation that she would return to Allenswood. She knew the disappointment that her failure to go back meant. She must have sensed, too, that in entering Society, although in rebellion against it, and in falling in love, she had abandoned the work at Allenswood and in some measure had gone against the grain of her reality. So silence in a way was her reply to Souvestre. But she gave another answer. Souvestre's portrait always stood on her desk or close to it. In 1902 she chose a path other than the one Souvestre had urged. She never spoke about it but it was always in her heart and Sou's photograph was there to remind her.

Marie Souvestre, said Alexandre Ribot, sought to teach her girls to be independent, to think for themselves, to be personalities, and at the same time "to keep their grace, their freshness of sentiment, elegance, which are the charm and smile of life." She had fortified the thoughtful Bye in the skills and stratagems that enabled her through Theodore Roosevelt to play an important role in American life. She strengthened Eleanor's self-confidence and provided her with ways of persuasion that greatly influenced Franklin Roosevelt and the New Deal. But that was in the future.

Returned to her early surroundings, Eleanor evidently felt out of place as she tried to get her bearings in New York. Cousin Susie, Mrs. Henry Parish, the niece of Grandma Hall, a very proper woman, came to see Mrs. Robinson and told her that Eleanor was "beginning to take a great interest in people and that she looked very sweet in her low-necked gowns." But when Eleanor went down to Washington for the New Year's celebrations at the White House, Mrs. Robinson confided to her daughter unhappily:

> . . . I am sorry to say that Eleanor did not make as good an impression on your aunt and uncle as she apparently gave them the feeling that she had very little interest in anything American, and went out walking in the midst of the New Year's reception, did not want to receive at the Admiral of the Navy's and altogether made one or more rather unfortunate mistakes. Poor child!
>
> She has lived almost entirely alone with Pussie in 37th Street [New York] in a most erratic way, and I think insensibly she has become less careful about things on account of her environment. She is always sweet and thoughtful with me and I think has enjoyed her winter, though not wildly. I really am distressed about the Washington impression. . . .

Afterwards, Mrs. Robinson learned the reason for Eleanor's strangeness. It moved her deeply. She promptly wrote her confidante, young Corinne:

> . . . Eleanor came to see me. Do not say anything about it, but the child has had a hard winter in many ways. Mrs. Hall has been all the

time at Tivoli, and Pussie is so erratic and inconsiderate that Eleanor's path is not all roses. She burst into tears and said 'Auntie, I have no real home,' in such a pathetic way that my heart simply ached for her.

She had no home; no wonder a career at Allenswood, close to Souvestre, appealed to her, but she decided against it, probably because of Brudie and her obligation towards G'ma, and even more, because of the wooing of a certain young man.

Was Eleanor aware of Mlle. Souvestre's sexual preferences? There is no evidence to indicate she was, any more than were Bye or Corinne. Perhaps Eleanor's silence about this side of Souvestre is to be explained by the lapse of time. Close, ardent relationships among women were accepted as normal in the nineteenth century. It was left to later times to equate such intimacy with a sexual liaison. *Olivia* was written in such times.

She was seventeen when she left Allenswood. The two most important people in her life up to then had been her father and Mlle. Souvestre. Both were androgynous characters. Elliott was basically masculine with an admixture of tenderness, sensibility, and sympathy. Souvestre was equally passionate, even more sensitive. She was a woman but ruled those around her with her vivacity, intelligence, and ardency. Eleanor was innocent but the air she breathed, although the times were Victorian, was of natures that commingled "masculine" strength of mind with "feminine" sensibility. Elliott was flawed, but Souvestre had discovered the secret of how to use her powers to obtain emotional satisfaction and to excel and rule in a male-dominated world.

Eleanor's father and Mlle. Souvestre, especially the latter, encouraged her to develop those qualities of force and gentleness, of intelligence and intuition, of courage and sympathy that enabled her to stand inwardly against Society's expectations of a woman. It would take time. There would be detours. But in the end her personality prevailed. The circumstances of life, instead of shattering her, reinforced the native qualities upon which Elliott and Marie Souvestre had smiled. Outwardly she would conform to the standards of the conventional female role, even managing with respect to the latter, to preserve the grace and charm that were the hallmark of womanhood, to be a wife, daughter-in-law, mother, but inwardly she appraised and judged, resisted and encouraged according to her own standards.

III

A Fear to
Call It Loving

T HE NEED to be loved and to be affirmed as a person by another's choice is never so clamant as in the years of youth. Those needs had been partly fulfilled for Eleanor by her father and by Mlle. Souvestre. A young man now entered her life as suitor, fiancé, and husband. She had begun to go her own way and to develop her potentialities for service to others, but the story of her courtship and marriage was also the story of her turning her back on the possibilities that Souvestre had seen in her. To fulfill her destiny as wife and mother, she renounced her intense desire to serve and to be useful outside of the family. To the approving smiles of Franklin's mother and "Cousin Susie," perhaps even of Franklin, she gave up her settlement work on New York's East Side.

She could not have done otherwise. Even though Society's rituals were an agony, its standards had no more obedient a practitioner. What Society demanded, her temperament and her breeding ordered, not to mention her knowledge of her father's outlaw life at the end. Her Uncle Eddie, who like Uncle Vallie had been a national tennis champion, had married Josie Zabriskie, a current belle. Eleanor described a party at Josie's:

> . . . we had the queerest time at Joe's. I don't go there often and in
> between times I forget the impression it always makes on me to see Joe

and all the other women there smoking and I find myself constantly
the only one who does not do one thing or another, which makes me
uncomfortable as they always say 'oh! well, Totty hasn't been here
enough to fall into our ways' and I dare not say that I hope I never
shall! Somehow I can't bear to see women act as men do and I wish
Joe wouldn't do it—

Eleanor was no virago, not even a bluestocking. But she was different
from the other girls who came out in the autumn of 1902. A sense of
solicitude for others, a readiness to be of help, a kind of coltlike vitality
marked her off. She returned to the United States in early summer of
1902, torn between two life goals: to return to Allenswood, to
Souvestre, to becoming a teacher herself; or to follow Society's code for
young women of eighteen, which prepared them to be wives, mothers,
nurturers—to make one's debut, to attend teas, dinners, and balls, to
find a marriageable man, and to raise children. Souvestre had cautioned
her against the corruptions of conformity and urged her to listen to the
promptings of her own nature. But inner voices usually are contradictory. She continued to live with her grandmother at Tivoli and with
Pussie in town, but there were frictions. Everyone was afraid of Uncle
Vallie, who was turning into an alcoholic. Although her family called
her "Totty," she was as adult as any of them and wanted to be recognized as such by her aunts, Tissie, Pussie, and Maude, especially in relation to her brother Hall (Brudie), who was seven years her junior,
bright and engaging.

She decided soon after her return to the United States to cut herself
free from Pussie when she was in town. She continued to live at Tivoli,
but when she went to New York she lived with Mr. and Mrs. Henry
Parish, "Cousin Susie," at East Seventy-sixth Street. It was a twin
house, one entrance opened into the house of Mrs. Ludlow, who was
Cousin Susie's mother and Grandma Hall's sister; the other into the
childless house of the Parishes. The drawing rooms of the two houses
opened into each other, as Sara Delano Roosevelt, of whom Cousin
Susie approved, noted. Cousin Susie was tall and sedate and, as Eleanor
indicated, attentive to the code that applied to nineteen-year-old
women in Society—the man made the advances. Only if one knew him
well was a letter to him appropriate. The signature "very sincerely
yours" maintained the proper distance and to permit a man to kiss you
before you were engaged was intolerable. "My grandmother," said
Eleanor, and this was equally true of the very proper Cousin Susie, "always made me a little self-conscious when I received a letter from a
man." By such rituals Society inculcated its women with a proper posture of passivity in thought and behavior.

Eleanor also decided upon her return from Allenswood to volunteer
as a worker at the Rivington Street settlement house on the Lower East

Side. She did it in association with other young women of debutante age, working through the newly organized Junior League. She enjoyed work; even more she responded to the affection of her young East Siders. Her class at Rivington Street, she said, was "the nicest part of the day." She quickly displayed her organizational competence to her fellow Junior Leaguers, was disagreeing with Mary Harriman, older sister of Averell Harriman, and one of its founders, about policies, and taking on all sorts of organizational tasks. "A box of reports have just come to me to send out & I'm looking forward to an awful day's work!" she complained to a friend.

Not long after she had returned to the United States, she became the responsible one, at the center of family, friends, and co-workers. Aunt Tissie, married to the wealthy Stanley Mortimer, going abroad, sent Eleanor an eight-page letter on her duties towards her grandmother. Usually Eleanor was able to make the violent Vallie purr, and she welcomed looking after Hall. In her autobiography she grips the reader with the account of the inner terrors she suffered when she came out, but two years later she is counseling a cousin and friend on how to take it all in stride:

> Corinne and Sylvia are sitting in my room discussing next winter's gaieties and incidentally the Tuxedo ball! They are both terrified, but not half as terrified as I am and yet I've been preaching hard at them and assuring them that very soon they will not be at all worried!

She would always present a serene face to the world no matter how agitated she was inwardly. She complained that hostesses at dinners seated her next to much older hosts. "I suppose I must resign myself to being considered twenty-five, however," she complained, preferring the company of the nineteen- and twenty-year-olds. But of course one can hear the host advising his wife, "Put Eleanor next to me. At least I can talk with her."

Then there was Franklin to ensure her against the fate of a bluestocking. They had not corresponded while she was at Allenswood, although they had met at Auntie Corinne's. In the weekly letters that Franklin had sent home from Groton and afterwards, although less frequently, from Harvard, there was only one reference to Eleanor. But now in 1902, finding themselves on the same train going up the Hudson, he tall, debonair, and handsome, to get off at Hyde Park, she tall, very much the self-possessed woman, to get off a few miles farther north at Tivoli, he ran into her and bid her to come forward to the parlor car to greet his mother, still in widow's weeds. Whatever Eleanor's personal convictions that she was the most unbecoming of the Hall women, she interested young Franklin. And soon in his line-a-diary there were references to Eleanor.

From the first of the courtship letters that they exchanged it was clear that she was uncertain about his intentions. But if she had any doubts about the path she should take, she concealed them well. He preserved her letters; she, unfortunately, destroyed his, probably in a moment when his behavior seemed to betray the youthful commitments and pledges they contained.

She had gentleness and grace and Society had no more loyal an adherent. She observed its rules of chaperonage meticulously. Since Cousin Susie would not be in, Franklin could not call upon her. Even the straitlaced Cousin Susie advised her to read First Corinthians 13 and lectured her on humility. "Then Cousin Susie talked to me a long time on the subject of forgiveness. She says I do not know the higher meaning of the word, because I never forget." At issue was her dislike of her Aunt Pussie, who was living with Aunt Maggie (Mrs. Ludlow), Cousin Susie's mother, in the twin houses at East Seventy-sixth Street. Her censoriousness also extended to Cousin Alice, Uncle Ted's daughter. Others in the family, including Uncle Ted, shared her views on Alice.

Together with members of Franklin's family she went to Cambridge the weekend of the Harvard-Yale game. She visited his rooms at Westmorely Court on the "Gold Coast" and together they went on to Groton, where he proposed to her.

"I have been thinking of many things which you & I must talk over on Sunday," she wrote him when she was back in New York, and then added a plea that underscored her own daunting insistence on absolute truthfulness:

. . . only one thing I want to tell you now. Please don't tell your Mother you have to come down to see Mr. Marvin on Sunday, because I never want her to feel that she has been deceived & if you have to tell her I would rather you said you were coming to see me for she need not know why. Don't be angry with me Franklin for saying this, & of course you must do as you think best.

Despite her misgivings about Franklin's mother, Sara, who opposed their marriage, her letters were filled with gentle reminders to Franklin that she knew his mother preferred to have him alone.

She accepted his offer of marriage:

Do you remember that verse I tried to recite to you last Sunday? I found it today & I am going to write it out for you, because it is in part what it all means to me:
    Unless you can think when the song is done
      No other is left in the rhythm;
    Unless you can feel when left by one,
      That all men else go with him;

> Unless you can know, when unpraised by his breath,
>   That your beauty itself wants proving;
> Unless you can swear, 'For life, for death!'
>   Oh, fear to call it loving!

She went on to write out the next stanza of Elizabeth Barrett Browning's poem and added:

> I wondered if it meant 'for life, for death' to you at first but I know it does now. I cannot write what I want. I can only wait & long for Sunday when I shall tell you all I feel I cannot write.

Franklin was at the Delano place in Fairhaven, Massachusetts, for Thanksgiving with his mother. There he told her about his wish to marry Eleanor. She was deeply upset and opposed. Back in Cambridge he sought to console her. "And for you, dear Mummy, you know that nothing can ever change what we have always been & always will be to each other—only now you have two children to love & to love you—and Eleanor as you know will always be a daughter to you in every way—" Eleanor's note to Sara, written from Cousin Susie's, reinforced Franklin's:

> I must write you & thank you for being so good to me yesterday. I know just how you feel & how hard it must be, but I do so want you to learn to love me a little. You must know that I will always try to do what you wish for I have grown to love you very dearly during the past summer.

There is no letter to Souvestre on these developments. That poor woman was dying of cancer. Perhaps she had been too deeply disappointed over Eleanor's failure to return to Allenswood. Perhaps she feared that Eleanor had been caught up in a course that was contrary to her potentialities.

There is a revealing plea from Eleanor that Franklin take more seriously her work with the Rivington Street settlement. Together with Rosey's daughter, Helen Roosevelt, Eleanor had taken a preparatory course for work on the Lower East Side. "Now don't laugh," she begged Franklin. "It *was* interesting & very practical & if we are going down to the settlement we ought to know something. I know you are laughing at this & if you were only here to take up all my time I would not be going I'm afraid, but one must do something or not having the one person who is all the world to one would be unbearable." Her work on the East Side, which reflected the joy of service, the compassion, the energy, and the competence that Souvestre had spotted and that in time would make her one of the world's heroines, amused Franklin and it bothered Cousin Susie, and in time she abandoned it as if to say the world was well lost for Franklin.

In today's more feminist atmosphere her disparagement of settlement house work makes poignant reading. Twenty years later the needs and competencies that went underground in her marriage to Franklin, re-emerged in her work and friendships.

Eleanor herself, writing in the late Thirties in her autobiography, *This Is My Story*, explained her readiness to marry:

> I had a great curiosity about life and a desire to participate in every ex-perience that might be the lot of women. There seemed to be a neces-sity for hurry; without rhyme or reason I felt the urge to be part of the stream of life. . . .

So she said yes to Franklin, who together with his mother were the epitome of the taboos and rigidities as well as strengths of New York Society, which was Victorian in its ethos. Eleanor's Cousin Corinne, in her unpublished memoir, wrote that it was Society's view that "To per-form a duty was right, but to have zest for living—joy in living was not very nice," and of the marriage bed, she told her children, "I always laughed with your Father and maintained that this purebred New Eng-land woman, when she finally married, knew her duty, lay on her bed, and murmured to herself as the husband approached 'for God, for Country and for Yale!'" Sex was an ordeal to be borne, Eleanor once confided to her daughter Anna.

Marriage to Franklin meant acceptance of the code. That code was embodied, among other places, in Groton and in its headmaster, the Reverend Endicott Peabody. In his novelistic account of the founder and headmaster of Groton, *The Rector of Justin*, Louis Auchincloss conveys the Rector's austere, absolute support of conventional heter-osexuality. He discouraged friendships between the boys, wrote Au-chincloss, "'Because, sir,' he exclaimed loudly, driving his stick into the snow, 'I did not think a hundred examples of David and Jonathan was worth one of sodomy.'" When George Biddle, a first-former whose years at Groton overlapped those of Franklin, became too chummy with his older brother, Moncure Biddle, a fourth-former, classmates in both forms let them know they felt they were "queer." "After that I kept away from him," wrote Biddle. Peabody filled up the hours of the day with recitations, religious exercises (Episcopalian) at the chapel and in Sacred Studies, a class that he personally taught, and above all with sports. The boys, except for the prefects, slept in cubicles, narrow alcoves about six feet wide and ten feet deep, with curtains rather than doors and with walls that reached only part way to the ceiling, an ar-rangement designed to reinforce the Rector's emphasis on discipline and obedience, manliness and achievement. Groton graduates looked back to their years under Peabody with awe, reverence, and affection.

Certainly F.D.R. did. As he wrote "My darling Mama and Papa," June 25, 1900:

'The strife is o'er, the battle won!' What a joyful yet sad day this has been. Never again will we hold recitations in the old School, and scarce a boy but wishes he were a 1st former again.

Nowhere in Franklin's letters home from Groton was there a hint of sadness or failure. One can only surmise that the presence in the form ahead of him of his nephew, James Roosevelt, Jr., "Taddy," an object of fun among his fellow fourth-formers, because of his queer ways, was a trial. Tad was the son of Franklin's half brother "Rosey." His grandmother was *the* Mrs. Astor. Tad finished Groton and went on to Harvard but soon was put on probation there. Franklin wrote his parents, and what a burden of suffering lay behind his words:

. . . but I think I should tell you now that I *know* that Taddy has been on to N.Y. several times without letting anyone know of it. . . . I think the very strictest measures sh'd be taken, but of course Papa must not worry in the least, as after all it is no affair of ours. Some measures should be taken to prevent his having his full allowance next year, as even this year he has had just *twice* too much.

Worse was yet to come. Taddy dropped out of Harvard and, reaching the age of twenty-one, came into an annual income of $100,000. The newspapers, which described him as the son of James R. Roosevelt, the cousin of Governor Theodore Roosevelt, and the nephew of John Jacob Astor, disclosed that he met, wooed, and married a very stout, blond Hungarian girl of the Tenderloin, "Dutch Sadie." In a rare explosion of excommunicatory rage, Franklin, who had entered Harvard, advised his mother:

The disgusting business about Taddy did not come as a very great surprise to me or anyone in Cambridge. I have heard the rumor ever since I have been here but in the absence of facts the best course has been silence. I do not wonder that it has upset Papa but although the disgrace to the name has been the worst part of the affair one can never again consider him a true Roosevelt. It will be well for him not only to go to parts unknown, but to stay there and begin life anew.

Rosey Roosevelt, an Edwardian American, who drove his own four-in-hand and considered himself a man of the world, sophisticated and agreeable, twenty-eight years older than Franklin, broke up the marriage and Taddy disappeared from sight.

It never is clear what demons tormented Taddy. One of the girls he had pursued and been rejected by, while still at Groton, had been Theodore's Alice. Taddy's sister Helen, a sweet and comely girl, had been brought up by Bye when she went over to London. Helen married

Corinne's eldest child, Theodore Douglas Robinson, in 1904 in one of Society's most elegant weddings. For several years, on and off, between 1904 and 1945 she kept a detailed diary filled with homely family detail. She never mentioned Taddy. After he broke with "Dutch Sadie," he became a recluse, lived in a shabby Kew Gardens apartment, and at his death after World War II left his fortune to the Salvation Army.

In few matters was Society, which aped Britain's class-conscious aristocracy, more harshly observant of the code than in insistence that its members not contract what it considered an "unfortunate" association. When Sara Delano's girlhood friend Maggie Carey remarried in circumstances towards which Society was critical, James Roosevelt forbade his wife to see her again. "It is not easy to make up my mind," Sara admitted to her journal, but she complied. So did Flora Payne Whitney, the wife of Cleveland's Secretary of the Navy, accept his caution not to discuss "the Henry Ward Beecher case with men." And when Taddy contracted his "unfortunate" alliance, his name dropped from the records.

The "Taddy" letter is one of the few F.D.R. letters among the hundreds from Groton in which Roosevelt disclosed himself and showed a strong-willed implacability behind the good manners and gaiety. In another case he advises his mother, who had informed the Theodore Roosevelts that Franklin was unable to accept their invitation to come to Oyster Bay, "Please don't make any more arrangements for my future happiness." He greatly admired his distant cousin Theodore. The real feelings were there, but it was part of the social code to conceal them. As Eleanor much later said of Franklin, "If something was unpleasant and he didn't want to know about it, he just ignored it and never talked about it. . . . I think he always thought that if you ignored a thing long enough, it would settle itself." For twenty-five years, from January 4, 1881, on, Sara kept a daily journal, but a sympathetic biographer says, "Unfortunately it is not very introspective or analytical . . . gives little recognition of her nature except by implication." By contrast, Eleanor liked to look at facts about herself and confront situations. She lived for intimacy and getting things done. "Alice Draper and I then had a chatty walk together," Eleanor wrote Franklin from Dark Harbor, Maine:

> She told me all her heart secrets, which quite overcame me and I am growing rather encouraged for I must be developing the long wished for quality!

She had the ability to listen and to encourage, and her sympathy spurred openness and confidence in return, but Franklin, although debonair, was more reserved. He had learned from boyhood on that if his doting but overwhelming mother were not to work her will on him he had to conceal his real intentions if they clashed with hers. Because he loved his mother, he pursued his way by indirection, one aspect of which was not to talk about what one really wanted. Eleanor wanted him to open his heart to her. Was he ever able to? We don't have his courtship letters.

One searches vainly through Franklin's Groton letters for an acknowledgment or disappointment he felt in not having starred in athletics, never made "Prefect," or shone as a scholar. When his parents left him at Groton, he was pictured by many, said his mother, "for a lonely little boy." George Biddle later wrote that he had heard from another Grotonian that "Franklin Roosevelt had always felt at Groton that he was unsuccessful and had not attained the prestige he would have liked." At Harvard, too, he was not elected to its most prestigious club, the Porcellian, and one of Eleanor's attractions to him was her thoughtful interest in his success. He wanted very much to be elected a class marshal in his senior year at Harvard. "Tomorrow is the day for your elections, isn't it?" she wrote in a characteristic letter of sympathy and sustenance. "Well, I wish you the very best of luck boy dear, as you know & I shall think of you often 'hanging round the polls'!" And when he lost, the compassionate Eleanor comforted him: "I was sorry to see by the papers this morning that you had been defeated but hope you will have better luck on Friday if you are nominated to one of the committees." He had better luck with the committees, and when commencement came and he spoke at the class dinner, her request was precise, flattering, and foretold the future, ". . . don't forget you are to bring me the rough copy of your speech."

She was protective, sympathetic, solicitous. She was about to give up her settlement work at Rivington Street, to Cousin Susie's relief. The side of her nature that sought serious work, which Souvestre had spotted, and the appreciation that came with it, she would satisfy through assisting Franklin in his career. Although some of her Oyster Bay cousins considered him something of a sissy, "the kind of boy you invited to the dance but not to the dinner," said Alice—a "hypocrite," suggested little Corinne—Eleanor sensed that he was a young man with large visions and determination and she could be helpful to him.

The Rector was a shaping influence on Franklin's life. He officiated at his wedding and prayed for the success of his presidency at the 1933 Inaugural. Peabody stressed the supportive role of a good woman, and when he married his childhood friend he exulted to the Reverend Julius W. Atwood, later Bishop:

> What a help she will be to me in every way and how she will enable me I trust, to make the school almost what I should like it to be. She is such a strong and beautiful character that I shall be more than twice the man I am with her by my side.

Strong as Sara was, she accepted this role for women. There is a drawing by Warren Delano, her brother, its caption reading, "Warren illustrates a Conversation with his (older) sisters." It shows three sisters in their teens and the somewhat younger boy, and he wrote in the drawing:

A Very Just Remark!

"History and Mathematics oh! all very well for us, but not at all the thing for women. You should read Cooking Books and Housekeeping Manuals and try to make home agreeable to us men."

The helpmate role that Groton assigned to women was also reflected in the marriage congratulations of the Reverend Sherrard Billings, second only to the Rector in authority and affection. "It has been a dream of mine for some years that you would be a man widely useful to your country," and since Billings knew Eleanor, whose brother, Hall, was about to win the highest honors at Groton, his added words took on special meaning, "and a sympathetic wife will be a great help to you on the road to realizing my dream and I am thankful and glad."

That conception of a wife's supportive role appealed to Eleanor. In the two and a half years between her return from Allenswood and her marriage she had become indispensable to the people around her, and though she complained of the many things she had to do, she loved the busyness. She was the nurturing mother. "Do be good to Grandma," her Aunt Maude begged her. "I think she will miss you frightfully." The reserved and reticent Henry Parish felt similarly about the place Eleanor had taken in Cousin Susie's heart: "Much as I am to Susie, you are more and I pray that you will always be."

In 1936 when Eleanor was at work on the first volume of her autobiography, she told the somewhat enigmatic story that, when she had broken the news of her secret engagement to Franklin, Mrs. Hall had asked her "if I was sure I was really in love. I solemnly answered 'yes,' and yet I know now that it was years later before I understood what being in love was or what loving really meant."

Did she mean that later she understood that love meant to be swept by physical as well as emotional passion? Yet her courtship letters contained avowals that were those of a lover. "My dearest, dearest Boy," she wrote him from Tivoli, and used the affectionate appellation her father's Aunt Ella Bulloch had bestowed on him:

I have missed you so all day. I cannot tell what a lonely feeling I have had to find myself alone after two such happy days. Sweetheart, I realize more & more how much fuller my life has become in the last six months & I lay & wondered this afternoon how life could have seemed worth living before I knew what 'love' and 'happiness' really meant.

The love letter she sent him Christmas Eve to open Christmas Day in Hyde Park, where he would be with his mother, showed the intensity of her feelings and was a forerunner of the ardent letters she would send in the future to all those who awakened and touched her emotional life:

Christmas Eve 1903
Tivoli

Darling,

I am sending this in the hope that you may get it on Christmas day as I want you to have a line from me. You know dearest all that I wish you and I only hope that your Christmas will be very, very happy dearest & that the New Year will bring you more joy than you have ever known before. I could never tell you how much happiness you have brought to me my dearest boy, but I can never remember feeling half so happy before. I haven't opened your package yet, as I wanted to have something from you in the morning, so I can't thank you really now but I will on Saturday!

I must stop now but Merry Xmas again dear, think of me often tomorrow & miss me as much as I shall miss you, then you will be really glad to see me on Saturday—

Ever your loving
'Little Nell'

She was loving, but also, as Franklin had realized, serious and high-minded. Also, as she made clear to him, in her gentle but emphatic way, she rebelled against the pomp and ceremony that high society required. "One thing I am glad of every minute I stay here," she wrote Franklin from an elegant Long Island mansion where she was a weekend guest, "is that we won't ever have a house half so beautiful or half so overwhelming! I'm afraid I wasn't born to be a high life lady, dear, so you'll just have to be content with a simple existence, unless you teach me how to change!"

Franklin, as brain truster Rexford G. Tugwell later observed, had that little "black box" in his mind that no one penetrated, where his most private observations, judgments, and decisions went on; so evidently did Eleanor. At the time of her wedding, however, she willingly subordinated herself to her dominating mother-in-law. Those were the years, said a close friend of hers, of "yes Mama, no Mama." When during their honeymoon Sara offered to find a house for them, she joined Franklin in welcoming Sara's selection and furnishing of a place to live around the corner from her. They moved into it upon their return. As she wrote Sara in the letters that she alternated with Franklin in sending home from shipboard, "I shall want to be kissed all the time!"

For the time being, Franklin, Mama, Hall, her family engrossed her thought and feeling. By no means, however, did they exhaust Eleanor's strength and vitality. The family came first, but she still maintained a correspondence with her closest Allenswood classmates, whom she had informed about her engagement and marriage. A German girl her age, Carola von Passavant, with whom she had shared a year at Allenswood, wrote that she had heard from Bennett that Eleanor was to be married. She was too, to a Fritz von Schäffer. Then Carola added, "You have probably heard that Sou has been very ill." Souvestre and Signorina had not left Allenswood "even" during Christmas. "The last news I had in the beginning of January sounded a little better, they hoped they could bring her to France. But it still seemed rather serious, and any illness is in Sou's age." Eleanor promptly sent a long letter to "Dearest Carola." "I was very, very glad to hear that this greatest of all happiness had come into your life Carola dearest, for I know of no one more worthy of it than you & I only wish that I knew your fiancé so that I could tell him how lucky I think him!" She told of her own approaching marriage and was glad that Bennett was going to Frankfurt for Carola's wedding. "We have not done much in the society way this winter, because going out every night made it very hard ever to see Franklin & so we have refused all the things which we did not feel obliged to go to." The letter, signed "Affectionately always, Eleanor Roosevelt," contained no mention of Mlle. Souvestre. Another Allenswood girl, Dorothy Alexander, who knew Franklin and to whom Eleanor had written of their engagement, wrote about the same time: "Sou has been very ill. I expect she will have to give up the School." Eleanor's enthusiastic correspondence with Allenswood classmates makes the absence of letters with Souvestre after October 1902 inexplicable. That remarkable Frenchwoman was much on the minds of many people. In December 1904, Lytton Strachey wrote to Leonard Woolf: "Marie Souvestre—the eminent woman —is ill with no one knows what. She refuses to let any doctor examine her—no one knows why—but they guess it may be because she's afraid she's got cancer—and writhes in agony. They think she hasn't got cancer but can't tell. It would be a sad loss if so eminent a person were to die." Souvestre's friends, especially the large Strachey family, visited her those last months, but not a word about her condition, if Eleanor knew of it, appears in her almost daily letters to Franklin.

Yet she must have talked with Franklin about the remarkable woman. "Tell Eleanor to be sure to write Mlle. Souvestre, if she has not done so already," Margaret Bradley, a Boston friend, wrote to him after receiving announcement of their engagement. "For when I saw Mlle. in London last autumn, we were speaking of Eleanor & Mlle. said that the thing she would like to hear most of all was that Eleanor had made a good match so that she will be delighted to hear the good news." The day Eleanor was married a cable arrived from Souvestre with one word, "Bonheur." Two days later she died.

There is a sharp but affectionate entry in Beatrice Webb's diary after Souvestre's death on March 19:

> Unable to comprehend a deity who would pay any regard to such insignificant creatures as human beings, she was a declared atheist, a humanist and, in politics, a fervently pro-Boer.

Eleanor met the Webbs during her and Franklin's honeymoon trip in Scotland. "They write books on sociology," was Eleanor's meager comment, "and Franklin discussed methods of learning at Harvard while I discussed servant problems with his wife." If Souvestre figured in her conversation, Eleanor did not mention it. Earlier she had written "Mama" that she had gone out to Allenswood and seen its new headmistress, the tiny Mlle. Samaia, to whom Souvestre had left the school, and she had added, "but it was dreadful without Mlle. Souvestre."

The "Marie Souvestre Memorial" Committee, which was announced in October 1905, did include Eleanor as well as Mrs. Cowles and Mrs. Douglas Robinson. The distinguished group numbered Beatrice Chamberlain, John Morley, Alexandre Ribot, Frau Dr. von Siemens, Mrs. Humphrey Ward, Sidney Webb, and several Stracheys. It began as a scholarship fund and ended up in 1908 in the construction in Paris of a "Maison Marie Souvestre," a workers' lodging house with inexpensive apartments, a restaurant, workrooms. Alexandre Ribot spoke at its dedication in 1908 on behalf of Marie Souvestre's friends. Allenswood and the "Maison Marie Souvestre" would help preserve the memory of "One of the noblest women" they had ever known, but buildings and bricks, he went on, were unable to catch

> l'originalité d'un esprit supérieur: c'est le charme de ces conversations où elle mettait toute l'impétuousité, toute la fougue de son esprit; c'est ce de qu'elle avait d'exciter les esprits par la contradiction même, et c'est cette foi profonde, ardente, qu'elle avait dans le progrès de l'humanité qu'elle entre voyait, un jour, pacifiée, élargie, délivrée de tout les servitudes, de la servitude, de la misère, de l'ignorance et de la haîne.

Beatrice Webb had complained that her friend Souvestre was "without personal experience of religious feeling or public spirit," so Ribot's emphasis in this tribute on Souvestre's faith in human progress was noteworthy. That credo would find expression in one of Souvestre's pupils and friends—Eleanor. Beatrice Webb also said of Souvestre in her entry of March 31, 1905: "Veracity, an undeviating directness of intelligence, faithfulness and warmth of affection, were her most delightful qualities."

Those qualities also found their echo in Eleanor. That was why Allenswood had been such a liberating experience. In 1905 their whole strength was turned inward toward the family. In time they would again assert themselves in the wider world. It would take a personal tragedy and a world war to cause her, as her cousin Alice put it, to "go public." But the key quality, "veracity," had been reinforced by Souvestre. With it as a guide, Eleanor would give her answer to the question that Alice James, the invalid sister of William and Henry, had asked:

> When will women begin to have the first glimmer that above all other loyalties is the loyalty to truth, i.e., to yourself, that husband, children, friends and country are nothing to that.

IV

Eleanor and Her Bridesmaids

A LMOST ALL of Eleanor's bridesmaids were either her or Franklin's cousins. For most of them the twelve years from Eleanor's marriage up to America's entry into the World War was the period in which they found husbands, adapted to their careers, established homes, gave birth to children—and repressed the promptings of independence and autonomy. Far from being different, Eleanor was among the most conventional of young Society's matrons. There was, however, something more, and the most perceptive among her contemporaries sensed it—the strength and vitality that she applied to fulfilling the role that Society expected. There were hints of what a formidable force these qualities might become if released into wider channels.

These qualities were to be seen in her relationship to Isabella Selmes, one of her bridesmaids, beneath whose beauty and impulsiveness was a seriousness of purpose that attracted Eleanor. Isabella became a bride of Robert Ferguson soon after Eleanor's marriage. In Scotland the Fergusons were a bulwark of the Liberal Party establishment. The youngest "Fergie," Robert, tall and taciturn, had emigrated to the United States, where he had been one of Theodore's Rough Riders. He had also been one of the gallants who paid court to Bye before her marriage. The links between the Fergusons and Roosevelts had included Eleanor's parents. In 1895, shortly after Bye had telegraphed Theodore the stunning news that she intended to marry the embassy's naval attaché, Will Cowles, even though she was, as her niece Corinne noted, a "ripe forty," she promptly went up to Scotland to apprise the Fergusons of the event.

Roosevelt links with the Selmeses were equally close. Before Theodore was thirty, while he was still widowed, on his way to his Dakota ranch he had met and been enchanted by Isabella's mother. Hailing from Kentucky, she was then Mrs. Tilden Selmes, married to a fellow rancher. She is "singularly attractive . . . very well read . . . a delicious sense of humor, and is extremely fond of poetry—including that of my new favorite, Browning, as well as of my old one, Swinburne," Theodore had written in 1886. To him she represented the "noble" female.

So did Isabella have nobility in Eleanor's eyes. Although Bob was eighteen years Isabella's senior, she married him in the summer of 1905, much to the surprise of most who knew them. Young Corinne, who considered Isabella a "perfect darling," wrote excitedly about the event in her diary:

> So unusual but oh! so like Isabella and Bob. Her career of success before the eyes of the world is ended & how extraordinary it all was. Taken up and admired & worshipped by all New York—that happily did not blind her, and she chose the better part. It is interesting though, the question of her future. . . .

Eleanor wrote Mama when she heard about Isabella's marriage: "Cousin Susie writes that Mrs. Selmes was ill and broken-hearted because she felt she had nothing left now to live for, but she is very fond of Mr. Ferguson and I think she will soon find that Isabella still needs her a great deal." Eleanor had not progressed to the stage where mother, or mother's surrogate in the form of mother-in-law, might be too close or too possessive.

Eleanor and Franklin caught up with Bob and Isabella at the family ancestral stronghold in Scotland, to which Bob had immediately brought his bride, and in the first years after their marriages the two young couples saw each other often. In 1910, however, the Fergusons abandoned New York and homesteaded in Cat Cañon, New Mexico, amid cactus, dwarf evergreen, and desert sands. Bob's health spurred the move. "The air is marvelous & still, sunshine indeed too good to be true. . . ." Isabella wrote to Eleanor. The latter envied Isabella the hard pioneer life, away from the comforts and protections of the East, and admired especially her ability to make her own life.

In 1912, when Franklin and her brother Hall took ship to see the nearly completed Panama Canal, Eleanor let them go alone, but joined Franklin afterwards in New Orleans for a visit with Bob and Isabella in New Mexico. They were still living in tents, to which, said Eleanor, they had imparted a characteristic charm. Their two children and Mrs. Selmes lived with them and all ate pork and beans and canned foods that would have been considered "absolute death" in the East. Altogether, Isabella seemed a gallant and devoted figure to Eleanor.

That was still the impression she made upon Eleanor in 1915, when she and Franklin, after visiting San Francisco and the Panama-Pacific Exposition, traveled south to the Burro Mountain Homestead, as the spacious adobe house of the Fergusons was called. Its large living room was filled with Adams and Chippendale pieces and it might well have been a living room on Long Island, said Eleanor. Isabella had a gift for vivid phrasing, as well as her mother's infectious gaiety. When a friend complained in 1916 of the onerousness of running a household, her comment was: "I know one Eleanor Roosevelt who has four children and moves them all six times a year—and does everything else besides!"

It was the tribute of one earth goddess to another. Eleanor wrote of Isabella: "When I think now of the endless care that went into the upbringing of two children in the same house with a man who was slowly dying of tuberculosis, I marvel at the fact that Isabella was able to create the impression that life was joyous, that the burdens were not heavy, and that anyone who was not living that kind of life was missing something."

Isabella had created one style of life, Eleanor another, but each perceived in the other fundamental feminine traits, nurture and endurance, that, backed by executive ability, made both remarkable to their friends.

Eleanor's first years of marriage were devoted to Franklin and his mother. Orphaned at the age of ten, she yearned to have her mother-in-law close and intimate. Sara scarcely was able to believe her good fortune. She claimed, may even have believed, that she did not interfere in her children's lives. A little inconsistently, she also told Eleanor that she had been advised by her late husband always to be economically independent of her children. She kept the reins of Hyde Park's management in her own hands. With an affectionate Eleanor's complicity, and because Franklin loved her, she wove unbreakable bonds between her household and her son's. She knew, moreover, how to use her money—"the golden loop," one of her grandsons would call it—as well as how to use her charm and Victorian strength to accomplish her wishes.

Another of Eleanor's bridesmaids, young Corinne, whose first semester at Souvestre's overlapped Eleanor's last, and who had found a "new" Eleanor there, "self-confident, much beloved," puzzled over the competent Eleanor's relationship to the imperial Mama:

Eleanor seemed to me such a slave to her dominant, demanding mother-in-law. . . . Perhaps Eleanor was trying to do what Franklin wished. He may have wanted her to 'placate' Mama, and probably preferred luxurious peace that was bought at a heavy price that Eleanor had to pay. . . . Nobody could say whether Eleanor was doing what Franklin wanted her to do, or whether her strong sense of duty made her feel that she owed this attitude of subservience. . . .

Duty, the stern daughter of the gods, was Eleanor's watchword. . . .

Eleanor and Franklin settled into a routine where they lived with Sara at Hyde Park in a mansion that overlooked the Hudson, shared a house, and later lived next door to her at Campobello, "the blessed isle" between Maine and New Brunswick, during the summer, and in 1907 they moved into the East Sixty-fifth Street house that Mama presented to them as a Christmas present. She had financed and planned the construction of two buildings cheek by jowl, consulting Franklin but not Eleanor. The latter had bowed out because, she said, she disliked any discussion, especially one that resulted in scolding. A fragment that *McCall's* published posthumously under the title "I Remember Hyde Park: A Final Reminiscence" showed how fiercely she came to dislike the arrangement: "You were never quite sure when she would appear, day or night," she said of Sara's appearances through the connecting doors. That was what she wrote later, but at the time she seemed content or at most withdrawn, and when a few weeks after moving into East Sixty-fifth Street her young husband found her in tears and asked her what the matter was, she lamented that this was not her house or the way she wanted to live. A nonplussed Franklin told her she was "quite mad" and left the room.

Perhaps Franklin did not notice; perhaps he did not wish to. In any case she did not put her foot down. Quietly she accepted the values and standards of her husband and mother-in-law. She dropped her remaining links with settlement house and Consumers' League work: she quickly understood Mama's feeling that really close attachments should be limited to the family, and while she did not comply, she took pains not to affront her unnecessarily. She liked Franklin's law partner, slim, tall Harry Hooker, and informed Franklin with amusement of Mama's obvious vigilance during Harry's visit to Campobello in Franklin's absence. She corresponded sporadically with a few of her Allenswood classmates, but in the main she subordinated herself to the needs of her family, which in a few years, in addition to Franklin, Mama, and her brother Hall, included Anna (1906), James (1907), a first Franklin, Jr. (1909), who died after a few months, and Elliott (1910).

The mildness of her submission was deceptive; her goodwill and courtesy concealed an inexorable will. At the moment that will upheld the rules of Society as interpreted by Mama and Cousin Susie. Every household had to have a handful of servants—a nurse for each child, a cook, butler, chauffeur, maid, and laundress. Between her and her children was a layer of nurses and governesses. "I am to take charge of her," she wrote of baby Anna almost exultantly to Sara, who was in Europe, "and put her to bed tonight as Nurse is going to Eastport to say good-bye to her son." She was surprised, she informed Mama later that summer, "I never knew before how easy it was to take care of Anna." And still later, she confided that although Anna was very happy to have Nurse Watson back, "I am glad to say that I think she missed me a little last night."

This avowal of solicitude for her own tiny daughter was as pathetic as the social convention that denied the possibilities for nurture with which men as well as women were endowed. She would have been much better off, she later wrote, had she asserted her primary relationship to her children and not deferred to Mama and Society. Occasionally her willpower and stamina did not produce the behavior that Mama wanted. There were stirrings of rebellion. But instead of protest she retired into silence—her "Griselda" mood, she called it, all submission on the surface, all restrained fury underneath.

That was not the first time among the Oyster Bay Roosevelts that "Griselda" was used as a deprecatory description. Theodore Roosevelt, writing about *Anna Karenina* to his "Darling Pussie" from Dickinson in Dakota Territory in 1886, said of "poor Dolly" in that novel that "she should have been less of a patient Griselda with her husband. You know how I abominate the Griselda type." He expanded on what he meant in his letter to Bamie the same day: ". . . Stiva, Dolly's husband, is to me one of the most repulsive characters in the book; he is to me complete proof of my theory that it is criminal folly for a woman to forgive her husband's infidelity and go on living with him; it comes from weakness and wrongheadedness, I do not think it can possibly be other than harmful, certainly not beneficial, to the children." "I've told you, and I say it again," says the admirable Kitty to her sister Dolly in *Anna Karenina*, "that I have some pride, and never, *never* would I do as you're doing—go back to a man who deceived you, who has cared for another woman. I can't understand it. You may, but I can't."

To call someone a Griselda was to suggest meekness, not to praise her, at least among the Roosevelts. Yet the Griselda legend, as told by Boccaccio, Petrarch, and Chaucer, carries a different lesson than Theodore drew. Griselda, although not the greatest beauty, took hold of her princely husband's household, and in time the kingdom recognized and valued her "rype and sad corage." Trained psychiatrists are unable to agree on whether there is "a special affinity between feminity and certain forms of masochism," between the masochistic style, which can roughly be translated as "self-punishing," and the "caring" pattern, which is characteristic of women. Dr. Helene Deutsch speaks of masochism as "the outcome of the feminine constitution," and warns that the term should not be confused with "perversion." "Aggression is renounced," she wrote further on in her classic *The Psychology of Women,* "for the sake of being loved." It well described Eleanor's subordination to Franklin and his mother.

In the medieval legend Griselda's self-sacrifice and generosity lead to recognition and acceptance as the Prince's true consort. Griselda's care did not turn into self-abasement because of her tact and wisdom. The same was true of Eleanor. Young Corinne had marveled at Allenswood to find that Eleanor was Souvestre's "supreme favorite and what was remarkable was that she had made no enemies through this favoritism."

But Griselda's triumph was not what Eleanor had in mind when she wrote of her Griselda moods. That she misread the Griselda legend as she did suggested that her knowledge of it originated with the family, especially T.R. It also suggested that beneath the "sweet" submission there were strong promptings of rebellion. The misreading testified to the power of the will that enabled her to suppress such stirrings. She knew what was expected of women, and to gain the love that she craved she conformed. In 1902 her Aunt Edith, after a few months of being the First Lady, wrote to Cecil Spring-Rice from the White House: "I count on misty moonlight evenings on the White House porch, Theodore in his rocking 'chair,' you and Cabot [Lodge] settling world affairs over your cigars while Mrs. Lodge and I meekly listen as becomes our sex and position." Basically it was not Eleanor's conception of woman's role to "meekly listen." "I could not at any age," she later said, "be content to take my place in a corner by the fireside and simply look on." But that was said after World War II. In the first years of her marriage she stifled her feelings of independence and *in extremis* took refuge in her "Griselda moods." She did her best to conceal them. Only those who knew her well saw the tightening of the mouth and sensed the meaning of the withdrawal. Mama was superb at not taking notice of the disagreeable. Her son, who long ago had learned the ways of his mother and usually could work his will with her, sympathized with Eleanor, but he preferred to avoid direct confrontation.

Two traits warred in her breast—the desire to run her own household and the desire to be accepted by Mama and Franklin. In pursuit of the latter she even allowed Mama to feel that the grandchildren were hers, not Eleanor's. Unable to prevent the marriage between Franklin and herself, Eleanor wrote in the 1930s in an article she did not publish, "she determined to bend the marriage to the way she wanted it to be. What she wanted was to hold onto Franklin and his children; she wanted them to grow as she wished. As it turned out, Franklin's children were more my mother-in-law's children than they were mine." She was unable, she did not wish, to rebel. There was another reason. Her own sense of personal inadequacy. "I was certainly not an ideal mother," she later explained. "It did not come naturally to me to understand little children or to enjoy them. Playing with children was difficult for me because play had not been an important part of my own childhood."

In bringing up her children, especially the older ones, she was the conventional society matron. Was it her nature or the way that she had been trained and taught? Later she realized her shortcomings as a mother and tried to remedy them in regard to her youngest children, Franklin, Jr., born 1914, and John the last, born in 1916. To young Corinne she seemed only partially successful. "Again she answered the call of duty," thought the young Corinne about Eleanor's relationship with her growing brood, "but I never felt that she truly enjoyed her young family."

Questions of nature and/or convention arose also in respect to the young Eleanor's zeal, or lack of it, for sports and dancing. Society smiled on such diversions, but she felt herself ungainly, inadequate and allowed herself too easily to prefer a book to the hockey field. Intellectual interests had been one of her links with Souvestre. After a rough game of hockey in the wind, an exultant Corinne reported from Allenswood: "Mlle. S. on our entering said that she could not understand how girls could make such sights of themselves for a game of hockey. She hates sports of any kind you know."

At Allenswood, Eleanor played hockey and danced with earnestness but without young Corinne's zest. In the early years of her marriage she tried to play golf, one of Franklin's passions, and to overcome her fear of water in order to sail and fish with him. She joined him on the tennis court and at bridge, and by 1908 she had made one of the first of many efforts, including a collision, to learn to drive. All came to little because of her own hesitancies and because it seemed to her that Franklin too quickly accepted her reasons for not going on. "I was shy and plain," wrote young Corinne, by contrast, "but I played games easily and well, and seemed to have at least some mysterious charm" for boys, and by 1912, when women were scarcely able to crank the motor, she was driving a Model T Ford.

Young Eleanor accepted the male attitude that men were the doers, but she resented it. That became clear in the Thirties when as an independent woman she built a swimming pool in which she swam and "dived," owned a car and drove it, played deck tennis daily, enjoyed being asked to dance. As she told Emma Bugbee of the New York *Herald Tribune* in 1935, when she took Emma sailing at Campobello, "I never get a chance to sail the boat myself. There are always so many men around. . . . One has always to let the man do the sailing."

She had been discouraged too easily, and deep down she yearned for more strenuous challenges. The description that her friends most often used about her at the time was that she was "sweet." She specialized in picnics, in making comfortable the guests who visited them, in provisioning the *Half Moon*, a sixty-foot auxiliary schooner, for jaunts to Bar Harbor in Maine or St. Andrews in New Brunswick. She made a home for Hall, especially during summers. He often accompanied Franklin on hunting and sailing expeditions. He was tall, robust, brilliant. He had been made senior prefect at Groton. She enjoyed his company and abetted his romances, spoke of him as son as well as brother. She was a considerate hostess, whether the guest was a friend of Hall, Cousin Susie, Aunt Maude, or Franklin's classmates Livingston Davis, Owen Wister, and their wives.

She and Franklin loved one another and that was what counted. "Dearest Babbie," he wrote out of the loneliness of separation in 1908, "I really miss you more than I can say and it is going to seem a very long time . . . Love to Mama." And when he was at Hyde Park with Mama and Eleanor was at Campobello, his mother's presence did not console him for Eleanor's absence: "I can't tell you how I miss you and Mama does not in the least make up." She expressed herself similarly: "I miss you dreadfully and feel very lonely, but please don't think it is because I am alone, having other people wouldn't do any good for I just want you!"

She loved Franklin. At the back of her mind was the unbudgeable notion that those women were happiest who were able to sink their fates into those of their husbands. That glowing faith in the mutual attraction, the love, that ideally came before motherhood and housewifery had been best stated in President Theodore's congratulations to young Franklin on the announcement of his engagement to Eleanor:

> No other success in life—not the Presidency, or anything else—begins to compare with the happiness and joy that comes in and from the love of the true man and the true woman, the love which never sinks lover and sweetheart in man and wife.

How much of a part Eleanor played in Franklin's memorable decision to run for the State Senate from Dutchess County is uncertain. Unlike the other young Roosevelt kinsfolk who made their beginnings in Republican politics that year, Franklin became a Democratic candidate. His own family tradition as well as temperament and ambition were at work. Whatever the roots of that decision, Franklin's victory transformed her life as well as his. "We are thinking of your move to Albany," Isabella Ferguson wrote her understandingly from New Mexico. Their rental of a house in Albany and Franklin's moving his family there for part of the year were less a measure of his affluence than a sign of their decision to get out from under Mama. While Mama would be a welcome visitor, she no longer was a constant presence. Mama came to see them installed in their Albany house and then returned to

Hyde Park. Eleanor was on her own and she loved it. Emotionally she was beginning to stand up to Mama.

There was another broadening aspect to the Albany experience. Franklin's fight to keep Blue-Eyed "Billy" Sheehan, Tammany's designee as senator, from nomination by the Democratic caucus was conducted from the Roosevelt living room. The nightly meetings were held there and Eleanor became good friends with some of the legislators. She had always been politically interested—it would have been difficult for an intelligent niece of T.R. to desregard politics—and her responsibilities as a hostess in Albany were a welcome political chore.

She was a very proper, almost prissy young society matron. But there is nothing like politics to shake class insularity. Some of the men in the anti-Sheehan caucus interested her. Her tolerance grew. She did not at first take to the New York *Herald's* upstate correspondent Louis Howe, who with his vest speckled with cigarette ashes and his skin-and-bones face was not an easy man to embrace. But she did begin to work with him after he joined Franklin's staff, and almost grudgingly to benefit from his analysis of political trends.

As Eleanor moved her family to Albany and through her husband began to move into politics, so some fifty miles east in Avon, Connecticut, her cousin Corinne, two years her junior, was making her start on a family of her own and, through her husband, taking an interest in Republican politics. Corinne had relished her debutante year and the years of dinners, dances, and weekends on the tennis courts that followed. There was, however, some self-doubt and self-reproach. On New Year's Day, 1905, she had resolved: "No. I. That the tiny things in society are going to mean very little to me. No. II. To put down self. No. III. Not to enter the competition one finds everywhere." She would enjoy Society but not be tied to it. Her schooling had been limited to the Roser Classes in New York and a year at Allenswood, but at the White House with Uncle Ted and Aunt Edith she felt it was "nice to be down here where each man is interested in a new thing—not all in the game of money . . ." She declined to get married simply to learn unselfishness or because it was "a real life to lead." But then her future came along in the shape of Joseph Alsop of an old New England family. He was ten years Corinne's senior, had attended Groton, Yale, and a German university. Like "Fergie" he had been one of Auntie Bye's faithful "Joe-Bobs." He had a "deep love of the land," "looked distinguished even covered with fertilizer," and was "a man through and through."

Corinne's destiny, like Eleanor's, was determined by the man she married. In her first three years in Avon "I learnt to be alone." She was either having a baby, she wrote of those years, or nursing a baby. She missed the companionship of women:

> It is what I miss here for Joe is essentially a man—a very masculine man—and I miss the times when one talks of people and things and abstract questions, for though one knows they are futile, one gets nowhere by talking of them, they are delightful (?) and there are not many men who have sympathy and enjoyment in these times.
>
> . . . .
>
> Yes women here are the only things I miss and I do not suppose they will be a thing I shall ever find here and I shall have to make up my mind not to wish to express unnecessary thoughts. And yet a life with only facts expressed seems rather cut & dried and then also Joe loves me to express the unnecessary but if there is no give and take in that direction it is difficult to continue. I hope I shan't forget how to bubble! I know it will be a mistake. . . .

Joe was elected to the State Legislature by the Republicans, but then in 1912 he and Corinne, as followers of Uncle Ted, attended the Progressive Party convention in Chicago that nominated him as head of its ticket. "We were in an exciting, religious but not very practical fervor," recalled Corinne. Joe organized the Progressive Party in Connecticut, just as Bob and Isabella were doing in the Southwest. "It eliminated Joe as a potential force in the Republican Party," Corinne realized, and it took years for them to re-establish themselves with the Party and then Corinne, as the women gained the vote, was the one elected town chairman and later to the State Legislature.

Uncle Ted's 1912 campaign had a devastating effect on his daughter Alice's relationship to her husband and to her understanding of politics. Alice had also been one of Eleanor's bridesmaids. She was eight months older than Eleanor and was as aggressive and restless as Eleanor was gentle and enduring. Her mother had died at childbirth. For three years she had been raised by Auntie Bye, whom she adored second only to her father. Auntie Bye had wanted to continue as Alice's surrogate mother, but Edith wanted her as part of her family, in part to diminish the influence of Bye and Corinne over Theodore. Edith was a firm taskmistress, a woman in the mold of Sara Roosevelt and Susie Parish. She loved her stepchild, but the latter was conscious that neither father nor stepmother ever spoke the name of her mother to her, and Edith wrote in her diary of Alice's amazement "that I was not papa's sister."

Alice had a quick mind, read widely, never forgetting what she had read, was witty and entertaining, and played far better than Eleanor at all sports. "While I always admired her, I always was afraid of her," Eleanor confessed.

Alice had neither intellectual training nor discipline. Her politics were those of her father, insofar as she understood them, and soon after T.R. became President, the country named her "Princess Alice." Some in the family felt that the White House spoiled her. Mrs. Robinson was worried, as she wrote her daughter:

> . . . Alice is dear but I deplore the change in her. She cannot be interested in anything unless it happens to excite her and she is terribly bored unless she is the center of everything. Poor child it is the natural result of her unfortunate position.
>
> She is always madly gay, or bored to death, & wishes to be *outre* in every way. Her father had to forbid her wearing a live snake on her arm, that kind of thing!
>
> She is always sweet to me; & I do not mean to be disloyal to her but I am so sorry to see the kind of attitude she has toward every thing. . . .

Young Corinne on her return from Allenswood found Alice a world away from Eleanor. She did not directly compare the two, but her diary entries speak for themselves. "Eleanor and I again intellectual reading Materlinck & having violent discussions," she wrote of Eleanor's visit seven months before she and Franklin were married. ". . . [W]hat fun it was," she said of their marriage. "Eleanor looked perfectly charming and was so sweet with every body. I do hope they will be very happy for if any one deserves it it is Eleanor." There was a colder, harsher judgment of Alice when Corinne saw her in Washington:

> Alice and I went out to Bennings in the afternoon and going & coming I had a very frank talk with her. She was perfectly furious with Uncle Ted as before lunch he had forbidden her betting which sent her in a rage of revenge. She certainly is absolutely selfish never thinking of any one but herself and her own pleasure but I liked her about fifty times better than ever before. I felt oh so sorry for her for though she seems to have a life absolutely free from what is generally considered unhappiness and a life certainly full of the greatest advantages, I think I would rather be any one on this earth than the person Alice is—craving always for unnatural excitement & eccentric in many ways—Power, notoriety & money are the things Alice really wishes for & she cares nothing about any of the greater things. I only hope it will be possible for her to change, for there is something fine I hope underneath all the superficialities. She cares however for no one in a real way and without the power of loving I am afraid it will be difficult to soften her.

Alice had the egotism, combativeness, and showmanship of her father. But she was a woman and although tutored by Auntie Bye she had not learned how to subdue her defiance and aggressiveness. She never learned the art of ruling men by deferring to them. "I wish she had some serious taste," her father wrote to young Ted. "Perhaps she will develop one later." She never did. It was not a matter of schooling, although some semesters with Mlle. Souvestre might have helped. Defiance was in her. She had never forgiven her father, although she adored him, nor her stepmother, for their silence about her dead mother, and she signed herself "Alice Lee Roosevelt" to make unmistakable her relationship to the Lees.

In Alice's diary, which belongs to her granddaughter, and which has yet to be published, there is an entry that helps explain her posture of cynicism tipped with malice:

> Father doesn't care for me, that is to say one eighth as much as he does for the other children. It is perfectly true that he doesn't, and Lord, why *should* he. We are not in the least congenial, and if I don't care overmuch for him and don't take an interest in the things he likes, why should he pay any attention to me or the things I live for, except to look on them with disapproval.

"Bah" was Alice's reaction to Eleanor's stern sense of obligation, to her acknowledgment of rules and morality that sometimes shaded into primness. Eleanor's prudery was not unlike T.R.'s self-reproaches for remarrying two years after the death of Alice's mother. When Eleanor was secretly engaged to Franklin, in other words after she had abandoned thoughts of a career and committed herself to his love, she spotted Alice one day in New York, and, she wrote Franklin, "looking well but crazier than ever. I saw her this morning in Bobbie Goelet's auto quite alone with three other men! I wonder how you would like my tearing around like that. I'm seriously thinking of taking it up, it seems to be the fashion nowadays."

Alice was brilliant. Men, as well as the press, pursued her, but, as young Corinne noted, she lacked the power of loving. In 1906 she married Nicholas Longworth, a second-term congressman from Cincinnati. He had breeding, charm, and money, had been selected by Porcellian at Harvard, and was an accomplished violinist, "the best," T.R. wrote to King Edward, that ever came from Harvard. He was fifteen years older than Alice and, although he had a shiny bald head, was a *bon vivant*, a good poker player, and a hard drinker, he had "worked his way along in politics," T.R.'s letter to King Edward went on, "and has shown that he has good stuff in him and I hope he can continue. I believe that my daughter will be of some assistance to him for she gets along well with politicians, is interested in public matters, and showed to real advantage under trying conditions when she visited the Philippines, Japan and China this summer. . . . But whether Longworth will be able to go in politics, neither I nor anyone else can say."

If T.R. hoped that Nick would be able to turn his daughter to domesticity, to motherhood and homemaking, he was disappointed. Who and what were responsible are not yet clear. Perhaps the papers she left to her granddaughter will shed light on what happened. In 1908, T.R. announced his decision not to seek another term and supported William Taft as his successor. Alice regretted that and subsequently, when her father turned on Taft, she enthusiastically supported his decision to contest the presidency, even though it subjected her husband, a fellow Ohioan and faithful Taft supporter, to intense strain. Longworth did his best to remain loyal to his father-in-law and wife and to Taft, a straddle that T.R. understood and accepted, but that became almost impossible after T.R. accepted the nomination of the Progressives. "Poor Alice is here," Theodore wrote Ethel, his other daughter. "It is horrid for her; she would feel better if Nick were strong for Taft."

After Alice left the GOP convention in Chicago that renominated Taft in 1912, she returned to Washington and went on to Baltimore, where the Democrats were deadlocked between Senator Champ Clark, the candidate of the conservatives, and Woodrow Wilson. Eleanor had accompanied Franklin to Baltimore. He was chairman of the New York State Wilson Conference. She had lunched with Uncle Ted and Auntie Bye in March. Almost all her friends supported T.R.'s third party candidacy. But she did not demur from Franklin's support as a Democrat of Wilson. Alice looked bad, Eleanor thought; almost all of T.R.'s supporters who turned up at Baltimore seemed to her "restless and unhappy." "Pops been praying for Clark," T.R.'s son told Franklin. Whatever Eleanor's private sympathies for Uncle Ted, she stood at her husband's side. "If we are not going to find remedies in Progressivism then I feel sure the next step will be Socialism," she wrote her Aunt Maude. That point of view enabled her to support either Uncle Ted or Wilson, but Franklin was a Democrat and she was a supportive wife. Women, moreover, did not vote; she did not even favor woman suffrage, and was content to accept Franklin's leadership.

Wilson was chosen on the forty-eighth ballot. "Splendid triumph," Franklin telegraphed Eleanor, who had decided to leave the convention and take her children to Campobello. In August the Bull Moosers met in Chicago and nominated Theodore. Alice wanted desperately to go, but said she would agree to whatever her father and husband decided. They decided it was best she stay away. Any appearance by Alice at the Bull Moose convention might defeat Nick. They were apologetic and Alice began to cry. "It was a bitter disappointment," she confided to Auntie Bye. It was a wrenching campaign. Except for Alice, the Longworth ladies—his mother and sisters—were for Taft. Nick kept silent but lost anyway by ninety-seven votes. Wilson won, T.R. came in second. Nick was out of Congress for a term. They closed up their house and settled in Cincinnati. Alice applied herself to the appreciation of chamber music and to making a friend of Nick's mother. The latter was "an amazing old female," "outrageous about Father," and sometimes Alice thought of turning suffragette "just to spite her."

When she and Nick returned to Washington in 1914, they found Eleanor and Franklin there, the latter serving as Assistant Secretary of the Navy and the family living in Auntie Bye's N Street house.

Eleanor's progress as a household manager and serious Washington hostess is recorded in her letters to Auntie Bye beginning with one a few days after Wilson's inauguration:

> You probably saw in the papers that Franklin has been appointed Ass. Sec. of the Navy. Of course he is delighted as it is the thing of all things he's most interested in.
>
> Now, I have to write & bother you for all kinds of advice & information. We don't want to take a house until the autumn & we thought at once of yours if it isn't taken . . .
>
> Will you tell me if there are any people I ought to call on at once for I don't know a soul in Washington & I am afraid of all kinds of stupid mistakes. There are lots of other things I want to talk about but they can wait until you are here.

Six weeks later she had taken on the chore of calling with vengeance, a virtue that Alice had promptly defied, calling it a form of insanity.

> Dearest Auntie Bye
>
> This is just a line to tell you that I feel more grateful to you every day for all you have done for us here. We had such a nice dinner last night at Mr. Biddle's & they were so sweet to me, all for love of you. . . .
>
> I'm trying to keep up with my calls but it is quite strenuous. I've done all the Cabinet, Pres. & V. Pres., justices, speaker, N.Y. Senators & some others, also some Congressmen. All embassies, counsellors, naval attachés & there are only a few less important ministers & the military attachés left. Besides I've paid dozens of calls on people who've called on me! When I come to you I'm going to bring my book & try to find out something about the people who haven't been at home & are just names to me!

After the beginning of world war, T.R. turned from momentary support of Wilson to fierce criticism of what he called his "spiritless neutrality." Alice agreed with him. "I was panting after my parent," she said afterwards, "longing to get into the First World War." Eleanor was ardently pro-Allied, but busy primarily with her children—Alice still childless—and her calls and other duties as an Assistant Secretary's wife. Pacifist stirrings were subordinated to loyalty to her husband. When Secretary of State William Jennings Bryan recast some old swords into plowshare-shaped paperweights, she used one, but subsequently agreed with her husband's militant criticism of Bryan as well as of his chief, Secretary Josephus Daniels.

She saw Alice from time to time but did not know that Alice was doing her best to encourage romance between Franklin and Lucy Mercer, Eleanor's social secretary.

V

Turning Point

E TALKED about it a little last night," she wrote to this writer in 1943, one of the rare times she spoke about the Lucy Mercer episode,

and suddenly it struck me what I went through the year I was Trude's age. There was a war then too & the bottom dropped out of my own particular world & I faced myself, my surroundings, my world, honestly for the first time. I really grew up that year, & I've been trying to think what I could drag up out of it all that might help you & Trude. I guess the most important thing I learned was that you can live thro' anything & when things are deep & true they last through anything. . . .

Earlier she had written to Trude, who later became my wife, from Campobello about that turning point in her life:

Ever since our talk at lunch on Friday, I have wished that I could help you for you are struggling with a feeling that you are responsible for unhappiness which you have brought to others. I do not think you are, for background, bringing up, circumstances shape us when we are young. Somewhere along the line of development we discover what we really are & then we make our real decision for which we are responsible. Make that decision primarily for yourself because you can never really live anyone else's life not even your child's. The influence you exert is through your own life & what you become yourself. No matter what you decide to do you may be a fine person but perhaps not as happy a person. There was a time when I thought happiness didn't matter but I think differently today.

I am no more given than you to burdening others with personal biography or ideas, but if out of a long life any experience of mine could
help you, I'd gladly tell you why I believe as I do to-day.

The ordeal she was talking about was the Lucy Mercer episode.
When she first began to talk with Lorena Hickok at the end of 1932,
she put it differently. Hickok then was a reporter for the Associated
Press and was assigned to cover her. "The war," she said, "was my
emancipation and education." Her elaboration of that remark was a
partial explanation, true as far as it went:

Then we went into the war. Instead of making calls, I found myself
spending three days a week in a canteen down at the railroad yards,
one afternoon a week distributing free work for the Navy League, two
days a week visiting the naval hospital, and contributing whatever time
I had left to the Navy Red Cross and the Navy Relief Society.
    I loved it. I simply ate it up. When Franklin went over on the de-
stroyer in 1918 I sent the children to their grandmother in Hyde Park,
and spent the summer in Washington, living alone in the house with
one servant and going every day to the canteen.

By 1918 she was deeply involved in war work. Long days at the
Union Station canteen in Washington, an enterprise that was staffed
by Washington ladies of good breeding, alternated with the supervision
of knitting woollies for the Navy. She steeled herself to make her first
speech. With America's entry into the war, as her cousin Alice phrased
it, Eleanor had gone "public." She even tried, unsuccessfully, to get
Alice, whom she and Franklin saw from time to time, to join the
women at the canteen. Both women were thirty-four, Alice was still
childless; Eleanor was the mother of five of whom John, the youngest,
was two.

Eleanor was the "dynamo" behind the canteen service, presided over
Navy Department rallies, was tempted to go abroad for the Red Cross,
the "real thing," as she put it, managed her household, served as wife,
mother, daughter-in-law, but she still spoke the language of male su-
premacy, and "did not believe in knowing things which your husband
did not wish you to know." It took the shattering discovery of her husband's affair with Lucy Mercer to change this attitude.

She had begun to suspect the nature of the relationship between
Franklin and her lovely social secretary, the well-born but impoverished
Lucy, the summer before (1917) when her letters showed that she
resented being bundled off with the children to Campobello. Franklin
rarely referred to family disagreements in his letters to his wife. One of
the few relates to her reluctant departure for Campobello in 1917. Like
countless cocky husbands before and after, he derides her fears that she

was being bundled off to be out of his way. "A goosy girl," he called her, and bespoke his envy of her chance to have a solid six weeks at Campo while he toiled in Washington's heat and humidity. But a few weeks later, when he came down with a throat infection, she bolted to Washington, however torrid its summer, to nurse him and after two weeks left with the stern warning that she expected to see him in Campo on the twenty-sixth. "My threat was no idle one," her farewell note warned.

Her language was vigorous, whatever her threat may have been. It reflected fears and suspicions, however, not certainties. In 1918 Franklin went to Europe on a naval inspection tour. His almost daily letters to Eleanor were in effect a journal that he hoped with her help to convert into a book. She wrote to him with equal regularity. He returned in September, having come down, on his way home, with double pneumonia. Alerted by the Navy Department, she brought an ambulance to the pier to which he was carried on a stretcher. She took care of him and in going through his things came upon Lucy's letters. Fears confirmed turned into despair that crushed.

She had built her life around her family and Franklin was its hub. With the coming of the war she had added, to management of the household, entertainment of the Allied missions that descended upon Washington and other war duties. The war, she later wrote, had awakened her long dormant executive abilities. Or as Isabella in her impetuous, accented way stated it at the time, "You doubtless dashing to give some canteen soup to soldiers—or wool to knitters—with every moment mapped for the next six months."

She welcomed work. It satisfied her need to be of use. She was happiest when she had a job to do, "the willing work horse," Mama's sister described her. She played her part in wartime Washington as ably as she had at Allenswood, and as at the school, so at the canteen and in the Navy auxiliaries her co-workers had come to depend upon her. Any tendency to suspect what might be going on between her husband and Lucy she kept to herself. She had continued to invite her to dinner parties when she needed an extra woman. But Lucy's letters made it impossible to ignore the situation. Also, according to her son James, "there came to light during this time a register from a motel in Virginia Beach showing that father and Lucy had checked in as man and wife and spent the night."

The romance was no surprise to some of Eleanor's and Franklin's friends. Alice had encouraged it. In 1917 he was thirty-five, Lucy ten years younger. He was patrician, gay, and despite narrow, sloping shoulders and an austere pince-nez was considered one of Washington's handsomest men. It was conventional, said Alice, for politicians in the summertime to bundle their families off to the mountains or seashore,

and for the "paterfamilias to accumulate something attractive." Alice
spotted Franklin motoring with Lucy. She telephoned him afterwards:
"I saw you twenty miles out in the country," she teased. "You didn't
see me. Your hands were on the wheel, but your eyes were on that perfectly lovely lady."

Alice and Franklin were both fun-loving and his reply was in the
spirit of the occasion: "Isn't she perfectly lovely," he answered. Alice
had the "lovely lady" to dinner along with Franklin. Booth Tarkington
was another guest. As Alice put it on the CBS show "60 Minutes," she
was "delighted to see him [Franklin] having a good time. He deserved
a good time. He was married to Eleanor." Eleanor was hurt, but in
Alice's view "partly to blame for being overly noble. . . . The Lucy
Mercer affair was a great blow to her."

There are several accounts of the romance and its effect upon
Eleanor. Alice's was one. She knew of Franklin's attachment to Lucy
from her own knowledge. Another part she learned from Mrs. Douglas
Robinson, her Auntie Corinne, who had stood by Eleanor's father even
in his final dissipated days. Corinne and Elliott had inherited more of
their mother's, Mittie Bulloch's, Southern softness and wit than had
Theodore and Bye.

"Never forget," Auntie Corinne told Alice, "Eleanor offered Franklin
his freedom."

"Darling Aunt," retorted Alice, "that's what I always wanted to
know." Auntie Corinne told her there had been "much conferring.
Eleanor said, 'Very well, I will give Franklin a divorce.'" But after a
family conference they "finally decided it affected the children and
there was Lucy Mercer, a Catholic, and so it was called off." And Alice
added, and whether she had heard this from Mrs. Robinson or elsewhere is unclear: "Cousin Sallie [Sara Delano Roosevelt] made too
much of it. It was she who came to Eleanor and wanted to know what
she was going to do about Franklin and Lucy."

Mrs. Robinson's daughter Corinne, cousin both of Eleanor and Alice,
said she had heard the story from Cousin Susie and gave her account of
it in her unpublished memoir. When told that Alice had Franklin and
Lucy to dinner while Eleanor was away from Washington, she called
Alice a "minx" who undoubtedly enjoyed Franklin's sense of humor
and would have considered it great fun to invite him together with
Lucy.

The affair should not be interpreted "as something scandalous," wrote
Corinne Alsop in her memoir. Franklin married "when he was young
and immature, and had led a life sheltered by 'Mama.' Rochefoucauld
has said 'il y a plein de bons mariages mais point de délicieux.'* Eleanor

* The original quotation read: "*Il y a de bons mariages, mais il n'y en a point de
délicieux.*"

and Franklin were both intelligent, they produced many children and on the whole it was a good marriage, but in my opinion it lacked the 'délicieux.'" With Lucy Mercer "lightning struck, but there was no scandal. Everybody behaved well and exactly as one would expect each of the protagonists in the drama to behave. From what I could gather at the time Lucy Mercer, a Catholic, could not make up her mind to destroy the family and she would not marry a divorced man. Eleanor was tolerant, understanding, troubled, but very kind, and was willing to give Franklin his freedom. Mama was regal, autocratic, and adamant. She refused to give a penny if he got a divorce. . . ."

The romance in Corinne Alsop's view had a "profound effect on Franklin. It is difficult to describe, but to me it seemed to release something in him." He seemed to gain a passion and commitment that were usually lacking. Although Franklin was handsome and debonair, he seemed to her, like his mother, "loveless. . . . Up to the time that Lucy Mercer came into Franklin's life he seemed to look at human relationships coolly, calmly, and without depth. He viewed his family dispassionately, and enjoyed them, but he had in my opinion a loveless quality as if he were incapable of emotion."

Corinne and Joe Alsop were political opponents of Eleanor and Franklin, but they tried to remain on good terms personally. That was easy with Eleanor, she wrote, but even with Franklin, Corinne was always on "a humorous, bantering, teasing basis of friendship." They treasured a fund of "funny memories," but she would never vote for him, because, as she said to him once when he taxed her with that failure, "How could I vote for a man without convictions and not capable of loving anything except the United States Navy and our great big beautiful country."

Alice and Corinne were partisans, dyed-in-the-wool Republicans, for whom Theodore Roosevelt was "the President," Franklin D. Roosevelt, a "Miss Nancy." Their testimony on the bare bones of the Lucy Mercer episode is important especially as the principals spoke of it, if at all, only with reticence. None of Eleanor's and Franklin's sons ever heard the story from the parents. However, because Alice and Corinne were partisans, their evaluations, their analyses of motivations, were less compelling. Franklin Roosevelt had a seriousness of purpose, a steadiness of commitment, a capacity for patience, especially after his siege with polio, that they never were able to acknowledge. Eleanor successfully concealed from them her deepest emotions, including anger and jealousy, as well as her sense of mortification over her failure as a woman. Work, sweetness, consideration for others were the ways she met the world, but other passions stirred deep down. "I have the memory of an elephant," she later said to intimates. "I can forgive but never forget."

Her attitude towards Mama and Cousin Susie and their values began to change. At first she turned to Mama instinctively, although silently, for protection. When Franklin sent from Europe his long letters about his activities, including a reception at Buckingham Palace, Eleanor begged him to include endearments for Mama, since she read her his letters. Please, she implored, "when you don't write Mama, send messages to her otherwise I have to invent and that is painful! . . . I hate not being with you and seeing it all. Isn't that horrid of me!" It was the summer of 1918. She spent part of it at Hyde Park. Earlier she had written Mama almost daily from Washington. Those letters were as full of regard as her honeymoon letters had been. "Much love always dearest Mummy," she wrote at beginning of the year. ". . . Very few mothers I know mean as much to their daughters as you do to me." And a few weeks later her words almost hymned with love: "I wish you were always here. There are so many things I want to talk over and ask you about and letters are not very satisfactory are they?" A storm threatened and she turned to the older woman for protection.

In the silent storms of the Lucy Mercer affair, Eleanor had been alone, unable because of inner scruples and restraints to turn to anyone. Mama had been a support of sorts, Louis Howe, who had moved his family to Washington and worked as Franklin's assistant on the Navy payroll, would soon become a confidant, but outside of a few people in her immediate family there had been no one in whom she confided, and, as far as Mama and Cousin Susie were concerned, it was part of the crisis that she was breaking free from them.

It is difficult to say what her domestic arrangements were with her husband before this episode. Her son Elliott, who in 1918 was age eight, whom she had named after her father, and towards whom she was always partial, at least until the final years of her life paints his mother in those years as a Mrs. Grundy, straitlaced and squeamish. He asserts that after the birth of John in March 1916, she decided that she had had enough of child-bearing and, since she knew of no other way to ward off pregnancy, his parents stopped living together as man and wife. Elliott's implication is that this birth control by abstinence explains his father's turning elsewhere. It seems unlikely his parents did not know there were other ways besides abstinence to avoid pregnancy. In any case after her discovery two years later of the Lucy Mercer affair, she no longer shared a marriage bed with him. The solemnity of her decision, the inexorable will with which she carried it out, show the absoluteness with which she invested the vows of marriage and the mastery of self that enabled her to live according to her code of what is right. One is struck by the words of James Roosevelt writing about his parents' agreement to continue as man and wife.

After that father and mother had an armed truce that endured to the day he died, despite several occasions I was to observe in which he

in one way or another held out his arms to mother and she flatly refused to enter his embrace. There was always an affection between
them. . . .

As part of the new arrangement he agreed not to see Lucy again. Perhaps Eleanor was unrealistic, as her sister-in-law, Margaret, then married
to Hall, wryly maintained. But she took it seriously. Could a woman do
otherwise and maintain her self-respect? Eleanor's Uncle Ted had
bluntly advised her mother not to have anything to do with her father
unless he broke off with his mistress. She had similar puritanical standards. "Men make these promises," Margaret (then Mrs. Cutter) commented in 1967, "but I think they are very seldom kept." However,
Eleanor "would not stay where she wasn't wanted." But she must have
realized that continence was scarcely the way Franklin, not yet forty,
would end his sexual life. Eleanor often had teased him about his flirta-
tiousness and gaiety, and their closest friends emphasized her forbearance and tolerance in this respect. But the romance with Lucy clearly
bespoke her own inadequacy, as she saw it, as a sexual partner—at least
to him. She began to school herself in the toughest discipline of all—to
accept his getting elsewhere the satisfaction, adulation, companionship,
and sexual stimulation he was unable to get from her.

The marriage continued. She remained the manager of the household, the mother of five children, the thoughtful and affectionate
spouse of a highly regarded Wilson Administration official. As a letter
that she wrote to Auntie Bye on a "United States Ship George Washington" letterhead showed, even more than Franklin she was the pivot
of a busy family life. She had accompanied him on the journey that
took President Wilson to the Paris Peace Conference, and wrote afterwards:

You have been very constantly in my thought ever since we heard of
Uncle Ted's death for I knew what a shock & sorrow it would be to
you. We just missed seeing Aunt Edith to our great regret as we left
Paris the evening she was due to arrive. We did however see Ted &
Kermit & Belle & Munro during our first five days in Paris. Sheffield
could not get up that time so on our return Franklin ordered him up as
his aide & by now you know that he is home. I hope that you & Uncle
Will will be glad for aside from our own pleasure in having him it did
seem the best for him as long as he did not want to stay in the service.
He was doing nothing at Rochefort & Paris is no place for any of our
boys & if he is returning to college, this year may be of great value to
him. It is the first time in a good many years that we've seen much of
Sheffield & every minute with him is a pleasure. We both think he is
the very nicest young man we know & we expect great things from him.
He's fine all through with an amount of character which I only hope
my own boys will have too some day. You must be very proud both

you & Uncle Will if you could hear him talk about you I know you would be very happy.

We've had an interesting trip & Franklin thinks he succeeded very well with his demobilization of all possible stations in Europe, settling of claims etc. He says now he expects to go into business this summer for a time so we may be in New York next year & there may be a little more time which we can call our own in which case I hope we are going to see a little more of you dearest Auntie Bye.

I do hope you are better & if Auntie Corinne is with you give her our dearest love.

The affectionate shipboard relationship between young Sheffield Cowles and Eleanor and Franklin had an unforeseen consequence. Franklin told Sheffield during one of their shipboard talks that his failure to make Porcellian at Harvard had been "the greatest disappointment in his life. That made a great impression on me," added Sheffield. "I thought he was quite successful. After all, as Assistant Secretary of the Navy he rated a 19-gun salute."

It would become settled doctrine with the Oyster Bay Roosevelts that in the 1933 crisis F.D.R. was particularly hard on Wall Street because of his exclusion from Porcellian. "This was a blow to his pride and a frustration to a very ambitious nature," Corinne wrote. "As Franklin had the proverbial memory of an elephant of anyone that harmed him he always hated members of the Porcellian Club particularly George Whitney, the master mind of J. P. Morgan who not only was a Porcellian but a brilliant financier which Franklin was not." But Eleanor drew a different conclusion and it was evidence of the service of love she continued to render him although she insisted she no longer loved him. Exclusion from Porcellian, like other rebuffs at Harvard, and before that at Groton, which he rarely acknowledged, had widened his sympathies, she said, had helped him to understand what it was not to be part of the in-group.

Evidently after their return from Paris, Franklin thought that for the time being he was finished with politics. He became vice-president of the Fidelity & Deposit Company of Maryland, in charge of the New York office.

Although she was outwardly unruffled, clinging to old landmarks, Eleanor's inner world collapsed. "I do not think I have ever felt so strangely as in the past year," she wrote in her diary at the end of 1919, "perhaps it is that I have never noticed little things before but all my self-confidence is gone & I am on edge though I never was better physically I am sure." She was humiliated, hated herself, was unable to eat, unable even to take Communion, although she was the one who went to church every Sunday. Sometimes she gave way to tears before a party. Life, she thought at the time, was draining away, but her consciousness, she later realized, was being forged anew.

A poem entitled "Psyche," by Virginia Moore, which she clipped out of a newspaper and marked simply "1918," was among her bedside papers when she died. It graphically bespoke her spiritual situation during those years:

The soul that has believed/ And is deceived/ Thinks nothing for a while/ All thoughts are vile.

And then because the sun/ Is mute persuasion,/ And hope in Spring and Fall/ Most natural,

The soul grows calm and mild/ A little child,

Finding the pull of breath/ Better than death . . . The soul that had believed/ And was deceived/ Ends by believing more/ Than ever before.

Franklin's practical arrangements with Fidelity & Deposit to head their New York office fitted in with his political interests. He began touring New York State in the company of the Democratic National Chairman, laying a groundwork to bid either for the senatorship or the governorship. When he went out to San Francisco, the possibility he might be chosen to run for national Vice-President did not figure in his thoughts. As for Eleanor, she would have preferred that he stay out of politics for a while. Her own plans on her return to New York were to learn to cook, to go to business school for shorthand and typing, and to take on only the jobs where there was work to do, not simply to serve on boards.

A letter to Sara said without explanation: "Did you know Lucy Mercer married Mr. Wintie Rutherfurd two days ago?" It was one of the few times in thousands of letters to family and intimates that she mentioned Lucy's name. Winthrop Rutherfurd, well descended, wealthy, a sportsman, had been a widower for three years. He was fifty-seven, Lucy scarcely twenty-five.

There were the world of convention and the world of real feeling. Her letters to Sara continued to be affectionate, but she was moving towards independence. When she left Mama's dominating presence, she confessed to Franklin of "feeling as though someone had taken a ton of bricks off me." The split between convention and reality was again underlined when Franklin wrote her: "It will amuse you as she says everything is going smoothly." She no longer was obsessed with Mama's sense of values, nor with Cousin Susie's. There were stormy sessions with both. After an evening with Sara and her two sisters, she commented to Franklin: "They all in their serene assurance and absolute judgments on people and affairs going on in the world make me want to squirm and turn bolshevik." Grandma Hall had died in 1919. Her life had been hard, Eleanor commented sadly, but it was a sign of her own growing independence that she added Grandma would have been better off had she made herself independent of her children and had remarried. It was Eleanor's lot, when tragedy struck in 1920, to accompany to Tivoli for burial the bodies of her Aunt Pussie and her two little girls, who had been burned to death in their house on Ninth Street. "In all our contacts," she wrote of this period in her life, "it is probably the sense of being really needed which gives us the greatest satisfaction and creates the most lasting bond."

This meaningful observation she buried in the passage in her autobiography that dealt with Pussie's death, but it was to become central in her relationships. She began actively to seek out the people who really needed her.

Among the first was Louis Howe. Her attitude towards him changed dramatically in the course of the 1920 vice-presidential campaign. For Franklin emerged from the San Francisco convention as its nominee for Vice-President. "A world of surprises," she commented dryly. When Louis at the Navy Department sought a picture of her for the press, she telegraphed back there were no pictures of her. Press accounts portrayed the candidate's wife as a "home woman" who disliked the "official limelight. . . . Just how she would endure the Vice-Presidential status . . . remains to be seen." But the Poughkeepsie newspaper in the only interview she granted, after agreeing that she was "first of all a domestic woman," uncovered a personality with forceful political views: "My politics? Oh yes, I am a Democrat, but, (pause) I was brought up a staunch Republican,—and turned Democrat. . . . I am particularly interested in the League of Nations issue. . . . We fought for it, and we should adopt it. If we don't adopt it, it will be useless. . . ."

It was a sign of women's progress that she was much in evidence at the notification ceremonies that took place on the terrace of the Hyde Park house. Reporters noted her presence, a tall, lithe figure, in a plain blue and white dress, who, perched on a balustrade, listened to her husband intently. By contrast in 1900, when her Uncle Ted had been notified at Sagamore, on Oyster Bay, Long Island, of his selection as vice-presidential candidate, there were no women on the platform and his wife Edith and daughter Alice had to stay off the terrace discreetly screened in order to listen.

The Hyde Park notification ceremonies were conducted by a Dutchess County neighbor, Henry Morgenthau, Jr. His father had been an influential and lavish Wilson supporter and Ambassador to Turkey. His son, Henry, seeking to make his own way, purchased a large farm near Fishkill. He was married to Elinor Fatman, dark-eyed, dark-haired. Her mother was a Lehman and she was a Vassar graduate. Mama had had the Morgenthaus for tea and afterwards wrote approvingly to

Eleanor: "Young Morgenthau and his wife called this p.m. . . . we had a pleasant tea. Young Morgenthau was easy and yet modest and serious and intelligent. The wife is very Jewish but appeared very well." All the Roosevelts at the time shared the social anti-Semitism of their class. But the Morgenthaus were exempt, and the more deeply Eleanor got into politics, the more she worked with them, especially Elinor, whose Vassar education she envied and increasingly valued.

Eleanor was a detached if observant participant, writing to Franklin's campaign manager: "Personally, I had wanted Franklin out of government service for a few years at least, so in spite of the honor I really feel rather unselfish when I wish for his success!" Her feelings henceforth would be mixed about his success in politics, wishing for it because he wanted it and because it was good for the country, but quietly making evident to those close to her that she doubted it was best for her. But she definitely wanted for him what he wanted for himself. It is a mistake to minimize the powerful bonds of affection and warmth that continued to flow between the two. "Dearest, dear Honey," she wrote him on August 27, "I am positively hungry for news of you and it seems a long time since your last telegram and they are meagre enough."

Suffrage had been finally enacted and for the first time in 1920 women had the vote nationally. Suffrage leaders hoped that it would be cast for peace. Although in Eleanor's interview with the Poughkeepsie newspaper she asserted she had never been active in politics, and never had campaigned for her husband, he wanted her by his side in the 1920 race. At the end of September both she and Louis Howe joined the campaign train.

Eleanor had kept this "gargoyle" of a man, his countenance rutted, his shabby suit flecked with Sweet Caporal ashes, at arm's length. Now she discovered a man of sensibility. No longer distant allies, they turned into the fastest of friends. She wired ahead to Sara to invite Louis Howe's daughter Mary, who was at Vassar, to come to Hyde Park for the weekend. She had begun to turn co-workers into intimates. Relationships that touched her emotions were the ones that counted. That a person lacked high social standing added zest to the encounter. Corinne Alsop, Eleanor's bridesmaid and cousin, a shrewd observer and vivid writer, described Howe in the unpublished memoir that her family deposited at the Houghton Library at Harvard. He seemed to be a "strange, powerful little gnome . . . a beneficent Svengali with both Eleanor and Franklin. . . ." In an expressive passage she pointed out that "Louis Howe was not only the 'kingmaker' for Franklin, but he was the inspiration for Eleanor to find the substitutes outside of the home which in the end made her a great world figure."

Eleanor's first campaign trek lasted a month, and although characteristically she played down her role, she learned a great deal, as her reports to Sara dutifully informed her. "This is the most killing thing for the candidate I ever knew," was her first observation from Franklin's campaign car, the Westboro. She noted that Franklin had improved as a speaker. "I never will be able to do without four large cups of black coffee again every day," another letter lamented. "I really don't see that I'm of the least use on this trip." Yet she satisfied people's curiosity about the candidate's wife and, also, if all else failed, she was depended upon to restrain his flow of oratory: "It is becoming almost impossible to stop F. now when he begins to speak. 10 minutes is always 20, 30 is always 45 & the evening speeches are now about 2 hours! The men all get out & wave at him in front & when nothing succeeds I yank his coat tails!"

On Election Day, Eleanor and Sara joined Franklin at the Hyde Park polling place to cast their ballots. By then it was clear that Warren Harding would win the presidency handsomely. "We all feel very badly over the result of the elections," Eleanor wrote Franklin commiseratingly a few days later. She herself prepared to embark on a new, more emancipated course. The hopes of suffragist leaders like Carrie Chapman Catt that the newly enfranchised women would cast a peace vote had been disappointed, but in Eleanor's own psychic evolution from complete dependence on her husband and mother-in-law to resolute self-reliance were the makings of a vast revolution that before her death would foretell the end of the dogma of male superiority.

Fifteen years earlier she had committed herself to love of a distant cousin. She would continue to take care of him and his children. But her womanhood was being reshaped. A force of character that had made her a leader at Allenswood, that in the intervening years she had confined to her family and a few friends, emerged onto a wider stage.

In the mythical tale of Amor and Psyche it is the latter's disregard of her invisible and divine lover's injunction to look upon him in the light of day, as her envious sisters had advised her to do, that led to her liberation and redemption from masculine dominance.* The Lucy Mercer affair holds a position in Eleanor's development comparable to Psyche's disobedience of Amor's command. In modern analysis Erik Erickson defines a crisis as "a turning point, a crucial period of heightened vulnerability and heightened potential."

Even without the pain brought on by the discovery of the Lucy Mercer letters, Eleanor's openness to the sufferings of others and her vitality were bound to have shattered the confines of the family because of her wartime work if for no other reason. But through the Lucy

* See *Amor and Psyche*, by Erich Neumann (New York: Bollingen Foundation, 1956).

Mercer affair Franklin had freed her for self-realization. She reenacted
Eurydice's marriage to death:

> Hidden in herself she went. And her being dead
> Fulfilled her even to fullness.
> Full as a fruit with sweetness and with darkness
> Was she with her great death, which was so new
> That for the time she comprehended nothing.
>
> She had attained a new virginity
> And was intangible; her sex had closed
> As a young flower closes towards evening,
> And her pale hands were from the rites of marriage
> So far estranged that even the slim god's
> Endlessly gentle contacts as he led her
> Repelled her as a too great intimacy.*

But death was only on the level of consciousness. She was no longer
submissive, and a new force had been released in herself and in the
world, and in a different way she began to love.

* Rilke, Rainer Maria. *Poems*. Translated from German by J. B. Leishman.
"Orpheus, Eurydice, Hermes" (London, 1934, page 43).

VI

Shared Work

F OR ELEANOR the return to New York was more of a new beginning. She did not act abruptly; for example, she rejoined the "Monday Sewing Class," a group of socially select ladies whose mothers and grandmothers had lunched weekly since 1872. But she was in rebellion against old New York's values and ways of doing things. She avoided boards that wanted her just for her name.

She made her first ventures into politics. She agreed to serve as vice-president of the New York State branch of the League of Women Voters. The League was the successor of the National American Woman Suffrage Association. Its president, Narcissa Vanderlip, a veteran of the suffrage battles, asked her to head the League's legislative work. She agreed but with misgivings, for all this was new to her. Mrs. Vanderlip said she could have the help of Elizabeth Read, a tall, soft-spoken woman and a lawyer. With Esther Everett Lape, educator and publicist, Elizabeth shared a Greenwich Village apartment and with her edited the League's legislative bulletin, *City-State-Nation.*

Franklin encouraged her to work for the League, and when she brought him problems that had come up in her legislative committee enjoyed the role of tutor.

Both political parties had begun to be concerned with the women's vote. Eleanor, the niece of Theodore and the wife of Franklin, knew that politics was where power rested—but in tandem with, not opposition to, the men, as she indicated to Franklin from Cleveland, where she attended the League's second national convention as a Dutchess County delegate.

Elizabeth and Esther, although not essentially political, had been active in the suffrage movement and they, too, enjoyed and appreciated Franklin's coaching. Political loyalty to Franklin and unspoken acceptance of Eleanor's reserve about him personally became a characteristic of the friends she now began to make. They were not told of the Lucy Mercer affair, but she particularly appreciated the friends who sensed the reticences in her relationship to Franklin yet shared her willingness to promote his fortunes.

Her tentative steps into politics in the winter and spring of 1921 were a groping towards independence as well as support of Franklin. The final years in Washington had been ones of anguish and humiliation. Like the fabled phoenix she had been restored from the ashes of degradation. She emerged from that nightmare determined to be and do the things that made life worth living. As she wrote later, "Out of a long experience I have decided that to me lasting friendships and intimate contacts with people mean more than any other things in life." She had long ago concluded that one did not try for happiness, but the self-effacement that came with doing well a job worth doing and making friends of the people involved were a pretty good substitute.

It is a matter of conjecture whether her agreement to continue to share Franklin's life but not his bed might have worked for long were it not for the polio that in the summer of 1921 paralyzed him from the waist down. In any event, when his fever mounted and his limbs turned numb, she nursed him, slept on a cot at the foot of his bed, and single-handedly, or with Louis Howe's help, turned his heavy frame. Most important of all, she supported him against Mama in his decision not to retire to Hyde Park to the life of an invalided squire. "She is one of my heroines," an attending physician told Roosevelt. As for Eleanor, the period after Franklin came out of the hospital became the "most trying winter" in her life.

Her refusal to yield to Sara's efforts to have a crippled Franklin withdraw to Hyde Park always marked in her mind her final liberation from her mother-in-law's domination. Had she yielded to Sara, she later wrote, she would have become "a completely colorless echo of my husband and mother-in-law and torn between them. I might have stayed a weak character forever if I had not found that out."

Either she or Franklin, probably both, decided on their return to New York that Louis should live with them in Manhattan at the East Sixty-fifth Street house. It was left to her to inform a fifteen-year-old Anna that she would have to give up her room to him. Eleanor slept on a cot in one of the boys' rooms, but Anna, not thinking of her mother, was too young to resist Granny's efforts to turn her against Louis and the new arrangement. She went to her mother to demand a switch in rooms, but her mother was firm. Only when Eleanor thought she was not being seen did she give way to depression and sometimes tears. Louis sustained her against surrender to total despair. He alone was able to cope with her moods. She was grateful to him as it was part of her new feeling about herself not to give herself airs. She liked to sit at Louis's feet in a gesture of companionship, although her children, certainly Mama, might take it amiss.

Corinne Alsop came to see them soon after Franklin's return from the hospital. She had telephoned Eleanor to ask if she could. She met Louis Howe:

> I went into the library first. Eleanor, two children and a little man whom she introduced as Mr. Howe were in the room, and I was intrigued immediately. He seemed to be the dominant person in the group. He justly disciplined the rather recalcitrant children and spoke with authority to Eleanor. After a while she asked if he thought I could then go in to see Franklin. After going into the other room he came back to say that Franklin was ready to see me. Louis Howe took me in and stayed with us while Franklin, lying in the bed brave as a lion, talked of the books he was reading and asked about the family.

Eleanor credited Louis with her decision to become active in New York State Democratic affairs, but she had already shown talent in her work with the League of Women Voters. She had impressed her co-workers in the League and it was not simply her name. The vitality, practical sense, the willingness to accept responsibility, including the most menial of jobs, the things that had attracted Mlle. Souvestre, that Isabella Ferguson, herself a dynamo, had sensed and that had won Eleanor a position of leadership among the canteen workers, were moving into wider fields. The desire to act, which was accompanied by the desire to know the details and above all to do what was needed to remedy a situation, now found a broader focus. Her new friends Esther and Elizabeth were impressed at state board meetings of the League with the way she always asked "to know exactly what she could do before the next monthly meeting." Her composure as well as her ability to keep the board's eyes on larger goals inspired all of them. "The rest of us," recalled Esther, herself a model of precise knowledge as well as of completing whatever she undertook, "were inclined to do a good deal of theorizing. She would look puzzled and ask why we didn't do what we had in mind and get it out of the way. As you may imagine, she was given many jobs to do."

As part of the process of getting to know the League, she had made friends of Esther and Elizabeth. She spent one evening a week with them at their Greenwich Village apartment reading French literature, something she had not done since the days of Mlle. Souvestre. They admired her insistence on doing her own work and not trading on her name. She admired their professional competence and general cultivation. Elizabeth was an accomplished lawyer at a time when women were uncommon in that profession, and a scholarly student of international law. Esther was a boyish, pucklike figure with quick, penetrating eyes and dark hair. She had taught English at Swarthmore and Barnard and written numerous articles on women's rights and immigrants. The two women's love of nature and solitude interested Eleanor, as did their philosophy of life, which Esther conveyed with a quotation from Plato —his invocation to Pan, god of the woods and fields:

> Beloved Pan, and all ye other gods that haunt this place, give me beauty in the inward soul; and may the outward + inward man be as one. May I reckon the wise to be wealthy (and) may I have such a quantity of gold as a temperate man and he only can bear and carry.

They were among a number of pairs of women, most of whom lived in the Village, most of them veterans of the suffrage battles. Their fastidious domestic arrangements did not include men and their tenderness towards each other achieved a solicitude few men could attain. Their relationship might best be described by the once-fashionable New England expression "Boston marriage."

These veterans of the suffrage wars played a considerable role in the education of Eleanor Roosevelt. They ran many of the movements that shaped the thinking of the Twenties and kept alive many of the programs that flowered into the New Deal. Another organization that Eleanor joined at the time was the Women's Trade Union League. She had met many of its leaders at the International Congress of Working Women, which had been held in Washington at the end of 1919. Now she pitched into the League's efforts to raise money for a clubhouse. Rose Schneiderman, red-haired, tiny, a fiery orator with a heavy Eastern European accent, had, as a member of Alex Rose's Cap Makers Union, headed suffrage work among women unionists. Now as director of the WTUL, she helped Eleanor find her way among the issues and personalities of the labor movement.

One day in the spring of 1922 a call came from a Nancy Cook, who introduced herself as the executive secretary of the fledgling Women's Division under Harriet May Mills of the state Democratic Party. Would Eleanor speak and make the appeal for funds at a luncheon? Spurred on by Louis and Franklin, she overcame her first impulse to say no and agreed. She arrived at the midtown hotel with a posy of violets which she gave to competent Miss Cook, whom she had not met before. Outwardly calm and self-possessed, inwardly she quaked. When she spoke she thought she had scarcely made herself heard, a self-described shyness that was belied by the successful drive for contributions that was to follow. That was the start of her involvement in

Democratic Party affairs. At the beginning of the summer she invited
Nancy Cook and her lifelong companion, Marion Dickerman, with
whom Nancy shared an apartment in Greenwich Village, to visit her at
Hyde Park. It was the beginning of a friendship that for several years
dominated her life.

Nancy, roughly Eleanor's age, lively, with tight curly hair and brown
eyes that bulged, who could, said Eleanor, "do almost anything" with
hands that were never still, had met, at a Syracuse student board-
inghouse, the tall, quiet-spoken, somewhat solemn Marion, who was
seven years younger and a candidate for an advanced degree in education. They had formed what also can be described as a "Boston marriage." Together they had campaigned actively for votes for women,
fought for the abolition of child labor and better minimum standards
for workingwomen, and against war. They had taught at the same
school in upstate New York, Marion history, Nancy arts and crafts, but
with America's entry into the World War, despite their pacifism, had
gone overseas as nursing orderlies. They had worked in a London hospital and returned home in 1919 just in time for Marion, at the request of
women's groups, to run against the Assembly Speaker, a reactionary Republican who had blocked all progressive legislation in the state. The
first woman to run for the New York legislature, she ran better than expected and finished her opponent's chances for higher office.

Nancy was her campaign manager and, finding politics exciting,
abandoned teaching to go to work for Harriet May Mills while Marion
served as dean at a normal school in New Jersey. That summer they
journeyed up the Hudson to visit Mrs. Gordon Norrie, a political cru-
sader whose Hudson River estate was in Staatsburgh just north of Hyde
Park. "Eleanor Roosevelt is expecting you," she told them.

Eleanor's youngest boys, John six and Franklin eight, were with her
when they reached Hyde Park. Although Franklin was absent, the conversation revolved around him. He had issued a letter to former Governor Alfred E. Smith asking him to run again, and Smith had just
replied in a "Dear Frank" letter agreeing and a big reception at Hyde
Park was being planned for him.* Eleanor had indicated that Franklin
was unable to campaign as yet, but she was ready to work for Smith.
She had also agreed to Nancy's plan to reorganize and put some life
into the Women's Division. The two women fitted her own needs. She
invited them to return when Franklin would be there as well as Mama,
"a regal" woman, they thought, and Franklin's private secretary, attractive Marguerite LeHand, "Missy," almost a member of the family. At
dinner on this second occasion Marion, who had spent the summer at
the newly established Bryn Mawr Summer School for Women Workers,

* Roosevelt's letter to Smith is dated August 6, 1922.

described a tour of the struck coalfields in West Virginia. Franklin listened intently, but "Granny," as Marion later called Sara, turned cool. Afterwards Franklin asked her if she had known there were Delano mines among those they had visited. Marion was a little dismayed by what she had said, but Eleanor liked this tall, earnest woman all the more for having brought the breath of reality into Mama's dining room.

By September, Eleanor and her new friends had begun to set up women's Democratic clubs throughout upstate New York. The letterhead of the Women's Division listed Harriet May Mills at the top as "Associate Chairman," followed by the four vice-chairmen, Mrs. Daniel O'Day, Mrs. Franklin D. Roosevelt, Miss Marion Dickerman, and Miss Nancy Cook. Through Nancy and Marion, Eleanor had met Caroline O'Day. The latter had been born on a Georgia plantation and was the widow of a liberal-minded Standard Oil vice-president. She had been a militant suffragist and now was an active Democrat. Like Nancy and Marion, she was also a pacifist and had held anti-war meetings in her home during the World War. She added to the progressive cast of the group of women who had begun to surround Eleanor and now moved into the leadership of the Democratic women's organization.

Eleanor's entry into politics, especially Dutchess County politics, brought her closer to neighbors who lived a few miles south of Hyde Park in Hopewell Junction, young Elinor and Henry Morgenthau.

She and the Morgenthaus and other Roosevelt loyalists lined up a Dutchess County delegation committed to Smith. Elinor introduced the resolution at a Democratic luncheon that committed the delegation to Smith against William Randolph Hearst, his opponent. Together with Louis and the Morgenthaus she went to Syracuse, where the state convention met, and Louis telegraphed the Boss at Hyde Park: "AL NOMINATED WITH GREAT ENTHUSIASM. MORGENTHAU AND YOUR MISSUS LED THE DUTCHESS COUNTY DELEGATION WITH THE BANNER THREE TIMES AROUND THE HALL. . . ."

"I had quite a session with our lady politicians as Mrs. Roosevelt no doubt told you," Smith wrote Franklin after the convention. "I was delighted to see her taking an active part and I am really sorry that you could not be there but take care of yourself—there is another day coming." The women had yielded on their demand for two places on the ticket when Smith agreed to appoint women to important posts in his administration. He also undertook to replace the venerable Miss Harriet May Mills as head of the Women's Division by Caroline O'Day. Henceforth five women, Eleanor, Caroline, Nancy, Marion, and Elinor Morgenthau, dominated women's Democratic activities in New York State. Shared work, Eleanor later wrote of her friendships, particularly with Nancy and Marion, was "one of the most satisfactory ways of making and keeping friends."

Eleanor not only made friends but she learned by doing, a title she used in one of her last books. These friendships and activities did not replace but supplemented her life at home, running a large household and bringing up five children to whom she had to be father as well as mother. Franklin often was away on a houseboat, the *Weona II* in early 1923 and the *Larooco* in 1924, drifting in the waters of the Florida Keys, or working in the summer with the neurologist Dr. William McDonald in Marion, Massachusetts, seeking to recover the use of his crippled limbs. Franklin's note in the *Weona II* log suggested that life on a houseboat was not Eleanor's preference: "Eleanor, Louis Howe, Esther Lape went fishing along the viaduct and caught 20 'Jacks.' They packed each other's belongs [*sic*] and none of their own. From 3 p.m. till 5 they paced the hurricane deck in store clothes, waiting anxiously for the train bearing the relief crew (all of which were 2 hours late)." Another woman might have been daunted but she welcomed the multiplication of duties.

Whenever Eleanor's name was mentioned, wrote Isabella, now Mrs. John Greenway, and one of the few old friends with whom she remained in touch, people say "'there is probably the greatest woman of this generation.'" Eleanor kept in touch, too, with Auntie Bye and Auntie Corinne, whose experience she valued and whom she visited, the first at Farmington, and Auntie Corinne at Henderson House in the Mohawk Valley. "Dearest Auntie Corinne," she wrote as she began to emerge as a public figure:

Thank you so much for letting me see Isabella's letter. I feel encouraged about Mrs. Selmes, but it is terribly hard for all those around her. Slow things are hard but Isabella is a wonder & in the end I'm sure all will be well. You are the most wonderful person in the world, to do all you have done, give pleasure & health to so many & create a cheerful, happy atmosphere when your eyes are growing worse. Dear Auntie Corinne you just are an inspiration as Auntie Bye is. One thing is certain none of us who are a generation younger can hope to be or to do what you have done but we can try I suppose.

Mama & Anna & James are home & they all look well. Anna & James very well, the latter 6 ft. & both seem to have gained so much from their trip. Anna is looking forward to seeing the girls here the end of Sept.

I am sending you a letter from Hall as you said you wanted to hear from him & this tells all the real news. Please return it to me.

Many thanks & much love,

Devotedly
Eleanor

Auntie Corinne was on Eleanor's list to receive tickets to hear Frances Perkins, member of the New York State Industrial Board, speak at one of the first Women's Trade Union League meetings on "Changing Aspects of the Problems of Women in Industry." Membership in the League was another of Eleanor's links with Nancy Cook and Marion Dickerman. Accompanied often by them, Eleanor read to the League girls one night a week, and when she began to organize an annual Christmas Party for the League, Nancy trimmed the tree.

People spoke of the composure and serenity in which she enfolded her energy. She explained it to friends with a line from David Grayson, a favorite author: "Behind tranquillity lies conquered unhappiness." She later said, "In all the years I only lost my temper with my Mother-in-law once and that was over the training of the children. I made up my mind then I would never lose it again. She forgot all about it the next day, but I have remembered it all my life."

One day a week in late 1923 she spent with Esther and Elizabeth going over the thousands of entries that poured in as a result of Edward W. Bok's offer, managed by Esther, of $100,000 for the "most practicable" peace plan. Franklin submitted a plan, and while the women disqualified it because of Eleanor's involvement as a judge, it showed his thinking about how to adapt American membership in a world organization to America's isolationism. The publicity for the competition was enormous and resulted in a Senate investigation led by the isolationists. Esther handled the senators with aplomb. Eleanor went to Washington "to hold Esther's hand," Franklin wrote, and though she was only a spectator in the Senate hearing room, that, too, was part of learning by doing. Peace was "the question of the hour," she said in a speech afterwards, and for the women "this should be a crusade. . . . Cannot the women rise to this great opportunity and work now, and not have the double horror if another war comes, of losing their loved ones, and knowing that they lifted no finger when they might have worked hard?"

"I told her [Esther] after Election I'd devote my major activities to her and let up a bit on the Democrats," Eleanor explained to Franklin. But politics remained her major activity. Together with Caroline, Elinor, and especially Marion and Nan, she toured the state setting up clubs in every county. With Louis's help they began to issue a monthly news bulletin. She listed herself as Finance Chairman, but as in the canteen work, she was the dynamo. Howe was a co-conspirator. He coached her in speaking, edited her speeches, suggested areas in which to concentrate.

By 1924 she had become one of the state's leading politicians in her own right. Rosey teased Franklin about her activity. "It's only beginning," he warned his younger half brother. "Once they mount the soapbox, mark my words, they never get off." But Eleanor was also ambivalent. The more deeply she became involved in political activity, the more staunchly she disclaimed that it really interested her. "You need not be proud of me, dear," she protested to Franklin, who was off on the houseboat *Larooco:*

> I'm only being active till you can be again—it isn't such a great desire on my part to serve the world and I'll fall back into habits of sloth quite easily! Hurry up, for as you know my ever present sense of the uselessness of all things will overwhelm me sooner or later.

A fatalist on the level of personal satisfaction and happiness, nevertheless in April she led the women's forces at a Democratic state convention convened to promote Smith for the presidential nomination. She presented the resolution pledging the state's delegates to the Governor; she also led the fight against Tammany leader Charles F. Murphy for the right of women to name the two delegates and their alternates, who would be women. If women were to gain real equality with men, she told cheering women at a dinner the night of the convention, and it was not the speech of a stoic, that meant working "with" not "for" men. In impassioned phrases, for they echoed her experience in personal life, she went on:

> It is always disagreeable to take stands. It is always easier to compromise, always easier to let things go. To many women, and I am one of them, it is extraordinarily difficult to care about anything enough to cause disagreement or unpleasant feelings, but I have come to the conclusion that this must be done for a time until we can prove our strength and demand respect for our wishes. . . .

She headed the committee that called on Governor Smith. Murphy capitulated and Eleanor told the press, "We go into the campaign feeling that our party has recognized us as an independent part of the organization and are encouraged accordingly."

But the New York State Democratic Party was in advance of the party nationally. The Platform Committee of the national convention was dominated by the men, and they turned down the progressive planks that the women's subcommittee of which Eleanor was chairman submitted, including a resolution calling on the states to ratify the child-labor amendment. All night long Eleanor and her subcommittee sat outside the doors of the Resolutions Committee with their demand that it reconsider. The committee refused; Eleanor and her subcommittee were not even admitted.

The convention also heard Franklin make his first public speech since he had been felled by polio. He was wearing steel braces and supported himself on a cane, as he advanced to the podium on the arm of his son James. He had rehearsed his speech in the library of the East

Sixty-fifth Street house. Eleanor and Sara were in the gallery as he made his "happy warrior" nomination of Governor Smith. So were Nancy and Marion, a measure of their closeness. John W. Davis, a conservative Wall Street lawyer, emerged as the Democratic nominee. Franklin again vanished from public view. Eleanor did not follow the example of Caroline O'Day and support Senator Robert M. La Follette's third party Progressive candidacy. Instead, at the state convention that renominated Smith for Governor, speaking for thirty women's organizations she persuaded the Platform Committee to include a child-labor plank as well as recommendations for an eight-hour day and minimum wages for women.

"Of course he [Smith] can win," Eleanor said in her seconding speech. She brought to every activity a sturdy optimism. It was especially valuable in politics and men responded to it as well as women.

She had begun to live the life of an independent woman. Some women chose the "perfection of work" to the "consolations of family."* She tried to do both. "I am so sorry you are miserable but get well by the 14th!" she wrote her daughter Anna, then aged eighteen. It was the end of the 1924 campaign and she was trying to turn a rebellious daughter into a friend. "Granny lays it to my letting you go campaigning."

* See interview with Katharine Hepburn, by Michiko Kakutani, New York *Times*, December 22, 1980.

VII

An Extended Family

NAN AND MARION often were at Hyde Park as were Esther and Elizabeth. Eleanor still lacked the courage to invite the Russian-born Rose Schneiderman. Although Nan and Marion had come to call Sara "Granny," Eleanor sensed beneath the good manners Sara's hostility to her friends. "She judged people almost solely by their social position," she wrote in "A Final Reminiscence." Eleanor was inclined "to worry too much about such things," Marion insisted in an interview after Eleanor's death. She doubted that Granny's hauteur meant that Eleanor could not have had Rose at Hyde Park, and felt it certainly did not extend to herself and Nancy.

Eleanor thought it did, and so in the summer of 1924 when the three women, F.D.R., Fjr., or "Brud," as they all called him, and John were picnicking at a favorite spot near Val-Kill, some two miles east of the Big House, Eleanor, Nan, and Marion listened eagerly when F.D.R. said he owned the land on which they were and why didn't they build a place on it to which they could come in the fall after Mama closed the Big House.* He would give them a life interest in it.

Franklin liked Nan and Marion. He appreciated their importance to Eleanor and her affection for them. He realized her importance to him and appreciated her effort to remain at his side. He accepted her need to be independent of the Big House. At the cottage Eleanor could live as she, not Mama, wanted. By 1925 they were talking of a sizable house, not a "shack," and he was deeply involved in the project. "Dear

* Eleanor began to capitalize these words only in the late Thirties.

Nan:—also Marion," he wrote from the *Larooco* off Longboat Key in
Florida:

> It is grand about the cottage. I *knew* you would adore Elliott.* He is
> one of the nicest people in the world and I certainly vote for including
> him in our gang! It seems to me that the suggestions are all to the
> good and I am particularly pleased that Elliott's figure of $8,000 is so
> low.

The long letter, which was typed by Missy, who had her own quarters
on the *Larooco*, was filled with architectural suggestions to which he
added some thoughts about Eleanor that showed he considered her two
friends practically members of the family:

> We await Eleanor on Sunday and I only wish that she would stay more
> than 10 days. She will certainly get lots of sleep and reading down
> here. There is no possibility of keeping her from getting tired in New
> York. The only way is to plan to get her away from N.Y. and when the
> cottage is built that will be one means towards the end.
>   A great deal of love to you both—I wish you could be here too. Per-
> haps next year we can make it a real family party.

He signed the letter "Affectionately yours," and Missy added a post-
script that underscored "the extended family" relationship that she,
Nancy and Marion, and, though Louis is not mentioned, he too had to
Eleanor and Franklin. "Dear Nan and Marion," Missy typed, "I just
want to send my love to you both, also. I wish you were both coming.
It will be nice to have Mrs. Roosevelt."

On the train to Florida, Eleanor read *The Constant Nymph* and
made some terse philosophic entries in her engagement book. Some of
them were about the woman across the aisle with whom she dined. She
was on her way to Cuba, and her husband "won't mind," she recorded.
"He's busy evenings being an active Mason and Elk and works all day.
An unconscious tragedy told!" Life had not measured up to her own expectations, but she had made another kind of adjustment. She had continued to serve her husband. He needed her more than ever. But she
did not cling to him. She had her own vital interests, but the line she
cited from the book she was reading reflected her own tragedy. "No
form of love is to be despised," she wrote as she journeyed through
what to her was "desolate and depressing country."

The more completely Eleanor went into Democratic politics, the
more attached she became to the Morgenthaus, who were active in
county affairs. Eleanor was intrigued by Elinor Morgenthau's sense of
style and an air of cultivation that reflected her Vassar education.

* Elliott Brown, a contractor and friend of Franklin.

Eleanor's envy of her friend's college degree carried that extra measure of regret for an accomplishment one does not have oneself.

Louis arrived and there was "much conversation . . . four beds arranged on the deck after violent discussion as to where which snore would annoy the least." The log for March 17, 1925, recorded a feast in the evening to celebrate Franklin's and Eleanor's twentieth wedding anniversary. "Moving speech by H.M. Jr. and a presentation to the Hon. FDR of a pair of *linnen* panties." The next day there was "heavy gloom at the departure of E.R. and Missy," and Eleanor wrote into her little book: "Missy weeps because last A.M. on boat!" Her exclamation point, as usual, said more than the letter itself about her feelings, especially her pleasure at being back on land, on the way to rejoin her friends, Nan and Marion in particular. The final Florida entry in her engagement book said simply: "I have satisfactory talk with F. about cottage affairs."

Eleanor's visit to Franklin on the *Larooco* provided a vivid glimpse of the relationship of camaraderie, shadowed by reserve, that was to characterize the remainder of their lives together. Franklin was forty-two, Eleanor forty. Despite paralysis he remained a magnetic, usually buoyant figure with a political future, and friends were willing to pay a price to stay close to him. Her stamina enabled her to continue to serve him, her household, and at the same time to lead a life of her own.

After she left, Franklin wrote her that he might sell the *Larooco* and concentrate on Warm Springs, Georgia, which he had visited the year before and whose natural waters seemed to have a tonic effect upon his limbs. He had seen its possibilities as a therapeutic center and had begun negotiations to purchase it. But Eleanor worried lest he let himself in for "too much money" for its purchase and development. Although she was determined to lead an independent life, as she knew *he* always had, she and Franklin remained indispensable to each other:

> I am sorry you ever thought of giving up the boat. I think you must have had a touch of that sadness which in spite of all its sunshine the Florida landscape always gives me! It is a bit dreary as a country but I liked the life better this time than ever before and tho' I'd like to find an ideal spot where you could swim daily still I do feel it is the best thing now to do. I do think you gain more at Warm Springs but it won't be practical in winter for a long time if it ever is and Florida does you *general* good which is important. I thought watching you swim you used your legs more than last summer. Don't worry about being selfish, it is more important that you have all you need and wish than anything else and you always give the chicks more than they need and you know I always do just what I want!

Back in New York, Eleanor plunged into a myriad of activities. Supper and theater with Esther and Elizabeth alternated with evenings with Nancy and Marion. There were frequent talks with Democratic politicians and, encouraged by Louis, they decided to expand the bulletin of the Women's Division into a respectable magazine.

A letter to Elinor Morgenthau, one of the first to her friends that have survived, showed how domestic preoccupations intermingled with political, and how strongly enterprises shared formed the basis of her relationships to people:

Dearest Elinor,

Of course I understood your wire and I think you are a brick when you feel ill to do any work of this kind—Marion and I have just been making out your itinerary and she thinks she'd better start for home on Sunday the 28th. So she is sending you the plans and if you feel ill you must leave her anytime and Nan can go and join her and I'll go to the office an extra day—I'm planning not to go much that week because the big boys will be home before going West but if necessary I can go down for an extra day—

I think we've had a fairly encouraging time for these counties. I hate to leave Marion alone for the weekend however in this Co. for it is a discouraging job and it is always so much worse alone—Tell Henry he should have more signs up in these parts we only saw one today but between Auburn and Ithaca they were everywhere!

I hope you'll surely be in Albany on the 19th for the Governor's conference.

Good luck with the new tutor. I always hate the first few days! Much love and thanks for all you are doing.

Affectionately,
E.R.

On July 7 she set out on a camping trip in the family's seven-passenger Buick with Nan and Marion. They took Franklin, Jr., and John with them as well as Hall's son Henry, and a contemporary of the boys, Dr. Draper's son, George. They made camp the first night near Lake George. The next night they set up tents at Ausable River. "Bad road down lovely spot but mosquitoes!" she observed succinctly. They pushed on to Montreal, raising their tents about eighteen miles outside the city in the yard of a French-Canadian farmer. The farmer looked with suspicion at the women without men. One even had inquired "Where are your husbands?" Perhaps to reassure the rural folk, she had young John sleep in the same tent with Nan, Marion, and herself. Quebec was their next stop and it was "interesting country." They climbed Mount Willard on donkeys, "all but Nan swam in pool," and ended up in Castine, Maine, where Molly Dewson gave them supper.

She had made Molly's acquaintance that winter in New York when Molly had taken over as civic secretary of the Women's City Club. Eleanor immediately took to this clear-sighted, resourceful woman who for twelve years had served as superintendent of parole for girls in Massachusetts, gone to France with the Red Cross, helped Felix Frankfurter prepare the economic briefs in the District of Columbia and California minimum wage cases, and who, with another woman, lived in the same cooperative house on West Twelfth Street as Nan and Marion.

The next day Molly showed them the road to Ellsworth, Maine, and Campobello Island, and off they went with Marion driving. They went into a ditch and were pulled out, hit a cart just before Lubec, Maine, and "reached home," meaning Campobello, at nightfall. Handling the boys, as Franklin feared, was a major undertaking in itself. Johnny was nine and Franklin, Jr., eleven and all four boys constantly embarked upon mad pranks. In addition there was a steady flow of visitors. "Miss Dewson came," as did Mrs. Simkhovitch, a forceful settlement house leader in Greenwich Village, and despite the fog and rain "we had a picnic." On August 1, Maud Swartz and Rose Schneiderman of the WTUL arrived by boat, and there was much trade union talk. On July 18, Eleanor wrote: "We marked out first towels," in reference to linen for the new cottage. Henceforth all of it carried the initials "EMN." The next entry said that "F's letter with bid came." Franklin had sent them off on their camping trip with the self-confident masculine injunction that he and Henry Toombs, an architectural draftsman and a relative of Caroline O'Day, would see that the cottage was built. "Dear Val-Kill Industries Founders," he wrote them:

> You got a wire today making firm bid of $12,000. Henry [Toombs] spent all of yesterday here and seems delighted with the whole plan. We had the stone man and the carpenter on the site, also the Poughkeepsie City Engineer. The forms for the concrete foundations were put accurately in place and as soon as Clinton has lowered the foundation levels, etc. he will pour concrete. This should be by Wednesday or Thursday.

The details followed as well as an enumeration of the advantages of the new bid over the one they had. "The swimming pool is completed," he went on, and closed: "I can only suggest that hereafter you call Father the 'Cascaret'—he works while you sleep. Affectionately, FDR"

Eleanor often discussed with Nan and Marion her problems with Franklin, her children, and Louis, another sign of how much she valued the women's friendship. Letters between Franklin and herself, even those he marked "Private—in part" and that he addressed to "Dearest E.," or "Dearest Babs," ended up in their possession perhaps because they contained references to the fieldstone cottage that he was building for them at Val-Kill. "Those kids are made of steel and rubber," he comforted his wife about her travails with the boys. He reassured her about Anna. She had sounded "perfectly cheerful" over the telephone. "She will work out of this nonsense. It is because she is 19." The letter went on to political and cottage affairs:

> I have raised cain in Dutchess County politics. I hope to get a real campaign and real candidates. I was offered $2500 to the campaign if I endorsed one of the Republican nominees. Don't breathe this even.
> I have had a long talk with Henry Toombs. He comes to H.P. Sat. to lay foundations & approves concrete. Here is estimate.

Franklin's figures showed the women how to save $1610 and he added:

> So if I don't get an indignant telegram I propose to go ahead with foundations & walls at once as soon as I find if the carpentry bid shows an equivalent saving over the Babcock figures.
> Why waste $4,000? That's what I figure I can save you *with Henry's* [Toombs's] *approval!!*

Presumably she discussed with Nan and Marion at least parts of the reply that she sent off July 23. "Dearest Franklin," she began:

> Thanks for your long letter of the 21st. I was glad you telephoned Sister, it may make her think about writing. I haven't heard since the letter I sent you but I thought she might have been angry at my answer. I am glad you feel it is just being 19 as you are usually right.
> I am glad to know all about Louis. I had a kind of last will & testament letter after his wire. He certainly has had a bad time & I'm not sure he wouldn't have been happier if he'd gone. If he can get out the "News" none of us will have to begin to fuss about it, but I must see to it when I get down.
> I'll look for Calder's check tomorrow. How about Mr. Bracken's?
> I've stopped the lassoing of sheep. F jr. cut his finger badly today & fell over the see saw & made his leg bleed again! I threaten to keep him in bed 3 days to see if we can't get him mended up! The finger happened thus. They were all working on the porch on their boats & they got to playing & Henry threw a pillow at George & it hit Franklin's hand & he cut himself. I had a talk with all & they promised not to play when they were working again.
> If fine we 3 ladies plan a trip to St. Stephens tomorrow & I hope all goes well there but I will try out Mr. Bracken!
> I'm glad you are doing so much politically in Dutchess but I don't see how anyone *dared* offer you money for the campaign fund with a string to it. They had nerve!
> We are so excited to think the foundations are poured!
> Much love from all. I enclose a kodak John took of Mama & Fjr. which I think rather sweet. His kodaks of this trip are good & I'm giving all a set to illustrate their diaries & have one for you.
> Ever so much love.
> Love to Missy.
>
> 		E.R.

Henry Morgenthau had suggested Cornell and the experimental farm at Geneva as courses that might interest Anna. But Sara feared that a college education might reduce Anna's chances of marriage. Henry did not wish to run afoul of the redoubtable Mama and through his wife urged Eleanor to keep him out of it. Eleanor complied with his wishes. She valued candor and appreciated the errands that wives had to perform for husbands who wanted to remain out of the line of fire.

"Louis brought me to beach," Eleanor recorded soon after her arrival at Fall River, Massachusetts, where Louis's family lived. "Franklin seems well." After three days at neighboring Westport Beach, where Franklin had a beach shack and daily hauled himself on his strong hands across the sand into the water, she took the Fall River boat to New York. She promptly left for Geneva, where Anna, in rebellion against her mother, was taking what she called the "short-horn agricultural course." An apologetic letter to Marion about the mess Louis had made with the "News" showed a clear-eyed detachment about Louis as well as the strength of her feeling for Nan and Marion.

Dearest Marion,

I think you've been the one to have the hard time, but don't worry dear, it is all right if only people don't take life too seriously! I hope Nan will soon get things back into shape & then she'll be happy. I feel I owe Caroline an apology for injecting such a disturbing element as Louis into the office, particularly as I know how fussily he worked & how interfering he was & how full of work for other people & improvements on what everyone else was doing. It was pure laziness on my part but families & jobs really don't go & I am getting it at last. I hope with all I said to Louis before he left at one today that the Sept. no. can be done without trouble but of course no one realizes their own faults— Louis no more than I & we all hide behind the cloak of good intentions! However my written 'memo' should remind him!

One thing at least this week should prove to you dear, that Nan needs your protection from the world.

Please give Nan the enclosed to give Mrs. Stevenson to enclose in a letter I told her to hold for a check.

Darling, don't be unhappy because you've grown to care for me. I have the power of dissociating myself from things because I've had to do it so often, & I'm not unhappy that way. Both you & Nan should cultivate it, you won't be so happy, but you won't be unhappy, & now let's all forget about this week & I'll be so glad to see Nan on Monday evening & you & Caroline Sunday. All my love dearest to you & Nan too.

E.R.

Eleanor's warmest letters were addressed to Marion, but, according to Marion, and she said this several years after the two women had quit

Val-Kill, moved to Connecticut, and Nan had died, it was Nancy to whom Eleanor was attracted. "Esther and Elizabeth were closer to Eleanor than Rose [Schneiderman]," Marion insisted, "but not as close as Nan and I were, particularly Nan, whom Eleanor loved." Repeatedly Marion returned to this subject in later conversations: "Eleanor loved Nan much more than she did me. She was very very devoted to Nan. Eleanor loved me but not with the devotion that she had for Nan. I was not jealous." Yet the care with which Eleanor addressed her most intimate letters to Marion suggested a hunch that Marion might indeed resent her relationship with Nan, whose aggressive attachments were often flaunted. Eleanor wanted both women to remain close and sending her letters to Marion rather than to Nan measured the delicacy of her instinct.

Met by Anna in Geneva, she noted in her diary: "She looks well & quite herself again mentally & spiritually." She left the same day, proceeded to Henderson House, spent the night with Auntie Corinne, and, after going to church with her, moved on to Hyde Park for what she called "cottage business & local politics," returned to Cape Cod, this time with Anna, to see Franklin work at his exercises with Dr. McDonald, and on August 23 was back at Campo. Nan and Marion were at work upstate and Eleanor wrote to "Marion dearest," that "The Meredith Inn sounds wonderful, sometimes when you & Nan & I need a rest we'll take the car & go there." Then she sounded a note of female resentment of male superiority that was interlaced with deep affection for her feminine friends:

> Today is glorious & Rose & I are going to walk. I wish you & Nan were here. I feel I'd like to go off with you and forget the rest of the world existed.
>
> Maud left last night for Portland [Maine]. At lunch we had a discussion on trade unions & I was left as I always am with the boys, feeling quite impotent to make a dent, because they regard me as a woman to be dutifully & affectionately thought of because I am their mother but even tho' I hold queer opinions they can't be considered seriously as against those of their usual male environment!
>
> Marion dearest I love & miss you & no amount of excitement could make me miss you less. I'll get to N.Y. the 10th & be anxiously awaiting your letter. Let me know your second route.
>
> Much, much love
>
> > Eleanor

Eleanor's letters were in longhand, as were Marion's and Nan's, but none of the pair's letters have survived. Nor did their letters to each other, which makes it difficult to chart the nature of their intimate affectional relationship. Franklin, who had encouraged their ties to Eleanor and was eager to keep their goodwill, wrote to Nan from Massa-

chusetts at the beginning of September, not only about the progress of
the cottage:

> Old legs are coming on finely. I can almost stand up without braces.
> Another two weeks will win that trick I think & then comes the effort
> to learn to walk.
>
> . . . .

Affectionately FDR

Eleanor was at the County Committee banquet in Poughkeepsie that
Henry Morgenthau organized and he reported to Franklin, who was
still in Marion, Massachusetts, that Eleanor made "a very good address." Afterwards the Morgenthaus sailed for Europe. Eleanor's letter
to Elinor was affectionate and newsy:

> Tomorrow being Thanksgiving Day I must write you a line to catch
> you I hope before you sail for home. You are one of the many things I
> am being thankful for tonight & I shall be so very glad to see you
> again.
>
> Your letter came just the day before Nan was going to buy china for
> the cottage so I restrained her & I think you & Henry were too dear for
> sending them such a lovely & useful present. We all received the deli-
> cious candies, we'll tell you later what a narrow escape these same can-
> dies had!

On New Year's Day the cottage was well enough along for the three
women to have their first meal in it. When Eleanor went south with
Franklin to be with him on the *Larooco*, the ardent letter she addressed
to Marion undoubtedly was meant to be shared with Nan:

> Dearest Marion,
>
> So many thanks for the pillow which I've enjoyed all day & the choco-
> lates which F & I have been eating! Nan's cigarettes made me laugh &
> I assure you when I left I felt anything but merry. I would be having
> such a good time if you two & my two little boys were along & as it is
> I've just tried hard to forget how much I am missing you. "Thunder on
> the Left" is finished, strange and imaginative, giving me a horrid feel-
> ing of impotence & unrest as tho' the web of life must beat us all & yet
> I read every word which you know is strange for me! I'm sending it
> back & I'll be interested in how you feel about it.
>
> Mr. Hart found us at Savannah & F & he have talked "Warm
> Springs" every minute & will till we reach Jacksonville at 10 p.m.! Ap-
> parently Washington was a success and F is entirely satisfied with his
> visit.
>
> The country was desolate this a.m. & it is sad still but more interest-
> ing since noon. Floods everywhere but not bad enough to bother the
> train.

Dear Marion, I love you & miss you sadly. Some day we must all go on a real pleasure trip. I'm so tired of doing just what I'm doing now! Much much love,

> Devotedly
> E.R.

Feb. 1st.

She resisted being caught up in the natural flow of things that Christopher Morley portrayed in *Thunder on the Left*. The stoic trait in her makeup was resigned to unhappiness as part of the natural order, yet she rebelled against the view that anything shaped by human beings could not be reshaped by them, so in the end she did not like Morley's book:

> Feb. 2d On board Larooco

i

Dearest Eleanor [as handwritten], (I'm too accustomed to my own name)

So many thanks for "Thunder on the Left." I read it on the way down and was much interested and charmed by the real imaginative quality but in another way I don't like it—He gives me such a feeling that we're all caught in a web, the web of life, and it is almost impossible to control the circumstances which seem to sweep so many poor human beings with their big or little emotions along willy-nilly. . . .

I didn't say half I wanted to when we were talking the other day, I've grown to love you and to feel that you and Henry were not only "our" but "my" real true friends and tho I can't take away the feeling you have it makes me unhappy to feel that it is worrying you and I want to put my arms about you and keep away all the disagreeable things which have made you feel this way.

> Much, much love always,
> Eleanor

Her serenity and calm sometimes were mistaken for indifference. This was true particularly of friends like the Morgenthaus, who tended to be overly sensitive.

Another handwritten letter went to Nan and Marion five days later postmarked Miami:

Marion dearest,

We are having a killing time with our engines & are now on our way to Miami but tied up to the mango bushes in one of the passages while they find out why the clutch is slipping. My face is covered with mosquito bites in spite of citronella & my only fear is that when we reach Miami they'll think I have small pox!

Florida is queerer each year & the people make me long to know why they are here. We have a mechanic on the boat today who brought his wife because they're living in a tent & I suspect she wouldn't be left alone. Well, she's a little German dressmaker & the most unhappy, out of place person for what is she doing here?

We're off again! I wish you were here, it would do you good & I should enjoy it. The canal comes out right here on the ocean & even I have to acknowledge it is pretty! There is just the strip of sand & palm trees & a few bushes between us & the ocean & on the other side they've cut the mangroves & are drying the land & I suppose people will build houses there!

Franklin is trying to walk on the deck & it seems to go quite well so I hope he'll do it every day.

I don't like "Stranger than Fiction." Haven't quite fathomed yet why it upset Elinor [Morgenthau] so much. "Thunder on the Left" will go tomorrow. I'm getting all my long neglected letters written & lots of reading done.

Much love to Nan & to you, life is quite empty without your dear presence.

E.R.

Feb. 5th. We just hit bottom but seem to progress.

Nancy ran the Women's Division and supervised the fledgling Val-Kill Industries. Marion taught and was vice-principal at Todhunter, a private school for girls in New York City. She approached Eleanor about assuming a responsible place in the school. Eleanor, who revered the memory of Mlle. Souvestre, wanted to try her hand at teaching. She helped Marion buy the school. She wrote to her on February 9, 1926, from Miami:

Marion dearest. I got your Monday letter when I finally got into Miami yesterday. I think you ought to take the 1st place for the first year with the understanding that you have no financial responsibility. It will be easier for you to settle in that way & when Miss Todhunter & Miss Burrell depart, then I'll have to slip in & do all I can for you but I feel strongly that you have to find out gradually what I can do. The one or two afternoons a week sound easy & I'll talk over the course with you but associate principals for the good of the school should have college degrees & I think I'd better be something less high sounding! I'd rather not have any financial consideration enter into it the first year as I would consider that I was being paid in experience and the next year if we assumed joint financial responsibility then we could arrange some percent of profit after your salary & all expenses were paid. I think it will be quite thrilling for it is your gift & it would be a crime for you not to use it & I know you can make a great success. It is going to be such fun to work with you & Nan & you are dears to let me join in it all for I'd never have had the initiative or the ability in any one line to have done anything interesting alone! . . .

The Val-Kill cottage and Nan and Marion's participation in her life at Hyde Park made it easier for her to establish a life independent of

Mama. "I wish you could read Mama's last letter to me," Eleanor had written to her husband from Campobello the previous summer: "She is afraid of everything in it! Afraid of your going over bad & unfrequented roads, afraid I'll let the children dive in shallow water & break their necks, afraid they'll get more cuts! She must suffer more than we dream is possible!" But Sara had the ability not to be aware of what she did not want to know and to go on behaving just as she always had. Mama, Anna, and Curtis Dall, the Wall Street stockbroker whom Anna had married, were at the Big House. Eleanor and the two little boys were at the cottage. So Sara serenely informed Franklin, who was at Warm Springs,

> but they came over here for some hours today and tomorrow they lunch here. We three are invited for supper tomorrow at the cottage and they all lunch here on Sunday. Eleanor is so happy over there that she looks well and plump, don't tell her so, it is very becoming, and I hope she will not grow thin.

"The cottage is beginning to look sweet," Eleanor informed Franklin on "Val-Kill Cottage" stationery.

A few weeks later she wrote to Marion and Nan from Warm Springs. She had gone there because Franklin was preparing to purchase the place. She did not approve of his decision and he wanted her support:

> I had a long talk with Franklin yesterday p.m. & he feels just as I expected that no one has helped him, that he's trying to do a big thing which may be a financial success & a medical & philanthropic opportunity for infantile & that all of us have raised our eyebrows & thrown cold water on it. There is nothing to do but make him feel that one is interested & try to keep his points before him 1st that he must use it in winter himself 2d that he cannot honorably neglect the F[idelity] & D[eposit] because of Mr. [Van Lear] Black's kindness to him. After much talk I told him I felt he should do this summer what he thought would help him to walk most quickly but of course he must decide & he said that going to Dr. McDonald at Marion would undoubtedly get him walking faster than anything else & he didn't think that 3 months would hurt now that he understood from Dr. Abbott what exercises might do for him!
>
> . . . .
>
> I enclose a line for Nan. I may have to go to H.P. for the day next week as Franklin wants a number of things done but I don't think I can go till Tuesday.
>
> I want so much to hear what you have decided about the school & Miss Todhunter. Do write when you know.
>
> Much, much love dear
E.R.

April 25th

Her letter of reassurance to Franklin (May 4, 1926) showed that in some respects he was the romantic, she the realist:

. . . I know you love creative work, my only feeling is that Georgia is somewhat distant for you to keep in touch with what is really a big undertaking. One cannot, it seems to me, have *vital* interests in widely separated places, but that may be because I'm old & rather overwhelmed by what there is to do in one place & it wearies me to think of even undertaking to make new ties. Don't be discouraged by me; I have great confidence in your extraordinary interest & enthusiasm. It is just that I couldn't do it, but then I couldn't contemplate doing what Nan is proposing at Hyde Park! . . .

"Sixty one patients is grand but I don't see where you put them," Eleanor was writing a year later.

She had asked Nan and Marion to put up Missy at Val-Kill for Anna's wedding to Curtis Dall, which took place in June 1926. She was grateful to Missy for giving up her independence to serve Franklin, whether it was on the *Larooco*, at Marion's, or now at Warm Springs. That made life easier for her and she treated Missy almost as one of her children. Whatever pangs of jealousy she may have suffered over Missy's relationship to him she suppressed. "I am so relieved that Missy can be in Georgia all the time," she wrote her husband at the end of 1926.

Franklin came north not only for Anna's wedding but to rent a house near Marion, Willowbud Farm, where he would be close to Dr. McDonald, whose strenuous exercises included several hours on the "walking board."

A letter to Marion showed how much she suffered from Mama's and especially Franklin's blindness to her feelings:

Marion dearest, I have just a minute & want to send you a line. I hate to think that you've been unhappy dear. It is new for me to have anyone know when I have "moods" much less have it make any real difference & if you'll try not to take them too seriously I'll try not to let myself have them!

I wish you were coming with Nan tomorrow, it doesn't seem quite right to be seeing things without you. I'll go straight to the office from the train on Thursday & hope to have a glimpse of you dear.

The house in Marion is cunning but I think will be hot & it is going to take some managing to get everyone in. The water supply is uncertain as to quantity I gather & it is quite a way into Marion & will require much going back & forth, but of course it can be made possible as it is really very comfortable for Franklin but I can't say that I look forward to it as restfull! [*sic*]

Much, much love dearest,

Eleanor

To have friends who worried about her moods, who were concerned with her well-being, was a new experience and she liked it. She needed appreciation and craved a feeling of indispensability to others. Nan and Marion gave her such reinforcement, so did Esther and Elizabeth, and Louis, and so did Elinor.

A good deal of the 1926 summer she spent at Willowbud Farm. Occasionally Eleanor longed for a less hectic life, as she confided to Elinor Morgenthau:

> How very dear of you to offer to help me when your own hands are so full and I do know you would do anything but for the moment all seems serene.
>
> James' prize day was a great success and he was happy and I'm driving myself back there on Wed as he wants me to be there the last night of school and I shall bring Elliott and a friend back on Thursday and send them off to the New London races at dawn on Friday! Nan and Marion were very active angels and helped me so much the first day here that I am very well settled. Mama came back with us yesterday and we've been very busy and this coming week promises to be hectic but I hope gradually to catch up with a much neglected correspondence. . . .
>
> I'm so glad you occasionally long for a mountain top. I often do in similar circumstances to those which you describe! I think every mother, wife and housekeeper should take 2 weeks holiday every year, sometimes more but I rarely do it! . . .

She longed to escape to a mountaintop, but usually she was reassuring friends who found her pace too strenuous.

Work came first. "It takes 2 evenings to really paste up the 'News,'" she explains to Elinor Morgenthau, "and Louis can only help me evenings so I fear that very delightful plan of yours wouldn't work very well." She was glad Elinor and Henry were "both having a vacation at last!" Next year she and Franklin would "stay in Dutchess County and help with some of the work! I can just hear Mrs. Norrie, how easy to talk, isn't it? I shall miss all of you terribly next Tuesday and Wednesday at the office but probably do a good deal of work!"

At the end of the summer she took James to Harvard. "Nancy darling," she scratched out hurriedly from Cambridge:

> . . . We got here at 6:30 & had a good trip over & no rain. Louis has done a lot & is pathetically glad to have anyone enthusiastic!
>
> You have been a peach & I am ever grateful for all you've done to make this summer pleasant.
>
> A world of love.
>
> E.R.

She and Franklin were much in evidence at the Democratic State Convention in Albany, which renominated Al Smith as governor and kept him in the limelight as the leading candidate for the Democratic presidential nomination in 1928. Franklin was the keynoter and Eleanor served on the Platform Committee and was spokeswoman for the women. She had criticized the men for their "inability to comprehend the value of sustained organization," and she spoke with the authority of a strong women's organization behind her. "Men think they can organize the vote six weeks before election, but women generally believe in all-year-round active political work." Franklin wrote teasingly to Henry Morgenthau: "You know, if you and I handle these things right, we can some day be the powers behind the throne in D.C. and let our better halves do all the interviewing, campaigning and speechmaking for us." Whether intended so or not, that was more than a jest. Both men were the beneficiaries of strong-willed wives.

The ever-present doubt of her ability to do things intensified her deep devotion to the women with whom she worked. "If I had to go out and earn my own living," she would say, "I doubt whether I'd even make a very good cleaning woman. I have no talents, no experience, no training for anything." Her friends gave her the courage, provided the expertise to carry off such ventures as Val-Kill Industries, Todhunter School in which she began to teach, to solicit advertisements for the "News," which she edited, and to send up buyers for the furniture pieces they had begun to turn out under Nan's direction.

When neither Franklin nor the children were at the Big House, she went to the cottage. As she wrote Franklin in October 1926:

I was delighted after I took all to the train at five to go back and say goodbye [to Mama] and come over here for a quiet evening with Nan. I've written two editorials & three letters & we have had supper & the peace of it is divine, but we have to take the 10:05 down tomorrow.

The first pieces of Val-Kill furniture that Nan turned out went to Warm Springs. "Nan dearest," she wrote from there:

I put all the beds up yesterday, & today the table & box came & they are both in the room & you can't think how lovely they all look. Franklin is delighted with them & can hardly wait to get in. . . .

She described a chest of drawers "for Missy's room," drawing a small diagram of it, and also a bed table.

We all bathed this morning & the air is very soft, daffodils in bloom! I think what I hate down here is the untidiness & shiftlessness all about one, the hotel, cottages, woods, pools everything untidy & everyone oblivious to tin cans & dirt! However, it is better than it used to be & when the road's dry & harder the new ones F. has built & the golf course will be very pretty.

I miss you so much dear & I do hope all is going very well at the "shop" & shall be keen to hear about everything.

All my love dearest & take good care of yourself.

Devotedly
Eleanor

Franklin was the beneficiary, not only of the "Shop's" furniture but of the help and advice of Eleanor's friends. Rose Schneiderman's Women's Trade Union League had its annual outing at Hyde Park, as did the state's League of Women Voters, and Eleanor and Franklin were the magnets for the admiring women. Esther and Elizabeth, after the completion of the Bok Peace Award competition, continued with the American Foundation as a two-woman lobby for United States entrance into the World Court. When Esther firmly nudged Franklin on the issue, he protested that he and Al Smith were doing the best they could. He teased them for their aloofness from politics:

> If there were more women like you and Elizabeth and Eleanor active in politics, you would make us dot our Is and cross our Ts more carefully.
>
> But there again! You and Elizabeth both decline to rub shoulders with the common herd of us dirty politicians!

Eleanor did not share their disdain for politicians. Encouraged by Louis as well as by her husband, abetted by Nan and Marion, allied with Elinor Morgenthau, she had become a superb one herself. Her first article, "What I Want Most Out of Life," which appeared in *Success Magazine* in May 1927, regretted that more women were not in politics: "More than anything else, it [politics] may serve to guard against the emptiness and loneliness that enter some women's lives after their children are grown." Mothers should become

> accustomed gradually and while they are still comparatively youthful, to having lives, interests and personalities of their own apart from their households . . . Home comes first. But—in second and third and last place there is room for countless other concerns. . . . And so if anyone were to ask me what I want out of life I would say—the opportunity for doing something useful, for in no other way, I am convinced, can true happiness be obtained.

Her reasons for being in politics, however, were not that she was a forty-year-old woman with empty hours to fill, or that she was the surrogate for a crippled husband. She had her own vision of a better world and was attracted to the people who shared that vision. An article that she wrote in 1927 and that was never published described a fictitious "Jim," who had "all the money needed to live a life of expensive idleness," and though generous and a gentleman who lived up to the code of his father and mother, "unless something from without rudely awakened him, he'd never lead his fellow human beings in some great cause, he'd never fight for an ideal and a vision of a new life on earth."

Did she have Franklin and the rude jolt of polio in mind? She and her friends all served Franklin, but it was her vision as well as executive abilities that pushed all of them.

That was the secret bond with Elinor Morgenthau, whose strength and determination were behind Henry, as hers were behind Franklin. Elinor managed Henry's household, mothered his three children— Henry born 1916; Bob, 1918; Joan, 1922—encouraged him in activities that made him the state's leading agriculturist, and on her own became an associate of Eleanor's in the Women's Division of the Democratic Party. She had become sufficiently intimate with Eleanor for the latter to discuss with her worries such as those over her Uncle Vallie:

> I came up last night to speak at a League of Women Voters meeting in Rhinebeck & devoted today to a trip to Tivoli as the woman who lives with my uncle writes me he'd been drinking for a month & something must be done. He's getting it from Patsy . . . & I'm wondering how I can get the place raided as not only Vallie but some young boys on the farm under 20 whom he influences are getting drunk constantly & their mother has tuberculosis & is at her wit's end! Isn't it too annoying? Tonight I want the Volstead Law enforced unmodified & I want to get rid of all state police who connive with bootleggers!

Eleanor sounded like her Uncle Theodore when he was New York's Police Commissioner or when he sternly sought to break up her alcoholic father's dalliance with a series of mistresses. "In some respects," Alice Longworth conceded,* Eleanor was more like T.R. than she was herself.

Eleanor does not explain the meaning of her next paragraph to Elinor. What did Elinor not want Louis to see in her letters to Eleanor? To make "an extended family" out of friends and helpers required tact and solicitude:

> By the way set your mind at rest. Louis never opens personal letters when I am South! I'd hate you to write me censored letters! Nan & Marion are so touched by what you did for them. You are the sweetest person.
>
> Anna & the baby are well & everything seems serene with all the boys. They had eight cases of scarlet fever at Groton but all were given the Schick test and so far Elliott is in perfect health so I start South on Tuesday with a quiet mind. Your boys are well I hear, also Joan, but they haven't yet seen the baby but Anna said she was going to telephone & try to arrange it next week.
>
> Nothing of interest here politically. I saw the Governor he evidently thinks as long as he is in a State Com. is not needed & he intends to

---

* *Mrs. L*, by Michael Teague (Garden City: Doubleday, 1981), page 155.

reserve Mr. Lehman for more useful things.* Caroline & I feel under the circumstances our work may seem unnecessary but we decided to wait and see him again the end of May when I get back.

Your furniture I think lovely & I do hope you will like it.

I think of you daily dear & miss you sadly.

All my love, E.R.

Anna's baby to which this letter refers was born March 25, 1927. Mama marveled at Eleanor's ability to sit up all night with Anna awaiting the baby's arrival (she was named Eleanor) and in the morning appear as fresh as a daisy. Her vitality and courtesy continued to astonish her even though she never accepted Eleanor's liberation from her own possessiveness and genteel values. A year later, when Sara went to tea at 10 Downing Street, she wrote home that Prime Minister Stanley Baldwin looked "honest and strong," but Mrs. Baldwin was "the healthy, stuffed doll type, no grade or breeding." Distance lent enchantment: "I thought of my gracious Eleanor." Eleanor had a stormy passage with her own nineteen-year-old daughter who had married the stockbroker Curtis Dall partly to escape the parental yoke. Eleanor sought to shift the mother-daughter relationship to a more companionable level. She helped Anna and Curtis move into their own apartment. She did not want to be the interferer, she wrote Franklin, "I want to help her but not be about & do the superintending for I'm too executive not to do it all & then she'd never feel it was her own. . . . Mama says I'm cruel to 'leave the poor child alone!' "

After carefully sounding out Franklin and hearing no objection from him, she accepted Marion's invitation and began to give two and a half days a week to teaching at Todhunter. She taught the older girls a course in American history, another in English and American literature, and later one in current events. Until she went to the White House, she stuck faithfully to her Todhunter schedule although she managed to sandwich in several other duties.

Some friends were startled by the interlinked monogram "EMN" that adorned the linen at the Val-Kill Cottage, but she seemed to transcend any suggestion they were a sexual threesome. She loved Nan and Marion. In the intimacy of the Val-Kill Cottage she told them about the Lucy Mercer affair. The cottage made it easier for her to pursue the difficult course of rendering Franklin a service of love while not loving him. Once while Franklin was at the Big House she abandoned her usual practice of being there while he was and took refuge at Val-Kill. For three days she refused to talk to him. Finally on Nan's advice he drove over in the Ford with hand controls and she went out and sat

---

* "Saw the Gov. yesterday," she wrote to Franklin. "He looks better than I've ever seen him look! Lehman is not to be state chairman. Nothing will be done & from our point of view [the women's] the organization is unsatisfactory."

with him in the car for more than two hours and then went back with him to the Big House.

In June 1928, Franklin was slated again to place Al Smith in nomination at the Democratic Convention in Houston. This time, his son Elliott instead of James, who went to Europe with Sara, accompanied him, as did Louis and Nan. Marion also went, later, as did the Morgenthaus. "Elinor & Henry Morgenthau are like children in their joy that she [Elinor] should be made a delegate-at-large," Eleanor wrote Franklin a few weeks before the convention. "I never realized that anyone could care so much and only hope that nothing happens to change the minds of the mighty!" Was she as resigned and as able to walk calmly away from politics as she meant to indicate?

Long ago she had written Franklin about the "uselessness of all things." Yet as Molly Dewson, whose executive abilities Eleanor admired, said of her: "If Mrs. Roosevelt did not hit two birds with every one stone, she never could have carried out her schedule." When Marion, Elinor, and Henry boarded the train for Houston, Eleanor was at the station. She intended to listen on the radio, she informed her husband, "and expire if it doesn't work!" "LISTENED TILL 3 A.M. . . . CONGRATULATIONS," she wired her husband. And when Al Smith received the nomination, she sent him a telegram of congratulations in her own name. Her actions belied her readiness to stay behind.

After the convention she checked in at Democratic state headquarters and reported to Franklin that "everyone was talking of your speech & feel you did untold good to the Governor's cause." But the women were dissatisfied because they had not been consulted

by the men leaders as to what women from New York should be given this or that place. It would be so easy for the men to do I can't understand why they prefer to stir up this current of discontent! However it is none of my business. I'm doing just what Mrs. Moskowitz asks me to do & asking no questions, the most perfect little machine you ever saw & after the National Committee meets & they appoint permanent people I'm going to get out & retire.

Instead she was drafted by the Democratic National Committee along with Wyoming's Nellie Tayloe Ross to head women's work in the campaign. "Gov. Ross arrived yesterday," she informed Elinor Morgenthau:

I think she finds it hard to understand the way we have to function but she will see Mr. Raskob this morning. I doubt if she will know much more when she is through! She will be much better in the long run as V. Ch. than in the campaign for she is like you in one way. She wants perfection and it tries her to see what *could* be done & is not done. However, my dear, that is your only point of similarity! Do rest & get very well for October is going to be a strenuous month for you.

My dearest love to you always,
E.R.

Mr. Lehman is the nicest, calmest person at h'd'q't's!

"Both offices are so busy that we are not even going out to lunch," she reported to Elinor two weeks later, as she divided her time between state and national. Two weeks later she filled in Elinor more fully:

It was nice to get your long letter & to know that you had really enjoyed your holiday & felt better.

There is plenty of work for everyone at the State office. I rather hope if you feel like it you will just take over the Jr. car and have a stenographer of your own and run it from next week on. You are, as you know, on the Natl. College Leagues group. Miss Ely is V.Ch. but does not return till Sept. 12th & they told me that beginning this week they would hold weekly meetings so I hope you will be able to be there as Miss Wooley who is ex. sec. isn't old enough to be without guidance & I haven't been able to help her much.

Mr. [Henry] Morgenthau* came in to see me and I was so glad to see him. He thinks we have done a good job on the maps & for our state cars I told him we would need the money the last three weeks of the campaign. I am asking Mr. Lehman for our first $5,000. this week but presenting him with a full account of our receipts & expenditures since Jan. 1st so he will know just what we are doing. We have a good report from the boys this last week & the car looks *very* conspicuous! No one is going out this week as we could make no plans for them over Labor Day & the signs on the car need repairs and the car needs going over but next week is all planned.

I will be in town all day Tuesday & Wednesday & again on Friday. Thursday I have to take a trip with my sister-in-law Margaret Roosevelt for the day & Saturday Franklin & I have to spend the morning in Fall River as we are godparents to Louis Howe's grandson & Franklin speaks that evening in Bridgeport & then motors home.

If you are in town on Wed. & can lunch with me I will go out to lunch (I never do anymore!) or if you are not coming so soon I will leave early Wed. & stop off for supper with you, but lunch would really be better if possible for you. It will be good to see you again. There is just one drawback to being busy as I am now & that is that you become so much of a machine that you forget you have feelings & it is nice to really look forward to seeing you!

I'm down here just to meet Mama who docks this a.m. & then I'm going back to H.P. & coming down early to-morrow.

Mrs. Morgenthau brought me the most exquisite lace table scarf. I

---

* Henry Morgenthau, Sr., Woodrow Wilson's ambassador to Turkey and an elder statesman of the Democratic Party.

can't get over her doing it, for she must have so many of her own to think about & I must try before long to go & see her.

I'm reading a book you'll enjoy, Burdik's "Gladstone," a bit hard on him but very clever.

Much, much love to you dear & welcome home

Devotedly,
Eleanor

Sept. 3d [1928]

Eleanor's education of Franklin, with the help of her friends, on the subject of women's rights had not been wasted. For the "Election Number" of the Women's City Club *Quarterly* he projected some ideas on "Women's Field in Politics":

It is my firm belief that had women had equal share in making the laws in years past, the unspeakable conditions in crowded tenement districts, the neglect of the poor, the unwillingness to spend money for hospitals and sanitariums, the whole underlying cynical attitude towards human life and happiness as compared to material prosperity, which has reached its height under the present Republican administration, would never have come about.

He stated a basic conviction that would shape his attitude as Governor and later as President:

I have always believed in giving women an equal share in the making of our laws. I have regarded their entry into politics—for they must enter politics if they are to have a voice in our legislative halls—the most noteworthy step toward securing greater happiness and greater prosperity for the individual that we have ever taken.

Until the state convention at the beginning of October that nominated Franklin for governor he made himself scarce and led a relatively relaxed life at Warm Springs, but Eleanor's schedule was hectic:

I worked till 4:30 a.m. on account of the radio speech this morning. Tonight I go to speak at Beacon & spend the night with Elinor & Henry & return to N.Y. tomorrow but go to Hyde Park with Miss Thompson Sat. night!

That was her first reference in her letters to Franklin to Malvina Thompson. Later she became "Tommy," and one of "Mrs. R's" (as she called her) closest friends. Daughter of a Vermont railroad engineer, she taught herself typing and stenography and had worked for the American Red Cross during and after the war. She had gone to work for the Democratic state committee in 1922 and from 1924 on worked increasingly for Mrs. Roosevelt. She had a strong chin, brown hair, a sense of humor and was an indefatigable worker. In time she would have Eleanor's confidence as few others.

In the seven years that ended with Franklin's return to the political fray, her friendship with Nan and Marion and the building of the cottage at Val-Kill were central to her emotional life and her emergence as a forceful, independent woman. She had come to rely on the two friends and the cottage as a buffer not only against Mama and the Big House, but as a safety valve for her feelings about Franklin. That reliance enabled her to carry through her consciously chosen role of companion and helpmate, although not lover, of Franklin, and to resign herself to places such as Warm Springs and Marion on Cape Cod, which though important to Franklin were considerably less attractive to her. "We always tried to help her in every way we could and also to build bridges back to him," Marion later recorded in reference to Eleanor's insistence that she and Nancy should be "*his* friends as well as hers."

The relationship of Nan and Marion to Eleanor was no one-way affair. "It is no loss of liberty to subordinate ourselves to a natural leader," says Santayana. Eleanor ennobled her friends' lives and made them more productive and fulfilling emotionally. Being politically minded, they sensed Franklin's possibilities and, though feminists, were prepared to hitch their wagons to his star, more so even than Eleanor, who always insisted politics was a matter of duty rather than enjoyment.

Franklin's willingness to set land aside at Val-Kill and help Nan, Marion, and Eleanor build a cottage there and start the Val-Kill Industries showed the lengths to which he was prepared to go to keep Eleanor at his side. A masterful personality, he did not feel threatened by rivals for Eleanor's attention, particularly if those rivals were women. So he welcomed them and joined Eleanor in making them part of their "extended" family. Nan and Marion, Louis, Missy, and Tommy were helpers, but also they were friends, and, driven by a shared purpose, they formed an unusual "family," one that was very different from the kinship Mama and Cousin Susie had in mind when they invoked that word but one that was more in accord with the spirit's search for new forms of community.

Eleanor's friends meant more to her than support, companionship, affection. When she wrote Marion in 1926 that it was "new" for her to have anyone recognize and care when she had moods, she betrayed how arid had been her world of love and friendship before she had been liberated from Mama and Franklin. That was all changed now. She had discovered the joys of openness and self-disclosure that came with real intimacy.

VIII

Eleanor and the Corporal

A S THE ELECTION night returns showed that despite Smith's defeat Roosevelt had squeaked in as governor, the spotlight also shifted to Eleanor. A reporter caught up with her at the Roosevelt-Lehman headquarters in the Biltmore Hotel in New York. He was startled by her reaction to the returns:

"If the rest of the ticket didn't get in, what does it matter?" she asked.

"No, I am not excited about my husband's election. I don't care. What difference does it make to me?"

For almost a decade she had built her own life, developed her own point of view, infused her actions with a self-confident, and at the same time anxious-to-please personality that immediately attracted everyone's attention. And now, she feared that as a result of her husband's election she would have to conform to the public's expectation, not to mention Franklin's, that she behave in a discreet, decorous, well-bred way. She had been propelled into political activity by her husband's illness, but his election as governor meant, she felt, an end, not only to the political work that she valued, but to voicing her own opinions.

She explained her reaction to Franklin's election in a letter to an aggrieved Elinor Morgenthau, who had worked in the Women's Division of the state campaign and was upset because Eleanor had paid scant attention to her. Work had swallowed up everything, explained

Eleanor, who had spent part of her time with the state campaign and part with the national. Work was "always interesting in itself." But it was not only the demands of the job to be done.

> I felt Gov. Smith's election meant something but whether Franklin spends 2 years in Albany or not matters as you know comparatively little. It will have pleasant and unpleasant sides for him & the good to the State is problematical. Crowds, newspapers, etc. mean so little, it does not even stir me but I know it does others. I simply haven't had time to spend with anyone.

Henry Morgenthau, Jr., had annoyed her with a telegram that had asked certain things of her in the state campaign. "I quite realize now that he was trying to do his job in an exceptional way & wanted things which I did not understand but my real annoyance was with Franklin because he did not answer my first telegram however I straightened that out with him & I should not have been surprised."

All seemed to get caught up in the hostilities between Eleanor and Franklin, and if they were sensitive people, as the Morgenthaus were, their feelings suffered. That was true of all the members of the "extended family," for Louis, and Nan and Marion, and Esther and Elizabeth were the "children" as well as the helpers of Eleanor and Franklin, and, as in all "families," a great deal of manipulation went on.

She realized that Elinor had been upset with Nancy at the state committee, but she did not intend to referee between the two of them, certainly not to reshuffle her loyalties. "I am devoted to her & it will be wiser for you not to talk to me about it as you cannot expect me to agree with you or to be influenced by your feelings." Although Eleanor's feelings about Nancy and Elinor changed subsequently, for the moment Nancy and Marion were her closest friends. "I have worked more years than you have with Caroline, Nan & Marion & enjoyed it & had no real difficulties & I resign now [from the Women's Division of the Democratic State Committee] with regret, only because I know if I take any part in politics everyone will attribute anything I say or do to Franklin & that wouldn't be fair to him."

She loved Elinor but would not permit possessiveness:

> I have always felt that you were hurt often by imaginary things & have wanted to protect you but if one is to have a healthy, normal relationship I realize it must be on some kind of equal basis, you simply cannot be so easily hurt, life is too short to cope with it! Cheer up & forget about it all, do what you enjoy doing & be happy! I'll be home for lunch tomorrow & Thursday at 1:30 but must work from 3 on tomorrow afternoon. Anna may be home but she may be out!
>
> Much love dear,
> Devotedly,
> Eleanor

Despite Eleanor's rebellious outburst the day after election, she realized that her own "it-makes-no-difference-to-me" attitude towards Franklin's becoming governor was untenable. How she was reconciled to her fate is unclear, although Marion says she and Nancy knew of Eleanor's reservations and may have helped.

In retrospect, Marion contended that the relationship she and Nancy had with Franklin had become almost as close as that with Eleanor, an illusion that Franklin did little to upset, despite its inaccuracy. He liked the two women but their primary attraction for him rested in the channel that they provided to Eleanor. Moreover Eleanor insisted that he treat her friends with the same consideration, courtesy, and solicitude that she showed for his, beginning with Missy and Louis. We can't live apart, she wrote to Franklin on one occasion during the Twenties, adding, nor do we seem able to live together.

Sometimes she felt the same way about her friends. "I hated not going yesterday," she would write to him in Warm Springs after his sensational victory in the 1930 gubernatorial reelection. It would immediately make him front-runner for the 1932 Democratic presidential nomination. She was off to Groton for visits with the boys and then would join him:

> On the whole I think we had better let Nan have the little room with me which has two beds in the cottage. I'm quite rested & don't feel as I did a few days ago that I couldn't stand rooming with the Angel Gabriel! If you'd rather have her in the hotel however put her there. . . . I would rather have gone alone & had no one on my mind! I fear in my old age I'm growing Cousin Susie like so I am not indulging myself! . . . Dear love to Missy & to you dear. . . . Remember me to Gus [Gennerich] & the Sergeant [Earl Miller].

She valued friends who appreciated the tugs on her to go it alone but who abetted her in her determination to stick with Franklin, even though at the times that he was especially self-centered and distant she resented their pressures. She could not summon up the initiative to break with Franklin, even though less and less did he give her the intimacy, companionship, and love that her nature craved, yet even as she held the household together, she was clear in her own mind who were "her" friends and who were "his."

The upshot at the end of 1928 was that she conformed to his wishes and needs. She resigned not only from the Democratic State Committee but from the boards of organizations such as the Women's Trade Union League, the League of Women Voters, and the editorship of the *Women's Democratic News*. On November 16, 1928, the New York

Evening Post carried a story that corrected that of the week before. It was headlined:

ROOSEVELT'S WIFE
IS HIS COL. HOUSE

She had never been called a "political adviser" before, she told the *Post's* reporter:

> I have always done what was needful. I will continue to do all that is required, of course. When we were in Washington for eight years, and in Albany three, I always knew what was going on and discussed public affairs with my husband.
>
> But this is part of any educated person's life, isn't it? The discussion of politics? I shouldn't dare to advise my husband what to do when he has a regular staff of fact-finders at his service. He would resent feeling he was not doing all his own thinking. No one has ever done my husband's thinking for him.

She went to Albany to look over the Governor's mansion and assigned to Missy a larger bedroom than to herself, "as if," wrote Marion later, "to emphasize that she considered her 'first lady' duties to be less important than others she performed in her own right, as Eleanor Roosevelt." She intended to spend two and a half days in New York City meeting with her Todhunter classes, returning to Albany on the noon train on Wednesday. If she had been asked at the time what was her vocation, she probably would have said teacher, for the gleaming image of Mlle. Souvestre was always before her. "I teach because I love it. I cannot give it up," she said. But she was a natural leader, as was suggested by a comment of Elizabeth Marbury. That legendary woman had been the Democratic national committeewoman from New York since the beginning of the decade, when women's suffrage had been enacted. Now she bowed out, saying, "They won't need people like me. They've got their Mrs. Roosevelt now."

Miss Marbury was not wholly resigned to giving up her preeminence, and in 1931, when Franklin began to bid for the presidency, he thought it prudent to have Eleanor, accompanied by Missy, appear at Elizabeth Marbury's Maine clambake. On the way up they stayed with Cousin Susie in Newport, stopped over in Portland to see Eleanor's Aunt Maude and her husband, David Gray, and, Eleanor reported to her husband as if about one of their children, Missy "smoked less today and I thought seemed more ready to sleep tonight. She is eating fairly well." After they arrived, Miss Marbury "talked politics ever since except for a brief time when Missy & I went in swimming. Molly Dewson is here too for the night & tomorrow there is a grand jamboree!"

Miss Marbury always looked on "all of us as novices," Marion recalled. "We wanted women in the party because we thought they stood for definite things that we could work for. She was not concerned with those things." Marion's dislike of Miss Marbury had a personal side. "She said to me, 'I feel holy in your presence. You look like a church window.' I didn't much like that."

Although Eleanor withdrew from committees and direct political activity, the appeals for help continued, and before long she had worked out ways of indirect assistance that kept her busier than ever and presaged the methods she would employ when she was in the White House. Every letter was answered, every request for assistance directed to some agency, public or private. She and Franklin presided over the picnic of the Women's Trade Union League to celebrate the paying off of their mortgage. Everyone came to Hyde Park. Eleanor, as much as Franklin, was the attraction. The women responded to his male magnetism. As governor he had the power to do things they wished. But Eleanor had her own force and allure. At gatherings such as the picnic, some clustered about him, others arranged themselves around her, listened carefully to what she said and awaited her marching orders. Married to Franklin or not, she would have the ear of the Governor. Of course being married to the Governor added to the powers that were imputed to her, powers that she learned to apply, always remembering that he was in command and that the public expected him to be in command. Eleanor's door was always open to the League of Women Voters, whose state chairman was Agnes [Mrs. Henry Goddard] Leach. Molly Dewson came to Albany once a week as head of the Joint Legislative Committee. Eleanor had enlisted Molly in the Al Smith campaign and when Molly wanted to cash in on her services and plead the case for the appointment of Frances Perkins as state labor commissioner, Eleanor immediately advised her, "Go to Warm Springs and see Franklin before others see him." Although she took her name off the masthead of the *News*, she continued to supervise its publication, working on the galleys with Louis. That "gnomic eminence" had decided to remain in New York City, where he unobtrusively promoted Franklin's presidential ambitions. And though Franklin had his staff of "factfinders," as she put it, he also encouraged his wife to visit the state institutions that because of his paralyzed legs he was unable to tour. He coached her on how to find out what he wanted to know. It was an assignment that she appreciated. By 1932, when the Brain Trust began to work with Roosevelt on his national program, his law partner, "Doc" O'Connor, one of its charter members, remarked that it should be among their first jobs "to get the pants off Eleanor and onto Franklin."

On Franklin's orders Eleanor was often accompanied on her journeys around the state by Corporal Earl Miller. A handsome state trooper, he was inordinately proud of his prowess as a marksman, boxer, and rider.

He had been Al Smith's personal bodyguard and soon was among Eleanor's most intimate companions, on a par with Nancy and Marion. When two old friends, Bill and Caroline Phillips, visited the Roosevelts in Albany, Earl's status puzzled the inquisitive Caroline. She had known Eleanor since debutante days and had seen her weekly while the husbands of both were assistant secretaries in Washington. When Earl came to tea, a puzzled Caroline gave him the rank of "Major." The observant diarist also noted the presence of "a secretary whom everyone called Missie [sic]," who was "a very sweet woman." They motored down to Hyde Park for luncheon and there they were met by Nancy Cook. "Eleanor's great friend," commented Caroline, "short, stocky Miss Cooke [sic], with her poppy-out blue eyes and short wiry grey hair . . . was as always warmly embraced by Eleanor. She is a most determined person who began by being a paid worker at some Democratic organization and then a sort of political secretary to Franklin and she now runs the Val-Kill furniture factory at Hyde Park as well as the Roosevelt family."

Marion and Nan did not like Earl, but they recognized and accepted the special relationship between him and Eleanor. As Marion recalled:

> He gave something to Eleanor. . . . You know it was a very deep attachment. I went with Eleanor to see his first girl. He was married at Hyde Park and the night before the wedding everyone gathered around the piano to sing. It was very, very deep. Eleanor always created a special Christmas for Earl. The four of us would celebrate. Eleanor and Earl and Nan and me. He used to annoy me the way he talked to her. I didn't like his tone of voice sometimes when he told her what to do, or when he did not like what was being served at table. . . . When Earl first came to the Big House with the Troopers he would eat out with the servants. That changed and he was later eating with the family. . . .
>
> Eleanor played with the idea of marriage with Earl. We had a perfectly ridiculous game. We would kid back and forth on what we would do under certain circumstances. When you go on a long drive with people, you talk of many things. How seriously she ever considered it I cannot honestly say.

What did Earl have to say about this? He was alive when I researched *Eleanor and Franklin*. He was then seventy years old, living alone in retirement in Hollywood, Florida. The text of that interview as I took it down in longhand will convey Earl's impression of the extended family of which he had become a member during the Albany years of the Roosevelts. The recorded text will also have to serve as an unsatisfactory substitute for Eleanor's many letters to Earl, which have disappeared.

The author stopped off to visit Earl in Hollywood, Florida. His hair was combed and glistening as of old. He was in shorts and the air conditioning was going full blast although it was a lovely day outside. The apartment was full of Roosevelt memos and curios, including a pair of bestockinged girl's legs (made out of plastic) high in the air behind the sofa as if she had been tumbled into the corner—a practical joke of a friend of Earl who had stayed with him.

He keeps a big correspondence going and types away on a machine perched in the middle of his bedroom.

I asked whether E.R. had ever spoken with him about her father and mother. She adored her father—there was an aloofness there that her mother had towards both of them—her father and herself. Her mother favored Hall.

When I heard that story of Lucy Mercer my heart went out to her—that he should have hurt her so.

I'm positive I met her, Lucy Mercer, at Josephus Daniels when the Governor and I were there, but she never visited Warm Springs until F.D.R. became President.

The Lucy Mercer story was known in the Navy during World War I. It came down through the ranks.

In those days I remember how at the barracks we saw pictures of the lady* before we ever saw her. They were in the Albany papers. She hadn't learned how to smile. Her expression was as if she hated photographers—"Please don't let them take my picture," she would plead with me. I said to her, "Now, listen, try to smile for just one picture." As soon as she did and saw how the pictures came out, her attitude changed and after that she never forgot to smile. I used to stand behind the photographers and make funny faces at her. But to go back to the boys in the barracks—when they saw her picture their reaction was "We don't envy you having to live with that old crab."

She credits me with that—the business of smiling.

I never was a card player. On these trips the Boss would like to play cards, especially gin. One time en route to the Governors' Conference in Salt Lake City, Charles E. Walsh, the Adjutant General, who had charge of the state militia, was with us. Three of us in uniform when we hit St. Thomas, Canada—Walsh, myself and a captain in charge of the Naval Reserve. Four of us were shooting craps, E.R., Missy, the Boss, and I—when we hit St. Thomas. The train stopped and immigration came in. I met them at the door. They wanted to pay their respects. The immigration official spotted the men in uniform. "Gentlemen," he said, "you will have to get into your civilian clothes." They made them go in and doff their uniforms and assigned an officer to go with them until out of the country. "Well what about him?" F.D.R. asked, pointing at me. I was wearing a forty-five. "Oh, he's the police,"

* Earl's expression for Eleanor Roosevelt.

was the way I was shrugged off. The Boss got more laughs out of that. He couldn't wait to tell the story to Governor Dern, who was host at the conference.

Yes, he was with F.D.R. and E.R. at the White House, he answered in reply to a question about the governors' delegation to President Hoover:

We left the Governors' Conference in Richmond—was it 1930 or '31?* and stopped off to visit Hoover to inform him on what the governors proposed to do about unemployment and find out what cooperation they could expect from the President. Hoover kept them waiting one and a half hours.

Missy's sister wrote a scathing letter to E.R. that Missy had been shabbily treated. The sister was quite cognizant of the affair between Missy and F.

That was the beginning of my trying to run interference for the lady as far as Missy was concerned. Missy played up to me a great deal. When Mrs. R. told me about the situation, I said I would break it up. I played up to Missy—carried on an affair with her for two years. At that time she was not having anything to do with the Governor. Missy had me put on night duty so that I could come to her room. [This was in Warm Springs.] My main purpose in playing up to Missy was because I knew the lady was being hurt. Missy knew I was playing around with one of the girls in the Executive Office. Missy found out and was quite upset and cried. In bed for three days. Told Mrs. R. the reason and Mrs. R. made me go up to her room and see her and make amends.

I had no home after I was twelve. I was an acrobat in a circus. I transferred the affection I would have felt for my parents to the Roosevelts. As I sat in back of the Packard and saw the back of F.D.R.'s head, I thought it was my dad. They gave me the first home I knew.

I took F.D.R. to his first professional wrestling match in 1929. We hit it off fine, he and I did. That's kind of saying something because after you get to know that guy, you knew he was an actor to the nth degree. Department heads came in fighting like hell. He would start off asking about their families, then told them one of his anecdotes. Had them laughing. They would all leave smiling and he hadn't committed himself to a damn thing. After they'd go, he would say "How'd I do, Sergeant?" You couldn't help but love the guy. . . .

I brought Earl back to E.R. What did she think of F.D.R.'s handling of people, his acting?

She did not think he was frank with people. . . .

* It was April 1932.

How did Earl get to know Mrs. R.?

When the Boss was in office he'd ask me to drive her here and there in her small car instead of the big state car. She got to know my family. She had my niece down. Next thing that brought us together was George Marvin* and Val Hall. I had to go over to Tivoli and put him under wraps two or three times. He was really scared of me. She told me I was the only one who could do anything with him. The first run-in—as I wrestled him down, the cords stood out in his head. "Hey, you're quite a strong fellow," he finally conceded.

I did all the Christmas shopping for people in Executive Department and for troopers. She was at a loss what to get people and was very pleased with that. One confidence led to another. She spoke at a women's club up in Elizabethtown [New York]. It was midway in his first term. I overheard these women talking. I could have strangled them. "I wish someone would teach her how to dress." "She certainly knows how to pick handsome troopers to drive her around." Towards the end of the second term common gossip all over Albany that Mrs. R. was going to stick with Governor until he was elected and then she and Sergeant were going to get married. That's why I got married in 1932 with plenty of publicity. I got married with someone I wasn't in love with. Same with second marriage. But I was never successful in killing the gossip. The girl I married was kowtowed to too much at Hyde Park. They gave us a piece of land at Hyde Park. Ruth Bellinger—she was a second cousin to my first wife. She wanted things I could not afford. One thing led to another. She was pregnant and had a miscarriage. One thing I did want was children. You know who talked her out of having children? Anna Dall. Anna was bridesmaid and Elliott best man. This girl still writes me. What a fool she was.

She, the lady, wanted F.D.R. to run for President. She had the strongest sense of loyalty I have ever known. [I asked about a letter to Nan Cook that Marion Dickerman told me about. The letter she was supposed to have sent to Chicago saying she did not want F.D.R. to run and which Louis tore to pieces.] She may have been down in the depths. [He warned me to be wary of what Dickerman said.]

Earl reciprocated Nan and Marion's dislike of him. The jealousies of the people around Eleanor were phenomenal. They made her impatient and the culprits sought to shield her from them by a veneer of civility and good manners. It is doubtful they succeeded. The complaints they did not utter she sensed anyway, and continued on her own way. Whatever Earl may have told Eleanor about them, it does not appear to have affected his behavior in the presence of the two women. Often, especially after Eleanor was in the White House, when she stopped over to see Earl's house outside Albany, Nan went along. It

* A former Groton tutor, writer, and, like Val Hall, addicted to alcohol.

was almost as if the possessiveness and envy among her friends were a price she had to pay for their help in her escape from loneliness.

The Boss was quite a traveler. He wanted to know what I thought about taking a trip through the old Erie Canal on *Inspector*. "You being a sailor, would enjoy it." There were only three people at the Mansion that summer of 1929. Only three people on duty in our absence, yet the bills were very high. I went through those bills. They sent her only the totals. No itemization. I hightailed it over to the butcher and I went back three months. They must have eaten a ton of filet mignons while we were not there. I don't know whether they ate them or whether they were being charged and splitting. That made me check the gasoline pumps. When we left fourteen hundred gallons. When we came back three hundred. I made out a detailed report, and it knocked the lady right out of her chair.

Those people, just the name of Roosevelt was enough for them to go up another fifty percent. I don't know how much money went through my hands as her purchasing agent. I went to the same people that Elliott did on building a tennis court.* I got a price of $1250 compared to Elliott's $1850. It was in my name. I paid with my check.

I gave her all the spirea. It was no good around Loudonville [New York]. She sent the truck up for it.

She was never one to check on those dunning her. I would say to her, "People aren't all good." She would say, "They don't ask for very much." A woman wrote for twenty-five dollars, said she was pregnant. Had an acre of land in Texas. The check was in the letter to go to her. Tommy showed it to me. She had enclosed the deed for this acre of land. I sent it to Jimmy Jackson of the Secret Service stationed there. A fake deed. Jimmy sent it to a man stationed in L.A., where the letter came from. Woman wasn't pregnant at all. The Secret Service scared the pants off her. E.R. said we were just lucky on that one. "Here's a woman who certainly needs help though I don't know how I can help her." Claimed her father was a rare coin collector. Father away and she had dipped into collection in order to eat. She wanted Mrs. R. to get coins through mint to replace those she had taken before father got back. Her father would beat her up. She talked with H.M., Jr. [Henry Morgenthau, Jr.] He said the coins were easy to obtain. So she said she would purchase them. I sent a memo to Jimmy. It developed the woman was a coin collector and was lacking these particular coins.

But it was not easy to protect the "Lady." Often she rejected my warnings with—"the trouble with you, Earl, is you're too much of a cop. You don't trust anybody."

The reason why Louis never liked me very much was that she transferred from Louis to me. She felt she lost Louis to F.D.R. She would ask Louis: "What did F.D.R. say? What did he think of that? What was his reaction?" She asked those things before she went in and sat on his bed. I think they were two conspirators against F.D.R.

* This was built at Val-Kill after World War II.

Both in Albany and Washington the staffs of Eleanor and Franklin were consciously loyal to one or the other. They might team up against outsiders, but among themselves their attachments in the final analysis were either to master or to mistress. Eleanor in this regard expected as much from her friends as Franklin did from his. Louis was a rare exception, despite Earl's claim. Although Roosevelt's election as president was Louis's primary ambition, he served as a link between Eleanor and Franklin and knew her well enough to get her to do things for Franklin that the latter could not himself get her to do. The interview with Earl went on:

I would hear him give a guy an awful argument and then an hour later he [F.D.R.] would say, "You know what I think I will do?" and then give this guy's plan. He wanted to be the originator. Three of us on a train. She gave her opinion. He then said, "Let's ask Sergeant what he thinks about it." He wanted the reaction of the man in the street. He would discuss things with her.

Her influence with him was great. I don't think he ever gave her credit to her face—ever.

I think she would have made a better president than he if she had someone to control her liberality. She had a keener insight into what people of the country needed. Unless F.D.R. saw a return in the voting booth, he would not go for something like this. She had a helluva time on the child labor business. He thought he might antagonize important groups. Only thing he didn't pull any punches on was Wall Street.

She and Miss Perkins had a lot of huddles. When Miss Perkins couldn't influence F.D.R., she would go to E.R. Her depressions were brought on by absolute fatigue. Elliott was her favorite. . . .

E.R. got the house on Eleventh Street in the Village in 1935. The lady didn't have a nervous breakdown, but she did have a case of nerves. I sent her to a neurologist. He gave her garlic pills. June Rhodes* brought Mrs. R. here [Hollywood, Florida] once. She spoke about her legs giving out. I told her not to worry abut that, Jack Dempsey's legs gave out. She had enough disappointments and heartaches. She was being treated with B-1 and garlic tablets. . . .

While I was stationed at Pensacola, there was a Jewish refugee ship from Cuba. I wrote her a long letter. The Boss didn't know too much about that. State Department handling it. By the time he did know it was too late. . . .

Earl let me look at some pictures and photographs. Many taken at Chazy Lake, New York, in 1934: Mrs. R. erect in a sweater, holster slung over hip, knickers, hand out straight with pistol. Target practice.

Leo Casey—up in Massena. Leo hit a chunk of ice. The troopers should not have sent out solo motorcycles. He was paralyzed from the waist

* Fashion publicist, witty and good friend of Eleanor, who had first met her when she had directed publicity for the women in Governor Smith's campaign for the presidency in 1928.

down. He wrote me first that he wanted to go to Warm Springs but it wasn't polio. I told E.R. about him. She had to go to Ithaca for Home Week and said she would go to Syracuse to see him. That was the beginning of their friendship.

She did not like Warm Springs. It was Missy's territory, she felt. W.S. people would condemn her for not being there, not realizing it was Missy's territory. I told her she ought to come down more. People are talking about it. You ought to be here more instead of Missy being around the Boss's neck.

It was Tommy who replaced [Grace] Tully. Tommy said "I hope Mrs. R. keeps me with her." We made a play at Chazy Lake: *The Kidnapping of the First Lady*. Tiny and Eddie Fox there and Nancy Cook. We made a film of the play. Sixteen-millimeter, 450 feet of it. I brought it down from Loudonville so that Simone [his second wife] could not get hold of it. I was dressed up in a Captain Kidd outfit, knife in my mouth. I kidnapped the First Lady and tied her to a stone. I had two troopers stationed there to protect the place. They came in on a rowboat to rescue her—while Nancy on the porch knitting and saying, "Now I can be the First Lady."

We then went in Earl's Corvette to a restaurant where he knew the proprietor. I bought steaks for both of us. On the way over in the car we got onto the subject of Missy again. He emphasized how demonstrative she was about her affection for F.D.R. and how this occasioned many rumors around Albany. I said at one point, "Wouldn't Mrs. R. have married you?" "Me?" he asked. "I never asked her or would have done so." "But might she have asked you?" I persisted. "You don't sleep with someone you call Mrs. Roosevelt," he replied. "Anyway my taste was for young and pretty things." "The Lucy Mercer thing finished any feeling Mrs. R. had for F.D.R."—she told him so. "Was Mrs. R. jealous?" I asked him. "No," he said. "Not even of Lucy Mercer?" "No." He thought she knew that Lucy Rutherfurd came to the White House after Winthrop died and also that she knew Mrs. Rutherfurd was at Warm Springs when F.D.R. died.

Earl owns a house in Hollywood which he rents for two hundred dollars a month, as well as owning his apartment. He bought them with proceeds from the Loudonville house. He is still vain about his looks— stalking around the house in a jockstrap, pulling up his shirt for me to feel scars from his many operations. Steel appliances in his body—spine and hip—cobalt treatment for skin cancers. Leg discolored. In his scrapbook many place cards in E.R.'s hand—doggerel verse.

As Eleanor's years in Albany came to an end, her attachment to Earl was as warm, intimate, and loving as she had with anyone. In the 1930s she acquired an apartment on East Eleventh Street in Greenwich Village. It was just above the apartment shared by Esther and Elizabeth in a house owned by them. She always had a room there available for Earl. At Val-Kill, too, she always had a room for him. And, as Marion observed, she organized a "special Christmas" for Earl. He had helped her, not only to conquer her job as first lady of the state, but to ride, to swim, to drive a car, even to practice shooting with a revolver.

But what did love for Earl mean? He interested her physically. It pleased her to have this handsome state trooper squire her about, even to "manhandle" her, as one of Eleanor's friends put it disdainfully. But neither physical yearning nor curiosity turned such encounters into more than exercises in altruism. She loved deeply—Earl, Nan and Marion, Louis, Elinor, Esther and Elizabeth, her children, but she was unable to let herself go.

IX

"Hick, My Dearest"

T HE MORE ELEANOR'S powers matured, the less she looked forward to the possibility that she might become the nation's First Lady and would indeed be the creature of pomp and custom. At the same time, a little inconsistently, as Franklin's drive towards the presidency showed every prospect of success, she pressed the issues that might give his candidacy a basis beyond the naked pursuit of political office. He, intent on being his own man who had his own set of values, became more withdrawn than ever. Instead of shared intimacy there were tension and hostility between them. He found her so difficult that when he conferred in Albany with a few top Democratic leaders about the political hazards of the Seabury investigation into Mayor Walker's amiable but corrupt rule of New York City, he asked Marion to stay and listen to him explain why he would not summarily remove Walker even though to do so would solidify his support with the anti-Tammany wing of the party. "You must let me be myself," Marion recalled him saying to her after the others had left the mansion. "Only when I am myself can I fit into my own pattern and find my way." He was determined, he angrily made clear to her, to follow his own star and intuitions. Why, then, did he want Marion there? She was neither political potentate nor mastermind, but she was Eleanor's friend. Unable to face Eleanor, who was in revolt against becoming First Lady, he used this indirect channel of speaking to her through Marion.

"Eleanor had very strong feelings about his running for the presidency," Marion recalled in 1967. "She didn't like that at all. I know she didn't want him to run. She wrote a letter to Nan in Chicago saying that she could not live in the White House. Nan showed it to Louis and he tore it into a thousand pieces. . . . There were times when life became too much for her."

On the fourth and final ballot California switched to Roosevelt and broke the deadlock. Roosevelt smiled contentedly. The rest of his study, said Grace Tully, a secretary who was assisting Missy and Mrs. Roosevelt, was a bedlam. The women reporters, including an owlish-looking Lorena Hickok, who was at the mansion for the Associated Press, found Mrs. Roosevelt scrambling eggs.

"That woman's unhappy about something," she already had observed to herself. And when another reporter asked Mrs. Roosevelt whether she wasn't "thrilled" at the prospect of moving into the White House, Mrs. Roosevelt cut her short with a severe stare.

"I'm a middle-aged woman," she later said to Hickok, who had been assigned to cover her on the campaign and was with her on her forty-eighth birthday. "It's good to be middle-aged. Things don't matter so much. You don't take it hard when things happen to you that you don't like."

Eleanor's resistance to the White House drew little sympathy from Louis or even from Nancy and Marion. She acquired a more responsive listener, however, in Lorena Hickok. When a few weeks later she learned from her level-headed secretary, Tommy, that Hickok's childhood, while so unlike Eleanor's in its sordidness, had been very much like hers in its unhappiness, she began to thaw out to "Hick," as she began to call her. Admiration united with sympathy when she also learned that Hick had made it on her own as a woman to the top of a profession that was dominated by men. Eleanor began to talk about her own problems, and that, as happened so often in the Twenties, was a prerequisite to their solution. By Election Day, 1932, when Hick arrived at the East Sixty-fifth Street house for the buffet supper that was an Election Night tradition with the Roosevelts, before going down to the Biltmore headquarters to hear the returns, she was rubbing shoulders with family, friends, as well as other reporters. She always remembered the embrace with which Mrs. Roosevelt greeted her. "It's good to have you around tonight." Later, as the election returns poured in, Hick perhaps alone understood the ambivalence of Mrs. Roosevelt's feelings over Franklin's impending victory.

Eleanor felt this ambivalence so strongly that in the exclusive she gave Hick the next day her strong feminist feelings were there for all to see. Hick portrayed her as a woman with a mind of her own, purposeful and resolute, not at all sure how she would reconcile her hard-earned independence with the subordination to ritual that the country expected of the First Lady, not to mention an acquiescence in the views of the strong-minded President-Elect, her husband.

"If I had wanted to be selfish," Hick's first story about Eleanor began, "I could wish that he had not been elected." She intended to remain "plain, ordinary Mrs. Roosevelt," Eleanor went on. There was not going to be "any 'First Lady of the Land.'" She looked quizzically at Hick, who was scratching away furiously in her pad:

> I never wanted it. Even though people have said my ambition for myself drove him on—even that I had some such idea in the back of my mind when I married him.
>
> I never wanted to be a President's wife, and I don't want it now. You don't quite believe me, do you? Very likely no one would—except perhaps some woman who had had the job. Well, I don't anyway.
>
> For him, of course, I'm glad—sincerely. I couldn't really have wanted it to go the other way. I am a Democrat, too. Being a Democrat, I believe this change is for the better.
>
> And now—I shall have to work out my own salvation.

Hick's next story, which described Mrs. Roosevelt's "truly Spartan life," talked of her as a "whirlwind" who got along on five or six hours of sleep, drove a blue roadster (whose ownership she shared with Nan and Marion), taught school two and a half days a week, used buses and taxicabs in town, wore a ten-dollar dress as well as more expensive ones, edited a magazine, was an indefatigable walker with a long, swinging stride, often alone and unrecognized, ate happily at drugstore fountains, but enjoyed taking friends to expensive restaurants. "She is never hurried," added Hickok, "apparently never harassed, and is seldom, her secretary says, even slightly irritable. . . . 'The only thing I notice is that sometimes, if she's bothered about something, she gets sort of remote.'"

The solemn recipient of Eleanor's confidences was a first-class reporter but an eccentric. She was squarish, moonfaced, non-athletic. Even as a youngish woman of thirty-nine, she was without sexual attraction. She was five foot eight but weighed almost two hundred pounds. Having made her way in the man's world of newspapers on the basis of journalistic competence, she preferred to be considered "one of the boys," an identity that she emphasized by the cache of cigars and pipes that she stored in her desk. Her serviceable attire of shirtwaist, dark blue or brown skirt, oxfords also attested to her wish to be considered a no-nonsense woman. Her biographer would later say that she dressed like a police matron. In any case she was no vamp, and in an autobiographical fragment where she wrote of her hatred for a violent, irascible father who had shouted, whipped, even abused her—her mother had died in South Dakota when she was thirteen—she said that her anger against her father had made her "dislike and distrust all men."

In flight from her father's rages, she became a hired girl at fourteen in South Dakota. Somehow she managed to acquire some schooling and to save up enough money to enter Lawrence University in Appleton, Wisconsin, but abandoned college at twenty-one, to go to work as society editor for the Milwaukee *Sentinel*. She briefly tried her fortunes in New York, but after being fired from the New York *Tribune*, decided to return to college, this time at the University of Minnesota. Again university classes yielded to the city room and soon she was writing by-lined feature stories for the Minneapolis *Tribune*. Although she was then in her early twenties, men held no interest for her except as fellow journalists. She had the first of her crushes, a tiny colleague, Ella Morse, two years her senior, with a sunny disposition that offset Hickok's own dourness. Ella wrote poetry and held a minor job on the *Tribune*. She was also a minor heiress, an only child, who when her father remarried left the family mansion on Pillsbury Street for a hotel apartment, which she shared with Hick and for whom she was soon doing the cooking.

The two women lived together happily in what might have been called a "Boston marriage" or "sisterhood." For many years the two were inseparable.

In 1926, Hick learned that she had diabetes. Ellie came to her rescue. She proposed they take a year off and settle in San Francisco. There Hick was to work on her novel. But in San Francisco, Ellie ran into an old friend with whom she promptly eloped to Yuma. Hick, thirty-three, was shaken. Deciding to give New York another try, she went to work for Hearst's *Mirror* and in August 1928 joined the New York bureau of the Associated Press. Her beat included the Democratic National Committee, where Malvina Thompson introduced her to Eleanor Roosevelt in a casual encounter. But a few weeks later, when she covered a Republican meeting where the speaker was Mrs. Douglas Robinson, one of Theodore Roosevelt's sisters, she asked her about Eleanor Roosevelt. She remembered Mrs. Robinson's comment: "Eleanor was my brother Ted's favorite niece. She is more like him than any of his children." That would have made her a formidable force indeed, and Eleanor's vivacity and charm, which Hick sampled in an interview the day after Franklin was elected Governor, added to her interest.

But their paths did not cross again until the 1932 campaign. On the campaign train Tommy made it a point to talk at length with Hick, including, said Hick, "about her childhood and mine." That became a turning point in her relationship with Mrs. Roosevelt. So Eleanor told her when they shared a drawing room towards the end of the campaign on the train back from the funeral of Missy's mother.

Suddenly, out of the blue, or so it seemed to Hickok, Tommy had telephoned her to ask whether she cared to go along with Mrs. Roosevelt, who was leaving Albany in order to accompany Missy. The latter's mother had died at her home in Potsdam, New York, and it was characteristic of Eleanor's solicitude for everyone in the extended Roosevelt family that she undertook to accompany Missy. Hick had noted in Chicago that when Bobby Fitzmaurice, who was in charge of the travel arrangements for the Governor and his staff, had been taken ill, it was Mrs. Roosevelt who accompanied him in the ambulance that met the train at the station to take him to the hospital. Eleanor had asked Hickok to come along with her on that hectic day. She now may have suggested to Louis that the trip to Potsdam would be easier if Hickok joined her. Hickok's first note to Mrs. Roosevelt, penciled on a New York Central letterhead, suggested that Mrs. Roosevelt had become more than an assignment. "About those reporters and cameramen— If there are any at the station, I can probably get rid of them without any hard feelings if I tell them you'll see them when you get back from Cambridge." So the unusual correspondence between the two began, and Eleanor's first note, although it started "Dear Miss Hickok," ended with an invitation: "Will you come up to my room for breakfast at 8:30 anyway?" And it was signed "Affly Eleanor Roosevelt."

On the way back from the funeral Mrs. Roosevelt insisted that Hickok take the lower berth.

'I'm longer than you are,' she [Eleanor] said when I protested. 'And,' she added with a smile, 'not quite so broad!'

It was early, neither of us was sleepy, and so we started talking. It was then she told me that I could thank Tommy for the fact that she had accepted me and permitted me to follow her about.

'She's very fond of you,' Mrs. Roosevelt said, 'and Tommy is a good judge of people. So I decided you must be all right.

'It was hard for me at first. I was brought up by a very strict grandmother, who thought no lady should ever have stories written about her, except in the society columns.

'To be frank with you, I don't like being interviewed. And that applied especially to you. For Franklin used to tease me about you. He'd say: "You better watch out for that Hickok woman. She's smart." He wasn't criticizing you in any way—he likes you. He was only teasing me.'

She then proceeded to tell me about her own unhappy childhood and girlhood, the tragic death of her father, whom she loved so much, her strict Grandmother Hall and her aunts who called her 'the ugly duckling.'

'May I write some of that?' I asked her fearfully before we finally said good-night.

'If you like,' she said softly. 'I trust you.'

As Hick was to learn, Eleanor saw herself as a prisoner of her husband's ambition. She was unable to acknowledge to herself that she was also a beneficiary, although that was the way it had worked out when she became first lady of New York State. Marion and Nan had been instrumental in reconciling her to the two roles of first lady of the state and to being herself. Hickok would now perform a similar service in her transition to the White House.

Had Eleanor had a different relationship to Franklin, had she been able to obtain from him the intimacy, consideration, and love her nature demanded, the pressures for independence might have been less clamant. But he was not able to give himself to any person—his mother, Eleanor, his children. He had loved Lucy Mercer. The extent of the personal commitment of that love can only be guessed at until his letters to her become public—if they ever do. He did not seem to mind when Earl had courted Missy, often sharing a bed with her. That may have reflected not only his essentially self-centered nature, but the restraints imposed by polio. ". . . [I]t would have been difficult for him to function sexually after he became crippled from the waist down by polio," wrote his son James. "He had some use of his lower body and some sensation there, but it was extremely limited."

James has also written that his father made several overtures to Eleanor, only to be rebuffed. He does not say whether such efforts at reconciliation included his giving up a style of life in which everyone served as an instrument of his purposes, purposes that always remained his own affair. No one was allowed to be privy to his innermost thoughts and feelings. They could only guess what was in that little "black box" in his head.

In early September 1932, just before Franklin set out on the campaign trail, Earl Miller married Ruth Bellinger* at Hyde Park, in a ceremony attended not only by Eleanor and Franklin, but by Anna, who was estranged from Curtis Dall and who was bridesmaid, and by Elliott, who was best man and separated from his wife Betty. Earl was close to Eleanor. Whatever his roughness and crudity, he had treated her as a woman. How far their intimacy had gone must remain a matter of speculation. But he had encouraged her to ride, to swim, to play, to feel as a woman. She had, according to Marion, even mused out loud about marrying him.

It had been a momentary impulse. "Sometimes," she told Hickok as she considered her future life as mistress of the White House, "I daresay I shall feel a little as one of my boys—after I lectured him on the responsibilities incumbent on the son of a man in public life—felt when he said:

" 'Wouldn't it be fun to do things just because you wanted to do them?' "

She might well have been referring to marriage to Earl among other things. How serious she had been about it, she nowhere said. James and

---

* See page 119.

Elliott both confirm the picture of a romantic attachment; neither advances the idea of a marriage. But gossips, according to Earl, did consider it a possibility and his well-publicized marriage to Ruth was meant to allay such rumors. For Eleanor, despite her silence, the marriage may have been a jolt. Earl had given her what her husband and sons in part had failed to do—masculine admiration, approval, affection. Now he stayed behind in New York State in charge of personnel for the Department of Correction. The loss of Earl made Hick's affection even more welcome.

James speaks of his father's holding out his arms to Eleanor but that she rebuffed his embraces. He does not say whether during the interval between Franklin's election as president and his inauguration on March 4 there was one such time, but Eleanor does describe in *This I Remember*, written after Franklin's death, an overture that she made to him. She had begun to speak around the country about the letters that were pouring in on her during the interregnum between election and inauguration. The Depression was at its worst, and these letters described its ravages upon individuals, high and low. She reminded her audiences of the "grave danger" former President Calvin Coolidge had warned against, of presidents, because of the "atmosphere of adulation and exaltation," becoming "careless and arrogant." Presidents "never hear the truth," Mrs. Roosevelt continued. ". . . [E]veryone says 'Yes' to you." She thought she might best help the President-Elect by serving as his "listening post." She screwed up her courage and finally proposed to Franklin that he give her a real job and that she handle part of his mail. He turned her aside, she wrote, with the remark that Missy would consider that interference. "I knew that he was right and that it would not work, but it was a last effort to keep in close touch and to feel I had a real job to do."

How keenly she felt her husband's lack of tenderness and companionship was suggested to a young friend in the service to whom she wrote many years later:*

There is one thing I've always wanted to say to you, when you do come home and get engulfed in work, will you stop long enough now and then even if T. is working with you to make her feel she is first in your life even more important than saving the world! Every woman wants to be first to someone sometimes in her life and the desire is the explanation for many strange things women do, if, only men understood it!

Her desire for a real job had been underscored in the final weeks of the campaign when she had taken the stump, not for the national ticket, but for Elinor Morgenthau's uncle, the Lieutenant Governor,

* This was written to the author in 1942. The "T" was Trude Pratt, who later became his wife.

Herbert H. Lehman, who was running to succeed Franklin as Governor. "I don't think it would be proper," she explained, "for the wife of the candidate to appeal to voters on his behalf. My speech last night was the first political speech I've made since Franklin became Governor, and I am not going to mention him in any speech I make." Strongly feminist, she had a clear concept of what was fitting in a democracy for a public official's wife.

She enjoyed politics. Little wonder that Theodore Roosevelt had considered her his favorite niece. She especially enjoyed promoting woman's role in politics. When two thousand persons joined to bid her farewell at the Waldorf-Astoria, her emphasis, as Hickok reported the next day, was on woman's responsibility: "We want women in politics to stand for the things we feel are important, and I believe we are going to need women in politics to accomplish the things we believe they have much at heart." Hickok's lead described her creed as First Lady:

I will make a prayer and ask for power to see what women may accomplish, and for courage to follow the light as it is given to me.

Talking to Hick helped her to work out her course of action. There were others to whom she turned, Nan and Marion, Earl, Louis, Elinor, Esther and Elizabeth, Tommy, but none meant to her at the moment as much as this gruff-tempered, essentially lonely woman. Hick accompanied her on her annual trip to Cornell to attend the Home Economics Department's Institute, and when Mrs. Roosevelt asked her to come with her in her roadster to Groton, Hick informed the AP bureau that there would be no story. Friendship was becoming dearer than her obligations as a reporter. Hick joined Eleanor on the trip she made to Washington in response to Mrs. Hoover's invitation to look over the White House. Louis and Elliott also came along, but at the Mayflower, after Eleanor declined Mrs. Hoover's tender of a limousine and a military aide and the offer of Warren Delano Robbins and his wife—he was the Chief of Protocol at the State Department—to drive her to the White House, it was Hick who hurried at her side when she traversed the few blocks from the Mayflower.

There were many with whom she had worked and who had come to realize that here was no ordinary woman. The farewell dinner of the Women's Trade Union League was crowded with civic leaders who wanted to testify to how important she had become in her own right. Heywood Broun defended her right to be herself in his column: "I would hold it against her rather than in her favor if she quit certain causes with which she had been associated simply on account of the fortuitous circumstances that he happens to have been chosen President." Broun was "delighted to know that we are going to have a woman in the White House who feels that like Ibsen's Nora, she is before all else a human being and that she has a right to her own individual career regardless of the prominence of her husband."

"Perhaps I have acquired more education than some of you [who] have educated me realize," she said at the Women's Trade Union League farewell. "I truly believe that I understand what faces the great masses of people in the country today. I have no illusions that any one can change the world in a short time. Things cannot be completely changed in five minutes. Yet I do believe that even a few people, who want to understand, to help and to do the right thing for the great numbers of the people instead of for the few can help."

How much Franklin had hurt her by his refusal to allow her to handle some of his mail was suggested in her invitation to Hick to pick her up at the Mayflower the day before Inauguration and to go with her to the cemetery in Rock Creek Park. Hick had come to Washington on her last assignment with Mrs. Roosevelt before Bess Furman, another top-flight reporter, took over. The two women alighted after they reached the cemetery and Mrs. Roosevelt guided Hick to a pine-shrouded grove in which stood the larger-than-life bronze figure of a cowled woman. It was the Saint-Gaudens memorial to Henry Adams' wife, who had committed suicide.

"In the old days when we lived here, I was much younger and not so very wise," she said almost in a soliloquy as the two women sat on the stone bench that faced the statue. "Sometimes I'd be very unhappy and sorry for myself. When I was feeling that way, if I could manage, I'd come here alone, and sit and look at that woman. And I'd always come away somehow feeling better. And stronger. I've been here many, many times." Henry Adams called the statue *Grief*, but for her it represented a woman who had transcended pain and hurt to achieve serenity.

That night Eleanor again had Hick dine with her at the Mayflower. She showed her a copy of the Inaugural speech that Franklin was to deliver the next day at the Capitol. Mrs. Roosevelt told Hick to wait for her in her big sitting room. It was at the northwest corner of the White House and had been Lincoln's bedroom. Eleanor had begun to furnish it to her own taste. Nancy and Marion had come down to Washington and presumably were at the Capitol for Franklin's speech. Nancy stayed on for eight days to help Eleanor "make the second floor into a living quarter for the Roosevelt family," said Marion. Hick did not mention their presence in her account of the Inaugural. She was a woman of moods, jealousies, and resentments. Eleanor understood this but she wanted her old friends with her as well as her new.

Although the room was filling up with Mrs. Roosevelt's things and photographs, it seemed empty to the waiting Hick. Finally Mrs. Roosevelt returned and much of what she proceeded to tell Hickok made the latter's story. "It was very, very solemn," she said, "and a little terrifying.

"The crowds were so tremendous, and you felt that they would do *anything*—if only someone would tell them *what* to do! . . .

"What I wanted to say," she ventured after many interruptions by members of the family, "is that one has a feeling of going it blindly. We are in a tremendous stream, and none of us knows where we are going to land.

"The important thing, it seems to me, is our attitude toward whatever may happen. It must be willingness to accept and share with others whatever may come and to meet the future courageously, with a cheerful spirit."

There was a family party that first evening. The guests numbered seventy-five and Eleanor met them at the front entrance. Hick was not among them, but she had secured a promise from Mrs. Roosevelt to keep a diary, which Eleanor began to do as soon as Hick returned to New York. The house was full of children and family, so that even people like Louis and Missy found rooms elsewhere during the Inauguration festivities. With Franklin's consent she assigned to Louis the large bedroom across the West Hall from her own sitting room. In time his photographs of Eleanor outnumbered those of the Boss. It was he who warned Hickok that "a reporter should never get too close to a news source." Was it concern for Mrs. Roosevelt and Hickok or jealousy?

Franklin had a bedroom next to Eleanor's sitting room, but it opened the other way into an oval study. Above the latter's door he hung a pastel painting of Eleanor of which he was particularly fond. Missy, when she moved over to the White House, was given a bedroom and tiny sitting room on the third floor. It was she who saw to it that there were tickets and a limousine for Mrs. Rutherfurd at the Inaugural. Tommy secured an apartment away from the White House. Henry and Elinor Morgenthau were also in the capital, he having been appointed Chairman of the Federal Farm Board.

Eleanor's diary testified to the strength and tenderness of her attachment to Hick. It came to form a unique chronicle of Eleanor's role at the center of government. Her first letter was dated "Sunday night, March 5th." Washington in the first days of the New Deal was bedlam, even the still precincts of the White House were invaded by the scurryings of government officials. There she sat at the end of the day in a pool of quiet at her desk in the sitting room, overlooking the White House grounds in the rear and the Washington monument. She wrote in longhand to Hick, as she did to all of her closest friends. She was forty-nine, but the emotions were those of a passionate, lovelorn woman:

> Hick my dearest. I cannot go to bed tonight without a word to you. I felt a little as though a part of me was leaving to-night. You have grown so much to be a part of my life that it is empty without you even though I'm busy every minute.
>
> These are strange days & very odd to me but I'll remember the Fay's* & try to plan pleasant things & count the days between our times together.
>
> To begin my diary, after you left I went to supper taking FJr. and John Mama & Betsy & we were followed by FDR & James just before the boys left. I went to station with them & left the Secret Service man at home. (1st assertion of independence!) Saw the boys on train. Gov. Ely† took trouble to come up to me & tell me he thought F's speech was great. Quite a change! Returned, had a short talk with F.D.R. James & Betsy, read Proclamation. Tommy came & we arranged tomorrow's work. At ten Meggy & I took her to the gate & I thought of you & 'Prince.'‡ She seemed very happy & said everyone had had a good time, also that you looked 'stunning' dressed up! I then went back & devoted ¾ of an hour talking to Mama, then listened to F.D.R. broadcast, sorted mail & am now preparing for bed. So endeth my first Sunday.
>
> I'll call you to-morrow night & this should reach you Tuesday a.m.
>
> Oh! darling. I hope on the whole you will be happier for my friendship. I felt I had brought you so much discomfort & hardship to-day & almost more heartache than you could bear & I don't want to make you unhappy—All my love I shall be saying to you over thought waves in a few minutes
>
> > Good night my dear one
> > Angels guard thee
> > God protect thee
> > My love enfold thee
> > All the night through
>
> > > Always yours
> > > E.R.

She had not wanted to make Hick "unhappy," the last part of her letter said. Hick's expectations clearly no longer were those of a reporter, for no other reporter had been given the advantages she had. She had become a friend and more than a friend, but the bliss of her

* The Elton Fays were friends of Hickok.

† Governor Joseph B. Ely of Massachusetts had supported Al Smith in that state's primary in which Smith had gained a stunning victory.

‡ Prinz was a German shepherd. Hick was devoted to him and from her meager weekly salary of fifty dollars paid not only a substantial food bill for him but for the services of an auxiliary dog walker. She enjoyed dogs; also, she was lonesome. Meggy was a female Scotty that belonged to Eleanor and had to be exiled after she bit a reporter on the lip.

intimacy with Eleanor Roosevelt sharpened the pangs of jealousy and loneliness when she was not with her. Eleanor had made her the closest of her friends, but she was also the newest, and she quickly sensed, and Eleanor understood that she did so, that there were others, Nan and Marion with Nan bustling about helping Eleanor with picture and furniture arrangements, and Louis, who was as much her political mentor as Franklin's, and Elinor Morgenthau, with whom she arranged to ride in Rock Creek Park, and Earl, who although married and in New York was always on her mind.

Hick would have preferred a world well lost for love, but that was not to be. She had to accept Eleanor's friends as well as her freely offered avowals of love on Eleanor's terms. Eleanor was the "First Lady," a natural aristocrat, whose very interest in her was a mystery but a marvelous one. Eleanor's acute awareness enabled her to understand, however, her friend's "heartaches," and she arranged for the times when she could phone, trips where they might be alone together, and she kept Hick in touch by sending her the diary she had begun to keep.

The next day, March 6, another long letter went off, postmarked "Monday night":

Hick darling,

Oh! how good it was to hear your voice. It was so inadequate to try to tell you what it meant. Jimmy was near & I couldn't say je t'aime et je t'adore as I longed to do but always remember I am saying it & that I go to sleep thinking of you & repeating our little saying.

Well, now for the diary! Got up at 7:15 walk with Meggie, breakfast in my room and suddenly Missy appeared half asleep from the Powhatan to announce Cermak's* death. Then she had breakfast in my room & I began to unpack & move furniture. Tommy & Nan came about nine & I left them in charge & went off with F.D.R. and James at 9:45 to Sen. Walsh's funeral. I sat in the Senate gallery & the coffin with the candles & lovely flowers looked impressive but I thought the service very unimpressive & the people in the gallery seemed to have come to a show rather than to mourn someone they cared about. I saw Frances Perkins for a minute in F.D.R.'s room. She is a little startled to find how many purely social people invite her for purely exhibition purposes!

Back by 11 & moved furniture till 12 then press conference of which I told you. I had all governors at conference and their wives to lunch, then a little more furniture moved . . . 4:20 Nat. Women's Press Ass tea, then home to find a mixture at tea with Mama & Miss Mills came. 7:30 Isabella† came to dine with me & we had a short talk about her

* Mayor Anton J. Cermak of Chicago was killed by the assassin's bullet intended for Roosevelt.

† The former Isabella Selmes had married John Greenway after Robert Ferguson's death.

children & Congress & Anna & Elliott. At last 12:10 bed & a talk with you, the nicest time of the day. A week from tomorrow! I came back from the telephone & began marking my calendar, Tuesday week is so much better than Thursday!

Nan has been such a help & Tommy too. I should be lost without them. Anna is enjoying life & I am a little afraid of gossip! Poor children! Make her show you her spectacles. She goes home Wednesday.

My room is nearly in order & my bed is in the little room & I can see the monument from it. A great comfort the monument has always been to me. Why, I wonder.

Give Jean* my love. She is a sweet person. No one is like you though Hick. I love you & good night.

Devotedly ER

Hick had suggested that Eleanor hold press conferences and, after clearing it with Franklin and Louis, she held her first, limiting it to women reporters so as to encourage the papers to employ more women. The women assembled in the Red Room and she came in, outwardly serene, inwardly a-tremble. She had been brought up to avoid the press. She handed around a box of chocolates and proceeded to field questions like a veteran. The conference produced little news but set a significant precedent especially for women. Hick chortled when Eleanor described the scene to her. Franklin was to hold his first press conference the next day. Hick could not have asked for a better pupil, even though it was Bess Furman of the AP's Washington Bureau who covered the conference.

Hick also had been made privy to Eleanor's problems with her children, although as she was unmarried and childless her advice would have lacked a certain reality. Eleanor had talked with her about her children during the campaign. She had never opposed her husband's public career, she explained: "Public office is a duty to those qualified to fill it," but it was certainly bad for the children, I remember Theodore [Theodore Roosevelt, Jr., her first cousin] saying once that he thought his father's being President was the worst thing that could have happened to him [T.R., Jr.]. "And I rather think he was right." Children of a public man learned early, she went on, that they cannot be "first" with their father. They are robbed of much of his time and companionship and he of theirs.

Because of his polio Franklin had been even less available to his children than the normal public official. Eleanor felt this keenly, particularly at the time. Her eldest child, Anna, whose marriage to the stockbroker Curtis Dall in 1926 had been in part an effort to escape the tensions between her father and mother, had found Curtis difficult

* Jean Dixon, actress, an old Minneapolis friend of Hick.

to live with, and had fallen in love secretly with a young reporter covering her father in Albany for the Chicago *Tribune*, John Boettiger.
Eleanor liked him, often teased Anna that she had known John before
Anna did, and, although he was married, smiled on the romance and
shielded it from public view. She even undertook to edit a McFadden
magazine with the melodramatic title of *Babies Just Babies* because it
provided a job for Anna. The latter's two children, Sistie and Buzzie
Dall, often were with her at the White House and became favorites of
the photographers and newspaper people. But discreet as John and
Anna were, Eleanor, as she wrote Hick, was "a little afraid of gossip."

Elliott's problems disturbed her even more, she confessed to Hick.
He was only twenty-two, had married a Pennsylvania heiress, Betty
Donner, when he was scarcely twenty, fathered a son, and now had decided to seek his fortunes out west without wife or son. Anna and his
mother were the only ones in whom he had confidence, and it was a
measure of Eleanor's trust in Hick that she made her privy to her worries about the son whom the other children felt she favored.

Her daily letters to Hick chronicled her efforts to seat herself firmly
on what she called the "merry-go-round" constituted by life in the
White House. The Depression was touching bottom. Banks everywhere
were closed. Even middle-class families were being forced into ram-
shackle "Hoovervilles." The bonus veterans driven out of Washington
by General MacArthur and President Hoover were converging on the
capital for another try. Soviet Russia, with the most successful propa-
ganda hoax in history, pretended, even as millions of its "kulaks" were
being slaughtered, that Stalin with his five-year plans had discovered
how to immunize Soviet society from the ravages of the Depression.
But even Moscow, as did the other world capitals, looked to the new
administration for a lead.

At the heart of that administration was a group of human beings
confronting almost Sisyphean tasks with poise, serenity, and an infectious buoyancy. In Eleanor's letters, especially to Hick, we get some picture of how the extended Roosevelt family embraced its new responsibilities.

> March 7 (?) 1933
>
> Hick darling, All day I've thought of you & another birthday I *will* be
> with you & yet to-night you sounded so far away & formal. Oh! I want
> to put my arms around you. I ache to hold you close. Your ring is a
> great comfort. I look at it & think she does love me, or I wouldn't be
> wearing it!
>
> Well, here goes the diary (let me know when you get bored!) Break-
> fast downstairs Nan & I joined, very late, by James. Then ER inter-
> views Mrs. Nesbitt & begins at the top of the house, meets all the do-
> mestics & talks over work. Then (?) with Tommy to meet Secretarial

force & 11:30 Sioux Indians, at 11:45 the exec. sec. of the Girl Scouts & must go to a meeting (minus? uniform) on Saturday at five. Then lunch & a tour of the White House, then take Mama to train & have tea & take a party to the concert. There I thought only of you & wanted you even more than I do as a rule. Home at seven & Tommy & I worked till 11:15 & then I put all my children to bed. Elliott & Ralph Hitchcock go West to-morrow a.m. Louis moved in & Mary Howe came to stay to-day. Missy moves in to-morrow.

Nan has been the greatest help and has done most of the furniture moving etc. She stays till Thursday night & I hope all the pictures will be hung by then.

By Saturday I hope to begin to read, & write, & think & feel again. What shall we read Hick? You choose first.

It is late 1:15 & I am very weary, so goodnight my dearest one, a world of love & how happy I will be to see you Tuesday.

Ever yours,
E.R.

Tuesday night we talked and on March 8th

Hick dearest I know just how happy you are & I'm glad you'll be with Jean to-morrow night & so glad you have Prinz. Give him my love. My thoughts are around you!

Wednesday, 8th
12:30 a.m.

Dearest, Your two letters this morning were such a joy & I loved your letter to Miss Furman. She was outside Justice Holmes' when we went there to-day & I walked Meggie home, so she walked along with me & told me she was sending me your letter & you were coming on the 20th!

Just telephoned you, oh! it is good to hear your voice, when it sounds right no one can make me so happy! *Diary* 8:30 a.m. breakfast & saw Elliott & Ralph Hitchcock off for the West in a Plymouth roadster packed with bags so the top couldn't close. What a gamble it is. I wish I felt surer about Elliott. Saw the housekeeper at 9:30 and Colonel Grant* about accounts at 10. Was presented by a California man named Staley with a box of dates at 10:45 in the Red Room, and at 11 the Cabinet ladies came. We agreed on no entertaining till autumn except for children's egg rolling at Easter & veterans garden party. I told them I would receive at tea once a week (Saturday p.m. we meet the diplomats) and otherwise we would only have people in informally & Mrs. Garner was much relieved. Mrs. Farley is overcome by it, but willing to do her duty! They left at 12:15 & I did a little picture hanging & at one my lunch party came, Isabella & Jackie, Louis Ruppel, Elton & Mrs. Fay, John Boettiger, Anna, James, Missy, Tommy, Mary

* Colonel Ulysses S. Grant III, in charge of public buildings and grounds.

Baker & Nan. After showing them around at 2:45 Nan & I went to Sloane's to choose some lamps, then I went for [Leo] Casey & toured the town with him & brought him here for tea.

At 5:30 Franklin, James & I went to Justice Holmes. He is a fine old man with flashes of his old wit & incisiveness. We got back about the same time though I walked Meggie & was almost rude to Miss Furman! She's nice though & she likes you which melted my heart! We dined 8 'en famille' & it is now 12 & I am going soon to find out if F is staying up all night or not! I think when things settle I'll have some privacy & leisure & I have better hopes than I had of getting away & of cutting red tape & pomp & ceremony! Perhaps we'll be almost human by the time you come!

I miss you so much & I love you so much & please never apologize. I always know & understand. One does if one cares enough. My dear love to you.

E.R.

[March 9, 1933]

Hick dearest, It was good to talk to you & you sounded a bit happier. I hated to have Nan go to-night & yet it is rather nice to have a few hours alone, so I know how you feel but I shall miss Nan to-morrow. She has been such a help & apparently enjoyed herself. The one thing which reconciles me to this job is the fact that I think I can give a great many people pleasure & I begin to think there may be ways in which I can be useful. I am getting some ideas which I want to talk over with you.

Life is pretty strenuous. One or two a.m. last night & 12:15 now, & people still with F.D.R. but this should settle things more or less.

I liked the article 'The Forgotten Man to his President' which I read last night and much of it is so pat. You or I might have said it.

My pictures are nearly all up & I have you in my sitting room where I can look at you most of my waking hours! I can't kiss you so I kiss your picture good-night & good morning! Don't laugh! This is the first day I've had no letters & I missed it sadly but it is good discipline.

Now for the diary! Out with Meggie as usual. Breakfast at 8:30, housekeeper at 9:30, Mr. [Ike] Hoover at 10:30 & settled reductions in garage [staff]. Then visited the doctor who is still in the basement & got splint for my finger & went to kitchen. Put books and ornaments around & left at 11:40 for the Capitol. Back at 1:40. Casey for lunch. James brought a California Congressman, making us ten instead of eight at the last minute which was good training in our ways for the staff! After lunch, some went back to the Capitol. I took Nan & Casey to Mount Vernon & back. At 4:40 saw 2 ladies for 5 minutes each. One brought gifts & one wanted to reorganize all the government cafeterias!

Tea took Casey home & Louis to the garage to see his car. Back, dressed for dinner, & tonight dictated to Tommy & signed oodles of mail. Took Nan to train & Tommy home. Gus paid me a long visit while I signed mail & now 12:35 to bed!*

Anna & the children left today at 2, so I have asked John to go for a drive with me tomorrow morning. Remind me to show you a note he wrote me. He is pretty sweet & I am so sorry for them. James left at 3:30 by plane for Boston & returns with Betsy & Sara Saturday night. Betty wires that Elliott has reached Little Rock! Here is the chronicle of my family. A bit varied, isn't it? Mary Baker also left for Urbana this evening.

One more day marked off my dear. My dear may I forget there are other reporters present or must I behave? I shall want to hug you to death. I can hardly wait!

A world of love to you & goodnight & God bless you 'light of my life.'

E.R.

Hick darling, The air mail, special delivery letter has never come, but the next one came this morning & my dear I was glad. Remember one thing always no one is just what you are to me. I'd rather be with you this minute than anyone else & yet I love many other people & some of them can do things for me probably better than you could, but I've never enjoyed being with anyone the way I enjoy being with you.

Eleanor's pleasure in Hick's presence, her images of endearment, showed a depth of passion reminiscent of the immortal description of love as a form of madness in Plato's *Symposium:*

. . . The whole soul, stung in every part, rages with pain; and then again remembering the beautiful one, it rejoices. . . . It is perplexed and maddened, and in its madness it cannot sleep at night or stay in any one place by day, but is filled with longing and hastens wherever it hopes to see the beautiful one. And when it sees him and is bathed with the waters of yearning the passages that were sealed are opened, the soul has respite from the stings and is eased of its pain, and this pleasure which it enjoys is the sweetest of pleasures at the time. Therefore the soul will not if it can help it, be left alone by the beautiful one, but esteems him above all others, forgets for him mother and brothers and all friends, neglects property and cares not for its loss, and despising all the customs and proprieties in which it formerly took pride, it is ready to be a slave and to sleep wherever it is allowed, as near as possible to the beloved; for it not only reveres him who possesses beauty, but finds in him the only healer of its greatest woes. Now this condition, fair boy, about which I am speaking, is called Love by men.

* Gus Gennerich, a former New York policeman, succeeded Earl Miller as F.D.R.'s bodyguard and was a family favorite.

Was this love, or the infatuation stage of love, which this passage renders so reliably? In any case there are echoes of Eleanor's feelings for Hick in it. But not altogether, for always there were others and other commitments and even more the stern voices of duty and discipline that had taught her to transform desire into tenderness, solicitude, and serenity, which were the faces she presented to all around her.

Diary March 10th
Out with Meggie at 8:30, a cold, clear, beautiful day. Breakfast in the west sitting room [hall] much brighter than downstairs. Just Louis, Missy, and I, as Doc O'Connor,* who spent the night, breakfasted in his room. 9:30 Mrs. Nesbitt, 10:10, Mr. Hoover, 10:30, picture hangers & furniture movers. At 11:25 went off from back door in my car, picked John up at the Washington. He drove out to the Elton Fays' for me, as I wanted to leave some candy & magazines. I saw the baby & their cunning house & I longed to go to work in the kitchen. She's a sweet thing. Poor John, he's worried to death. I hope I imparted some of the philosophy of old age!

Back in time for lunch. Admiral and Mrs. Byrd & Margaret Donnelly who goes back to Albany today, & Tully were my guests. He's very proud of an organized committee he has formed to back FDR. I patted him on the back. Tommy & I moved books & furniture till 4, when we drove to the Congressional Club to meet the new Congressmen's wives, & then I dashed in to see Elinor Morgenthau. She's feeling better, but was sick over her calls!

Back here at 5 and had the Parishes, Denmans (here from California) Sheldon Whitehouses (on their way back to Guatemala, where he is our minister), and the Adolph Millers to tea. FDR appeared about 5:30 & brought Admiral Grayson, & everyone seemed to enjoy everyone else. The rooms begin to look homelike.†

My tea party left at 6:30. Dressed and dined at 7:30, just ourselves, and had a movie of FDR which Pathe is giving us and, of course, a "Krazy Kat" & then FDR told me where to hang all his pictures, so I ought to be all settled tomorrow.

We have our first official diplomatic tea tomorrow, & I'm just a bit scared!

I walked to the gate with Tommy & Meggie tonight, & she (Meggie, I mean) is getting very obstreperous (is that the way you spell it?) so we returned barking loudly & running after a rather terrified woman with a little boy, who was peacefully walking home past the White House.

* Basil O'Connor, Roosevelt's law partner, and one of his closest associates in law and politics; he became head of the National Infantile Paralysis Foundation.
† Adolph Miller, appointed to the Federal Reserve Board by Woodrow Wilson, had been a member of the Sunday night group that met weekly when Roosevelt was Assistant Navy Secretary. Admiral Cary Grayson had been Wilson's personal physician.

Did I tell you that the first day in his office, at 5 p.m. FDR found himself with nothing to do. Horrors! Nothing like that had happened to him in years! So he reached under his desk & rang all five bells, & people ran in from every side to find him calmly demanding something to do! He had the start of a cold yesterday. I fed him a pill. At the conference in the evening he took a senatorial pill, a congressional pill, a treasury one, an attorney general one, & today he is cured! He is having such a good time that his mood is amusing most of the time! We all watched the bill signed last night.

Darling I must stop writing nonsense, but it is good to hear your voice & I love you dearly. Goodnight & good morning if you get it in the morning.

Devotedly*

E.R.

Friday or rather Sat. 12:20 a.m.

* The Franklin D. Roosevelt Library dated the part of this letter that begins "F.D.R. told me where . . ." March 4, 1933. Hickok in transcripts of the letters that she began at one time to prepare for publication, minus, however, the personal parts, made it part of this letter. The internal evidence suggests that it belongs here.

X

Eleanor in the "Goldfish Bowl"

THUS FAR the author has grouped the materials that show
Eleanor in relation to her friends as a story that belongs
mainly to the annals of feminism. Unlike some feminists she
neither hated men nor preferred the company of women. Nor did she
deny the differences both physical and emotional between the sexes.
Her temperament was weighted towards finding the good in all people,
towards appraising their strengths and building on them, but she never
denied the differences among them.

Her relationship to Hickok and the letters growing out of it are
unique. But do those letters tell the tale of a friendship touched with
lesbianism, whatever that word may mean? Or are they the chronicle of
a quasi-spiritual figure, the set-apart kind whom William James dealt
with apologetically, lest he be considered sanctimonious. Even Sigmund
Freud did not reject saintliness, saying, however, that saints "were saved
from severe neuroses by their sainthood, their faith."* A perceptive
woman who read this paragraph commented, "These possibilities do
not exclude one another. Eleanor could have been *both* a spiritual being
and a woman who felt drawn to another woman. Especially if she disciplined her longings and channeled some of that energy into what you
call her 'service of love' to the country." And of course she was right.

* Gregory Zilboorg in an Introduction to *Beyond the Pleasure Principle*, Sigmund
Freud (New York: W. W. Norton, 1961), page x.

In the 1960s Hickok turned over her correspondence with Eleanor Roosevelt to the Franklin D. Roosevelt Library. It numbered 2,336 letters from Mrs. Roosevelt to Hickok and 1,024 from Hickok to Mrs. Roosevelt. At one time Hickok had herself begun a book based on Eleanor's letters and laboriously had transcribed to the typewriter some of those written in 1933. As a result she turned over to the library not the originals of many 1933 letters but her transcriptions, which omitted the expressions of endearment and closeness with which they usually began. The originals disappeared. In addition she burned some letters in the 1970s. Esther Lape told the author that Hick had wanted her as a witness of such a burning, even though Esther was not told what was in the letters. After Hick's death her sister burned a handful.

It would tax the reader's patience to publish textually all the letters to Hick that have survived as well as the thousands that Eleanor wrote mostly in longhand to other intimate friends usually at the end of a long day. The chronicler can only assure the reader that he is publishing whatever is of historical interest, whatever expresses Eleanor Roosevelt's character, and, especially for the purposes of this book, whatever shows the intensity of her relations with these closest friends.

As one seeks to understand the letters to Hickok, there is less help to be found, as we suggested earlier, in our knowledge of Sappho than of Gandhi and Tolstoy and of a book such as William James's *The Varieties of Religious Experience*.

Both Tolstoy and Gandhi went through their early lives as successes by conventional standards, the former as a great literary artist, the latter as a widely consulted lawyer. Both fell into crises of faith from which they emerged purified and sanctified. Worldly goods and praise became meaningless. They developed life styles of abnegation and austerity. Tolstoy encapsulated his salvation and teaching in the discovery that "the kingdom of God is within you," a conception that Gandhi, who kept an autographed picture of Tolstoy on his wall, embraced. Although aristocrats, they advocated a radical egalitarianism and the satisfactions of manual labor. They preached and practiced sexual continence. They had gotten their "souls in order," to use an expression of William James, and their escape from the falsehoods of polite society had released new energies.

Eleanor's flight from falsehood had begun with the Lucy Mercer affair. Her struggle against despair and the impulses to suicide turned into an effort to forge a new personality at whose center were her desire to love and her passion to be of use. Some people, wrote William James, had "a genius for love." Eleanor was one of them. Such people, said James, live in a "state of grace" and to read of them "is to feel encouraged and uplifted and washed in a better moral air." People who had "an inborn genius for certain emotions" differed from "ordinary people" in that "magnanimities once impossible are now easy; paltry conventionalities and mean incentives once tyrannical hold no sway. . . ." That was the case with persons for whom "spiritual emotions are the habitual centres of [their] personal energy. . . ." James employed a striking analogy to describe how the "passion of love" endowed the person loved with new looks, values, attitudes. He spoke of the way the sunrise on Mount Blanc transforms it from a "corpse-like grey to a rosy enchantment." Such passions were non-logical, beyond our control, and were a "gift."

Eleanor later wrote in *This I Remember* that she lived through the White House years "very impersonally. It was almost as though I had erected someone a little outside of myself who was the president's wife." Under the impact of the duties imposed upon her as White House chatelaine her vital center retreated deeper and deeper within herself. Perhaps it was the desperate effort to hold onto that vital center that produced the explosion of love for Hick. It was as if the self-surrender involved in her love of Hick released the softness of heart and magnanimity, as well as calmness and courage with which she met the new demands upon her and instead of being defeated by them used them to make herself the nation's conscience.

Eleanor's next letter to Hickok was filled with chitchat about Franklin, about Jimmy and his wife, "Bets," Elliott's "swell time on his way West," Missy, John Boettiger's "rather interestingly told" book on the Lingle* murder, "more pictures hung," her meeting in the D.A.R. building with the Girl Scouts, "E.R. not in uniform," how together with Mrs. Irene Robbins, Mrs. Edith Helm and Mrs. Early she poured for the diplomatic reception and managed some personal exchange with almost everyone there. She also ventured a few brisk maternal admonitions to Hickok: "Stick to your desk, lose 20 lbs more & you'll forget you are forty & please go to see the doctor next week." She ended on a note of serenity and yearning:

> I miss you greatly my dear. The nicest time of the day is when I write you. You have a stormier time than I do but I miss you as much I think. I couldn't bear to think of you crying yourself to sleep. Oh! how I wanted to put my arms around you in reality instead of in spirit. I went & kissed your photograph instead & the tears were in my eyes. Please keep most of your heart in Washington as long as I'm here for most of mine is with you!
>
> A world of love & good night my dear one.
>
> E.R.

Eleanor was forty-nine in 1933, but there is something schoolgirlish in this self-portrait of a kiss bestowed upon Hick's photograph with

---

* Boettiger covered the story and helped apprehend the killer of Jake Lingle, a fellow reporter.

tears in her eyes. Her cousin Corinne had spoken of the Saturday Putney afternoons when the girls at Allenswood filled the rooms of the girls on whom they had crushes with posies and other small gifts. Eleanor's had led the rest. It was as if she now had to regress to the intensity of her Allenswood days to find ways to express the intensity of the love that she felt.

Carroll Smith-Rosenberg in "The Female World of Love and Ritual: Relations Between Women in Nineteenth Century America" described "the long-lived, intimate, loving friendships" between women in the nineteenth century as an aspect of the female experience that historians have chosen to ignore. The adoration of photographs, the use of noms de plume, the ardent letters, the domestic embraces, the closeness with which women shared their sorrows, anxieties, joys, were all considered "both socially acceptable and fully compatible" with married life. The issue of genital contact seemed irrelevant.

A year later Nancy Sahli in "Changing Patterns of Sexuality and Female Interaction in Late Nineteenth Century America"* examined, also by the use of letters and diaries, why the network of "female support and intimacy" described by Smith-Rosenberg had turned more guarded, restrained, and less acceptable as the century ended. She blamed the increasing secularization of American society, urbanism, the triumph of science and technology, and an easing of earlier intense religiosity. Her speculation is suggestive. Equally pertinent to this effort to understand Eleanor Roosevelt's relationship to Hickok is Nancy Sahli's discussion of the custom of "smashing" another nineteenth-century custom. It was practiced at the handful of women's colleges that existed at the time. "We would probably call it lesbianism," writes Nancy Sahli, "although sensual homoemotional behavior is a more accurate definition." She used an 1873 letter that appeared in the *Yale Courant* to describe it:

> There is a term in general use at Vassar, truly calculated to awaken within the *ima penetralia* of our souls all that love for the noble and the aesthetic of which our natures are capable. The term in question is 'smashing.' When a Vassar girl takes a shine to another, she straightway enters upon a regular course of bouquet sendings, interspersed with tinted notes, mysterious packages of 'Ridgeley's Mixed Candies,' locks of hair perhaps, and many other tender tokens, until at last the object of her attentions is captured, the two become inseparable, and the aggressor is considered by her circle of acquaintances as—smashed. The mortality, so to speak, resulting from these smashups, is frightful to contemplate. One young lady, The 'Irrepressible,' rejoices in more than thirty. She keeps a list of them, in illuminated text, framed and hung up in her room like a Society poster. How 'In the name of the

* Third Berkshire Conference on the History of Women, June 1976.

hogshead of banter/ Devoured at each breakfast at Vassar,' such a custom should have come into vogue, passes masculine comprehension. But the solemn fact remains, and Vassar numbers her smashes by the score.

The custom of "smashing" bothered college authorities, especially as there was a masculine prejudice against higher education for women on the spurious ground that it harmed them physically. One of the first reports of the Association of Collegiate Alumnae, later known as the American Association of University Women, was on physical education. It challenged the masculine notion that academic rigors resulted in poor health among women students. Alice Stone Blackwell, the daughter of Lucy Stone and herself a pioneer in the women's movement, was a member of the committee. She had graduated from Boston University in 1881 and in a letter commented on the committee's consideration of smashing:

We did have such a delightful time, talking over the needs of the different colleges, the various things that injured the girls's health, & what could be done about it. And you will be surprised but the girls gave it as their strong opinion that one thing which damaged the health of the girls seriously was 'smashes'—an extraordinary habit which they have of falling violently in love with each other, and suffering all the pangs of unrequited attachment, desperate jealousy &c &c, with as much energy as if one of them were a man. I could hardly have believed that the things they told were not exaggerations, if Maria Mitchell hadn't told me, when I was visiting at Vassar, what a pest the 'smashing' was to the teachers there—how it kept the girls from studying, & sometimes made a girl drop behind her class from year after year. Miss Brown, of the committee, told us of her own experience, evidently not without some embarrassment, but for the general good; how she, at Smith, though not at all given to that sort of thing, had been a victim. 'A veteran smasher' attacked her, & captured her, & soon deserted her for someone else; & she used to cry herself to sleep night after night, & wake up with a headache in the morning. And they write all sorts of things, like a real courting of the Shakesperian style. If the 'smash' is mutual, they monopolize each other & 'spoon' continually, & sleep together & lie awake all night talking instead of going to sleep; & if it isn't mutual the unrequited one cries herself sick & endures pangs unspeakable. I listened with undisguised curiosity & amazement, for we had very little of that sort of thing at B.U. My theory is that it comes of massing hundreds of nervous young girls together, & shutting them up from the outside world. They are just at the romantic age, they see only each other, & so their sentimentality has no other outlet. The coeducational colleges don't suffer much from 'smashes.' . . . There are plenty of cases of 'particular friends,' but few or none of 'smashes.'

Havelock Ellis's book *Sexual Inversion* appeared in 1897.* He did not consider that feminine closeness, including "smashes," meant lesbianism or even that lesbianism necessarily meant either physical involvement or sexual activity.

Eleanor's letter of March 12 was a Hick transcript; the original is missing. It lacks the personal endearments which Hick must have omitted. It was dated "Sunday" and Franklin was to deliver his first Fireside Address that evening. Eleanor may have been "smashed" on Hick, but to the world, especially those about her at the White House, she was a poised and accomplished hostess:

> My diary tonight will be short & simple! Walked with Meggie at 9 this morning, had breakfast. Mrs. Nesbitt at 9:30, then Mr. Hoover. Then signed mail with Tommy. I left at 10:40 and walked to church, home again, accompanied by Emma Bugbee. The Woodins, Derns, Morgenthaus, Parishes, William Phillips, Miss Patten here for lunch. Very pleasant until poor Mrs. W. realized she must move, & then she nearly died. Finally she came & asked whether F. dismissed her or she left & we sent her home!
>
> 3:15 I started off with Meggie & Louis in his car for Great Falls, ending up at Ruby Black's about 5. Her baby is a beauty & I wished he liked strangers but he may get accustomed to me if he comes & plays with the grandchildren later. I liked her & her husband, & their house is sweet.
>
> Got home at 6, signed more mail, dressed, & Martin Conboy, Sam Rosenman & Ernest Lindley came to supper. Afterwards, while we waited for F's broadcast, we lit the fire in my room & sat there. Ernest says he has worked so hard he hasn't had time enough even to sleep. I asked him to bring Betty for lunch when he comes down. We listened to the broadcast, I saw Tommy on her way home, & now I am on my way to bed.

She flew to New York, accompanied by Tommy and the faithful Emma Bugbee of the *Herald Tribune*. She had, we assume, the usual flurry of appointments, as well as engagements with Hick, but it all was tranquil compared to the round of activities that greeted her on her return to the White House:

> Thursday night
> 12:25 a.m. (March 16)
>
> Hick darling, I've just said 'goodnight' & you are right we should not do it every night so I'll probably put a 'special' on this & not call you tomorrow in the hope that I won't mind not hearing your voice when I know I'm going to hear it on Saturday. Oh! dear, I can hardly wait!
>
> Well, we had a very bumpy trip but I was fine & poor Tommy upchucked all day & so did Emma at least on the plane.

* It was reprinted by the Arno Press, New York, 1975.

Arrived here & John Sargent met me & Maude was at the house. The horses have come & Chief is settling down. I had Frances Perkins, Grace Abbott, Elinor Morgenthau, Ruth Bryan Owen, Mary Miller & Mrs. Denman to lunch. Saw a man about the welfare of Tenn. Mountain children, took Maude to the Senate to hear some dull speeches on beer and listened to F's message on farm relief. It is not very profitable for me to go to the Senate or Congress as I hear so badly. Got home, dressed & received the Supreme Court & I think they enjoyed their tea. Had a talk with John Boettiger on the telephone, did some mail, & dressed for dinner. Fred Hall (Senator fr. Maine & an old friend of Maude's) and Steve Early to dinner & then were given a private showing of the movie 'Gabriel Over the White House.' Some of it is raw & silly but oh! some of it is swell & I have so much more faith in the people than Fred Hall type. He'd have soldiers out if a million unemployed marched on Washington & I'd do what the President does in the picture! So we argued & I finally took the dogs for their evening walk & we are going to bed after a goodnight to you.

I love you & seeing you again was such joy. Bless you my dearest.

ER

In *Gabriel Over the White House*, the President, portrayed by Walter Huston, begins as a weak man dominated by his cabinet. After an automobile accident, however, inspired by Archangel Gabriel, he becomes earnest and strong-minded, dismisses his cabinet, and when an army of a million unemployed march on Washington, he decides to go to Baltimore to meet them, a gesture of identification and reconciliation of which Eleanor thoroughly approved and which she emulated in her own expedition under Louis Howe's guidance to the veterans' bonus camp.

The next day was her wedding anniversary, and there was essentially a family dinner to celebrate it that night. But Eleanor does not mention the anniversary, at least not in the typescript that Hick has left us of "the diary of a long day," which was chiefly of people received and social events lived through.

The March 21 letter vividly described Eleanor's adjustment to the White House, especially the dinner for the Prime Minister of Poland, Ignace Paderewski, who also happened to be the most noted pianist of the time; her use of Mrs. Sheila Hibben, a well-known nutritionist, to educate her housekeeper, Mrs. Nesbitt, whom she had brought down from Hyde Park, where Mrs. Nesbitt had also been head of the local League of Women Voters; Eleanor's experiment with a "7½ cent" menu; and her canter on horseback followed by a covey of still and moving-picture cameramen.

Tuesday, March 21
[Hickok's transcript]

Driving rain this morning, so lazily sent the dogs out. Breakfast at 8:30, Mrs. Nesbitt at 9:30, Tommy getting people for dinner with

Paderewski, telephoned. Ike Hoover, then a Dr. Taylor, expert in vocational guidance who had tested FJr., requested an interview, & I had to see him for 20 minutes. Then a Mr. Black from California, a friend of Mrs. Greenway's must talk to me about an unemployment scheme for 15 minutes & then got him an appointment with Frances Perkins which was what he wanted. Next Mrs. Hibben, who is to educate Mrs. Nesbitt & the cooks in American menus, and lo & behold it was 11:45 & time to visit the amaryllis show. Tommy & Missy went, too. I never saw one before. Do you know them? Huge flowers like lillies on a stiff stem. Red is the foundation color, but there are all kinds of variations, even to one pure white with a tinge of green in the center, but all the other whites had at least a streak of red. A good color show, but not a flower I would enjoy! Mrs. Wallace there to meet me, & Mrs. Hull & Mrs. Roper.

Lunch at home at 12:30 (7-½ cent, Miss Rose menu). Mrs. Cummings & Mrs. Hibben to lunch. Then took Mrs. C (who went home this afternoon for some weeks) to see the house & offices & was reminded that I hadn't had my nose treated, so bade her goodbye & had it done. From 2:30 to 3:15 dictated to Tommy. Seated the dinner, etc., dressed & went riding at 3:30. Cameras & movies followed us nearly a mile. After I'd been out a while I began to enjoy it (I'd been really scared to begin) and I think I'm going to love it, & I did feel so much fitter.

Confession is good for the soul, so I'll tell you my sin of the day! I forgot to put down a verbal invitation which I accepted for Tommy & me to lunch with Mrs. Walsh (the widow) & so I had to go, hot & muddy, at 4:30 to call & apologize, & we'll lunch there tomorrow. Home, cooled off by this time, & no time to change & received Mrs. Garner & her two friends for tea, but they were dear about it (my riding clothes, I mean) & thrilled when F. came in. After he & James had tea, Tommy & I worked on mail (signing, mostly) till 7:20. Then she went home & I dressed & went down at 7:50 & received like a lady, & Ike Hoover approved! We had the Polish Ambassador (he's an old dear, we got on very well, & I am to read poetry to him when he comes to tea!) Mr. P. is always a joy, and his secretary very nice. Secretary of State & Mrs. Hull, Senator & Mrs. Robinson, Senator & Mrs. McNary, Representative & Mrs. Snell, L.H., Missy, Jimmy, Sunshine Robbins, Mrs. Fort (an old friend of J's), Eddie Melcher, Mr. & Mrs. Bill Hard, Anne O'Hare McCormick, Mrs. Hugh Wallace. Food was good, but service very slow. Must do a bit of ordering tomorrow. The really important part, however, was that I think people talked & enjoyed each other, except for Mrs. McNary, who was heavy! We had a short & very light movie, which I could have done without. Everyone left, & Mr. P. went to bed, and I walked dogs. I had to wait awhile for James, who left for Boston at 1:55 & now in a minute I'll be off to bed. Elliott has written me twice and is positively lyrical and sounds so happy!

A world of love & good night, my dear, dear friend!

Devotedly—ER

Eleanor was an ascetic. She showed it not only by her lack of interest in food, her ten-dollar dresses, her few hours of sleep, long walks, and hard rides, but the book she undertook to do, *It's Up to the Women,** stressed austerity and spartanism. The women who had borne hardship and privation in the conquest of the wilderness excited her admiration. "Perhaps we need again a little of that stern stuff our ancestors were made of," she wrote. She needed risk and harshness to challenge the soul's energy. "Some austerity and wintry negativity," insisted William James, "some roughness, danger, stringency, and effort, some 'no! no!' must be mixed in, to produce the sense of an existence with character and texture and power." An icy bath before breakfast after having slept in the coldest of rooms was Eleanor's way of habituating herself to toughness.

"Anna called tonight & that helped," she wrote Hick the next day, and after settling with Louis Howe "who should work in Dem. Hdqts. Women's Div." devoted most of the rest of the letter to Paderewski, whom she was turning into a friend:

> Dictated till we went at 4:30 to Paderewski concert. Too beautiful. Tommy really enjoyed it. Missy was glad to hear a celebrity! Home at 7, dressed. Dinner with Paderewski & his secretary, Sam Rosenman, & Tully as our only guests. F. at work all evening. I sat with P until he left at 10:30, then had John [Roosevelt] for ¾ of an hour, poor kid. Now must go to bed.

So the letters that Hickok transcribed went. There was a horseback ride with Marion "under the bluest of skies & through woods that spoke of Spring on every side." She visited the Corcoran Gallery and doubted that her offer for one of the watercolors would be accepted. Two newspaperwomen came in to discuss how to make her weekly press conference "more interesting & useful." Four hundred "lady chemists or wives of chemists" came to tea, then she dashed upstairs to a more select tea party. She complained mildly of an overlong interview: "Oh, dear, I wish Governor [Nellie Tayloe] Ross would learn to talk to the point & think fast! Not very kind, am I & she is such a sweet nice woman!" She took Aunt Maude and her husband, David Gray, to the Folger Memorial Shakespeare Library "& that was a treat. Sometime you & I must go there." She came back to the White House for "an interview which Cissy Patterson had asked for & which I dreaded." Eleanor explained her anxiety. "She is bitter & can be malicious & untruthful. But I felt sorry for her before we finished our interview, & I suppose I'll writhe over what she writes."

Cissy had known Eleanor since debutante days, when her racy behavior had startled a very correct and somewhat prudish Eleanor. So had

* Published in New York by Frederick A. Stokes, 1933.

Alice Roosevelt. Alice and Cissy were competitors for men, for the limelight, and both loved to scandalize society. Cissy, an heiress of the Chicago Patterson newspaper clan, was now editor of the Washington *Herald,* a considerable power. Eleanor Roosevelt may have quaked inwardly, but outwardly she was all poise and disinterestedness, and the story that Mrs. Patterson, who had known her so long, wrote reflected her surprise at the ability of the once-diffident Eleanor to move through "these cram-crowded days of hers with a sure, serene and blithe spirit." Eleanor's first answer about her robust constitution did not satisfy Cissy. Nor would she accept the sequel: "When I have something to do—I just do it." A narcissistic woman herself, Cissy wanted to know how she escaped the "sick vanity" and "wounded ego" that sapped other people's energies. "You are never angry, for instance?"

"Oh, no, I really don't get angry. . . . You see I try to understand people."

"But when you were young, were you free like this? So free—so free of yourself?"

"No. When I was young I was very self-conscious."

Then how had she achieved her remarkable self-mastery? Cissy persisted. Eleanor evaded a specific reply. "Little by little. As life developed I faced each problem as it came along. As my activities and work broadened and reached out, I never tried to shirk. I tried never to evade an issue. When I found I had something to do—I just did it. Really, I don't know . . ."

Cissy abandoned her effort to get Eleanor to be more specific about her adjustment to the Lucy Mercer affair, about which Cissy would surely have known. Regardless of how Eleanor had managed to achieve her tranquillity and self-command, Cissy was certain: "Mrs. Roosevelt has solved the problem of living better than any woman I know."

Eleanor reported more comings and goings at the White House to Hick, who always pressed for additional news. "Sometimes I think I am the Washington 'Merry-Go-Round'!" she said of her busyness, which, in fact, she loved although she always denied that, to herself as well as to others. She was particularly worried about Anna, who was being secretly courted by John Boettiger. The latter was married. So was Anna. "She's been lost without John and no word from him & very anxious, poor kid, but she's swell. I wonder if you bear it better at her age?" She was solicitous for Hick, trying to strengthen her friend's spirits with a dash of her own:

Hick, darling: I hate you to say 'I'm only a reporter.' You are a very good one, & you will some day be as good a journalist as Anne O'Hare McCormick. Her things are good, but her hold is that she has a reputation & she can get to see important people. She doesn't hesitate to use her friends. She did get to me & through me to FDR & there is no one you couldn't see! If I take a trip to Mexico will you go with me? We might get some good materials. I have an idea even Gaspé [a peninsula in Quebec Province to which they were planning a trip together] may yield some. Wouldn't the AP let you write for a magazine? By the way, can you get off June 17th? F wants to go off on a cruise from Groton to Marblehead & the next Friday Campobello for the weekend (This is a secret.) I'll have to go up if he goes, & if you can't go, I'll arrange for you to take a train from N.Y. to Ellsworth & meet you there.

She had reported Elliott's progress westward with some relief. She now learned he was on the point of divorce:

Just talked to Anna on the telephone, & she told me Elliott telephoned her today that Betty was angry at the job he had taken & wanted a divorce. She [Betty] phoned me this a.m. & is coming here tomorrow with Bill [her baby]. If she is willing to go down, I think he should let her go & talk it out, but far be it from me to settle anyone else's lives! Anna was preparing for a talk with Curt and dreading it. Well, my dear, there will be no misunderstandings between us.

This last was a tantalizing phrase. Did she mean that her relationship to Hick was tantamount to marriage, or just the opposite, that, untrammeled by institutional ties and legal undertakings, the spirit of caring and intimacy that animated it had a better chance of survival?

She next reported that Elliott was calling her from Texas "collect!" and the note that she added showed how much she had come to rely upon Hickok. "Later—I'm to talk to Betty & find out their future. Oh, dear! I'd like to run to you. I want to lean on you. . . ." There Hick's transcript broke off.

Although Hickok was intensely jealous of Eleanor's other friends, all of whom had known her years before Hick did, Eleanor went serenely on her own way, determined to remain mistress of her own destiny. "Arranged everyone's occupations. Nan was busy with photos, so Meggie & I drove miles out 16th Street to call on the mother of a little jr. lt. [junior lieutenant] lost on the Akron*. . . . At 6:30 I drove Nan around the basin to see the cherries, & oh, they are lovely. Then home, fell into my clothes for early dinner. Greeted Curtis Bok & Esther Lape who came to see F. on Russia & the World Court."

Evidently Hickok had protested any suggestion she did not relish her role as newspaperwoman. "I do understand your joy & pride in your job & I have a deep respect for it," she assured Hick. "I know I'd glory in the newspapermen. I like to watch people I'm fond of & be proud of them. A world of love to you. I hated to have Nan go. . . . ER."

The emphasis she repeatedly placed on "hating" to have Nan go

* The lighter-than-air craft *Akron* after several test flights had crashed at sea off Barnegat Light in April 1933 and seventy-three were lost.

reflected a spontaneity of feeling, but it also may have been a warning to Hick that no one could possess her. Hick's discovery of this, as becomes clear in the correspondence, occasioned much heartache on Hick's part and regret on Eleanor's.

Feminist, diplomatist, campaigner against poverty and for equal rights, manager of the White House, she was all these things, but the family was always in her thoughts. "Came home to greet Fjr & friends." She drove to Union Station to spend "15 minutes" with James, who was on his way to Thomasville, Georgia, to join his wife Bets. "A wire from Elliott to me today demands to know the results of my conversation with Betty as he wants *all* settled at once! Isn't youth priceless? As though anything could ever be settled pronto with no loose ends & no regrets & no suffering! . . . Had a talk with Anna. Poor kid, blind faith in a kindly providence keeps her up but I fear a break sometime."

Hickok replied sympathetically and it comforted Eleanor to share her worries about her children with her:

Hick darling: What a dear you are! Your letter warmed my heart & made me a little ashamed. What have I to be depressed about! I hate to see the kids suffer, but I know one has to, & I suspect they suffer less than I sometimes think. Especially Elliott & Betty. I never talked to anyone. Perhaps that was why it all ate into my soul, & I look upon so many emotions more seriously than do the younger generation. In other words, I was a morbid idiot for many years! Only in the last ten years or so have I made friends to whom I have talked!

The last sentence might serve as an introduction to a book about "friendships of women," except that Eleanor's circle of friends included Earl and Louis, but the striking point was that she had discovered the joys of sharing work and intimacies only in the last ten years and what a difference that had made to her.

Elinor Morgenthau was one of those with whom she talked, and they rode almost daily. Spring had rarely seemed as alive as that April, and though it was in the middle of the historic series of events that have come to be known as the "Hundred Days," she had Franklin sitting next to her as one Sunday afternoon she headed her runabout into the country:

We had a glorious day, Hick, dear. Spring was in the air, & I drove my car, top down, leaving at 10:30, taking F.D.R. & John [Roosevelt] & Gus [Gennerich] in the rumble seat. We had a caravan, but the roads were not crowded, & the last part was lovely. The camp is enchanting, simple & beautiful.* Very shut in, therefore I cannot understand going

* The Rapidan camp used by Herbert Hoover.

as they did with a crowd, for shut in places to me need only a few intimate people. I'd like to spend a week there, & I'm not sure it isn't the
place for Tommy & me to go & write this darn book.

The book *It's Up to the Women,* which Eleanor referred to here,
came out in October. It was a feminist call to arms. "There have been
other great crises in our country and I think if we read our history carefully, we will find that the success of our meeting them was largely due
to the women in those trying times. . . . And I hold it is equally true
that in this present crisis it is going to be the women who will tip the
scale and bring us safely out of it."
The book had a chapter on parents and their children. It reflected
some of her own agony. "Each generation must learn by its own experience and though it may be hard to watch our children go through the
same mistakes which we went through, it will do no good to pursue
them with warnings drawn from our own experience. All we can do is
be worthy of their confidence and to refrain from criticism and recriminations and then in the words of the Scriptures we may be 'a very present help in time of trouble.' "
She was not so sure about Elliott's behavior. She and Franklin tried
to restrain that headstrong young man:

Elliott is meeting Betty in Memphis on Wednesday. Franklin talked
to him & then he called her. I dread it for her, & yet I see how she may
annoy him. Oh, dear, I am an old woman! At least they none of them
know it.

Eleanor began to send Elliott's letters to Hick, while her own letters
continued to detail daily life at the White House. "A rather nice day,"
she reported on Friday the thirteenth. She rode regularly in Rock Creek
Park, usually with Elinor, often with Missy, on Dot, the horse that Earl
had given her. At tea on the thirteenth the guests were a little unusual,
even for her. Present were only Sistie, age six, Buzz, age three, and the
Polish Ambassador:

Then I read poetry till 6:30, with the Polish Ambassador & Maude
Gray as audience: Ode to the Nightingale, Ode to the Grecian Urn, the
Highwayman, Milton's Sonnet on his Blindness, Danny Deever, the
Blessed Damozel. I enjoyed it & I think they did!

There was other, more worldly news: "I'd give something to know
anything authentic on Germany or Russia.
"F.D.R. is having a grand time, a conference today with Com[mit-
tee] on Agriculture, & he thinks he won them to support of the bill."
[The Triple A]
A reference to Mama, whom she had asked to supervise the rental of

their house on East Sixty-fifth Street: "A letter from Mama & no word about the house! I think she knows I want to know & is holding off!"

Her thoughts kept reverting to Elliott and Betty:

> I'm feeling tonight that the greatest responsibility anyone can have is that of making someone else suffer, & I suppose we all do it. Lord, keep me from it ever again is going to be my daily prayer. Betty just came in to tell me she had telephoned Elliott, & he wanted her to go ahead & didn't seem to care. She looks so white, but she's very self-controlled, & my heart aches!

Hick sent her a cynical quotation about human nature from George Bernard Shaw that evoked a more hopeful view from her: "He picks the flaws in us neatly but he does fail to see the virtues & there are many!" She believed in human perfectibility, but after a long talk with Anna she was not so sure: "It is so easy when you are not doing the suffering to see what one *should* do." When she saw Betty off "she offered to give me back my pearls (which I did not take) & was so sweet in ways which I must tell you about sometime that I just felt I couldn't bear it." She was in conflict over how she should deal with Elliott and when she took Louis for a drive "he told me what he thought should be done. . . ." Then she received the French Ambassador, had tea. ". . . more mail, & 14 for dinner & a movie ahead & I must dress."

Easter Sunday she attended services at the Tomb of the Unknown Soldier at 7:30 in the pouring rain and three hours later went to the cathedral. In between she wrote letters to her four boys: "I am praying for wisdom in my letter to Elliott."

Working for the AP, Hickok began to discover, interfered with her relationship with E.R. The AP had assigned Bess Furman to cover the First Lady in Washington. Hickok had introduced Bess to Mrs. Roosevelt, and helped her, but she did not like the separation for herself. She tried her hand at magazine pieces. Eleanor encouraged her:

> When you haven't the feeling of responsibility to the AP I know you have a happier time. I hope that, whatever your decision, it may be the right one for you. I want you to be happy in your work, but I want you to be free from this worry over finances. So I would find out if you could make good arrangements with Brandt* which would mean both more money & interesting work of the kind you love.

She had talked with Franklin and "it is settled that I go to Arizona if Elliott wants me to June 1st & join F.D.R. the 15th in Boston."

At the end of April her letter-diary was filled with comments about the visit of British Prime Minister Ramsay MacDonald and his daughter Ishbel. "F.D.R. & the P.M. have talked all evening, & when I went in to urge bed upon them I could see content reigned between them."

* Carl Brandt, a literary agent.

"Hick, darling," her next letter continued, "I like MacDonald & I think he is a great man. What delightfully well-read, cultured people some Englishmen are! He keeps on insisting on belonging to the people, but his tastes, we feel, would denote the gentleman of leisure." She talked for an hour with Frances Perkins, the Secretary of Labor, "on the chances of camps for unemployed women," and at 6:30 took "H.H. [Was it Harry Hopkins, the head of emergency relief, or Harry Hooker, an old friend and Franklin's former law partner?] to see the darker pink double cherry blossoms."

The statesmen went down the Potomac on the *Sequoia*, talking uninterruptedly. Hitler had come to power in Germany, Roosevelt was launched on the "Hundred Days" that took the United States down an opposite path. Eleanor sought a longer view: "Is history being made? What road is the world going to take? And will this day count? It is interesting, Hick."

The MacDonalds prepared to leave, and the French delegation, headed by Premier Edouard Herriot, arrived. "Honestly, Hick, these are dreadful days from the point of view of time, but most interesting." She squeezed in a ride with Elinor before breakfast, conferred with Molly Dewson, and then had James Farley and his aides in "& start them off on patronage for women. . . . I hope I didn't preach too much to Elliott."

Spurred on by Eleanor, Hickok, like Louis, counseled her about Elliott. "You said just the right thing," Eleanor assured her afterwards, "& I entirely agree & have tried to do what you suggest, though my letter may have sounded too austere. . . . By the way did I leave my sponge in your bathtub? If so, please bring! . . . I'll meet you & Anna at the airport."

The sedentary life was not for her. "Ruby Black [reporter for the United Press and *La Democracia* in Puerto Rico] with a man from Porto Rico who was interesting, I must go there. . . . At 10 Louis & I do the News, & I hope to get to bed at 12:30." Hick sent her encouraging news about Carl Brandt's reaction to her story ideas:

> I think Brandt sounds grand & the Ike Hoover story would be wonderful, but FDR would have to be consulted. I think he'd consent if you were doing it. What a story it would be! McCall's is good, too, though I don't see why you couldn't do both. I am glad to have you feel encouraged.

That letter was mailed from upstate New York. Together with Nan she journeyed north to Massena, New York, where Nan's father lived. Nan drove the roadster a third of the way, Eleanor the rest. The latter became drowsy towards the end "& Nan insisted on singing from then on!" On the way to Massena they also stopped in Syracuse to see Leo

Casey, the paralyzed state trooper who occupied a special place in Eleanor's heart.* He was driving to Malone State Police headquarters, in his specially fitted car, so Eleanor drove with him. She promised to see his captain on her return. When they did reach Malone, Earl and Ruth "blew in," and Earl drove her car while Nan went in the other. "I'm riding this morning with Earl & going over his lecture outline for him this p.m. to correct his grammar." They rode for three hours and visited a camp on nearby Chazy Lake which Earl was intent on renting. "I had promised to spend two weeks with them, & if they get this camp, it will be very restful & yet plenty to do. . . . Then I corrected Earl's speech outlines till supper & all of us listened to F.D.R. on the radio & went to bed. . . . I love you on Elliott & you are just right."

Elliott began to soften:

I have a funny wire from Elliott! 'Hope the remembrance of Mother's Day will not cause fainting spells to overcome the W.H. staff. Love & affection & hope that you will arrive out here as soon as you can for visit. Life will survive my rushing tactics & maybe I will, too. Elliott.' So, my dear, I will be going & I'll make definite plans tomorrow, but as he's in Los Angeles, with plenty of people around, I shall only go to stay a few days with him, just to see him. I'm going to urge Nan not to go, for she would see so little for the money spent. However, if she goes, I'll arrange to show her more than I will do if I go alone and probably I will be gone two or three days longer in consequence.

A quick note to Nan after she returned to Washington:

Many thanks for your letter & check, though I hate to take the latter.

At last I can make some definite plans! F is not going to Chicago so I'll be up for graduation [Todhunter] & spend the night with Elinor M. [Morgenthau] & go to Bear Mt. the next day [to see a newly-opened camp for unemployed girls] & a little school A. [Auntie] Corinne was interested in at Garrison for tea, then home to you for Sunday & perhaps if you ask Earl & Ruth they could come for Saturday night & Sunday. Elliott does want me to come out. . . .

She made a trip to New York. That meant, in the first place, time with Hick and more discussion of her desire to leave the AP. Eleanor was sure there was work in the Government she might do. It is unclear whether Harry Hopkins, head of the new Federal Emergency Relief Administration (FERA), whom Eleanor had known as an energetic social reformer in New York, came to her or she to him. The suggestion came up that Hickok, in view of her experience as a reporter, might fill the slot of chief field investigator for Hopkins.

"The worst of having a good time is one's lack of desire to give it

* See Earl Miller's comments on Leo Casey, page 121.

up!" she wrote Hick afterwards. She had been late returning to Washington and found "the girls"—they were the members of her press conference—"very sweet." She chatted about her "tramp," as the family called Al Kresse, an unemployed hitchhiker to whom she had given a lift and then her card with her New York address, where he would be given a meal. Like many others, though young and eager to work, he was starving: ". . . I have another nice letter from my tramp. He's going to picnic lunch with me next Friday. His letters are amusing. He used to hate the leaders of the nation, but he loves his mother!" She later obtained work for Kresse with the Civilian Conservation Corps (CCC) and she would see him through various of life's small crises. She was so glad, her note to Hickok ended, that the latter had sought out her unhappy Anna. "It seems nearer to being with her myself. You are a peach."

Anna's despair over her love of the married John Boettiger, and Elliott's abandonment of Betty saddened her. She appeared composed in the middle of her duties as First Lady, but self-reproach tugged at her:

> I don't seem to be able to shake the feeling of responsibility for Elliott & Anna. I guess I was a pretty unwise teacher as to how to go about living. Too late to do anything now, however, & I'm rather disgusted with myself. I feel soiled, but you won't understand that.

The trip to Los Angeles loomed over her: "My first day back & I did feel low just walking in the house. Wonder if it was just missing my freedom & you or other things? I'll be different when I return from the West." Some senators came to dinner. It "would have been dull, but I threw bomb shells at them about federal control & setting minimum standards . . ." Jefferson's Monticello was lovely,

> but my zest in life is rather gone for the time being. If anyone looks at me, I want to weep, & the sooner this Western trip is over, the better all around, I guess. I get like this sometimes. It makes me feel like a dead weight & my mind goes round & round like a squirrel in a cage. I want to run, & I can't, & I despise myself. I can't get away from thinking about myself. Even though I know I'm a fool, I can't help it! Does that describe my state of mind satisfactorily?

Writing to Hick helped. "You are my rock, & I shall be so glad to see you Sat. night. I need you very much as a refuge just now."

She had learned that Elliott not only wanted a divorce but that he was wooing a Texas girl, Ruth Googins. Franklin seemed less ruffled than she, perhaps because presidents were not permitted to have personal feelings, especially when Congress had not yet adjourned. "I've just been to say good night to Franklin & tell him about Elliott's call, & he really is so sweet about everything, but quite philosophical."

She put on a brave front. "I rode with Elinor & Esther this morning. Frances [Perkins] & I had a press conference on work camps for women. . . ." She had the usual teas and dinners. A few days later she flew out to Los Angeles. She would talk with Elliott about his plans to remarry and, if he insisted, she would meet his new girl. The transcontinental flight by the First Lady made air travel history. One burden was off her mind. Hickok's future had been settled. The latter notified Harry Hopkins that she would report in as soon as she finished covering the tax evasion trial of banker Charles E. Mitchell. It saddened Hickok to leave journalism, but Hopkins' job was "the only thing that has come along since I began contemplating the possibility of getting out of the AP that has really interested me."

Eleanor sent Hick a running account of her dash to Los Angeles by air. She advised Elliott and Ruth not to communicate with each other until Elliott had his divorce. An evening was spent with Isabella Greenway in Tucson: ". . . bath in one of Isabella's little houses, next her own. Pink adobe . . . Then dinner in the late dusk on Isabella's porch. . . . A full moon & bright stars unbelievably beautiful & also conducive to making our troubles sink to proper perspective!" A word of comfort for Hick: "Poor Hick, I know how you hate to leave Bill* & the life I do hope there will be enough interest in the next years to compensate."

Soon after her return to the White House she went to Orange, New Jersey, to visit the Parishes, at whose home in New York she and Franklin had been married. Cousin Susie represented the life from which she had broken free, yet she had no wish to hurt her. Cousin Susie's attitude towards incompatibility in marriage, like Mama's, was that "since you had made your bed, you must lie in it." Eleanor no longer was sure. She abetted Anna in her affair with John, but Elliott's divorce distressed her. She felt obliged to break the news about Elliott to Cousin Susie. "A quiet day," she wrote Hick, "& on the whole little said by either Cousin Henry or Susie. I really think they are very sweet & understanding, & I am much surprised & not a little relieved." There was Mama, too, to represent the old world of custom and propriety: "We got home at 12 & found two irritating letters from my mother-in-law & have just called her up & been my most agreeable superficially, but really horrid, so I am not proud of myself!"

The flush of activity into which she plunged on her return to the White House irked her. She wanted to do a serious, sustained job. "I'm filled with horror at the mass of detail which render my days so full, & yet nothing accomplished to show for the passing hours!" It was a frequent complaint, and she needed people like Hick with whom she was

* W. W. Chapin of the Associated Press news desk.

able to converse quietly. In spite of her complaints the same intimates also appreciated her status and authority, the poise, competence, and verve with which she handled the "details" of her day. As she wrote: "I have cleaned up mail & done a little on the book & had a press conference & now I'm going to be pretty weary after talking to everyone & trying to seem interested, when I was not much."

The "Hundred Days" came to an end. Eleanor held her last press conference. A sensitive note from the AP's Bess Furman, "It is exceptionally hard to find words to express appreciation for the sort of thing you are doing for women of the press," she sent on to Hick. The latter evidently had thanked Eleanor for the job with Hopkins, but Eleanor wanted no thanks for doing what a friend might be expected to do. "I loved your letter, but hated the note. It is so nice to do anything for you, &, Lord knows, you won't be spoiled by a little ease of life now."

"Be nice to Louis," she urged Franklin as she left on trips out of Washington. "He's much upset." She did not say what about, but the frailer he became, the more he depended on her. "Hick wanted me to tell you," her note to Franklin went on, "how much she appreciated your being so nice about her taking this job for Hopkins. I think she'll do it very well & she felt she must get out of the A.P. with all the Elliott & Anna troubles coming."

Up at Hyde Park she was met by Nan, who was "so pleased" with her operations on the shop, the grounds, the cottage. They swam in the brook. Then it rained intermittently, "so while Earl is working on his reports I'm writing, & then we'll go up to see Vallie* and perhaps take a walk late."

With Nan and Marion she headed upstate again to Massena with a stop in Syracuse to see Leo Casey. "I drove up in the capacity of ER today & only on arriving became FDR's wife," she wrote Hick en route. Hick could do no wrong; Eleanor was ambivalent about her own efforts. "I should work as you do, but I can't. I am more apt to disappoint you, dear, than you are to disappoint me." She reached Southwest Harbor on Mount Desert Island in Maine to stay with Mary Dreier, a pioneer in the Women's Trade Union League, and a good friend of Nan and Marion: "Mary Dreier is having a party tomorrow afternoon, & I don't dare tell Nan, but this is not my idea of a holiday!" she confessed to Hick. After a White House season she wanted privacy. Franklin pulled in on a boat he had chartered after Congress adjourned:

I was just doing my exercises this morning when Nan rushed in to say FDR & the whole fleet had come in late last night, & by the time I was down, James, Fjr, & John had come to breakfast, rather overpowering for Mary Dreier, but she seemed pleased. We all went out, & I visited

* Her alcoholic uncle at Tivoli.

the press also. Very comfortable they all are. John seems to be happier as a sailor. F. informed me he was staying at Campo till the 1st, so I must stay.

The *Amberjack II*, skippered by a relaxed President, was headed for Campobello, his first visit to the island since he had been stricken with polio. Eleanor, Nan, and Marion were also headed there to get the house ready for him:

I hope we have good weather so I can give Nan & Marion some nice trips, & especially do I want good weather when Franklin and his fleet are there. I love the place & like people I like to see it at its best. Fog is nice if you know a place & are with someone you like. It is like a winter storm. It shuts you in & gives you a close & intimate feeling & adds to the joy of your fire. But you don't want to meet a new place in a fog any more than you want to be intimate with a new acquaintance.

They covered the stretch from Southwest Harbor to Lubec across the water from Campobello the next day "& were soon home in the house I really like." In another letter: "Lunch & a trip to Eastport to buy essentials, with the engine breaking down as usual, & the rain in our faces for a time. . . . We came in to tea before the fire. No telephone. Absolute peace. It is a joy!"

She risked the same sputtering engine to go up to St. Andrews in New Brunswick. The joys of the trip made her lyrical: "The sun is out, & the fog is rolling out to sea, & I'm sitting in the bottom of the boat, sniffing salt air & every now & then looking over the water to my green islands & grey rocky shores. I do think it is lovely, & I wonder if you will." Tommy had wired her that Hick, having left the AP, was staying at the White House. Eleanor wished Tommy would do the same.

She prepared for the inundation of people who would arrive with Franklin. After a peaceful walk through the woods, "I got back at 5 to find the house swarming with people & all my peace gone." The guests included her brother Hall's former wife, Margaret Cutter, and her brother Henry. Margaret's husband also was coming. Betty, who was divorcing Elliott, was there. Then Missy, who was expected, arrived, and so did her brother, who was not, "so I had to hurriedly rearrange." They waited for Franklin and that was not a new experience for her.

Reports kept coming of FDR being here or there, but, as the fog outside was thick, I felt sure he would be late. At 4 he came & we went to meet him. After speeches he came home & I think happy. Marion & I drove Mr. [Norman] Davis & John to the evening train in East Machias & drove home watching the sunset, & I recaptured a little serenity!

The President left Campobello on the cruiser *Indianapolis*, and Eleanor hastened to Washington, where she found Hick in the middle of an indoctrination course at FERA headquarters. Hick had a talk with the President on her forthcoming duties. Eleanor had arranged this rather august briefing, then she drove off with her on their long-awaited holiday. It took them through upstate New York and New England, up to Quebec and around the Gaspé Peninsula. "We've done quite a bit of walking," she wrote to Franklin from Quebec, "& as most of it has been up & down Hick was a bit lame but she is recovering & her sun burn & my sun burned lip are our only concern." Later both she and Hickok wrote accounts of this trip. Hick was enormously impressed with Eleanor's detailed interest in the problems of the potato farmer in Aroostook County in Maine and in her later report to Franklin.

After the Gaspé and Aroostook, Eleanor ended up at Skowhegan, Maine. "Dearest Honey," she began a letter to Franklin. (She rarely addressed him now in that way, although his letters to her invariably started: "Dearest Babs.") "I'm enclosing a letter from Elliott":

> He sent it in one to me which sounds a trifle discouraged. I can't believe he's getting married for he has no job but I'm writing Anna to find out if he actually needs money. I think it is better to let him fend for himself but I don't want him to borrow from others or to give the impression to others that we won't give him anything. . . .
>
> . . . .
>
> We all went to the play here last night & tonight all the others have gone but I stayed home to sit on the balcony & to watch the sunset over the lake & listen to the waves a few feet away on the stones & catch up on mail. It has been a wonderful trip & Hick is grand to travel with, nothing bothers her. She isn't afraid, she doesn't get tired & she's always interested!

Hickok, after the twenty-one-day trip, left for Pennsylvania. Her graphic accounts of life and views in the mining and steel communities soon found their way to F.D.R.'s desk, sent to him by Hopkins as well as by Eleanor. "I know you are going to do a swell job, please let me share it," she wrote Hick the day she left, "for I shall have an interest in what you are doing & then twice as much interest & pride in the way you are doing it." The two weeks while Hick was away were going to be "hard in spots. Mama annoyed me on the telephone this evening, & I thought I was all set for complete serenity. Well, I must do my best."

A letter went off to Marion, who was in Europe. It was loving, also anxious about Elliott:

> . . . I quite understand your wanting to be here & yet wanting to go. Life is often like that. . . . Elliott asked Anna to meet him in Chi-

cago & in spite of her arguments (and Ruth Googins) they [Elliott and Ruth] decided to get married & were married last Saturday in Burlington.

They got Franklin's consent & perhaps they were right & one can only hope they will be happy. . . .

The Gaspé trip is a beautiful trip & you would not know you were on this continent, only French spoken & very primitive people. . . . It was hard telling Mama & Betty at Campo of Elliott's impending marriage but Betty was a brick. There is good stuff there & she'll make some man happy in the future.

I agree with you it would be much nicer to feel nothing! I don't really mean that, for one would miss so much happiness. . . . I love you always & very dearly.

Guided by the Quakers in Philadelphia, who had been working among the displaced miners in Appalachia, Hickok had gone there. Eleanor went to Hyde Park to finish the book *It's Up to the Women*, and as usual entertain "shoals of people." She scrawled a note to Marion describing her Hyde Park life:

Here we are in Hyde Park & I miss you very much at the cottage for as I work over there with Malvina I go over every morning & afternoon & on hot days we take from 12–1 to swim & again when Franklin comes over in the afternoon. We have had some very hot weather & Nan felt it a good deal after Maine but I do think she seems better. Of course there is a great deal of coming and going & everyone who comes wants to see the shop. I only hope it brings us some orders!

Then she fell asleep and finished the letter the next day. Another part of the Hyde Park chronicle went off to Hickok: "Louis arrived today & we make a start on the 'News' tonight. . . . Anna, he and I dine at the cottage, while the others go to Laura [Delano]. I'm just going over to tell Mama I'm not going with them & I can hear the row!" She and Franklin were both concerned over Anna: "FDR is now talking with Curt and wanted me here 'in case' he needed me," she wrote a few days later.

General Hugh Johnson, the colorful and energetic administrator of the National Industrial Recovery Administration, arrived with codes for steel and coal. She wrote Hick about them. The latter's shocked letters from Appalachia led Eleanor to promise to join her in Morgantown, West Virginia. "I read parts of your letter to Franklin, & he read the report and was much interested."

Esther Lape arrived at Hyde Park to see the President on Russian recognition. She lunched with Eleanor and Franklin. He wanted her information on Russia. He sought information where he could get it, and as on many problems Eleanor and her friends provided a missing slant.

Anna returned to Hyde Park after a talk with her estranged husband,

Curtis Dall, in New York. She needed her father's counsel, and he wanted to give it, but the Cordell Hulls were at the Big House, and he had to be attentive to them. The Secretary of State was reporting to the President on the London Economic Conference, for which he had headed the American delegation:

> She [Anna] is now hoping FDR can talk to her tonight if Mr. Hull doesn't talk too late. Mr. Hull says it [the conference] was a great strain. He is a lovely person & very gentle but F hasn't told me yet how he feels. He said at lunch the Tories led by Chamberlain, had never meant the conference to succeed & they had taken the lead at the start.

Franklin did talk with his daughter. He was affectionate but firm. He advised her to tell John Boettiger she could not see him until after the divorce.

Al Kresse, the "tramp," arrived. He now worked at the newly established Camp Tera at Bear Mountain, New York. Eleanor drove him around Hyde Park and later went with him to inspect the camp. She acquired a secondhand roadster, Bluette, and gave it to Hickok: "You saw us some weeks ago discussing her and said innocently: 'That is just the kind of car I want.'" Without comment she forwarded a news item about Hick that had been sent to her: "This lady, a buxom, businesslike individual whose every move indicated efficiency, started with a barbecued sandwich, a dish of baked beans, a glass of buttermilk, and wound up with a topper of ice cream on a piece of apple pie and well-creamed coffee for a chaser, with utter disregard for the effect on the girth."

There were teas, picnics, dinners to be arranged and presided over at Hyde Park and in between she and Tommy worked on the mail and the book, *It's Up to the Women*, ". . . all but 1,000 words were done!" A picnic at the Val-Kill Cottage, with a big fire roaring against a background of dark cedars, moved her to reflect: "So safe & quiet—& the world tottering." Although she often complained about the busyness of her life, she now rather welcomed it: "Work is a good thing & I have plenty of that which keeps me away from Mama, which is also a good thing!"

She took several newspaperwomen down to Camp Tera. "Such an improvement." They picnicked and Al Kresse joined them. She drove to Elinor Morgenthau's "and we went to Miss [Lillian] Wald for supper. I was happy to see her looking so well & enjoyed Jane Addams & Dr. Alice Hamilton, too."

Extraordinary encounter. The three women—Jane Addams, Alice Hamilton, Lillian Wald—were outstanding social reformers. All had been involved in pacifist activity during the World War. All had found intellectual stimulation, support in the battle for progress, and companionship in other women. The evening with Eleanor and Elinor, who represented a new generation of reform, should have been recorded. Elinor Morgenthau in her own quiet, fastidious way was one of Eleanor's friends who enabled her to survive in the "goldfish bowl" and sustained her increasing authority and influence.

Eleanor, when she joined Hick in Morgantown, West Virginia, was driving her own car. She saw unimagined scenes of poverty at places like Scotts Run, where the displaced miners and their families lived in tents, the sewage ran in the gullies, and the miners, who hadn't worked for years, were close to starvation. Franklin and Louis on her return were as appalled by what she had seen as she had been. The President said the displaced miners had to be gotten into houses. Louis said he would take it on, and the idea of Arthurdale, the first Subsistence Homestead project near Morgantown, West Virginia, was born. It would be a unit of the Subsistence Homestead Program, established during the "Hundred Days," an experimental plan that might help with the problems of urban congestion and rural decay.

The President talked with the steel magnates, who were balking against the code. "F. describes his talk with Schwab & Myron Taylor, ending with: 'Myron is a moron.'" Eleanor was struck by Franklin's inability to tell Curtis the truth while being so tough with the steel men. She worried over her own capacity to give Anna wise counsel: "Do say a prayer for me. I love her & I will be tempted to want what she wants, but I must be fair to all. Even if she suffers, the children must not." Mother and daughter had several long talks "& tonight we agreed we were a pretty good team & see almost any situation through together. Just pray that I will be wise, Hick. I need it as I've never needed it before."

Earl Miller went to Bermuda for a holiday. There he met two exhibition dancers. Eddie Fox and Mayris Chaney. He liked them, especially "Tiny" Chaney. She was blond, pert, and, as her name indicated, diminutive. Dancing engagements were difficult to obtain at the time, even for the ablest of performers. He introduced them to "the Lady." Before going to a tea at Fishkill with Elinor and "270 women," she met them. "Earl brought the two little dancers, Eddie Fox & Tiny Chaney." Tiny's waiflike aspect, coupled with a crisp common sense, attracted her. It was the beginning of a lifelong relationship.

August at Hyde Park drew to a hectic end. She completed the book; also an article that ended up in *Redbook*: "But I finally did that article on the shop that Nan has been wanting to go with her pictures, so I hope it can be sold & repay her for what she spent on the book. I'm giving it to her for her birthday, with money enough for the German camera she wants & some little odds & ends." Leo Casey came. She talked long into the night with Anna, but, "how futile it all seems in comparison with what you are doing in Appalachia, but we have to do what we are let to do, don't we." She began a question-and-answer column for the *Woman's Home Companion*. The summer ended with the traditional clambake at the Morgenthaus'. Everyone, including the newspaper people, went. "Very good & everyone enjoyed it. They had singing & dancing afterwards."

She then went off to fulfill her promise to Louis to spend several days at Horseneck Beach just outside of Fall River. "He is pathetically eager to show me his improvements & I get the impression I am the first person who has been enthusiastic except the man who is cook & nurse & chauffeur to small Bobby [Howe]!" She played with the latter, who was Louis's grandson. She bathed and sunned on the beach. Always intent on killing several birds with one stone, she drove to nearby Newport to spend a couple of days with Cousin Susie. "This is nice country but Newport depresses me, it is so smug." Louis had driven back in his own car, which had followed hers:

> This is like another world from what I live in as a rule. At Hyde Park & in Washington I feel much closer to the grim realities of life, & all the rest of my life I feel a part of the life of the most insignificant citizen, but here I feel far away, like a dream—& that they don't know it is a dream & that soon it will be over.

She wanted Hick to see Cape Cod with her, but she was glad she took this trip. "It would have been easy to stay put but I think it is a pleasure to Louis."

Frequently she sent Hick words of encouragement: "How funny you are about your reports. Of course they are good, absorbingly interesting. FDR told me he wished your letters could be published. He is hard to please & he always *asks* me if I've anything to read him from you."

By Doris Faber's count there were 129 letters between mid-March and mid-November that Hick transcribed and turned over in that form as part of her correspondence with E.R. to the Roosevelt Library. A letter dated September 6, 1933, is one of the few original letters from that period. Its ending is reminiscent of her kissing Hick's photograph in an earlier one: "Only Friday, Sat., Sun. & Mon. & we will be together! I can hardly wait."

The next letter date, "10 Sept," had "Dannemora" as its return address. The main state prison was located there, and mail that Tommy sent her was forwarded to Chazy Lake, the secluded bungalow camp nearby that Earl had shown her in July. She and Nan, Earl and Ruth, joined for part of the time by Eddie Fox and Tiny, spent the next two weeks there:

> Yesterday I had two good walks. Though there has been quite a wind, & it is cold, still the sun is warm, & the air makes you feel grand. I read

a little before the big fire last night, & this morning I rode with Earl at 7:30. From 11 to 12:30 I had a shooting lesson. I'm being taught like a prison guard. It is interesting, though, because there is so much more than I thought to learn. I did improve.

Since she refused to allow the Secret Service to guard her, she had to learn how to use a revolver, Earl had insisted. She even boasted a little:

Beautiful day again & a grand ride. Shooting better daily. I'll be an expert dish washer & housemaid, too! We are having a dinner tonight. Eight to dine. Nan got out in a boat to fish this morning, but only caught two small fish.

Only a few weeks earlier she had been at Newport. She had come a long way from the "coming out" days and the assemblies that it all represented. The slightly bizarre crew who surrounded her at Chazy Lake would have jarred Cousin Susie as much as Eleanor's practice shooting with a revolver would have frightened her. Mrs. Parish, and many other Americans, had they known about her Chazy Lake friends, would have considered them scarcely fit company for a president's wife. But she loved them all, and the tentative efforts she made to satisfy such earthly tastes as she had discovered in herself as cleaning the house and making breakfast were to her a measure of personal progress rather than social decline.
She was troubled about Nan:

I don't think Nan has ever been through such a test of friendship. She doesn't like to do any of the things we do. She's away from home, which she hates & has to cook, which she used to like, but doesn't any more. Another time I'll bring someone to cook, but I won't ask Nan for I can see how unhappy she is, though she wouldn't say so. It is partly that I do so much with the others. Yesterday Earl & Ruth slept all afternoon, so Tiny, Eddie & I hiked to the cross roads, an hour's walk, at a quick pace. Nan of course can't do it, and I am really sorry for her. When she's home she is happy with her own things to do. Well, you always have to try these things out once to know, don't you. I wish I didn't like so many different kinds of things!

Bess Furman, of the Associated Press, and Martha Strayer, of the *Washington Daily News*, were doing a book about the President's mother and sent the manuscript to Eleanor. Newspaper salaries were low and both had financial troubles. "I read and returned their manuscript & offered to loan her & Martha money if they needed it." Oh, time of innocence! Eleanor forwarded to Hick Bess Furman's note of thanks: "It just so happens that I've been earning my own living ever since I was fifteen years old, & you are the first one who has ever said to me, 'You can have a loan if you need it.' Someday, I myself am going to have the pleasure of putting down in printer's ink just what a swell person you are—in the first person singular, not bound by AP rules." The book about Sara never appeared. The two women desisted when they learned that a book on the subject by Rita Halle* was about to come out.

Eleanor liked to travel. She had the stamina for it. Also it gave her a chance to visit her children. She went up to Boston to see James, and that enabled her to inspect Franklin, Jr.'s, rooms at Harvard, where he was newly installed as a freshman:

> I got in this morning & had a bath & breakfast & then James appeared & a little later Fjr not having had breakfast. We fed him & then I went with him to Cambridge. The rooms aren't bad. No private bath but an open fireplace, & I think they will look nice, & I am glad it is one of the simple places. The poor kid is wild as reporters try to catch him every time he moves, & though I came in as unostentatiously as possible, I didn't get beyond the first floor in the shop before people were whispering. Oh, Lord, how I hate it! After I left Brother I took the subway into Boston, ordered all he needed, did an errand for James & met Mrs. Cushing, Mary C., James, Fjr., & John Sargent for lunch. Then bought James an overcoat & back to the Statler to wait until James comes to take me to Cambridge from where Fjr., & Bobby Delano are going with me to Groton to have supper with John. When I get back I will call Louis, who is much excited because Hartley (his son) had a temperature when he left the beach yesterday. I hope it is nothing.

Among her first visitors when she got back to the White House was "Mrs. Bourne from Puerto Rico." James and Dorothy Bourne were Dutchess County neighbors. Dorothy had worked with the League of Women Voters; he was now in charge of Puerto Rican relief for Harry Hopkins. "She's come up for the Child Welfare Conference tomorrow, & she is an interesting person, not too enthusiastic about Gov. Gore [an F.D.R. appointee], so I asked her to come back for dinner & told FDR about conditions."

The conference on child welfare was run by Grace Abbott, the head of the Children's Bureau, a Republican who had served under Hoover but who now had Eleanor's backing. She went with Elinor. ". . . spoke briefly, made a suggestion, listened to a lot of generalities, which tried my soul, for we certainly don't need them at present." Her dislike of wordiness echoed in her comment about an afternoon conference, ". . . from 3 to 5 I spent in Louis's office on this subsistence farm scheme. They say women don't talk to the point. I could have done all

* *Gracious Lady*, by Rita Halle Kleeman (New York: Appleton-Century, 1935).

we actually did in one half hour! Mr. Hopkins and Ickes* are good to work with & not verbose, but the others were!"

Earl's marriage to Ruth broke up, and he kept Mrs. Roosevelt informed about that as well as the furnishing of rooms that he had taken at Glens Falls north of Albany. "Nan darling," she wrote:

> Will you order the mattress & springs & 2 pillows for Earl tomorrow? Things have come to a head & Ruth has told him she is going out with another boy & having a good time & felt she gave up too much in marrying so she wants ½ of everything, an annulment! of her marriage & $50 a month for 3 years. Isn't it strange to be so calmly mercenary? She asked him *after having* told him this, for her birthday present ahead of time as she wanted to buy a jewelled sorority pin & she took $25 from him! She also wishes to be friends & feel she can depend on him & retain all his friends! He therefore wants to hurry his own home & he wants the simplest possible bookcase to go with his furniture 5 ft high 24 in. wide & 9 inches deep & has his desk & chair. I'll give him those things for Xmas & birthday so send the bill to me!

Hickok at this time was in Washington getting ready for a six-week trip through the Midwest. Eleanor filled another letter to Nan with directions on moving things for Anna, whose house in Tarrytown, New York, was being vacated. She herself went to Chicago to speak at the Century of Progress Exposition. On the way she stopped to see Al Kresse at Bear Mountain, Grace Tully, who was recuperating from t.b. not far away, Earl at Glens Falls, Leo Casey in Syracuse, and at Hyde Park she went to see Rosey's widow, Betty, whose house was next to Mama's:

> Grace Tully looked well & is thrilled to be going to Maryland. Bear Mountain was satisfactory. Camp TERA was being made comfortable, & this winter I think I'll go up for a night. Kresse's cabin made us want to scrub & furnish, but he is happy. We'll gradually do something about it.

About her visit with Earl:

> We had a nice day, & he's got two nice rooms with sun pouring in, & I think we can make them very nice, though some of the things he wants are a bit startling, for instance a tiger rug on the floor!

"Tommy is so nice & companionable," she observed when they finally boarded the train for Chicago. Eleanor made two speeches on the way and in Chicago appealed to the women of the nation to cooperate with the Government in ensuring the success of the new programs that F.D.R. had started. Her important news, however, was about Harry

---

* Harold Ickes, former Bull Mooser, feisty Secretary of the Interior and head of the Public Works Administration.

Hopkins and Hick's advocacy of a program for unemployed women. "Your boss spoke so well & then came here & told me all about the letter & said he was telephoning Henry [Morgenthau]. I showed no sign that I knew anything. We are going to get something done for the single women, I think."

She wanted her friends to appreciate the things that she liked and to be involved in the programs that she sought to further. Louis's interest in speeding the creation of Arthurdale delighted her, for she dreaded what might happen as the pace and complexity of government in Washington proved too much for his flagging energies:

> Louis & I had dinner together last night & we went up to Poughkeepsie on the train this morning, & I drove him down, & I think he had a happy day. He seemed very cheerful & full of chat, &, though he made me take a long road—325 miles—it was very lovely. But I nearly died of sleep the last ten miles!

Nan, whose competence as a craftsman she respected, came in to help with Arthurdale. "From 11:30 to 1, Subsistence Homesteads W. Va., & they seem to be really getting under way & Nan & Mr. [Clarence] Pickett* & Dan Hulston got a lot of detailed work done." She saw a good deal of Hopkins: "He's also talking to the Red Cross for me & if he approves, I shall spring a suggestion in opening my course at the Junior League on Wednesday for Mobilization of Girls as in war time." Hopkins cultivated Eleanor. He wanted her support for some larger goals that he had in mind. "Mr. Hopkins's new idea is going to be put into effect, & he hopes to put 2,000,000 men back to work & then 2,000,000 more. Let's hope it works. It will cost $400,000,000."†

She dashed up to New York:

> Bought Louis some clothes, started my class, spoke at the Junior League lunch, tried on two dresses at Milgrim's, was at my furniture sale for an hour, the usual photographs & press & 5 to 6:30 spent with Cousin Susie. Then went & dined with Louis. Nan is happy because in two days we've sold $3,000 worth of stuff!

She shared her intense curiosity about Russia with Hick:

> Litvinoff, who has been a bit arrogant in conversation with Mr. Hull, listened to FDR today & changed much. FDR said at dinner, however, that using your mind so hard was tiring, & he looked it. I'm glad he's soon going to Warm Springs.‡

* Executive secretary, American Friends Service Committee.
† The Civil Works Administration succeeded the Federal Emergency Relief Administration with Hopkins as Administrator on November 9, 1933.
‡ Maxim Litvinov, People's Commissar for Foreign Affairs, came to Washington in November for negotiations that resulted in United States recognition of the Soviet Union.

Her big news was that John Boettiger "has his divorce & returned after a very successful week in Chicago, very cheerful. Anna is also cheerful." Although John had his divorce, "there are complications on the business side however as Col. McCormick might not approve too much intimacy with the enemy camp! John is much in favor however. I hope Earl's announcement goes off as quietly & smoothly next Saturday."

Emma Bugbee of the *Herald Tribune* took her to the train while she was in New York:

> . . . & as I'd promised to go to see Tiny Chaney on the way to the train, & she came, too, I was well seen off. Emma wanted to know about doing a book on me, & I was quite frank & told her I wouldn't want one now, & I had promised to work with you on it, & because I couldn't keep a diary, I was sending you daily doings for future reference. She was very nice about it & said she quite understood.

But it was more than "doings" that she sent Hick. "I'm glad I'm not making speeches for a while," she confessed in mid-November, "for I've been saying silly things & getting into trouble of late, nothing to worry about but I should have known better."

At this point, the bowdlerized letters that Hick turned over to the Roosevelt Library end. The remainder of the massive correspondence includes the personal references that give them their special savor. Eleanor took the train for Boston. "I'm glad I'm not motoring I'd miss you too much!" A crisp paragraph that mixed momentous events with a little gossip:

> It was a busy & rather fruitless day. I started to ride & then Litvinoff was late & Henry Morgenthau wanted a ceremony to swear him in so by 12 that took place & it was too late to ride. Well Russia is recognized, Bullitt goes as Ambassador. I wonder if that is why F.D.R. has been so content to let Missy play with him! She'll have another embassy to visit next summer anyway! I hope Henry [Morgenthau] will do well in the Treasury, it is a big responsibility.

The public's reaction interested her. She knew how hard F.D.R. had worked to get recognition terms that were acceptable to American opinion. He had told them at dinner a few days earlier that after two hours with Litvinov, he had "two-thirds of the essentials, but every session is like pulling teeth. Russia wanted recognition & then arrangements. She doesn't like having to settle certain things first." Now what impressed her was: "How quietly everyone takes resumption of intercourse with Russia. Also Henry M in charge of the Treasury."

She began to count the days till Hick's return. The temptation to call was irresistible: "It seems to me that on Thanksgiving Day from Georgia it wouldn't cost so much. . . . Have you been good about your diet?" She had seen Tiny Chaney and Eddie Fox, who were playing at the Hippodrome in New York. "I would give a good deal to put my arms around you & to feel yours around me," that letter ended.

Eva Le Gallienne, Frances Perkins, and Isabella Greenway came to lunch. "Much talk on a national theatre & she's anxious of course to be subsidized. I asked her to write out her ideas & I'd try to arrange a meeting with F.D.R. on his return." Whatever her reservations about speaking, a few days later she appeared for Carrie Chapman Catt. "She is a busy old lady & I hope at 76 I can still speak as well if I still encumber the earth!" Speaking still gave her problems, however: "I dread tomorrow morning's speech," she wrote later in the day, "but that will be the last & I am looking forward to taking Tiny up & hanging Earl's pictures! I love settling houses even someone else's."

She arranged a special Christmas for the friends to whom she felt particularly close. She had done so for Earl, for Nan and Marion. There would be a Christmas tree, a festive meal, and an exchange of presents, which on her side she had been collecting over the whole year. "Well, perhaps you'll come up [to East Sixty-fifth Street] & spend the night of Dec. 21st here with me," she wrote to Hick. "It is sentimental & I didn't mean to tell you but I'd like to have you here that night & celebrate a little Xmas of our own! Probably you can't do it but perhaps— who knows!" An analogy she used indicated how close she considered Hick and herself to be: "Louis tells me one of the newspapermen casually mentioned the other day to a group of them 'Now that John B. has his divorce I suppose we'll soon hear of Mrs. Dall getting hers'! One cannot hide things in this world can one? How lucky you are not a man!" John and Anna sat on her sofa at the White House "all evening & seemed to have a swell time while I worked. Dear one, & so you think they gossip about us, well they must at least think we stand separations rather well! I am always so much more optimistic than you are. I suppose because I care so little what 'they' say!"

She lunched with Harry Hopkins before leaving for Warm Springs to join Franklin. A letter from Hick in Iowa gingerly reflected the latter's jealousy: "I suppose you arrived in Warm Springs today. Well—I'd probably not be happy there, anyway. Oh, I guess I'm probably a little jealous. Forgive me. Forgive me. I know I shouldn't be—and it's only because it's been so long since I've seen you. I'll be good."

Even before she received that letter, Eleanor wrote as if in telepathic response: "I had a little longing (secretly) that F.D.R. might think I'd like you to be here & insist on your coming to report to him. You know how one dreams? I knew it wouldn't be true but it was nice to think about!" Her days at Warm Springs were almost as hectic as those at the White House: "I swallowed lunch, went to speak to a Federation of Women's Clubs meeting in the village some 1600 strong & was nearly mobbed & when Franklin came to get me his car was buried & I couldn't find it!" She sought to console Hick, who complained of her own growing status as a minor celebrity: "Darling, I know they bother you to death because you are my friend, but will forget it & think only that someday I'll be back in obscurity again & no one will care except ourselves!" Nan and Marion were with her in Warm Springs. Marion walked and rode, but Nan begged off because of an injured leg. "We've had a chance to talk these few days & I'm relieved to find that F.D.R. is thinking in terms of the next five years. He was interesting about the hotels & apartment & manufacturing plants which were all overbuilt & had to be written off or buying power in general sufficiently increased to use them."

Mail and social duties accumulated at the White House while she was away, and that, combined with getting ready for Christmas, made for some busy days when she returned:

> I will try not to be 'distant' with Tommy but I have felt driven & that always makes me feel queer! She enjoyed Thanksgiving I hope at home but she feels driven, too I think and Mrs. [Edith] Helm does take up so much time on our parties & teas & I know I'm not fair in the way I hurry her.

She had shielded Anna and John, who had been together: ". . . I've been glibly telling F.D.R. she spent her holiday in N.Y. May I be forgiven! Tommy & I have worked all evening. I must write Earl & sign a mountain of mail so goodnight sweet one. Eleven days from now!"

Their letters now became a litany of longing for the moment when they would again see each other. Hick wrote her from northern Minnesota:

> Tonight it's Bemidji, away up in Timber country, not a bad hotel, and one day nearer you. Only eight more days. Twenty-four hours from now it will be only seven more—just a week! I've been trying today to bring back your face—to remember just *how* you look. Funny how even the dearest face will fade away in time. Most clearly I remember your eyes, with a kind of teasing smile in them, and the feeling of that soft spot just northeast of the corner of your mouth against my lips. I wonder what we'll do when we meet—what we'll say when we meet. Well— I'm rather proud of us, aren't you. I think we've done rather well.

And Eleanor's letter was much in the same tenor:

> We went to hear F. speak to the Federated Council of Churches & it really was a good speech. I wonder if by any chance you were listening in. Funny everything I do my thoughts fly to you, never are you out of them dear & just one week from tomorrow I hope I'll be meeting you. Of course the long separation has been hardest on you because so much of the time you've been with strangers but on the other hand

your job is more stimulating than mine. Both jobs are rather tiring & we'll both enjoy two days rest won't we?

She brought together Eva Le Gallienne with Harry Hopkins about a federal theater program, and met with museum directors from all over the country "who are to form the advisory committee on helping artists." She felt she had really "made a start on Xmas things," but:

Dear, nothing is important except that my last trip will be over tomorrow morning before you come & then I hope the next will be with you. Less than a week now. Take care of yourself. I know I won't be able to talk when we first meet but though I can remember just how you look I shall want to look long & very lovingly at you.

Hick's letter that same day was indignant with the elevator boy at the hotel in Hibbing, Minnesota. Was she a "Girl Scout Leader," he wanted to know, wearing as she did a "dark grey skirt," a "gray sweater," "low-heeled gold shoes," and slouch hat? A "uniform," he dubbed it. The long letter from Hibbing ended, "Oh, my dear—I can hardly wait to see you! Day after tomorrow, Minneapolis and letters from you. A week from now—right this minute—I'll be with you! Good night, my dear. God keep you."

So the letters continued. The emotional meaning is clear. Who is to say what they meant physically? They saw each other. They had their weekends together. Hick, a woman alone, wanted to shut out the world. Eleanor had a large family and was especially close to Anna, who needed her. Moreover, she cherished people like Earl, Louis, Nan and Marion, Esther and Elizabeth. They also needed her. She was unable to make herself available to Hick the way Hick wanted. "Hick, dearest," she wrote after she had been in New York just before Christmas:

It was good to have a few minutes with you last night & I went to sleep saying a little prayer, 'God give me depth enough not to hurt Hick again.' Darling, I know I'm not up to you in many ways but I love you dearly & I do learn sometimes.

Christmas Day she wrote again at "1 a.m.":

Darling, I'm just back from the midnight service & it was lovely & I was glad I went alone & now dear I will call you in a minute—tho' I almost hate to do it for I hate to break in on your party. I wished & prayed for many things for you as I knelt in the dark tonight. May you have your heart's desire & be happy & at peace this day & forever more!
Anna read me part of your letter this morning & she said she hadn't been able to understand it & thought we must have had a fearful fight but I told her no you were just feeling very low. Darling the love one has for one's children is different & not even Anna could be to me what you are. I love her. I want to protect her, but I know her life must

claim her & I must only touch it where I can help. There is a difference with friends of our own age & with you there is a much deeper understanding and quality of companionship not possible with youth. . . .

Anna's relationship with Hick and intimate knowledge of the two women's feelings for each other indicated to the Roosevelt Library archivists that on Eleanor's side they lacked a lesbian component, if that word is taken to mean sexual intimacy.*

Eleanor was particularly close to her good-looking twenty-seven-year-old daughter, especially in this period of estrangement from her husband, Curtis Dall, and romance with John Boettiger. Both Anna and John would have considered lesbianism not nice, a form of morbidity. Eleanor had "a genius for love," but it was a passion that was more striking because it was altruistic and sublimated.

Eleanor spent part of her Christmas Day thanking friends for presents. She was grateful to Nan for the coat, gloves, and bathing suit she had sent, and went on to ask, "Now dear when will you come down & is Molly [Goodwin] really coming as well as Marion? I think all my young people will be gone on New Year's day so you can arrive the 2nd if you wish. . . ." She thanked Hick for underclothes, a little lemon fork, and "most of all the notes." She gave her the news and sought to assuage her jealousy:

> Franklin said I could ask Harry Hopkins about Puerto Rico & he said nothing about not flying when I said we'd go that way. I only wonder if I'll be a nuisance for you for of course we can't keep it quiet & there will be reporters & press. Would you rather I didn't try to go with you? Be honest, I won't be hurt. . . .
>
> We drank a toast to absent friends whom we would like to have with us at dinner & I thought of you dear one as I proposed it. We started with stockings, then breakfast, church & Anna & the boys & I walked home. After lunch which the kids had with us we opened presents nearly all afternoon. I went down to see Hackie [operator of the White House switchboard] & give her presents when she came on at 4:30 but we saw & spoke to her in church as she sat in a pew ahead of us, I don't think she was really sad. Dinner was jolly & then F.D.R. read parts of the Christmas Carol & John B. whispered to me it was the nicest day he ever had & he would never forget it! The young ones then went dancing including Fjr. who has had & still has a sore throat! John didn't go & he went out with the dogs & with me & at last I got him to bed. I must go too. It was good to hear your voice & you shall dine in bed & sleep all you want if you'll just stay here & be happy. Don't think I don't know what it is like to be jealous, or to want to be alone, because I know both emotions tho' I succeed as a rule in subdu-

* Doris Faber, *The Life of Lorena Hickok* (New York: William Morrow, 1980), page 155.

ing them with laughter! When I don't, I give you & myself a pretty bad time, don't I, but I promise I'll be quite reasonable & in hand before you get here Friday!

"Washington has never seen the likes of Eleanor Roosevelt," wrote Bess Furman of the Associated Press after Eleanor's first day in the White House. She had no reason to alter her judgment at the end of 1933. Eleanor in the White House had become a benison. She gave hope to the desperate and defeated, seeking out the underdog and the eccentric and enveloping them in her love and solicitude. Who can measure the extent of her love by conventional standards? The more singular her children and the old crowd considered some of her affections, the more determined she was to pursue them. "No form of love is to be despised," she had noted almost ten years before, and she reached out to give and receive love everywhere. It was as if she engaged in a dialogue that was always invested with love. Religion and tradition bolstered it. At midnight service she falls to her knees and prays for her friends. She toasts to the "absent" ones at Christmas dinner and thinks of Hick and Earl, of Nan and Marion, of Elinor Morgenthau. Some gossips chattered of a lesbian relationship; others of an affair with Earl. Both relationships enabled her to remain human and to plumb depths of feeling from which she had long been absent. She was grateful and did not care what the papers wrote.

She did not achieve happiness in marriage. Yet she continued to serve Franklin and loved those particularly who also served him and made it easier for her to fulfill her compact with him to stay at his side. The broken marriages of her children caused bad moments of guilt and self-reproach and many discussions with her friends about the ways she had brought them up, but always the nurturing mother, she tried in her White House years to walk the thin line between meddlesomeness and solicitude.

To move into the White House was to move into a great goldfish bowl on which the white light of public attention always blazed. Yet she managed, as her letters to her friends indicate, to live an inner life of love that had little to do with power, popularity, and publicity. With her entry into the White House, she would always maintain, her real self was buried deep down inside her. But as one reviews her first year, one is struck by how well she managed.

She was almost fifty, but as a woman who read this manuscript commented, she was coming into the most productive time of her life, able to integrate her emotional and spiritual yearnings.

XI

"Something locked me up...."

HICK REACHED the White House a little before New Year's, and for a week the two women enjoyed each other's company, but on January 5, Eleanor, a little self-reproachfully, boarded the New York–Washington train to New York again. She began her penciled note with an amused reference to the indefatigable lobbyists: "The pair of gentlemen who drove me to the station proved to be Ford agents who asked me to tell FDR they appreciated all he was doing for business & one of them had the opportunity last spring of giving Mrs. Hoover a similar ride! It was funny, wasn't it?"

In her loneliness and insecurity, Hick might have quoted Shakespeare's sonnet: "Being your slave, what should I do but tend/ Upon the hours and times of your desire?" But Hopkins was sending her south. At the end of Eleanor's note were words of comfort: "I've slept and worked all the way up & dear one, I can't help hating to let you go but we have had a good time & we will have other good times, very soon at that & I am going to try to be more at home."

One occasion for getting together again might be when she went to Puerto Rico in March. ". . . I am going to speak to Mr. Hopkins to find out if there might be a time when he would want you to go to Puerto Rico." Before that, with the consent of Franklin and Sanford Bates, the head of the Federal prison system, she planned to visit the penitentiary in Atlanta, after which she and Hick could join up for a long weekend at Warm Springs.

She, Tommy, and Missy went to see Tiny and Eddie on the stage, and since it was now Sunday, "We all slept late this a.m. & Tiny, Louis & I had breakfast in my room at 9:30 but I went swimming & did exercises first! I was lazy. Read the papers & talked with Esther Lape & Elizabeth Read who came late last evening. Curtis Bok came for lunch to talk about World Court, & Alice Longworth & Paulina [her daughter] a good combination wasn't it? Later Alice took me off on the radio & did some other very clever impersonations. Sometime you must see her for you wld enjoy her!"

Her nonchalance about Alice's mimicry was a pose. "I am so set up that you liked my speech," her next letter confessed. "Alice took me off so well that she made me feel a sappy sentimentalist & yet I don't think I really am."

She had found room at the White House for Hick on December 29 but had deferred Nan's visit until after New Year's, when she said the children would have left. Her affection for Nan and Marion, nevertheless, continued. "It was good to have you here," a postscript dated January 13 said:

> I'm going to Atlanta after the reception next Thursday night. Hick will be back there & I want to show her W.S. & visit 2 prisons. I'm going to write some prison articles so try to come down the 23d when I'll be back. I think we have a nice dinner that night. Feb. 2d & 3d I'm visiting more prisons & camps & spending the night in Williamsburg. I think Elinor Morgenthau will go. I hope you will meet me in Ithaca the 15th & spend that weekend visiting N.Y. State prisons, Casey & Earl. The latter wants you to see his place. . . .
>
> Marion said she would come on the 30th but she'd probably have to go back at midnight but you'll stay a day or so won't you?

Hick rebelled against acceptance of Eleanor as she was—a woman who loved many and served even more, whose sense of duty, position, and tradition controlled her almost as strongly as did her love. Even as Eleanor in her daily letters was planning their weekend in Warm Springs and filled her letters with endearments, Hick was lamenting their separation. Eleanor did not know how to change that. In any case she envied Hick's abilities as a writer, even more her opportunity to move around the country semi-anonymously, getting to know its many shapes and peoples. She went to New York to attend the funeral of the mother of Gus Gennerich, the New York policeman who was Franklin's personal bodyguard and had become a part of the Roosevelt household. "Gus has changed," Eleanor wrote afterwards, "& I don't know how to cheer him up. Someone always seems to be suffering, don't ever let's hurt each other again." She was concerned about Hick, but also felt guilty about not having done anything for Mama, who was staying at the White House, and Hick should wire Louis, whose birthday was on Sunday and who she feared was "failing fast." She helped furnish Tommy's apartment and was solicitous about Nan, who, in and out of the White House, was busy with the subsistence homesteads. "Dearest one," her letter to Hick of January 14 ends, "Your picture smiles at me & I love you & bid you godspeed."

She went to Cousin Susie's for lunch. "She looks badly & I am sorry for her but, well. She must have ten times your income even now & we spent 1½ hours talking chiefly about what 'she couldn't do' because 'they were so poor!' "

Hick should not drive so rashly: "Remember as you drive better not to get over-confident that is the way accidents happen." When Hick reported an unpleasant encounter with a hitchhiker, her advice became stronger: "I'm glad you will beware in the future & not drive after dark & I will take my pistol & leave it with you!"

Often she lunched or dined with Isabella Greenway, who had been appointed to Lewis Douglas's seat in Congress, and Mary Rumsey, Averell Harriman's older sister and head of consumer work in the NRA, and Frances Perkins. Their friendships went back a long way. They too were women who were making it in a man's world, and that added to the spice of such occasions. It was one of the ways that all of them kept in touch with what was going on in Washington. Just before she left for Atlanta, she lunched again with Isabella in the House Office Building "& we had a grand time." Later she walked to Harry Hopkins' office "& had a brief but grand talk with him. He looks tired & I wish we could kidnap him. Such nice things as he said about you & he always meant to send you to Porto Rico so I guess when this trip is over we will go."

Eleanor inspected the Atlanta penitentiary and then proceeded to Warm Springs to spend three days with Hick. "Dearest, it was a lovely weekend," Hick wrote afterwards, for the moment content. "I shall have it to think about for a long time. Each time we have together that way brings us closer, doesn't it? And I believe those days and long pleasant hours together each time make it perhaps a little less possible for us to hurt each other. They give us better understanding of each other, give us more faith, draw us closer." Hick sent her a woman who had been head of the Georgia Public Welfare system. "She's a most unusual woman, truly attractive and feminine, yet she has the breadth of viewpoint and the impersonal attitude of a man."

Eleanor wrote the same day. "It seems years since we sat & read & read & were alone together. I loved every minute & I am going to live in it these next few weeks." She did not then challenge Hick's assumption of men's distinctive intellectual powers, but a few months later she did. "The one thing I want to take you to task for is that phrase 'she has the mind of a man.' Why can't a woman think, be practical & a good business woman & still have a mind of her own?"

She had talked with Hick's "boss" about Puerto Rico ". . . & he wants me to go & return, then they'll call a meeting of sugar owners, Nat. City Bank etc. & dramatise the whole situation. I imagine you'll go down to get data for that meeting." Anna, who had decided to go to Reno in the summer to get her divorce, wanted to go with them to Puerto Rico. "I'd rather go alone with you but I can't hurt her feelings & we do have fun together but I may suggest she take Betty [Lindley]." Not upsetting Hick was like walking on hot stones: "Darling, I love you deeply. I never want to hurt you. You are dearer to me than you can guess. I kiss your photograph & ask every blessing for you." Such expressions were becoming a kind of ritual. They were sincere, as were all her endearments to her close friends, but they were also a form of self-therapy, their utterance kept alive the feelings of innocence, purity, and love of her youth.

Elliott turned up. She did not expect to "get down to anything beyond being glad to see each other. Funny world!" And behind Elliott came her "poor old colored laundress of years ago. . . . She's been on relief & the rate is pathetic. I've got to try & help her but she is old & it will be hard. Cousin Susie is worried about finances. I wondered how they'd like to change places."

When Harry Hopkins arranged for children to get better school lunches, she was enthusiastic. "He is a swell person to work with!" Hick's report from Florida led her to exclaim, "How you can write!" The pace in the White House began to tire her again. It helped to fall back on "so many happy memories! I love you deeply, tenderly, darling & I would like to put my arms around you."

She remembered bad trips south to visit Franklin on his houseboat. "How well I know that Florida landscape. I might like it with you, it may just be that I knew it best in my stormy years & the associations are not so pleasant." When Florida reliefers set up picket lines demanding more money, Hick was furious. She was not a "savior of humanity," she protested to Eleanor. The latter took it more calmly: "People are never satisfied Hick dear, when things are done for them. It is unfortunate that we have to do it, they like doing for themselves." One should put oneself in the other's shoes. "Human beings are poor things. Think how much discipline we need ourselves & don't get too discouraged."

January 30, the President's birthday, became the occasion for a double celebration, birthday balls throughout the country, the proceeds of which were to be used to aid crippled children, primarily through the Warm Springs Foundation, and a dinner party of the Cuff Links Club, most of whose members had been with the President since the 1920 vice-presidential campaign. Eleanor attended three birthday balls in Washington. Together with Louis Howe she was also the impresario of the private Cuff Links party that preceded them. That meant preparing not only the menu and favors, but place cards and skits. Louis proposed the theme, which burlesqued reactionary cries that F.D.R. was becoming a dictator. The photograph of the occasion shows him in a purple toga, garlanded with laurel, as a Roman emperor. Louis called his skit "Dear Caesar." Eleanor played a Delphic oracle. The men were in steel helmets and togas, the women in seraphic gowns. Nan and Marion were there, as were Missy and Tommy. Participants received photographs of the occasion with Steve Early's stern rejoinder to guard them against leakage. Marion's copy only surfaced in the 1970s.

"Dearest Hick," Eleanor wrote amid the busyness of that day:

> No letter today. I imagine because Franklin's wire & mail have swamped them to such an extent that they have sent up no mail! I feel a bit aggrieved which is foolish! You have gathered I expect that all the preparations for F's party etc. are a bit on my nerves & I am missing you far away. What shall I do when you are West, oh! well, sufficient unto the day etc.!

Not only would she go to the after-dinner balls:

> I finally wrote two stunts. Louis was paraphrasing hymns & that seemed to me possible so we will have something to do when called on.

The party had "gone off well," she reported the next day, "& I think Louis enjoyed it!" She said nothing about Franklin. "Evidently the ladies stunts were acceptable. I'll show you the songs & I was a Delphic oracle & evidently answered to their satisfaction at least they seemed amused!"

Hopkins was not at the dinner. His chief entrée to the White House at that time was through Eleanor. "I had a grand time with Mr. Hopkins today. Our trip to Porto Rico is set for March 5th." Hick also was being asked to help with publicity at Reedsville, West Virginia, where the Arthurdale project was located. It was an assignment that Hick did not like, as she later indicated. One threat, however, abated. John Boettiger vetoed Anna's going to Puerto Rico. She would be away too long; moreover, Anna hated to fly.

A telephone call to Hick showed that she again needed reassurance:

> I just talked to you darling, it was so good to hear your voice. If I could just take you in my arms. Dear, I often feel rebellious too & yet I know we get more joy when we are together than we would have if we lived apart in the same city & I could only meet for short periods now and then. Some day perhaps fate will be kind & let us arrange a life more to

our liking for the time being we are lucky to have what we have. Dearest, we are happy together & strong relationships have to grow deep roots. We're growing them now, partly because we are separated. The foliage & the flowers will come, somehow I'm sure of it.

After Puerto Rico, Hick was scheduled to go to the Far West, and Eleanor dreaded that, but Ella, the woman with whom Hick had shared an apartment in Minneapolis and later in San Francisco, "can be with you," and Eleanor was

glad . . . tho' I'll dread that too just a little, but I know I've got to fit in gradually to your past, meet your friends & like them so there won't be closed doors between us later on & some of this we'll do this summer perhaps. I shall feel you are terribly far away & [it] makes me lonely but if you are happy I can bear that & be happy too. Love is a queer thing, it hurts one but it gives one so much more in return!

Corinne Alsop came to stay. They did many things together and Eleanor took her to visit Isabella. Nan arrived. "Quite a household when everyone has trays! Louis is in his bedroom still all the time. He insists he is coming to N.Y. Wednesday & going to Fall River Thursday & that he needs a change, but I can't see how he will stand the trip." All her friends had claims on her solicitude, but the one that perhaps involved her most was that with Earl, and that was the one about which she said the least, so powerfully did she feel her relationship to him. Her actions spoke. Among her many activities, she reported one hectic day, was to "cut Earl's coupons on the bonds I have in my safe deposit box," a domestic chore that suggested the intimacy of the two.

She went up to Ithaca with Elinor Morgenthau for her annual appearance at Flora Rose's institute at Cornell and "called FDR to find out if he had signed C.W.A.," the bill that would keep Hopkins' agency alive. The opposition was trying to kill the bill through amendments, and Roosevelt decided to let C.W.A. lapse and to continue work relief through the FERA, of which Hopkins was also the head. After the 1934 midterm elections he planned a new, more ambitious program. Hick was coming back to Washington: "Only 10 more days. Dear one, I love you & the nicest part about my desk is looking at your picture & kissing it goodnight."

Despite wintry roads Eleanor was driven to Lewisburg in Pennsylvania to inspect the federal prison there. "Much the best I've seen & the man in charge is grand." From there to Ithaca and a postscript: "And will you be my valentine?" A few days later she sensed that Hick was not feeling well. "Dear one, I don't think you'll need to go to Reedsville. What you've seen will be all you need to write the stories Mr. Hopkins wants & I think N.Y. needs you much more & a rest with me in Washington is absolutely essential." She had forgotten while she was in Harrisburg to mail her daily letter. "I know it is worse to feel neglected when one is ill." She and Nan traveled to Glens Falls with Earl. He was "enjoying life & so proud of his rooms." They would go for a hike: "Nan says she'll stay home!"

From March 4 to March 15 Eleanor made what Bess Furman of the AP, one of several newspaperwomen who accompanied her, called a "flying trip" to Puerto Rico and the Virgin Islands. Hick went along, and Rexford Tugwell turned up for the Department of Agriculture, where he was Undersecretary. "This is the most delightful flying I ever did," Eleanor wrote en route to Anna, who was also a confidante:

> Hick is bearing up under the crowds & the 'girls' fairly well. Her only outbreak came as the train man said good night last evening telling me he'd send a train order to be autographed. As the door closed Hick said 'I hope he chokes on the way!'

For Bess Furman the most telling moment of the trip came as they inspected one of the worst slums in San Juan with the near-naked children screaming "*La Presidenta! La Presidenta!*" Suddenly, Mrs. Roosevelt halted in a street that ran with sewage and swarmed with flies, and called to the pool photographer who accompanied them, "Sammee! [Sammy Schulman] You can take this! For really showing what it is like, I want you to get this!" Eleanor gave many reasons why she was there but always stressed that the President wanted Puerto Rico to know he was really interested in it. From her letters to Hick, however, and her promptings and conspirings with Hopkins, it also appears she wanted to stir the mainland up about the island's plight and to help bring it the New Deal.

As separation from Hick approached, she soothed her:

> I believe it gets harder to let you go each time but that is because you grow closer. It seems as though you belonged near me, but even if we lived together we would have to separate sometime & just now what you do is of such value to the country that we ought not to complain only that doesn't make me miss you less or feel less lonely.

Usually she avoided doctors, but, having persuaded Hick to see the White House physician, Dr. McIntire, she was left without argument not to see him herself.

> He is going to give me a diet. He found some signs of arthritis & I must drink lots of water. He will try my blood pressure again in a month but he feels 105 is normal for me, it would be 130 ordinarily. He is going to treat my ear twice a week beginning tomorrow at 10 a.m. So now you have my whole history! He says few people would have so little the matter at 50!

Hick's moodiness was unappeasable, but Eleanor kept at it, for bolstering Hick also helped her:

You are not childish only I get swallowed up by duties and am not so sensible in doing what I want to do & forgetting what I think is my duty! I need to learn to do that & we will both be happier!

She took the Hopkinses, the Tugwells, Jim Bourne of Puerto Rico, John and Anna to the opera to hear Maria Jeritza: "Your boss was very fit & more cheerful." A vivid glimpse of F.D.R. followed:

Didn't F get walloped in both the House and Senate? Louis seems complacent, but Anna says F was wild over the House vote. Louis just says 'a defeat will be good for the young man' & 'he must see more of the heads of Committees'!*

Isabella took a more relaxed view of the House defeat, but the men in the White House were not as relaxed about her:

Rainey [Speaker of the House] had been in & told Louis she was the greatest influence against the administration & Louis stormed in to me & said if she wanted to defeat F. she could & would be responsible for his downfall. I laughed & said it was flattering that they felt a woman had gained that influence in so short a time. *She* came in to tell me Rainey had said this to her plus the statement that F. was the greatest man who had ever lived & everyone must do just as he said, on every subject! Doesn't it seem unbelievable? Well I took her in & let her talk to Louis & then at 3:15 I took him for a drive & let him tell me all his worries.

The harassed feeling returned as Easter approached: "Oh! Lord I'm getting to feel more like a goldfish every day!" At the Easter dawn services at Arlington National Cemetery she nearly froze and came back to the White House to sit in front of the fire. Later she went to church but was unable to hear the sermon because of her defective hearing:

I sat & thought about you & prayed I might make you happy & care in the way which would make me plan & foresee enough so as to never make those I love unhappy. I think my real trouble is not that I don't care enough, but that for so many years I've let my work engulf me so as to have no time to think & now when I should know how & shake it it has become my master!

She found time "Easter Sunday" to send off a letter to "Nan dearest":

How very sweet of you to want to give me the "Frog Baby" [a cement figure] and of course I've always wanted 'us' to have one in a fountain but we've always shared everything at the cottage & don't let's change.

* F.D.R. had vetoed the Independent Offices Appropriations, which had, contrary to his economy wishes, restored salaries he had reduced and several veterans' benefits. The House overrode his veto, March 28, 1934; two days later the Senate did the same.

I feel everything belonged to you & Marion, also we'll christen it for us all please! Our bedrooms we may want individually & perhaps now & then a sitting room to work in & retire to if we want to be alone or have some friend who needs solitude but on the whole what is mine is thine & I'll hang a 'do not disturb' sign out & you must do the same when you wish complete isolation temporarily!

Louis drove with her almost daily, but when they tried walking, he only managed to go ten yards. Anna and John came in: "Anna & I had quite a talk yesterday & it is grand to be young. You still trust so much in the future, or rather I suppose there just seems to be so much future!"

Nan's father, who lived in Massena, died. She decided to go through with her speech in Columbus, Ohio, get herself to Syracuse, where Earl would meet her and drive her to Massena. "Louis is low but I think it is just my going away & I hope he goes home tomorrow." She had news about Hopkins. "He is worried about white collar people & his own staff the country over for he feels they are discouraged & that bothers him. He's got a new plan . . . it is still nebulous but his mind is working."

Hick's friendship with Eleanor was becoming known generally and the attendant publicity caused Hick problems. Eleanor commiserated: "Poor dear, I am so sorry that I pursue you so unpleasantly all over the country but of course unimportant things like the Porto Rican trip are played up in all these local papers!"

She put her trip to Columbus to good use. Tommy went along and Eleanor managed to write three syndicated articles on the way out and part of a piece for the *Woman's Home Companion*. In Columbus she found Tiny waiting. She spoke to a large audience: "I've been very much 'Mrs. R.'—all day!" but when she began to speak, she wrote of herself in the third person. ". . . she suddenly felt like herself & not like the first lady & said several things the first lady shouldn't have said."

She attended Mr. Cook's funeral in Massena. Her coming meant a great deal to Nan. Although Nan and Marion did not approve of Earl, even they agreed that he "has been a dear & understanding soul." She stopped to see Leo Casey on the way back and then went on to Hyde Park. Hick, in the meantime, had been in New Orleans and described her final dinner at Arnaud's: "I made it a memorable one: two gin fizzes, some kind of a marvelous shrimp concoction known as shrimp Arnaud, pompano baked in a paper bag, potato souffle, a pint of sauterne, crepes suzettes (I think I'll never order them anywhere else!) and black coffee." She wished she was able to enjoy food, Eleanor replied sadly, perhaps she might be able to with Hick.

Some day we'll lead a leisurely life & write, so we can take our work with us & do all the things we want to do. Now and then we'll take

Earl along because he seemed so lonely yesterday when we left him that my heart ached! Women do get along better than men. Even you dear settle down to work & I drown my longings in routine but a man has something the quality of a lost animal.

She even had had mint juleps, she noted, "made just right, but it was in the days when my conscience bothered me as I drank & I don't think I could have enjoyed nectar!"

Hick reported an off-color story about prostitution in Houston. Unemployed single women were being driven to it because of poverty. A male social worker who investigated the transient setup was solicited by several girls. To one of them he said, "I can't. I have no money." "Oh, that's alright," she replied. "It only costs a dime."

Eleanor did not comment on this story unless her brisk "I shan't show it [Hick's letter] to Franklin!" was in her view comment enough. The depiction of some aspects of life, such as a sexuality that was not attached to love, caused her to squirm. When later she went with Elinor Morgenthau to see *Tobacco Road*, its realistic portrayal of the South's lower depths disgusted her:

> Never have I seen on the stage a more revolting 1st act, the 2d & 3rd were horrible but interesting but I don't really think that type of play helps even the 'poor white.'

It was spring again in Washington and her calendar overflowed:

> One of my bad days, not one minute to breathe! Met F. together with most of the Democratic members of Congress & all the children & Missy. My sense of humor was tickled! Came home & ordered meals etc. went & met Marion & my graduate class at the Freer Gallery, went with them to the Folger Library, then to Bureau of Engraving & Printing & 'said a few words' about the Mother's Day stamps.
>
> Had a grand lunch at Isabella's with Mary Rumsey, Frances Perkins & Lady Lindsay, rushed home to say goodbye to Elliott & found he was staying over till tomorrow. Saw people from 3:45–5, went to Wilson Teachers College, 'said a few words.' Came back & saw Clarence Pickett, took L.H. for a drive stopping at the Naval Hospital to see what had happened to Joan Morgenthau, who fell off her horse jumping. Found just a broken collar bone, & drove around the basin very lovely at that time of evening & got home in time to fall into my clothes. Have had my graduate class to dine & write while a movie goes on!
>
> No letter from you today which would happen when I'm going away! Well, I'll find more on my return.
>
> You may have gathered I am missing you tonight but dear one I will be all right on Sunday, it is just because I am rushed & hate this trip!
>
> Much, much love darling. I'd like to put my arms around you & shut out the world.

Her cousin Theodore Douglas Robinson, the eldest child of Auntie Corinne and married to Rosey's daughter, Helen, died, "bronchial pneumonia, & a heavy drinker always a fatal combination. Poor Helen, she always was in love with him I think & what he put her through!" She journeyed up to Herkimer, the family seat of the Robinsons in Mohawk Valley, a "cold & gloomy day. Helen & Corinne & all the children were grand & the service was in the old hall at Henderson." She wished that the "life eternal," pronounced by the minister, "meant at least the spirits of those who have gone before could communicate with us easily here."

She worried about Louis's health and how she might help him. "Louis is begging me to spend a weekend in May at the beach as Grace [his wife] is going to Europe about the 5th for a month. I don't think I can manage it but I promised to consider it if he'd go home for two weeks & rest, I'd do it for I think it would do him a world of good."

She returned to a White House full of people: "I'm oppressed by my calendar the next two weeks & fussing about things I can't help & I shouldn't be writing you for I'm in the mood when I shouldn't be, also it is 2 a.m."

The publicity stemming from Hick's association with Eleanor had eased off. Eleanor was pleased: ". . . we must be careful this summer to keep it out of the papers when we are off together. No, I am *always* glad you were assigned to me in 1932 & I am glad if you feel the same way. . . ." Her weariness had begun to abate. "We are funny, I think I was worried because they told me how annoyed Fjr. was with me & I realize how he never comes home & yet I know one can never do anything for one's children." Rose Schneiderman and the Women's Trade Union League wanted the workingwomen of the country to present her portrait to the White House: "I put off decision for a year. It may not have to be done!"

She and Hick had begun to discuss sharing a "camp or cottage" on a semi-permanent basis that was theirs. That meant leaving the stone cottage at Val-Kill that she shared with Nan and Marion. How serious she was is never clear, but the idea kept recurring. She went to New York to look in on Val-Kill's annual furniture display. "One corner cupboard I long to have for our camp or cottage or home, which is it to be? I've always thought of it in the country but I don't think we ever decided on the variety of abode nor the furniture. We probably won't agree."

Separations were becoming easier, Hick confessed, and that led Eleanor to talk about herself. She had not been

> very good this time but that is purely myself & you know me well enough to know I will have moods, don't you? Remember you must never worry about my being depressed or cross for it is just a passing mood with me & it never tires me the way it does you!

An "interesting talk" with Walter White of the National Association for the Advancement of Colored People about the anti-lynching bill. She became his great administration bulwark in that fight. As an afterthought she added: "I am sorely tempted to make a radio contract, $3,000 a week & picked up wherever I am! Tommy & I have worked all evening & FDR has 80 publishers still downstairs firing questions at him!"

Hick, on Eleanor's instigation and Elliott's invitation, made it a point while in Texas to see Elliott and Ruth. She found Elliott "quieter, not so restless, *much* more mature . . . as for Ruth—she really is a *vast* improvement over Betty, I should say. She's the neatest sort of person and darned attractive even when pregnant." She was going to bed, Hick went on, in hopes she might dream about the absent E.R. She rarely did dream, but once when she had a Mexican dinner she had dreamt "that I was going to marry Earl and your mother-in-law was simply furious!"

The D.A.R. came to Washington "& at 3:35 [she] began to shake hands . . . & by 5:10 the line was past & 2,555 had gone by!" She thought she had made "a good speech on peace" to them that morning and "a lot of the D.A.R.'s as they shook my hand this p.m. murmured 'I admire your courage.' It didn't take any courage but it was rather fun."

Perhaps it was Franklin's defeat in Congress on the CWA, perhaps the impoverishment she had seen in West Virginia and Hick's reports to the same effect from around the country, but she kept up the pressure inside the White House for real change. "Franklin looks well & is cheerful but last night I told him it appeared to me fundamental thinking was lacking & he agreed." She attended a CWA artists' exhibition at the Corcoran Gallery:

> One portrait of a young working man is the most stirring thing I've seen. There is tenderness in the face but bewilderment & discouragement & a certain resentment growing in the eyes. It is the unemployed youth of America. I've got the Tugwells & the Hopkins' coming to dine tonight & I hope we'll have a real talk of some ideas I think we should work on. I wish you were to be here but you would probably refuse to talk!

Rex Tugwell's name began to appear more frequently in her letters. "Rex Tugwell has sent me his report on Porto Rico & it is grand, also he made a grand speech to the newspaper people."

Hick's approval of Elliott and Ruth stirred a sympathetic chord in her: "I feel just as you do about Elliott, he is steadier & older & happier . . . she [Ruth] must have a lot of character & I take my hat off to her for what she's done for Elliott." Earl worried her: "He's much upset because the doctor tells him he's on the verge of a nervous breakdown with a blood pressure of 95. I told him to stop worrying & rest & he'd be all right."

She called on a woman who had worked for her many years earlier:

> It is sad to be helpless & poor & old, isn't it? I hope you & I together have enough to make it gracious & attractive! . . . Will Rogers gave both F. & me a little puff this a.m. so I feel quite set up tho' I had stern reproof from an anonymous D.A.R. on my speech! Fifteen more days! Dear one, I would give a great deal to put my arms about you tonight!

As E.R. had feared, Hick was involved in a smashup. Hick emerged unscathed but the car was demolished. "Oh! dear one I love you & long to be with you when things go wrong but I'm glad Ella will be there tomorrow. Give her my love & tell her I am so relieved to have her with you." Eleanor undertook to get Hick a new car and to advance the money for it while the insurance claims were being settled.

She went with Franklin to hear Josephus Daniels dedicate a statue to William Jennings Bryan, "& as I listened to Mr. Daniels I decided he accomplished a great deal, but I did not like him." She and Franklin returned to Anna's birthday party, "& the kids enjoyed seeing 'Papa' spank her. She is 28 & how much further ahead than I was at her age. . . . Rex Tugwell delivered a speech to the Nat. Dem. Women's Club here & called it 'Wine, Women & Song' & the Methodists & W.C.T.U.'s are out for his scalp."

One of Hick's companions for dinner out West was a recent Vassar graduate who was doing a statistical survey of transients. "She is afraid there won't be a revolution and I'm afraid there will be—so our argument was rather amusing. She admires the President greatly, but doesn't think he'll be able to put his reforms over because of Congress." On a trip East, Hick stayed at the White House. When she left for Ohio to visit her first subsistence homestead, she drove Eleanor's Buick. They had had a stormy as well as happy time together:

> Hick dearest, I know how you felt today—you couldn't let go for fear of losing control & being with me was hard & I imagine I made it worse by sending you to say goodbye to Missy & Tommy but she spoke of it at breakfast & I was so afraid she'd come & stay & spoil our little time together. Darling I love you dearly & I am sorry for letting my foolish temperament make you unhappy & sorry that your temperament does bad things to you too but we'll have years of happy times so bad times will be forgotten.

Among Eleanor's recipes for the restoration of serenity was a visit to the Saint-Gaudens memorial in Rock Creek Park.

I took the kids out to see the Sargent Memorial [did she mean Saint-Gaudens?] this a.m. & it had its usual effect on me & they loved it. Louis has been feeling badly & very depressed & there was another Reedsville attack brewing & I knew I was getting nervous but that visit gave me back my perspective. I have to remember that in the future you & I have to go there at least once everytime you are here!

Unable to find a Buick convertible or roadster, she recommended that Hick "stick to" a Plymouth.

Hick's positive reaction to the subsistence homesteads in Dayton relieved her: "I think you must be seeing what Nan went out to see & she was thrilled too." Hopkins and his wife came to the White House to dine, "& we will all go on the *Sequoia* for lunch tomorrow if it's fine." But it rained, "so no boat. . . . Your boss looked much better last night & he's going to think over my idea for young people." F.D.R.'s programs were beginning to have an effect, but the benefits went chiefly to the wage earner, the businessman, the head of the household. She was groping for a way to meet the needs of the young.

Another federal prison. This time she went with Elinor to Alderson, West Virginia. "It isn't a prison & they are doing rehabilitation & Dr. Harris is a wonder." The two women drove on to White Sulphur Springs, West Virginia, to visit Elinor's mother. Then, wending their way northward, they ended up at Elinor's farm in Fishkill, had a walk, "a *very* cold dip in the pool," and went over to Camp Tera, but Al Kresse was out. "The Hudson River is lovely & I guess it is bred in me to love it." She returned to the question of a home of her own, but no longer seemed to think of it as a place to be shared with Hick:

> I've been wondering the last few days what I really want for my declining years. I could completely take over the cottage at Campo & make that the place to turn to when I want to be 'at home' but it is far away not only for me but for my friends & quite out of the question for winter. Shall I build a cottage at Hyde Park? Perhaps I won't ever use it but I could lend it to people if so where shall I build? Oh! well, I won't have to decide for years as I'll have to save thousands of dollars first!

Hick should not give up her own apartment in New York City, for "it is home."

Hyde Park was home for Eleanor and it is doubtful that she ever might have settled elsewhere. She sent Hick a rose from there:

> I wonder if any of the sweetness of this little favorite rose of mine will linger by the time it reaches you? My bush at the cottage was a lovely sight in full bloom & unconsciously I wanted you to see it with me.
>
> We got here at 9:15 and at 10:30 I went out with F. in his car & drove over all the little roads on this side of the place & some over the

other. I hope Franklin has a few years here, he would really enjoy it & I believe he would enjoy it even with Mama here. I kept thinking of the mess we had made of our young lives here & how strange it was that after all these years I return here as indifferent & uninterested as a stranger & I doubt if any child has any feeling about it because nothing has ever been his or her own here. It is a pity one cannot have one's life over again but at least one can try to keep one's children from making the same mistakes & if you cannot help them much financially one can at least leave them free! We got in at 12:30 & I wasn't giving vent to these thoughts so poor F. doesn't have such a bad time! The Astors & Morgans lunched here. Anna escaped to the cottage for the day & John was there too. I walked over, getting there about 4 & Molly & I had a swim & then Mama & Betty & F came to tea & Nan & I drove around the new road with him back of the cottage. Anna & I took John back to Poughkeepsie & came home to dine & then at 10 we drove up & saw Anna & F. off & I talked with Mama for an hour. She is unhappy & I see why & yet I feel so strongly she brought it on herself but she can't help it for she doesn't understand. She'll be 80 in Sept. & I must make it a happy day for her. I've been such an unsatisfactory daughter-in-law!

She, Franklin, and Mama drove to Groton, where Franklin was to speak on its fiftieth anniversary. Johnny, their last son to go there, was graduating and he received permission to dine with them "& what do you think he ate? Tomato juice, 1 quart milk, 1 hot dog, 1 sirloin steak, asparagus, 1 chicken sandwich, 1 vanilla ice cream, 1 strawberries!"

Franklin was the star but she also was busy:

Lunched with the graduates a few of whom I knew. Then went to the river for a race, sat under a tree & talked to people I knew slightly, many of whom belonged to my dim & distant past, paid some calls with F., had tea at the Rector's. Agnes Leach & I went over to the chapel at 6 for the organ recital which we enjoyed & then I dressed & went to the dinner. F. spoke well & it was a nice evening with well deserved praise for the Rector & Mrs. Peabody. 451 graduates were back, a good record for 50 years.

She intended to join Hick in the West for their three-week holiday: "It has the great advantage of letting you be longer near 'Ellie.' It was sweet of her to suggest it."

Harry Hopkins came to dinner and as usual was full of praise for the "grand reports" Hick wrote.

We're praying Congress will adjourn Saturday but no one knows & they spent 5 hrs. talking about Tugwell today! Isn't it maddening? . . . Frances, Mary & I had lunch & things good & bad are happening in both their bailiwicks but they are happening at last! Your boss is thinking about my young people & we may put a plan over in Oct. & I feel far from stagnation tonight.

Tomorrow Anna leaves [for Reno] & then Oh! how I dread it.

She saw Anna off "and we made it unnoticed, but it will break tomorrow. Poor child, she was lonely & sad & I felt like a beast to let her fare forth alone. I'm riding with John tomorrow morning at 8 so as to write her afterwards!" Later she drove with Louis "& dinner with just Mr. [Clarence] Pickett to give F. his impressions & now all of us at work."

The story of Anna's impending divorce broke. Eleanor felt the "papers have been fairly decent," but an evening with Cousin Susie left her so low in mind she thought she might weep. She "made a scene & I became cold & calm. She's spent the evening after a few more home truths saying she was sorry but somehow I never can thaw." She felt more charitable the next day. She visited Cousin Henry who was in the hospital. "He is an angel & how he stands his life I don't know."

Jimmy and Betsy and Rosey's wife, Betty, joined her in New York at the steamship pier to see "Mama safely in her palatial quarters & for once I did not want to go in the least. She's staying at the Embassy in London, going to stay with the King & Queen of England. Lord how I would hate it & how she will love it!"

"Remember even disagreeable things come to an end," she advised Anna. "Granny is staying at the Embassy & couldn't understand why I had no desire to go with her!"

Nan and Marion joined her on the *Sequoia* at New Haven. The two women had the large cabin. She had Missy's. F.D.R. spoke at Yale and then they weighed anchor for New London to watch the Harvard-Yale boat races there. "Fjr.'s crew lost." That caused great gloom among the young. They had twenty aboard for lunch,

among them Ethel duPont whom Fjr. is playing with. . . . Of course, I'm not a proper parent. I don't care who wins but I hate to see the boys flop over & to hear Fjr saying everything was red & black the last half mile. It all seems needless strain but I do think it is good to learn to take defeat.

Public and private affairs commingled. She and Franklin returned to Hyde Park, where she prepared for a trip to the TVA* with Nan and Marion. Elliott and Ruth and their baby were there. "I do like Ruth. . . . I don't feel frozen with her so far & I must tell her sometimes what wonders she had done for Elliott." Earl was at the cottage and the next day drove her to Tivoli. "He looks better but is still pretty nervous. It is hard for me ever to believe in anyone having a nervous

* Tennessee Valley Authority, established 1933 for development of the Tennessee River basin.

breakdown but I can see Earl has had one & is working hard to pull out."

Grace Falke, who was Rex Tugwell's aide, joined Hick in the West. "I noticed she was none too happy when the Senate Committee had Rex Tugwell on the pan." Did Eleanor catch the implication? Later Tugwell divorced his wife and married Grace.

Eleanor found the Big House "peaceful" with Mama away. It was an idyllic June evening. All went up to Laura Delano's "for a grand dinner, taking Elliott & Ruth. She has great poise & fits in remarkably with the younger ones & does not seem ruffled by name or wealth. I drove Franklin up & back in my car which was rather fun & I think he has enjoyed his day tho' it has been busy."

Her manifest pleasure in driving Franklin in her own car up to Laura's seemed to belie the arm's-length attitude she often assumed in approaching him. So did her cordiality, good humor, and concern with him on other evenings and drives. But as in her conflicted attitude towards Hyde Park, which on the surface she managed almost in the same breath to love and not to love, some friends suspected that just as she could never bear to move away from Hyde Park she never ceased loving him. To maintain his respect, she had learned she could not afford to be taken for granted. She had come to prize her independence above all. Hick was learning that, too, but autonomy carried a price for Eleanor. In Hick's case Eleanor worried over her everlasting complaints of being hurt. In Franklin's case her marriage to a man who preferred deference and tractability in a woman, even the most beautiful, meant sometimes being on the outside.

She stopped over at the White House before setting out for TVA country. Hick had seen Ella:

> I am so happy that Ellie met you & that the old companionship is there & I do hope she stays with you right along. Yes, dear, I think you will remember that I once told you I wished you had been happy with a man or that it might still be. I rather think that the lack of that relationship does create 'emotional instability' but people do seem to weather it in time & who knows what the future holds. In the meantime Ellie & I will try to do a little stabilizing or at least help you to do it!

Hick's letter that produced this statement has disappeared. She and Hick had different approaches to men. If one had to, their absence could be "weathered," but their presence in life added a kind of psychic balance. Hick knew and resented that for Eleanor the fulfilling relationship was that between a man and a woman.

She enjoyed helping Anna and John over the rough spots. Anna was in Nevada and she had John to dinner and to ride, and then wrote to her daughter:

He told me some things he wants to discuss with you & he doesn't want you to delay any longer than you have to on the way home! He said he was lonely but I told him that was a good sign!

I am a little weary of adjusting everybody, officials, secretaries, desks, so I'll be glad to get out on the road next Monday & I can hardly wait to see you.

With Congress in adjournment, Roosevelt, the midterm congressional elections in mind, went on the air and delivered a "fireside chat." His legislative strength lay in his ability to appeal to the people over the heads of the Congress. Now he asked them, "Are you better off than you were last year?" and indicated the ways in which the Government had sought to help. A few days later, taking Franklin, Jr., and John with him, he boarded the U.S.S. *Houston* at Annapolis for a ten-thousand-mile cruise that would last four weeks, take him through the Panama Canal, to the Cocos Islands and Hawaii. On July 28 it would end up at Portland, Oregon, where Eleanor and members of his staff would be waiting. "I liked F.'s speech tonight. He isn't leaving till Sunday so I go to Reedsville for the day Sat. . . ." Franklin, Jr., and Johnny accompanied her.

Bernard Baruch came to tea. He offered to look into the budgetary soundness of Reedsville. ". . . got out clothes, talked long with Fjr. & John on what is a successful life! No less!" Hick sounded happy. "I am glad. Ellie must have a good effect on you for you to be calm about that California mess." Affirmative references to Ellie were now a steady refrain in her letters. "I love you & feel content about you when you are with 'Ellie,'" the next one said. She also reported the trip to Reedsville: "I drove Louis in his car & led the procession & we made good time about 200 miles in 6 hrs. . . . Isabella, Mary Rumsey, Bill Astor went for the day & all were thrilled. 32 homesteaders are in their homes & we stopped to talk to them." A couple of days later she was on the road through the succession of valleys and mountains that led to Norris in TVA country, and she exclaimed, perhaps not the first to do so, "Man is vile but nature is glorious!"

In Norris she, Nan, and Marion spent a day looking at houses "& seeing the dam from every angle. It is stupendous & interesting but they are still looking for industries. Did I tell you there are no tent colonies in West Virginia, also that the relief loads have dropped in Williamson & Logan?"

She disagreed with Hickok's assessment of F.D.R.'s fireside chat pointing out the help that government had given people. Although she called herself the agitator and him the politician, she shared some of

F.D.R.'s intuition for timing in politics. "I quite understand what you felt about F's speech & yet I think it was good & reassuring. No one can give you a definite plan with any hope of carrying it out after he's given it. The nearest was F's message to Congress 2 or 3 weeks before adjournment & I'm not sure that was wise tho' he felt it was needed to help the Economic Planning Committee. Well, thank heaven if you do listen to me Monday evening you won't be expecting much so you won't be disturbed & perhaps you'll go to bed early instead which I would prefer."

She drove to Chicago from Norris: "Dear, I've been seeing such grand people & tho' I know what a mixed-up world we have, still somehow I have faith in the ultimate solution."

She visited the World's Fair again, this time in the company of her brother, Hall. She also sought to reassure Hick, who had developed a bad case of nerves over Eleanor's impending visit:

> Dear one, why should you feel shy & worried about seeing me. You don't feel that way about your old friends. I suppose it is just that you haven't known me long enough. Well, try to feel you just saw me yesterday & we will pick up just where we left off.

She returned to the subject of Hick's jitters the next day:

> I can't quite understand why you are so worried dear, why can't you just be natural? Of course we are going to have a good time together & neither of us is going to be upset.

Mrs. Roosevelt flew from Chicago to Sacramento. Her destination was supposedly a secret, but on arrival, to Hick's dismay and hers, the press was there. It is difficult to understand how they imagined they might elude the press. As Eleanor wrote "Darling Nan" in a note that Nan transcribed but itself disappeared with part of the contents missing:

> The trip out was smooth & pleasant except for the fact that they wired I was on the plane from Chicago but I got [out] nowhere till Salt Lake tho' I had doubts at Des Moines & in Salt Lake at 3 a.m. I had to because the Gov. & his wife & all kinds of officials were there but they sent the photographers away first—Hick met me in Sacramento—but we . . .

She had seen John Boettiger in Chicago and sent him a vexed account of her encounters with the press:

> . . . The trip coming out was horrid, papers had it & tho' I wouldn't be photographed or interviewed it seemed so ungracious not to go out & say 'hello' to the people who had come out to see me. . . . When they followed me out of Sacramento I pulled up & told the boys they could just telephone their editors from the next town I was either

going to be free or I was going to leave *any* state where the press followed me & of course if I went back East I would not meet the President [and] he would probably be somewhat annoyed. In the next town
with Hick scowling I invited our two pursuers to breakfast in a coffee
shop till their editors could be reached & we had a pleasant meal & the
editors let them 'lay off'! . . .

I loved seeing you in Chicago, John dear. I've grown to love you like
one of my dear ones & I'm grateful beyond words for the happiness
you've already given Anna & I trust you for the future.

Hick's account of their three weeks' holiday, which began with a stay
at the home of Ellie Morse Dickenson and her husband, was a continuous story of efforts to elude the press. At Ella's, Eleanor read from
the *Oxford Book of English Verse*. She was a dramatic reader of poetry,
in that respect following in the footsteps of Mlle. Souvestre and her
Uncle Ted. At Warm Springs she had treated Hick hour after hour to
another favorite, Stephen Vincent Benét's *John Brown's Body*.

The two women journeyed to the Nevada ranch of the William
Danas, where Anna was waiting for her divorce. They were leaving
"very early," she informed Nan, "& praying no one will see us here! Rex
Tugwell & Miss Falke [who toured with Hick most of her last trip]
come for tomorrow night." The Danas, who owned the Arrowhead D
Ranch, about fifty miles from Reno, where Anna was staying, were particular friends of Marion:

I feared you suffered at 'Tobacco Road.' I did for that first act seemed
so unnecessary & there is some beauty—even in that life & it shouldn't
be left out.

Mr. & Mrs. Dana are very nice & hospitality could not be more cor-
dial & sweet. It has been wonderful for Anna & even better for the
chicks but Nan will tell you about that. Mr. D. & I ride in the mornings
very quietly but with great pleasure & in the afternoons we swim & lie
on the beach in the sun. The wild sage is delicious & the desert beautiful but the blue lake makes it more wonderful than anything I've ever
seen of this kind. I arrived with a particularly vicious stye on my eye
but I hope it will soon come to a head. It hasn't bothered me much in
any case.

Hick & I go to the Yosemite Sunday but beyond that our plans
depend on the strike [the general strike in San Francisco] & I'll wire
Nan.

She wrote to Nan the same day:

Anna & the chicks are fine physically & another two weeks & this ordeal
will be over for Anna. The kids have gained a lot in other ways. It is
good to be where human beings count on their worth & not for what
they have & here we all eat together even Katie & after a few startled
questions they have accepted the boys who cook & the old horse trainer

as friends. I tremble a little at some of the things they'll tell Mama but it has been good for them.

She and Hick camped in Yosemite under the watchful eye of the rangers and picked their way over its trails on horseback, a lark for Eleanor, a trial for Hick.

"San Francisco went off pretty well," she wrote to Nan:

> & the drive up thro' the Redwoods & by the sea was beautiful. We spent last night at Crater Lake but the altitude bothered Hick as much or more than in the Yosemite so I walked about this morning & we left after lunch & are spending the night here & going on tomorrow to Portland.

Hick left Portland before the President's ship docked, their efforts to elude the press a failure. Eleanor shook her head: "Franklin said I'd never get away with it, and I can't."

Tiny, Louis, and Steve Early also were in Portland. Louis was angry with Eleanor. She had promised to meet him in San Francisco for the drive up to Portland. They had not connected. Was Hick's passion for being alone with Eleanor to blame? It took all of Eleanor's persuasiveness to calm Louis down. Hick, meanwhile, had left: "Darling, how I hated to have you go! It is still a pretty bad ache & I've thought of you all day especially as we drove along the road we had covered yesterday & which you drove over this morning."

She sought to comfort Hick, but new responsibilities, new occasions, swallowed her up as she traveled eastward on the presidential train. "Sec. Dern [Secretary of War], Ickes & Sen. Wheeler came to dine & I staged a grand conservative youth argument versus radical elders!" They were en route to Glacier National Park after the President's speech at Bonneville Dam in Oregon. Hick had returned to San Francisco, and Eleanor hoped that Ella was with her. "The place & the person together should help."

With Tommy on hand she caught up on her mail and did an issue of the "News" for the New York State Women's Division. In script a little more erratic than usual because of the "jiggly" train she caught up on correspondence with Elinor. Had she had a "lovely time on the ranch & I heard Bob shot a grizzly. Was he thrilled? I also saw Henry 3rd was home. . . . Franklin & the boys seem to have had a perfect trip." That was another side to her existence. She was devoted to Elinor; even more she admired her—her solicitude for Henry, the intelligence with which she brought up her children, her feeling for the arts. She was overly sensitive, but that, too, she understood in view of Elinor's Jewish background.

Social and political life on the train was almost the way it was in the White House, she wrote to Hick:

We have guests for every meal. Sen. & Mrs. Nye tonight. Luckily I've rather enjoyed the various dignitaries tho' the Indians are a bit dirty. F. has acquired 2 rather nice Indian titles, 'Love-Chief,' & 'Fearless Blue Eagle.' I have one 'Medicine Pipe Woman!' The boys say it was given me because of my excessive smoking.

Ella was no substitute for E.R., Hick made clear in a letter from San Francisco:

Although I shall miss Ella greatly when I no longer have her with me, it seems good to be here alone, in my dressing gown, for a quiet talk with you. I hate being hurried or interrupted when I'm writing to you just as I hate it when we're together.

In Chicago, Ray Moley, who was still considered one of F.D.R.'s chief advisers, "asked to talk to me after breakfast & said he was worried about certain things in the Wisconsin speech & said he'd go back & join the train & I think he did! One remark amused me. 'It's easier if he's [meaning F.D.R.] tired to let him say things & not argue & do as Missy & Tully do just let him think he's always right, but I think I ought to go back & argue this out!' "

F.D.R. seems to have taken Moley's advice. In any case Moley approved the Green Bay, Wisconsin, speech, but the business community rejected the olive branch. "How did you like FDR's speech?" she asked Hick. Big business had begun to clamor for an easing of government control and regulations. The speech urged a restoration of "confidence." "Those who would measure confidence in this country in the future," Roosevelt said, "must look first to the average citizen." Eleanor commented: "The reaction in papers & financial circles is interesting." The reaction was adverse. "I read the Wisconsin speech & thought it was good," she wrote to Franklin, addressing him as "Dearest Honey." "Even the Tribune could only be mildly disagreeable. . . ."

Tiny and Eddie drove her to Hyde Park when she returned to the East. "I talked with Anna & she sounds happy." The next day she reached Earl's camp at Chazy Lake. Tiny and Eddie were there, as were Nan and Marion, also her German shepherd dog, Major, who had been banned from the White House: "At first he didn't seem to know me but he's slipped quickly back into familiarity & follows me around as usual & no doubt will sleep with me or with Earl." She had some firm words about her relationship with Hick:

Your letter today was a joy & I am glad it was easier on the whole but I'm afraid you & I are always going to have times when we ache for each other & yet we are not always going to be happy when we are together. Somehow we must find the things we can do & do them so that what time we have together is as happy as it can be in an imperfect world!

All the activities she had been too shy to undertake with Franklin at Campobello when she was young she now did with her friends. Calisthenics at 7:30, shooting, riding, reading in the sun, doing the beds, writing on the porch. When Elinor Morgenthau arrived at Loon Lake in the Adirondacks, she drove over. Elinor's mother was "far from well," she wrote Hick, "and for once I could be sympathetic." She thought Elinor was overly protective of her mother. Elinor had interpreted some remark of Eleanor's at the beginning of the summer to mean she did not want to be worried by mail, and Eleanor, for whom receiving and responding to letters was a vital part of being alive, had "missed having no letters," she assured her after her visit:

> I'm so sorry about your mother & I know how you are feeling for it is much worse to watch someone you love suffer than to suffer yourself. Poor darling, you have so many troubles & never seem to get a real rest. I'm going to try to plan in early Nov. to take you away for a long weekend!
>
> Friendships are always important to me & please don't ever think the opposite no matter what stupid things I do which hurt your feelings. It is never intentional.

"Yes, I am happy here," she wrote Hick almost defiantly, from Chazy Lake, "& one reason, of course, is the place but there are other reasons & I was analyzing them today. Perhaps the main one is that I think I am needed & wanted. I suppose that is why I enjoy being with Anna & John, so often with the boys I feel tolerated!"

So deeply did she cherish her friends at Chazy that she agreed to take part in a movie skit, filmed with Nan's newly acquired camera, "The Kidnapping of the First Lady." In it Earl dressed as a pirate, properly mustachioed, picks her up and carries her away in a rowboat. He ties her to a tree while Nan impersonated the First Lady. The scene ends with Eleanor's rescue. What she did not say in her letter to Hick was that she liked being manhandled by Earl, and felt strangely aroused, to a point where she felt guilty. "These foolish young people are acting a movie play & as it develops I hope it never reaches the press!" The amateurish filming went on for several days. "They are spending the afternoon doing the movie & soon I'll have to go & be tied & gagged."

A news item that said a boat she had been on had run aground in Chazy Lake brought an admonitory telegram from "L," presumably Louis: "FRANKLIN TRYING TO LIVE DOWN DISGRACE OF A ROOSEVELT RUNNING AGROUND IN A BOAT BUT IT COMES HARD. SUGGEST YOU STAY ASHORE OR KEEP OUT OF THE NEWSPAPERS FOR BALANCE OF VISIT. GOOD LUCK. L."

She did things for other people because she felt needed and that gratified her. But her response to Earl's touch was another kind of gratification. She yearned for affection and whatever Earl's roughness, perhaps because of it, he gave it to her. But to Hick she wrote in the usual vein:

Yes, dear, you are right. I give everyone the feeling that you have that I've 'taken them on' & don't need anything from them & then when they naturally resent it & don't like to accept it from me, I wonder why! It is funny I know & I can't help it something locked me up & I can't unlock!

The ten days at Chazy Lake ended. Earl drove her and Nan to Hyde Park. "I'm a little low in my mind as I always am when I return from the company of people I like to the atmosphere here but it will pass & I wish I could see with the eyes of Rita Halle in 'Good Housekeeping.' Do read it you will enjoy it."

She met Franklin at the train at the Hyde Park station. "Earl came down in time for Nan's birthday dinner & Franklin read 'Frankie in Wonderland' & then 'Alice' herself & we talked till 10:30." The Tory parody "Frankie in Wonderland" was modeled on *Alice in Wonderland* and mocked the New Deal. Marion gave it to the President, who had roared with laughter as he read it aloud. The next day he read it again to the newsmen who had assembled at Val-Kill for the annual picnic.

F seems in a militant mood & I think is preparing to say real things which will be a satisfaction. Whether it is wise or not remains to be seen! He says however he has some good facts & figures & that Donald Richberg has done a grand job [at the NRA] this summer.

There was an interesting footnote to Eleanor's description of Earl's presence at Hyde Park for Nan's party: "I think he [Earl] had a happy day & was pleased Franklin wanted him."

Did Earl feel that Franklin resented him? A suggestion that this was the case was contained in a letter that Eleanor had sent to Franklin from Chazy:

Earl wants me to tell you that all arrangements are made for the 29th at Wal-Kill [a state prison that the President was going to inspect]. . . . Would you like Earl to go with you from Hyde Park? He'll be at Hyde Park Sunday night for Nan's birthday anyway & would like to go if you want him but wants you to be entirely frank.

Franklin evidently was glad to have Earl along, for Eleanor's next letter went into the arrangements for Earl's going, and a birthday telegram from Hyde Park to Steve Early at the White House listed both the President and Earl among the signatories:

MANY HAPPY RETURNS OF THE DAY. WE ALL THOUGHT OF YOU AT NAN'S PARTY LAST NIGHT AND SO ALL JOIN IN SIGNING THIS BEST WISHES FOR MANY HAPPY YEARS TO COME. MRS. JAMES ROOSEVELT, FRANKLIN D. ROOSEVELT AND ELEANOR ROOSEVELT, NAN, MARION, MOLLY, MISSY, GUS, EARL AND TOMMY.

Important officials arrived and left: "Everyone now applauds whatever Franklin says. I only hope it isn't the same when they retire to talk in his study!" Henry Morgenthau came, as did the Hopkinses and Tugwells. Eleanor enjoyed talking with them. At the same time she worried about Hick, who was not well. "I always feel that you & Earl need me more than anyone when things go wrong for neither of you have anyone much nearer to whom to turn & to whom I must remember not to offend."

The end of the summer at Hyde Park showed Roosevelt's commitment to the direction that history subsequently has labeled as the New Deal. Not only were Hopkins and Tugwell in constant attendance, but Lewis W. Douglas, whom Roosevelt had described as the "find" of his early administration, resigned as Director of the Budget because of the thrust of Roosevelt's policies. He joined the ranks of the newly formed American Liberty League. In a letter to Ambassador William Bullitt in Moscow, Roosevelt dubbed the league the "I Can't Take It Club." At the Morgenthau clambake, "It was a grand party & Franklin was in grand form. He is very angry with Lewis Douglas for choosing this moment to resign tho' he's glad to have him out & somehow he worked his rage out by having a good time."

Hopkins had told her that Hick's reports "would be the best history of the depression in future years." He wanted Hick to drive all the way back from the Coast so she could report on conditions to him, but "I fear this means you won't get back quite so soon." Her letters would wait for Hick in Cheyenne, "but they take you worlds of love & I wish I could lie down beside you tonight & take you in my arms."

Everyone in the presidential party came to Val-Kill to swim. She served them lunch and there was a baseball game played by press and government officials. The newsmen then went off while she sat on the lawn "till 7 & supper, beer & much talk. Gee! I like Harry Hopkins, Rex Tugwell & Oscar Chapman.* The wives are nice too."

In New York for her radio broadcast, she spent "an hour" preparing her script, "ordered my winter clothes. . . . Dined with Anna & John & then went to broadcast & Emma [Bugbee] was there & I went back &

---

* Oscar Chapman, a Western progressive, was Assistant Secretary of Interior, working for Harold Ickes.

dropped her at the *Tribune* to escape being taken home by all the men!" Devoted as she was to John Boettiger, she worried over how Sistie and Buzzie were taking to Anna's marrying him. But they accepted him easily and that baffled her: "It is queer but the kids accept the changes in their lives very calmly. No questions or comment & apparent easy adjustment!"

Hick's new Plymouth acted up. She should have it overhauled in Kansas City, Eleanor advised. "I am complaining bitterly about her to the Plymouth people." She took Franklin to visit a CCC camp and Camp Tera at Bear Mountain. "The girls there looked healthier than last year." Tommy's marriage had broken up. "She was depressed today, it was her wedding anniversary just as it was Earl's & I think she took it harder than he did. What a pity everyone can't be happy!" She spoke in Syracuse and with Nan and Earl paid a "nice visit" to Casey. Earl drove her back to Hyde Park. There was a scare that weekend. She went down to the Morgenthaus' for dinner, where James's wife, Betsy, reached her:

> James had started in an ocean race & all the other boats were in but the one he was on was then seven hours late & there was a terrible storm last night. Well, we almost lived on the telephone, getting Coast Guard & naval boats out & we didn't want to tell Mama & at midnight he was reported in Portland & we just talked to him, 180 miles away from the place he was supposed to be! It's funny—how calm you are when you feel as tho' something serious is hanging over you. I felt queer in the pit of my tummy but perfectly fatalistic & numb.

In New York for her weekly broadcast, she had "tea with Tiny & Jane Brett, dinner with Louis, broadcast, cool drink with Hall & Tiny & Eddie & soon to bed for Tommy & I leave at 8:30." She was off for Newport to visit Cousin Susie, then to Louis at Horseneck Beach, Maude and David Gray in Portland, and Cambridge to see that freshman John was installed in his rooms. In advance of dinner at Cousin Susie's, she wrote:

> I will try to behave tonight, but Myron Taylor one side of me & Peter Gerry & Gov. Green* & a few such combinations are something to handle & Harry Hooker wants me to drive tomorrow. I'm so afraid I'll say what I shouldn't to someone that I am getting nervous of seeing anyone!

She and Tommy lunched with Esther and Elizabeth in Westbrook, Connecticut, on the way to Newport "& Tommy liked their house as much as I do & she likes them too I think. Perhaps you'd like them.

---

* Myron Taylor was head of U.S. Steel; Peter Gerry was a senator from Rhode Island; Theodore Francis Green was Governor of Rhode Island, later senator from that state.

They are intelligent." Maine had reelected the first Democrat as governor in sixteen years. "I talked to F.D.R. & he is delighted over Maine & said he gave Louis [Howe] lots of praise, which he deserved. [Donald R.] Richberg was there & Johnson is being moved out of N.R.A." A quip about Anna's suitors. Now that she was divorced she had to convince C. finally "he has no chance . . . he's been married 20 yrs. & a man falls for romance where marriage becomes an old shoe!" Was she thinking about herself and Franklin's romance with Lucy in 1917? If the institution of matrimony was itself usually subject to strain, as this quip suggests, why did she keep Franklin "at arm's length" and punish him for his one romance? Was it her inability to forget, or her yearning for intimacy and concern that he was unable to give her—or anyone else?

"I lived thro' the dinner," she reported after her evening at Cousin Susie's, "& liked talking to Myron Taylor last night. Peter Gerry after dinner was not so interesting. The strikes are bad & I hate seeing soldiers & guns used, it makes me sick. The Governor was due here for dinner last night & gave it up as he felt he might be needed."

On her way to Portland, Maine, she stopped at Horseneck Beach with Louis and his family. "Their house is very nice (of course I never liked near neighbors, but that is early life at Tivoli). . . . Louis seems much better to me but still he has to be very careful & I doubt if he is ever able to lead a really free & easy life & it irks him sadly, but he can be so useful as he was in Maine, & as I feel he will be thro' his political acumen in the next years. So I hope he will be reconciled to his physical limitations." She and Hick might drive through the Cape and Provincetown areas sometime in the future: "I think you'd like it. I've not been bothered at all on this trip by reporters so we might get away with it!"

Anna and John were at Maude's when she reached Portland. "They sat on my bed last night & talked & tho' you know that kind of happiness can't last, it is nice to have it for a time!"

Back in New York after her stop in Cambridge: "Tiny to lunch as she still has no work & I know needed cheering. Shopped for the boys & finished trying on my clothes & got in just in time to dress & go down & dine with Esther Lape & Elizabeth Read. Then broadcast & now to bed."

Although Eleanor was still at Hyde Park when Hick reached New York, she was unable to get down to meet her. "Franklin has decided to stay over till Monday night so I don't like to leave too early Sunday afternoon. . . . Darling try to save lunch & dinner for me on Monday." Their reunion was affectionate, but it also had tempestuous moments, presumably because of Hick's possessiveness. For the first time Hick undertook to help her with an article she was writing: ". . . I am terribly grateful for all the work you did on that article. I meant to cut out those two stories because I cut out all the part that said 'why illiteracy' & I forgot. I mean to do another article on that point. I'll try to do in N.Y. or H.P. next week."

She often felt insecure about her writing. Her punctuation was erratic, the syntax in her longhand letters even more so. She appreciated suggestions and criticism, but writing was an activity she enjoyed. It was truly her own and she intended to keep it that way.

Hick was full of gloom over what she had seen of the Democratic organization in Ohio. "I am not at all surprised about Ohio and you won't get into trouble telling Charlie West & Wayne Coy* if you don't tell everyone else down the line & don't say there is no chance in '36 etc. that makes them all mad but the bare facts today won't! It will be good too!"

She was in New York on her fiftieth birthday, but she liked celebrating the birthdays of others, not her own:

> I wish I had not had to leave you last night, tho' of course I wanted to come & see Anna. You are a grand person dear, & don't ever think I don't appreciate what you are going thro' for me. . . . I do love presents & I love you to give them to me but I can't let go & be natural & that's all. I will try dear to do better work as long as it matters to you! You see I care so little at times, other times I realize if one does anything one should do it as well as one can & having failed in Mrs. Edison's conception of a woman's real duty (did you see her interview?) I might at least do these other things to the best of my ability which however is far more mediocre than you can imagine!

Eleanor had to fight to make herself believe that life was worth the candle. The conflict seems to have gone on ever since the death of her parents, especially her adored father, a hurt that had been reopened by the Lucy Mercer affair. She had learned to compensate for her inability to let herself go by doing things for her friends. She loved them and the least she could do for them was to vindicate their faith in her.

Hick had forceful views, feelings, moods. She declined Eleanor's invitation to accompany her to the Reedsville Project, West Virginia. "I miss you!" Eleanor said in a quick note from the White House, "& tho' I know you would hate the crowd I'm sorry you're not going." On a trip to Cambridge to see Franklin, Jr., and Johnny, the latter's complaint reminded her of Hick's: "I just talked to John & he demanded in a tone similar to yours whether I had on my Girl Scout uniform."

Hick was in and out of New York that October on missions for Harry Hopkins. Could they meet, Eleanor inquired, when she came up

---

* Charles West, congressman from Ohio, later went on to F.D.R.'s staff after he lost a primary fight for a senatorial nomination. Wayne Coy, New Dealer, was administrative aide to Governor Paul V. McNutt of Indiana.

from Washington? "I have every minute filled Monday but I told Earl I'd take him to dinner & the play & I'd love to have you too unless it would just be a trial!"

Eleanor's Auntie Bye used to amuse her sister, Corinne, by the systematic way in which she budgeted her time and activities even when she came to New York to visit the ill Corinne. The latter had a similar reputation within the family. Both aunts had died, Bye in August 1931, her last visitors having included Eleanor and Franklin, as well as a contemporary, Mama; and Corinne shortly after the 1932 campaign, from which, though a regular Republican, she had abstained, largely because of affection for Eleanor. Both beloved aunts had passed on to Eleanor an almost impersonal, tightly organized approach to each day's calendar as well as enjoyment of all varieties of people. Hick found it difficult to reconcile her relationship to "Dear You," as she addressed Eleanor in her letters, to the impersonality of a calendar that gave her a sliver of time, as is clear from Eleanor's defense of her style of living:

> I am sorry that you were hurt dear, but weren't you a bit hasty? I was back at 6:45 & lay on the sofa & read from 7:15–7:45 which was the time I had planned for you. I do plan times dear one to be with you but you have been here a good deal & the steady routine gets on your nerves, in the old days when it was only a day now & then, we broke routine & you pine for that & we must do it more often!
>
> You must not think so long of things I say which I really do not mean so seriously. I want you to be happy because I love you, & when I've hurt [you] I am sorry & cross with myself for not thinking ahead & preventing it but I wouldn't give up our times together & our happiness for these little troubles. You have been a brick & don't think that I don't know how hard it is.

Although couched lovingly, it was a rebuke in a similar vein to those of several previous letters. All were affectionate in tone but carried the same message—that, deeply as she loved Hick, the latter would have to bear in mind Eleanor's temperament and ways of doing things as well as her own. As long as she and Franklin were in the White House, she would continue to protest the goldfish-bowl aspects of her life there. Yet it was in these years that her sense of duty and the satisfactions of altruism came together in work that had to be done and that resulted, even after she was fifty years old, though this was not usually the case, in some of the most productive years of her life. She helped Hick wherever possible, but Hick had to adjust to her style of life too.

An angry letter from Hick, although it dealt with another subject, may have been affected by Eleanor's assertions of independence. She did not like Mrs. Roosevelt's style of campaigning. Unable to find out what Eleanor had said at a windup dinner for Caroline O'Day, who was running for Congress, Hick exploded against the press coverage of the event. "Damn the newspapers," she wrote; perhaps she also resented Caroline's association with Eleanor long before Hick had known the latter, and her close association with Nan, Marion, and Elinor Morgenthau, who also had been close to Eleanor before she appeared on the scene. Her letter was furious:

> As the President's wife, you were out of politics, of course! But the minute one of your friends becomes a candidate—and the fact that she is the widow of a Standard Oil man, socially of some consequence, and supposedly wealthy, doesn't help any—you change your mind. Don't you see how it might look to an outsider? Lord, I'll be glad when this campaign is over! But I *do* wish I knew what you *said* last night.

Although the papers did not quote Eleanor's speech, the stories did describe how, when she had finished, Hick's letter said, "the toastmaster immediately cut in, giving neither Miss Frook [the Republican candidate] nor anyone else a chance to ask any questions. One of them [the stories] described you in a blue velvet dinner gown, described all the prominent people present, described Miss Frook in street clothes 'crashing the gate,' and had 'Mrs. Roosevelt' leaving after her speech 'surrounded by a party of friends.' Damn it—I hated it. It made you sound like a rotten sport."

Eleanor cared about what Hick thought, but she did not defend her decision to campaign for Caroline. She carefully described what had happened in regard to Miss Frook:

> Your letter has just come. Miss Frook borrowed a U.P. press pass to get into the dinner & Mrs. Whitney when she first saw her was unduly excited & insisted to her that she must not speak. When I heard it I asked her to tell her I did not mind her asking any questions she wished to ask. She never asked one. She could have several times during my speech for I paused & spoke slowly. There was a pause at the end. When I went out, I passed next to her & she could have stopped me. I do not know what she looks like or I would have stopped but I stood in the hall right outside the door for 15 minutes waiting to find my coat & many people came to talk & she could have done so. She's crazy & I did not want to go on the radio with her or continue answering what I've answered several times so I'm writing her to reach her after election & not answering her wires.
>
> Darling, if we all stopped wearing velvet dresses there would be worse times than there are. If you have money you must spend it now, so I don't feel as guilty as you do. Of course if you could give it all where it would do the most good that would be grand but we can't always do that! Don't think me heartless but your vehemence always makes [me?] calm.

She had other news for Hick that she would not like:

I find that Louis wants to be here & go to headquarters on Tuesday evening if he feels well enough & if so I think I'll have to devote my evening to him. I will try to be at the house at 6 & I'll go to your apartment at 6 so you & I can have an hour alone & then we can all dine together but if Louis is here he will want to come back & talk & I think you'd better stay the night at the apartment. . . . My dear I know you will be disappointed & I am distressed but Louis seems so miserable I would feel horrible to tell him I wouldn't look after him that evening. You know I'd rather be with you.

All she managed on election night was a short note:

I felt terribly leaving you tonight. I do know how the world must seem to you & I feel painfully smug when I try not to get emotional with you but if one feels too acutely the misery around one, life becomes unbearable & one's ability to be useful is really impaired. *Wed. a.m.* It was terribly hard not to have you here last night & put my arms about you & try to comfort you but Thursday, tomorrow, is not far off. . . .
Last night made the Lehmans happy I think, it should & Caroline seems to have got a good vote. I couldn't find out a thing about Isabella.

Isabella was elected, as was Caroline. The midterm elections gave an unparalleled vote of confidence to the Administration. Republican representation in the House fell from 117 to 102 and in the Senate from 35 to 25.

A few days later Eleanor was off with Franklin to visit the TVA, terrain she had scouted several months before with Nan and Marion. He would also go to a subsistence homestead project in northern Mississippi.

An interesting day but somewhat tantalizing to me for driving thro' cheering thousands doesn't make me feel I know much about the people & that is what really interests me.

She ended up in Warm Springs, as did Franklin, for the two weeks through Thanksgiving. She had sought to persuade Elinor Morgenthau to come down with Henry, but Elinor was unable to do so. Eleanor described her stay there:

I spend the morning riding & swimming & the afternoon down in Missy's little cottage which Tommy and Nan have & where we can work in peace. I dictated 4 things today & at this rate will have much for the winter months done which will make the 'Season' somewhat easier. . . .

Hick in the meantime, having things to do in Washington, stayed at the White House and had Mrs. Helm for company, and Anna and John. Eleanor wrote:

> I knew you'd have a nice evening with Mrs. Helm. You poor dear with those two young things but just be comforted, for Anna at least can't control her emotions & she knows it. They are sure of themselves for the moment just wait until their confidence is shaken ever so little. You are right, there are only two ways to treat jealousy, one is not to love enough so as to care if someone gives less than you thought they might, the other is to love so much that you are happy in their happiness & have no more room for thoughts of yourself, but that is only possible to the old!

But having declared what was possible only for the old, among whom she included herself, although she was only fifty, she reported a run-in with Nan and F.D.R. whose specifics she was too embarrassed to describe to Hick:

> I behaved very badly last night & this a.m. to F.D.R. so I am not exactly 'persona grata' to him or to myself & the sooner I can get away gracefully the happier I shall be. I'll tell you about it some day but it is too stupid to write about. Train quarters & this cottage are a bit cramped for me!

A letter to Anna went into much greater detail. Her reticence to Hick in this instance, compared with the fullness of her confession to Anna, indicated there were aspects of her personality and relation to F.D.R. she preferred to keep within the family:

> I will probably fly home in a day or two. I'd like to leave at once but I injudiciously told Father that I always felt like a spoilsport & policeman here & at times elsewhere because I lost my temper last night. He's been giving Nan a cocktail every night & for two nights it went only a little to her head but it was so strong last night that she not only talked incessantly much to their amusement but couldn't talk straight & I felt he did it on purpose tho' he swore he didn't. Anyway, he needn't make them so strong & the others could all have two or three if necessary. I just revolt physically from anyone in that condition & that makes her unhappy & yet I hate to be the one that keeps her from taking anything so I'd give the world and all to be out of the way quite aside from the fact that I'd like to be where I could have an eye on you young lady! Father says how puritan & I wish I had the right kind of sense of humor & could enjoy certain things, at least, thank God, none of you children have inherited that streak in me, it is as well to have some of Father's ease & balance in these things!

Hick protested E.R.'s self-reproaches:

> I don't know what you did to Nan and the President but I don't believe you behaved very badly. Because it simply isn't in you to behave

very badly. The trouble is dear, that most of us demand and expect too much of you—and this despite the fact that you really do give more of yourself to your friends than almost anyone else I ever knew. I suspect that at one time or another you've spoiled most of us. You did me. I say all this perfectly aware that I am the worst of the lot in the business of expecting & asking too much.

Hick's words of comfort, like the presents and honors given to her, were not what she wanted. The fault was in herself, she insisted, not in her friends. "Wouldn't you, like everyone else spoil me if you could! Tommy will tell you however just how disagreeable I was. Nobody was demanding anything of me. I was just lacking in a sense of humor." However, Hick's declaration that she was the worst sinner of the lot in leaning on Eleanor brought words of reassurance:

> If only it could be proved to you that as a reporter & holding successfully the job you do you had earned recognition & that knowing me had nothing to do with it, you would get some satisfaction out of your well-deserved recognition but as it is you can't. I doubt if anyone can ever make up to you for having saddled you with such a burden. Oh! well, there is nothing I can do about it!

She was talking as much about herself as of Hick. Until Franklin's death she firmly believed that most people sought her out only because of him. Hick had been a good newspaperwoman, but what journalistic accolade was equal to having one's reports read by Roosevelt and Hopkins and dubbed by them a priceless record of the Depression? Hick was thin-skinned and demanding, and somewhere had realized that the more she bared her vulnerabilities to Eleanor, the closer she held Eleanor to her. And for Eleanor, afflicted by a sense that it was Franklin, not she, the world cared about, total loyalty, which people like Hick and Earl gave her, was a priceless compensation.

Rex Tugwell arrived at Warm Springs after several weeks in Europe. She enjoyed the play of his mind. All listened in on a presidential press conference:

> F.D.R. gave them background off the record on foreign trade & utilities, mostly stuff I knew but I kept wondering why they didn't ask a lot of questions & at the end I had to & if we had not had to leave to see a new machine I think we would still be discussing!

Another gloomy report from Hick caused Eleanor to comment:

> . . . I don't wonder your notes make you red! Well, much of it I've known but it seems to take so long to educate people! Rex Tugwell, F.D.R. & I all lunched with Nan & Tommy & they agree as to where

we are trying to go but accept the possibility that what may be needed to get us there is more wars, whereas I rebel at the thought!

She looked forward to seeing Hick on her return. "I have your photograph on my desk & every time I look at it I think how I'd like to hear your voice & put my arms around you. I'm all calmed down & well-disciplined again but it will be peaceful to get to my own room & to you."

There were few letters in December, presumably because Hick and Eleanor saw a good deal of each other. At Christmastime there were the usual letters thanking for gifts and reporting on activities, but an undated anguished note, written probably on Eleanor's return from the special Christmas that she had with Hick, underscored the tensions and pleasures that, although diminished, continued to surround their relationship:

> The cry of 'I want something all my own' is the cry of the homeless & I was so near to tears last night. You told me once it was hard to let go but I found it was harder to let go & yet hold on. Love as much & yet share. Gosh! I sound horrible but I mean that you taught me more than you know & it brought me happiness & I wish I could bring it to you. I bring unhappiness & if I didn't think in the end it would make you happier I'd be desperately unhappy for I love you & you've made of me so much more of a person just to be worthy of you—*je t'aime & je t'adore.*
>
> E.R.
>
> P.S. I hope you overslept but I fear you had a bad night. If you can come on so I can put my arms around you tonight!

Although other of her friends were much more self-sufficient, her letters to them were equally affectionate.

> Nan darling, This is just to say goodnight & tell you what a happy time I have had & I wish it could have been longer! Gee! I wish you were here or rather I wish we were at Hyde Park!

And to Elinor an undated letter was suffused with concern for her:

> Of course bring Mrs. Lehman. I'll have the invitation sent here. I'm glad you are having treatment if it will make you feel better but sorry I can't be nearby to go to see you. Let me know when you will be back as I want to see you soon!

By the end of 1934, as Eleanor shows in these letters, her closest friends had structured themselves about her in a constellation of love and power that was unique in the history of American women. Those who worried her the most were those, like Hick and Earl, who needed her most. Each wanted something from her, and they used their needs to manipulate her. That was all right with her. To be useful, rather than to use, seemed to be her governing principle. Something "locked" her up, she grieved, referring to her inability actively to seek self-fulfillment, especially physical, for its own sake. ". . . [Y]ou see I care so little at times," she said of passing events, and perhaps that is the fate of those who have had to live through psychological disasters such as loss of their parents when they are young. Seeking to explain her credo of self-denial, even when it was addressed to people she cared about, she had explained to Hick there were only two ways to treat jealousy, ". . . one is not to love enough so as to care if someone gives less than you thought they might," and that in her mind might have applied to Franklin; and "the other is to love so much that you are happy in their happiness & have no more room for thoughts of yourself, but that is only possible to the old."

Not to have room for thoughts of oneself was indeed a difficult self-discipline. Her self-abnegation had a paradoxical outcome. What she was, did, and said radiated with ever-increasing power and influence. Consciously she sought to be of use to people, but the objective result was that they served her needs and purposes as much as she did theirs.

She might be manipulated but she could not be bought. At her personality's core was the poised, independent woman who had emerged since the Lucy Mercer crisis in her life. A person's duty was goodness, Eleanor said repeatedly, but that meant there was a person who accepted and performed obligations. In *Candida* George Bernard Shaw has his heroine rebuff the choice that the two men who loved her presented to her. "Oh! I am to choose, am I?" she exclaims. "I suppose it's quite settled that I must belong to one or the other." Her husband agrees, but Candida's young lover, as Michiko Kakutani noted,* gets Candida's point. "She means," he explains, "that she belongs to herself."

It was painful for Eleanor to defend her independence against Hick, but that was its nature, and Hick, like others, had to adapt and to adjust.

* "G. B. Shaw and the Women in His Life and Art," by Michiko Kakutani, New York *Times*, September 27, 1981.

XII

Triumph over Loneliness

O F THE MEMORIAL service for Mary Harriman Rumsey, Averell's older and more progressive sister, who had led the consumers' movement and had been killed in an automobile crash, Eleanor remarked at the end of 1934, "There was a triumphant note in it [the service] & perhaps death is just one more thing conquered, who knows?"

Stoicism lent her power. "Think as if one were dead," a Japanese saying goes. She had arrived at the Eastern teaching that acceptance of death strengthened one for life, over its fears, physical limitation, the shadows of the past. She constantly told an unbelieving Hick that the latter had taught her more than she realized. Hick's insecurities gave Eleanor a bench mark against which to measure her own ability to transcend fear.

Her first Monday in 1935, January 7, was jam-packed and typical, she reported to Hick. She breakfasted with her old friend Harry Hooker, a helpful lawyer and "society gallant," whose non-aggressiveness appealed to her. Then she had "my interviewers," meaning a steady succession of meetings—with the head usher, on goings and comings in the White House that day; Edith Helm on her social calendar; and the housekeeper, Mrs. Nesbitt. Plans were changed, new orders issued, all done crisply and speedily. Then she was off to a Civic Association meeting from which she returned for her weekly press conference, which she handled with aplomb. A light lunch with Tommy in her sitting room, a half-hour drive with Louis, a talk with Clarence Pickett of the American Friends Service Committee:

> . . . & from 3–5 we locked our doors, lit the fire & settled down to do speeches & articles & actually got the dictation done on 3 radio speeches & 1 article. Nan arrived at five & we 3 had tea in my room & I went swimming at six with F.D.R. & then lay down & read for half an hour. I've started Pearl Buck's last book & it is fascinating but I wished I had not missed the one in between.
>
> We dined at 7:15. Elliott & Ruth have four western friends & Bill Bullitt, Missy & Tommy & Nan made up the party & after dinner all but Bullitt who was to talk to F.D.R. went to hear Cornelia Otis Skinner. She did 'Mansions on the Hudson' extremely well & I hope Mama never sees it or she will have the future of Hyde Park completely visualized, even to callow me it was a bit depressing!
>
> Nan has gone to the train, & now I'm writing you & when I've talked to you I'll go to bed.
>
> Bless you dear. I love you & wish you were here so I could put my arms about you as I say it. Goodnight.
>
> E.R.

Hick's restless soul constantly sought proof from Eleanor that she was Hick's "one and only," a possessiveness that Eleanor, as she realized the full dimension of Hick's claims and needs, apologetically and gently began to ward off. Eleanor was torn between an affectionate nature that was starved for Hick's attentiveness and a sturdy self-reliance that rebelled against being hemmed in.

At the end of 1934, Hick sent her "boss," Harry Hopkins, a review of the jobless situation as she saw it. Despite industrial revival, technological advances had left a substantial part of the labor force idle in lumber, steel, coal, and agriculture. She urged the government shift from the FERA (Federal Employment Relief Administration) to a work relief program and cited a bitter and ominous last stanza of a poem written by an FERA client in Ohio:

> Will there not come a great, a glittering Man
> . . . .
> We care not if Thy flag be white or red,
> Come, restless Savior, messenger of God,
> Lenin or Christ, we follow Thy bright sword.

Hick knew from Eleanor, as well as from Hopkins, that F.D.R. was planning the program that in April was launched as the Work Progress Administration with a congressional appropriation of 4.8 billion dollars. Hick wanted to help with that program, but she was tired of travel. She would like to do a book based on her reports. (The report finally came out in 1981 as *One Third of a Nation*.) Above all she wanted an assignment that might keep her close to Eleanor. The latter encouraged her: "I trust when you talk to Harry Hopkins things will straighten out but whatever happens it is best to have it over with." Eleanor herself was depressed, and Hick was one of the few people to whom she acknowledged such moods: "I've felt better physically today but a little low in my mind, well, that will pass too."

Hick's efforts to change her assignment were much on E.R.'s mind: "I've thought so much about you & do hope things will be straightened out by tomorrow evening," she wrote from Val-Kill. Nan and Marion were there but Hick's presence was felt so strongly by Eleanor that it did not allow her to enjoy the cottage: "Dear I miss you & always wish you could be happy here for it is a peaceful spot."

Hopkins felt unable to change Hick's assignment: "You won't have to tell me," Eleanor wrote from New York. "I can imagine most of Mr. Hopkins's difficulties! I'm glad you are settled in your mind & having you here will be grand. I'll miss you but you will be happier!" Presumably Hick contemplated a move to New York. Despite occasional moodiness Eleanor turned a serene and composed face to the outside world while with Hick "things are always serious . . . & I ought to know it." She did her best to persuade Harry to find work for Hick:

> Had a good talk with your boss last night, who does seem to know what F.D.R. wants him to do & likes it. He says he'll probably have work for you by the end of the week so I hope you will be healed & well. . . .

She mentioned Nan's arrival at the White House. Nan was on her way to Reedsville, another of Eleanor's pilot projects, this one an effort to find homes and jobs for the "homesteaders," as the displaced miners in Appalachia were called. Hick resolutely refused to share Eleanor's interest in Arthurdale, or Reedsville, a boycott that was odd since it was Hick who originally had steered Eleanor to Appalachia and the relief work of the Quakers. But Eleanor understood Hick's jealousy of Nan and Louis, both of whom were deeply involved in Arthurdale. Hick did not wish to compete with those around Eleanor whose friendship predated hers.

So far and no further, Eleanor's letters to Hick seemed to say:

> Here I hardly count anything in the way of personal interests pleasant! Dear, I wish it would be a joy when we meet & are together & not such keen unhappiness at other times but there is always the balance to everything until one gets to a certain kind of numbness. I saw my Grandmother reach that after repeated blows & she retained her sweetness & ability to enjoy sun & flowers & children & whatever good things came to her. I suppose that is what we all should pray for.

Much as Eleanor resented the routines thrust upon her as First Lady, she rarely said no to the opportunities to be useful that the position facilitated. "I am going to do 10 more broadcasts beginning Feb 15th & it has complicated my life a bit but I think I've worked it out." The half-hour broadcasts would be lucrative. The fees were paid into an account kept for her by the American Friends Service Committee and used for public purposes.

She scolded Hick for considering it "egoism" to tell her about her aches and pains. "I would hate it if you didn't & always wonder what really went on & what you hid!" One should not clam up:

> It is what I do so much down here & what makes life hard for those around me! Don't worry over the Reedsville stories. I don't bother at all about them except in the fear that they will hurt the homesteaders or Louis. It is more fun to help a few people & stick to a job & see results but again life carries you & you must take what chances it gives you & not kick against the pricks! I do it all the time but I know it is futile!

Despite an influx of people at the White House she managed to write an article, go with Elinor to view some watercolors at the Smithsonian, entertain her brother, Hall, and tend to her mail. "One of my broadcasts is to be a day in the White House. Wld you like to write it?" Hick was not sure that she could do a decent script:

> Dear, I know how you felt about the W.H. & it is partly my fault because I have no enjoyment in my life here & you feel it & think I mind more than I really do. I've lived so much of my life 'going thro' & being relieved when certain periods are over & yet I don't really mind. I'm just kind of cold about it & that makes me cold to those around! Yesterday for instance I looked forward to seeing Anna but never saw her till 6 p.m. & will not see them except in their crowd at supper tomorrow but she's happy & that is the important thing!

She hated the White House routine, but it had advantages:

> F.D.R. thinks the 4 billion will go thro' in another 2 weeks in the Senate & then he'll settle where homesteaders go & then we can try to do something again. The 'Sun' story last night sounded as tho' I were trying to shirk responsibility!

She was not one to evade duties, and if she accepted Franklin's advice to stay in the background on Reedsville while the Senate debated the work relief appropriation, it was in deference to his political tact. Moreover he was in command of the Government and he never allowed anyone, including his family, to forget that. She too, although she pushed harder for certain objectives, had a superb sense of political tact. When Martha Gellhorn, spirited, talented, and beautiful, fresh out of Vassar, was befriended by Hick, she also became a friend of Eleanor's. "She comes to lunch today," Eleanor informed Hick. "She must learn patience & not have a critical attitude towards what others do for she must remember that to them it is just as important as her dreams are to her. . . ."

In early 1935 the Administration made a major effort to combat American isolationism through a Senate resolution for adherence to the World Court. A last-minute radio and newspaper blitz by isolationists such as Father Coughlin, William Randolph Hearst, and Representative McReynolds inundated the Senate with demands that the resolution be voted down. Adherents of the court sought unsuccessfully to get a figure of national prominence to go on the radio to combat the blitz. "I wanted to do well because Mr. [John Nevin] Sayre called me yesterday p.m. & said they could get no man to do it & the guns (Father Coughlin, Will Rogers & Rep. McReynolds) were pretty heavy against it. I listened to McReynolds, & he made me angry but I haven't an idea whether I was good or not." Her speech failed to stem the tide. The adherents fell seven votes short of the needed two thirds. After the defeat she commented on her role. She rarely spoke so plainly on such matters:

> Enclosed is a copy of the useless speech. I rather expected the vote to go as it did. We are so prone to be led by the Hearsts & the Coughlins & the Longs & I am only really sorry that I pushed F.D.R. to try to pass it. Let us hope that it doesn't imperil other things! F. says the price may be over as it goes in 3's & the child labor amendment was killed in Albany & in Kentucky they refused to hold a primary which he advocated!

But she continued to hold onto her faith. Revolutionary spirits like Martha Gellhorn must learn tolerance; older, more pragmatic people must hold onto their dreams:

> How I envied Elliott & Ruth their youth & their dreams this morning. . . . I have a curious feeling of being through with dreams, old age really setting in. Old age is really nothing more than that, having no faith in the future, no dreams! I guess it is the day [it was, she said, 'gray & gloomy'] for as you well know no one plans farther into the future than I do & that requires faith!

But she did not allow herself to be discouraged by the isolationists. A group of the American Legion Auxiliary came for tea, "so I delivered a dissertation on peace."

Hick's new assignment still had not come through at the end of January: "You sounded so down this morning & I know how you feel but I wouldn't worry about the salary, everyone would think that was fair, only I do want you to get to work for I know how you feel . . ." She herself was trying to find time in which to do some articles and sample broadcasts:

> When I get them in shape I'll send them to you. I really am trying to do better work, but it is hard to find the time.
>
> Hick darling, I want you too but you would be more unhappy, as you were, hanging round here while I went thro' this deadly round. At least in N.Y. you've got people you like & a city you enjoy.

What did Eleanor make of Hick's passionate attachment to her? Was she aware of Hick's lesbian orientation, or for that matter, Nan's and some of her other friends? She had an odd prescription for Hick's unhappiness if it was caused by lesbian yearnings:

> Of course you should have had a husband & children & it would have made you happy if you loved him & in any case it would have satisfied certain cravings & given you someone on whom to lavish the love & devotion you have to keep down all the time. Yours is a rich nature with so much to give that the outlets always seem meagre. Dear one, I do love you & appreciate the fight you make not to make me unhappy, but there is no use trying to hide things from me because I know just how you feel!

Eleanor sometimes conveyed the feeling that she was only able to savor pleasure if it came wrapped in duty or, as she put it, that to be of service was a sure source of pleasure. But she also rebelled at the necessity:

> Your weekend sounds nice to me. Wherever I go there are always 'duties.' There must always be an excuse for going so one really works all the time! I am keeping March 6 & 7 free in the hopes that you will be near enough so I can join you without any duties attached, just for the pleasure of being with you.

She lunched with Isabella and Frances Perkins:

> Frances is a fine person. Many people would be resigning on account of fancied slights—but she tries to understand people & not to be sensitive which is unusual in both men & women. . . .
>
> . . . a long argument with Elliott & Ruth over the World Court, debts, foreign trade, S. America et al which ended at 10. You can imagine Mrs. Nesbitt & Mrs. Helm got little attention!

Her comment on her neglect of the housekeeper and the social secretary carried an undertone of pleasure.

Molly Dewson, who had chaired the Women's Division for Franklin, came as a guest

& had a grand time at dinner finding out things from F.D.R. He gets much less annoyed at her when she tells him things are wrong than he does at me!

She and Hick exchanged valentines. Eleanor's doggerel read:

> May the world be full of sunshine,
> And our meetings frequent be,
> Hours of joy & quiet time,
> Take us over life's rough sea.

She took her annual pilgrimage to Flora Rose's Institute at Cornell, as usual with Elinor and Nan. The trip to upstate New York gave her a chance to see Earl and Leo Casey:

> I was homesick for you in Ithaca but you would hate the crowds & the telephones & the fawning. Oh! Well, it is really just as well you are not. The icy drive from Elmira to Ithaca would have terrified you as much as it did Elinor!
>
> I can't get my brief case because it is in the bedroom & Nan has gone to bed. She decided an hour ago she was weary & Earl might like to talk to me alone so she went to bed & I just looked in & she is sound asleep! Earl just left, after showing us his cruise pictures & talking to me on prison problems for an hour with a little family troubles thrown in. . . . I have had a nice time & I love seeing Earl, but I miss you too. One never seems to have everything at once!

She paired Hick with Earl as equally her intimate friends. But there also was the ailing Louis, whom she took for drives every day that she was in Washington and often in New York. "The reason I may have to spend Monday night in town," she advised Hick, "is because Louis may be there & he always looks forward so much to dinner that I couldn't disappoint him. However, we will have Tuesday night here all to ourselves!"

She saw James for half an hour between trains: "I'm a little low in my mind about some things there but I say to myself 'even if you see your own mistakes being made, don't interfere, it is not your life.'"

A mischievous comment on Earl followed: "Earl has a new girl he thinks he is or may be in love with, but he is a skeptic on anything lasting & his state of mind while I was there & his letters are reminiscent of others I have known! What a nuisance hearts are & yet without them life would hardly be worth while!"

Hick went to Washington and although she stayed at the White House was lonely because Eleanor was in New York:

> Poor dear, I have an idea there are a number of lonely people in the world fighting just your kind of battle but it is easier for you here [in New York] because you have many old friends & in Washington your

sense of loneliness is intensified by having few old friends & being in a place you don't like with the only person you would like to see tied down to a very exacting job most of the time!

I've just taken Louis out to dinner & he was so short of breath I didn't think I'd get him home. He does seem worse. I must have another talk with the doctor on my return. . . .

Eleanor's children disagreed with her critical appraisal of the President's mother, Sara. All of them had been spoiled by "Granny," as they called her, an appellation in which they were joined by Marion Dickerman, who shared their, rather than Eleanor's, view of the *grande dame*. Mama rarely acknowledged her jealousy of her daughter-in-law, but occasionally betrayed her true attitude.

I've had a most disturbing day. My day began last night when James told me that after I told Mama it would not break my heart if Franklin were not reelected & left, she turned to him & said 'Do you think Mother will do anything to defeat Father? Is that why she stays in politics, just to hurt his chances of re-election?' Now I ask you after all these years?

Then he told me Fjr said if we didn't make any more effort to understand him he thought he would just as lief leave college & so would I make a little effort! This a.m. comes a letter from John. He thinks he may come home the 11th & Fjr will row at Annapolis the 25th & come home afterwards! This last is the most disconcerting for that is the one week end in Long Island [with Hick]. Could you delay a week & go the next week end? . . . I don't want you to give up the L.I. week end & I ought to be here to see Fjr. row. Let me know what you can manage & please don't be upset because I am just as tired as I can be.

Eleanor's chagrin over Mama's lack of sympathy after almost two decades of what she called her "service of love" to Franklin was equaled only by her sense of failure over her efforts to stay close to her children. The last was a familiar parent-child complaint. Not every family, however, in which such a defeat took place had a "Pa" who was President of the United States and a "Ma" who was a fiercely independent spirit. Her daughter Anna alone had become a friend and every reunion with her and John Boettiger, whom Anna married at the beginning of 1935, was a joyous occasion for all three.

"John dear," she wrote to him on the eve of his marriage to Anna:

I won't get a chance to talk tomorrow so this is a last word of motherly advice. You know I shall always want to help you both to be happy but never let me interfere & remember that Anna is I think rather like me. She'd always rather have the truth even if it is painful & never let a doubt or a suspicion grow up between you two which honest facing can dispel. I love Anna so dearly that I don't need to tell you that my willingness to let her go to you speaks much for my trust &

love of you. Bless you both, live so you keep the precious thing you now have, have patience in the daily rubs of life with each other & enjoy life together & with those you love.

My love to you,
L.L.

"L.L." was John Boettiger's private name for Eleanor. The initials stood for "Lovely Lady."

She was almost lyrical to Hick about Anna and John, who it seemed to her were safely launched. She felt differently about James's future, she reported to Hick, who was in Detroit for Hopkins. She was glad Hick sounded "cheerful . . . for I've been ready to chew everyone's head off." Her letter to Hick made her "feel better for blowing off to you." F.D.R.'s backings and fillings on the use of James at the White House vexed her. She had talked with the President, who was leaving to go down the Potomac:

He calmly tells me that the doctors think the heat will be bad here for J. as he still has a small ulcer so he is only having him down for visits till autumn. James looking upset & bewildered meets me outside & says his health has nothing to do with it but he thinks FDR is afraid if he gives up his work it will bring more stories, so having spent $1,000 on legally getting out of business he's been told by Pa to go back on a 3-day week basis & buy his business back. He's going back to N.Y. tomorrow, etc. I think he's hurt but I who knew something wld happen am so mad with F.D.R. It seems to me now he should have gone thro' with it & I wonder a little if Missy, Mac, Steve & Louis have [text unclear] & the girls off & it is a blessed relief to have this house to myself!

She was so furious with Franklin that a day later even Hick was informed she better keep away:

I'm too darn busy these days to be any good to anyone & also too deeply upset I think. I'm glad I'm going to be away for a bit before you come home for I'm so on edge it is all I can do to hold myself together just now. That is not a good mood for you to return to, is it? Darling, I wish I could give you emotional security but I guess that is one thing we have to get for ourselves!

A revealing note about Louis. At the end of the usually busy day except that this one made her "too late to swim," she found "a demand from Louis to come & see him at once & spent 15 minutes there, signed mail & now must dress for a little dinner of 70!" Although Franklin demanded that his staff be considerate of the increasingly disabled Louis, were it not for Eleanor he would have been ignored in the rush of events through the White House. Hick was a responsibility too, but thinking of her still was a relief. "I'd like to put my arms around you, instead I'll kiss your photograph."

A day later she was finally able to announce: "My calm has returned & my goat has ceased bleating!" She attributed to Hick's willingness to change her plans, so they might see each other, her becoming "much more cheerful. . . . I have got myself in hand again. Why do I let myself go in that way?"

Hick had cautioned her friend not to allow her anger to spill over into rashness. Eleanor reassured her:

Your Tuesday night letter made me happy this morning & I'm sorry I worried you so much. I know I've got to stick. I know I'll never make an open break & I never tell F.D.R. how I feel. He still thinks I accepted & believed his story & he has probably persuaded himself by now that that was his real reason. I blow off to you but never to F.! Of course it is better for James not to be here & I knew that from the start but it was done in a way which hurt him because he wanted to come & I hate to see so sweet a person hurt. However, dear one, I am quite in hand again so don't worry & I love you very much.

Elliott and Ruth and the latter's mother arrived at the White House and Eleanor's worries and criticism of Elliott yielded to admiration:

I really am finding dear what I always know, that a mother always loves her children & when they are in trouble fights for them even tho' when all goes well with them she realizes their faults & limitations.

Darling I do take happiness in many ways & I'm never likely to fight with F. I always 'shut up.'

She held back in order not to cause an open break with Franklin. Her forbearance and self-control seemed limitless.

Hick should not try to gauge Eleanor's reaction by what her own might have been:

I'm only unhappy [in] spots & heaven knows, most people are! I'm not a bit sorry for myself. There are plenty of people would enjoy what I dislike & discipline is good for us all so while I like you to be sympathetic & grieve over me don't let it really worry you for I get over it quickly & I don't suffer the way you would.

She and Hick did not agree about happiness:

One thing I differ with you on, the thing which counts in the long run is never any one person's happiness, it is that of the greatest number of people. If you pick up happiness by the way well & good but remember always you are darned unimportant! No, dear, we won't have scenes. I made up my mind to that last time & I never have spoken to him about this but this burying things in your heart makes certain things look pretty odd in the future & I think a little plain talk there will be a violent shock. . . .

Like all great moralists the subject of happiness fascinated her. Hick must understand how she felt, and for herself, too, it was essential to formulate what she really thought:

> I think it is this way. To most of us happiness comes thro' the love we give & the return love we feel comes to us from those we love. There does not have to be a balance however, we may love more or less since there is no measure of love. Over the years the type of love felt on either side may change but if the fundamental love is there I believe in the end the relationship adjusts to something deep & satisfying to both people. For instance I know you often have a feeling for me which for one reason or another I may not return in kind but I feel I love you just the same & so often we entirely satisfy each other that I feel there is a fundamental basis on which our relationship stands. I love other people the same way or differently but each one has their place & one cannot compare them. I do know for myself that if I know someone I love is unhappy I can't be happy & I would be happier to see or to know they were happy even if it meant giving up my own relationship to them in whole or in part. I'd probably hope to get it back enriched some day but if not, well, I know no one I love I wouldn't rather see happy & I hope they wouldn't worry about my hurt because it would be so much less than watching them hurt. I don't think I'd run away either, unless they wanted me to! I'm always worried tho' for this means that I am a person of little depth & really don't know what suffering such as you go thro' is really like.

The selfless love that Eleanor described here was powered by a benevolence so earnest and persistent that it almost seemed driven. Love had to come enfolded in selfless devotion just as pleasure had to come wrapped in duty. Was it, as she often thought, her early experience? Or was the shallowness that she worries about here in reality the detached, or non-attached, frame of mind in which she had schooled herself and that was an unconscious echo of Stoic or Eastern philosophy?

Congress had finally approved the WPA, and Eleanor was brimful with new plans. A new administration personality began to figure in her letters, Aubrey Williams. A former social worker, courageous and far-seeing, he was Harry Hopkins' assistant. "Saw Aubrey Williams this p.m.," she wrote on May 17, "& they have a good youth programme ready to submit to FDR I think." The next day she was even more enthusiastic: "I think we are going to get a youth programme started & one for artists far more far reaching than I dared hope!"

She had invited Hick to join her in Ohio on the way East. She and Clarence Pickett were planning to go down a coal mine, "a 2 hr. trip & we will get dirty. So wear suitable clothes, if you know what is suitable.

I confess I am stumped!" As she prepared to meet Hick and go down the mine, the prospect excited her: "There is no doubt about it, part of one's joy in life is anticipation, if only one doesn't suffer as you do when fulfillment doesn't come up to the anticipation!"

After the trip down the mine she and Hick spent several days together at the end of which Eleanor wrote: "Last weekend seems a beautiful dream, but it gave me so much that it is a joy to think about." Her intimate talks with Hick were therapy as well as love. They agreed to read John Cowper Powys' *The Art of Happiness* (1935): "I've finished the chapter on 'Woman with Man' & I think Powys ignores the disciplined woman. He also has a low estimate of woman's love except in its possessive manifestations. I'm half way thro' the 'Man with Woman' chapter which is almost equally poor. Write me what you thought when you read them."*

A social work conference in Montreal gave her a chance to team up with Nan and Earl and to pay a fleeting visit on the way north to Earl's living quarters in Glens Falls:

> Yesterday we had a good drive back tho' it rained a little. Nan's family & a lady friend of Earl's lunched with us in Plattsburg & then Nan & I sat peacefully & talked & read while he washed his car. . . .

On her return to Hyde Park she found Anna and her children:

> Though I had such a little time F. drove us over to look at the pool & it is practically finished & Nan had things started for toys in the shop. F seems to be in good spirits.

She had some advice for Marty Gellhorn, whom Hick was trying to help through an unhappy love affair:

> Poor Marty! I'm sorry for her but all you could do for her is to sympathize & suggest if you love one person, others you don't love won't help, but if you can get to care for people in a large sense & work for them some of your own pain may be absorbed in theirs. Don't let her get sorry for herself & become just another useless, pretty broken butterfly. She has too much charm & real ability for that. Hard on you dear, but I guess you've got to take her on & be her 'tower of strength.'

* This particular chapter begins: "When one is no longer 'in love' " and asserts: "The following remarks then are addressed to the type of woman who, though she and her mate still love each other in the sense of affection and respect, is no longer under the spell cast by that radiant condition called 'being in love.' " In Powys' view, women's two most basic desires are to have lives of their own and to possess a man. The latter clearly did not recommend itself to Eleanor, neither, although she did not say so, did the subheading "Happiness is not a by-product." She believed profoundly that one did not try for happiness as such, but realized only after a job had been done or a relationship nurtured that one had been happy.

Hick, in Missouri, had run into the Pendergast machine, which sought to get WPA operations under its control. She described her problems to Eleanor, who replied:

I know Pendergast & all that situation and hate it but you are right, one is practical in these circumstances! That is one reason why I wouldn't run for office under any circumstances. . . .

An editorial in the Richmond *Times-Dispatch* suggested that the speeches she made all over the country meant that she was preparing to run for president. That amused her and she agreed with the paper's editorial on the subject, which it entitled "Fantasy in Carolina." When she saw Franklin at Hyde Park transport a great many of his belongings from the Big House to Washington, her reaction was anti-political: "I can't help wondering what he will do with it when we leave the W.H. perhaps next year."

Earl drove with her in July to Portland, Maine, where she stopped off to see Maude and David and then drove on to Campobello. Tommy even joined in the shooting "& seemed to enjoy it." "Nan darling," Eleanor wrote back to Hyde Park:

We had two good days coming up & made record time. Here at the house yesterday at 3:30. Today is a bit foggy but they are seining a weir after lunch & we are going to see that & we shot this morning, even Tommy tried her hand!

She was "settling down again into this quietest of places and loving it," but Earl was "a restless creature when he cannot be out & doing every minute." She reported of a children's guide to Washington she had agreed to write: "We've done quite a bit of work on the book." She interrupted her stay in Campobello for a quick trip to Hyde Park and Washington. On the way back she stopped in Castine, Maine, for lunch with Molly Dewson and Polly Porter, who were a twosome.

Eleanor always maintained that life and politics were enhanced by marriage to a man and that those men and women were luckiest whose lives together included work as well as conjugality, but she had a significant number of women as friends who were doing important work and had long-standing emotional relationships with each other. In addition to Molly Dewson and Polly Porter, there were Nan and Marion, and Esther and Elizabeth, into whose Village house she would move, in her network of friends.

"It is beautiful and peaceful here," she wrote to Elinor Morgenthau. "We had a good sail yesterday afternoon & this morning Marion & I walked down to the quaint little church. How I wish you could come even for a few days!" She wished too that Hick were with them but realized that was not to be, that Hick "wouldn't be happy" despite Campo's loveliness. Neither was Hick happy to be back in the field:

> I realize that it would be easier for you to go where new sights & duties offered distraction. I blame myself for you through all this & offering you so little when I hoped to really help. You need not fear however that my love is less or that your suffering will alter my feelings, it just makes me very sorry.

Hick had no wish to play what she considered to be a supernumerary role at Campo:

> The sunset at Campo Sunday night must have been very lovely & it was nice to think that you wished I were there. You're probably right, though when you say I'd not be very happy. I'd probably feel like a fifth wheel. Well—never mind, darling! The time will come when it won't matter to me that there are so many others who have priority rights to your interest & affection. Then I daresay we'll be one nice big happy family. You must admit, though the possibility of it's being sometimes rather tough to be the most recent of the people who have any claims on you! I have no seniority rating at all! I am so very much an outsider. But when the time comes when I don't care so much—or at least not in the way I care now—it will be easier. Anyway, I'm glad you're up there & enjoying it. And we'll have our time together later on.

Eleanor refused to take offense:

> No dear, we won't ever be a happy family here! We might spend a night or even a week in close proximity now & then but never more, somebody's feelings would be hurt & I'm too old to live under a strain. You & I will always want to have some time alone together when we spend any length of time in a place where life is not just routine like Washington.

"Life has been very quiet," she wrote to Elinor, "but Tommy & I have had plenty of work to do" and "Marion & I have had lots of exercise."

She had done substantial work during her Campo stay managing to complete not only the children's guide to Washington but a thoughtful piece "Can a Woman Be Elected President?" She read it to Marion and Tommy. "I know it is controversial & will cause violent differences of opinion." She sent it to Hick to read but not to revise.

"Certainly, a woman can be elected President," she wrote, "in all probability some time a woman will be, but she *may* not, in my opinion be elected at the present time or in the near future." Not that she underestimated woman's capability. "Time will show, I think that women are more capable of attending to detail & are able to think clearly even when their emotions are involved & to use common sense, just as do men, but until this has been perceived, there is very little use in pushing women into positions which will be made untenable for them by prejudice."

Her views about the qualities required of a President, whether man or woman, reflected a First Lady's vantage point of observation. First she looked for "complete self-mastery"; after that the ability to "inspire people who may not be able to understand his objectives, to believe in his integrity, and in his interest in their welfare." She had high praise for women, ". . . for instance, women will understand human suffering better than men & they will work harder and faster to eliminate it. Women bear pain better than men, but they have greater sympathy for those in pain." Praise, however, was not unmixed. "They must stand on their own feet and make no excuses. They should come up from the bottom and learn their jobs in public life step by step, and above all, they must learn to take other women with them . . ." Women still have some distance to travel, her article concluded. "The editors seem very pleased," she informed Hick, but "the feminists will be down on me & a lot of people will say it is camouflaged political partisan material, & in a way it is!"

"I took Louis to the hospital yesterday," she wrote to Anna from Washington. "He is no better & no worse. It is like a living death. Very pathetic." A week later a note to Anna about her father also underlined the pathos of Louis' situation:

Pa telephoned me at 1:30 a.m. about Huey Long's filibuster & seemed much excited & on the whole rather pleased! I was sound asleep & thought something terrible had happened so I think at first he thought me a little crazy. Poor Louis is in the hospital & has convinced himself that the utility people put him there to separate him from Pa & I think he thinks I am connected with their machinations. He can only have a telephone part of the day & that adds to his grievances.

At the end of the summer she and Hick finally got together. Yearnings for intimacy and warmth were fulfilled on both sides and both were able, as they put it, to blow off steam to each other. Afterwards, Eleanor wrote:

You don't know it dear, but you did a grand thing for me Sunday night by showing me that I should never be sorry for myself. I have so much more in life than most people & I am really never unhappy except when I begin to whine & feel sorry for myself & God knows I've no right to do it. You are putting up such a grand fight & have so little to make you happy that you make me feel ashamed.

She wrote to Elinor Morgenthau about the reports of rearmament and repression pouring out of Hitler Germany:

> German news is horrible & I don't wonder you feel as you do for I feel much the same. The Italian news too is dreadful & I feel keenly that if we were in the League we might stop this conflagration & if it starts even if we remain neutral we will suffer in the end. It makes me sick.

Hick dreamt of becoming a newspaperwoman again. She thought she might like to be a war correspondent. Mussolini's invasion of Ethiopia was about to be launched. "I think the war [correspondent] idea is a good one," counseled Eleanor, who thought there might be some role for her, too, "& a woman writing will be a new thing in war journalism. I'll be tempted to join you if war comes in some capacity if by chance F.D.R. doesn't get in but I think he will by a small margin."

Hick's reputation in the newsrooms remained creditable:

> I'm so glad you found that your A.P. work was really what you could stand on & now if you could just stop talking about your friendship for me & ignore it I think you would find it is practically forgotten & no one would think of it twice. I don't think you have to go to Europe to do newspaper work tho' I can see why it would be interesting & why you want to go but if you get a job in N.Y. I don't think you need to fear their demands for I think they don't need you now to get any story they want.

The job of correspondent in Europe tempted Hick because she feared that in the United States the wire services inevitably would seek to exploit her connection with Eleanor to get stories on the Roosevelt Administration. Although she was a little corpulent and not exactly spry, she preferred assignment in Ethiopia to New York or Washington. Eleanor, meanwhile, confronted Mussolini's invasion on another level. "That Ethiopian development does put some questions up to us, doesn't it?" Could the United States stand aloof while Britain and France at the League of Nations tried to restrain Mussolini? "F.D.R. thinks war in Europe is very near," she noted at the end of August, "but I still hope Mussolini will come to his senses."

Magazines were clamoring for articles by Eleanor and she asked George Bye, one of New York's most successful literary agents, to represent her. He was full of ideas for articles she might do for the *Saturday Evening Post* and other mass circulation magazines. Despite her lack of technical preparation, she embraced such ideas with alacrity. She sought Hick's help:

> It is a grand criticism & has given me a way to analyze what I am thinking which is most helpful. Mr. Bye did not say just the same things from Lorimers [of the *Saturday Evening Post*] (he hadn't read

it) but you need not have been afraid that your or their criticism would discourage me. You see, I haven't the feeling that things are good in themselves. I've always felt it was largely name & I'm glad to have it back because it shows they are wanting something besides name. If I can't do this after giving it a good try then I must do something else that is all & one can only find out by trying.

She wanted Hick to speak her mind about the pieces she was sending her:

Dearest, you can be as tough as you like in your criticism. I know my tendency to write speeches & Mr. Bye said just that too. I want to do good work & I want the help which you can give me, no one else is half as good as a critic & I'm very grateful to you & don't mind at all!

Setting up a date with Hick, who insisted on being alone with her, could be complicated: "If I don't get in till the 6th which I think is probable, why don't we sleep in the W.H.? We will be alone & could take a picnic lunch & go off on Monday & be quiet both evenings & alone for no one else will be there. I'll do whatever you like however & this is just a suggestion."

When Hick sent in a major report to Harry Hopkins, she sent a copy to Eleanor, knowing that increased the chances of its being read by Harry. At the time, however, Hopkins was involved in a violent feud with Harold Ickes over the administration of work relief funds and had little time for his chief field investigator. The Hopkinses were in Michigan, Eleanor wrote to Anna at the end of August, "& I hope [he] is getting a rest for I think the constant strain of fighting Sec. Ickes & appearing to be friendly is beginning to tell!" Harry came to Hyde Park before Eleanor and Franklin took off on the transcontinental trip that ended with F.D.R.'s boarding the U.S.S. *Houston* in San Diego:

I liked your report & I am sure Harry will also. I didn't see him on Tuesday when he was up. F.D.R. is taking Ickes as well as Harry on the cruise with him. I don't think anything will be accomplished & I doubt if anyone except F.D.R. has a good time but this is not my trip!

As Eleanor feared, Hick protested a change in plans and Eleanor answered crisply: "I could shake you for your letter of the 19th. I've never even thought of not being in Washington with you. . . . I know you felt badly & are tired, but I'd give an awful lot if you weren't so sensitive. You are worse than Elinor Morgenthau & haven't her reason!" Such a "shaking" was undeserved, Hick protested. "I was only trying not to be selfish—to treat you as I would Jean, Howard or any of my other friends! . . . Please don't be cross with me. I'm not in most of my relationships with people, 'worse than Elinor Morgenthau.'"

Eleanor did not permit Hick's protest to go unanswered:

Your letter made me feel that in some ways I'd given you the impression I really didn't care to see you in early Oct. That I thought more of something or someone in N.Y. than I did of you & that you would go about your business & not burden me. Now one likes to be burdened by one's friends. Sometimes one can't do things, but one wants to do them & I wouldn't give up seeing you after all these weeks for anything except an emergency illness or crisis of some kind & you ought to know it by this time! Darling, I sound like an old scold. Forgive me, I treat you badly lots of times I know when I don't realize it!

She wrote to Hick as the presidential train traveled westward: ". . . [W]e've only had to go out on the platform now & then. Crowds however at most stops but then it is Indiana. . . . Harold & Harry lunched with us & behaved like lambs! Harry looks better already. F.D.R. is feeling in good spirits too."

But Hick, who was in Toledo, was concerned with the black despair of the unemployed. Harry needed a vacation, her letter admitted, but, "Darling, it is so hard even for me not to feel a little bitter at the 'big shots' these days":

The President, Ickes, Harry Hopkins, all well fed, well clothed, warm and comfortable complacently starting off on a vacation, while out here in places like Cleveland and Toledo thousands of people *aren't* getting enough to eat, are facing evictions, begging for little jobs at a 'security wage' that none of us could live on. . . . My bitterness is directed at your husband, Ickes, and yes, to a certain extent, at Harry. Months and months of rowing about who is going to run the show. And hence—no show running. . . . I feel a good deal as if I were shouting into space.

The presidential party stopped at Boulder Dam, where Franklin spoke. "Harry & I slipped off when everyone was gone," Eleanor wrote to Anna, "& went down to the bottom in the bucket & got a grand impression." In Northern California, Tiny caught up with her. "F.D.R. has had a marvellous reception, how much it all means I don't know." Hick's complaint about the "vacations" of the President, Ickes, and Hopkins was viewed more equably by Eleanor. "Don't get too bitter dear. I tend to get that way but age has taught me some things which I will expound to you by word of mouth!" Hick defended herself:

Oh, I know you all think this is temperamental with me—that it's impossible for me to see anything but the dark side. But, God, I wish some of the rest of you had to listen to this day in & day out. I bet you'd all feel gloomy too.

The next day Hick felt more tolerant:

Gee, I'll bet you get tired of my blowing off one day and apologizing the next. I'll try to keep on a more even keel.

The President, Ickes, and Hopkins boarded the *Houston* for a trip that took them through the Panama Canal to the East Coast.

"Nan darling," Eleanor began after F.D.R. had boarded the *Houston:*

> I've thought of you so often on this trip & wondered if I should have let you come & go back with Tommy for we went thro' cheerful places & F.D.R. really went away pleased & content. How much it means in the future Lord knows!

She flew back for a reunion with Hick and to learn that Johnny and James had been in a cab that collided with a train: "Gee how quickly life could change from calm to chaos," she commented.

The opportunity to be of service that her occupancy of the White House presented did clash, and it had so often, with the public life she was obliged to live. When a story that John Roosevelt might work for the TVA leaked into the press, he almost decided not to go, and Eleanor commented: "What a price one pays when a revered parent decides to serve his country! I'm beginning to think obscurity the greatest boon that we can ask for in this world!"

Nan and Marion continued to be an intimate part of her life, although she was branching out into activities—writing, lecturing, broadcasting—which meant personal growth and to some extent separation from the Todhunter School and the Val-Kill Industries. Though the two women had a smaller part in her new life, she continued to cherish them. She lunched with Nan at the Waldorf and afterwards wrote Hick:

> Nan broke the news that Marion had awakened voiceless & she was to speak for pay at 4 p.m. at the Brooklyn Academy of Music & would I go? So at 2:45 I spoke on Housing, heard the Mayor talk very well, took the subway, spent an hour speaking & answering questions & got home at 5:40.

"Home" now was a small apartment that she had rented at 20 East Eleventh Street in Greenwich Village in the house owned by Esther and Elizabeth. Anna inquired: Would Hick join her and John in giving "Ma" some cocktail glasses for the new apartment on Christmas?

> Ma is really getting quite a kick out of her apartment & having people come there who will sit around & feel at home—& have a drink—on her. In a funny way I think she has always wanted to feel included in such parties, & so many old inhibitions have kept her from it until now.

The tiny apartment would be full, Eleanor wrote to Elinor at Thanksgiving. Could they get together at Elinor's mother's?

> I am thankful today for your friendship & I love you & I look forward to Monday afternoon & evening. Tuesday won't be quite so nice! If

you are free would you like to do slum clearance with me Tuesday or must you go Xmas shop?

In December, Eleanor made a leap in her development as publicist for the New Deal. She agreed to do a daily diary for the United Features Syndicate. It was to be called "My Day." She sent in some sample columns with trepidation. "The writing is easy so far. They just want one incident out of my day & so far I've had no trouble." She signed the contract on December 20.

The anniversary of Mary Harriman Rumsey's death inspired some realistic *caveats* to Hick about such events:

Darling, don't let anyone hold memorial meetings for me after I leave you. It is cruel to those who really love you & miss you & means nothing to the others except an obligation fulfilled & certainly it can mean nothing to the spirit in another sphere if it is there at all! I'd like to be remembered happily if that is possible, if that can't be I'd rather be forgotten.

She celebrated Christmas with Hick on the twenty-third. Then on Christmas Eve she wrote to her:

The busy day is nearly over & I want to send this line which I hope will reach you sometime tomorrow to tell you how much I have thought of you. I hope Prinz [Hick's German shepherd] proved a joy & healed the feeling of loneliness a bit. This is a bad time of the year to be lonely!

At the same time she also wrote to Anna:

Perhaps I needed to have you away this Xmas to realize just how much it means to have you & so I think I'll try to tell you in these few minutes before dinner just how much I miss you. The dogs & I have felt sad every time we passed your door. It was hard to decorate the tree & get things distributed at the afternoon party without you & I dread dinner tomorrow night for so many of your friends will miss you & if anyone says much I shall weep for I've had a queer feeling in my throat whenever I've thought of you. Anyway I'm happy that you & John are together for I know you will be happy. . . .

XIII

A Great Man—
and a Stranger

RODE EARLY & again spent much of the day in the pool," she wrote from Hyde Park, "& finally achieved jumping in off the diving board, so one more fear is destroyed & I may dive yet." Without such struggles life would be dull: "Darling, no matter how hard living is," she advised Hick, "as long as one has the necessities of life, I wonder if our hardships are not better than so much smooth sailing that life would hold no interest? There is something worth tackling in a struggle even if it is with ourselves."

Spectator sports left her indifferent. "Got in at 4:10 & as L[ouis] H[owe] couldn't see me took my bath & had tea in my room with James & John to the tune of football games in Miami & then Pasadena. You would have understood it better than I did." At Hyde Park in June the fight in which Joe Louis was knocked out by Max Schmeling of Germany in the sports upset of the year left her as unmoved as the football games: "A quiet evening & Nan turned on the radio & we heard the fight which meant nothing to us."

After Congress adjourned and before the presidential campaign began, Roosevelt sailed down east with his sons, except Elliott, as crew. Eleanor already was at Campobello. Nan, Marion, and Tommy were with her. The Hopkinses also arrived. "The 'boys' sailed in for an hour today just to show off their beards. F. has side burns & looks just like his Father's portrait. Funny how men love to grow hair. I think it makes them feel virile!" Usually the most indulgent of persons, her comment carried undertones of tartness. Did she resent Franklin's exclusion of her from the men's world of yachting and the like?

She yearned to have her strength tested: she also dreamed of domesticity. Her attentions to Earl—and his girls—became idylls of homemaking. She went often to Albany to watch and help the progress of a house that he was building at nearby Loudonville. He, in turn, came to New York, where she celebrated his birthday in 1936 with dinner and the inevitable girl and a play. "She's a sweet child," she wrote Hick about Roberta Jonay, Earl's new lady friend, "obsessed by the thought that she might be an artist & yet in love with him. Well, she can but try & decide which is most important to her & in the meantime it won't hurt either of them to be very sure for she says 'to be hurt once again wld be too much for him' & I entirely agree." She went up the river, filed her column in Poughkeepsie, and traveled on to Albany. "He & Roberta came & took us to see his cellar which is dug & ready for the foundations." A week later: "I got up early enough to go with Earl & Roberta to his house site & the foundations are being poured & we had a picnic lunch up there under a tree before I went to my meeting."

At the end of the summer, she informed Hick that from September 4 to 14 she was to be reached at Earl's, care of the State Police Barracks at Newtonville, New York "& don't put my name or Tommy's on the envelope." She and Tommy went shopping for him and the two women "were most domestic all morning as Earl had to go to the office. I did the ironing, renewing my youth & made popovers which came out well & so feel very satisfied with myself." A few days later she announced triumphantly: ". . . I've actually learned to get breakfast if no one eats anything." For the first time "I've even learned to feel a tinge of confidence in a kitchen."

She was feeling unusually lighthearted. Mrs. Helm at the end of August was on holiday at her Grayville farm in Illinois and forwarded to Hick a telegram signed by Eleanor and Tommy, commenting: "Those two gals were evidently in a gay humor. . . ." Their telegram had read: "WE ARE BACK IN WASHINGTON FOR TWENTY-FOUR HOURS. YOUR FACES MAY BE LIFTED BY LAUGHTER. OUR SOULS ARE LIFTED BY DOING OUR CHRISTIAN DUTY ALL OF WHICH IS SOUR GRAPES. OUR POOLED LOVE TO YOU BOTH."

Eleanor did not like women who were social butterflies. An encounter with Jimmy Walker, the popular ex-Mayor of New York who had resigned under Franklin's investigatorial pressure, brought a strange compliment. It was at a luncheon in Brooklyn:

That was a tremendous gathering of ladies & I sat next to Jimmy Walker! He was always easy to talk with & I enjoyed myself & he confided in me England had taught him to live at a slower pace & then that his wife admired me! How about that for a compliment, dear? 'Betty Compton's ideal.' I never thought of myself quite in that light before, did you?

She welcomed domesticity and quiet but only as counterpoints to the "worst verge of tears condition," which is what she called the round of entertainments and campaign treks that 1936 forced upon her.

She agreed with Nan that Val-Kill Industries should be sold to the men who worked for them:

> Nan's room is lovely & we had a grand, quiet time yesterday. Lots of work going on today but moving the shop out & giving the furniture to Otto & machinery, & the other two boys the pewter and other things is really a great relief to her & will mean a more peaceful life.

She inspected the vacated space with Tommy and Henry Osthagen, a Treasury Department employee who became Tommy's companion after she and her husband separated: ". . . & now Tommy, Henry & I have been going over her apartment. I'll have definite estimates this week. It is fun to build or change things over."

The decision to give up Val-Kill Industries also was spurred by her personal growth and self-confidence as a writer and as a speaker. In March she went out for the Colston Leigh lecture agency for a series of speeches in Michigan and Ohio. The series began in Grand Rapids. "Now it is about time to go," she wrote to Hick. "Tommy & I have dined & I am as usual scared."

By the next day she was able to say,

> The speech went well last night, the trip over was comfy, but I've been sleepy today! It is warm, but the projects are interesting & so are the people! I spend most of my time during the day doing things & talking. It would be easy to be either the President's wife or the paid lecturer but the combination is exhausting!

In Dayton, "the last time on this subject for a while, thank heavens!" She was gone less than a week and the trip was lucrative: "Back in New York with no fuss & feathers & $3,000 to my credit! It has to go out at once in income tax however!"

Elinor Morgenthau's mother died and she was full of sympathy:

> I wish I had gone back last night for I might have been of some help to you this morning. Now the first shock is over you are probably able to be grateful that for your Mother the struggle is over. . . .
> I know you will miss your Mother for she was so constantly on your mind & there is a sense of insecurity that comes to us with every loss & no matter what we have done when we really loved people as you did your Mother you wish you could have done more. You gave her so much pleasure, however, & so did your children, & at least you know she is at rest.

A note to Franklin at Warm Springs: "Dearest Honey," it began:

Got back today after three busy days in N.Y. in which I bought all my spring clothes, had a dentist app., spent one afternoon & evening with the Institute of Women's Prof. Relations, one taking Earl to dinner (his school at Ossining is going well) & one taking Anna & John to dinner & the play (a good one but depressing). Had tea with Mama & Cousin Susie on separate occasions, had Esther & Elizabeth to lunch, Nan & I went out one day. . . . Saw several people who wanted to save the world & one man has an interesting educational idea which will appeal to you I think. . . . Louis is more awake & stronger but very hazy still. He must be kept very quiet. . . . Lots of love. E.R.

A few weeks later Louis Howe died. She had long expected it. As she wrote Elinor: "Louis was a fine person & a loyal, true friend, but it was merciful to go now as he did—we will miss him but in a curious way I have felt for a long time that the real person was gone."

"Saw Louis who seems like himself yesterday & today," she had written to Hick in January, "but it is a mental life I think. I only hope F. goes over tomorrow. L.H. feeling better is because he feels F. followed his advice in his speech."

Finally on April 18, as she wrote Hick, Louis breathed his last:

I got in from speaking last night & Dr. McIntire called me to tell me Louis has died in his sleep. They just noticed his breathing was changing, called the doctor who did what he could but he never responded & never was conscious. A merciful way for him. We got Franklin as soon as the Gridiron dinner was over & I spent hours getting Mrs. Howe & Hartley on the telephone but finally succeeded & they took it calmly, thank Heavens! I've been doing a thousand & one little things, changes in dates, etc., but until Grace gets here we won't know what she will want to do. . . . In an hour I shall meet Grace & Hartley & go with them to the undertaker.

I think I felt Louis would always be an invalid but still always there & tho' for a long time the real person has been gone I shall miss some of the things that made one at times almost resentful. He was like a pitiful, querulous child but even when I complained, I loved him & no one will ever be more loyal & devoted than he was.

There was much to be done and much of it fell on her. Exhaustion set in, though it rarely did: "I really am not weary, but the innumerable little arrangements for funerals always recall previous experiences and depress me immeasurably. I hate funeral parlors. I hope I get put rapidly in the ground in the least expensive of coffins. It all seems so unimportant when 'you' no longer exist." "This has been a long day," she wrote to Hick of the funeral services in the East Room:

I got up early & met Mary Baker [Louis's daughter] and various other members of the family arrived. Then there have been endless questions all day, seating, flowers, etc. but the services were nice I think & as he would have wanted them to be. Rabbit* is the one I am most sorry for just as if I should outlive F.D.R. I know Missy would be the one I should worry about! I rather hope however that I will be the one to go, before I go through this again. It would seem so logical & so restful! However I feel well so don't be alarmed!

"It was a trying trip," she wrote of the burial journey to Fall River, "but the service in the cemetery was lovely & the place itself is beautiful."

Just before Louis's death she had accompanied Franklin to Baltimore for his address to the Young Democrats on what the Administration was doing to widen employment and opportunity for America's youth. The situation of youth was one of her major preoccupations. In connection with it she had recently had her first meeting with the American Youth Congress in Washington, a fateful meeting, and she became increasingly involved with the congress. The Baltimore youth audience that heard F.D.R. that night was congenial, and Franklin's words, which Judge Rosenman, the editor of his public papers, placed under the rubric "The Period of Social Pioneering Is Only at Its Beginning," were meaningful. Yet writing about the speech to Hick, Eleanor confessed that she had slept through it:

I slept all the way to Baltimore & back with FDR last night & was too sleepy to know whether his speech was good or bad. I fear I'm going to sleep thro' the Pan American concert tonight!

After a lifetime of listening to political speeches Eleanor might be forgiven for treating another as less than sacred writ. Or was there more to her drowsiness—an inability to treat Franklin as a savior and dispenser of the Truth? Mama had wondered to James whether Mother wanted to defeat Franklin. Sometimes Hick had the same heretical question in her mind. In 1932, Eleanor had given Nan and Marion a letter to take to Louis Howe at the Chicago convention that nominated Franklin. It said she was opposed to his running and Louis had calmly ripped it up. He was dead now and Hick was the recipient of such daydreams and revulsions.

At the Jefferson Day dinner in New York City, Roosevelt portrayed the crisis that had hit the United States in 1929 as one in buying power and urged that "nationwide thinking, nationwide planning and nationwide action are the three great essentials to prevent nationwide crises." "I am glad you liked the Sat night speech," she wrote to Hick, "it was good tho' I did want to say 'how' once or twice & he confessed he wanted to also & wasn't sure he could answer."

The technological advances that were allied with industrial recovery

* Margaret Durand, Louis's secretary.

had not produced a comparable restoration of jobs. Unemployment continued to be one of the reviving economy's chief problems, he said. Youngstown, Ohio, pointed up this situation for Hick when she went there for Harry Hopkins:

> The steel mills are running full blast, 80 percent of capacity as good as 1929. . . . And yet— In the last three years they've spent 10 million dollars modernizing these plants, and the result is that in 1936, with the mills operating at 1929 production, they are employing 10,000 fewer men than in 1929!

Eleanor read Hick's letter to Franklin and to Scripps-Howard publisher Roy Howard, who was a White House guest at dinner. She reported the consequences to Hick:

> From your Youngstown letter, taking out the name of place & industry I've written my Monday piece at Franklin's & Roy Howard's suggestion. If you mind, I'm terribly sorry. I wanted to wire for your consent but Franklin won't let me. I think he wants me to be whipping boy & tho' he can't bring the question out he wants it out.

She usually lent herself willingly to purposes such as floating a trial balloon. But she did not allow him to take her for granted, so helpfulness was combined with defiance as she tried to walk the thin line between appreciation of the qualities that were good for the country and worry lest her personal independence and self-esteem be destroyed. She made Hick the confidante of her efforts to keep Franklin at a distance and yet be helpful to him, and Hick, more a Roosevelt loyalist than she, helped keep her on an even keel.

There was a sequel to the Youngstown story. A few weeks later Franklin sent her a memo: "I wish you would read this. It seems to show that the figures which interested you and me so much were almost wholly incorrect." Eleanor questioned his acceptance of the new figures and wrote on the memo he had sent her:

> It seems to me the Chamber of Commerce of Youngstown from whom the former figures were obtained should either have more accurate figures or not give them to anyone! I wonder if *any* figures are accurate, everyone colors to please themselves. Perhaps the Chamber of Commerce did not want to say anything was nearly as good as in 1929.

During a quick trip into Arkansas and Texas in June, Eleanor wrote from the presidential train:

> He purrs like a cat under the enthusiasm & friendly welcomes, but I begin to understand why Hoover drove unresponsively thro' streets when he felt hostility about him!

The next day: "I'm weary of cheering crowds (I'd like them less if they booed but I'd be more interested)!" When someone handed her a copy of the Republican platform, she brushed it aside as "the same old bunk. I hope ours is not so long but it is foolish to hope it will be any less 'bunk-ish.'" She loathed pompousness and egotism: "By the way I was photographed with the Girl Scouts," she confessed to Hick from Indianapolis, "& came in behind open sirens so perhaps it is as well you were not with us! Even Tommy remarked 'what an unobtrusive entry you are making.'" A ceremony for Dr. Alice Hamilton, a pioneer in industrial toxicology, at White Sulphur Springs, West Virginia, caused her to praise the non-aggressive virtues:

This evening has been nice because I could talk to Dr. Alice Hamilton & she is such a dear, so gentle & unassuming & yet look what she's done! A lesson to most of us who think we have to assert ourselves to be useful & particularly good for me as I was feeling rather annoyed with F.D.R. Nothing unusual just a little feeling on his part that he was abused because I didn't cooperate with his plans about H.P. [Hyde Park] when I wasn't asked at the time to sit in or express an idea! Then my pride was injured at his perfect forgetfulness of part of a political suggestion I had made on a train & I was annoyed until I realized how small it all was sitting by the sweet-faced woman who has probably given the impetus to workmen's compensation & research into industrial diseases & saved countless lives & heart breaks.

There was a shy, unassuming quality about John Boettiger. She had liked that, and when John sent her a note of gratitude, she sent it on to Hick and it ended up among Hick's papers. "Dearest L.L." John began, again using the old shorthand expression for "Lovely Lady":

The year is up and I'm deeper in love than ever! You know, of course, that it's been the happiest and shortest year I've ever known.

I've often wondered how things would have gone with us if we hadn't found you so blessed with a wonderful understanding and faith. I'm glad I don't have to worry about that too much!

The year's been happy, too, in giving the three of US many grand frolics together though there weren't nearly enough of them. . . .

Her relationship with Anna and John, as with Hick and Earl, made it easier to accommodate herself to the role that Franklin expected of her. Politics seemed to her often matters of boast and brag. She listened to the Democratic convention in Philadelphia:

The magnolias out of my window are in bloom & they look beautiful at night. I listened to the bitter end last night & wondered if in 1783 they whooped it up so much. It seems undignified & meaningless but perhaps we need it!

It has always been too sober a business for me (living I mean) & I guess this quality of abandon is a grand thing to have.

She felt almost as withdrawn the next night when she journeyed to Philadelphia with Franklin and heard him throw down the gauntlet to the "economic royalists":

> I felt entirely detached last night & as an onlooker it was a wonderful sight. I think F. *felt* every word of his speech. We drove around the Stadium afterwards & it was a mob of enthusiastic people but they were 'the people.'

A few weeks later Franklin skippered the boat he was sailing with his sons as crew into Campobello. Her letter to Hick that described the scene and discussed Franklin's election chances could not have been more aloof: "I feel, as usual, completely objective & oh! Lord, so indifferent!"

Hick, in South Dakota, objected violently to Eleanor's aloofness:

> Your Monday night letter came today & I'm wondering if you—or I—or any other enlightened person really has any right to be so indifferent about the outcome of this election as you are. Oh, I know—you hate it all. The 'position' and so do I when I'm with you. I can't even be polite about it. I know that you at least would be happier if you were not in Washington. . . . Well, it all boils down to this: all your personal inclinations would be to rejoice in defeat. And, so far as evaluating the President, and his administration go—you 'can't see the woods for the trees'. . . . I still think he is a very great man. His defeat—and I'm awfully afraid, he will be defeated—will be a terrible calamity for millions of people in this country. The kind of people you, of all people, are supposed to care about. The poor and the lonely. Forgive me if I have offended you . . .

Hick's angry letter caused Eleanor to say more about her own attitude towards Franklin and also about the personal pursuit of happiness:

> The letter sounded like an effort to convert me but really my dear I'm doing all I can do without being accused of trying to run F.D.R. One can be personally indifferent & yet do one's duty. As a matter of fact it is only when one is in oneself very unhappy that one even thinks about the individual right to the pursuit of happiness. . . .
>
> Let me tell you a secret dear, I know I'll not be happy in Washington nor out of it so the surroundings don't matter much. I'll get on alright anyhow & tho' I'm not sure anyone is very important, I agree one must make an effort for what is apparently best!

But Hick's rebuke stung and Eleanor expanded on what she meant by happiness:

> I'm afraid my reasons for thinking I will probably never be much happier than I am are different from yours dear. You think some one thing could make you happy. I know it never does! We are not happy be-

cause we don't know what would make us happy. I know it never does! We may want something & when we have it, it is not what we dreamed it would be, the thing lies in oneself. . . .

She had taught herself how to quiet the longings of the will and achieved an almost Buddhist understanding of how to combine "universal sympathy with perfect spirituality." Long ago she had concluded that the kingdom of heaven was not of this world and the prayer book of her childhood not only bespoke a lifelong piety towards the sources of her being but in her maturer years kept her true to ideal ends and reconciled her to what Santayana calls "the mysteries and pathos of mortal existence."

Earlier in June, when Hick had announced that she would not return to New York till September, Eleanor had taken it calmly and underscored her own adaptability to the circumstances imposed on her. "Well, dear it is for you to decide for you are the one who suffers & I just enjoy what I can have & learned long ago to accept what had to be." She combined the stoic's acceptance of natural fact with the moralist's sense of urgency and feeling—a paradox, also a universal human condition.

It seemed sometimes that her sharpest barbs were reserved for Franklin. A telegram to him on board the "Presidential Special Train" in Salt Lake City at the beginning of September bristled: "ALMOST IMPOSSIBLE TO GET ANY INFORMATION AS TO YOUR PLANS OR WHEREABOUTS FROM STEVE. APPARENTLY HE IS AS MUCH IN THE DARK AS THE REST OF US. WHAT HAS HAPPENED TO MAC AND YOU? IS IT UNCOMMUNICATIVENESS ON HIS PART OR LACK OF DECISION ON YOURS? . . . OUR LOVE TO YOU. E.R."

In October she was again on the presidential campaign train and the trip at its end wrung an astringent definition of her attitude towards Franklin. But first she recorded the plaudits for the President. They had gone through St. Paul and Minneapolis: "The streets were very crowded in spots . . . F is entirely confident tho' I put in a word of pessimism at dinner last night." He addressed huge crowds throughout the corn belt, lent a hand to the progressive Senator George Norris, went as far as Denver, returned through Kansas and ended up at Chicago and Detroit:

I have never seen on any trip such crowds or such enthusiasm. If it doesn't mean votes then we are a dissembling people for they answer F.D.R.'s questions with a roar. I begin to feel the ground swell is growing & they are getting on the band wagon & if they really have all this faith I hope he can do a good job for them.

up my childhood for the kids. That would have more about people no one else can remember." She made enough progress to talk to her agent, George Bye, about the "memoir," as she sometimes called it: "Mr. Bye has two firms of publishers bidding for my autobiography up to 1920!" she informed Hick in early September, amazed evidently that people outside of her family might be interested. "I told them you were writing my biography but the most interesting time for that comes after 1920 I think." By October she was dictating to Tommy the first draft of the "2nd instalment." Thoughts and memories were pouring out and a few days later from the campaign train she was promising Hick the "3rd instalment." She had only three platform talks scheduled for that afternoon, she said, and hoped to get some more dictated. Like every budding author she waited anxiously for her agent's reaction: "No word yet from Mr. Bye," her letters repeated. "I'm so glad you liked the second instalment, no word from Mr. Bye & I'm getting nervous! The third is very long & I do a little more description. . . . I've been honest so far about everything & I dread the grown up years."

Finally the fateful telephone call came, and she wrote to Hick:

> Mr. Bye called up & said Ladies Home Journal said on basis of what they had seen of Memoir if it went on like that they'd give $50,000, & he thought he'd get $75,000. I shall invest ½ & spend ½ if I get it.

Publication now seemed sufficiently likely to mention it to Mama. "Told her about the book & she is horrified!" She remembered so much she was afraid it might become boring. A week before the campaign ended, "I've been in all evening & correcting the 4th instalment. We've sent in 18,000 words & they want 90,000 so I need not have been afraid of being too long!" She read parts to Marty Gellhorn and Joe Alsop, both of whom liked it "apparently." She wanted Earl's reaction:

> . . . when one knows so much oneself it is hard to realize what is not sufficiently explained & even you & Tommy can't be very helpful there for I've told you so much. I think I'll have to let Earl read it & mark the parts that he finds ambiguous!

The campaign over, she embarked on another paid lecture trip. It began in Minneapolis, which was where Hick had started her journalistic career and where she still had many friends. When Eleanor surprised her with the news that she would be lecturing there, Hick created a scene over Eleanor's failure—so she thought it—to check with her the people who might expect to be called by Hick's best friend. Eleanor smoothed Hick's ruffled feathers: "I hope you will be glad to learn that we tried to reach all the friends you mentioned. . . ." Hick was penitent: "Oh, you always do the nice thing—and I always blunder. How you can ever *like* me is beyond me."

Eleanor's rebuke was gentle but firm: "You offer yourself up too often as the sacrificial lamb! Next time you want me to see someone say so!" She did not wholly appreciate Hick's *mea culpas.* "How you do castigate yourself! Do learn to be a little simple, free & natural & do what you want to do! I have such a hard time teaching all of you that I don't need to be protected!"

Hick's WPA job was finished and she asked Eleanor to get an interview for her with Grover Whalen, who was heading the preparations for the New York World's Fair, scheduled to open in 1939. Whalen did see her and by the end of the year had employed her. Eleanor also introduced her friend, whose reports, she thought, would make a book, to her agent George Bye: ". . . a letter came from Mr. Bye thanking me for sending you to him & saying he thought you had a good book in mind."

In Milwaukee on her lecture stint she briefly panicked over the prospect of having to fill its huge auditorium. She thought of writing to Colston Leigh to limit the size of her audiences in the future. "I'm told I'll have no audience tonight because the old lady who is running the show has a communist introducing me . . . it is in the auditorium which at best F.D.R. would fill. I dread it." Her fright was needless: "I think last night's speech went well. I was scared. That big auditorium was full, 16,000 people the manager said, were there, & enormous tho' it seemed I was glad not to be faced by rows of empty seats!" Her letter to Anna indicated progress rather than pleasure:

> Colston Leigh seems to be satisfied even if I wasn't & even I think the last lectures have been better & so does Tommy. Tonight is first night on a new subject & I tremble! I'm lunching with Laura & Lawrence Houghteling & Tommy is typing & sending Mr. Bye our 4th instalment. . . . I promised to have Hick for dinner that night alone. She thinks I'm an ogre because I'm insisting she write now while she is fresh with the story of her four years investigations!

Earl's house near Albany was finished, and on her return East she gave him a helping hand: "Like a young bride he's having a bad time with his servant problem!" She enjoyed performing housewifely chores for him:

> I am very busy doing things I know nothing about! Earl wants me to try & watch John make a cake to find out what he does wrong! Then I'm to show him about ironing shirts! In the meantime Earl's nerves are about like yours for different reasons so it is probably a good thing I'm here!

She frolicked in the snow with him and contentedly made biscuits for his lunch and an applesauce cake:

> It is so peaceful here but he is another person like you in whose soul there is no peace. He has to attain it himself but I think it is harder

for him than for you because he has no intellectual resources which he has developed.

A postelection meeting with Molly Dewson was fraught with plans and projects for women: "Molly Dewson came to lunch at one & we talked till 3:30 & I have my work cut out with FDR & Jim on the women!"

James was off with his father on the *Indianapolis* to Latin America. Franklin, Jr., and John were at Harvard, Elliott on his ranch in Texas. Of all her children, Anna alone at the moment seemed close. Now that, too, was threatened, as she wrote to Hick and F.D.R.:

I talked with Anna last night & it is a dead secret but they are going to take W.R.'s [William Randolph Hearst's] paper in Seattle that has had all that trouble. John gets a written agreement that he controls the editorial page & doesn't even publish Mr. Hearst's editorials when he doesn't want to do so. Of course John & Anna are blissful, $30,000 for him, $10,000 for her & she is to edit the woman's page which will mean working with him, just what she wants, you see. It now loses $200,000 a year. If he can make it pay he gets 5% of profit. I feel a bit sad for it means complete separation, even worse than with Elliott but I'll get used to it & I wouldn't spoil their joy by ever saying a word about it. . . .

She admitted her dejection to Elinor:

I hate Anna & John going so far away but it is better than Europe for one can at least fly. I might as well confess to being depressed but such is life!

To her husband in South America her resigned acceptance of life's ebb and flow, which seemed austere in its detachment and egolessness, she wrote, ". . . [S]o life is life, not always very pleasant."

Nor did James's news when he returned from Latin America in mid-December particularly cheer her: "Do let me know," she had written to Franklin on his departure, "if you've decided anything about Harry Hopkins, Ed Flynn or Eddie Roddan."* She unburdened herself to Anna:

Pa and Jimmy got home last night & this is just a hurried line to tell you that both looked well & rested. J. says Pa was much upset about Gus [Gennerich, his bodyguard] but he thinks he tries not to think about it & J. says he has a state policeman he's sending down to try out. James himself is coming down to act as Sec. on Jan 15th. They are taking a house. . . . I was amused & surprised but made no comments.

* Edward J. Flynn, Democratic political leader of The Bronx, close associate of the Roosevelts and later chairman of the Democratic National Committee. Edward L. Roddan, White House correspondent of International News Service, who had worked for the Democratic National Committee during the 1936 campaign.

"Somehow it was always he and I." Sketch of Eleanor's father, Elliott, that was drawn by a camp-mate on a hunting trip to Texas that he took at the age of sixteen. The journal of this trip, including its sketches, was turned over by Eleanor Roosevelt to the Franklin D. Roosevelt Library.

L. to R. Eleanor, Marion Dickerman, and Nancy Cook at Campobello in the summer of 1926. (Courtesy of the National Park Service/Franklin D. Roosevelt Library)

Marie Souvestre, headmistress of Allenwood. She was "the very soul of veracity and keen-witted," Beatrice Webb said of her, Eleanor became her favorite during her three years at the school. (Courtesy of the Franklin D. Roosevelt Library)

L. to R. Eleanor, F.D.R., "Missy," and Earl Miller at Val-Kill swimming pool, around 1930, during F.D.R.'s governorship years. (Courtesy of the National Park Service/Franklin D. Roosevelt Library)

Eleanor with Malvina Thompson and Elizabeth Read at Salt Meadow, the 147-acre estate on the Connecticut shore owned by Elizabeth and Esther Lape. (Courtesy of the Franklin D. Roosevelt Library)

Esther Everett Lape, c. 1945. She and Elizabeth were among the pairs of women, veterans of the suffrage battle, who lived in Greenwich Village and who in the Twenties helped educate Eleanor Roosevelt. (Credit: Pach Brothers. Courtesy of the Franklin D. Roosevelt Library)

Top, center, bottom. Three of the frames from "The Kidnapping of the First Lady," a home movie made by Nancy Cook at Chazy Lake in the Adirondacks, where Eleanor and her friends were holidaying. The "pirate" is Earl Miller. (Copyrighted by Marion Dickerman. Courtesy of the Franklin D. Roosevelt Library)

"I got married with plenty of publicity to kill the gossip that 'the Lady' was going to divorce the Governor and marry me." F.D.R. standing with Earl Miller and Ruth Bellinger, whom Earl had just married. (Credit: UPI. Courtesy of the Franklin D. Roosevelt Library)

I am saying nothing these days & Pa has no time to be talked to except on matters of business! J. told me, & if true I think it diverting, they plan to make Harry Hopkins Sec. of War to reorganize the Dept. till Congress creates a Dept. of Welfare or what not when Harry will go in there! A pacifist in the War Dept. is funny, now isn't it?

Anna had a different worry. "By the way, have you ever heard Pa express any opinions on our new job? We are both a bit curious along this line! It might amuse you to know that I (nor John) have ever heard a word from Jimmy since we decided to come out here."

As 1936 ended she was closest to Anna, but among her children her chief anxiety at the moment was Franklin, Jr. In September she had twice accompanied him to the dentist's office, where four wisdom teeth had been extracted. Now, at the end of November, he began to have nosebleeds. She dropped everything to be with him. He had told her that he wanted to marry Ethel duPont, and Eleanor left his bedside when Ethel arrived: "The duPonts have asked him to go to S. Carolina so he will do that & recover faster than the Doctor expects." But two weeks later she returned to Boston "to find Fjr. achy & his temp. back to 100. Nothing to be done on his nose until everything quiets down." Another quick trip to New York and back to Boston: "I am getting old. I hate these trips, hospitals, hotels, etc."

There was the usual Christmas week activity—the tree at the Women's Trade Union League, the party and presents for the people at Hyde Park. She and Nan made a late train journey to the latter: "I then realized I'd been all day without food & not ever noticed it!" Daily she telephoned Franklin, Jr., and was reassured by the heartiness of his voice, but as Christmas Eve approached, "I telephoned him & he was terribly upset & proceeded to have a hemorrhage. I imagine it is just a good nose bleed but that settled it & I go to Boston either tomorrow night or Thursday night & probably stay till Sunday night." She canceled all Christmas activities, even the party with Tommy and Henry. Hick decided that the best she could do for her friend was to accompany her on the train to Boston.

It was a sober Christmas Eve and night. ". . . the doctors came to fuss with his nose. . . . I think I'm here for quite a time. Ethel arrives tomorrow morning & that doesn't please the doctor but I think I can make her do the things he wants, like not staying evenings etc. If it looks like most of next week here I'll have Tommy come up for we can do lots on the book." The crisis came the weekend of December 26–27:

Fjr has had seven (3 severe, 5 slight) hemmorhages [sic] from that wretched nosebleed these last two days. No more since last evening at 8 but he is packed tight & most uncomfortable. . . . They want him to make no effort so they want us to be here & always within call for fear something goes wrong but not much in his room. . . . I think I'll be here till Friday anyway.

Hemmorhaging stopped and oozing started.

The poor child is afraid to move & truth to tell I'm afraid to have him turn his head for fear I will be the cause of starting it. After many refusals I am moving into Mr. Filene's house tomorrow. . . .

"No form of love is to be despised," she had written in her diary at the beginning of the 1920s, quoting a line from the novel *The Constant Nymph*, but her mother's love for her children overruled all the others. "Circumstances force your children from you," she later wrote, but whatever distance there was between them and herself it was rarely because of her lack of trying. Franklin, Jr., wanted and welcomed his mother's presence, but he was a senior at Harvard, handsome and full of spirits, and his thoughts were with Ethel. Eleanor accepted that if for no other reason than that she and Franklin had leaned over backwards in order not to interfere in their children's lives as Mama had in theirs. ". . . [Y]ou cannot live at all if you do not learn to adapt yourself to your life as it happens to be," she observed stoically in *This I Remember*.

As the year drew to an end, she wrote to Hick from Boston: "My first two galley proofs are here & I must buckle down to final things on the book." "How is yours coming?" she went on the next day. "They gave mine a title I didn't like & we are now squabbling about it."

XIV

The Second Four Years in the White House

"U MBRELLAS & more umbrellas!" was Eleanor's physical impression of the second Inaugural. It poured, and on the drive back from the Capitol F.D.R. insisted that the top be down and they pulled into the White House portico drenched. At the Capitol, she had searched out and seen to it that a few friends were able to stand out of the rain—Nan and Marion, Molly Dewson, Laura Delano, and old Dr. Peabody of Groton. She had listened to F.D.R. deliver his inaugural in the rain. "I see one-third of a nation ill-housed, ill-clad, ill-nourished," and she thought his speech "good." From 11 A.M. on she stood, tall, gracious, and cheerful, welcoming first the 710 who came to lunch and afterwards, 2,700 who arrived for tea and whom she greeted individually. At the end of the strenuous day she wrote to Hick her real feelings as she faced four more years:

> I confess that arrangements & people bothered me beforehand but even more my sense of 4 yrs more beginning bothered me. Why can't someone have this job who'd like it & do something worth while with it? I've always been content to hide behind someone else's willingness to take responsibility & work behind them & I'd rather be doing that now, instead I've got to use my opportunities & I'm weary just thinking about it! Well, we'll live thro' it & worry along & see the irony of it & laugh at ourselves!

Hick had begun to work at the New York World's Fair, and as she wrote to Eleanor a few days after reporting to Grover Whalen, its president, she also was expected to be a discreet liaison with the White House. She would help to arrange events involving the President and the First Lady, but any pictures that might result should show the Roosevelts with Grover. Eleanor willingly lent herself to her friend's stratagem, for it meant well-paid and secure employment. It meant also that Hick could live in her small apartment in Manhattan and from April through November commute between the fair's offices on Long Island and a little house in Moriches, farther out on Long Island, a part of the Dana estate which Hick rented. Hick and her German shepherd, Prinz, lived happily there, sharing the cottage with a young writer friend, Howard Haycraft, with whom she got on splendidly, without any suggestion of sexual involvement on either side. ". . . I certainly love this place," she wrote of Moriches. "More than any other place in the world, I think." Both she and Eleanor accepted the separation that made mail and telephone their main communication.

Eleanor's correspondence with Hick continued unabated. The Franklin D. Roosevelt Library records that the correspondence deposited by Hickok listed:

	E.R. to L.H.	L.H. to E.R.
1937	293	227
1938	289	195
1939	292	241
1940	213	137

On Eleanor's side these letters continued to constitute one of the most remarkable diaries of the Thirties. Whether she registered her feelings as frankly and meticulously as she did because she expected Hick someday to write her biography or whether writing to people she trusted enabled her to clarify to herself how she felt, or whether she hoped to write her own account of the White House years someday, nowhere else did she write as frankly and in such detail. To the extent that writing conveys personality, her letters did. Yet the size of the correspondence did not reflect the vehemence of her attachment to Hick. The latter continued but long since had ceased to be a governing passion. In early 1937 they were planning a week together in April. Why did Eleanor not come down to the country? Hick suggested. She wanted her to come alone, not even with Tommy, because the latter's presence, Hick explained, meant that the two of them would work and leave her "bored and miserable."

Eleanor gently turned the notion aside:

Of course I could settle down for a week or a month alone with you & be happy but I really want to see Charleston, S.C. with you. We needn't drive further than we want any day for we don't have to reach a given spot.

Even before she had received Eleanor's reply, Hick was apologizing for having been "too blunt & arbitrary," and when she had read Eleanor's letter, she quickly yielded: ". . . I gather you would rather make the trip. Let's wind up in New Orleans," which is what they did.

A reckless, driven soul, Hick vented her dissatisfactions on Eleanor, and that first year at the World's Fair she decided that Grover Whalen did not like her and the work was a bore. She complained because people identified her with Eleanor and ignored her real merit as a newspaperwoman. She also was unhappy because she was separated from Eleanor and had a non-political job. Eleanor did not mind her discontents. It strengthened her to calm Hick:

> I have thought so much of you & your weariness & hoped you got quickly & safely home & to bed. It seems so hard that life should be so little worth living to you when so many people love & depend on you but I have felt as you do & I keep hoping that someday things will change for you & seem more worthwhile.

As usual Hick was apologetic:

> I'm sorry I talked to you with such bitterness the other night. It wasn't fair. But—since I did say it—it's true. I've felt this way for nearly a year. I'm much *calmer* about it than I was last Spring & Summer though.

Eleanor commiserated and rightly guessed that Hick's unresolved relationship with the White House was at the heart of her discontent:

> I hate all this you are going thro' & I know in some ways it is connected with us. Somehow I hope you get another job soon & that it is so remote from our influence that you will be relieved from that blight!

The misunderstandings with Grover Whalen were quickly cleared up, if indeed they ever existed, and when Hick persuaded the President to address a preview session of the National Education Association at the fair in June 1938, Hick's anxiety shifted to the fear she might be "murdered" by feuding education officials if her involvement ever was suspected, and as for the fair, "Grover thinks he did it himself."

Eleanor had introduced Hick to George Bye in the belief that Hick's reports to Harry Hopkins might be shaped into a book.* She prodded Hick to get on with her writing and at the same time worked on her own: ". . . [I]f we [Tommy and herself] do as much on the train tomorrow as we did today it will be swell for I won't feel so guilty about

---

* Published in 1981 under the title *One Third of a Nation*. Urbana, Illinois: University of Illinois Press.

'my' book. I hope you feel as guilty as Hell." But Hick, as she began work for the fair, decided to put aside her book: "I chuckled over your hoping I felt 'guilty as Hell' about the book. It always amuses me so when you get profane! And I also chuckled over the President's reception of Alice Longworth.* He was bad, of course—but, oh, she so richly deserved it! Your indifference and your poise simply are more than human!"

It was not indifference. She had ruled out as an objective happiness in the sense of gratification of personal need. She obtained her own satisfaction in helping others achieve what they thought they wanted. After their week together, when Hick went on to the Ozarks and she returned to Washington, her wish for Hick had been: "I hope you will get some joy out of the trip if only the feeling you are making some one else happy!" The same altruistic note colored her reaction to the film *Lost Horizon.* "Shangri-La" meant, she wrote in "My Day," "the attainment of that peace and contentment which one can only have within oneself if one feels that whatever ideals of happiness one has created for those one truly loves is actually attained. To Hick she wrote: "Sat thro' 'Lost Horizon' last night & I wonder if everyone's 'Shangri La' must not eventually be within themselves."

She went to the wedding of Franklin, Jr., and Ethel duPont in Wilmington, Delaware. It represented a kind of "grandeur" from which she shrank. She insisted, nevertheless: "The wedding won't get me down. Nothing but something that really hurt the people I loved would bother me. Personally, I'm pretty immune." Her acceptance of what had to be was sometimes stoical; at other times it clashed with a vitality that welcomed challenge and refused to allow fear or pain to deter her from effort. It was the saints' time-honored protest against the world coupled with their indifference to the passing show. On a more mundane level it made us into "contradictory" creatures, as she explained to Hick, and never more than in relationships with men.

The newspapers reported that Hick's old boss, Harry Hopkins, although his wife Barbara had died only recently, intended to marry an actress. "How could he forget so quickly?" an indignant Hick asked, noting: "It's only about six months." The newspaper story had "upset" Harry, Eleanor replied, "but I told him if he isn't stampeded by it into doing something he doesn't mean to do, it will not matter long!" And when she received Hick's angry protest, Eleanor read her a lesson in the vagaries of human feeling:

> You don't know much about men do you? Harry was happy with Barbara & so he is lonelier than if he hadn't been. Women are sorry for

---

* At the diplomatic reception, wrote Eleanor, "Alice came & F.D.R. was rude, looked straight at Col. Watson & said 'I won my bet [that she would come]'! Johnny didn't recognize her & was affable!"

him. They like to be seen with men whose names are in the papers &
it helps him to forget. He isn't serious but he did openly go out with
Mrs. H . . . & of course can't *say* he doesn't intend to marry her. He
was disturbed but I told him if he didn't let himself get bluffed into
marrying someone he really didn't care for no permanent harm was
done. I'm afraid Diana is more apt to be left alone than to have a
stepmother tho' of course that may happen!

Her day-long attendance at the wedding of Ethel and Franklin, Jr.,
ended on a resigned note: "Well, it's over & the future will be what it
will be." The same detached note sounded again, six months later.
Franklin asked her to go with him and call at Justice Cardozo's: "I fear
he is dying which is a great loss but he makes no fight to live. Another
one who has not found this world too entrancing."

She had devised several personal stratagems to keep herself from
yielding to the sense that life was not worth living. The most important
was the realization of the number of people who depended on her and
to whom she gave some security and contentment. Another vitalizing
device was her attitude towards gifts. She resisted being a recipient. Her
pleasure came in giving to others. On Christmas Eve her sitting room
at the White House turned into a cheery madhouse. In one corner she
calmly wrote last-minute gift cards while children, spouses, and older
grandchildren sat on the floor wrapping, writing, and filling stockings.
Hick called Eleanor's attitude a "generosity of soul":

It isn't the things you give people—and I'm using 'you' in the personal
sense now, meaning you yourself—but the thought and care you put
into it all that means so much. All the little details, like the artichokes
for supper, the candles and Christmas tree, the warmth and cozyness
of it all, the expression on your face when one is opening the presents and is pleased—oh, darling, you are swell! It's a kind of generosity
of the soul that you have, that is above your truly magnificent generosity about material things.

Hick's appreciation caused Eleanor again to dwell on the ambiguity
of happiness:

Your dear letter came today & I wish you a quiet heart & a sense of
security. Few of us know what our heart's desire is dear, & if we had
what we fancied it would probably turn to dust & ashes so security &
peace are safer wishes, dear!

She did surprising things for her friends, she once acknowledged.
Hick should not feel embarrassed at asking whether Howard might stay
at the White House, "for who should know better than I do the things
one must do for one's friends." Physical exertion was the easiest. She
often complained of her hectic life, yet always left others exhausted as
she went cheerfully on, arranging a trip upstate in order to see friends

like Leo Casey or Al Kresse. After Esther and Elizabeth repaired to Westbrook on the Connecticut shore, she often journeyed there with Tommy for an overnight visit. She entertained Elinor at her own cottage, going equally often to the Morgenthau farm at Fishkill.

The expenditure of energy for the people one cared about was easy; equally so was her awareness but indifference to public reaction. She drove regularly to Loudonville outside of Albany to stay with Earl in his new house, to help him with his many girls. She was "off" with Earl, she wrote from Hyde Park, "who can hardly wait to get home & see if his grass has grown since he was there on Wed.!" Ensconced in Earl's house in Loudonville, she was "doing some sewing for Earl while he was working on his hedge." She was deeply involved in his relationships with his girls and once when she heard that he had holed up in her apartment in New York, to which he, like her brother Hall, had a key, she decided to go up there after a speech in Philadelphia and postpone her return to Washington: "I may be of some use however in helping decide what to do. I think he'd better take a rest cure!" But six months later she records: "Earl & Miss von Haver are here & I've spent a long evening teaching her to knit."

Often, however much as she tried to help her friends, the more discontented they seemed to become and no one more so than Hick. The latter, on one such occasion when she had been unable to help herself, begged Eleanor to be patient:

> So don't, please feel—as you seem to feel sometimes—that you have failed in your relationship with me. . . . As I look back on these five years—I don't think anyone tried harder to make another human being happy & contented than you have tried with me.

Eleanor had come to realize that too much help, especially coming from her, overpowered the recipient and resulted in more dependence rather than self-sufficiency:

> Of course dear, I never meant to hurt you in any way but that is no excuse for having done it. It won't help you any but I'll never do to anyone else what I did to you. I'm pulling myself back in all my contacts now. I've always done it with the children & why I didn't know I couldn't give you (or anyone else who wanted or needed what you did) any real food, I can't now understand. Such cruelty & stupidity is unpardonable when you reach my age. Heaven knows I hope in some small & unimportant ways I have made life a little easier for you but that doesn't compensate.

In answer to Hick's repeated query as to why Eleanor was unable to let go emotionally, she tried again to explain herself: "I am *not* unhappy. Life may be somewhat negative with me, but that is nothing new. I think it was when I was a child & is now a habit, but there is much peace & calm about it!"

Her childhood, as was suggested at the beginning of this book* had spoiled her for happiness—that indelible scene after her mother's death when her exiled and adored father, dressed in black, visited her and promised they would be together in the future, in her child's eye replacing her mother, and since that nirvana could never be achieved, forever coloring all pleasures with sadness.

She was no partisan of Sigmund Freud, as we have noted, yet his explanation of the process of "sublimation" seems appropriate here:

> A small minority are enabled . . . to find happiness along the path of love; but far-reaching mental transformations of the erotic function are necessary before this is possible. These people make themselves independent of their object's acquiescence by transferring the main value from the fact of being loved to their own act of loving; they protect themselves against loss of it by attaching their love not to individual objects but to all men equally, and they avoid the uncertainties and disappointments of genital love by turning away from its sexual aim and modifying the instinct into an impulse with *inhibited aim*. The state which they induce in themselves by this process—an unchangeable, undeviating, tender attitude—has little superficial likeness to the stormy vicissitudes of genital love from which it is nevertheless derived.†

Although Freud insisted that benevolent love was rooted in desire and self-interest, he also acknowledged that the renunciation of instinctual satisfaction not only was achievable, but that civilization was made possible by the transmutation of "egoistic trends into altruistic and social ones. . . ."

The biggest physical change in Eleanor's personal life came with the removal by Otto Berger, its chief craftsman, of the Val-Kill factory to the village of East Park. First she installed Tommy in an apartment in the vacated structure. Then in 1937 her own cottage took shape. She, Tommy, and Henry Osthagen went to Hyde Park in May, "and I am now getting excited over my own apartment. It seems to be really coming on and I think in June I'll be able to move furniture in." She was back in June: "A lovely day & over my ears in furniture moving & list making! What a lot of things there are to get to start even a small house! I love it however." The carpenters were at work and the upstairs began to look in order. "It is going to be a good refuge I think eventu-

* See pages 1–2.
† *Civilization and Its Discontents*, by Sigmund Freud, translated by Joan Riviere, as quoted in *The Idea of Love*, by Robert G. Hazo (New York: Prager, 1967), page 305.

ally but I am impatient to get it finished." Earl drove her up from New
York: "They have done much here in two days in the way of little
things, shelves, etc. This week they will paint & finish the woodwork &
if only the windows & screens come for my upstairs porch I'll really be
able to settle when I come next week." "I am sure you will rest if you
come up here to me in this peaceful abode," she coaxed Elinor. "If necessary we'll make Henry go and stay at the Big House with F.D.R. &
have them over for a swim & tea with us!"

After young Franklin's wedding she had her fellow columnists, including Westbrook Pegler and Heywood Broun, for a picnic at Val-Kill.
She loved picnics. They enabled her to be gregarious and motherly.
Henry Osthagen took over some of the landscaping: "Henry's lake is
beautiful & when the banks get done & the dam in, it will be very nice."
Now she was able to have Earl and Tiny stay with her. Nan and
Marion were always about. Elinor Morgenthau was dragooned into
helping paint chairs. "I've been learning that there is skill even in
painting!" Shirley Temple appeared with her mother and father.
Eleanor made sure that Sistie and Buzz were present. ". . . [I]t was fun
& rather strenuous. That child is a wonder, well brought up & so reasonable." The foundation stone was laid for the first presidential library
next to the Big House:

> The party to give F. the check brought so many to the Big House that
> all the kids & Joe Kennedy came for a picnic lunch with me & I was
> amused hearing of the latter's impressions of England. He says 'Rose'
> is very close to the Queen, it is quite the talk of London & he finds the
> Queen very nice!

She was unable to get Hick to come. "No thanks," Hick said, too
many tensions, too many guests. Eleanor accepted her friend's foibles:
"Sometimes when we can be alone at Hyde Park we'll try it & I think
you'd like my house but oh! not when I have to run to the Big House
or when we are overrun with guests!" The cottage might often be
crowded, but it was her house and these were her friends. She went up
to Syracuse for a paid lecture. First she dined with Leo Casey. "He is
such a dear & what courage!" After the speech she caught a train back
that left her at Poughkeepsie at 5:09 A.M., only to be greeted by her
"whole household," Nan and Tommy, Henry and Earl. They had left
sleeping "the poor girl who came to meet Earl" the night before. "I was
so mad for that is an hour when one does not want to be met. . . .
Rest of the day I have bought food & have done mail but I sat in my
upstairs porch & it was fun."

Archery, badminton, horses—later she built a tennis court—were all
sports in which she now joined and tried to master. Her progress in
learning to dive tested her mettle; the performance was something else.

The summer of 1938 was the first that she made the Hyde Park cottage her "headquarters" when Franklin was not at the Big House. She was fifty-four and a half, she humorously complained: "Again I've done no work. Too many social obligations & too much outdoor exercise!" Riding was a constant theme. Even more so the efforts to dive, which produced some mighty splashes. "I've learned at last to stand on my hands in the shallow end of the pool & put my feet in the air & I see a faint glimmer of hope for learning to dive!" A few weeks later:

> The weather is gorgeous & someday by dint of working every day I am going to be able to dive! I never worked so hard on any real work in my life!

That was August 21, 1938, at Hyde Park. Another week passed:

> I've got some articles that must be written & I just can't find the time! However, I am at last learning to dive & I can stand on my hands on the bottom of the pool!

At the White House pool the following winter she felt that she had progressed but wondered whether the fears that had become habits were to be overcome:

> . . . I had a swim tonight & I've got so I go in head first quite easily but I don't know if I'll ever learn to really dive!

That 1939 summer she thought she had triumphed:

> Had a swim & I can dive off the board at last!

And a month later announced:

> I've finally learned to dive & enjoy it!

The conversion of "The Shop," as the Val-Kill Industries structure was called, into a cottage for herself, and Eleanor's insistence on "clear title" to it, occasioned a break with Nan and Marion. The breach is difficult to trace. I heard about it from Tommy. Marion Dickerman coolly denied any role in it and declined to discuss it when I asked about it in the course of research for *Eleanor and Franklin*. The letters between Eleanor and Hick confirm the rupture. Eleanor talked about it to her, as she did to Tommy and Elizabeth Read, who did her taxes. But it is also clear that Eleanor had no desire to hurt the two women and sought to preserve an atmosphere of civility and kindness in the relationship between two households that only a stone's throw separated.

There were several issues, one being Marion's need for Eleanor's support in Todhunter's expansion drive. Although Eleanor all through the Thirties continued to attend Todhunter's opening exercises and to have the graduating class at the White House, she gave up teaching there soon after Franklin entered the White House. When in 1938 the school sought to project Todhunter as her chief interest after Franklin would leave the White House, Eleanor refused and soon afterwards asked that her name be dropped from all Todhunter promotional material.

She became even more determined to separate herself from the school when Marion and Nan insisted that the Todhunter Trust Fund, to which the three women had contributed, was a "school fund" and that Eleanor could not give up her share of the fund to the two women in partial recompense for obtaining clear title to The Shop at Val-Kill. Their insistence on this shocked her, as did their reluctance to accept her renunciation of her share in the Stone Cottage, in which they had lived together since 1926. The negotiations were painful. Eleanor's independence, as reflected in her transformation of The Shop into a cottage for herself, also represented a growing away from Nan and Marion. In the end, the separation involved lawyers, and as Eleanor wrote to Harry Hooker, who represented her, she insisted on paying a gift tax on her renunciation of her share of the school fund, "as I want to have it registered that I gave up something which I had possessed. It is not a school fund. It belonged to the three of us jointly."

Eleanor's disenchantment with Nan and Marion was evident in Hick's letter in November 1938:

> It was so good to see you last night, dear, and I enjoyed our talk a great deal. . . . But the situation about the cottage is too bad. I hate to see you disillusioned that way. I cannot see how they can be such damned fools. . . . Well, it's all settled now for you anyway, and I hope you'll enjoy your place up there for many, many years. Please do try to get some fun out of it. For yourself.

A few months later, while Eleanor was in Los Angeles on a lecture trip, she wrote: "Tommy told me about Marion's letter & I was horrified. Poor Marion, her desire to have a school swamps everything else." A month later she was again on the West Coast, this time in Seattle for the birth of Anna's baby. She was working on the revisions of an article, she informed Hick, "& a diplomatic note to Marion to remind her to remove my name from the school papers this spring." Hick's exasperation reflected the reaction of the few friends who knew the situation, an exasperation that Eleanor was too kind to entertain herself: "Won't Marion Dickerman take a hint, *ever*? She's amazing."

1939 was the last peacetime summer at the cottage. She was still resolutely practicing her dives. She went horseback riding with two officials of the American Youth Congress of whom she had grown especially fond, Joe Cadden and Frances Williams. Aubrey Williams, the head of the National Youth Administration from its establishment in 1935, arrived. Earl turned up:

> He had arrived with a young lady in the p.m. & he didn't leave till nearly 11 this morning which slowed me up as much as a ride would have done, but it was nice to see him. Kresse is coming down on Saturday with the young lady he thinks he wants to marry!

Then she added a quiet note about Nan and Marion.

> Betty Roosevelt, Grace Greene & Marion & Nan came to lunch. The first time the last two have been here except to picnics. They asked me to lunch tomorrow & Tommy thinks me weak to go but it is the first time this year & I felt as long as I wanted to live in pleasant fashion I should go on occasion.

"My lunch with Marion & Nan was pleasant & uneventful!" she commented the next day.

Her success as a lecturer and writer enabled her to help friends like Hick and Earl, and to finance activities such as the conversion of The Shop: "I've done a better job on the whole," she wrote after a Midwest tour in the fall of 1938. "It ought to be better at the price & probably will have to be after 1940!" Hick suggested that it would be nice to travel together without being official. Eleanor's realistic reply showed how she envisioned her own future:

> I don't know dear, if I'll ever have the money to travel except on a money-making basis such as lecturing or writing & I cannot imagine that you would enjoy it, even if I were not the President's wife for one does of necessity so much one does not want to do. We can take short motor trips when I have more time some day & those, when I am no longer recognized wherever I go you will enjoy again.

She did two or three lecture tours each year, and at least one of them took her to the West Coast, where she was able to see James after he left Washington, Tiny in San Francisco, and Anna and John and their children in Seattle. On the way out or back she managed a stopover in Fort Worth to be with Elliott and his family on their ranch. In the beginning she drew audiences because she was First Lady, but in Roosevelt's second term people listened to her because they sensed that she was on the side of the angels and validated her crisp, often moving utterances by the way she lived.

Her writings strengthened that impression, not only her column "My Day," but the publication in 1937 of the autobiographical *This Is My Story*. The book's acclamation exceeded George Bye's expectations, not to mention her publishers' and certainly her own. Despite lack of academic training, her mind was so well organized that she became somewhat impatient when editors wanted revisions at the beginning of 1937, although she had begun the manuscript only six months earlier. She checked her earlier memories with Alice Longworth and Maude Gray. ". . . Alice Longworth alone till 6:30!" a note at the beginning of 1937 read. "Maude made numerous corrections in the manuscript so in off moments we've been correcting that." She went through old letters "thinking I'd find one at least from Mlle. Souvestre to use, which I did. A few other things may be of interest . . ." She selected photographs of herself in 1937 that might be used by the *Ladies' Home Journal* which would serialize the book. "I hate them all because they take all the lines out & you look smooth but characterless!" In April she was looking over the "next to last installment. They are going to be through in Oct. so it can be a Xmas book & I'm very glad & hope it will sell."

The editor of the *Ladies' Home Journal*, Bruce Gould, was dissatisfied with the final installments: "It is not enough of a story yet [of] 'a soul' so next week I'll see him & see if I *can* do what he wants. That means work ahead & I thought I was done which is a bit annoying!" Hick put her finger on the shortcoming of the last chapters:

> I'm sorry the L.H.J. doesn't like those installments of your book. I haven't read them, but I suspect by that time you have come close to the period where you can no longer be wholly truthful. And it shows in your story. That's the trouble with autobiographies.

Gould's misgivings were offset by the jump in the magazine's circulation, due chiefly to Eleanor's installments:

> Mr. Gould writes that the April L.H.J. went over the 300,000 mark, a gain of 85,000 over the previous April & 95,000 over the month before. I wonder how much will be sustained? In view of his fears over the 7th and 10th installments (he's only just received the 11th and 12th). I'm glad anyway they made an initial gain. I'm wondering whether he'll dislike the last two more or less.

She settled happily into her cottage as she revised the galleys: "Life is pretty busy for me but I revised the first galley yesterday & will get it off so I can see if it meets with their approval." Two weeks later:

> I've received 2 more galleys but I haven't sent them to you because they are clamoring to get them back. I may be able to send you the last two which are not yet done, I mean revised. They reported back that they were satisfied with the first one received.

The autobiography not only boosted the circulation of the *Ladies' Home Journal*, but the book when it appeared in the fall was greeted as a minor American classic. George Bye happily reported that the mass circulation magazines were clamoring for articles, as many as she would do. She willingly complied but insisted on writing her own material. In November, George Bye wired her that *McCall's* was pleased with her article "My Home," meaning the White House, but wanted more color in the piece on "My Job . . . They will not believe tho' I'll write it myself or not at all! He says the reviews of the autobiography coming out Sunday in the Times and Tribune are good which is nice!"

She had sent a copy of the article on the White House to Hick, who liked it. Eleanor was glad, and added:

I didn't put in anything but what is at present my job, the W.H. end. The rest is not my job just my preference & stolen from the times I can get away from 'the job!' No one is interested in my part of it, they are only interested in a first lady! As I wrote you they want more color so I'll get in Memphis & redo.

The "audiences are bigger than ever before," she had noted in Ohio in mid-November 1937, and with success came self-confidence. Once she listened almost awestruck to Rex Tugwell when he came to dinner. Now she felt that she had a better sense of how to make complex problems intelligible than he did:

I had a speech of Rex Tugwell's among other things & if he could write with a little less erudition it seems to me that every American citizen should read it. In its present form, however, I have difficulty in understanding many of the words. Perhaps I have been writing down to my public too much till I don't use words beyond the one syllable variety.

She had advanced steadily in the public's esteem as a lecturer and writer. "I hear less & less," she sighed when taking some young people to the theater. "My voice gets worse & worse too." The decline in those faculties, she comforted herself, might compel her to become a better writer. In fact, assiduous training of her high-pitched voice was turning it into a finely modulated organ of expression, and she charmed audiences with the smile and glow of her presence.

The lecture tours appealed to her because they helped her to know what people were thinking, and they brought in money; they also enabled her to see her children, who as the decade went on settled in scattered parts of the country. She loved them without stint or hesitancy, tried her best without interfering in their lives to keep them from mistakes, and, as mothers did generally, forgave them their failures. Her affection for her children was selfless and unconditional, and both love and duty prepared her to drop everything to be at their side when one of them needed her. "I hated to leave," she wrote Elinor after a stay in

Seattle, "but you know my theory about long visits specially when Anna & John are working so hard on the paper."

When any of the children or their spouses became seriously ill, they turned to her. Christmas of 1936 she had spent with Franklin, Jr., in a Boston hospital. Christmas Eve of 1937 she flew out to Seattle to be with Anna, who had to check into the hospital. "I'm damned glad you're going, dear," wrote Hick. "I think you'll be much happier there." A few months later she was back in Seattle for the birth of Johnny Boettiger, and in July (1938) she went to Philadelphia to be with Ethel and Fjr. after the birth of their son, Franklin III, returning to Hyde Park, "for this is Sis and Buzz's last week & I want to see them all I can." When in 1939 Anne's first baby was born prematurely and dead, Eleanor went to Boston to comfort the young parents and at Johnny's request to meet with the press and explain what had happened.

James, who worked for his father and was married to Betsy, from whom he was estranged, gave Eleanor and Franklin their worst scare. In May 1938 he went to the Mayo Clinic in Rochester, Minnesota, for what turned into a three-week stay. The doctors found a small gastric ulcer. "He has to stay an extra week because he has not progressed as much as they hoped. I may fly out for two days," she advised Hick, and a week later, "I hate leaving the kids . . ." She had been in Hyde Park. F.D.R., after a transcontinental tour, was on the *Houston.* "James looks well but he'll have to come back in Sept. tho' he is going home with me on Monday."

In early September, Fjr. telephoned her from Eastport, Maine, opposite Campobello. He said, "I had better go out with James to Rochester on Monday so though it rather upsets my plans I'm going." That was Sunday. She thought the next day she would be back East on Tuesday. She and James waited in Rochester for the results of the X-rays: "They treat you here like an old friend & the atmosphere is very kindly! Nevertheless I am glad I do not have to stay." To help her while away the time, Dr. and Mrs. Mayo took her and James to the movies. As always there were letters to be written. "Poor Tommy is upset I know about the publicity on her divorce but it will soon be over." The X-rays came and the doctors decided to operate immediately.

Betsy arrives tomorrow a.m. early & I go to meet her, after that I expect to feel somewhat out of place! F.D.R. gets in Sunday a.m. I hate these long drawn out preparations. May the Lord be kind & let me go without any fuss & if I ever have an operation I'd rather have everyone wait & come to see me when I'm getting well & need entertainment!

I'm reading aloud a most amusing book to James called 'With Malice towards Some'—The lady [Margaret Halsey] will not be able to return to England but her diary is most entertaining. . . .

P.S. We'll be here anyway till Thursday the 15th . . .

James and Betsy were playing bridge with one of the doctors and his wife. Betsy had arrived the day before: "the situation is most confusing to me. I've come to the conclusion that I like facing facts & I hate living unrealities!" That, in a manner of speaking, was her chief count against Franklin. He permitted no one to get near to him. He arrived on Sunday, the eleventh,

> with his retinue & I dread it but I'm glad Tommy is coming. I've dodged reporters & cameras ever since I've been here & think of the influx tomorrow! Elliott is coming which will be nice, tho' a bit hard on him for he's opening his new network on the 15th. . . . I'm glad he's doing it tho' & that FDR asked him for he gets a 'left out' feeling so often that it will be good for him.

Sunday Franklin arrived:

> Well, they decided yesterday p.m. to operate today after FDR gets in so I met the train at 9:30. He saw the doctors & the X-rays, saw Jimmy & by 10:40 they began. It was over at 1:30 & nothing malignant found & his condition is good. Betsy has had the jitters & I've felt 1000 & as cold as ice which is always my reaction.

They began to relax:

> We are all lunching in the [railroad] car today & I'm taking a cake for Missy's birthday. James is doing very well but while I spend a good deal of time in the hospital I don't go in much for there are so many doctors & F's visits & Betsy flitting in & out that I feel he must make a great deal of effort. The less now the better for his future. He really ought to be quite well after he has completely got over the effects of this operation.

After the surgery everyone prepared to leave, but "James wants me to stay till tomorrow night." The family scare was superseded by the war crisis, and her comments to Hick, while not strictly speaking part of *Love, Eleanor*, have historical value. "Hitler patting himself on the back because Chamberlain is going to see him makes me sick. Just the same if war can be averted by flattering him why it is worth doing."

The week after Rochester she spent at Hyde Park except for visits to Elinor Morgenthau at Val-Kill and to Earl in Loudonville. Coincident with the buildup to the Munich crisis was the 1938 hurricane: "Our cellars here are flooded & no furnace but it isn't very cold!" She, Tommy, and Harry's daughter, little Diana Hopkins, who had been staying with her, went to Washington: "It was warm when we got here & I found FDR better but much troubled about Europe. No one can think of much else these days." A letter from Hick was full of the damage the hurricane had done to her little house on Long Island. "Here the hurricane is eclipsed by the world situation," Eleanor replied. It "keeps FDR on edge all the time. He is not going to H.P. tomorrow & of course he is right but if we are in for a long pull, we'll have to do many of these normal things or everyone will go under." Hick apologized for dwelling on her troubles: "After all, with another world war imminent, little things like a house in the country & trees . . . aren't so very important, are they?"

The previous day Roosevelt had sent a second appeal to Hitler urging a settlement of the Czech crisis by negotiation rather than force and proposing an immediate conference in some neutral spot. "We all feel a bit happier over the foreign situation tonight," Eleanor wrote on September 28, after Hitler had invited Chamberlain, Daladier, and Mussolini to meet with him in Munich the following day, "but F says he's done the last thing he could do & we all pray some thing moves Hitler tomorrow. What a mad man!" The following day the Munich Pact was signed, which Chamberlain hailed as meaning "peace in our time." "The European war seems to be averted," Eleanor wrote from Boston, where she saw Johnny and Anne, also Elliott, who had come East. "I suppose everyone's concern is a sign of improvement & perhaps we will have a fair adjustment tho' it does not seem probable now." She visited Esther and Elizabeth at nearby Westbrook, which had been devastated by the hurricane. She took their views on foreign affairs very seriously and perhaps her sharper recoil from the Munich settlement reflected talks with them: "No one could be objective about a war who had ever seen the results of one. I am greatly relieved that we haven't a war going on this minute. On the other hand it seems to me a very unsatisfactory peace & I am afraid it is not permanent."

Two weeks later on a lecture tour in the Midwest with "two speeches over but 11 more to go," she touched on foreign affairs. "It is 'peace' again & that is interesting these days but difficult." She had been reading Anne Morrow Lindbergh's *Listen! the Wind,* which she thought a "gem" of a book. But she wondered about Lindbergh. When Nazi authorities gave the signal for the pogrom against the German Jews who remained in Germany that became known as *"Kristallnacht,"* she wrote from Cincinnati. "The German-Jewish business makes me sick & when F.D.R. called tonight I was glad to know [Ambassador Hugh R.] Wilson was being recalled & we were protesting. How could Lindbergh take that Hitler decoration!"

The approach of war, the World's Fair, Roosevelt's ever-present pleasure in self-dramatization brought an influx of royalty. Eleanor performed as White House hostess with her usual grace and dignity. The royal visits, moreover, added color to her columns, but in her letters to Hick she disclosed a constant effort to get to know the human beings behind the public faces. That was intriguing about others who had to live in a goldfish bowl. The Swedes were the first to come. The World's

Fair, of whose progress Hick kept her informed in detail, unofficially opened in late spring 1938. "On Friday I began the Swedish royal visit badly," she wrote Hick in July, "by being late to receive them, but, they were early! We drove them around then a dinner & movie & the picnic, hot dogs & all was a success yesterday & then they left! They were very nice & simple but Lord it must be awful to be royalty. They gave everyone presents & how do you suppose one manages to travel with so many?"

Other Scandinavian royalties followed the Swedes the next spring. "When I next return," she recorded after a contented April weekend at the cottage, "I will be at the Big House & we will have Norwegians & Danes on our hands!" F.D.R. telephoned her from Warm Springs. He "sounded very gloomy over Europe."

Roosevelt also worried over Japan's moves to set up "a new order in East Asia." The U. S. Fleet was ordered to the Pacific. Not wishing to alarm public opinion, the Navy portrayed it as a call on the San Francisco Exposition. Grover Whalen, presiding over New York World's Fair, wanted the fleet as a backdrop to his fair and was upset, as Hick indicated to Eleanor. "Grover can't have any idea of the international situation if he thinks the fleet was moved to help any fair," commented Eleanor.

"I had 2 Youth Congress leaders to lunch at the cottage," she wrote on her return from a flight to Seattle. Afterwards she drove to the Big House "& went with FDR to meet the Norwegians at the dock. They are nice young people but how bored they must be!" Her cottage became a feature of the royal entertainments: "I worked like a dog over the picnic this a.m. & it went well. Then we all drove to the Astors for tea. Another dinner went well this evening, with at the end gifts & good night. One is over!" The next day she barely reached the Big House in time to meet the Danes: "A pleasant evening" but "a day tomorrow & 2 visits are over! These are all nice, simple young people & one can't help liking them."

The following week in the White House she received another foreign visitor, this one alone. "Constancia de la Mora, the Spanish Loyalist, I liked better & better. She is a real person. . . ." De la Mora returned, this time to Eleanor's New York apartment, and brought Dr. Juan Negrín, physiologist and statesman, who had just been forced to resign as Premier. "They were interesting, tragic, but gallant & great people. . . ."

Mama presented a problem when royalty was to be received and protocol became paramount. A grande dame, she insisted on recognition, and diplomatic events, especially the visits of royal personages when all was style and punctilio, gave her an opportunity to shine. A vignette at the beginning of 1939 illustrated the different worlds that Sara and Eleanor now inhabited. It happened at the White House:

> I've played rather a mean trick tonight, pleaded a headache & sent Mama down to sit as hostess at the Diplomatic dinner! She told everyone at lunch today how much she disliked having to sit so far down the table so I thought this was a good way to put her at the top & I've had 1½ hrs of sleep so I'll really be able to enjoy the music for a change! It is rather nice music tonight too!

Mama's son loved her, but she created problems for him, too, especially when he refused to allow her to interfere in visits of state. On the eve of the visit of their Britannic Majesties, George VI and Elizabeth, part of which was to take place at Hyde Park, Franklin had to go to bed with a sinus, Eleanor noted eight days before the arrival of the King and Queen: "F.D.R. is convinced his sinus is due to being cross with his Mother from Sat. a.m. to Tuesday night! I'll tell you about it!" she promised Hick. Some things she did not wish to put on paper.

There were repeated brushes between Eleanor and Mama over the impending visit of the British King and Queen. It was as if Eleanor were enacting an Emersonian role in her insistence that Americans should be themselves in meeting the British. They should be courteous but self-trusting. American non-conformity, she insisted, was a virtue. Mama's emphasis on traditional usage and grandeur represented a delicate counterpoint that was appreciated by a few:

> Oh dear, oh dear, so many people are worried that 'the dignity of our country will be imperilled' by inviting Royalty to a picnic, particularly a hot dog picnic! My mother-in-law has sent me a letter which begs that she control me in some way and in order to spare my feelings, she has written on the back a little message: 'Only one of many such.' But she did not know, poor darling, that I have 'many such' right here in Washington. Let me assure you, dear readers, [this was written in "My Day," May 25, 1939] that if it is hot there will be no hot dogs, and even if it is cool there will be plenty of other food, and the elder members of the family and the more important guests will be served with due formality.

She underscored with gentle courtesy the importance of not aping the British: "I should not be at all surprised if some of the things which the King and Queen will remember and laugh over, when they return to their own fireside, are the differences between the English way of doing certain things and the way they are done here. . . ."

F.D.R.'s willingness to send the U. S. Fleet to the Pacific, so distressing to Grover Whalen, reflected an unspoken naval alliance with Great Britain, which he had slowly been forging in the Thirties despite American neutrality. The visit of the King and Queen powerfully reinforced that unofficial entente. F.D.R. was the helmsman for the American side on that occasion and Eleanor a willing accomplice, stamping the visit with her own brand of dignified naturalness.

Franklin had all the lines in his hands but she worked hard on her end of the preparations. "I've just been housekeeping hard ever since I got here [Hyde Park], inside & out! . . . [the cottage will] need a good check up before the house is filled with my children over the King & Queen's visit. James telephoned me the Queen wanted to attend a press conference & not to ask the Embassy as they would veto it! Won't the news gals be glad!" One of the newspaper reporters did query the Embassy and the Queen's attendance was eliminated. "Gee! I will be glad when the K&Q have been here & gone!" she confessed to Hick in the midst of the preparations:

A good ride this a.m. after going over lists with F.D.R. which I think pretty well finish up all arrangements for the K&Q! Then an hour with Henry Morgenthau who is in the dumps!

There were still matters to be looked over ten days before the royal visit, "Lord! what details!" she exclaimed. Three days before their arrival, "F. telephoned that I must tell Elliott not to comment in his broadcasts on the K&Q!" Her letter-diary to Hick on the eve:

I'm glad you liked the article on tolerance & what you say about there being 'meat' in what I write pleases me. *Look* took the article but hasn't yet paid, George Bye said.

I've got quite a bit of work lined up for the summer.

Busy day. Looked over everything this a.m. 11 press. Spoke at Worker's Alliance 'Right to Work' Congress 12:30 Ad. Byrd for lunch. Hair & nails 2:30–4. At 4:30 five people to tea at 5. Out to the Newspaper Women's Club, then a visit to Cousin Susie at the Mayflower, & 8 of the newsgals for a goodbye picnic supper from 6:45–10 p.m. Now mail & late bed.

'Grapes of Wrath' is a wonderful piece of work but I can hardly bear to read it. I dread to start each new chapter.

Then she wrote:

I am glad the next year will be the last year!

The next day, Thursday, she wrote:

Well, one day is over & fairly well over. The Queen reminds me of Queen Victoria! He is very nice & doesn't stutter *badly* when speaking aloud & not at all in quiet conversation. The entertainment went well tonight I think & Marion Anderson was divine.

The heat is oppressive & I am weary. Four hours of sleep last night! Swam tonight & hanker for a regular regime of exercise, little food & work, with a good bit of reading wedged in!

She recorded on Friday:

> This day is also over & has gone well.
>   . . . even F.D.R. is content & I am glad for him. The young royal-
> ties are most intelligent. At the tea they asked everyone questions & left
> them with a feeling that their subject was of interest & well understood.
> At dinner the King told me he felt that he had learned a great deal.
> She seems equally interested. I begin to think there is something in
> training.
>   I'm glad to be leaving tonight, it is hot & the air is heavy! I shall feel
> really free when Monday is over! I think my column has been good &
> innocuous!

The deprecatory reference to her column masked a concern that it
should be well received. Her syndicate's praise pleased her:

> I got a nice wire from Mr. Carlin about my column. London cabled
> they were well satisfied & so is he & don't you think for the N.Y. Times
> to take them from the World Telegram for the next morning is quite
> a feather in my cap?

"Dammit, you have got a journalistic sense," Hick replied, and for
"the august Times to pick up your column and run it after it had been
run in the W-T" was an achievement. On the way north the King and
Queen visited the World's Fair while the President and First Lady
went on to Hyde Park to prepare to receive them there. "Well, I saw
'em too—in spite of myself," Hick wrote. Her job had been to get the
schools to turn out for the occasion. "I had the kids there and I guess
everybody was happy." Then she added irreverently: "I finally got back
to my office about 4:30, sighed, 'God damn the King and Queen,' and
took off my shoes."

Eleanor filled her in on the British reaction to Grover Whalen, who
had escorted them around the pavilions:

> The King & Queen did not fall for Grover. They themselves were nice
> & I wish you could have *talked* to him especially. She is a bit self-
> conscious, but who wouldn't be? Turning on graciousness like water is
> bound to affect one in time!

That was it. That summed up her whole struggle in the White
House to know what she really felt and to insist upon saying what she
thought even if it meant being indicted for unconventionality. She had
royalty's ability to turn on "graciousness like water." She also knew its
dangers and was always on guard against them. On Sunday the visit was
over and she, the President, and Mama escorted Their Majesties down
the long hill to the Hyde Park Station:

> The crowd suddenly began to sing 'Auld Lang Syne' . . . We stood
> and waved, but my mother-in-law reminded us of the old superstition

that one must not watch people out of sight, and so before they turned the bend we were back in our cars and on our way home.

To Hick she wrote:

I was too weary to write last night but F.D.R. was satisfied & all went well. I liked them both but what a life! They are happy together however & that must make a difference even in the life they have to lead. MacKenzie King is jubilant over the whole trip. I should think it might give Hitler & Mussolini food for thought. They undoubtedly made friends. . . .

This [Hyde Park] will be headquarters now but I expect I will be away as much as here.

Although a major participant in the reception of the King and Queen, she had declined to accompany Franklin to Canada in August 1938, when the visit had originated in his discussions with Mackenzie King. The contradictoriness of human beings that she had mentioned to Hick also reflected her own attitudes, especially in relation to F.D.R. It had begun at the Inaugural when she had wished someone else had the job of First Ladyship but being in the White House at Franklin's side felt a duty to use her opportunities.

She cultivated the people with ideas she might use in her continuing battle with him to do more on behalf of the disadvantaged one third of a nation that had keynoted his second Inaugural, the people identified with the Workers Alliance, the American Youth Congress, the blacks, the resettlement camps and Arthurdale. They fed her ideas that she used to good purpose, while denying she did so. "Everyone tells me how they feel thinking it will seep thro' to F.D.R. & of course I never tell him!" That was said at a moment of irritation, for, of course, she was always telling him, or giving others a chance to tell him.

She fed him ideas and usually performed the duties that he wanted done, but she saw him coolly, letting a few of her intimates know that she opposed a third term. Mrs. William Brown Meloney, the organizer of the *Herald-Tribune* Forum, asked her to get the President for the October 1939 Forum. "She wants you for a 3rd term and I thought this most unwise," a memo in the summer of 1938 read. "You know I do not believe in it. . . ."

She worked with the organizations who considered F.D.R. their leader, and she cultivated the people in the White House who were not as dispassionate as she about Franklin's leadership. They included Hickok as well as Harry Hopkins. After she listened to Franklin at the Pan American Union, she wrote:

We've just come up from F's speech & I think it was good if a bit arrogant in spots. He did not stir me but I may have been too tired or perhaps he can't.

That final resigned phrase said a world about her distrust of the histrionic role assumed by almost all politicians, including Franklin. She admired self-reliance, directness, and moral courage, virtues that were in short supply among the men and women who bid for the public's votes. Hick demurred from Eleanor's dim view of F.D.R.'s speech to the Pan American Union. It was "one of the finest things he has ever done," and she expressed "a wish to God she could help him." Eleanor did not argue. It was as if she appreciated and sought out as friends those who kept her from acting out her exasperations with Franklin.

She liked Harry Hopkins. She hoped, in vain, that he would be a link between her and Franklin, as Louis had been. "To me Harry looks very thin," she wrote from Warm Springs in March 1938. "He's gone to take a nap & he must be weary. I don't feel happy about him but for Diana's sake I hope I am all wrong." The next day she wrote again: "Harry has been at work all day with Aubrey & others & he's going to appear before Congress on Tuesday. Quite an ordeal I should think." She counseled him on his romances after the death of his wife Barbara and made Hyde Park and the White House into second homes for the orphaned Diana. At the end of the 1938 summer Harry came with Franklin to Hyde Park:

> I had a most interesting talk with Harry this morning. He is a swell person & I hope he keeps his head & continues to feel as well as he does at present.

When Harry had to check into the hospital she and Missy were among his constant visitors.

Early in February 1938 for the first time she mentioned that F.D.R. was building his own cottage, on a hill behind Eleanor's at Val-Kill and like hers away from the Big House. "We all lunched with Nan & Marion & FDR took the Backers* to go over their lot & Henry Toombs [F.D.R.'s favorite architect] is there discussing F.D.R.'s house & Mrs. Backer's."

Eleanor and Franklin both wanted to stay in touch with each other, and perhaps the mile of country road that separated her cottage from his, and both from Sara, represented not only the aloofness and exasperations that separated the two, but the warmth and indispensability that bound them. On March 15, 1938, she writes from Fresno, California:

> Dearest Franklin,

> Just a line to tell you that I sent Missy a check for part of the picture you wanted as a 17th of March present & the rest will be yours at Xmas!

* Dorothy Schiff and George Backer had become publishers of the New York *Post*.

Eleanor with Lorena Hickok on the right; woman in the center and left not identified.
C. 1933 (Courtesy of the Franklin D. Roosevelt Library)

". . . . Nan rushed in to say F.D.R. and the whole fleet had come in late last night." *Amberjack II*, skippered by a relaxed President at the end of the "100 Days," is visited by Eleanor and her friends. Back row, l. to r., Frances Keller, Mary Dreier, Marion Dickerman, Antonia Novotny. Middle row, l. to r., Nancy Cook, F.D.R., Jr., John Roosevelt. Front row, l. to r., Eleanor, F.D.R., James Roosevelt. (Courtesy of the Franklin D. Roosevelt Library)

Tableau, F.D.R. as Roman Emperor, staged at his birthday party, January 30, 1934, by Louis Howe and Eleanor. Conservatives who in March 1933 had begged F.D.R. to act, and to act decisively, were beginning to charge him with dictatorial ambitions. Eleanor as Delphic oracle.

Seated 1. to r., Marguerite Le Hand, Malvina Thompson, Margaret Durand, Stanley Prenosil. Standing, Marvin McIntyre, Grace Tully, Thomas Lynch, Kirke Simpson, Nancy Cook, Eleanor, Irwin McDuffie, Anna Roosevelt Dall, Charles McCarthy, James Sullivan, Marion Dickerman, Louis Howe, and Steve Early, who was the President's press secretary. He enjoined those who received copies of the photograph to keep them out of the hands of the press. (Courtesy of the Franklin D. Roosevelt Library)

Eleanor with Elinor Morgenthau in Rock Creek Park. Elinor was friend and confidante as well as a member of the official family. (Courtesy of the Franklin D. Roosevelt Library)

Anna wrestling with her mother beside the pool at Val-Kill, summer of 1932. Woman in background on left is Caroline O'Day. (Courtesy of the National Park Service/Franklin D. Roosevelt Library)

Anna married John Boettiger, the correspondent of the Chicago *Tribune*, in January 1935, after a secret courtship that Eleanor had protected. (Credit: UPI. Courtesy of the Franklin D. Roosevelt Library)

Eleanor with Mayris Chaney, "Tiny," at the Ambassador Hotel, New York City, 1938. When Eleanor employed "Tiny" in the OCD's physical fitness program, she was denounced for hiring a "fan dancer." (Credit: UPI. Courtesy of the Franklin D. Roosevelt Library)

Eleanor with Trude and Joe Lash on a bench on the White House grounds, October 1941. Mrs. Roosevelt was in mourning for her brother Hall and had just begun to work at the Office of Civilian Defense. (Credit: Harris & Ewing)

I fear this European situation has you all worried pink & I fear work is pretty bad but hope you'll get away by the 20th.

Miss S. was glad to sell the miniature of Anna for $100, so I sent Missy my check for $50. & told her to send a check to Miss S. & have miniature sent on for John's birthday if you agreed.

Lovely weather now but signs of flood everywhere & they have been hard hit. Mr. Creel's* ceremonies went off well yesterday. This trip has been interesting & seeing so much work at first hand has been very enlightening.

The lectures have seemed to go well & the audiences are very good. What do you suppose happened to Richard Whitney?† It seems incredible.

Best wishes for the 17th & much love.

E.R.

A letter from Anna says she feels much better.

But the next day from Los Angeles she is irked by the silence of the White House: "I've not had a line from the W.H., no letter, no wire, nothing since I left a week ago Sunday. I've wired & written twice & now I'm going on strike!" But an assuaging letter from Franklin arrived, and she responded:

Dearest Franklin,

I was glad to get your letter this morning & sorry about the wisdom tooth. I hope it gives you as little trouble as mine gave me.

Evidently Europe is not giving you deep concern & you plan to get away. I note you get to W.S. the 23d does that mean you stay there after the 2d?

From the point of view of work projects both N.Y.A. & W.P.A. have interesting & varied things to meet different climatic conditions & the needs of different racial groups.

The trip goes well but it is very busy.

Much love
E.R.

Who is going with you to W.S.?

"Everyone well and send their love," her telegram from Seattle announced on March 20. A few days later she wrote in greater detail:

Dearest Franklin,

You will be reaching Warm Springs this p.m. & I was glad to see by the papers you actually got off.

* George Creel had been chairman of Woodrow Wilson's Committee on Public Information during World War I and since then high in the ranks of Democratic leaders in California.

† Richard Whitney, Groton, Harvard, Porcellian, former president of the New York Stock Exchange, and leader of the opposition to securities legislation, was in 1938 indicted and sent to prison for stock manipulation by young District Attorney Thomas E. Dewey.

Everyone here is well & Anna has gained 5 lbs in spite of a heavy programme of work. Having me here is adding to it because I've always refused to do outside things & this time I decided I'd better do W.P.A. & N.Y.A. projects. We lunched at a practice house yesterday & spend two hours tomorrow & Friday a.m. on projects & in addition visit two hospitals! This p.m. Anna has a big meeting in the Civic auditorium on household employment, then a tea & then people for dinner!

Sis & Buzz look well & are much excited about coming East. Buzz can now ride a bicycle & roller skate which was the first thing he told me.

Remember that I will be gone all the 29th from Warm Springs.

Tommy wrote Missy about our arrival & she told Mac she would have to have a room in the hotel. If my plane is on time I should land at 4:55 & reach Warm Springs for supper. If we are late I'll go in to Atlanta, eat & come out afterwards but I'll wire Tommy & she can let you know. She leaves here tonight.

> Love to Missy & all.
> Devotedly
> E.R.

A few weeks later F.D.R. addressed the teachers at the New York World's Fair. He stressed the need for federal assistance to schools where states and private sources were no longer able to finance them. He made a ringing plea, too, for civil liberties: "If the fires of freedom and civil liberties burn low in other lands, they must be made brighter in our own." In contrast to her reaction to the Pan American Union speech, Eleanor did not find this one dull: "It will bring repercussions from abroad I think & even Mayor Hague* & the Legion might not like it!"

F.D.R. took off on a barnstorming trip across the country in connection with the ill-fated effort to "purge" the Democratic Party; Eleanor stayed at Hyde Park, her messages reporting the progress on his cottage. "Most of the excavating for your house is finished," she wired him in Texas, "but not part for your heater." When he boarded the U.S.S. *Houston* for some fishing in the Galápagos and Cocos Islands, she wired him assuringly: "Walls of your house up everything moving satisfactorily. . . ." He wired back: "Glad everything progressing well." She reserved the family news for a longhand letter:

Dearest Franklin,

The enclosed will show you that Maude & David like the little farmhouse but you will have to talk it over on your return.

Wasn't it nice Ethel had a boy since they both wanted one? Fjr. said both were well. I'll go down for a day to see them next week.

* The Mayor of Jersey City, who threw civil libertarians into jail with the autocratic dictum: "I am the law."

James looks well but has to follow a strict regime & go back September. He should live in Framingham [Massachusetts] for a year or two but Dr. May says they could tell more after his next visit.

It was nice to get your notes & the papers say the fishing is fair.

Mama writes happily. The two children here are well & very happy & much pleased because Curt does not want them till August 1st.

I'm swamped with work & people since I went away & there is no rest for the weary! Tommy is fine & so am I however & I hope you are having a grand time.

> Much love,
> Eleanor.

F.D.R. sent her two letters from the *Houston* addressed to "Dearest Babs," full of fishing news in the Galápagos and both of them ending with requests that she accompany him to Canada on August 18:

> By the way, will you go to Canada with me for the 18th? I hope so. I get to W. the 12th & thought I would go direct from there the eve. of the 17th to Kingston, Ontario (the 18th) get a degree, lunch, motor to the Thousand Islands, and dedicate the bridge. Mackenzie King will be along—leave that even. and get to H.P. the a.m. of the 19th and stay there 10 days.

His second plea that she accompany him to Canada was written from the Canal Zone: "I wired you today about the plans for Canada the 18th. I do so hope you can come."

But before she received these letters she had already written him her own plans and they did not include accompanying him to Canada:

> Dearest Franklin,
>
> I would not live on Long Island [where she had been visiting Hick] for all the world! Everything sticks & I don't want to move! I've improved much in typing however having to do my own column every day here! Harry [Hooker] asked me over to the Piping Rock Club to spend another week with him & I said I was sorry I couldn't but I wasn't sorry at all!
>
> A letter from John says they want to come to Hyde Park before he starts work & will you be there the 20th? The papers say the Tweedsmuirs* are away & you have curtailed your plans. John would like to meet me in N.Y. the 18th & spend the 19th getting what he wants out of storage. If you don't have to have me in Canada will you wire *at once* & I will arrange to meet John & Anne in N.Y. They want the side board [that] used to be in our front hall & Bets has that in the dining room but I'll write & ask her if she wants to keep it there.
>
> I've sent you some mail to read & there is no news but if you have any definite plans as to trips & times at Hyde Park I'd like to know to arrange for servants etc. I don't want to go anywhere I don't have to go

---

* Lord Tweedsmuir was Governor General of Canada.

until my lecture trip which starts Oct. 13th & takes me into Middle
West & South to Alabama. I go early in Oct. to Kentucky & Tenn. for
2 days & Sept. 30th to Portland, Maine & from there to please Sen.
Green for a noon speech in R.I.

Much love,
E.R.

She received Franklin's messages about Canada but adhered to her
plans not to join him. "Franklin has curtailed his Canadian trip and
the Tweedsmuirs won't be there," she wrote to Elinor Morgenthau,
who was abroad, "so I am not going & instead I am meeting Johnnie &
Anne in N.Y. to go through the things in storage!" She did arrange to
be at Hyde Park when F.D.R. returned:

Dearest Franklin,

Two letters this morning are grand & tell so much that is interesting
about the trip. What a big shark!

I am writing Johnnie to try to go through the storage on the 18th so
we can be here that night & meet you the 19th & I'll call you when you
get to Washington if you will wire me what would be a good time.

I am so glad you are staying here till the 29th, do you think you will
get back here for the next week & Labor Day?

Mama writes all is well in Campo & James very faithful to his regime.

Do you care to have the Woodstock dancers the evening of the 27th
or any other time? If they come will ask the crowd to a picnic supper
here. That is the day of the Home Club meeting & I thought we would
do the whole thing in one day!

The rain, damp & heat have been trying but it must improve. I am
afraid you won't find the South or Washington very pleasant however.

Your house has reached the point of having window panes set. The
stone work is very nice I think.

Much love
E.R.

Maude & David come today & will give your message.

Roosevelt's speeches in Canada created a sensation, since he extended to that British dominion the protection of the United States.
"The President arrived this a.m.," Eleanor wrote after his return to
Hyde Park on August 19, "& tomorrow the flow of visitors begins, but
on the whole it is calmer than usual."

Although she was against a third term, she pressed F.D.R. vigorously
to get more from Congress, especially for work relief. Ever since his legislative setback on his proposals to change the Supreme Court, and the
failure of his efforts to purge conservative Democrats, he had moved
cautiously, but at the Jackson Day dinner he declared boldly that

"every true follower of Jackson asks that the Democratic Party continue to make democracy work."

> FDR told his stories at the Jackson Day dinner tonight very well but Lord, he served notice on recalcitrant Democrats as to what he intended to do in certain eventualities. I'm not sure it was wise but it was honest & certainly fearless.

Despite Roosevelt's plea that the Democratic Party had to remain a liberal party if it were to win in 1940, conservative Democrats joined the Republicans to slash the WPA appropriation.

> The cut went thro' by one vote & F.D.R. heard & read it out in Cabinet looking straight at Jack Garner he said. The latter has begged every Senator to vote for the cut & was responsible for the final outcome. I wish there could be a real demonstration at the Capitol but of course there won't be.

It was a moment of discouragement for both of them:

> F.D.R. announced tonight that he could run the country successfully as a Dictator but doubted if the country could ever do it for itself! I begin to be a bit discouraged by the democratic process too & yet it should work!

Had F.D.R. talked "seriously" about being a dictator? Hick wanted to know.

Eleanor cleared that up quickly:

> No, F.D.R. wasn't serious. He was just pointing out how easy it wld be to cure certain ills (mainly economic) if he were a dictator & how the democratic process makes it practically impossible. The trouble lies with human nature I guess!

More perhaps than anyone else in the Government because of her contacts with the unemployed, the blacks, and the young people, she knew how far the Roosevelt revolution still had to go. A speech that she made to a meeting of the American Youth Congress, in which she described the Roosevelt recovery and reform legislation as having given the nation time to think, was widely remarked and she had Tommy type up copies to send to Hick and others. When she was with Anne and John in Seattle, she noted: "I did answer some idiot who asked me if I wld run for President, that 'nothing on God's green earth could make me run!'" The very asking of the question was a measure of how strongly she had taken hold of the public consciousness.

Women had made progress, especially during the New Deal, but as she noted to Hick after the Secretary of Labor, Frances Perkins, had come to her, as she often did, with her troubles: "How men hate a woman in a position of real power!" Though she stoutly maintained that what little she had managed to do had been done for her, she was a force in her own right:

> I've been talking to F.D.R. like a Dutch uncle lately & he's been good about it but I can't bear to have Congress go home with nothing done!

Contradictory? She genially admitted to the indictment. When Bill Dana, who owned the Dana Place at Little Moriches, died suddenly and his widow, Ella, turned up with a young cowboy, Hick's eyes filled with tears. "How could she do such a thing?"

She was sad for Ella, Mrs. Roosevelt wrote back. "She misses Bill & the very things that bothered her in Bill she probably has in this boy. How contradictory we are!" Was she thinking of her own relationship to F.D.R. and her tolerance in others what she was unable to abide in him? Poor man! He complained about the food served him by the housekeeper, Mrs. Nesbitt, whom Eleanor had brought down to the White House. The story is an old one, Eleanor's reaction less well known:

> I could be low in my mind but I'm not going to be for I realize it is a question of annoyance! I simply can't get F.D.R.'s food organized to suit him! I'm trying a new plan when he returns on Thursday.

Annoyance, yes, but a powerful bond of affection, too. She ended her note to him about her "strenuous" fall lecture trip: "Hope you are having a grand week. Everyone asks for you & your 'dream house!' Much love." And a few weeks later after she had dashed out to Seattle to be with the Boettigers, her letter filled with family news ended on the usual benign note: "Hope you & Missy are having a restful time! Much love to Missy. Love to you from all the family here with mine. E.R."

A steady glow of affection and kindness suffused her actions. The moods that reflected an almost existential sadness and loneliness only a few were permitted to see. She was always striving to see the world in a better light. In one of those flashes that made her letters to her friends such rewarding reading, she had remarked to Hick on her return once to the White House, after the tranquillity of Hyde Park: "A real Washington day, much doing but nothing done!" That was the way she often seemed to herself, not conscious that from her life she was creating a rare model of self-reliance, directness, and moral courage.

XV

The Unfinished Revolution

THE FIRST BIOGRAPHY of Eleanor Roosevelt appeared at the end of 1940. It was written by Ruby Black, a newswoman who had covered Eleanor for the United Press from the beginning of her tenure at the White House. *Eleanor Roosevelt*, as the book was called, occasioned an interesting exchange between Hick, who had always wanted to do Eleanor's story, and Eleanor, who had encouraged her in such hopes and whose letters to her constituted a diary of the New Deal years. In them Eleanor speaks in a voice that in terseness, realism, a wit that often bordered on wickedness, and psychological understanding represented the way she really saw the world.

It was six days after Franklin's election to a third term and Hick wrote: ". . . I'd never have believed it possible for a woman to develop after 50 as you have in the last six years. My God, you've learned to do surpassingly well, two of the most difficult things in the world—to write and to speak. I'd not worry about a 'life of ease' or getting old if I were you." Hick then addressed Ruby Black's book directly. She did not like Ruby's treatment of Mrs. Roosevelt's early life and personal development, but the

> chapters on your career in the W.H. are excellent. I think—much better than I could do. My trouble, I suspect, has always been that I've been so much more interested in the *person* than in the *personage*. I

resented the personage and fought for years an anguished and losing fight against the development of the *person* into the *personage*. I still prefer the *person*, but I admire and respect the *personage* with all my heart. But all this explains why I shall never write your biography. I can think of only one other person who undoubtedly felt about this as I have—or would have felt so, increasingly, had he lived, Louis Howe.

In her reply Eleanor told a story about Louis Howe and herself that Ruby did not have. How could she? Not even Hick had known.

You are wrong about Louis. He always wanted to make me President when FDR was thro' & insisted he could do it. You see he was interested in his power to create personages more than in a person, tho' I think he probably cared more for me as a person as much as he cared for anyone & more than anyone else ever has! Sheer need on his part I imagine! I used to laugh at him & tell him I had no interest in the job & I still think the personage is an accident & I only like the part of life in which I am a person!

This exchange was illuminating also about Hick's early years with Eleanor. She had resented the personage, wrote Hick. She had fought the claims of public, family, and other friends upon Mrs. Roosevelt, but, as she admits in her letter about Ruby Black's book, her impassioned effort to gain Eleanor's undivided attention had not succeeded. Their close relationship continued, but Eleanor's letters and endearments had long lost some of their earlier intensity. The fear that Hick's possessiveness would limit her autonomy and independence had subsided and so had her dread of becoming First Lady.

That realization was beginning to dawn even upon her as the doubting expression "I still think the personage is an accident" suggests. She had entered the White House a fatalist: the real person would be subjugated by a public person known as the First Lady. Instead she had placed her individual stamp upon the job. Her intimate friends had all contributed towards the overcoming of fears that would have kept her in a conventional mold. But once the fears were overcome, there had flashed on an ever-widening scene the grace, purity of spirit, devotion to truth and service that had been manifest to people like her father and Mlle. Souvestre, her aunts Corinne and Bye, and to Franklin, qualities that had been there all the time. The personage had become the person.

The transformation was reflected in the drumfire of activities that beat through her letters despite bouts of exhaustion with herself as much as with the calls upon her. On a paid lecture trip in Kansas and Missouri in November 1939, she and Tommy appropriated a dining table on the train and worked on her column and on the magazine pieces for which her agent, George Bye, had a never-ending market. There were other signs of her growing personal popularity on that trip.

As she diffidently put it: "For some strange reason at these stations people have gathered and in St. Jo the Mayor had wired that he wishes to give me a bouquet which I suppose means a crowd."

Paradoxically the more the country responded to her as a person in her own right the less sometimes she seemed to care. There were moments when even her cottage at Val-Kill, which was where she preferred to stay when the President was not at the Big House, left her strangely apathetic. "The grounds look nice here," she observed on her return to the cottage in May 1940, "& everyone has worked hard but I'm ashamed how little I care about it. If I never came here again it wouldn't matter to me!" She paid scant attention to press misrepresentations of her. "Tell her not to worry about inaccuracies where I'm concerned," she advised Hick in regard to Ruby Black. "The newspapers said I bought 100 doz. hankies for Xmas & the world & all has been writing in for them ever since."

What did such indifference signify—a passing mood, a deep strain that all is "vanity" that warred with an even stronger sense that everything had meaning and posed choices? Other words and actions showed how much she cared to be appreciated for herself, not just as an appendage to Franklin. She was, moreover, deeply attached to Hyde Park's paths and walks through the woods, the pool, the cottage, which was the place where Earl and her other friends could stay, the place that she considered her home. A few months earlier she had gone down to the Poughkeepsie station to meet Anna and John Boettiger and their children. They had come East for the holidays, and afterwards she wrote: "Tonight I'll stay at the Big House & tomorrow I'll come back here to sleep." The previous evening alone at the cottage had meant everything: "I loved being over here last night. It was so quiet & peaceful. I hope it is just a taste of what it will be in the future!"

The historian is tempted to read into Eleanor's fitfulness about Val-Kill her hopes that F.D.R. would not be a candidate for a third term. While Anna and John were with them she reported: "We had a talk with F.D.R. John [Boettiger] was floored because F.D.R. said he wouldn't run again & tried out on him the [Cordell] Hull idea." This puzzled Hick, to whom this was addressed, because she thought Mrs. Roosevelt had written "Hall" not "Hull." Eleanor set her straight: "I meant HULL & John is horrified because he does not consider him [Hull] a liberal & John has become a good left-winger in many ways." Although Eleanor considered herself a left-winger, she did not particularly oppose the Hull candidacy. She opposed a third term even more, but that only a few friends like Hick were allowed to see. When trainmen came up to her on her travels to tell her how much they hoped F.D.R. would be a candidate, she smiled kindly and said she would convey their feelings to the President. She kept to herself the conviction that leadership in a democracy needs periodic revitalization through the introduction of new and younger people.

There were strong personal reasons as well which occasionally came to the surface as they had in 1928, when Franklin had been elected Governor, while her candidate, Al Smith, whose women's organization she had directed, was defeated. "What does it matter to me?" she had said of Franklin's victory. She had rebelled similarly, and vainly, in 1932, when Franklin's candidacy for the presidential nomination seemed to be on the point of success. Then she had feared that success for him meant self-subordination for her, no job of her own to do. She still felt that way. ". . . [Y]esterday was a pleasant day in Arthurdale," she wrote in 1939 after a visit to the resettlement community in which she had invested a great deal of herself, and she added tellingly: "To be honest I don't feel anything I do has much point. I suppose because I realize how important are the things F.D.R. does & I feel there is nothing I seem able to do."

The President might have served his purpose in history, she told me in early February. At that time I was becoming a real friend. Youth should not cling to him for leadership. New leadership was needed for the next step ahead. "Unless," she added, "the international crisis made him indispensable as a stabilizing force because the people had faith in him."

During Franklin's second term she gave her support to many movements that served a useful purpose, but to no youth organization more than to the American Youth Congress. She was no ideological radical. Marxism had little interest for her, although radicals like Anna Louise Strong did,* even when the latter took almost two hours to explain "the Soviet point of view" after the Nazi-Soviet pact. At the time of her humbling by the Lucy Mercer affair she had embraced a radical egalitarianism that, coupled with an instinctive commitment to fairness and justice, had made her the champion of many popular front causes such as aid to Republican Spain, the unemployed and the Workers Alliance, the new CIO unions, and, above all, the American Youth Congress.

The last also reflected her faith in youth, a sense that the generation of her children—and here she thought first of all of her cherished Anna —were so much more advanced than she had been at their age. There was, too, the mess that she believed she and Franklin had made of their own young lives because they had allowed themselves to be dominated by the customs and values of Mama's generation. Her private history had reinforced the public nightmare of a Depression youth that was out of work and out of school, and in countries such as Germany and Italy was filling the ranks of Storm Trooper and Black Shirt. In 1934, consistent with her interest in people rather than movements and ideologies,

* She had been sent to her by Lillian Wald.

she had periodically assembled a group of young people at her East Sixty-fifth Street home in New York in an effort to elicit from them some ideas for tackling youths' problems. Against the advice of some of her husband's more cautious advisers she had appeared in early 1936 at a meeting in Washington of the National Council of the American Youth Congress and from that time on had become increasingly involved in its affairs. She had counseled its leaders to take a more rational approach if they wanted a hearing on the Hill, and her interest encouraged Administration officials to be cooperative.

She befriended its leaders, helped a few with a personal stipend, appeared at their weddings, and those whom she had come to know well often stayed with her at the White House. She enjoyed having them at dinner with the President. Unlike many of the people he saw, the young people stood up to him. A few people warned her that organizations like the American Youth Congress and the American Student Union were controlled by the Communists. She sent copies of their warnings to the leaders of the American Youth Congress and was satisfied with the latter's explanations.

With Franklin's concurrence she had accepted to be a sponsor of the Second World Youth Congress, which was held at Vassar in August 1938. "Every Catholic organization is deploring my association with such a communist organization!" she wrote Hick. "I don't think F.D.R. will be able to go unless he's prepared to offend the church!"

F.D.R. stayed away, but she went to several sessions, her knitting needles busy, always congenial, quietly observant, seeking a sharper feeling for what the young delegates really believed:

> Since lunch I've done the column & some notes for tomorrow's speech at the Youth Congress. I have been bombarded with protests from Catholics & others saying they are communist controlled & believe me I'm going to watch & ask Dr. McCracken [sic]* to report to me but I think they are wrong.

At one session she answered questions for an hour and a half from the 800 delegates and returned later in the evening to join in the dancing. To Hick she wrote at the end of the day:

> We came back a short time ago from the World Youth Congress & I for one felt sad at the sight of all those young people & so earnest & full of hope—54 countries represented—Did you see them in N.Y.? They asked me tough questions but I tried to answer truthfully.

The President was the "politician," she later explained to me, as our friendship began to deepen, while she was the "agitator." "Where to draw the line was the real problem," she went on, and she "frequently

---

* Henry Noble MacCracken, president of Vassar College 1915–46.

disagreed with Franklin about that." In the continuing conflict between them the Youth Congress people were welcome allies. It was fitting, therefore, that it was at an American Youth Congress dinner that her answer about the New Deal as an unfinished revolution should have become a bench mark with historians in measuring New Deal reforms.

The Republican speaker had criticized the National Youth Administration and other New Deal agencies as having "molly-coddled" youth. She believed in the National Youth Administration, she replied with great deliberation, as she did in Social Security and other New Deal measures. "But never," she went on, "as fundamental answers simply as something which has given us hope. . . . We have bought ourselves time in which to think, that is what we have done."

"Am I just going into an impulsive handspring," asked columnist Heywood Broun, who was in the audience, "or is this one of the finest short speeches ever made in our time?" People realized a definitive statement had been made about the New Deal and the brief remarks, which were not in her prepared statement, were quoted in the New York *Times* and the *Herald Tribune*, and she had them typed to be sent to her children and others whom she wanted to know what she was thinking. Another accolade came from Mary Beard, the wife of Charles and a historian in her own right—she was chairman of the World Center of Women's Archives. That historically minded woman and feminist suggested that Mrs. Roosevelt "write down and sign the statement you made at a meeting in New York of Youth a night or two ago to the effect that the Security and other New Deal legislation has been a stop-gap, giving democracy time to think about fundamentals, not being fundamental itself. This in my opinion is superb thinking on your part and highly courageous as pronouncement. Nothing could be more valuable as testimony to your mind and personality."

When Mrs. Roosevelt replied that her papers would have to go where the President and her children wanted, and, therefore, not to the Women's Archives—an interesting indication of how she herself envisaged her place in history—Mary Beard's response was a commentary on Eleanor's place as a leading feminist saw it: "It would be extremely appropriate and elegant for the Center [for Women's Archives] to have eventually, if it could be so favored, all the documents (perhaps newspaper clippings in the main) which show your rise in public favor through the hard years of your traveling and speaking and commenting in 'My Day.' . . . In whatever form this story appears, it ought to be kept together as an invaluable record of how you 'changed the mind of a nation.'"

"Might get her a set of clippings," Eleanor scratched on the corner of this letter to guide Tommy's reply. She thereby indicated not only some willingness to cooperate, but a tolerance, at least, of Mary Beard's estimation of her place in history. However strongly she rebelled against the role of First Lady, the duties it had imposed upon her had forged her public personality and, though she would not admit it, person and personage were becoming one.

As Franklin's second term was drawing to a close, she was most strongly identified in the public mind with her activities in support of youth and the Youth Congress. It pleased her when the 1939 summer meeting of the Youth Congress condemned communist as well as fascist dictatorships. She little imagined that the condemnation resolution had been sanctioned, although grudgingly, by the young communist leadership that lurked in the background. Nor could she know that the young people in the leadership of many of the youth groups whom she had befriended were members of a special Marxist group organized by the Communists, whose members, whether they carried cards or not, were sympathetic with Communist policies and responsive to its leadership. Until August 21, 1939, the date of the Nazi-Soviet pact, it did not seem to matter who was who—everyone spoke the language of the New Deal. Except for a few Socialist groups, these were the people, these the organizations, that were carrying forward the fight for a better world.

In mid-September, when the head of the Women's Division of the Democratic Party brought together the leaders of the Young Democrats with those of the Youth Congress in the hopes that the latter would encourage the former to speak out more boldly, Mrs. Roosevelt invited everyone for tea at the White House. She added to the pressure on the Young Democrats. As long as they echoed the older people, they would not be able to win the allegiance of the young, she advised them. The young woman who led the Young Democrats was enthusiastic but her male co-leader was non-committal.

Eleanor was a fighter for her beliefs. New Deal Washington at the end of 1939 was in retreat, but she was building for the future, an undertaking in which the Youth Congress seemed to her a willing, knowledgeable, and loyal ally. Then on November 30, while she was in New York to receive an award from *The Churchman*, a Protestant weekly, she received a telephone call from one of the leaders of the Youth Congress. They had been summoned to appear the next day in Washington at a hearing before the House Un-American Activities Committee. The Congress had been demanding such a hearing for over a year, and now there were some who urged it to stay away. She urged the leaders to go despite the short notice. She would be on the midnight train to Washington. Perhaps all might be able to meet at Pennsylvania Station and talk, even if briefly. As Executive Secretary of the American Student Union, I had also received a telegram to appear. I was a member of the Cabinet of the Youth Congress but I was not among those who had become her personal friends.

The note in my diary about that evening read:

Discussed for an hour with Mrs. R. our strategy before Committee. She urged us to volunteer information, undertake to cooperate with Committee and not assume a hostile attitude unless and until unfairness forced us into another position. Said she got cooler as she got angrier. She would try to get President's permission to be at hearing, which we all urged.

She then went to her berth in the sleeper; the young people sat up in the coach to work on their respective releases.

The next day, as she had promised, she appeared at the hearings and afterwards wrote to Hick:

Most of today has been spent at the Dies Committee & I think the Youth Congress people made a grand impression. Their testimony was clear & carried conviction. The Committee oozed encouragement & confidence in them!

At noon she had, as one newspaper put it, "scooped up" the Young Congress leaders, including myself, and taken us in her car to lunch at the White House. In the afternoon the Youth Congress finally had the hearing that it had sought for fifteen months. In Mrs. Roosevelt's presence the members of the committee were courteous. Representative Dies stayed away, and at the afternoon's end she invited the youth contingent to stay at the White House.

The next day she returned for my testimony, moving up to the press table to hear better when I began to testify. The questioning was being done by J. B. Matthews instead of the committee's counsel, Rhea Whitley. Matthews, a former radical minister and advocate of the united front, was the committee's specialist on left-wing activities. His prosecutorial manner towards a free American citizen seemed wrong to Mrs. Roosevelt, and she wrote in "My Day" that his "whole attitude, tone of voice and phraseology made one feel that a prisoner considered guilty was being tried at the bar."

But she found my testimony troublesome, perhaps because I gave the appearance of a troubled man as indeed I was. I had broken with the Communists at the time of the Nazi-Soviet pact. The other Youth Congress leaders had not. Few people, including Eleanor Roosevelt, outside the movement were aware of the cleavage and I was unwilling to sacrifice the young Communists in the Student Union and Youth Congress in order to gain favor either with Mrs. Roosevelt or the committee. I sought to resolve this quandary by fighting the sin, not the sinner, seeking to expose the gradually emerging changes in political line, not those who were bringing them about because they were young Communists.

When Representative Jerry Voorhis of California, the committee's most liberal member, said flatly that he thought Communists should not be permitted in the Student Union, my answer underscored the dilemma I was in.

"It's easy to say, let's not have anything to do with these people. But we have found it a good thing to discuss things with people you disagree with."

"That's all right if you can predict what they will think," commented Voorhis.

"Well, they can't predict what I'll think either," I replied. The *Daily Worker* correspondent at this point murmured an audible, "Hear, hear!"

It was easy to sacrifice the Communists, I went on. "But they have cooperated very ardently with the American Student Union. Now their policy is changing and no one has denounced that change more than I."

When I left Washington I did not know whether I would ever see Mrs. Roosevelt again. On her side, she had sensed there was something different in my testimony from that given by the other Young Congress leaders, but, having given her confidence to the latter, accepted their view that their friend Lash was depressed and emotionally unsettled because of the pact.

"It seems funny not to have the house full of young people!" she wrote to Hick. "Ten of them slept & ate here for two days!" Together with many other people of goodwill, Russia's invasion of Finland, which had begun on November 30, 1939, outraged her even more than Stalin's pact with Hitler. "Yes the Finnish business is bad, worse than anything, but surprise on our part does little good & we can hardly interfere with force!" Her next letter underlined anew the place that youth groups had assumed in her life: ". . . but life is interesting these days, so many young people come by my door . . ."

A Youth Congress official who saw Mrs. Roosevelt after the hearings told me that she wanted to know why I had appeared so uncertain. Would I consider it interference if she asked me to talk with her? What was the poor Youth Congress official who hated the idea of further contacts between Mrs. Roosevelt and me to say? All he could do was transmit her message. A typed note from Mrs. Roosevelt, the first letter she ever sent me, invited me to come in and talk: "I had a feeling that your political opinions were not completely clarified, but I think on the whole you did a pretty good job.

"If you ever feel that you would like to see me and talk things over, either in New York or here, I shall be glad to have you come either alone or bring anyone you want with you."

I accepted her offer immediately and sent her a copy of a "Save the ASU" statement that the liberals in the ASU had sent around to the chapters in anticipation of the national convention in Madison, Wisconsin. On her next trip to New York I joined an associate and friend, Agnes Reynolds, who had been with me at the Dies Committee hearings, and we went to Eleanor's little apartment on East Eleventh Street. She met us at the head of the stairs with the words, "Your statement is a grand one." Since the document stressed the need to insulate ASU policy from the twists and turns of the Soviet line, it was for us, two young people, an auspicious start.

We talked for about an hour. Here are my diary notes about that meeting:

> Said she could understand the basis of communism among young people who saw no way out—especially its base among young people in New York. I explained we might not win in Madison [convention] because YCLers [members of the Young Communist League] were volunteering as delegates.
>
> The problem for the YCLer, I said, was that on one side he saw the *status quo* and on the other the USSR. The latter seemed to offer some hope for the future. She had thought Russia should be sympathetically regarded and watched, she observed. But now it seemed to have exactly the same problems as other nations. She had had a talk with Anna Louise Strong's husband who seemed to describe "personal property" in such a liberal fashion that it seemed a basis for something approaching capitalism.
>
> She thought recent events beginning with the non-aggression pact should be disillusioning young people and asked whether the ASU could not adopt some generalizations on foreign policy and concentrate on domestic issues—a simple four or five point program. Especially since foreign policy developments were almost incomprehensible at this moment. I remarked that one of the difficulties was that young people could not see a liberal leadership emerging in Washington. She said it would come from Harry Hopkins who was getting better. She had a high regard for Ben Cohen but thought Tommy Corcoran temperamental. The real problem was to hold onto the gains we had made. We could not go ahead of the people. She pointed to the poll on the Dies Committee which had appeared the day before and showed that 75 percent of the people were for its continuance. The President was for a full NYA appropriation, but what would Congress do? She had been pressing President on a health bill. The President had replied—well, when it gets so that people will get mad, then we can go ahead again. The President felt he would have great influence from outside of the White House, implying to me thereby, that he would not run again. The problem, she went on, was whom to suggest as a successor.
>
> She asked me what I would do after leaving the ASU.* I wanted a

---

* I had just turned thirty and had declared my intention to leave after the Madison convention.

chance to think my position thru. Was there a third path? Said she had thought at times that revolution was unavoidable, but in the end decided you had to cover the same ground either way—that our generation was way ahead of hers in its thinking at the same age. I said it was less a matter of what one wanted than what objective circumstances allowed. I pointed to the almost anarchy that existed at the end of Hoover's regime. She said simply that when that happened, why we would have to meet it as it came.

She invited me to use her cottage at Hyde Park after the convention. It was a quiet place where I could figure out my beliefs. She wondered whether communists were not being used by reactionaries to break up the American Student Union. Reactionaries feared a student movement. Students were important because they influenced their families as well.

I said I favored a national [youth] leadership that was politically independent but felt that we ought not to set up political criteria as a general rule for ASU offices. She agreed emphatically.

The Madison convention showed the Communists to be completely in control of the American Student Union. The test vote was on the Finnish question. It came as an amendment to a resolution that said America should keep out of a war that was imperialist in nature and was silent about Soviet Russia's invasion. The students rejected the amendment 322 to 49. As the Associated Press story reported: "The one-sided vote of the delegates to the fifth annual convention surprised observers."

The account of the convention that I sent to Mrs. Roosevelt called the decision "fatal." I ended my letter a little forlornly. "I myself am going out of the youth movement. I am thirty. Youth movements should be led by young people." The transition to another form of activity would be difficult. Most of all I wanted to take a few months off to do some studying.

Mrs. Roosevelt was both amused by my sense of elderliness and concerned that I should take things so hard. My Youth Congress friends bore down hard on the latter. "He was always too emotional," they told her. She also was reserved about my analysis of what happened in Madison. "My dear Joe," she wrote to me:

I am very much interested in your letter as I am in all the accounts of what happened in the American Students Union Convention. I would like to talk about it with you some day.

I think you are wise, having reached the great age of thirty, to come out of the Youth Group and into some other work which is going on. I was talking yesterday with a Mr. [Louis] Weiss and a Mr. [Ralph] Ingersoll who are planning to get out a new paper [PM] which I think

has great possibilities from the youth point of view. I hope you will see
them sometime.*
    In the meantime, I really meant my offer of a haven for a few weeks.
If you want to go up to my cottage you are welcome to bed and board.
However, you would be pretty much isolated. The room which you
would have has two beds so you could take some one with you if you
wished to. There is only one maid there and except for occasional visitors you would be very much by yourself.

She signed it "very sincerely yours," and it left me unsure of where I
stood with her in regard to the politics of the youth movement. But
when I went down to Washington for a conference on "Children in a
Democracy," she promptly returned my call and invited me over for a
swim in the White House pool and dinner. "She seems absolutely persuaded," I noted unhappily in my diary, "that it was understandable
that the ASU had voted the [Finnish] resolution down out of other
than pro-Soviet reasons." I credited the Youth Congress officials, who
were much in evidence as they prepared for the "Youth Congress Pilgrimage" in February, with having done some good work from their
point of view.
    The President was at dinner that evening and was annoyed by the ar-
guments of Youth Congress leaders that the nation should spend less
on armaments and more on social services, and he asked to record his
protest for history. The United States had a stake, he said emphatically,
in preventing a Russo-German victory in Europe. Eleanor urged that he
should say those things to the Youth Congress Pilgrimage when he
spoke to it on the White House lawn in February. She asked me to
come back for lunch the next day so that she might tell me about Hyde
Park and where to find things.
    She trusted the Youth Congress leaders and assumed that their reluc-
tance to condemn Russia for what it was doing in Finland reflected a
fear that statements critical of the Soviet Union might be used to get
America into the war. Her own sympathies were made clear at lunch
the next day. She read a letter she had received from Martha Gellhorn,
who had just returned from covering the Russo-Finnish War for *Col-
lier's* magazine. Mrs. Roosevelt had smiled on her romance with Ernest
Hemingway and had helped her to arrange her trip to cover the war. It
was unmistakable, "Marty," as she called her, now wrote, that Finland
was fighting for its independence and would have fought irrespective of
the social regime in the Soviet Union. The United States should help
Finland with a loan, Mrs. Roosevelt commented, but she feared greater

* Louis Weiss, a distinguished attorney whose chief client was Marshall Field,
had interested the latter in P.M., which was to be a daily tabloid without ads. Ralph
Ingersoll, an innovative newspaperman, was to be its first editor.

intervention. "Her son Franklin would volunteer at the drop of a hat if she would seem at all sympathetic."

She detained me after the luncheon to talk to me about Hyde Park and also about the ASU convention. The opinions of young people should not be taken as seriously as many of her correspondents were doing; the real problem was that students lost their radicalism so quickly after graduation, she thought. When I expressed concern that the convention actions would destroy the ASU, she read it as a sign of how distraught I was inwardly. It was difficult to have one's followers refuse to follow one's advice, she assured me, but they would have to see for themselves.

Although she accepted the Youth Congress appraisal of what had happened at Madison, she increasingly felt a sympathy with my political position, and when I asked her to talk with a friend, Karl Frank, a leader of the German underground group *Neu Beginnen* (New Beginning), she quickly agreed.

A few days later, Bill, Mrs. Roosevelt's "groom," as she had described him, met me at the Poughkeepsie station and drove me to Val-Kill. There was a longhand note, the first she was to write me, waiting at the cottage:

Dear Joe

Just a line to say that I wish I could run in & make sure that you are comfortable & happy.

I forgot to tell you that telegrams should go to you c/o me at Poughkeepsie & letters be addressed like this one. Perhaps someone else told you.

I find the woods & the hill top conducive to thought & I hope you will find peace up there.

Eat & sleep well, the rest will come. Good luck to you & I hope I shall find when I go up to the Big House on Feb. 3rd & drop in to see you that you've enjoyed it.

Cordially yours,
Eleanor Roosevelt

A quiet-spoken Negro girl took care of the cottage, and she showed me to my room. When I came down I was greeted by Earl Miller, who introduced himself and said he happened to be in the vicinity and when I offered to divide the large helping of chops that Alice served, he cheerfully accepted. Earl returned later that day and took me for a walk that he said was "the Lady's" favorite, and as we hiked through the silent woods, an expression that Earl used when the subject of the President's speaking at the Youth Congress Pilgrimage came up, stuck in my mind. It was "about time," he said.

Evidently Earl promptly reported his impressions to "the Lady," for a handwritten note came from her:

Dear Joe,

It was good to know that you were comfortable & feeling at home. I hope you have a friend up for the weekends. Perhaps I'll drop in & lunch with you on the 3rd if you will have me?

Earl wrote me he'd enjoyed a walk with you. He radiates a bit too much activity if you want to rest!

I sent some recent magazines up to Alice. Ask her to unpack them if you would like them. Go on eating & sleeping & you will 'possess your soul.'

Cordially,
Eleanor Roosevelt

A week later Eleanor and the President arrived at the Big House, and soon afterwards she came to the cottage and tripped into the room where I was, propped herself on one of the beds, and after a few courtesies asked—"if it's not interfering"—what my prospects were and how soon did I need to earn some money? She was ready to help, she said, indicating that her question was not an idle one. The Youth Congress had been filling her with stories of my despondency. Did I still feel there was little point to life, she now asked. I had never questioned that, I replied, "but I was in doubt as to what was the correct political path."

The more we talked, the more sympathetic she seemed. We went down to the living room and she started a fire going in the fireplace and went to work on her knitting as we talked on. After a while she called the President at the Big House. Why did he and Missy not come over for lunch the next day? In answer to something he said, she replied— and it was my first indication of how she really felt—that she would be able to hear everything Mama had to say that evening. So that afternoon, one of the most extraordinary in my life, continued until she left to dress for dinner at the Big House.

My views, even my doubts, seemed closer to hers than those of the Youth Congress leadership. That, combined with the Youth Congress's whispering campaign against me, whetted her interest. The next morning she called and invited me to come over to the Big House and walk back to her cottage with her. First she took me through the library, then we started out through the icebound woods on what proved to be a forty-minute walk. Her views on foreign policy turned out to be miles apart from those of the Youth Congress leaders. I wrote in my diary:

She looks upon Finland as the barrier between an aggressor and the neutral democracies. If the big nations can gobble up the small ones whenever it is expedient, the world will be condemned to unending wars, armaments and anarchy. She does not excuse England's policy since Manchuria. She considers it contemptible and in the interests of England's ruling class. Nor does she spare the United States in her criticism of recent foreign policy. I questioned whether a privately raised loan would be enough to save Finland or whether Finland could be saved without military intervention. She said the Finns seem to believe they can hold Russia off if they were assured of arms and sue for peace.

We stopped to see some houses that her brother Hall was rehabilitating. The project had done the alcoholic Hall "a world of good," she observed. A little further on was a large house in which Nellie Johanssen, a local woman, had her loom and Mrs. Roosevelt was her best customer for the tweeds that she wove on it. She also took in lodgers. Nellie should be firm with Hall if he became obstreperous, Eleanor advised her.

We then took the long, winding road that led to the cottage, and reached it only minutes before the President drove up with Missy. The Secret Service people carried him in and a vigorous discussion soon ensued. Mrs. Roosevelt was interested in what he would say to the Youth Congress when he addressed it a week later, and he may have been probing to find out what he should say.

Lunch ended when a couple of local political allies came in to talk with the President. Mrs. Roosevelt, Missy, and I went to the next room where the two women chatted, mainly about Harry Hopkins, whom Missy had just seen and who despite his operation still thought he might run for the presidency in 1940.

The President and Missy drove off. Mrs. Roosevelt and I went to the railroad station to go down to New York together, talking animatedly—about presidential leadership, the Nazi-Soviet pact, about how far ahead in thinking and style of life her children's generation was from her own. When I brashly asked her whether she had done much reading in the social sciences, she laughed but was not annoyed. She wanted me to know she had read a great deal, even Ibsen, she said, responding gaily to another of my questions. That led her to tell me about Mlle. Souvestre. But the more she had to do, she went on, the less time she had for reading. She had to get everything from people. "I am very good at skimming the cream off a person's ideas."

XVI

"I knew we were going to be friends..."

THE YOUTH CONGRESS "pilgrimage" to Washington had been announced before the European war had broken out, before Stalin had made his pact with Hitler, before the Communist line had changed. Mrs. Roosevelt gave it her full backing, easing the way for Youth Congress officials who were engaged in the preparations, mobilizing many of her friends, including Cabinet wives, to provide housing, squeezing a considerable number into the White House, and even asking the Army to provide cots and meals for the delegate overflow. Because of her support the Labor Department Auditorium was at the disposal of the Youth Congress, and Administration officials from the President on addressed its sessions. But what had originally been slated as an "institute in government" was subtly transformed by the Youth Congress leaders into a political demonstration of a breach between youth and the Administration.

This was done by maneuver and indirection and none of the Youth Congress officials who were in touch with Mrs. Roosevelt on the preparations for the pilgrimage thought it necessary or right to tell her there had been a shift in Congress thinking. They later claimed they had been taken by surprise and that the President's pugnacious speech had contributed to the breakaway, but avowed Communists in the Congress said afterwards it had been necessary.

The events at the pilgrimage may be viewed on several levels. The one that rated the headlines was the "spanking," as the columnists put it, that the President administered to the several thousand young people who listened to him on the lawn of the White House. The second was the abrupt shift in loyalties of the Youth Congress from Roosevelt to the sonorously eloquent John L. Lewis, the president of the United Mine Workers. He was delighted to offer the cheering, stomping young people the "house of labor" as a new home. He told them that the Youth Congress resolution that the President had denounced as "twaddle," because it criticized a loan to Finland as forcing the United States into an imperialistic war, was identical with a resolution adopted by his own miners.

The third was Eleanor Roosevelt's firm but kindly hour of replies to the barrage of questions that were fired at her at the closing session of the pilgrimage. "The nation probably has not seen in all its history," wrote the correspondent for the Baltimore *Sun*, "such a debate between a President's wife and a critical, not to say, hostile auditorium full of politically minded youth of all races and creeds."

There was, however, another drama, hidden from public view, the tension between a strong President and an equally strong First Lady. Each had plans and purposes, and sometimes they did not march together. Earl Miller had hinted at the cross-purposes between Eleanor and Franklin when he made the startling statement to me as we walked in the Hyde Park woods that it was "about time" the President addressed the Youth Congress. Her willingness to tell me that the President might have served his place in history and that youth should not cling to him for leadership and her private opposition to his running again unless an international crisis made him indispensable, all demonstrated an independent woman whose long life with Franklin as well as her own well-developed sense of autonomy made her little disposed to worship at Franklin's altar.

I did not fully understand this. Indeed part of my attraction to her was my wide-eyed astonishment, as an outsider to the circles of power and privilege, at her coolness towards the perquisites and privileges that came with being First Lady. There was another factor: despite my radical background I had a lively sense of F.D.R.'s importance, and this helped her keep her own balance. Equally important, perhaps, to our growing relationship, was that I helped her disentangle herself from the Youth Congress with self-respect and dignity.

She had noticed at the pilgrimage how the Youth Congress leaders had cold-shouldered me, assigning me to stay at a house in suburban Bethesda, Maryland. When at the end of the pilgrimage she offered to take me and other Congress leaders to Washington's Union Station, she began to tell me how shaken she had been by some of the developments at the Congress, only to fall silent when the others climbed into the car. To my long letter the next day giving her my evaluation of the pilgrimage she replied quickly, before she left with Tommy for a two-week holiday in Florida:

> My dear Joe:
>
> I was very glad to get your letter. I have been mulling over my impressions ever since the Institute because, of course, I have to contend with the world in which I grew up, and that is not always easy.
>
> When I come back and go to New York, I should like to have a long talk with you and I am saving your letter until then to go over point by point with you, as well as to tell you some of the things which I have in mind and which as yet, I cannot formulate. I expect to be in New York on March 6th, and will see you before that. I hope you will let me know what you are doing and how you fare in job hunting. . . .

There had been several references to the Youth Congress in her letters to Hick during the pilgrimage. "I feel a bit depressed or at least disconnected about the American Youth Congress. I hate to see them being dragged into a political fight," she observed during the sessions, and when it was over she wrote at greater length:

> Sunday, I spent all day with the Youth Congress, ending with answering questions Sunday night in a way which was not too popular & there was considerable hissing. F.D.R. made them very sore, more by the way he said things than by the things he said & it is especially hard to stand in the rain & 'take it' when you feel as sensitive as youth does. John Lewis grasped his opportunity & walked away with them the next day & I brought them down to earth a bit which wasn't pleasant either. However, when all is said & done it was remarkable to have so many come & talk & listen & I think it was a great experience for them & I learned much myself. . . .

Tommy saw matters more matter-of-factly than Eleanor. Although she considered her boss the greatest woman in the world, she sometimes differed with her. She did so now over the American Youth Congress. On the day some of the pilgrimage delegates had booed the President, several of its leaders were at the White House later for tea. A caustic Tommy had let them know exactly what she thought: "How dare you insult the President of the United States?" she upbraided them. Evidently the President heard what Tommy had done. He sent for her and when she went into his study and stood mutely in front of his desk, not sure what to expect, he looked up and said only, "Thank you, Tommy."

Hick had just gone to work for the Democratic National Committee under Charley Michelson, a working reporter and since the end of the Twenties the committee's gifted director of publicity, an appointment that the chairman of the committee, James Farley, made as much because of Eleanor's support for Hick as because of Hick's merits. Hick wrote to her from the field:

I'm still very much distressed about the American Youth Congress. If it's true they hissed you last night, that is the most foolish thing they've done so far. Not that it would in any way change your attitude toward them—nor mine either, for that matter. . . . But [and here Hick mentioned an old-time Democrat] was simply wild at their having the nerve to hiss you—after all you've done for them! It does make them look sort of bad . . .

Young Franklin's wife, Ethel, "blew in," Eleanor wrote from Florida, "& I got a kick out of Ethel's saying she wished she had been at the Youth Congress meeting & that Fjr. had told her that I handled my questions & the crowd so well, I suppose one is always surprised by praise from one's children." Hick's letter from Cleveland cast an interesting light on her need for Eleanor in the first years of their friendship:

Honestly, my dear, this is one of the most interesting jobs I've ever had. Haven't had so much fun since I covered the Walker-Seabury story. The job with Harry was interesting—but as you know horribly depressing. I was so bitterly unhappy & emotionally unstable all through that period, or most of it.

When Hick reached Indiana, she had to report news that Eleanor did not want to hear: "Darling, I'm sorry, but it's all third term. Labor people—even those in the McNutt organization here—tell me privately they would much rather have the President run!"

Life in Florida, where Eleanor had rented a house on Golden Beach for a winter holiday, was made more agreeable by the presence of Earl and Tommy's friend Henry Osthagen. Earl had had several friends in, Eleanor reported to Hick, including Simone von Haver, whom he later married. When Eleanor was back at the White House she wrote: "Earl & Simone (one of his girl friends) spend the night of the 17th on their way to Albany & I'm going to have 'Gone with the Wind' for them & for F.D.R. who hasn't seen it. By the way F.D.R. finds what I give him from your letters *very* interesting."

She came to New York on March 6 and she and I had the promised long talk. Indignant as Eleanor had been over the booing of the President, she also had regretted his speech. It had been too much like a lecture, she said when I came to her apartment, and was based on the assumption that his audience had no brains.

Whatever her own feelings, most people seemed chiefly concerned with the third term, she was finding. "The train men have been in to hope FDR would run again," she wrote Hick from the Midwest, "and it is rather pathetic because people seem to feel helpless." Presidential politics interested her less than helping people. Vice-President John Nance Garner, the flinty conservative from Texas, had said to her, she told me, that if the Workers Alliance, an organization of the unemployed, staged a demonstration in Washington, the demonstrators should be dispersed by force. In such a case, she had replied to Garner, she would go down and join the demonstrators. The President was aware of the unfinished business of his administration. If business could not give people jobs, the Government would have to go into business, he had said to her.

She had wanted him to develop such considerations with the Youth Congress, but he felt that its members would not listen because it was under Communist influence. He should be indifferent to criticism, she felt, at least not personalize it.

I had been debating in my own mind what the claims of personal loyalty were—to the Youth Congress leaders of whom I had been one until the Nazi-Soviet pact and the staunchness of whose commitment to a pro-Soviet line I respected even as I disagreed with it, or to Mrs. Roosevelt, whose friendship seemed almost a miracle to me and whose stalwart democratic views fitted my own, especially now that I was disenchanted with the Communists. At the end of the eventful dinner in the White House during the Dies Committee hearings, the youth leaders had clustered around Aubrey Williams, the resolute director of the National Youth Administration, to sing the praises of Mrs. Roosevelt's courage in coming to the hearings. Williams stopped us with a fierce stare: "Don't let her down; it will break her heart." One participant, at least, was unable to erase the memory of that look.

In one of our talks after the "Institute" I told Mrs. Roosevelt about my own political development, how after I had left the Socialist Party in 1937 I had regarded myself as a non-party Communist, taken part in a Marxist study circle organized by the party, and had been waiting only until I left the ASU to formalize my relationship to the party.

It was against Eleanor Roosevelt's personal code to give up easily on people to whom she had given her confidence, nor would she ever appeal for help personally. She listened to my account: "What is to be done about the American Youth Congress?" was her immediate and practical reply. She was not afraid of the Communists or Communism. Conditions produced them. When I proposed a student leadership institute, an evening with the President when he would set forth his views to a selected group of youth leaders, and a handbook that through his public papers would show the progressive philosophy that had governed his administration, she readily agreed. She would take the suggestions up with Franklin, she said. "My dear Joe," she wrote two days later:

I talked over with the President your idea on his papers and he thinks
it is grand. . . .

I also talked to the President about the summer camp and he thinks
that is a very good idea. . . . He also was willing to give three hours of
an evening later in April or in May for a meeting with a group of
youth leaders. He does not want it to be wholly Youth Congress, but
to represent as many different groups as we can get together and whom
we trust not to go out and talk about it. I think that about twenty-five
would be a good number. . . .

It was grand to see you and I look forward to seeing you again soon.

Soon after this exchange Eleanor left on a Midwest trip of speeches.
The Communist issue troubled her. It was her profound conviction
that "communism succeeds only as we ourselves fail." That meant jobs
and schooling for young people. She had supported the Youth Congress
in part because it had enabled her to focus the attention of the country
and Administration on the issue. What she feared now was that the
country might turn repressive. She tried out a new theme on her
Midwest trip and wrote to Hick afterwards:

The speech I really dreaded on this trip is over & went well. It is the
first time I talked on civil liberties & of course I may find tomorrow
that I've said a lot of dangerous things but I believed them anyway.

Eleanor returned to the issue of the Communists and civil liberties in
discussing a new book about Finland by Martha Gellhorn. The book
had annoyed Hick, who had written: "She didn't need to use Communists. Lord knows there were plenty of other people beaten up and
killed by the Nazis. . . . I get bored with Marty's Communists."

She saw the issue differently, Eleanor wrote to her from Ohio: "I
think Marty used Communists to make us really [think] what we must
guard against Hick. I'm frightened by our fear of them, that is the way
terrorism started in Europe in many places." Hick stood fast: "Darling,
I'm not afraid of Communists and I certainly agree with you that bait-
ing them—or any other minority group—is bad business. But they bore
me, dammit!"

On Eleanor's return from the Midwest she startled me when she invited three Youth Congress leaders and me to breakfast at her New
York apartment and discussed with all four the steps I had proposed to
reduce Communist influence in the Youth Congress. Did she really
think, I asked in my diary, that these were the people whom, as she had
put it, "we could trust"?

She invited me to return that evening for dinner. For the first time,
she asked out loud whether her identification with the Congress served
only to highlight its mistakes. I decided I had better make explicit not
only that I disagreed with the growing isolationist policy of the

Congress but also with most of its leaders in whom she continued to believe. She was aware of the personal disagreements, she interrupted. The fight against the Communists should be carried on, she urged, but within the Congress. In public it should be defended.

A longhand note after my departure caused my heart to sing:

My dear Joe,

I hope you are getting to feel that I am going to be a good enough friend someday, for you to accept this little Easter present from me.

You see once upon a time I knew what it was like to need money & to be very uncertain & I know one needs time. I have great faith in you & I hope someday you will trust me as you would an old friend.

I enjoyed having you here with me so much too. You were a dear to come.

Affly yours,
Eleanor Roosevelt

Another longhand note from Chicago expressed the wish she could attend the Lake Geneva, Wisconsin, convention of the Congress in July "without being seen for I would be interested in the discussions." She had spoken for the Chicago Youth Council, "& I still disagree with some of their ideas & sometime soon I must find time to talk it out with some of you. I think I now know what I myself think!" She and Tommy had been in Yosemite and she wished I might have been there too. "Will you come in & see me the first time I am in New York? I want very much to see you." She sent me the draft of an article on youth which she had written for *Liberty* magazine. Would I have suggestions? "I cribbed a good bit from your letter which I hope you will forgive."

She had been doing her best, but unsuccessfully, to help me find a job and in the meantime insisted that I accept a loan from her. My efforts to get a Littauer fellowship at Harvard, despite her letter of recommendation, had failed. I decided to try the liberal weekly *The Nation*. "I will write Miss Kirchwey* about you," her note said, "and I will say my prayers!" The typist had put in "Very sincerely." She crossed that out and wrote "Affly." A follow-up note reporting uncertainty at *The Nation* over my qualifications, added warmly: "I want so much to see you. Would you feel like coming to breakfast this Wednesday the 8th at 8:30? I'll be getting in on the midnight. My thoughts have been [with] you. Affly. E.R."

She tried to get a contribution for the Congress from Dorothy Schiff Backer, the liberal publisher of the New York *Post*. Mrs. Backer not only refused to contribute because of the Communist control issue, but turned over to Eleanor a memorandum prepared by reporter Oliver

---

* Freda Kirchwey, publisher of *The Nation*.

Pilat on the Congress personnel. That evening Eleanor read part of it to me, including a paragraph that said I knew the score and, though not a Communist, because of loyalty to the Congress would never tell Mrs. Roosevelt.

I picked that up. I had a pretty fair idea of the political affiliations and loyalties of many of the people identified in the Pilat memorandum, but I had decided after my break with the Communists that I would fight them on the basis of policy. She must have been aware how I had been torn between loyalty to her and unwillingness to be an informer. I felt she should form her own judgments on the basis of what people said and did.

She was glad I did not tell her and preferred that I not do so, she said. She had given them every opportunity to tell her themselves. It would not have altered her personal relationship to them, but politically it would have, since she had fundamental disagreements with Communism and would not want to strengthen its position. But of course if now she were to discover some of them were Communists, that would affect her personal as well as political relation to them.

The President's meeting with the youth leaders was to take place on June 5, 1940. "If you are coming down with some particular friend for the meeting on the 5th of June, I will be delighted to have you both stay here. I shall be delighted to have you stay as long as you want to before or after the meeting, if you have other things to do." A postscript said: "I enjoyed City College but I'm so grateful that you took time off & went with me. I would have felt lost without you. I loved meeting your Mother too." The taxicab that had taken us downtown from City College went past my mother's grocery store on Morningside Heights. She had readily agreed to stop and meet my mother. She had never been able to interest me in becoming a businessman, my mother said to Mrs. Roosevelt when she had recovered her composure. Children rarely become what their parents want, Mrs. Roosevelt quietly replied. As she said goodbye she added that she had become very fond of me. Back in the taxi I expressed my gratitude because she had stopped to talk with my mother, but she halted me. "When you know your own weaknesses, you know that you are no better than other people, but because of your position have a greater chance to do good. You don't allow yourself false airs."

The Nazi armies had outflanked the Maginot Line and were racing towards Paris. Belgium and Holland lay prostrate. Roosevelt went before Congress to ask for a huge increase in defense expenditures. "My feelings were torn," my letter said, and also asked her to invite Agnes Reynolds, "between those of approval of his request for 50,000 planes as soon as possible and of sadness that it would have so little to do with the things that made life worth while and for which we have been concerned. I know the President could do and say little else. . . ."

She had little time for regrets for an anti-war position that she herself had put aside in the face of Hitler's aggressions: "Dear Joe," she wrote in longhand:

> I will write Aggie Reynolds & expect you both on the 3rd. I know how you felt for I've been feeling so much the same, but it is necessary to meet this particular force with force. Not being willing to face a situation & beclouding it with words that have little or no relation to reality doesn't help. I wrote Jean Horie [of the New York Youth Congress] today after reading the morning papers that I thought it only fair to warn her that next Sunday evening my speech could not be to the liking of the group & did she really want me. If she does I will go up by air & should get to them between 6:30 & 7. Do call up Stuyvesant 9-6848 (private number) on the morning of the 28th & perhaps we can get together.
>
> I start for West Virginia Wednesday morning & get back here Saturday morning.

She flew up to New York, leaving a very somber group around the President riveted to the bulletins reporting Nazi advances that poured in:

> Very foggy & we circled a long time & landed in Newark instead of Laguardia so I was very late for the Youth meeting. However, I got there & did rather badly & left before [Representative] Marcantonio spoke which probably looked as though I wouldn't listen to the other side! I wanted to hear FDR & just got in before he came on & I found the speech good.

"You don't want to go to war," she had said in defense of the President's rearmament program to the eleven hundred young people at Mecca Temple on West Fifty-fifth Street. "I don't want to go to war. But war may come to us." Marcantonio's attack on the defense program against which he had cast the only negative vote in the House of Representatives had brought the audience to its feet whistling and stamping. She was glad, she told me the next morning, that the President's speech had warned the conservatives that he would not undo "any of the great social gains we have made in these past years." She was not satisfied with her own speech. The Youth Congress applause, I commented, was probably meant to show appreciation for her personally, not for her views. "I was discouraged with those kids of the N.Y. Youth Council," she wrote to Hick. "Marcantonio's fervor & slogans appeal more than reason."

In retrospect, Mrs. Roosevelt's speech at the Mecca Temple was her last public appearance at a Youth Congress meeting, although she did bring its leaders together with the President, as she had promised. Half of the youth leaders who attended that meeting with the President were suggested by the Youth Congress,* the other half by myself and my friends. Eleanor was struck by the failure of the Youth Congress people to ask the President questions about his foreign policy after accusing him at public meetings of wanting to send troops to Europe.

During that troubled and tumultuous spring I had been telling her that the International Student Service (ISS), an organization that raised funds in the colleges for refugee students and helped place them there, was considering an expansion of its program. As a member of its board, I had been appointed to a small committee to plan that expansion. I told her about its new program—speakers and a conference bureau, work camps, and an organizational department—and said ISS might offset the Communist-dominated American Student Union. She would be willing to help, she told me.

When Aggie and I arrived at the White House before the meeting, Eleanor greeted us and showed us to our rooms. Tommy would fetch us at 4:30 for tea, she said, hastening off. In both rooms there were fresh roses. People came to unpack our bags. Bewildered, I said, "No, thank you." Tea was on the lawn. Several New Deal officials were guests, including Dr. Will Alexander, of the Farm Security Administration, and Arthur Altmeyer, head of the Social Security Board. When the latter remarked that the new Social Security building was about to be finished but might be preempted by the War Department, Eleanor's reply did not wholly reassure him. She hated to distract the President with problems that did not bear directly on the international crisis. As the tea ended she told us that we were free to go anywhere in the White House, but not to wander in on the President, who only wished to see the people he specifically asked for. She told us that Hick stayed in the White House when she was in Washington. One morning when Eleanor was away Hick had started determinedly towards the President's bedroom, telling the usher that she wanted only to say good morning to him. The usher gently led her away: "I do want to say good morning to the President. He was so nice to me last night."

It gave Eleanor pleasure, when Aggie and I came in at eleven that night, to take us to the mall so that we could see two of her favorite views, the reflection of the Washington Monument in the pool and the statue of a seated Lincoln, vibrant in the light. Back in her sitting room she spoke of how the second floor of the White House seemed alive

* See *Eleanor and Franklin,* page 609; *A Friend's Memoir,* pages 99–106.

with historical presences. Sometimes she imagined she heard Lincoln walking about. I realized that she kept her own joys and memories green by sharing them with people, particularly those she cared about. It was early morning when we said good-night. She was dressed brightly in a riding habit when we met the next morning for breakfast in the West Hall. She spoke more critically than ever about the leaders of the Youth Congress. Would I object to sharing my room with one of them that night?

We talked of leadership, as we did so often those days, not only because of the third term issue, but they were the days of Dunkirk and Winston Churchill's resolute effort to keep a collapsing France in the war. All great decisions have to be made alone, she said. Strong people have to be reconciled to going into eclipse temporarily. She had never asked the President his intentions in regard to a third term. That decision he had to make alone and she did not want to influence it by expressing her wishes.

Back in New York after the President's three-hour session with the youth leaders, many of whom asked hostile, rhetorical questions, I wrote to thank her. Had I given her the impression of skirting the problem of finding a job? "But where is one's post?" I asked. The defeat of Hitler was necessary, but it would not of itself assure a better world. I was worried about the way that reaction was using the emergency to get back into positions of command. And I said of many of the young people at the meeting with the President: "They weren't listening; they were telling the Government." The non-Communist group in the governing body of the Congress was meeting to plan its strategy for Geneva. If Mrs. Roosevelt wanted to reach me, I was spending a week in the country home of Mrs. Eliot Pratt, a fellow board member.

My questions helped her clarify her own thinking. My misgivings were those of many liberals. Yet important as it was to figure out what she herself thought, it wasn't easy amid the incessant calls on her. "Sometimes I think it is more hectic here," she wrote to Hick, and she was then at Hyde Park, "when FDR is home than in Wash . . . I feel as tho' a multitude of details obscured my ability to think about anything else!" She liked to think out loud with me. I was concerned with the larger issues: "I am devoted to the President and yourself for I consider you democracy's last best hope," I had written. Her continuing exchanges with me strengthened her for more public encounters. She answered my letter:

> I have been over your "Program for Democracy" and so has the President. I think it is very well arranged and very well done. The President was really pleased with it and so am I. Your choices seem to me excellent.
>
> Of course, you do not give the appearance of shirking the problem of

finding a job. I know exactly what you are going through and I think what the President said today in his speech* applies to you somewhat but I also think many of you young people are not recognizing the fact that while you cannot be sure of the future, there are immediate things that have to be handled now and we have to go on feeling confident in our ability to go on fighting for the other things in the future. I could tell you plenty of things about the way everyone of us here has to fight reaction every day and be on the look-out but that does not mean we must not use the people who sometimes unconsciously would push us back. They know nothing else and they may learn, and it keeps us alive trying to keep up with them!

I think you ought to be in some of the things down here and Mr. Hopkins and I have been talking about it. The President agrees but I am not perfectly sure that you want to be tied to a political party even temporarily. How would you feel about it?

I was surprised the other night that there were so few questions asked on foreign policy and I have a letter from Joe Cadden saying that he wished it had been a smaller meeting so certain questions could have been followed up.

I was amused by Elliott's reactions to the boy from Missouri. He said that he did not think him sincere and I am afraid that was my feeling too.

I had word from Mr. [Sumner] Welles [Under-Secretary of State] about Dr. Eliasberg and I asked him to cable at my expense for further information. I am terribly troubled because Italy has now declared war and I do not think the President's speech will make them feel any more kindly towards Americans or those we are trying to help.

Would you like to come up and spend some days with us at Hyde Park after we get settled? We will be driving up every Tuesday and Thursday so we could take you along if you feel like coming. You could work as much as you liked and in any case you would have to be prepared to look after yourself part of the time. I would be glad to ask anyone you wished to bring with you.

She sent me the note she had received from Sumner Welles on the case of Dr. Georg Eliasberg, one of the underground New Beginning people caught in Europe. That encouraged Karl Frank, the head of New Beginning, to ask to see her again—this time to ask her help to get a considerable number of labor and Socialist deputies away from the Continent. "Joe dear," she wrote me from Hyde Park:

I've written Mr. Frank & suggested that you & he come to breakfast at the apartment [in New York] next Tuesday at 8:30. I hope you can

---

* Roosevelt had spoken that day at the University of Virginia and in memorable words had denounced Mussolini: "On this tenth day of June, 1940, the hand that held the dagger has struck it into the back of its neighbor." Much of the speech, however, was addressed to youth: "It is right that each new generation should ask questions. But in recent months the principal question has been somewhat simplified. Once more the future of the nation and the American people is at stake."

come as that seems my only free time. The plight of the poor refugees in France is appalling but the chance of doing anything seems so slim. I've been working all week on some & see no results as yet. I think we got somewhere on children in England but I've not even seen how that will work out.

I'm enclosing the family ticket for you to take in coming up & will you come Saturday as I have to have a birthday party Friday for my brother & I don't think you would enjoy it—I don't always find it easy to manage myself. Do stay a week or more if you can & tell me if you want to bring anyone for all or part of the time.

I'm awfully glad you'd like to work in Washington & I'm beginning at once.

I've had a few intemperate letters but nothing to indicate much sympathy with the *Liberty* article [on youth].

Of course, if you'd like to come Friday in spite of Hall's party you are welcome, but be prepared for a good part of horse play & wildness!

I'm hoping to see you Tuesday, till then

> Affly yours,
> E.R.

She reported the outcome of the meeting with Karl Frank and his associate, Joseph Buttinger, to Hick:

Finally had Joe Lash & 2 German refugees for dinner. Poor people it is pitiful. They try to help their friends abroad & their hands are tied. I telephoned FDR but all he can say is that our people around are doing all they can.

At the end of June the Republicans met in Philadelphia and nominated Wendell Willkie, the colorful public utility executive and, it seemed, the grass-roots candidate of the Eastern internationalist wing of the party. But with France prostrate and Eleanor fearing that "it looks as tho' England might sue for peace," party politics seemed relatively far off. She reproached herself for her attitude: "Campaigns seem unimportant but perhaps it does matter." A few days later she was even more troubled: "The papers are discouraging to me since F. told me he really felt Willkie was a crook or words to that effect. I have a hunch he's going to win. What's yours? The lull in European news makes me dread the storm." Hick demurred:

No, I don't think Willkie is a crook, but I don't care for the crowd that is backing him . . . he will beat any Democrat except the President—& very likely the President. We are all having a bad time now at the office, trying not to get a defeatist attitude.

Defeat was not in Eleanor's code: every problem had a solution. Hick was on her way to the convention with Charley Michelson. She should get some fun out of it. "Don't get tired & don't get a defeatist attitude. Willkie can be beaten. The strategy must be good & the campaign well planned but he isn't so hard to beat—of that I feel sure." In particular it was necessary to get at "his essential indifference to labor."

Between the Republican and Democratic conventions, the sixth annual meeting of the American Youth Congress took place at Lake Geneva in Wisconsin. With the world awaiting Hitler's invasion of England and Roosevelt's decision on a third term, the youth meeting was a minor event, but it was important to Eleanor. She had refused the pleas of the Youth Congress leaders to speak at Lake Geneva: it would only draw more criticism on the Congress, she told them. In letters and talks with its leaders she repeatedly insisted that "the position of the AYC has got to be cleared up." She arranged to get reports from observers and participants of different backgrounds, especially her radio agent, Betty Lindley, and from me. Together with three others who shared my point of view we stopped off at Hyde Park on our way out to Lake Geneva. We went in Trude Pratt's car. We would find the atmosphere "cool," Eleanor predicted as she said goodbye, and, turning to me, whispered that I would find it "especially cool."

She sent me a note that I would receive on my return to New York:

If you are back in New York the 8th do call me at the apartment about 6:30 p.m. Would you care to come & stay here on Monday the 15th for a week & bring anyone you like? I'd love to have you & you can work or play as you wish.

I'm thinking of you this week & hoping it will not be a bitter experience for you. So far the first news stories have been fair & not hostile.

A long dispatch today from Bullitt & things look black in France. I'm doing what I can by reminding everyone about the refugees but I dread the true story of what is happening to them in German-occupied territory. The sinking of the British ship with refugees on board was horrible.

She had sensed that I seemed more than casually attracted by Trude Pratt, and her letter ended: "I liked Mrs. Pratt. She is not the one I had met before."

The Lake Geneva experience was not all that bad, I reported. The Communists and their allies were not prepared to abandon isolationism, and on key issues such as aid to England, support of the Administration, the need for universal service they voted down the opposition group. But they were chastened by the collapse of France, and leaned over backwards to give the opposition a hearing and elected several of us to the incoming Cabinet.

I returned East optimistic about the Congress's future. Eleanor was more reserved but confessed that she found Betty Lindley's report confusing. So incidentally did Hick, who had written to Eleanor from

Chicago that Betty had "hove in" on her on the way East: "She says that Abbot Simon, Joe Cadden, etc., were in full control and yet that everyone had a right to speak his mind, etc.—that the Communist crowd were running the show and yet they passed a resolution endorsing National Defense, and so on! I find it rather puzzling."

She had Betty's report, Eleanor replied, "& it is a good one but the confusing factors are what always have been confusing to me. They are so contradictory." Privately she continued to support the activities she agreed with, but avoided further public identification.

She was preoccupied with the Democratic convention. F.D.R. was in Washington, she at the cottage in Hyde Park when it took place. She still did not know his decision about a third term. "I do hope it won't be a long convention," she wrote to Hick, "but if it is I feel sure FDR won't run & that for me would be a pleasant certainty." A few months earlier she had wondered why she was so indifferent to Hyde Park's beauty. Now with Tommy there, Earl and myself moving in and out, it had become precisely the refuge she always had wanted. "Joe Lash came at noon for a week & in the afternoon Earl & his Albany young lady turned up, so we all played games & swam & sunned from about 4 p.m. on."

Mrs. Roosevelt has written about the nominating convention and her part in it, but for me, who spent the week at the cottage with her, the days had an idyllic, enchanted quality. Games, high politics, and the most astonishing insights into Eleanor's life seemed to chase each other all week long. "Mrs. R. tries to dive," I wrote in the diary that I carefully recorded at the end of each day, "takes a deep breath and plunges but invariably lands flat with her legs bent at the knees. Earl kids her mercilessly." The latter's little blond friend, Simone von Haver, would stand in the water legs akimbo. He swam under and threw her up in the air. Simone wanted Earl to do the same with Mrs. Roosevelt. "Not even for you two," she said laughingly. The four played ring tennis at the net beside the pool, Earl joining her, Simone with me. "We were defeated even tho' we had the advantage of Mrs. R.'s being on Earl's side."

After dinner she and I talked as the dusk thickened. I asked whether I might invite Trude over and she agreed, asking about her background. She never gave advice, she said. She had always tried to get her children to talk to her, but advice, no; one can never be certain one's advice is correct. When she was young she did not have anyone to whom she could talk.

My work with ISS had brought me increasingly into contact with Mrs. Eliot (Trude) Pratt. She was an attractive, German-born socialite, or so I thought her, blond, blue-eyed, vivacious, who seemed to know everyone, and who, it turned out, had her earned doctorate from Frei-

burg before she came to the United States in 1932 and married Eliot
D. Pratt.

Mrs. Roosevelt readily agreed to see Trude. We had gone on talking.
She asked about my friends, and whether I saw much of my family,
which I confessed I didn't. She spoke very fondly of Isabella Greenway,
but the only interesting women to talk with in Washington, she had
found, were the newspaper girls. Most of the wives were afraid of com-
promising their husbands. When I mentioned that my father had died
when I was nine, she recalled feelingly her own father. I recorded in my
diary:

> She did not like the idea of speaking because the President could say
> things so much more effectively, and if she said things that he later
> said the cry of 'petticoat' government would go up. She would be ac-
> cused of making up the President's mind and it could get under the
> President's skin. It would get under anyone's skin.
>
> She did not relish another four years of glaring publicity and big
> crowds. She liked to be with the people she really cared about, do the
> things she really was interested in and see a job to its conclusion. This
> way she had to champion many causes because her position imposed a
> duty and responsibility.
>
> She never could understand why she was called upon to do things
> like going to Chicago. She was not important or influential. I said I
> would like to read the history books a hundred years from now. I was
> not prepared to say the President's personal impact, as distinct from
> that of the office, would be greater than her own on the times. I was
> crazy she said. The function of women was to ease things along,
> smooth them over. They were not main movers.

I had the impression she was not wholly displeased with what I said,
even though she was not able to accept it consciously. She had been
brought up with the concept of woman as a nurturing presence who
gets her way by selflessness, and though she lived up to such ideals of
womanhood, she also believed in strong women, who lived and judged
independently. The head of the Democratic Women's Division, Mrs.
Dorothy McAllister, wanted her help to resist the convention's adop-
tion of a resolution in favor of the Equal Rights Amendment. From the
time at the end of World War I when she had become interested in
such matters she had battled the amendment as a manufacturers' plot
to get rid of the special legislation that protected women in regard to
wages, hours, and working conditions. Now she had begun to change
her position: ". . . I've sent her to Chicago the message she wanted on
the Equal Rights Amendment. I wish Industrial Women would get
fully organized so we didn't have to continue this fight."

After consulting Franklin, Jim Farley, and Hick, she flew out to
Chicago. It was an unruly, tumultuous convention in rebellion against

the President's insistence on Henry Wallace as his running mate. She calmed and inspired it, her speech eliciting a tribute from Senator George Norris, the dean of American progressives:

> Sen. George Norris has written me a letter which I think I shall always be proud of. I must have done better than I realized. It is just something to be thankful for, one might so easily fail!

She was gone less than a day from the cottage. The delegates were "like lambs," she told the little group at the cottage. I recorded: "Now she's taking a bath and will be ready for a full day again which includes a swim, a column, letters, picnic with 30 Hudson Shore Labor School people, and dinner with Mrs. James [Roosevelt]." When the Hudson Shore group arrived, they were full of questions for her. She had one request for them, to sing "Joe Hill."

"I am glad you were satisfied with my job in Chicago," she wrote to Hick. The next day there was a sense of relief. "All my guests have gone & quiet reigns. . . . I had a good walk & swim in the morning & I'm getting better at the ring-throwing game, tho' none too good." She and Tommy had taken Henry and me to the train and she had spoken with F.D.R., who arrived for the funeral of an aunt in Newburgh, New York:

> I tried to tell FDR about the feelings I thought Jim [Farley], Charlie [Michelson] etc. had & he agreed to see them all, map the campaign, etc. but he feels much worse because he thinks the newspapers decided to make Harry [Hopkins] the goat & his feelings are hurt! FDR is busy & happy in his library where cases have begun to arrive. He seems obsessed with the idea that the soothsayers say whoever is elected this year won't live out their time so he talks all the time of Wallace as successor.

Trude Pratt came over to talk with Mrs. Roosevelt. I had thought she wanted to talk about her personal affairs, but she had turned shy. Instead they discussed where she might serve in the campaign. She was a flirt and found my warnings that I might take her more seriously to be a challenge. "Have I ever thanked you for having taken me to Mrs. Roosevelt?" wrote Trude afterwards. "She makes the air seem fresher even on a sultry afternoon. It makes me happy that *you* introduced me."

My personal affairs were in a mess. So Eleanor discovered as she got to know me better. It seemed to her that I was taken with Trude, but planned to marry Aggie, and was not legally divorced from the girl I had married in 1935. Nancy and I had separated amiably in 1937, but neither could accumulate enough money to go out to Reno. When

Eleanor found that out, she told me it was up to Nancy and me to decide what we wanted to do, but the relationship should be straightened out and she would lend me the money to pay the fare out to Reno if that was what Nancy and I decided to do.

The book of Roosevelt extracts on which I had been working was rejected by the publisher who asked for his advance ($100) back. When I declared myself a "bust," she put me in touch with the Home Library publishers and sought to reassure me: "I am not as convinced as you are that it is your work. I think Mr. S. may have other influences." The new publisher took the manuscript, changed it drastically, and put it out without my name, as I requested.

The more troubles I had, the more she insisted on helping me, the closer she felt drawn to me. When I went down to Washington, she urged that I stay at the White House:

I thought this clipping might interest & amuse you in spots.

I hope the week is going well & the White House isn't too gloomy. I'll be there Sunday in time for 7:30 supper on the porch if you happen to be free to join me. The President says he won't get back till 8:30 or 9. Tommy & I will be coming back on the 3 p.m. train Monday & if you are coming that day we'll expect you to share our drawing room & to dine with us somewhere in N.Y. if you feel like it!

The President goes back tonight & I spend tomorrow at the headquarters in N.Y. again. Franklin jr. went to work there yesterday & I've had four telephones already on the 'young democrats' who seem to be causing quite a headache!

She invited me to spend August at Hyde Park and, having to be away, left a welcome note for me:

So sorry not to be here, but welcome back. When Mrs. Huntington leaves I'm putting you in her little room so whoever comes you will be undisturbed & please use my porch to work or read.

We found it easy to talk to each other. She showed me a copy of the speech that Lord Halifax, the British Foreign Secretary, had made to the students of Oxford University, and that led to the subject of bringing up children. I doubted my ability to do a good job. She questioned this. She had not done a good job herself because she had been so unsure in the early days of her marriage. She and the President had little money then. The President's mother, however, had a good deal, which she lavished upon the children, believing that it was a good way to hold their affection. Eleanor had resented it greatly. "The only thing you can do for people is to love them and thereby give them a sense of security so that they know they can come to you and get understanding and forgiveness, even though they know that you disapprove of what they have done."

She spoke of young Franklin's charm and wondered whether his marriage would last. Anna was the one among her children who had developed the most in understanding and compassion. "The Morgenthaus," she stressed, "have done a very good job with their children." The clock on the mantelpiece tolled midnight. "We locked the doors and said goodnight. Mrs. R. patted my head and said 'nice child.'"

Several Youth Congress leaders came to the cottage. Everyone swam, played ring tennis, but when they went over the resolution that the Congress had adopted at Lake Geneva the conversation occasionally became tense, especially in regard to conscription. The Youth Congress spokesmen picked away at the civil liberties aspects of it. When had any of them, I wanted to know, ever spoken in favor of selective service, or, for that matter, military preparedness, or a larger army? That was not their job, Joe Cadden argued. I subsequently chided them for refusing to acknowledge that there was a Communist problem in the Congress. That really made discussion pointless, I said. Mrs. Roosevelt looked surprised and said I had never before said the Congress was so heavily under Communist influence. That troubled me. When she stopped by my room at midnight, I remarked I had not been aware that I had spoken more sharply about Communist domination with the Youth Congress leaders than I had with her. I had no compunction about challenging them to their faces. She had reacted the way she did, she explained, because she did not want the Youth Congress people to feel I had said those things previously behind their backs. "Then she added that someone had to protect them even if they were all Communists. They had to feel some sense of security."

The Youth Congress gradually was receding as a matter of primary concern. Too much else was going on. The Morgenthaus were in and out, and, I noted with amusement, how the President and secretary commented about their "two Eleanors." There was an evening's discussion at the Big House about Charles Lindbergh, and when someone commented that anyway he was sincere, "Yes, sincere fascist," remarked the very respectable Alice Huntington. Afterwards Mrs. Roosevelt talked with me in the dark on the porch. She had never felt comfortable in the Big House. Mrs. James still did not approve of her. "Her concept of a woman's role was to be pleasing to men which was the way she, too, had been brought up by her grandmother. . . . Mrs. James was still not reconciled to her public activities. Feels she does not do for Franklin what she ought to be doing, yet somehow senses that she has been of real help." Eleanor had wanted to send their children to public school; Mrs. James had vetoed that.

They were fascinating comments, critical to an understanding of the Roosevelt household. None of them figured in the Ruby Black biography. That she made them to me was a measure of how much she had come to trust me. "She said I had become part of the family and hoped I didn't mind being considered such. Last night when she said goodnight she kissed me on the forehead and said again, 'nice child, so glad to have you here.' " We drove down to New York together, each with a separate mission, and returned at the end of the day. She talked with Ed Flynn, who had replaced Jim Farley as head of the campaign:

I lunched with Ed Flynn today & think he's going to be a tough boss but very satisfactory to work with. Things will be well organized or he'll know the reason why & he's going to put us all on our toes as to expenditures as he thinks it will be hard to raise money.

"Don't sound as if you will never see me again—unless you are voyaging off to remote and inaccessible places," I wrote to Trude. "I drove to New York yesterday with Mrs. Roosevelt and called you on the slight chance you might be in New York."

I told Mrs. Roosevelt of my call and also told her other news that Trude had communicated: "The first letter from my mother [in German] arrived—since the beginning of May. My oldest brother was not killed but taken prisoner and returned when France fell! My youngest brother was wounded in the battle of France. Sometimes the division that goes through my whole life is hard to bear.* As I can only wish German defeat, it would be better if I could hate the German people instead of only the idea of Naziism. It is stupid to think that way—I know!"

Elinor Morgenthau was often at Val-Kill. At Eleanor's picnic for Democratic women from the five adjacent counties, four hundred were expected, eight hundred came. Eleanor answered their questions with aplomb. After a while, Mrs. Morgenthau took refuge in the cottage, looking slightly battered. The next day, joined by the Clarence Picketts, we all went up to Tivoli, Eleanor's girlhood home, and she regaled her friends with stories of her life there. To Hick she wrote: "The house is falling down, but the place is still lovely."

Another sign of her increasing acceptance of me was Tommy's cordiality. Tommy was so suspicious that people might try to use Mrs. Roosevelt that she personally avoided making friends. By the summer she trusted me sufficiently to tell me about the rift between Eleanor's household and that of Nan and Marion. After she and Mrs. Roosevelt returned from an inspection trip with the President over the Labor Day weekend, she confided her worries about the Youth Congress to me.

---

* The division was there, although this information turned out to have been inaccurate. Her eldest brother had escaped from a prison camp in France and her youngest brother was not wounded in France but later blinded at Stalingrad.

Good reporters on the train, all of them, she said, and an enlightened woman like Mrs. Ickes had said to her that a lot of people were losing confidence in Mrs. Roosevelt's judgment because she still defended the Congress.

Once that summer, on the way to the Berkshire Festival, we picnicked in a pasture, and after Eleanor had shooed away a mild invasion of cows, she asked me what I had thought when she came to the Dies Committee hearings. I said that I had debated with myself whether I should urge her not to come, but decided she would resent it. She replied that she would not have resented it, but would have come.

Back at the cottage after the concert she brought out copies of David Grayson's *Adventures in Solitude*, *The Countryman's Year*, and Edna Ferber's *Nobody's in Town*. They were "great favorites," she explained, and I might like to read them.

When I came down to breakfast the next morning, Earl was there. He was constantly in and out, an obvious favorite of "the Lady's." A couple of weeks earlier, the electricity had gone out during a storm. "Alice, Tommy & I took it calmly while Earl dashed around lighting candles." This time he had arrived sporting a large Willkie button. It outraged Mrs. Roosevelt's chauffeur, but it did not ruffle her.

On the way to the Morgenthaus' for dinner, Ruby Black's biography again came up. Biography should be written only after a person is dead, Eleanor maintained. Only then could the truth be told. Tommy and Hick and her Aunt Maude would span her whole life, she went on, but not even Tommy knew everything because some things belonged to other people.

Later at the cottage she and I sat on her porch. I read while she worked on the mail. I wrote in my diary: "Again said I should consider myself part of her family and like her children could come to her with my joys and sorrows. I could come whenever I wanted to. But I should watch out—to be known as her friend was dangerous and life would be made difficult for me."

In her next letter to Hick she wrote:

I slept part of the way up yesterday p.m. & read the papers which are horrible to me these days. I have a deep discouragement about the world these days & would like to run away from having to face it. If I feel that way what must other less secure people feel.

She "had Franklin with Bill Donovan* doing most of the talking," during a picnic supper at Val-Kill. "FDR sent him on a secret mission

* A leading Irish-American, colonel with the Rainbow Division in World War I, a Republican and later head of the Office of Strategic Services (OSS), in World War II.

& he has come back with a conviction that England can hold out & will & that we ought to help."

On another trip to town to see Ed Flynn she was stopped by the reporter for the Republican *Herald Tribune:* "I wouldn't know anything about politics," she insisted blandly. "I never make any campaign speeches." She had discussed Fjr.'s role at campaign headquarters with Flynn, who very much wanted him there. She also put in a good word for me and with the women for Trude Pratt. "Fjr. has spent a tough day at your headquarters," she wrote to Hick, "but I think he is going to like it & be good at it. He is coming here tomorrow for lunch & to get a little more dope. I hope you'll see him now & then & steer him a bit." A week later she is querying Hick: "Do you hear about him at headquarters?" Isabella Greenway had come out for Willkie, and Eleanor's reaction was:

I'm a bit weary of having her reasoning always so pure but I know she thinks she is doing the right thing & with her new husband she could scarcely do otherwise.

In conversation with me later she was sharper. It had been reported to her that one reason Isabella was against the Roosevelts was that they were too much under the influence of the Jews. Mrs. Roosevelt said she was unable to believe this. She hoped it was not true. If it was she could not bring herself to speak to Isabella again.

She found it difficult to break down my reticences. Although she tried to get her friends to call her "Eleanor," they, including me, were not quite able to manage it. Hick took refuge in "Madam." My friend Aggie suggested "Aunt Eleanor":

I agree with you that Aggie's 'Aunt Eleanor' is nice & I wish you'd call me that. I'll like a sense of relationship with you even an adopted one!
I thought you would feel [Gustave] Regler's* letter. It is a horrible world but one has to fight for a better one or die, so we go on but one is tired at times. I've been in N.Y. all day, at headquarters, trying to help Franklin jr., to whom Mr. Flynn has given all youth activities to supervise, sort himself out a little. He's telephoning you tomorrow. I also saw the southern women, held Mrs. McAllister's hand, talked to Ed. Flynn & Hick & had Mr. Taussig for lunch & spent 3 hours on the way home with the Girl Scouts in camp.† They have girls from all the countries in this hemisphere & it was fun talking with them. Now I'm doing the mail, so you see I'm not twiddling my thumbs even if I don't write as I should! My love to you.

* German novelist and refugee. He had fought with the International Brigade in Spain and now was in Mexico seeking admission into the United States.
† Dorothy McAllister, headed women's work at Democratic headquarters. Charles Taussig, head of the American Molasses Company and chairman of the Advisory Committee of the National Youth Administration.

A week later she was worried about where to put the visiting Norwegians:

> We have a hat we think is yours since we've asked everyone else we can think of & no one claims it. Have you missed a nice straw hat?
>
> I was really sorry to miss you today but glad to see Molly Yard's little sister. I shall be most anxious to hear how things go next week. I'm going to be fairly busy here the next few days & just now I have no idea where I'm going to put everyone who is apparently coming to stay tomorrow. The President is delightfully bland & says 'oh! you'll find some place!' Nine Norwegians, plus 6 or 8 Americans seem to add up to more beds than the house contains! Did you read Ralph Ingersoll's page on the choice of governments we had before us? It was in yesterday's *P.M.* & I thought interesting. Anna's written me an interesting letter on politics out there which I'll read you as it may be of use even with your young people.
>
> I hope I'll see you next Wed. for breakfast.

For the first time she looked at Harry Hopkins critically. It seemed as though the closer he came to F.D.R., the farther he moved away from her. "Harry Hopkins amuses me, he would not have come this weekend had royalty not been here." The next day she was sharper: "I'm feeling a bit disillusioned in Harry Hopkins but I may be unjust."

After the Norwegians—"& I shall be glad for them when they are by themselves"—came the Austrians: "I've just been notified that on Sunday we have all the exiled Austrians for lunch. I find royalty heavy & boring. I long for my mother-in-law to do the honors tho' managing the house is far easier without her."

A group of undergraduates who were connected with the Roosevelt College Clubs and whom I shepherded to Washington for a meeting with Senator Norris on why he was for Roosevelt received no play in the press. Why did I not show the release to Hick? Mrs. Roosevelt suggested. "It's beautiful stuff," Hick advised her, and she would edit it for the young people. Eleanor wrote her:

> I'm glad you are going to help the kids with the Norris statement. It ought to get out. Joe Lash was depressed. He drove up with me to the ISS lunch & I could see it was a real disappointment & he feels it more than Fjr. who has had so much success that he never looks at anything as a setback! I agree with you that Fjr. is putting a lot into the campaign but now he's got to put a lot into passing his exams & Ethel is worried for fear he won't. I guess her family will make it hard if he fails!

Her next letter to Hick again contrasted me with her own children:

> I'm glad you like Joe & think well of him. It seems to me he has promise but so many ideals that earning a living is going to be hard! My

children could better afford the ideals & they are not touched with them!

My vulnerability together with a resolute adherence to my values touched her. Anything I asked of her she tried to do. She enjoyed counseling me about my domestic problems:

I never seem to get time to show you things which I think might interest you or to ask you things I really want to know!

I suppose you are wise to give up your apartment since you may be in N.Y. or Washington after the campaign but will you be happy at home? Don't do anything to make life any harder just now. Even if you took a single room somewhere it might be better than having less privacy at home, but I may be wrong, only I wanted you to think about it.

. . . .

I wish I could help you just now dear boy, but there is little one can do for one's children or one's friends but love them & stand back of them. As time goes I've known you a very short time but I have a real sense of kinship & understanding & I'd like you to feel you had a *right* to my love & interest & that my home was always yours when you needed it or anything else which I have. . . .

Perhaps I can see you for a little while next Wednesday—I'd like very much if we can find even a half hour when we are *both* free!

My dear love to you,

E.R.

She rather relished it when my friend Aggie and I stood up to Harry Hooker over conscription. He had supported conscription before World War I and was inordinately proud of a letter he had written to Woodrow Wilson to that effect. Although he now derided Aggie and me as "dreamers" when we spoke of young people wanting assurances that this war would be the last, Eleanor was with us:

Thanks for returning all the things I had sent you & for letting me see your letter to Mr. Hooker. I feel as you do that there must come a day such as we long for & only because I believe that, is it worth fighting on trying to keep the gains & add to them as we live our little lives.

Your own letter is very precious to me & I hope that you & I help each other to live up to 'our' beliefs, in ourselves & in each other. . . .

I wrote you a line to the office since I wasn't sure of your hotel. Do you want 2 tickets for the Dubinsky* play Sat. night & would you alone or with a friend like to join me for dinner beforehand & drive back to the cottage for Sunday? If you come up do plan to stay till the early train on Monday morning.

Tommy & I drove over here this afternoon. The colors are beautiful going on to Provincetown tomorrow & to Johnny & Anne for Wednes-

---

* David Dubinsky, president of the International Ladies' Garment Workers' Union.

day night & home on Thursday. I am glad to get here [Westbrook, Connecticut] for my friend Miss [Elizabeth] Read is far from well & she seems to enjoy seeing us. . . .

For a time she signed her letters "Aunt Eleanor," but both of us found that form of address stilted and after a few tries we gave it up for "E.R." and "Dearest E.R."

I did not quite understand her taking off in the middle of the campaign and spending a day in Provincetown, visiting Johnny and Anne in Nahant, Massachusetts, and coming back by way of the Mohawk Trail. Great as was her feeling for autumn foliage, I wondered whether her absence from Hyde Park and Washington was not some form of silent protest about her role in the campaign, connected perhaps with her remark to me when the President decided to campaign: "I wish now I could be with Franklin for his speeches but he said he wasn't going to campaign." The clue to his keeping her at arm's length may have rested in the next paragraph of her letter, which was written from the White House:

I think I am going to get into trouble over a colored convention of women which Mrs. [Mary] Bethune asked me to have for one session here this p.m. It appears that they are mainly Republicans & the Democrats are annoyed but I am having them because of their interest in youth problems & not because of their interest in politics!

You were a dear to come in & see me off last night. I do love having you around! Till tomorrow.

She wrote two letters that day, the second, for it was her fifty-sixth birthday, gently protested my extravagance in sending her Carl Sandburg's book about Lincoln:

Of course I'm delighted to have the "Prairie Years" & your friend's book but you shouldn't have been so extravagant. I wish you would remember that what I really enjoy & deeply appreciate is your thought & affection & I don't want you to spend hard earned money on me! Just the same a thousand thanks dear boy & say a little prayer that both you & I will have enough leisure to read *all* the Sandburg some day!

I'm enclosing an itinerary. You will wonder why & not want to be bothered with it, but I always, when I go away, give the people who have a right to reach me, if they wish, these lists! You are one of those people & you don't have to communicate with me. It is just in case you felt the need.

Meet me Sat. at the Hotel Algonquin West 44th St. at 1:15 & I'll try to be on time.

I saw some good N.Y.A. projects yesterday. A boy of 26 heads up the best one I've seen, it really was thrilling.

I've discovered one thing which makes me feel a bit better about Elliott's situation. Gen. Arnold* says he couldn't be accepted in the draft or in the army as a private because, without glasses, he can't see more than 10 ft. He can only get in on a commission on account of experience as a specialist of some kind, so resigning would do no good & he might as well stay put. Of course in case of war many of these regulations will go & then he could change. I am sorry for him & sorry for the effect on the young people but knowing he couldn't get in as a private makes me feel less badly about 'sitting tight.'

I talked with the President last night & he left me with the feeling that he might be called back for Japan's soft speech makes them all suspicious!

I wished for you to be here Wed. evening when young [Alan] Lomax spent the night & sang folk songs for us. I hope he can come in [word indecipherable] sometime when you are there. My love to you & thanks again.

A postscript from Tommy: "I was so pleased you did not over-look Mrs. R's birthday, although you were too extravagant. Not one of your AYC colleagues sent as much as a penny postcard!"

She had rarely seen a dirtier campaign, she wrote to Hick from the West Coast, where she visited James and his wife, watching the former drill and flying to Seattle to see Anna and the children. Hick had criticized Elliott's acceptance of a commission. The Republicans had turned it into a campaign issue with the issuance of buttons that read, I WANT TO BE A CAPTAIN TOO. "If I said anything that hurt you, please forgive me, I realize, as well as you do, I think, that Elliott has honestly tried not to take advantage of his father's position, and I'm awfully sorry for him now," wrote Hick. Eleanor also was contrite: "I probably sounded more vehement than I felt. All these things seem relatively academic to me even Pegler & wasn't he poisonous two days ago about all of us?"

She was remarkably detached about the possibility of Franklin's losing. She wrote to me:

Don't worry about Nov. 5th dear you have done your best for the things you believed in. If the Republicans win it will mean that the majority wanted Willkie & Ham Fish as Ch. of the Foreign Affairs Com. We are democrats & believe in the will of the people, don't we?

She again sounded the note about the people's will to Hick a few days later:

FDR has evidently been persuaded he must go out & see audiences. Perhaps it is as well, in any case, I like the out & out political speeches with no camouflage. I've never seen so much scurrilous stuff in print &

* General Henry "Hap" Arnold, head of the United States Army Air Force.

by hand since the Smith campaign but I don't get excited because the outcome rests with the people & if they want Wilkie [*sic*] I'm willing!

Back in New York she and Trude Pratt gave a dinner for the Work Camp program of ISS (International Student Service). It was "very nice & I hope will bring in some money." She had simplified her attitude towards the campaign to almost aphoristic brevity:

> Pegler & [General Hugh] Johnson were poisonous tonight. I'll be glad for the kids sake when the campaign is over! If FDR wins I'll be glad for him & for the country & if he loses I'll be glad for myself & the kids!

Hick filled her in on the turbid politics of the Women's Division, especially of the State Committee, where Nancy Cook was in control:

> Betty [Lindley] says Nan's latest is to have some sort of radio dictaphone installed in Jean Poletti's* office so she can hear everything that goes on. Can you beat it? She must be losing her senses.

She added that Mrs. Eliot Pratt, for whom this was the first campaign, "can't understand why the State Committee acts the way it does."

Nancy's divorce in Reno came through two weeks before Election Day. It evoked an article and a teasing editorial in the Republican *Sun* in New York, but my private fear that it might become a campaign issue abated when the press showed no interest in the item. Neither did it alarm Eleanor.

Hyde Park on Election Day was something special and she asked me to come up:

> I imagine you have to vote before you come up on election day for the night so I enclose the ticket & a time table & try to get the earliest train you can. I've marked the trains which are best & I'll probably meet you myself, if not look for Schaeffer.
>
> Now that election day draws near there are questions I long to ask you about your plans. Will you think me very impertinent! It was nice picking you & Aggie up last night but I wish you could have gone back to the Biltmore with us & talked a while. How did you like the speech? . . .

The next day she spoke at Colby College in Maine:

> As I listened to the radio yesterday noon & heard the draft numbers read I found myself thinking of you & hoping that your number would not come up. I want you so much to get started along lines which you can follow & develop into great influence & use to others of the younger generation & I would hate to see you put it off for a year of army train-

* Wife of Charles Poletti, Lieutenant Governor of New York.

ing. However if you have to we'll have to hope that you will find something developing in it. I don't feel the same about my boys, except Fjr. whom I would like to see take his bar exams in March.

I wish I had asked you to write me what happened. Oh! dear, I suppose I'm becoming a burden as a friend & I don't want to be. Forgive me, but I wanted you to know I was thinking about you. . . .

On Election Day my train was met by her chauffeur, whom all called "Schaeffer." A penciled note explained:

We have to go up to the polls at noon to please the press. Schaeffer will take you to the cottage where you have the double room which you can find I know & then will bring you on over to the big house to join us for lunch.

It's grand to have a chance to see you & have you with us today, no matter what happens! Love.

After lunch at the Big House she and I went on a long walk, and I recorded:

Talked about the next 4 years. Said she hoped Pres. would do all the things that he has wanted to do and knew had to be done but had not done because of political considerations. Again expressed anxiety that victory should be clearcut so that there would not be a repetition of the last 4 years. For herself she saw with horror 4 more years in the White House.

We went back to the Big House for tea. Later, on the way back to the cottage, she chided me—she had done it before—for my fears that I might hurt her by being seen with her. She could understand fear of "notoriety." Earl, who was at Hyde Park, shrank from being seen in public with her. She could also understand it if I was afraid that being seen with her might hurt my standing with young people, but I should not be concerned with hurting her. We went back to the Big House to listen to the returns. At 2:30 A.M. I went into the dining room to say good-night to the reelected President: "We seem to have averted a putsch, Joe," was his stark good-night.

Eleanor, Earl, and I drove back to the cottage. Tommy, Mrs. Helm, and Henry were still listening to the returns. Later I wrote: "E.R. went to work on mail. I to bed."

Hick, in a note explaining why she was glad the Democrats had won, added a revealing line: ". . . and hoped you were not too low in your mind." Eleanor replied the next day:

No, I don't look forward to the next four years for I will probably be too old for a new job at the end & I dread getting accustomed to 4 more years of easy living but perhaps I can keep from being too dependent on it. Anyway what is the use of worrying about tomorrow let alone 4 yrs from now.

In conferences with Ed Flynn, Molly Dewson, and others, Eleanor now set about trying to get jobs for Hick and myself. Hick thought she would do well as executive director of the Women's Division of the Democratic National Committee. Ed Flynn agreed to the appointment, but the support of Molly Dewson, who had been summoned from retirement in Maine to direct women's work during the campaign, was essential. Flynn was off to Santo Domingo for a holiday and did not want to decide until after his return, Eleanor informed Hick. And Molly Dewson, although she liked Hick, feared that the latter would have little time for the women who did not have a professional approach, yet whose support of the division was necessary. A little annoyed, Hick replied that neither Mrs. Roosevelt nor Molly should worry that she might "get bored or impatient with the ladies." She was forty-seven and unable to afford being choosy, she added.

Eleanor reassured Hick. Whatever Hick's drawbacks, she told Molly Dewson, Eleanor would work with her and stand behind her, and fortunately, Eleanor added to Hick, everyone agreed that whoever was chosen should have her confidence.

I constituted a more difficult problem. Government people were afraid to be identified with me. I took this more seriously than she did. Despite her plea on Election Day that I need not worry about embarrassing her because of my radical background, I remained deeply conscious of such a possibility. I had run into it too often during the campaign. When she had urged Ed Flynn to use me during the campaign, the National Chairman, although friendly, said he did not want me at Democratic headquarters and shunted me off to the Norris-LaGuardia Committee for independents. At that committee Tom Corcoran, while unwilling to finance a youth division, did put me on, but felt it prudent to keep me under cover as he did himself. Aubrey Williams, one of the most outspoken of progressives, had cautioned me that I would take an awful beating if I were to become a front man in a youth operation for F.D.R. "After election," he added, "you can write your own ticket."

When, therefore, the Board of International Student Service, a well-regarded non-governmental group in the world of education and student assistance, invited me to become its general secretary in connection with its expanded program, I decided to accept. The salary was four thousand dollars a year, which was generous for the time. I would not be responsible for raising the budget, and Trude Pratt, a key member of its board, eager herself to step out of the role of wealthy so-

cialite volunteer, strongly urged me to accept. I consulted Eleanor, who
said that she would help the new program in any way she could.

She and Tommy were off on a lecture trip in the Midwest when I
wired her the news that I had been appointed. "You'll do a grand job.
Much love," she telegraphed back, followed by a letter full of warm
counsel:

> It was grand to get your wire last night. You will do a fine, constructive
> job & I hope you will make me useful wherever you think it possible.
> Of course you will be worth the salary but start in & save some. You
> are so generous that it will be easy for you to spend it.
>
> I've thought of you often this week & hoped to hear from you. I'm
> spoiled by these past months when I've had a chance to see you often
> & I've grown to depend on you & enjoy being with you.
>
> Tommy sends her congratulations, she says warm ones & affectionate
> good wishes & if she is ever out of work, do you need a secretary? I'll
> tell you, so you won't be too hopeful that I see no prospect of her
> being without work! She's been busy as a whole hive of bees on this
> trip.
>
> It has been an easy trip, good audiences & I think the lectures have
> gone well. I've got to find some new lectures they will take however be-
> cause I get bored with the same subject. I've talked six times this
> trip on "The Individual's Responsibility to the Community," & it is
> very hard not to get stale.
>
> I suppose you are in your apartment & sent my wire there this morn-
> ing. Please send me your telephone number for if I knew it I would
> call you now & while my plans are a bit uncertain as the President
> hasn't told me whether we were surely going to H.P. I do want to see
> you the first chance that I have when you are not busy.
>
> We'll be back in Washington Wed. a.m. & if the President hasn't
> gone to H.P. & is going I'll go up with him that night, but he may be
> going ahead or he may not go at all! Anyhow I'm coming to N.Y. on
> Sunday the 24th for several days. Perhaps you'd take me to see your
> apartment that afternoon & could you keep Tuesday evening free if
> nothing very pleasant or important turns up? Mr. Robert Spivack*
> wants to see me & I think I want you there & there may be something
> pleasant I'd like you to do that evening.
>
> Monday afternoon I plan to get your things & mine from the 65th
> St. house & I'll take them to your apartment.
>
> I have two tickets if you care to have them for Marian Anderson's
> concert at Carnegie Hall on Dec. 1st in the evening.
>
> The 30,000,000 group asked me to hold Monday evening but I have
> heard nothing more, do you know if they are having a meeting?
>
> I mustn't wander on any more. You will have a hard enough time
> reading this! My heart is singing for you & I'm grateful you are to have
> this opportunity to help youth. Take care of yourself & much love dear
> boy.

* A former general secretary of ISS.

I immediately wrote and asked whether she'd be free to speak to the first ISS conference on students in politics over the Christmas holidays. I also described the pleasures of my new apartment, where I had started a fire in the fireplace, lit a pipe, and leisurely read the *Times* and *Daily Worker*. She telephoned, for I had included my new telephone number. Later she wrote:

> You sound so content & busy & happy & I'm so interested in all the plans. I'll keep your letters so I won't forget any of the things I want to talk over with you. I think I can plan to be with you Dec. 28th but I can't be sure yet awhile.
>
> . . . .
>
> I'm sorry about the A.Y.C. but there are too many constructive things to work on now to bother about unconstructive ones. I think some exciting things are coming along which I hope I can tell you about.

Would I pick her up on the twenty-fourth at Radio City, where she had to broadcast? Afterwards she wrote to Hick:

> I came to town this morning & spent from 1–3 getting ready & going on the Chicago radio hour, then Joe Lash called for me & we walked down town & he showed me his new apartment. Having got the job he liked he's in the seventh heaven. Then I came home & had two friends of Earl's for cocktails & dinner as he is down preparatory to going off for his naval reserve month's cruise tomorrow morning.

My diary read:

> She likes my apt. As I feared, she is going to send me many more things in addition to stuff she bestowed on me from the 65th Street house. Will send me a dropleaf table from HP and firewood. Said she had already gotten me my birthday gift, so there was nothing to be done about that.
>   Confessed she had not really been concerned about the outcome of the election, that is that she would gladly have left the White House, until the last 3 days. Before then she had favored a Democratic victory in an impersonal way because she considered it important to preserve the things that had been done, but the last 3 days she became really alarmed because of the nature of the forces backing Willkie.

A final note in my diary that day said that I had been awaiting a call from Trude, and ended, after detailing the things I had done: "It never came."

Some "little things" would come for my birthday, Eleanor advised me before she left on another lecture trip, this one to Texas. When Wanamaker's deposited a crate, it turned out to be a well-cushioned armchair. Did I have permission to sit in it before December 2? I wired her. She had left me a letter:

This is the first birthday letter I have ever written you & yet I feel as though you were very close to me & your concerns were mine. It is funny how quickly one knows about people. I think I knew we were going to be friends or rather that I wanted to be when I looked across the table at you about a year ago! Anyway my dear boy we can count on a growing understanding & I hope that all your birthdays will mark a deepening of that kind of understanding out of which enduring love & respect grow. Many, many happy returns of the day Joe dear & may the coming year bring you much joy.

I sent you the *Home Book of Verse* because sometime if you like to read aloud perhaps you'll let me come over & read some of my favorites in front of your fire. The little radio I hope you may find fun to carry around & listen, without disturbing others, to anything you really want to hear. I get the news in the morning on mine & I never cease to marvel that something so small can bring you a voice from Europe! Gifts don't mean much I know unless they represent real thought & these do that but I don't feel I know your likes & dislikes well enough yet to choose very well. They take you however much love & a promise of more knowledge sometime!

There will be delivered at your apartment from Wanamakers on Tuesday or Wed. a premature Xmas gift & just a gift to the apartment. You can change if you do not like but they seemed to me suitable. The table I had in the country was too light. Tommy is so pleased you asked her over & we've decided to come over & cook you a chafing dish supper in the near future. Of course you haven't asked us & we'll give you a chance to refuse!

This is growing too long & the purpose was brief just to say God bless & keep you & give increasingly happy & useful years.

With real love & devotion to you from

"Aunt Eleanor"

I thanked her for the way she had filled my little apartment with "magical influences" and what a "wonderful birthday" she had made it.

You once wrote that you hoped we would become friends, and I remember thinking with easy assurance that of course we would—as if real friendships were formed as casually as one takes a cup of tea! I did not then realize the fullness of feeling, sympathy and understanding that you meant by friendship, and which has so enriched my life.

I had always admired you greatly because you were courageous in behalf of great causes, and because there was no separation in your person between democracy as a political credo and democracy as a personal practice. But what really brought me close to you was the situation in the Youth Congress. I wanted desperately to help you by letting you know what the situation really was in the AYC, but I didn't want to discredit the kids with whom I had worked.

For a time I thought the only solution to the dilemma was to fight as hard as possible in the AYC to make it what you and liberals everywhere wanted it to be. That has not proven possible, but I am glad that you have remained fond of the kids.

As for me I have gained the most precious friend in the world who walks beside me all the time counselling me to be a better person, a kinder person, a happier person.

That is why this has been such a wonderful anniversary.

I only hope that in some way I am helping you.

　　　　　　　　　　　　　　　　　　With Much love,
　　　　　　　　　　　　　　　　　　Joe

XVII

Borrowed Love

A NOTE FROM HICK reported about Trude Pratt. During the campaign she had helped in the Women's Division, making her mark by joining Ellin (Mrs. Irving) Berlin on a Wall Street soapbox during lunch hour to challenge a crowd that was hell-bent on the election of Wendell Willkie.

"Trude took me to lunch at the Plaza, no less," Hick wrote to Eleanor:

> Isn't it swell about Joe Lash getting that job? I like Trude. Incidentally, she may give my sister a job. She asked me yesterday if I knew where she could get a good secretary—someone to handle her household and farm accounts, requests for money, etc. After I teased her properly about needing a secretary—the idea of that infant with a secretary is perfectly preposterous, and I think she'd be much more contented with life if she waited on herself—I recommended . . .

Mrs. Roosevelt responded in kind: "I'm glad you had such a good time with Mrs. Pratt. She is attractive & probably needs a secretary. . . ." She did not underline any special relationship between Trude and me. What Eleanor knew by conjecture and the frequency with which I had begun to mention Trude she was soon to learn directly. She invited Trude to attend the Gridiron Widows Party at the White House, which she held annually the same night the newspapermen had the President at their all-male party. "I did enjoy Mrs. Pratt & I hope she enjoyed being here," she wrote to me afterwards. "In repose her face is very sad but how really sensitive & beautiful."

When I went with Eleanor to Hyde Park, she learned more about Trude. Writing to me a few days earlier, Eleanor had said:

I have a little Xmas custom with the people I love dearly Tommy & Henry, Earl & Hick & I wonder if you would like to have me carry it out with you? I always fill them a stocking with odds & ends to open Xmas morning & then I call them up about 9:30 that day. If we can get together before for a dinner or celebration we do, Hick will be dining with me next Friday night & whatever day Earl comes home we'll try to get together. Tommy, Henry & I always get together about 11 p.m. Xmas eve in Tommy's apartment, I hope you & I will see each other this coming weekend but will you let me slip in & have the stocking by your fireplace for Xmas morning!

Her letter to Hick after their Christmas dinner together was warm and affectionate:

Dearest

It was such fun being with you last night & I love my Xmas gifts. I can hardly wait for the first cold night to use a log. The lunch set goes with me to Hyde Park this morning & my jellies will go with me to Washington in their cute basket on Monday morning. I shall try the relish here very soon.

I had a grand sleep last night. Earl blew in towards 2 a.m. I think but didn't bother me & now he is getting his car & will drop me at the cottage on his way home. Not very nice weather but a little snow in Hyde Park will be nice!

I hope this weekend & Xmas will be very nice for you. Much, much love.

Earl was off with "some of his girls," as she put it, and I joined Eleanor at Hyde Park, coming up by train. I helped her festoon and garland the cottage. I protested that she must be getting tired of my presence, but she replied:

I love to be with you dear boy. I never want to be alone when I'm with people I love. It is only under other circumstances I long for solitude! . . . You gathered from my last letter I hope that I like Mrs. Pratt *very* much.

We read Robert Louis Stevenson's "Christmas Sermon," which she had given me as an advance gift. "Mrs. R's tears at lunch," my diary read, "over inability of the world to settle human problems with less human suffering. Several times she reverted to the sorrowfulness of the day." Georgie, her maid and cook, whom she had brought up from New York, placed sprigs of holly around the pictures and served a Christmas-like dinner even though it was only December 22. I talked about Trude, with whom I confessed I was totally and fatally in love and who, I said, reciprocated my passion. She fetched out Elizabeth Barrett Browning's *Sonnets from the Portuguese* and read several. She offered the use of Hyde Park as a refuge, and wrote to me afterwards:

> It is always a joy to be with you dear boy & I enjoyed so much having you in H.P. & last night. I wish I could help you dear, for I know so well how hard & yet how glorious these days are. All I can do is to tell you that only those who love really live in spite of the pain loving so often brings. If having an older friend who loves you & will always understand is any help you have that at least to count on.

Christmas night she wrote to Hick and me, and probably Earl and Tommy. The last two letters, if they exist, are not available, but those to Hick and me again demonstrated the difference between fresh new feelings and a more settled emotion:

> Joe dearest,
>
> The little bronze boy* sits before me on my very crowded desk & is a joy, I've just eaten a cookie & soon I'll take the book of poems to bed. I loved all your cards & was deeply touched that you wanted me to have something you were fond of. You may be sure I will cherish it just for that reason. It was nice to hear your voice this morning & you sounded like a little boy & I wished you could have been with us here but I knew you must go to your own family, I told the President you liked his message & sent him your Xmas wishes & he said 'How nice of him, give him mine.'
>
> I had a sweet note from Mrs. Pratt & sent her a line in reply.
>
> We've had a good day here & we were fortunate in drawing in many friends this evening. We sang carols till 11 p.m. & then had a waltz & a virginia reel. Couldn't you come down for New Year's Eve? It always gives me a catch in my throat when Franklin drinks to the U.S. but it is the kind of thing does one good!
>
> Talking to all the children was heart warming too, in fact a very nice moment in the day!
>
> Tommy loved your brush(?) & showed it to me with great pleasure.
>
> I'll be going out to New Brunswick [New Jersey, for the ISS conference at the New Jersey College for Women] from New York & can leave at three or anytime thereafter. Could you find out the next train out & back for me? I'll take a bag & dress there as the Dean told me I could go to her house. You will all be in my thoughts Friday & I'll be wishing you well.
>
> My thanks again & I love you dear boy. Devotedly,
>
> Aunt Eleanor

* A little bronze figure that I had brought back from Republican Spain of a youthful Spanish militiaman in coveralls. It was a symbol of the Republican cause.

To Hick she wrote:

Dearest,

I've begun on the jelly & it is delicious.

Your Sunday letter sounded so contented. I just hope this last week will be one long joy & you will be looking forward to a time in Feb— after the teeth are out!

The day has been busy & yesterday was exhausting but on the whole I think it was one of the nicest days we have had. The party tonight was great fun & lots of the old crowd, Herricks, Lindleys, Storms, & Eddie Rodden were here. Mrs. Lindley Sr. was here but Betty & Ernest seemed to be together tho' I wasn't sure how comfortable Ernest [Lindley] was with FDR. I wish I could change that strain! Talking to all the children was grand too & they sounded happy.

I've got so many presents that I'm overwhelmed!

Now I must go to bed.

All my love & I will be looking for you on the 2d,

Ever devotedly,
E.R.

She spoke at the New Jersey College for Women, the intercollegiate meeting that inaugurated the new program of the ISS. "I think I did a good job at the I.S.S. conference last night," she wrote to Hick, "anyway a lot of kids asked if I would come to their campus! Leigh will die at my doing so much for them this winter but I think it is important."

Afterwards I brought Trude to see her in her apartment in New York, and Trude told her that from her side she was hopelessly in love, that her marriage had become purely formal, except for her three children. But she would never give them up, even if it meant giving me up. Eleanor listened. If her own experience might be of help she was ready to offer it.

A telegram from "E.R." at the White House shortly afterwards read simply: "If Mrs. Pratt wants to stay here at any time please tell her she is very welcome. Love."

At the White House on New Year's, the solemn moment came at midnight when the President toasted the United States and in turn his health was toasted. Then Mrs. Roosevelt toasted their children. Unobtrusively she came over to me, I having come in response to her invitation, and touched glasses with me in a toast to Trude. At dinner that night she had put a little figure at each place. At mine she had put two little rabbits under an umbrella. She had once given the same figures to Anna and John.

All that day we had talked, for she enjoyed having her friends close and at the time she responded particularly to my company. Fascination works mysteriously, absent particularly, the sexual element. How explain it? That I had enabled her to extricate herself with dignity and self-respect from the Youth Congress entanglement? If so she never acknowledged it to me. But she had had a deep involvement with the Congress and I still received letters from her lamenting her inability to come to the personal help of those leaders of whom she had been particularly fond. My commitment to F.D.R. may have helped reconcile her to the third term. She could talk about that. She told me that from things she had learned since the election she was more and more convinced that Willkie's election would have been a catastrophe. I had realized it earlier and felt it more keenly, she said. Perhaps she had been selfish and in wanting to get out of the White House had tended to underestimate the importance of the President's election. She said I had helped there.

She took me and some of her other guests out to Rock Creek Park to see the Saint-Gaudens Memorial, commissioned by Henry Adams after his wife had committed suicide. She again explained why the hooded figure meant so much to her. It gave the impression, she said, of a woman who had attained absolute self-mastery. That to her seemed a supreme virtue in a woman, committed as she herself was, although she did not say it at the time and I only realized it later, to giving a husband who had long ceased to love her a service of love, a service made easier by her special friends.

A few days afterwards when she was in New York, I confided to her that Trude and her husband had decided to separate. It was awfully rough on her, I commented, "but both of us have a sense of being driven on by fate." Eleanor was not as confident that the separation would go as evenly and uninterruptedly as I seemed to believe. The two of us should be careful, she cautioned, but when I spoke of prospects of happiness, she came over and kissed me, and when I said that Trude was going to Washington, she insisted that she stay with her at the White House. Georgie, her maid, had fed us dinner at the East Eleventh Street apartment. Afterwards we walked the few blocks to my apartment, where I played for her the "Six Songs of the International Brigade." They stirred her deeply. Would she be capable of such self-sacrifice? she kept on asking, and added, what a tremendous sense of fellowship there must have been in the brigade.

"Joe dearest," she wrote two days later from the White House:

Saturday evening is a very pleasant memory. I loved the music & the nice peaceful time.

I hope you liked the [F.D.R.] message. You will see if you read tomorrow's column that I was shocked by the partisan attitude. FDR says the increase in N.Y.A. will come from defense money. I hope it does. I see Carmody* tomorrow.

If you did not see these items in the "Daily Worker"† you may be amused. They are rather mild!

I've removed many unnecessary things from my desk so I can really see & enjoy the little Spanish boy in front of me!

I am immersed in lists & long talks with Mrs. Helm. This period before Inauguration has its comic side & it is also somewhat trying since Mrs. Helm meets me every time I turn around with a question!

I'll be so glad to see Trude Wednesday. I hope she gets here in time to attend a meeting of important ladies. I am scared about it for as a rule they discourage me very much!

Tommy's sister is better, but she was worried over the weekend & so depressed & tired yesterday that I tried to reorganize the work only to discover that I was making matters worse so now she has reorganized me & I shall try to live up to it & hope it will make life easier for her!

This letter is really just to tell you that I think of you often & love you so I think I'll say goodnight & bless you dear boy.

Both Trude and I stayed at the White House. I feared that I had offended Hick at dinner because I was so preoccupied with Trude, and I learned more of how Eleanor had fostered the relationship between Anna and John:

You need not worry about Hick. For the moment she is so engrossed in her job & all that touches it that she was quite unconscious of any lack of interest on your part. If she hadn't grabbed you I would have put John [Boettiger] with her for I knew you should have been near Trude.

I wish you could have overheard a talk John & I had while I was cooking eggs in the other room. He reminded me of the bad times he & Anna had lived thro', & that he was not divorced until long after she was, that the difficulties seemed insurmountable & sometimes I'll tell you about it for he felt often worse than you did & many a time I picked up the pieces of two very discouraged people after some hard blow! You'll be surer of Trude dear when she is free & can tell the world 'I love thee'. Now, for both your sakes, she must not & neither must you. Let me tell you one thing. No one of us is ever worthy of the real love of anyone else. No one ever lives up to the best in themselves all the time & nearly all of us love people because of their weaknesses rather than because of their strengths. Trude loves you more I'm sure because she knew you needed her. You are neither weak

* John Carmody, Federal Works Agency administrator.

† The *Daily Worker* correspondent at the ISS conference led with Eleanor's comment on work camps in which she had stated: "I believe that every boy and girl in this nation should give a year's service to the nation. I believe it should be compulsory." Although the *Worker* was isolationist in Europe, it was critical of her mild demurral from Japan's ability to buy war materials in the United States.

nor mean, just honorable & human, if that wasn't so neither Trude nor I would love you as we *both* do.

I send you two clippings which may interest you & a letter which is heartbreakingly lonely. Keep them for me.

The Thomas Manns have been here since Sunday & I have enjoyed knowing them a little better. I must tell you about dinner & a meeting last night but just now time flies. I've been so busy that I can only stay calm by being an automaton. At times like these I try to be a machine or I would break into tears or run away. I can hardly wait to get away on Thursday when I shall take the plane & try to forget what I leave behind here undone!

Trude says she is coming down Sat. do you want to come with her or will you come down with me on Sunday a.m.?

When do you both have to go back as I should make some reservations, the crowd will be great. Please wire me about these two points & I'll look forward to seeing you.

My love to Trude & you dear boy & remember bad times do come to an end.

The weekend before Inauguration she and the President were at Hyde Park. Anna and John, who had come East, were with them and their presence always buoyed her up. She took us all down to the Morgenthaus'. She cherished them. On New Year's Eve the Secretary had moved everyone with his toast about his gratefulness for having settled in Dutchess County before World War I and the opportunity it had given him to serve. Eleanor was fond of the tall dour-voiced Secretary. He had convictions and stood up for them, even to the President.

An exchange, emblematic of the tension between President and First Lady, took place at lunch at the Big House. Mrs. Roosevelt asked whether the man the President had appointed to supervise defense housing would be sensitive to problems of low-cost housing and schools. She had heard that he sided with the real estate interests. Roosevelt was impatient; she persisted. He would appoint an assistant to watch especially for those things, he said, and tried to end the argument. "Would he have any authority?" she pressed. The President's mother, meanwhile, noting the President's refractory mood, had gotten the butler to wheel up the President's chair. Now she stood behind the President and he was shifted to the wheelchair and thus gotten away from a discussion that Sara saw did not please him. Unable to pin Franklin down, Eleanor had gotten angry. "The family all congratulated her on having stuck to her guns," I noted.

But her judgment of the President was remarkably balanced. The next day when she and I flew down to Washington together, she remarked that the last two paragraphs of a *Times Magazine* article on the President were a good description of his frame of mind and temper as he began this third term. And she summed up the paragraphs as saying that "despite the arduous character of the times, there was still a sort of buoyancy about him."

Trude and I were at the White House for the Inauguration, and a few days later Eleanor wrote to me:

. . . I loved seeing you Monday as always & I'm going to miss you, seeing little of you this month. You have made me care so much for you young man, & I was going to make no new friends but perhaps we die when we do that & I'm not ready for death! I saw Rose Franken's play "Claudia" last night & I'd love to take you & Trude sometime. I think you'd enjoy it as I did.

Yale was a pleasant experience. I'm never sure that I'm adequate. When one has a chance to plant some seeds & it is so important, the sense of my own shortcoming always overcomes me & I wish for all the gifts which I don't possess! You'll hear when you go there what the criticisms are & I hope you'll tell me honestly for that is the only way I can do a better job. Henry Ford was not an issue & I'll tell you how he came in when we meet.

Elliott & Ruth haven't been able to get back so I am sending the children home this afternoon. I've had all the stars to lunch & enjoyed [Lauritz] Melchior & Wallace Beery my table companions. Remind me to tell you about a conversation with Mr. Beery because I think you will be amused.

To Hick, who was in New York, she wrote:

Then the stars lunched & we had the usual picture. . . . The party for F.D.R. went off well & I'm through with balls & going to bed by 12:30. It is hard to believe!

She had Trude and me at the White House during the February "town meeting" of the American Youth Congress. Five thousand strong, it was a demonstration against passage of the Lend-Lease Act. Mrs. Roosevelt gave it no assistance, but I felt obliged to put in an appearance to speak in favor of passage of the act; I was the only one to do so. Although Mrs. Roosevelt had long since withdrawn from active identification with the Youth Congress, veiled attacks on me at the "town meeting" as the recipient of White House favors angered her:

Feb. 19, 1941

Dear ———:

I read your News Cast of the Town Meeting with interest.

I am especially interested to note your feeling that people who happen to have convictions opposed to your own, have sold out to the White House because of favors.

I can assure you that no one else has received favors comparable to what you and the leaders of the AYC have received. It has suddenly occurred to me that perhaps all of you are made uncomfortable by the fact that you feel you have to accept things from me and that you have to appear friendly in order to further your cause.

I would not want in any way to have you feel the slightest obligation.

I have continued to give you my monthly check because I agreed to pay your salary for one year, and I could continue to do it with a clear conscience because I believe in some of the objectives you work for in this country.

I feel more strongly every day, that, with a Hitler victory in Europe, this type of objective would be far less easy to reach in this country and that one must face first things first.

I will, of course, continue to fulfill my promise for the balance of the year, which will mean that the last check is payable on August 1st but I cannot help resenting your feeling that other people have sold out to the White House. I think you should recognize that other people have convictions as well as you yourselves, and I consider that all of you are under far greater obligation, for, quite frankly, the White House has done nothing for any other group in a material way which compares with what has been done for the AYC. Friendship has been offered to many of you, but having an opposing conviction does not mean that you are in any way obligated because of this friendship.

Please remember that anytime I will understand perfectly if you feel you do not want to have any connection with me whatsoever. It will neither hurt my feelings nor make me feel any bitterness toward any of you. I have a personal affection for many of you and I think that perhaps some day some of you will change your conviction. Until that day arrives, I do not want you made uncomfortable by contact with me or what may be unwanted favors from me.

Sincerely yours
Eleanor Roosevelt

The more she withdrew from the Youth Congress, the more she helped ISS. She attended board meetings, raised money, spoke at conferences, held a monthly party for its staff, and had its members stay at the White House when they were in Washington.

When the organization decided on a summer student leadership training institute, she consulted the President and made available the house at Campobello Island as the site for it. "I'm so glad the Campo house will be used next summer & I hope it works out well. Perhaps you & Trude can come up & help me get it in order & start them off? . . . Don't thank me for things dear," her letter ended, "having you & Trude near is pure self indulgence on my part. I like to have you use Hyde Park whenever you wish."

She sent me, as she did Earl, Hick, and Tommy, stationery-store valentines, but when I responded with a lame verse,

And shall I not a valentine
Indite to her whose heart
like the sky

Takes in all men, yet not so high
As fails on special friends to shine.

she came back with verses of her own:

A lady read a valentine
Beneath a sky so blue
And spirits soared with every line
For words rang kind & true.

Your verse is better far than mine
But I ask that you take a bit of my heart
And share it with that Trude of thine,
And ever be grateful for Cupid's dart.

"I've wished for both you & Trude tonight," her letter went on, "for Eve Curie is here, a gallant & a tragic person & Harry Hopkins is really interesting. I'll tell you both more when I see you."

She also enclosed an American Student Union leaflet that attacked her advocacy of "forced labor camps," and quoted her statement to the ISS conference. "I do believe and have said so several times that every young person, boy or girl, in this nation should give a year of service to the nation. . . . I believe that work camps are good for us all."

Trude's resolve to separate from her husband had its ups and downs, as Eleanor learned from my glooms and despairs. If my laments bored her, she never let on. Instead she sought to steady me:

Joe dearest,

I am worried about you. You looked tired & not very happy tonight. Take care of yourself because so many people love you & you mean so much just to me, let alone anyone else! I've grown to depend on you, & my heart sings when I'm going to see you in much the same way as it does when Anna's coming! Bless you dear, I'll be up Thursday p.m. if you feel like dropping in at 5:30 for an hour, with or without Trude, do come & in any case, come to breakfast Friday morning at 8:30.

She had talked with Marshall Field about money for ISS but did not have his answer when she wrote to me:

I was glad that Trude's temperature was gone Saturday night & I hope she is a lot better. I've got some letters to show you but they will wait till Wed.

We had a very short day at H.P. & how I hated to leave but I'd promised to go to the Negro college in Petersburg, Va. today & I felt I must not back out. I think I was honest in what I said but talking about Youth & Defense to them was not easy.

Two articles have gone to George Bye [her agent], I hope you'll read them for you won't agree with me but I want you to know what I think now & why. You may in time persuade me to your point of view but if I get these published they will start people thinking & talking at least & I think that is important. Something better than my ideas will probably evolve!

Mr. Woollcott is back, acting in "The Man Who Came to Dinner" & I hope I can get the President to go & see it with me on Tuesday evening.

She reproached herself for not having tried to reach me in a moment of dejection over Trude:

I'm cross with myself for not having tried to reach you Saturday. Friends were meant for just such days as you describe & besides you would have kept me from doing my duty & I'm a much nicer person when I don't. I just took it for granted when I found Trude was still home that you were there having a happy time & so after Tommy & I had some food I went to see Mrs. Parish before we went to the plane.

I did not mean to be sharp with F. but I like her so much & the way they treat you seems to me so unfair that I feel she at least should see it.

I'll tell you tomorrow what Harry thinks about 'war aims.'

At the beginning of March she and Tommy and Henry Osthagen flew down to Golden Beach, Florida. Earl, although on active duty in Pensacola, was in and out. Trude was there too, and after a few days I joined them. Eleanor's letters to Hick described her stay: ". . . [W]e walked about 3 miles on the beach & then Trude Pratt & I went in the water. No one else would go but it wasn't a bit cold." Two days later: "Wasn't it grand the lend lease bill went thro' so well? Is it true that the opposition began feeling a change in the temper of the country?" They played some deck tennis, another report said, and then Paderewski "came to tea. How old he has grown & how sad he is!" They were reading a "rather interesting little book [by Harold Laski] about 'How to Win the War.'" She teased Hick about her sedentary ways: "The water is softer & warmer than I ever remember it & even you could enjoy it here for it is shallow for miles."

Her letters to me reported mainly on Trude's condition:

Trude will have written you about the trip down & her impressions. I think she is comfortable for the time being & she looks better already, *less white, & less strained*. We've worked a little on Dr. Cohn's article.* I hope he never knows that I had a hand in it for of course the ideas are all Trude's. I may just be able to help a little on the wording. I think the old gentleman seems to be able to exhaust both you & Trude but you must not let him. I'm sure we can make him see in the long

* Dr. Alfred Cohn, a heart researcher at the Rockefeller Institute, was a member of the ISS board. His draft pamphlet on the ISS was vigorously resisted by the younger members, including a unanimous staff.

run. He is too insistent on his ideas which is a fault many of us have as
we grow older. I fight it because I have to cope with it in my mother-
in-law & Cousin Susie & so I'm reminded to watch myself!

   . . . & when you come I think you'll find a rested Trude & I hope
you will both have a happy 3 days. I miss you & look forward to next
Friday with keen anticipation.

Trude's letter was graphic:

There is a great wind blowing and your skin gets wonderfully salty and
sticky—like the salt licks we used to put out for the deer in the Black
Forest. Mrs. Roosevelt is working over Dr. Cohn's piece. Earl has just
discovered that the grocer is trying to put one over on Mrs. R. and he
is 'that mad.'

Mrs. R. sends her love and says that 'it will be nicer when you get
here.' Your picture is on her dresser. I have no picture and I want one
so much. But every moment I know how you would look. . . .

They reworked Dr. Cohn's pamphlet version four times, Trude reported. "Mrs. R. said she could have written a new article in one tenth
of the time. No, Tommy said that. . . . It is wonderful to be with her.
She is so incredibly patient and understanding, and every hour I get
more devoted to her—if that is possible. Sometimes it is not necessary
at all to talk—she will know what troubles you."

"Earl is grouching," a later letter said, "because Mrs. R. and I talk
about your coming so much. What a nice, funny person he is! So much
in need of activity all the time. . . . Joe, dearest, never have I wanted
so terribly to push the hours."

While all were in Florida I decided that I ought to make myself
available for military service and not wait for the draft. Perhaps I
should consider enlisting in the Navy, Eleanor said. She would check
the possibilities with the President's naval aide. On her return from
Florida she sent me Captain Callaghan's memo. On it she wrote: "This
just came to me but FDR talked to him since & so did I so more explicit information may be mine by Thursday. Capt. Blackburn is in
charge in N.Y. 90 Church St." A letter accompanied the memo:

I'm going to N.Y. Thursday afternoon for Ingrid Warburg's dinner & I
will take the one o'clock plane back Friday. If you & Trude are going
to the dinner, could I pick you up & will you breakfast with me Friday
a.m. at 8:30?

Tell Trude if she wants to come back Friday it will be fine & if she
prefers to bring the children this weekend instead of at Easter it is
quite convenient for me.

I'll have to finish this tomorrow when I have the information both
of you want but I want to write you tonight & tell you how happy I've
been having you with me. I love seeing you & Trude happy together &
I am very fond of her. There is a look which is so sweet when she looks

up at you that I can well understand how you feel. You are the one I've grown to love very dearly however, & I hope so much I can help you dear & bring you some happiness. May God bless you dear boy & watch over you & the one you love.

Monday a.m. For Trude. I find Mrs. Tillett will only be here for the Jackson Day dinner on the 29th & not again for the day till the 1st. Hick leaves here this Friday night & won't be back till the 1st so Trude may not want to wait till that day as that is the stunt party night.

I can't find any school for 'non coms' except as they are enlisted men. Capt. Callaghan is exploring possibilities of all kinds & I'll let you know. FDR is taking 'How to Win the War' away with him on Wed. He leaves at 3 p.m. & I'll meet him on the 31st at Fort Bragg for the inspection of that camp. I imagine I'll be looking for some things he won't be! We will get back the morning of the 1st.

The next day she wrote again:

I think your chance for the Navy is going to be of necessity going in as a gob like Bobby Morgenthau & if they decide you are officer material you get a chance in the School for Ensigns. No groups are planned but they may be by autumn & Capt. Callaghan is looking into it. Remind me to tell you an amusing incident in our conversation.

I'm busy but I love you & I'll add a bit to this tomorrow.

Tuesday a.m. The President leaves tomorrow p.m. & I'll be glad to see him off as he looks tired. I liked his speech last night* but I disliked many things about that opening. How that rich group hate him! It all seemed a farce to me knowing that Mr. Mellon only did it to escape jail on his income tax!

She had approached Captain Callaghan about my Navy application as the President was having his nose swathed to fix his sinuses. The naval aide said that I should go to the officer in charge of the New York district and enlist there. The President piped up: Had Callaghan spoken to Captain Blackburn of the Third Naval District? If he hadn't, the Navy would conclude after an investigation of my record that I was a Communist and reject me. Callaghan was reluctant to do anything about it, preferred to leave it to his successor, but the President repeated that he had to call; otherwise I would not get in. The episode amused Mrs. Roosevelt. She did not know the obstacles I would encounter, despite the President's attitude.

Eleanor was thinking about her own role in the war effort. She wanted to serve actively. Long experience, however, had taught her to move cautiously. "A lot of people came to lunch," she wrote to Hick, "& then I worked on this home defence with the Committee. It is at

---

* Address at the dedication of the National Gallery of Art, March 17, 1941, established by joint resolution of Congress, which accepted Andrew W. Mellon's offer to give his art collection, a building, and an endowment fund to the United States.

last taking shape & I hope F. can get it started on his return." Community mobilization in the defense effort in such a way as to improve the national diet, health, and literacy interested her. She saw a special role for women in such a mobilization, perhaps even for herself. She took Trude and me to see Shaw's play *The Doctor's Dilemma* and afterwards commented that Mrs. Dubedat in the play "symbolized the worst traits in a woman, self-deception and playing up to men to get her ends." Such a woman clashed with her own ideal of sturdy, self-reliant, and autonomous womanhood. When Tommy at breakfast expressed misgivings about the First Lady saying that the moral code was man-made, as she had in an article she had turned over to George Bye, Mrs. Roosevelt replied simply, "Of course it is." Would a woman of her independent views have a place in home defense? she wondered, and when such friends as Tommy and I urged her to take it on, she listened while telling us that there was no chance.

"Here is your memo also on seeing Capt. Blackburn," she wrote to me. "If you knew how I hate to see you all swallowed up in the defense forces! By next fall however we may all be busy on it, who knows & I wouldn't have any of you doing anything different." Captain Blackburn appeared impatient to me. There seemed to be no place where I could fit in, the captain observed. "Thus my first effort to volunteer has bogged down," I wrote in my diary.

Eleanor left Washington at the end of March for a trip south that began with a stay at Bernard Baruch's plantation in South Carolina, "Hobcaw Barony." Her trip coincided with a "terrible weekend," as I described it, in which Trude had telegraphed me that she was not coming to town and I got "stone drunk." Mrs. R. sought to reassure me by citing her own experience:

> Your letter came before we left this noon & I wished I had telephoned you as I wanted to do last night. I begin to think you wouldn't mind if I was less restrained & sometimes made myself more of a nuisance! I know just the mood of lonely despair you were in, but you have to reach the point where you're sure of Trude. Time & trust in yourself is all that will bring that about. Sometimes I'm going to tell you just how lonely I can be in a crowd & it may help you to overcome the same type of thing which I've had to fight all my life. You don't believe in others because you don't believe in yourself. You have the strength for any self-discipline & faith that is required if the objective is worthwhile. We have to be preoccupied with 'self' when we are young otherwise the world would come to an end! Every experience will help you & others.
>
> I'm delighted you will be on the air the 13th & will be listening. It will be such fun to have you in Washington that weekend. Do come Friday & stay till Tuesday if you can for I'll be gone quite a time out

West. I miss you very much when we are not near enough so I can see you fairly often!

I'm looking forward to the book you sent but it hadn't come this morning so I brought along Laski's "The American Presidency" which I was asked to review months ago. I don't want anything which I gave you in N.Y. back only what I mailed you Sunday. I think I'll get those analyses regularly & if I do I'll mail them to you.

Flying down wasn't so good today but this is a beautiful place. Acres & acres of marvellous trees & so quiet. Not pretentious just very comfortable living. Mr. Baruch does much for his people. I'll tell you about it & his relationship with his children & friends. It is interesting. He assures me Walter White is wrong & Jim Byrnes is not anti-Semitic & that he would be fair to the Negro on the Supreme Court. I liked your statement on teachers & entirely agree & the Daily Worker performed true to type.

Goodnight my dearest boy, I love you dearly.

The subsequent two weeks before she embarked on a month-long lecture trip, Trude and I often were with her. Afterwards she wrote from Buffalo:

Your letter struck an answering chord in me for I had been thinking on my long trips how we had to snatch at beauty & joy & hug them close for hovering so near was hatred and ugliness & death & destruction. We must not let the walls close in Joe dear, each of us must manage to do our part in preventing it. . . .

I had a most glowing account from Betty Strevig of your broadcast & Tommy too told me you were very good & she thought Aggie* good. No matter how much the lady may wish you to sink she'll never outwish me on the other side! I say a prayer every night & many times in the day for my boys & for you & Earl. . . .

I like to think of you & Trude talking late in the moonlight in the park. I hope you've had some peaceful, happy times together since. Perhaps you will both save June 7th & 8th & we might go to Monticello. I'm enclosing a line for you to give Trude.

Will you call Georgie tomorrow & tell her you are coming to breakfast on Sat.? It saves Tommy a note, but if you forget it won't matter for she can add a plate & an egg when you arrive. . . .

A note in my diary about that Saturday read:

It was a good 24 hours with her in town. I went over to breakfast. I was quite gloomy because of T. and almost turned back outside of 20 East 11th Street not wanting to burden her with my gloom. I went up the stairs with leaden feet, although usually I bound up two or three

---

* Agnes Reynolds, then an organizer for the Student Defenders of Democracy, the author, and William Bundy of the Harvard Student Defense League upheld the affirmative in a debate over convoys against three isolationists. Aggie, to whom I had once been close, had not taken kindly to my romance with Trude.

steps at a time. Mrs. R. was on the phone to Earl so I went in and said
hello to Tommy and Tiny. Mrs. R. came in and threw her arms around
me in a great big hug. She had had a letter from T. Was it one, I wondered, after our bad session, or a thank you note for the WH weekend
with the children? We went out to breakfast on the porch. Soon I was
cheerful as it is so easy to become with her. She full of stories about
her last few days. She had been to Buffalo and Wilkes Barre for lectures. At Wilkes Barre she had tried a new lecture on Latin America.

That evening Eleanor and I went to see Lillian Hellman's *Watch on
the Rhine*. The audience stood and applauded when she came in. In
the play, Kurt, the hero, renounces a comfortable upper-class life in the
United States to return to underground work in Germany. When Kurt
played one of the songs of the International Brigade, Eleanor gripped
my hand, for it was at my apartment that she had first heard it. The
two talked about courage and commitment. Was it possible to have
Kurt's single-minded devotion to a cause outside of the Communist
Party? I asked. Kurt's courage and heroism in returning revived for her
the question she often asked herself, especially in those dark days.
Would she be able to stand up when the going really got tough? Could
she reconcile herself to death and meet it indifferently in the course of
doing her duty? Repeatedly she said, "We must do better than in 1918.
If people could be brought to understand we would do better." The
time for courage was now in the way the war was being fought, she
went on, not later. Perhaps the battle already was being lost over such
matters as the tax bill, health, housing, the rights of labor.

The next morning, when I returned for breakfast, she had reformu-
lated her anxieties: "If Hitler consolidates his power, if the war must be
fought for many years, will we be able to keep from Hitlerising ourselves in order to fight Hitler effectively? She wished she could feel
there was a solution. The President never lets on if he feels there isn't
one."

I drove with her to the airport. She scrawled a penciled note from the
plane: "You were such a dear to come out to the airport this morning.
I hate leaving people I love but I'd hate not seeing others & lecturing
not only pays the piper but seems a worthwhile job. I guess it is about
the only way I can help much anyway!"

On the way to Los Angeles she lectured in Chicago. Her poise there
showed her to be a level-headed trouper indeed:

> My first experience during the lecture last night with a man who had
> an epileptic fit. You've no idea how hard it is to talk sense when an
> audience is watching something else & yet it seemed best to go on talk-
> ing! After he was out I tried to be a bit dramatic to draw the audience
> back & Tommy thought I succeeded fairly well. The questions were
> good.

From Los Angeles she had cautious advice about "happiness":

Your letter of the 22d greeted me in Los Angeles yesterday & I was so glad to get it & I loved the 'very sure, very strong & very happy.' The first two you should always be, the last alas, is not given to us poor humans to be except in shining times & we should always grasp them & cherish them. It isn't your respective characters that bring you & Trude all your difficulties & troubles, though they might bring a few, but past experiences & present situations are responsible for the greater part I think.

Dear, the boy you talked to is in the situation my John is in. A year ago he told me nothing would make him take part in any war except to defend his home. In Boston the other day he told me that much as he hated leaving home & his job still he knew now that if Hitler dominated the world he couldn't be happy in it. It is no different for rich or poor fundamentally, you have the same thing at stake, preserving a world you can live & grow in.

. . . .

I think of you so much & wish you were with us Joe. I think we'd have fun travelling together. The desert is in bloom & so lovely. I wish you had enjoyed it with us yesterday.

A troubled letter about my relations with Trude reached her at the Melvyn Douglases'. She had become deeply involved in our love affair, so much so that she followed its ups and downs as if she were a participant. It was almost as if she loved vicariously:

Of course you & Trude are what I think much about & you are wrong Joe for it won't be the world or claims & habits of the past which will settle the future for you two. It will be what Trude & you *are* & want of each other & the future. If Trude wants the kind of life she had, only more personal freedom & expression & if you can't make yourself secure whether she loves you or not that may bring you to one conclusion. Whereas if you are sure & strong & want her desperately because life together will mean beauty & a wider opportunity for you both & she is willing to forget the world & all former claims (except her children) & sink herself in a life *with* you that will bring another result. I love you both & you both are fine but you are more sensitive & less selfish than Trude. She is therefore at times more effective! You appreciate all the difficulties except perhaps a few practical details & you may not quite realize how many ties she has built around her largely because she had no central, strong love to hold her. This is a hard time for her & you must manage to make her feel you believe in her but all relationships have obligations & she must learn how to build up your sense of security by showing her love for you & understanding. Of course lovers have the hardest time to build the kind of relationship you need because they are jealous & long for perfection which only comes on rare occasions!

. . . .

This is a lovely house but being with the Douglas' is what is nice. They are grand people & I've had an exciting time this afternoon. I met & really talked with James Hilton & liked him, & Dorothy Parker & Burgess Meredith & many other people & they think as we do about so many things. It is heartening!

Wasn't Churchill's speech a challenge & didn't it make you feel you had the courage to meet any difficulty? I've always loved Clough's poem but I hadn't read it for years. I must look for it next time I'm at Hyde Park & have my poetry books.

I must stop & go to dinner. Joe, dearest boy, I wish I could help you gain your security & your happiness but all I can do is send you loving thoughts many times a day. Bless you.

She sent me the draft of a radio speech: "Will you read it & if you have any suggestions make them so I can include? It will take as it is a little less than the time they gave me so I can leave & read slowly or add & read fast." (On the train Wednesday P.M.) By the time she reached Seattle, she had responded to my suggestion: "I think on your suggestion I have strengthened my speech quite a bit for the 13th & I have it for you to read in N.Y."

Seattle, above all, meant Anna and John and Sistie and Buzzie and little Johnny:

It was good to get here last night with all my work done & it is like coming home, nevertheless I read & reread your letter of the 29th before going to sleep & I will be so happy to see you soon. I'm counting on seeing you in N.Y. Come to breakfast on the 7th & if the spirit moves you meet us at the airport at 10:55 daylight. We take a 5 p.m. standard plane fr. Chicago.

You know that every detail that touches you & Trude interests me & I'm happy you had a good time together before she left. I hope you told each other some of the things you were proud of in your past however for I can't believe that either of you need to be really ashamed of much. You see it is only mean & cruel things one needs to be ashamed of & I don't think either of you have many such actions on your conscience. Mistakes, & what people call such, we've all committed but on occasion they arise from qualities which are far from reprehensible. I love the whole of people but I've often liked so-called 'sins' better than some kind of virtues.

. . . .

I'm so sorry you missed Churchill's speech. There is so much in *hearing* him. How interesting that you knew Clough, I thought he was more of my generation! There are many of his poems I like. James Hilton gave me a sequel to 'Mr. Chips' published in England but not here & autographed which I am looking forward to reading. I liked him so much.

Sis & Buzzie & Johnnie have grown & I always feel happier about their upbringing & the atmosphere in which they live than I do about any of the others. I think they will be better prepared to meet whatever the future holds.

A letter from Fjr. sounds as though he were feeling rather close to war. Poor Rommie is plunged in some of Jimmy's hurriedly left & somewhat tangled business affairs. I was both grieved for her & a bit worried but there is little I can do.

Tomorrow being Anna's birthday we have no engagements, which is our favorite form of celebration!

I do hope that Trude was satisfied with her work in Nashville & I hope to hear about it soon. Give her my dear love. . . .

Trude and Ellin Berlin had gone to Nashville, where the Women's Division of the Democratic Committee, whose executive secretary was Hick, was holding the first of its regional conferences. Hick wrote to Eleanor from Nashville: "Just left Trude and Ellin Berlin, who flew in from N.Y. They were interviewed at the airport about Lindbergh, and I gather, they took the hide off him, which is certainly all right with me." A week later Hick reported: "Trude made a terrific hit & she was swell. They are going to try to get her again on their own. She handled the economic side of the discussion and she was GOOD."

I teased Trude for the flowered hat she had worn in Nashville. In reply she gave me a copy of the curriculum vitae she had prepared for Hick:

I was born in 1908 in southern Germany from a mixture of serious religious Black Forest people and light-hearted wine-growing Huguenot descendants. As the oldest of five children, I spent my childhood resisting my father's determined efforts to turn me into a chemist and engineer (his own profession). In 1927 my father died, we became quite poor. I studied philology, philosophy and modern literature in Freiburg: Heidelberg, Berlin and Paris and journalism in Berlin. In 1927 I had passed a secretarial course and from then on held jobs while I studied (reporter, secretary, teacher, research assistant and translator).

After I had taken my PhD in Freiburg in 1930, I lectured Middle High German for one term and was for a year the head of the organization that took care of all foreigners studying at the University of Freiburg. Then I decided that I wanted to go to the United States. I was sent as an Exchange teacher (also as a delegate to the World Conference of the International Student Service, held at Mt. Holyoke in 1931) and taught for one year at Hunter College. At the end of that time I wrote a rather aggressive and not very mature report about education in the United States which was published by mistake and rather displeased my superiors at Hunter College. On my return to Germany in the fall of 1932, I started to work for the Taegliche Rundschau, a neo-liberal newspaper in Berlin. The paper was one of the first to be suppressed when Hitler came into power, some of the editors were shot. I had married Eliot Pratt in December of 1932 and was lucky enough not to be a German citizen any longer.

Since March, 1933 I have been living in this country trying to get under the surface of the United States and the Americans which is considerably harder than in any other country. I have been working with refugee organizations, with the International Student Service and other student organizations. This fall I took a rather active part in the national campaign. I also have three children and spend much too little time with them.

Eleanor also heard from Trude and she cheerfully passed the news on to me: "A letter from Trude written after Nashville sounds baffled but you would like her last sentence 'and whatever happens in I.S.S. Joe's way of solving the problems will be mine.' Dr. Cohn seems to have brought about this conviction which is hardly the result he intended I imagine."

She wrote to Trude from the Melvyn Douglases' aglow with Churchill's speech. "What a use of the English language, one almost feels Mussolini & Hitler wither!" Trude, like Joe, had apologized over allowing personal problems to press in upon the public at so critical a juncture in the world's history. Eleanor demurred:

I don't think you should feel that concern about personal problems is wrong for only as we solve our own problems can we give the best that is in us to the world problems. You have identified yourself so much with the whole Pratt family & have taken on so many other ties to fill a somewhat empty heart that it is hard to cut loose & decide whether any one thing is big enough to swallow up the other things. . . . I think of you often & will be happy to see you again dear. I hope that you & Joe can work out your problems so that you will both feel that you are progressing to some solution.

Her return flight to the East Coast was exhausting:

Got in after a good night at 7:40 standard but planes even when you lie down I don't find restful & on Northwestern you sit up, so I've been leisurely bathing & dressing.

Then her note to Hick sounded a grimmer note: "War looks nearer every day. Somehow I don't see how we can convoy & not declare war." Trude and I met her at LaGuardia and drove back into town with her for some talk and a bite. Trude had reached a decision not to see me while she settled her marriage with Eliot. She wrote to me a few days later. It was neither the first time nor the last:

When we saw Mrs. R. that Sunday night she looked at *you* and said 'It will be lonely and miserable for a while if it is to be good afterwards.' And now it is happening. I must now try not to hurt El too much—and help him wherever I can. —And you suffer. Also—I am sick and can do less because I get tired. And you suffer.

It is too complicated, and because of me, because I did not decide early enough, because I somehow hoped for a miracle, now it almost needs a miracle to prevent tragedies.

And I must deal with my past life alone. It's El's right to have to deal only with me. —And because he has no part in the future, I pray that I may be as fair and kind as I can, and unhurried and sympathetic. Please understand, I implore you! For now, just for now let suspicions rest—I love you more than anything else in this world. But the present is not yours and mine only.

And bless you, call me, tell me that dark hours are not too much to bear because you know they will pass.

And either on this occasion, or one like it, Eleanor sought to comfort me:

My dearest boy, I hated to leave you last night, but there is so little anyone can do to help in the difficult times of life but just to be physically near people you love means something I think.

The Maurois article I'm enclosing seemed to me interesting & if I hadn't shown you the old Quaker quotation this is a good moment for you to keep it in your pocket. The copy of the letter I meant to give you in case it would be useful to the 'Defenders of Democracy.'

Something I said to you last night has bothered me because it wasn't wholly true. It was that weak people turned quickly to other new emotions & people for consolation. There are always special circumstances surrounding any situation which make generalizations like that not true, but what I was trying to say to you was that if you & Trude cared enough & could trust each other enough even when more or less apart, I thought strong people won through to what is perhaps as near the perfect human relationship as we poor humans can achieve. You two seem to me to deserve it & to be capable of it. God grant you may have it. My love is with you both.

The Quaker quotation she enclosed had noted on it: "Written long ago in England by John Woolman, Quaker." It read:

How deeply soever men are involved in the most exquisite difficulties, sincerity of heart and upright walking before God, freely submitting to his providence, is the most sure remedy. He only is able to relieve, not only persons, but nations in their greatest calamities.

Mrs. Roosevelt arranged for me to see Bernard Baruch about a contribution to ISS. "Just a line to tell you that Mr. Baruch is sold on you! He thinks you able & honest & likes you very much," she reported. "He is still considering ISS & I think he fears I may be diverted from doing my job of real usefulness here. Of course that is nonsense. . . ." When I indicated alarm that she might indeed ease off in her support of ISS, she reassured me: "Don't worry I won't neglect anything I can really do here for I.S.S. or any other interest. Someday when we have time I'll have to explain to you a few things I don't usually talk about so you will know what I can & what I cannot do."

Later she explained that cryptic remark in the course of refusing to take a job with civilian defense. Tommy asked my opinion about Mrs. R's taking the chairmanship of the Women's Division of Home Defense. Mrs. Roosevelt had decided to turn it down, she added, saying that she herself was troubled by the decision. I agreed with her. It would give Mrs. Roosevelt official status, I commented, a national audience at her command, and she might make a weekly talk to women, whose trust she had as well as that of young people. But Eleanor replied that she was afraid she would embarrass the President. Everything she said and did would be construed as coming from him and she did not want to add to his troubles now. In my mind I recalled her reluctance at the time of the Democratic National Convention to go out lest it raise the cry of "petticoat government." Any suggestion that she helped make up the President's mind would get under his skin. Such considerations were never far from her mind.

May and June were difficult for Trude and me. She began seeing a psychoanalyst who reinforced her feeling that she owed it to her husband and children to work matters out at home without daily encounters with me. But that was easier said than done. First there was Eleanor, who accepted her decision to work things out with Eliot. Her unbounded love for me seemed an unspoken protest against Trude's vacillations. Trude knew, moreover, that Eleanor disapproved of psychoanalysis and was convinced it gave the analyst a dangerous hold over the patient. But more powerful than Eleanor, analyst, or anyone else was the passion that drove us towards each other. It was difficult not to postpone her decision to return to her husband in the face of my pleas that she join Eleanor, Tommy, and me in driving up to Campobello to get the house there in shape for the student leadership institute. The activities of ISS in which she had participated with such zest were coming into dramatic focus with the Campobello Institute, and she wanted to play as much a part in its success as she had in its preparation.

So on June 18 two cars set out from Hyde Park. Eleanor was in the lead, driving her convertible with Tommy in it, and behind her came Trude's little Chevy, with me, a beginning driver taking turns at the wheel. Eleanor had known Campobello since 1903, when Franklin had first invited her to visit him and his mother there. It grieved her that since Franklin's polio the house and pine-girt island had been so little used. "The air is grand & Tommy & I like it here!" she now wrote to Hick on their arrival. Many things had to be bought and she delighted in taking Tommy, Trude, and me to Eastport and to St. Andrews to shop and picnic. Gradually the large red clapboard house was gotten ready for the thirty students and the William Allan Neilsons.* ". . . & then Trude, Tommy & I arranged all the beds for occupancy," she wrote to Hick on the twenty-first.

In the midst of all their preparations, Hitler invaded Russia, a move that caught the world by surprise, but not Roosevelt or Churchill. As Mrs. Roosevelt sought to get information from the President over the island's single and very bad telephone connection, she wrote to Hick: "This last German move may be good or bad depending on whether the Russians can hold out." The next day she repeated her hesitation: "Will it be good or bad? If they hold out & retreat good, but what will they do? I saw Hull followed Churchill's lead & where will our Catholics go?"

The institute opened on Monday, June 30, and she and Tommy left on Saturday, Trude two days later. Trude went to Bailey Island, near Brunswick, Maine, where she would work with her analyst, an enterprise that filled me with foreboding. Eleanor, who was to return on the tenth bringing an ailing Mama who was eighty-six, to stay in her own next door house, left me a farewell note:

> You may be so busy on Monday that you won't feel as lonely as I fear you will be but in any case I want to tell you what a happy time you have given me. I've loved being with you & Trude & I hope you two have had a happy time on the whole & that it has been a helpful interlude in these trying months. Remember that if you want to spend any time in August at Hyde Park I will make it as easy for you as possible.
>
> Trude is a fascinating person & I think I understand her & only wish that I could help her. You, I love deeply & I would do anything I could to bring you happiness.
>
> This should be an interesting & useful few weeks. I'll be thinking of you constantly & wishing you luck. It will be something to look forward to, getting back here before long & watching you in action.

* William Allan Neilson, president emeritus of Smith College, noted editor of Shakespeare's plays, and genial Scotsman, head of the institute.

Her sympathetic note to Trude bared more of her innermost feelings than she usually did:

> I know Monday will be a hard evening for you & so I want you to know that you & Joe have given me such a happy time. I have loved being with you & only hope it will prove for both of you a helpful period in these trying months.

She then developed her views on the autonomous, self-reliant individual, views that were based on her personal experience and that are quoted on page 66 at the beginning of the Lucy Mercer chapter. One had to live one's own life because one could not live that of another—whether husband or child.

Back at Hyde Park she wrote to Trude about her plans to return to Campo:

> You will be amused to hear that my husband thinks his mother has just decided to be contrary & go when she likes to Campobello so he suggested I let Schaeffer take her & go whenever I want! So, I think I'll probably go up & spend the night of the 7th or 8th near you. I'd love to have you spend it with me & if Mama refuses to go with me it can be anywhere you would like, in fact Tommy & I could come to your boarding house!
>
> Please eat enough, don't just feed your mind & forget about your body. Is there anything I can send you? If Dr. Cohn & Dr. [Alvin] Johnson come to lunch I'll send you an account of that!

Eleanor's first letter to me from Hyde Park revealed interest in the burgeoning civilian defense effort that ran counter to her hesitation over assuming a formal role in it:

> We've dedicated the library today. Mrs. Kerr & Mrs. [Anna] Rosenberg have been here and we went over the Mayor's plans, before I go back some advances will be made. . . . I love being here but I long to be with you in Campo too, in fact I want that most!

To Hick, who was in Washington, she also reported progress on civilian defense matters but lamented her inability to find the time to do all that was needed: "The Norwegians are here till Saturday & very nice but I find it irksome to sit every evening with folded hands & converse, knowing that my desk is piled high!" Now that Russia had been invaded, she was being courted anew by American Youth Congress officials and other Communist sympathizers. The Youth Congress wanted her to discuss her ideas on conscription, which the Congress had opposed, from its platform. She wrote to Hick: "I have a wire from Anna Louise Strong asking for aid to Russia so that we can now take advantage of our greatest opportunity to crush Hitler. Also Don Stephens sent me a copy of the Constitution of the U.S.S.R. & a long dissertation to the President on the difference between Stalin as a dictator & Hitler!" To such items, whose irony she did not need to stress, she added a cryptic: "He [the President] tells me one of his 'hens' is laying an egg on Sunday so watch the news." A few days later U.S. troops landed in Iceland.

Always a believer in starting an idea by trying it out in her own community, she reported to me:

> Elinor Morgenthau & I went to see the county agent this a.m. to try to start a nutrition campaign in the county but I think it will move slowly. Sometimes I feel that people appear to be awake but are really asleep, they seem to move & think so slowly!

The Archibald MacLeishes, Justice Frankfurter, Dr. and Mrs. David M. Levy, Aubrey Williams and Floyd Reeves, Mrs. Albert Lasker, Mrs. Morgenthau, Captain James Roosevelt, and the James Wechslers were all about to descend on Campo when Eleanor returned. She wrote to me:

> I wired you about rooms at Miss Venell's because the numbers began to appall me! We must make Mrs. MacLeish sing! It ought to be a weekend almost too rich in stimulus but somehow we must get the most out of it for everyone! I've mainly worried for fear I won't get any chance to really see you. Will your reputation stand it if an old lady comes & converses with you after you've gone to bed? That looks to me about the only time I'll see you alone!
>
> I had a long letter from Trude today written on Wed. & she'll spend the night with me on Wed. near Bath [Maine].
>
> The Hudson Shore Labor School came for their picnic today & as we sat talking after lunch I noticed a man whose face I liked & who helped greatly by asking interesting & stimulating questions. The talk turned to I.S.S. & I said I thought we had a good many learned & high falluting people on the Com. & later he came over & said 'I'm afraid you'll class me with the learned people, I'm Max Lerner!' I liked him so much & he said he wished he could come to Campo but he had to be with his children & was leaving for Harvard tomorrow where he will be when I speak on the 16th. I'm getting more & more scared about it & wonder why I ever said I'd go!
>
> I must go to bed but I am looking forward so much to seeing you dear boy. I think you are right Trude belongs with you & there will be usefulness & love & happiness & I pray for you both that she feels it. Perhaps she's right to think things through alone if only she doesn't rely on the psychoanalyst.
>
> Bless you & take care of yourself & I do hope you are over your cold & that the fog is gone. A world of love.

Eleanor drove Mama to Campo. On the way there they spent the night at Bath, where Trude joined them. "Trude dearest," she wrote to her afterwards:

> It was hard to leave you yesterday. I wanted very much to take you with us & I shall be wanting very much to help you in any way I can these days to come. Don't let indecision on anyone's part drag the strain out too long. No one is spared pain in the long run.
>
> Joe looks tired but being so busy has kept him from thinking & he is a much stronger person. I have a growing admiration for Joe's heart & spirit. I think he wants to get away after school closes & Dr. [Remsen] Bird wants to see him so we may leave Sat. p.m. or Sunday morning & drive to N.Y. & do other things after we get to H.P. He needs a rest but I don't know if he can take one. However, I think, he'd rather be where, if you need him, he will be near & I feel much the same way.
>
> Bless you dear. May you have courage & clarity & I know that whatever you do is what you feel right for you. Much love.

But a letter from Trude reached me at Campobello at the same time and plunged me into deep gloom:

> I feel pulled and tugged to come to Campobello but unless an emergency arises I shall stay here—and in this rather difficult and strange way sort out what's important and find out what I have to do. I love you dearly and passionately but I won't come back unless I know beyond doubt that I cannot do anything else and be myself. . . .

Letters from Eleanor to Hick described the weekend at Campobello:

> Mama stood the trip up wonderfully & was so happy that I felt it was well worth while. It was a strain driving her because you couldn't do anything sudden!
>
> There are so many guests here that this weekend is strenuous & it began the moment I arrived. Aubrey & Floyd Reeves were here & we went to Quoddy [Passamaquoddy] yesterday & have been with them & their school here all the time. I'm glad I came for tho' we've kept Mama in bed till today I've been able to fill the house!
>
> I'm going to meet Dr. Cohn.

The next day, Sunday, she was again full of the institute:

> These have been the busiest days I've ever spent & I'm certainly not going to consider this trip a rest! I've spent hours talking & tonight I've read poetry for hours. Mr. MacLeish read this morning & it was a really moving experience. The details of so many guests made life hectic & they drop in at all hours.
>
> I like the young things & I think Dr. Neilson is happy but Mrs. N. is not. They make too much noise! Really they should be in a separate house. Joe Lash is wonderful but he is tired now & I should think

would be very weary by the time they depart. Luckily, I think the guests think well of the School! . . .

Frankfurter is talking tomorrow, but he is talking all the time! We all go to Quoddy in the afternoon & he speaks there. . . .

Her farewell note to me when she left for Hyde Park was full of affection and concern about Trude:

I shall be so happy for you & Trude when this month is over. It is so desperately hard for you but being busy is always best when one has to wait for something.

I had decided to apply formally for a commission in the Navy and filled out the application forms that Captain Blackburn had sent to me: "I can't bear to have you leave I.S.S. & go into the Navy," Eleanor wrote to me on the way back to Hyde Park, "but even that can be borne if Trude decides as you want for you won't feel so alone & somehow we'll keep your plans going till you can return. Mrs. Levy said such grand things about you this morning that I could have kissed her & she said Dr. L. was deeply impressed by you. She & I both hope against hope that some miracle may let you go on in I.S.S."

Back at Hyde Park she sent Trude, who still was on Bailey Island, a detailed account of the big weekend at Campo:

Your letter of the 12th didn't reach me before I left, so to my joy I found it here this evening. Joe & I wrote you because we both missed you & thought about you & wanted you to know it.

He will have written you all about the weekend from his point of view & probably has told you about his last talk with Dr. Cohn which I cannot report on. Dr. Cohn did tell me that he was pleased. Mr. Frankfurter said that he was most enthusiastic & would so report to both Mr. Baruch & Mr. Field which ought to help us. The Neilsons should be out of the house. He is a dear. I glanced through her book & watched her. She is too conscious of herself to help anyone & both are too old to be uncomfortable. Joe thought he might suggest they stay at Mrs. Gough's but I don't know what happened. Dr. & Mrs. Levy were enthusiastic. Elinor Morgenthau & Mrs. Lasker were both impressed & so were Dr. Reeves & Aubrey Williams. The evening on Monday at Quoddy was a success. The MacLeishes made Sunday memorable. Mr. Frankfurter was masterly on Monday but the kids didn't like him. Too self-conscious again I think. I think the kids are grand. I like the servants & dislike the dietician but of course the person who makes the school & carries it is Joe & the kids know it.

He has a marvellous influence & is wonderful with them. He is working too hard & is tired but I think the anxiety about you & your decision would break Joe if he were not so busy, so it is really a blessing.

Tommy, Elinor & I left Campo Tuesday morning & Mama was really well & cheerful. We spent the night at Whitefield, N.H. & I saw my cousin Mrs. Parish & then reached Boston at 3 p.m. on Wednesday to find Anne & Johnny waiting for me & Franklin jr. came in soon after & they left when I went to my dinner & lecture in Cambridge. Thursday we left at 7:15 & were here before one.

In the afternoon the Hampton quartette came & sang beautifully & they showed their film. I had all the neighbors over at the big house. Today I have flown in a sea plane to Auburn, N.Y. to dedicate a new N.Y.A. center & it looks to me very good. I shall go to Washington from Wed. to Friday & next Sunday I go to Alexander Woollcott for a night, to Camp William James for a night & I will reach Campo the afternoon of the 29th or by noon on the 30th. I think I'll stay in the house with the kids if Joe has room because one can know them so much better.

I didn't read "Darkness at Noon" [by Arthur Koestler] but I'll hope to next time I'm up there. I'm just now finishing Shirer* but I've read much government material & mail so I haven't been idle.

Dear, you are much in my thoughts & should you want me to spend the night of the 29th where you can join me, I'll gladly do it whether you are going to Campo or not. I hope you are.

Tommy sends her love. My prayers & good wishes & love are going to you daily.

The longer that Trude on Bailey Island pondered her course, the more strongly she felt she had not been just to her husband. She wrote to me:

Do you want me to write what goes on—how I realize more and more that even if there had been a chance of a relationship between El and me—it could not happen because I did not let it happen?

Bailey would not have been necessary if I had honestly faced my situation before. But when I knew in April that I would never do it as long as there was a chance of being with you—without having to settle my marriage—I was easily persuaded by you that I was wrong. I wasn't wrong—I was only afraid and weak and now these last months seem terribly wrong—like a life snatched from somebody else.

Then came the decision I had feared:

Going back includes the possibility of getting stuck there. It seems impossible now—but I cannot promise that I shall be free at a certain moment. The need to go back is not just the need to 'serve time' for a bad deed. I can promise that I shall be honest—and I pray for courage and insight.

You believed that I was free to love you—when I said I was—and now you are involved in something that belongs to my past and you suffer. A thousand times these days I have prayed for some way to help you—but I can only try to be a better person. Your love is true and

---

* William L. Shirer, who wrote *Berlin Diary*.

right—and strong. And because you love so much you have made it possible for me to believe again that I might become able to serve a belief I had long since given up.

I had no alternative but to accept her decision, I replied. I would do my best to respect it. Eleanor telegraphed: "I think you did the right thing," and by letter sought to console me:

I want to be with you & put my arms around you. We will hold our faith in Trude & in her love for you. I am happy you want to be with me at Hyde Park & will go back when the Campo house is in order & do just what you want. You are a strong person & will grow thro' this & always dear & Trude will be proud of you as I am.

Trouble piled upon the Campo venture. The presence on the island of New Deal personalities like Justice Frankfurter, Aubrey Williams, as well as Mrs. Roosevelt, drew the attention of Westbrook Pegler. He went after the galaxy in his column and with glee leapt on me. My past Communist affiliations and divorce hardly qualified this "inveterate and professional youth" to lead the young.

"Pegler seems to have written a very poisonous column which I haven't yet seen about me & Frankfurter & he draws you in," she wrote to me. "Sometimes I wish I could do things without attracting attention & drawing venom down on my friends. I'm sorry dear if it hurts you."

A few days later when she had returned to Campo for the end of the school, there was a second column: "Pegler has written another vicious column I hear. I really wonder why he takes such joy in being disagreeable." Again she told me she was sorry that she brought such attacks on me, but I felt that I was a handy stick with which to besmirch her.

On the drive down from Campo, I spelled her at the wheel of her car, a little surprised always that she was willing to trust the wheel to so inexperienced a driver. Tommy suffered but kept her silence. Eleanor persuaded me to spend a couple of weeks in Hyde Park. Her sympathy in my courtship of Trude was shared by Tommy. Ordinarily, she concealed the feelings beneath what she called her "rough exterior," but in this case she sought to comfort the hapless lover with an account of "similar experiences," in which "time and hard work [had] helped greatly. You are fortunate in having a friend like Mrs. R. who is so understanding and helpful. . . ."

They were historically momentous times: "How excited the papers are over FDR's cruise," she wrote to Hick, but if she knew he was about to meet Churchill at Argentia, Newfoundland, she kept it to herself.

As a result of that meeting, the first between the two leaders, the Atlantic Charter was written. A major concern that August was with the mounting pressure upon her from people like Harry Hopkins and Anna Rosenberg, as well as from friends like myself, that she take on the job with Civilian Defense. The President had established the Office of Civilian Defense in May and appointed New York's pugnacious mayor, F. H. LaGuardia to head it, but as Eleanor informed Hick, "I fear the Mayor is having a good bit of trouble. He isn't interested in volunteer work or the women's end of it but he won't delegate authority so he'll have to straighten it out himself."

The use of women and young people in the defense effort interested her, as did the mobilization of volunteers, but she hesitated. Would the Mayor give her the authority she would need? There was always the reluctance of the President to have her take on a key job because she might become a political issue.

To worry about me was almost a relief. She handed me a note to read when I was alone:

> It is futile to tell you that I love you & want to help when I know just now I can't help & there is only one love that matters, & that, is yours I believe, but is swamped by other considerations.
>
> I can only tell you that the hardest blows of fate, met with courage, somehow are bearable & I know you will come out a stronger & a more helpful man. I have unbounded confidence in you & I count so much on you. Your companionship & respect & trust mean so much to me that I can only beg you to be with me all you can be and let me be as close in every way as possible.

When she took me to the Poughkeepsie railroad station, she handed me a note to read on the way down and the family ticket to use on the train coming back:

> You will doubtless smile at all my concern for you, but I've grown to love you so much that your moods & anxieties & joys & sorrows seem very close to my own heart & you are very constantly in my thoughts. I'm happy always when I'm going to see you & I do want you to feel that with me, wherever I am, there is a home for you & those you love.

Another note greeted me in New York:

> I hope the excitement of getting back to New York dulled all your other feelings & I hope you didn't hate to go as much as I hated to have you go this evening.
>
> I came back & dictated hard to Tommy tomorrow's column & speech & several other short things & now I'm writing some of the children but I had to send you a line first for you are the child most in my heart at present. I could have wept when you left! I realize you want to work & it is better for you, but you forgive me for being selfish & missing your presence, don't you?

She was not wholly uncritical about the President's meeting with Churchill, and when I expressed anxiety over the morale of the Selective Service recruits in the camps and the desirability of the President speaking to them directly, she noted: "I told Franklin about your worries & he agreed that he'd like to talk the situation over at a meal at H.P." Hick voiced similar misgivings: "You expressed much of what I felt about the meeting on the high seas, but I do feel FDR is better able to handle foreign diplomats than Winston & we may get somewhere," she replied.

That fall she gave up her apartment on East Eleventh Street and moved her things to the East Sixty-fifth Street house. Hick would always have a room there, Eleanor told her, and she gave me, as I helped her rehang her pictures, a key. Had Earl not been in the naval reserve, he too would have had a place there. She flew down to Florida to visit him. "You & Tommy were right," she wrote to me, "I am dripping as I wait in Jacksonville for the plane to Pensacola. . . . Joe dear, I think of you so much & I hope Trude has already dispelled some of the resentment. If only all this can come to a happy solution soon, the scars will heal."

Trude wrote to her why she felt she had to make an honest effort to hold her family together. "I almost know Trude's letter by heart," she wrote. "I've reread it so much in an effort to understand her. I've written her & I hope I haven't been unkind, but I told her what I think. I am afraid for her & Eliot & the children because I still believe she gave you her heart. If not, then I would have no respect for her."

She was becoming reconciled to going into civilian defense. "I'm worried about the civilian defense job because I don't want to do it & am not sure I can do it but if the Mayor asks me I'll have to try. Just at this moment I feel very low but I will have recovered when we meet Friday a.m.!" The same note of tentativeness sounded in her letter to Hick: "I may try to help on that civilian defense job but I dread trying to tackle it."

Family anxieties now superseded. September became a harrowing month. Hall was sinking and Mama, who had been an invalid all summer, was home from Campo only a week when she died. "The endless details, clothes to go through, checks, books, papers. I began on Sat.," she wrote to Maude Gray. Eleanor was "of course attending to everything," reported Helen Robinson, who lived next door at Hyde Park. "I am so weary I cannot write," Eleanor explained to Hick. "I was up most last night, 1½ hours was the time I spent in bed & I've been seeing relatives all day." Franklin could push unpleasant memories out of his mind, but not she, she wrote to me:

It was so good to hear your voice tonight but I can't help worrying about you & Trude & I'll be anxious to talk to you about both of you on Friday. I loved your little note which Tommy brought & I miss you & want to talk many things out with you. I feel that you are putting your own troubles out of my sight for the time being & that worries me. What ironical things happen in life & how foolish it all seems. I looked at my mother-in-law's face after she was dead & understood so many things I had never seen before. It is dreadful to have lived so close to someone for 36 years & to feel no deep affection or sense of loss. It's hard on Franklin however & the material details are appalling & there of course I can be of some use.

With Hall I have an odd mixture of feelings but again I am enmeshed in details of things to do. The next few months are going to be a strain so I'm going to cling to all the hours I can steal to be with you & people that I love! Just don't let me be too demanding!

She arranged for Hall's transfer to Walter Reed Hospital in Washington. "Lord knows how long we can keep him, if he gets better," she wrote to Hick, "but it doesn't look very hopeful to me." A penciled letter to me from the hospital:

I loved your letter, it sounded content. When you are alone & happy I know all is well. Trude's letter is sweet & I return it & send you a very dear one she wrote me. Perhaps I should also have more faith & patience where I cannot understand. I will write her.

Your article I like immensely. May I subscribe to "Threshold"* & get several extra copies of this past number?

I am sitting with Zena† as we have sat almost constantly since Sunday in Hall's room. He is completely unconscious & just breathes heavily. I fear the end may be horrible, a struggle for breath & I do not want Zena to be alone so while I do go home for a few hours, I sleep here at night in my clothes & worry all the time I am gone in the day!

Tommy found a copy of my father's letters & I sent it to you today. If you like it enough to want to keep it I'll put your name in it.

I hope you will like the Sunday broadcast. It has been written under difficulties but I hope it is good. I'm not going to broadcast for the Democratic women on Sat. but write it & have it read.

I went home at 12, did the column, had Mrs. Leach for lunch & said goodbye to Diana who went off to school. Worked with Tommy & have been back since 3:15. Will go home at seven & return at 8:30.

I am glad for your sake you are keeping your apartment & I understand your wanting to be near Trude but I think you may sometimes find it hard & I rather dread some things that might happen. Well, perhaps they won't. I do love Trude also for herself but I think of her more with you & so when you & she are not together it does not seem possible to see her. I suppose both of you find that hard to understand. I don't know that I understand it myself. As you know much that one feels is unreasonable & analyses badly!

* Newly published magazine of ISS, edited by Irwin Ross.
† Zena Raset, Hall's devoted companion of his final years.

Her note to Trude said:

The President wants me to tell you how much he appreciates your message of sympathy.

You were sweet to write & you are strangely understanding about things which may come up & I appreciate it.

It seems a long time dear, since I've seen you & I think of you a great deal. Just your promise to try in the future not to add to my troubles & cares can't take you & Joe out of my heart. I love you both & want to share your joys & sorrows & even the struggles & hopes & defeats which I hope in the end may bring you both to a safe haven.

It was almost as if writing to Trude and me enabled her to bear the final searing hours with Hall:

I'm glad you don't mind my telephoning you because I do like to hear your voice. It tells me something about you but it also has a reassuring effect on me & I seem to want it very much now. I was happy to have yesterday with you & you were so dear this morning. [I had gone down to Washington.]

This has been a bad day. My idea of hell, if I believed in it, would be to sit or stand & watch someone breathing hard, struggling for words when a gleam of consciousness returns & thinking 'this was once the little boy I played with & scolded, he could have been so much & this is what he is.' It is a bitter thing & in spite of everything I've loved Hall, perhaps somewhat remissedly of late, but he is part of me. I do have a quieting effect on him & so I stood by his bed & held his hand & stroked his forehead & Zena stood beside me for hours. She won't give up hope of his recovery & keeps asking me if I don't think he's strong enough to pull through till I could weep.

Tommy came out to the hospital at noon & we did the column in the car. She is a brick too! Jimmy telephoned but there is nothing anyone can do just now. I'm waiting for Franklin to get back & when I've reported to him what I got done yesterday, I shall go to bed for I am pretty weary & I'm going out at 7:30 in the morning if they don't call me before.

Darling, you know I'm glad of anything which cheers you & if things are working out so Trude sees how things really are more clearly you will have justified your patience & fine faith. I'll be thinking of you both with love & hope.

"Some day you & I will be cheerful again!" her next letter said. It linked my unhappiness over Trude with her own over Hall. "Fjr. arrived this a.m. & stayed tonight because he thought I was upset which was rather sweet. He was a bad boy, however, before he came so I scolded all over again & wondered how much good it did!

"I love saying goodnight & because this is a hard time for me, it means a lot to talk to you."

To Hick she wrote: "Another visit to the hospital, & an almost violent argument with FDR & Elliott at dinner on our responsibility to our own boys & to defense. . . ." She had decided to take the job of Assistant Director of the Office of Civilian Defense in charge of volunteer participation and community organization. "A talk with Anna Rosenberg & I'll go in just to look over the office next Monday & the Mayor will announce my appointment as of the 29th."

Another long letter to reassure me underscored the importance of the "one" person:

> Your letter was waiting for me when I went home at 7:30 & you are right. I should indeed feel shut away & buried in my present horror if you did not write about yourself. I can never understand why you feel any proof is needed that you are loved for yourself & I feel you have had a fine faith in Trude. She herself or circumstances beyond your control shake it now & then but perhaps if it keeps returning you will win out. I've never doubted that Trude loved you, other things sometimes worry me. Where does this lead Joe? Two people not working towards *one* happy life but losing themselves in the joy of being together when they forget their other lives? You never could try my patience, dear, I know how elusive happiness is & how important the 'one' person is, worthy any effort & all inconsistencies. Of course you can say anything to me & out of my love for you I think I will always understand. I'm glad you are happy to be with me for that makes me happy. I want you to be as sure of me as my own children are. These days are hard because Hall was always a little my child & the waste of a life seems a bitter thing. This way of dying seems so unnecessarily hard & I am weary & heartsick for Zena. I'll tell you some of the things she said which make me want to weep but I shall not for I cannot let go. Jimmie & Romaine came for me this evening & drove me home. They have been very sweet. Tommy is an angel too & she has had a day of getting Elinor Morgenthau inducted into Civilian Defense & seeing the advertising man on the radio & doing all the other chores besides 1-½ hours here while we did the column & the script.
>
> I shall be anxious to see the pictures. I'm more interested in good ones of you than of me.
>
> Joe dear, I'm glad your voice sounds happy. I shall long to see you sometime this weekend, at the cottage or in N.Y. if you have the time. I feel sure this cannot last much longer tho' everyone has ceased making predictions & I may not see you till you are here again. I have slept in my clothes. Tonight will be the third night but we both sleep & I dare not leave. He is quieter tho' tonight which means weaker I imagine.
>
> Bless you dear boy, I love you very much.

The next day Hall died. She turned down my offer to come up. She and those in the family close to Hall would go to Tivoli, but she wrote to me:

Your wire touched me deeply this morning. I don't know why I couldn't talk this morning. I just couldn't control my voice & there didn't seem any good reason. I was quite alright in a minute & it was good to hear your voice both this morning & tonight. I love you dear for your thoughtfulness & it will be good to see you Saturday afternoon.

A few days later she assumed her duties at OCD. "I've been looking at the little Spanish boy on my desk tonight," she wrote as she examined the organization over which she had taken command, "& I'm glad I brought him down from H.P. for I'm going to need the kind of courage he symbolizes. Being actually in this show I find I'm uncovering some things that are never entirely truthful. Things are devious & I wonder if I have knowledge & courage enough to go on successfully."

Despite her many duties as assistant director of OCD, she continued to be as attentive to her friends. Her private life strengthened her for the other. Hick, as executive director of the Women's Division of the Democratic National Committee, continued to live at the White House although she spent weekends at her little house in Moriches, Long Island. Earl, together with Simone, to whom he was now married, was stationed in Pensacola, and Eleanor occasionally visited him there and corresponded with him faithfully. She would soon employ Tiny to work out a dance program for children as part of the community participation program of OCD, an appointment that would be derided by a hostile press as that of a "fan-dancer." Elinor Morgenthau came in as her associate. "Mrs. Morgenthau will confer when I am not available," her notes on the organization and its objectives stated.

Those notes on Val-Kill letterheads and in her handwriting she turned over to me. I was at Hyde Park that weekend and put them away with my own note:

> Mrs. R. woke up at 3 a.m. and found herself perfectly calm and rested. Said she lay until 6 thinking out her plans for Monday's induction at OCD and then arose and wrote them down as attached. She gave them to Tommy at breakfast to compose and type and then let me have them.

Written in pencil, the notes began with "Over-all objectives." They were followed by an enumeration of "Goals for Dept. Heads" which were to be achieved "by November 1." Tidily she followed this with "our first job to organize headquarters office," which required that the staff persons write out for her their respective duties, salary agreements, staffs in Washington and the field, and their salaries. She set aside 9:15 to 10 every morning for consultations with her staff. All policy letters were to be submitted to her "before" going out, and copies of all letters were to be sent to her secretary before the end of the day. She explained how press and publicity were to be handled, listed the people to be put through right away on the telephone. Visitors were to be screened by Mrs. Betty Lindley or Miss Dorothy Overlock. She detailed how she wanted fieldwork checked and said that policy would have to be established on "our responsibility to rest of org. & to Mayor."

"A great manager," commented Tommy after she typed out the notes.

She kept telling me that her relationship with me at the time was the one from which she received the deepest satisfaction. "I told you last night," she said to me during the days I was at the White House while Hall was ill, "how much your being here these days has meant to me. I love knowing you are in the house & we are going to meet now & then & I look forward to the moments & hours & days that we spend together."

She liked Trude but she was impatient at times over the latter's inability to come to terms with an unhappy marriage. When Trude told Eliot that she was unable to abide by her agreement not to see me and I unhappily accepted her remaining as head of Eliot's household, she reconciled herself to that arrangement too for my sake: "You are right to try for your happiness," she wrote, "& I hope you win for your courage & faith deserve it. God bless you & I'll be wishing you a happy evening Thursday. . . ."

That fall Eleanor's vitality was hard-pressed as she sought the time and energy on top of her duties to OCD to do her column, fulfill her lecture schedule, carry on her personal correspondence, do what she alone could do for a multiplicity of organizations, and meet a White House social calendar even if Mrs. Helm held it to its bare bones. At the President's request Anna and John came East to discuss the settlement of Mama's estate. "It was wonderful meeting Anna & John this morning & we are having snatches of fun but I have every moment taken so we talked late this evening." She reproached herself: "I wish I had no work & no engagements & could just be with Anna & it seems bad management on my part! I'll go out there in Jan."

After Mama's death she wanted to make changes in the Big House in order to make it more livable and more hers and Franklin's, but Franklin would not say yes or no. She only learned from Anna that the President wished to keep the house the way it had been during Mama's lifetime. That settled matters for her. She would stay at the Big House when the President was there, but was determined otherwise to live at Val-Kill. A very private person, she was willing to state to the world: "My mother-in-law owned the house and ran it herself up until a year ago, and it is exactly as she left it. It never was my home in the sense that I ever had anything to do with the furnishing or running of it." She said nothing about Franklin's attitude. At times he had shielded her against Mama's dominating ways, but at other times he refused to notice them, even sided with his mother. "I think Franklin will forget all the irritations," she wrote to Maude Gray at the time of Sara's death, "& remember only pleasant things which is just as well."

Between her father's death when she was ten, its pangs rekindled by Hall's tortured end, and Franklin's unwillingness to agree to her redoing the Big House, a sense of life's meaninglessness again seized her. "I am so weary," she confessed to Hick, "that I feel as you sometimes look & yet I know it is because I am letting myself be indifferent inside. You know how I get these moods, they pass but they are a nuisance." She was still depressed the next day: "I'm in a horrid frame of mind, but I think it will pass & I hope I don't show it." Hick wrote from Chicago: "Remember, even when you're feeling that way, you do a better job at whatever you're doing than most people do." Eleanor's work at OCD was taking shape. "I felt for the first time today that I could perhaps see light ahead & soon begin to see things happening!"

She discussed her OCD plans with Bernard Baruch. "He approved my setup as far as charts went but I don't think he realizes what Defense Councils are going to be like to deal with," she wrote to me from Washington. Her letter ended:

Somehow I wish that we could be in the same town these days so if you wanted me at any time I could be available. As it is I just want you to know that having you near makes me happy & I hope it helps you & when I can be in New York I want every minute you can spare!

She did not like to celebrate her birthday and drove her closest friends and family to distraction trying to figure out what to get her. She did not like birthdays because she sensed insincerity in what people said about her. The previous year Mama had made a speech about her which made her writhe, she said. She was fifty-seven. Whatever she thought, the President took the lead in celebrating it. He took her and the friends she asked him to invite down the river on the presidential yacht *Potomac*, confounding a previous statement she had made to me: "No party at all," when I had asked her whether there might not be one. Here were my diary notes on the trip:

It was thrilling to watch him being piped on board. It was a placid party. Mrs. R. worked on her mail for three hours, the President on his stamps. The rest of us sat around and chatted desultorily. Then we played gin rummy. At 6:30 we had old-fashioneds—which Mrs. R. is willing to take because with the fixings she can make herself believe it is a kind of fruit punch—and then a sumptuous dinner ending with champagne. Jimmy and Rommie had a gift for Mrs. R. at her place with a little dedication verse that played naughtily on the word 'asterisk.' It was passed around the table and Helen Gahagan Douglas began to read it out loud until she came to the key word, gulped and read "neck to risk" which was a brilliant recovery.

The President drank a toast pointing out this was the first time he had gotten Mrs. R. on a naval vessel, and that by next year at this time he and Mrs. R. would have met the Prime Minister of Japan on an island in the Pacific. Not unless she could fly there and back, Mrs. R. said, laughing. She would not be so restricted in her moments as traveling on a naval ship would mean.

The President's gift was Jo Davidson's original of the Inaugural Medal, inscribed: From Jo Davidson to F.D.R. to E.R.

Even for her the pace that October and November was unparalleled. She had to fit in Dorothy and Leonard Elmhirst* "for breakfast. They are here & the young Straights & Douglas Fairbanks." At Hyde Park: "We've been working on Mama's papers & clothes—doing a bit about entertaining royalty in between! I like [Princess] Juliana. She is simple & sweet & her children are Dutch dolls!" She wished, however, she might have been more with Tommy and Mrs. Helm "at the cottage," and suddenly the hecticness of it all made her think of 1917–18. "Funny, I'm living just as I did in the first war & I swore I'd never do it again. How little we know!"

From Detroit she wrote to me:

You will laugh, but there are so many people clamoring at me, on the plane, in the corridors, etc. that I've just decided to write a letter & let Tommy cope with it till everyone gets sorted out!

At that point I went to the press conference & in a half hour the Governor & defense officials will be here & at 4:15 a local of working girls & 4:30 the Democratic women & at 5 Dorothy Roosevelt & the 3 girls for tea & at 6:30 dinner with the ladies of the Forum & 8:30 talk on 'Women in Defense' & 11:45 train to Cincinnati! Tomorrow I'm going to be frivolous & have my hair done.

. . . .

Some belated press are at the door for one more picture & one question. So goodbye dear boy. It was so nice to see you this morning. It made my day start pleasantly & yet I hope it didn't mean real discomfort & effort for you.

"Shall we have our Xmas dinner 22nd or 23rd—in N.Y. or D.C.," she inquired of Hick on November 18. It was not yet Thanksgiving. The same day she wrote a note to me to be opened on Thanksgiving:

You will open this I hope on Thanksgiving Day & regardless of how you may feel about other things in your life I want you to know that you have given me much to be thankful for on this day.

I'm thankful for many things but one of the things I am most

---

* The former Dorothy Whitney had been married to Willard Straight before his death. They had helped found and fund *The New Republic*. With Leonard Elmhirst, Dorothy presided over Dartington, a school and creative arts center in England.

thankful for is that our friendship has deepened & means more to me as the days go by. I love being with you & I like to think that the future holds many opportunities for us to be together, sometimes in quiet contentment & sometimes in gay company. I hope we see & do many things that we enjoy together & with those we both love.

God grant that you may have some sense of thankfulness on this day & that every year in the future you may have more & more to bring you a sense of contentment & joy & peace.

Although she and Tommy had allowed me to drive them part of the way down from Campo in August, I only obtained a driver's license in November: "Schaeffer tells me he *knows* you passed your test!" she wrote after the examination. Two weeks later on my birthday she sent a card:

> A fire truck had glamor once,
> Later a dump truck was the thing.
> But now only an open car
> Maroon in color for the nonce
> And with an engine that will sing
> Will make me feel I've reached a star!

"I'm dying to see the car & hope you like it," another note said, referring to the Pontiac convertible she had gotten for me. There was another note on my birthday:

I'm writing this because it is always easier to say 'no' if you have time to think about it but I do want you to say 'yes' if you would like to do it!

Do come up whenever you are free. I'll be at the house soon after six & waiting to both kiss and spank you & I would love it if you have nothing else that calls, to have you stay the night. It would be nice to tuck you in & say goodnight on your birthday!

I'll call you in the morning about eight to say bless you & I'm so glad you were born on this day!

A few days later, December 7, life changed for everyone.

XVIII

"To know me is
a terrible thing..."

PEARL HARBOR changed everything. Eleanor as assistant director of OCD, together with its director, Mayor LaGuardia, immediately flew out to the West Coast, which expected, if not an invasion, at least bombing by Japanese planes. When over the phone I told her that I was due to speak at an intercollegiate conference in the Los Angeles area, she had the White House get me a seat on the same plane. "I'm so glad we are going together & I'm longing to see you," her note greeted me.

We saw each other during the two days she was in the Los Angeles area, speaking over the radio, meeting with civilian defense officials. It became a standing joke among the three of us, for Tommy was along, whether I would be able to shake a certain college president who was determined to gain Mrs. Roosevelt's favor. As she took the train northward, for the military had banned all commercial flights, and I returned East, she sounded an unusual note of self-approbation: "One thing among many others I've learned, if we have trouble anywhere I must go because it does seem to calm people down. I think I must wangle permission to go by army plane when necessary."

The officials in the coastal cities discovered, and the latter included Portland, Tacoma, and Seattle as well as Los Angeles, that she was calm and clearheaded:

We were only half an hour late this morning & I went to a meeting where the Mayor, the Sheriff & the head of the Fire Dept. sounded off on what a lot they had done & would do when the Federal government gave them the money. I hope that I showed them that getting the money was a remote possibility & doing was different from saying! Then we had 2 meetings where we all got down to business in small groups & I think something was accomplished. The Japanese problem seems to be increasingly difficult & the vegetables for the entire country will be curtailed if we can't get some assets 'unfrozen.'

While I was on the West Coast, Trude had stepped in at ISS as acting general secretary of International Student Service. It was a portent of things to come, for it was only a matter of weeks, I thought, before my draft classification of 1H would be changed to 1A and I would be drafted.* I hoped that Trude would be acceptable to the ISS Board as my replacement. She was more than willing. By training and temperament she liked professional responsibility. Moreover, although she was a United States citizen she was German-born, and felt a patriotic need to serve. She wrote to Mrs. Roosevelt:

This war does change the feeling of everything for me. Not because we are now actually at war against Germany and I am German born. That passed two years ago, when war broke out. Since then I have been praying every day that this country might not decide too late that we too must fight for our beliefs on the battlefield. And so when war came all the uncertainties and fears disappeared. What haunts me is the feeling that I am not doing my part—that all these years I have not done enough. But if goodwill helps then some day I shall find my place.

Although Trude was clear that she wanted to work, she continued to be torn between her love for her children and her love for me. She was determined above all to hold onto the children. Eleanor saw us in New York and afterwards wrote to me:

I wish I could take both you children in my arms & shield you from all the suffering but I fear few of us go through life without being burned. I can only hope that talking to me eases the strain a little & remember that I love you deeply & tenderly & will always be here for you to turn to.

"It seems like a completely changed world," she had written from the West Coast. That was again brought home to her in Washington when she and the President said goodbye to Jimmy, who had been ordered to Hawaii, and to Elliott, who had been assigned to a bomber squadron. Over the phone, on her arrival in New York, I had detected a

* 1H was a category established at the insistence of Congress. It included men ages twenty-eight to thirty-five who were deferred because of age. At the time I was thirty-two.

dispiritedness in her voice and rushed up to the Roosevelt house on East Sixty-fifth Street to see what was the matter. She spoke about her boys. She knew they had to go, but it was hard. Simply by the laws of chance not all of them would return. She wept, then regained control of herself, thanked me for having come, and told me to go back to my office.

She hated to have people see her when she was not in total control of herself, but though she scolded me, I felt that she had not minded. That Christmas season some of her deepest moments of pleasure, she said, came from thinking about how to be helpful to me. Christmas Eve, just as she was about to take Tommy's presents over to her and afterwards go to midnight service, she dashed off a note to me. A book she had read the previous night made her think of me "& your love for the Spanish songs. Bless you." She had given me an envelope marked "For Xmas morning." Winston Churchill was at the White House, and her fond letter was filled with the political detail that she knew I craved:

> I've just trimmed the little tree & with Diana [Hopkins] & my thoughts went flying to all my children & I found them coming back to you very often. I wish I could be with you dear, these days, not because I think I could be of much help to you but because it would be of so much help to me. I've grown to feel closer & closer to you & depend on you greatly & it's a great pleasure & a source of real contentment to be with you. Of course, I know I grow greedy for instead of just being thankful for the times I have you I always want more!
>
> The house is full of official business & official people. It is interesting & Franklin with his historic sense is enjoying it greatly. I never have much sense of being a part of history! The Prime Minister is jolly looking & interesting but I'd like to tell you about our conversation at dinner about the exiled governments & their people. I liked Mme. Litvinoff very much today & he is a wary diplomat who would not be led on tho' I tried hard! George Fischer* seemed to enjoy being at tea with them. He had to rent evening clothes because just now we dress every evening.
>
> I hope you enjoy opening the many foolish packages & if there are things you don't want to wear you can change them & if there are things you don't want to eat you can give them away. Whether you like them or not you will know that I enjoyed wrapping them & with them goes a very deep & tender love for you dear boy. May the day be happy as happy as it can be this year. Give your Mother my greetings & a world of love to you.

---

* Son of the political journalist Louis Fischer. Mrs. Roosevelt helped bring George and his brother and their Russian-born mother to the United States. George had been at the ISS institute in Campobello.

A Christmas Eve letter from Trude, who was in New Milford, Connecticut, with her family, added to my contentment:

There is one Christmas wish I have beyond all else—to be at peace with you. To know that our love is strong and good and a blessing from heaven because it is given to us. It never seems to me that I own it, that I can do with it wilfully what I please. Rather it is a happy state in which I dwell.

The decisions one has to make sometimes are directed by considerations outside that love—but love is not less true for them. I have had to learn everything about love because I had never experienced it before. And I have been crude and hurt you—because I did not know and struggled against something that was not in my power but I have not hurt you from ill will.

I don't know what this new year will bring, but whatever it is, I know we will be strong and devoted—and willing to take it on.

To you go my love and my thoughts and my confidence.

So often lately I have felt your presence even when you were far away. The knowledge of you and your love have changed my life and made it real—and now I have no words, dearest, to tell you how close you are to me, and how you fill the world by your presence.

I shall think of you tonight when you burn the red candle—and what people consider just a light in the sky will be a shimmering band between your house and mine.

I put my arms around you and kiss you and wish you a very Happy Christmas.

If Eleanor had misgivings about my unwillingness or inability to force matters to a showdown with Trude, she concealed them. She thanked me for my presents:

Your Xmas day letter made me happy. I'm so glad peace was with you dear & that Trude made you happy. The house sounds lovely & perhaps I can get a glimpse of it on Sunday. Shall I go down from the station & pick you up? . . . I feel peaceful too in one way Joe dear & I echo your wish that the coming year will bring us both joy. I am sure of one thing, the knowledge that you love me will bring me happiness no matter what else may come. . . .

A letter to Hick the same day enlarged on her views of Churchill:

Hick darling, Your letter of Thursday came today & I'm glad you stayed in N.Y. & had such a pleasant time seeing friends & helping them over bad places. You've had such hard times yourself that you are especially thoughtful & helpful to others.

I hope you had a happy day & will enjoy to the full the days in the country.

The day went off well here from an official point of view. The

Lindleys & Herricks decided to come to dinner & all seemed to enjoy it & there was nothing said that made 'news.' I've talked much with the P.M. & he is a forceful personality but the stress on what the English speaking peoples can do in the future worries me a little. I don't trust any of us with too much power & I want the other nations in too! I didn't go to Congress but listened from the office to the speech & that is the one thing that troubled me.

FDR says he'll have an answer on Sunday he hopes on the future of O.C.D. The Mayor seemed subdued when he came in to see me this p.m.

I'm dying to see your suit & the fox furs!

This has been a nice quiet day! Office all a.m. & time this p.m. to put away Xmas presents with only a few people for tea.

Ever so much love to you dear.

The OCD was not working satisfactorily. A strong element in the opposition was anti-New Deal feeling. Eleanor's efforts through the volunteer participation program to build up social standards in the local communities through programs of physical fitness, nutrition, and literacy were denounced as efforts to "socialize America" under the pretext of an emergency.

The programs were never attacked as such, but Eleanor's appointment of Mayris Chaney, "Tiny," the dancer, as an assistant in the physical fitness program, proved a bonanza for the cartoonists and hostile columnists and congressmen. The Hearst press uncovered the presence in the OCD of several individuals who had participated in the Thirties in organizations labeled subversive by the Dies Committee, and that too provided headlines. These appointments suggested that the organization harbored "pinkos." Melvyn Douglas, Malcolm Cowley, and I were among the individuals thus savaged. It did not matter that we had not been appointed by Mrs. Roosevelt and that Cowley and I were members of an advisory committee, not paid staff people.

The attacks on her leadership of OCD and the attacks on me because of my radical past seemed to interfuse in her mind. When Pegler had begun to attack me during the summer, Eleanor with characteristic self-depreciation took the blame. If he had not wanted to get at her—and Franklin—she told me, the columnist would not have bothered with me. It was a continuing argument between us—I insisting that were it not for my radical past I would not serve Pegler as a useful stick with which to belabor her.

Neither of us expected, however, the issue to arise in connection with my effort to enlist in the Navy. When she volunteered to join as references Dr. William Allan Neilson, president emeritus of Smith College; President Harry Gideonse of Brooklyn College; David Niles, who had been familiar with my work during the 1940 campaign; and Ulric Bell, director of the Fight for Freedom Committee, neither of us realized what a challenge Mrs. Roosevelt's backing meant to the ruling powers in the Navy. That was especially true of Naval Intelligence, to which division the Bureau of Personnel had recommended that I apply. Although Mrs. Roosevelt hated to see me go into the service, she was so unsuspecting of the Navy's reaction to my application that during a moment of intense troubles with Trude in September she had said I might be better off in the Navy.

But the admirals did not want me. Naval Intelligence did not want me. Their problem was how to confront Mrs. Roosevelt on the rejection? A quiet word to me would have sufficed to cause me to withdraw my application. They did not realize that or perhaps there were those in Naval Intelligence who relished the idea of turning me down and thus rebuking my sponsor, Eleanor Roosevelt, a leading spokesperson of American liberalism. Or perhaps it was just stupidity.

Many years later Charles Harding, the stockbroker, grandson of banker Jay Cooke, disclosed to friends the commotion caused in the Bureau of Personnel when my application was received. Harding was in a position to know. A member of the Naval Reserve, he had been called to duty before Pearl Harbor and was an officer assigned to Admiral Nimitz, who then headed the Bureau of Naval Personnel. According to Harding, who was a man of wit and learning, the admirals had asked Admiral McIntire, the Navy physician who served as Roosevelt's personal physician, "to whisper" in Roosevelt's ear that the Navy did not want Joe Lash.

Presumably the President had sent back word that it was the Navy's business. Suddenly in October stories appeared in the Scripps-Howard press concerning my application and Mrs. Roosevelt's sponsorship of it. The first said I was under investigation. The second quoted Dies Committee sources that Mrs. Roosevelt was a "backer" of the application. The third, again allegedly from the Dies Committee, reviewed my antiwar statements, and there were many during the early and mid-Thirties, including such colorful remarks as "American youth does not intend to lay down its life in shell holes around Shanghai or Timbuktoo." My support of the Oxford Pledge was emphasized. The moral was pretty explicit: how could such a man ask for a commission or be trusted with one?

To Eleanor, the moral seemed to be the opposite: my switch and decision to enter the service was a statement to other young people, many of whom were isolationist, of the need to rethink their position.

On November 26 a letter from Admiral Nimitz advised me that "after careful consideration, the Bureau is unable to approve your application for appointment in the United States Naval Reserve because of failure to meet all the requirements for a commission in the Naval Reserve." In retrospect there was more to this story than either Mrs. Roosevelt or I realized at the time. I would discover when I entered the Army as a draftee that I was a marked man by the intelligence services, many of whose members welcomed the opportunity to get at Mrs. Roosevelt. But at the end of November 1941, Mrs. Roosevelt was busy with OCD, and when I informed her that the Navy had enough problems without worrying about me and that I had decided to let the matter rest, she did not demur, and Pearl Harbor a few weeks later made it likely that my draft board would soon call me up.

Nevertheless, the episode had fixed in the public mind her sponsorship of my application, and when the Hearst press with the aid of the Dies Committee unearthed my membership on one of the many advisory committees of the OCD, it promoted that into a minor exposé.

Years later the Department of Justice supplied me the following letter, of whose contents and existence I had not known, that Eleanor Roosevelt had sent to Attorney General Biddle. Also included was J. Edgar Hoover's five-page answering memorandum to Biddle about me, which detailed my activities with left and Communist organizations in the Thirties, noted my break at the time of the Nazi-Soviet pact, and asserted: "The Federal Bureau of Investigation is conducting no investigation of Joseph P. Lash."

OFFICE OF CIVILIAN DEFENSE

Washington, D. C.

January 9, 1942

My dear Mr. Attorney General:

I wonder if it would be possible for you to run down for me through the Federal Bureau of Investigation, Colonel Donovan's Naval Inspectors, and the Dies Committee, what they really have on Joe Lash.

He turned in to the Navy the absolute truth on all his former connections—that he had never signed a Communist Party card, that he had, however, been very close to the Party, and he told them all that he had made a break with them at the time of the Nazi-Russian Pact, and since that time had never done anything but work for those who upheld the interests of this country. I know this to be so, both in his public and private situation. I think to hound someone who has lived up to his convictions is really unwise procedure. He was not accepted by the Navy, but was never told why. I feel quite sure it was because he was so honest in telling of his former connections.

His investigator told someone that the people who knew him, like Dr. William Allen Neilsen, ex-President of Smith, and Dr. Alvin Johnson, were high in their praise of him, but that others spoke of his former connections.

It has a very bad effect upon youth in general when they think something unjust is being done, where people have honestly lived up to their convictions. I am seriously worried, not about what will be done to Joe, for practically the whole board of International Student Service is back of him, because he has done such very good work for them as their General Secretary, but I am worried for the effect it will have on the groups with which he has been working.

Today, I got a message from our Youth Activities representative, Miss Jane Seaver, which reads as follows:

"I thought that you would want to know that Mr. Robert E. Stripling, who is Special Investigator for the Dies Committee, phoned to find out if Joe Lash were employed by us. I said no. He went on to ask if he were serving in any capacity at all with our division. I told him that Joe was serving in an advisory capacity on our Executive Committee along with the others (mentioning the names). He wanted to know if he were receiving remuneration. I told him he was getting expenses. I don't know what all this means, but I hope it doesn't mean trouble for Joe."

This kind of thing is bad for all young people, particularly if they know and admire the character of the person involved. I would stake everything I have, and so would my son, Franklin, Jr., who worked with Joe in the last campaign and who offered to write a letter to the Navy saying that he is a high, idealistic young man, thirty odd, who perhaps was too radical when he was young, but who will always work for the good of the majority of the people as far as all interests are concerned.

He is a Jew. Perhaps, that is one more reason why I am concerned not to see him unjustly treated.

If they have something convincing outside of the things which he wrote as a youngster when organizing the American Student Union, which he also left when it became controlled by the Communists, I would like to know what it is, and I certainly think it would be fair for him to know.

I am doing this not because of one individual. I am doing it because of its effect on many young people.

Very sincerely yours,

/s/ Eleanor Roosevelt,

Mrs. Franklin D. Roosevelt
Assistant Director

The Honorable Francis G. Biddle
The Attorney General
Department of Justice
Washington, D. C.

Being a forthright woman accustomed to confront realities, no matter how unpleasant, and to make decisions no matter how unpleasant, she decided to face Mr. Dies directly. Without informing me, she invited Dies to lunch at the White House. A tall, rangy man with political aspirations, the Texan was flattered by the invitation. There were rival members of his committee, however, in particular a right-wing Republican, Representative J. Parnell Thomas of New Jersey, whom he had to guard against. Dies came over to the White House, bringing his dossier on me. As he reviewed it with Mrs. Roosevelt, she indicated that she was familiar with its contents. Joe had held those views in the Thirties, she said, but had honestly renounced them. Why did Dies not talk with me directly? He was amenable and suggested that I come to see him when I was next in Washington.

He was equally amiable when I, accompanied by Dr. Neilson, came in a week later. In his own youth, he told us, he too had been a radical, having had to fight the Ku Klux Klan. I apologized for the irreverent ditty which I had sung before the committee when I had appeared before it in December 1939.*

The chairman could not have been more agreeable, insisted that he understood my political evolution as a young man, and suggested that he assemble a session of the committee to hear me immediately. That was done and J. B. Matthews did most of the questioning. I explained to the committee what had attracted me to Communism in the late Thirties and how I had practically become a member yet was not a member of the party.†

---

* If you see an un-American
  Lurking far or near
  Just alkalize with Martin Dies
  And he will disappear.
† I was inwardly startled when Matthews produced copies of minutes of meetings
of the National Board of the Young Communist League which listed the presence of

The only discordant note at the session was provided by J. Parnell Thomas. He had learned that the hearing had grown out of Dies's luncheon with Mrs. Roosevelt, and, already aiming at displacement of Dies as the nation's scourge of the Reds, was disinclined to follow the chairman's lead.*

To the surprise of both Mrs. Roosevelt and myself, stories began to leak into the press the next day about the so-called "executive" session. All the stories construed my appearance as a move to have the committee support a revived effort to get a Navy commission. Representative Jerry Voorhis, a liberal member of the committee, told me off the record:

> The Committee was convinced of the sincerity of my break. He said my testimony had not alienated them. The contrary was true of all of them except one whom I took to be Thomas. But everyone including himself was under the impression that the purpose of my visit was to get a letter from the Committee to the Navy. This the Committee did not want to do and he himself thought it would have been improper. He had proposed sending me a letter attesting to the Committee's conviction that the change was a sincere one. No one else supported it.

There was evidently a genuine misunderstanding about the Navy matter and I issued a statement:

> I was and am content to accept the Navy's decision . . . When recently I was informed that my application for a commission had been denied, I thought that the best thing for me to do was to wait until I am drafted. . . .

But J. Parnell Thomas scented a chance for headlines. He rose in the House to assert that my pursuit of a commission was designed to enable me to avoid the draft. He demanded that I be transferred out of the 1H category, which exempted men between the ages of twenty-eight and thirty-five, and be immediately drafted. "If the majority of the Committee does not take this action, I will," he cried.

Draft boards nationally were in the process of reviewing all 1H deferrals and were transferring to 1A all who were physically fit, had no dependents, and were not engaged in an essential military occupation. My local draft board informed me that although I was now 1A I was unlikely to be called before April. The intervening weeks were to be

---

a "J.L." "Wasn't that you?" I was asked. I replied I had been invited to a few meetings where student affairs were being discussed, but I was neither a member nor a frequent participant. Only later did it occur to me that "J.L." must have been the initials of John Little, an acknowledged member of the Young Communist League Board.

* Convicted later of payroll padding, he was obliged to resign from Congress and after imprisonment was pardoned by President Truman.

among the most difficult in my life. A member of my ISS board, Mrs. Dwight Morrow, a lifelong Republican and an internationalist, was quoted to me as saying, "I think it's outrageous what they're doing to Joe Lash." I appreciated the loyalty of the board and other friends. "Everyone compliments me on how well I've stood up under attack," I wrote in my diary. "But I know how badly I've reacted—wanting to commit suicide—to enlist immediately—unable to work—simply feeling badly. It makes me feel like a fraud—yet I am grateful for their support and would feel worse if people said nothing and accepted me at my own evaluation."

Eleanor's support helped above all. Beset though she was at OCD, beginning to feel it might best be served by her own withdrawal, her concern for me did not lessen. A letter reflected her sense of a common predicament:

> Your letter greeted me today & I'm sorry you are despairing, sorry too about Sunday but things on that are happening to me too! I'll tell you Tuesday when I know the whole story & we can decide what is best for us both & perhaps pick a better country week end.
> I wish so many things for you & Trude but they all come back to the fact that she must decide whether she wants to be your partner or not. . . .

Eleanor had come into OCD on the plea of people like Harry Hopkins and Anna Rosenberg that she alone had the energy and authority to give life to the volunteer participation program, but she had never overcome a premonition that whatever authority she had as the President's wife was offset by the target she offered the enemies of the President who did not dare attack him. And so it happened. "Please don't be disturbed. I love a fight," she sought to reassure friends who worried over the savagery and concentration of the attack upon her, but by the beginning of February 1942 she had begun to weigh the pluses and minuses of remaining head of the program. A one-hundred-million-dollar OCD appropriation became the vehicle in the House for a renewed assault upon her. Conservative congressmen, most of them Republicans and Southern Democrats, many of them pre-Pearl Harbor isolationists, exploded in wrath. There was a "Bundles for Eleanor" campaign to help her place "unfortunate idle rich people" in civilian defense jobs. Her office was denounced as "a haven for so-called liberals," who have long campaigned for America's active participation in war but who are now apparently seeking every means of avoiding the front-line trenches and doing any fighting. Even in the war effort, shouted an isolationist from Georgia, "reform still clings like a leech" to the civilian defense program.

Eleanor saw these attacks coolly for what they were: "I am not in the least disturbed by this latest attack," she wrote to a social work leader. "It is purely political and made by the same people who have fought NYA, CCC, WPA, Farm Security, etc."

At the beginning of February she left Washington on a civilian defense trip that took her to Chapel Hill, Atlanta, Pensacola, Urbana, and Chicago. It gave her a chance to touch base with Earl in Pensacola. She attended an ISS conference at Chapel Hill and afterwards Lou Harris, a Campobello alumnus, motored her to Greensboro, North Carolina. "The conference seemed so good to me but being with young people gives me a heartache these days. . . . We have had a quiet dinner with Earl & Simone but tomorrow sounds like a hectic day," she wrote to me. Then she went on to Atlanta:

> I spent yesterday morning with Earl viewing coast defenses from 9–11, then spent an hour with the civilian local defense council & ¾ of an hour with a coloured group who had been left out. I slept 2 hours in the afternoon for this southern air always gets me & we had people in for cocktails & dined with the Commandant & his wife. We left at 7:15 this morning & the ride was nice & I slept most of the time again! Missy* was out driving so we missed seeing her but from all accounts she's doing well & I spoke at a very big meeting here this evening & talked with our new regional director who seems grand.

Her letter ended: "These trips are worth while but of course I should have been in Washington too this week!" Not that it would have helped. The train journey to Chicago tired her, which was not surprising, although her admission of it "I'm probably feeling my age!" was. She worried about my going into the Army:

> I hate to see you go in to the army & I dread it & I know you must. I feel sadly responsible for the difficult position you are in & that probably makes me worry more about it. I'm good too as you know at visualizing all the dangers all you boys must run & what the whole thing may do to you physically mentally & spiritually & I dread it for you. It is not at all that I shall miss you selfishly tho' that does mean a lot to me for I enjoy being with you & doing things with you & I have come to depend on you for advice as well as companionship & enjoyment but I know what the last war did to people's souls & I dread it for you. I wish these last weeks before you leave could belong to you & Trude & you could feel she was with you & waiting for you, it would be a fund of happiness to draw on. If it can't be, draw what you can from the love & devotion & admiration of all your friends. They can't make up for the big thing you want but they may help.

* Missy had suffered a stroke in 1941 and was now a helpless invalid staying at Warm Springs, where Eleanor had stopped to see her on the way from Pensacola to Atlanta.

A few days after she returned to Washington, she went up to Cornell as she usually did for the Home and Farm exercises. She hoped to resign "very soon," she told a press conference, and in her speech said, "I realize how unwise it is for a vulnerable person like myself to try a government job." She added another reason, one that had burned itself into her soul: "To know me is a terrible thing." Her broadcast a week later after she formally resigned spoke of the "small and very vocal group of unenlightened men" who are now "able to renew, under the guise of patriotism and economy, the age-old fight of the privileged few against the good of the many. . . . Perhaps we must all stand up more and be counted in this fight, the virtuous Peglers on the one side, the boondogglers, so-called, on the other."

A long letter to Maude Gray, the youngest of her Hall aunts, whose husband F.D.R. had appointed as U. S. Minister to Ireland, encompassed her family world as she saw it at the moment of resignation from OCD:

> I owe you & David so many apologies. I don't know where to begin so I better just say that I've worked so hard for many months that I've been neglectful of everything else.
>
> First, thanks for all your dear letters & cables & F.D.R. tells me every now & then what a grand job David is doing & that means you too, Maude dear, for no one can do a diplomatic job alone.
>
> Now for all the family news. . . .
>
> Last time I saw Cousin Henry & Susie I did them more harm than good because I was undergoing one of Pegler's attacks & they were troubled. Both have been far from well this winter. . . .
>
> F.D.R. is grand. Stands up even under Singapore without a ripple in his serenity! Churchill's visit was interesting & he is a pleasant guest & a wonderful war leader but I don't want him to make the peace. I gave him Adamic's 'Two Way Passage' to help him understand the U.S. I'm sending you a copy too. I've had so little time to read I've not even read the book you sent me yet but now that I am getting out of the Civilian Defense Office I will have time to breathe again. Since Sept. I've worked all day at the office & every night on mail till 2 or 3 a.m.! It has agreed with me however!
>
> Elliott is now a navigator on a bomber. Based at Lake Muroc in the Mojave desert & patrolling the Pacific but apt to leave soon for parts unknown. James is back in the active Marine Corps training with a 'commando' regiment & expecting to shove off the end of March. Fjr. has seen some hard trips in the North Atlantic but before that had an easy convoy trip to Capetown, S.A. Just now he's recovering well from an appendix removal in the Brooklyn Hospital. I'm so thankful it could be done ashore. I saw him last Sat. & Sunday & go up tonight to see him again tomorrow but I'll be back Friday a.m. as it is my last day at the office. The new babies (Ethel's & Ruth's) both boys are very cunning & healthy.

We are working very slowly to 'all out' war but it will come.
Much love to David & a world of love to you Maude dear.

Devotedly always
Eleanor

I wish you were home so often. I'd give anything to have you here
now! I think the N.Y. houses are sold & I've found an apt. on Washington Sq. we can all use.

The Sixty-fifth Street houses were in the process of being sold to
Hunter College, and Eleanor, having rented an apartment on Washington Square, undertook to empty them of their contents. I, who was
daily expecting to be drafted, helped her move. The newspapers were
tipped off and we found ourselves on the front pages again. Trude, still
uncertain that she had given her relationship with her husband a
chance, again put off placing her relationship with me on a "business"
basis. "But everything has been changed," I noted, "because I am
going into the army in March. She said she would be with me as much
as possible until then." And when Trude swore that in her "heart of
hearts" she had not ruled out a divorce, I settled for that. "I have no
right to be severe with T.," I wrote in my diary. "I myself am bad, for
there is a strong pull in me so that if T. *has* decided I do not want to
know about it and let the army swallow me up."
But I pressed my suit assiduously by letter, telegram, and verse:

I know you hate sentimental stuff
And prefer the ditty that is rough
Or bawdy wit in whose confine
There is no room for Valentine.

But on this morn of our second year
Your lover, dear, has lost all fear
And says in accents of bold design
I am, forever, your Valentine.

Though I may be sent to distant lands
You will be true to him whose hands
Have taught you to worship at the shrine
Of the fierce and gentle Valentine.

Eleanor was unhappy with my acceptance of Trude's inability to decide. She flew out to Seattle to be with Anna and her family while
Anna checked into the hospital for an undescribed operation: "Now,
darling, to talk about you," she wrote to me from there:

The more I think it over the more I feel that if *you* make the decision
that the time has come for Trude to face herself & Eliot & the children
without you, & either urge her to go away or stop seeing her the stronger
you will feel. If you wait till you have to go the choice is not yours & I

think she will feel you are stronger if you decide. The situation for you is heartbreaking either way, but if the decision goes against you it will make it no easier that you did not give her this chance & perhaps your strength will be in your favor anyway I think it will help you. By now you are thinking I'm an old busybody & you know whatever you do I will understand, but I want you so much to feel strong inside, you are, but the long strain of this situation has sapped your strength.

So many of us depend on you for the future Joe. I know that is true of the friends you have that I know & so it must be true of those I don't know. You have to be strong for others, not for yourself alone. You know that I count on & dream dreams for you. Of course it is because I love you but also it is because I admire you & feel in you the possibilities for the leadership that the people of the country are going to need.

If you were not going away this might not seem very important to me as in time you would come to feel sure of me but now there seems an urgency about it because I want you to count on me no matter what the future holds. Both of us may have to go through things we don't even imagine as yet but if you know how I feel & I can feel that to you too it is a sure & an accepted thing somehow I feel it will help us both.

I did not accept her advice, and if she saw it as weakness, which she probably did, she forgave me, for, as she once had told me, she loved people for their frailties as much as for their strengths. Back East she joined Trude in planning ISS's farewell party for me. She undertook to be with me as much as possible those final weeks before I went into the Army, but with my inveterate feeling that I was a burden to her I seemed to back away from her gestures of companionship. She sought to put me at ease by spelling out what belonged to her children and what to me:

This is being written because you said something the other night that was so like the way I always feel & I want you so much not to feel that way with me. You will only not feel it if I can make you understand certain things. No matter what one's children are, one never loses the feeling, at least I can't, that they are mine, part of me, as they were when they were little & helpless in my arms & I love them dearly. With Anna I have grown to have something more, a mature understanding & sympathy, a feeling that we think & feel alike & can trust each other as friends & companions. Now & then I have moments of that with the boys but it is not the same secure relationship. With you I have that feeling of understanding & companionship. I know I enjoy just being with you, reading, talking, doing all kinds of things together. I'm sure that we will find new & mutual pleasures whatever we do because I like just being with you. In addition I have a bit of protective feeling one always has for one's children & that is why it has hurt & worried me when you have suffered through me. I'm always afraid of asking too much of you, because more than anything else I want you to have what makes you happy but I want you to know that you could never come too often or be around too much as far as I am concerned.

I had been notified to appear for induction on April 15. A few weeks earlier I drove Eleanor and Tommy up to Hyde Park. The President and Harry Hopkins were at the Big House. She invited them over to the cottage for dinner and at dusk they drove over. It was an evening of relaxed talk. "I am still terribly conscious," I wrote in my diary, "that I am in Hyde Park or the White House only because of my friendship with Mrs. R. and am grateful when others show some signs of friendliness. I want so much to prove Mrs. R's faith in me by works. Many times during these two days I wanted to disagree with the Pres.—when he scoffed at post-war planners, when he deprecated the split between labor and the boys in the armed services—but kept quiet. I felt he wanted to be let alone and that he wanted a rest from incessant argument and being on guard. Perhaps I am wrong. Mrs. R. goes after him because so few people disagree with him that it is important someone tell him how others are reacting. But even Mrs. R. these days wonders whether one has a right to."

After the dinner at the cottage and an evening of desultory talk in front of the fireplace, the party broke up. Eleanor, Tommy, and I sat around a little longer. "Mrs. R. said it was a godsend that the President could relax in this way, put all cares aside and not allow problems to sear into him. I remarked on how different he was in this regard from Lincoln. We have talked of this often. He treats all problems impersonally as if they had no organic relationship to him. He treats people the same way. Otherwise he could not have stood three terms in office —especially the last one."

Eleanor went out to Seattle again the third week in March, on the way stopping to see James and John in San Diego. The young, in particular, with their openness, as she wrote to me, attracted her:

> I thought of you so much on the plane & wished you were along! We were very late because at Fort Worth they took every one off, except me, to take on ferry pilots—so we & the ferry pilots owned the plane this morning. We got into long arguments, would we be able to prevent more wars? Was there a moral equivalent for war? What about Russia after the war? etc. etc. Those boys are certainly doing some talking & thinking. Johnny started in tonight on overtime for labor & the way the boys felt & I see there has been an organized barrage of letters to Congress. I partially convinced Johnnie but I expect James will start tomorrow. . . .

But James, who was serving under Major Evans Carlson in "Carlson's Raiders," a group of Marine volunteers, surprised her with the liberalism of his views. She was happy to write to me:

> You've been in my thoughts so much because yesterday afternoon & evening I spent a great part with James' boss Major Carlson. He be-

lieves in the Chinese cooperatives, those *not* government controlled, he thinks the profit motive must be eliminated & he's teaching his men that they must make all people their friends. They are fighting the system that forced all people to war, but they must not hate the people! His men are farm boys, many Southerners, C.C.C. boys but he talks to them. James gives them a 'news review' on Sunday & answers questions afterwards. He [Carlson] preaches race equality & has taught them a Chinese rallying cry meaning 'We cooperate.' He does everything they are asked to do & so does every officer. The Marine Corps thinks it is horrifying but the men think he & they are the finest things on earth. . . .

With the President occupied on public business, she was, more than ever, the hub of the family. "Dearest Franklin," she wrote to him from the West Coast:

A good trip out tho' delayed by the taking on of ferry pilots so I did not get here until yesterday afternoon.

I spent the night with Johnny as James couldn't get home till 11. Saw him just a minute & then he went home to bed. Both boys look well tho' James looked tired. The training is hard. Next week he is off on a 3 weeks practice for landing & then they go so I'm glad I came this week.

I have written Tommy to go ahead & plan on moving the 15th of April for if Hunter doesn't buy the houses the other offers wanted immediate possession.

> Much love,
> E.R.

You will have to explain to the army & the people why we should not destroy overtime. The feeling is running high.

By the time she reached Seattle, the feeling against overtime pay distressed her even more, and she felt she had better phone the President. "Dearest Franklin," she wrote to him on March 23:

I'm telephoning you tonight because one thing worries me too much to wait but both James & John told me enough to bother me greatly & if you are not going to Hyde Park I shall return that day to Washington.

Anna looks fairly well & is on the whole fairly strong tho' her balance is poor as yet. She gets tired quickly. She loves the star but wanted Granny's gold bangles because those were the things she remembered her as wearing most & I don't remember seeing them when we looked over the jewelry. I hope they are not lost or given to someone else.

John & the kids are well & we are preparing for the birthdays on Wed.

I think Helen Gahagan will run for Congress if the party really unites behind her. I spent a very pleasant 4-½ hrs with them yesterday & my trip up here was on schedule all the way.

I hated to say goodbye to Romaine & Jimmy but I am finding it harder & harder to talk to these groups of boys. We spend now to send them to die for a "way of life," & a few years ago the very men who spend so willingly & speed them on their way were afraid of taxes to make this same way of life give them a chance to earn a living.

Much love
E.R.

Her letter to Hick from Seattle was equally scorching about the reactionaries who wanted to empty the war of all meaning:

I went out to James' camp on Sat. & Major Carlson came in to dinner. He's an interesting man & all the men adore him but it is a hard training & James doesn't look too well. They are off soon & talking to them was hard. I grow deeply resentful inside when I look at these boys, that now we spend so much on, that they may go out & die for a way of life that a few years ago we didn't want to tax ourselves to give them a chance to make a living in. Will we do it all over again when those that live through it come back with McKellars & Byrds in power? I hate war & the selfishness of the rest of us who risk nothing & worry because of little discomforts.

As my induction approached, Eleanor and Trude footed the bill for the champagne at the going-away party that ISS gave me at the old Lafayette Hotel in New York. My friend James Wechsler, then a labor reporter for *PM*, spoke humorously but with passion about the fate of men who tried to steer a middle course between reactionaries and the Communists. Afterwards Trude and I and some of the young people went on to Café Society uptown, and Eleanor went home. I was now scheduled to report on April 29. Eleanor prepared a series of notes, each in a separately numbered envelope to be opened during my first week in the service.

"Joe dearest," the first letter, dated "April 6th," began:*

Just a week from tonight you will be out of reach & starting on this new life that I dread so much for you. I hope with all my heart that it brings you what you want & need at this time. In the long run all you have lived through & will live through will add to the enrichment of the spirit & heart & mind which is the real 'you' but for the time being we who love you must hope for numbness & physical weariness to help you start building up again.

A little bit of my heart seems to be with you always Joe. You'll carry it round wherever you go & in its place the thought of you will be with me wherever I go. This is just to say goodnight & I love you. Sometimes I think if we have *chosen* to love someone, we love them even

---

* This was still while I was slated to report on April 15.

more than we do the children of our bodies & so that is why I shall be looking forward to every chance of seeing you & longing for the day when you are home for good. God bless & keep you.

E.R.

Tuesday, April 7th. This is a nice day, you are here & it is spring & Trude is coming & I hope for you both a few happy hours. I want you to have happy hours to live over again in your mind these first days. When you do write tell me the truth dear, the details of life & what you think & feel & the boys you are with, otherwise I'll never feel I am able to see you in your surroundings & if things happen to you inside I'll have it all to find out later!

I've just been told that a gentleman coming to tea is a spy so if you & Trude come in I'll try to tip you off! I wish you could have talked to the Australian foreign minister at lunch. He has a marvellous cockney accent but he's a strong labor man & a believer in the New Deal.

I want to be close to you these days & put my arms about you often. They will feel empty for you until you come back. Goodnight my dear one.

Wednesday, April 8th. You & Trude have gone off to the State Department & you were sweet & asked me to drive to H.P. with you on Sunday. Perhaps you know how much I want to cling to you these days but I want even more for you two the feeling that these were your days. Whatever comes in the future Joe dear, you will feel that you have had a chance to be with her & see her & pray God the memory will be sweet. If you can keep it without bitterness, happy things will grow again & if the future is to belong to you both together you will be doubly glad of these opportunities. So, it isn't that I don't want to be with you every minute because I do but other things are more important for you.

One thing at least you may be sure of always, that is my love is here & I will be always waiting for you ready to go to you or welcome you wherever I can. No other engagement can't be given up, if there is a chance to see you!

The party last night was nice, but I think I'll enjoy more the ones we'll give to welcome you back.

She went down to Hampton Institute, where the Julius Rosenwald Fund board was meeting.

Just a minute—before I go down to start for Richmond & I'll write you a line.

It has rained all day but we've had a good meeting & decided to do some things which may be valuable. I didn't speak well tonight. I can't face these kids here without emotion & that is not good for talking! I voiced my faith in your generation however & when I do that I'm always thinking of you for what you are & what you stand for is responsible for much of my faith.

God bless you dear. Goodnight & my love is yours,

ER

P.S. I looked at many barracks this afternoon & thought of you!

She went to Nashville for the Southern Conference on Human Welfare:

This is for the second night when you will be gone. Oh! how I hope it will not be too far away! Having you ill at home, where I know Trude & Tommy will look after you makes me realize how I would feel if I thought of you ill somewhere far out of our reach! Anywhere in this country, of course if you beckoned I would fly!

There are a lot of interesting labor leaders at this conference. I like [James] Dombrowski better than ever & I like Clark Foreman very much.* The world has a great many people in it that are really very nice!

We had a rather rough trip down & a poor little naval officer across the aisle was very ill, but so tidily & unobtrusively! I felt very sorry for him for it will be worse when he gets on a ship!

I must go to bed for I breakfast at 7 with Dr. Homer Rainey† & I think tomorrow will be busy with little time to sleep since the plane is not a sleeper.

Lou Harris isn't here, in bed with a tummy ailment.

Wed. eve. April 22nd. Joe darling, You've just told me that you've heard from the draft board & you leave next Tuesday. My heart contracts. I hate to have you go. I dread so many things for you & so many for myself. I shall miss you very much & count the days till I can see you. I put the good luck horse shoe you gave me on my chain so it would be always with me as I like having something from you very near me always. I have so many good luck emblems they ought to bring those I love *very* much good luck too!

I hope you will be o.k. tomorrow morning but you weren't wise to go out tonight. You must be careful these next few days & get your strength back fully before Tuesday.

F.D.R. said tonight that last week he felt disturbed & depressed about the war but things now looked better from both military & productive aspects. If it only would mean a speedy ending!

April 23rd. Joe dearest, I've just said goodnight & I feel sad for you. I wish we could just blindly trust Trude & feel sure that the fine things in her were going to triumph as I hope so much they will. You see anyone's weaknesses I can understand but not once they have gained strength & independence. Of one thing I am sure Joe, don't accept a

* Left-wing Southern leaders.
† Former president of the University of Texas and now director of the American Youth Commission.

compromise. Trude must be all yours, otherwise you will never be happy.

Someday I'll tell you why I'm sure that is so, but just now no corroborating history is of interest to you & all the contribution I can think of which is helpful, is to beg you not to accept ½ a loaf of love. I know there is a future for you—of happiness in good work & of companionship & love with a fine woman—not to speak of the richness of your many friendships. This period has been lived through & some hard times may be ahead but I'm sure you'll make the future triumphant.

I'd be grateful beyond words if I could by my love for you just lighten the burden now enough to make the struggle seem a little more worth while. All my love & devotion seem to help me so little in being of use to you.

God bless & keep you darling. I do love you.

Friday night. Joe dearest, I just said goodnight to you & I hope so much if today has been a happy day that you will find peace from now on. There is nothing to do but trust that Trude's love will triumph & I think it will.

Now, I want to talk to you like the fussy & interfering old lady I am but please forgive me & believe it is done because I love you. I know the next two months there is bound to be waters of despair engulfing you at times & at such times we are apt to do things we later wish we hadn't done. Don't let yourself reach the depths where this happens, sit down & write to Trude or to me instead or call us & talk to one of us. I take it for granted that if for some reason Trude is not available I may be of some help. Another thing dear. Write often & about little things otherwise we will drift apart. We must know what we are mutually thinking & feeling & going through or the ties between us will loosen.

This is the last letter I am writing you for I hope you will have been able to let me know where you are & I'll send you a little daily note which is more up to date.

I love you with all my heart. Goodnight & bless you dear.

The night before I reported for induction, she wrote again:

Dearest one, That you have friends & influence over many people, nobody needs to prove to you. That you are deeply loved by the one person you care deeply about I think you must be sure of too. I can't help but feel that hope & trust should be in both our hearts.

I hope that even after I've said goodbye to you tomorrow, I will hear your voice during the day & know something of your moves. Do write & telephone whenever you can from wherever you are & let me know when you get off for if I possibly can be around I'll try to get wherever you plan to be! I've told you so often how much I love you that there is little left to tell but I'll write it here again because I won't dare trust myself to *say* much tomorrow. I am going to miss you more than you can know & so you will be constantly in my thoughts & my heart will be a bit empty always till you are back again. The prayers will be said night & morning as usual but with a little more fervor while you are gone. God bless & keep you & bring you back to welcoming arms & a happy & serene & busy & fruitful future. My love is with you.

The next morning Eleanor breakfasted with me and took me to within a block of the draft board office and said goodbye. There were twenty-four other inductees from Chelsea, a neighborhood in lower Manhattan, with their little suitcases for their civilian clothes at the office of Local Draft Board 19. Press and photographers were also there. They had not seen that Eleanor was with me. Make the interview short, the local draft board chairman snapped. "The Army can't wait and Japan won't." The photographers followed the little contingent into the subway all the way down to the Battery, where it boarded the ferry for Governors Island. They pressed me for my plans. The youth movement was behind me, I said. "My one idea is to be as good a soldier as possible."

Eleanor began a long letter that she would mail to me after I had a semi-permanent address:

Your voice had a confident sound tonight & I'm so happy you weren't upset by the papers. I will long remember your last words 'my spirit isn't broken' & I watched you walk down the block till I could see you no longer & your walk expressed the same feeling. My spirit hasn't been any too good for I'm very dependent on you & I know we are only beginning a long, hard pull but hearing your voice tonight helped a lot for I felt you were better off & happier than you had been for a long time. . . .

Do not "accept ½ a loaf of love," she had begged me in her letter of April 23. "Of one thing I am sure Joe, don't accept a compromise. Trude must be all yours, otherwise you will never be happy." There is the story I have been trying to tell. This rare woman had accepted such a compromise and she had lived up to it faithfully. It had meant an almost unbearable loneliness. She had sought to overcome her isolation by work and advancing the interest of others whom she loved. Her love for Trude and me and, it should be added, for her children, was the healing force and gave her the energy to go on. "The deepest need of man," wrote the psychoanalyst Erich Fromm in *The Art of Loving* (Chapter II, page 9), "is the need to overcome his separation, to leave the prison of his loneliness."

Seeking to explain what perhaps cannot be explained but can be described, she had written to me a few days earlier about escaping from such a "prison": "With you I have that feeling of understanding and companionship."

XIX

"Love is important to the person who gives it..."

THE DAY I reported for induction Eleanor began a letter she intended to mail to me when she had an address. She notified the White House switchboard that I was to be added to "the list of those whom I want to speak no matter what I am doing." Emotionally drained by my departure for the Army as well as by James's imminent movement overseas with his Marine Raiders, she was relieved to have speaking engagements to occupy her and happy to report that "Tiny & Earl were here for supper." Earl was being shifted from Pensacola to Floyd Bennett Field in Brooklyn. She was cheered, too, by the President's hopefulness:

> He [James] says they are all, including himself, in fine condition but— oh! how I hate to have them off. They have all the equipment however. To my joy I heard Franklin say today that he felt better about the war situation than he had three weeks ago & thought things would begin to happen next winter. I'm going to pray harder than ever!
>
> There is talk again of a Negro march on Washington & I can't see anything good to come from it.
>
> In a way I hope you are so physically tired for a time that you can't

have time to think, then as that wears off the thinking may be easier than any of us anticipate. You are so much a part of my daily life that I keep wanting to have you do things with me or to talk to you about them. So even writing you is a help to me & I hope it doesn't bore you.

She learned from Trude that after a day's stay at Governors Island my group was sent to Fort Dix, New Jersey. She immediately set about learning how Trude might reach Dix by train and taxi. She doubted she could be well enough disguised to go along: ". . . it would cause a riot & do you no good," she advised me, and added, "I love seeing her now because it is somehow being nearer to you." I described the exhausting day of all conscripts at Fort Dix, and ended, "It's very exciting watching the armies of America assembling. . . . You know fascism is finished." Before the first week of induction was over I was on a slow troop train bound for Miami. She could get a suite there, she wrote in a letter that waited for an address, "& when you say the word Trude & I or perhaps Trude can go at any time."

This episode lives the more vividly in my memory because of Eleanor's presence when the visit took place. But at the time I must confess that I harbored a hope I would never have dared admit to full consciousness that Trude would come alone. Two were nicer than three and Eleanor's presence, despite her tact, would turn the visit into an event and publicity was inevitable, a thought that had occurred to both of them. But I also knew that without Eleanor's protective presence Trude would find it difficult to visit me in Miami. Moreover Trude and I treasured her company and accepted at face value her declarations of pleasure in ours.

Eleanor's letter also reported that Trude had talked with Eliot,

> & she had told him she was yours but would run the house this summer & live there apart. He asked if she had promised you & she was glad to be able to say she had made no promises. The future will now be yours & I am so thankful, I could sing today.

I was at the Hotel Tudor, one of the Miami Beach hotels that the Army Air Corps had taken over to house the recruits, three and four to a room, while they were given basic training and tested for purposes of assignment—communications, maintenance, weather. "I'm a real private now," I notified Eleanor, "and will you please address letters to Private Joseph Lash (I lost my middle initial in Governor's Island because it didn't stand for anything)." At Hyde Park she applied herself to learning to ride a bicycle, ". . . it took me quite a while to make up my mind to take off! I imagined being laid up with a broken leg & then I never fell off at all!" There were echoes of the civilian defense brouhaha. "I had Cousin Henry & Susie & Earl & Tiny for lunch. The combination was perfect. I told Cousin Susie Tiny's name

twice & then in just the right tone of voice she said, 'Oh! the dancer!'
Cousin Henry was taken with her however!"

"Life is full of extraordinary ironies," I wrote to her after assignment
with two other draftees to a room at the Hotel Tudor:

> You remember we listened at Golden's Beach to the President's speech
> on the Lend-Lease Bill and I said at the time I wanted to go into some
> branch of the armed services. Well, here I am back in Miami where
> the Army Air Corps is taking over all the empty hotels and has con-
> verted Miami Beach into a Training and Replacement Center. I will
> be here for 22 days in which time one goes through further 'processing'
> i.e. testing for the kind of work for which one is best qualified, and one
> learns the basic drill formations . . . Well I've got to get ready for my
> 2-hour spell of guarding the portals of this hotel.

My letters told of having become two people in the Army, one for
the "guys," as I called my fellow draftees, the other for the people back
home, mainly Trude and Eleanor. That did not surprise the latter: "Of
course, you'll lead two lives in the army & be two people. You'll be
different as a result of it all when you are back." She begged me to do
my job in the Army "with as much absorption as you have done other
things in life! I loved your line 'fascism is finished.' It will be, but God
grant it is done fast enough & we have strength enough & determination
for the peace-time fight to follow."

A conservative coalition in Congress was riding roughshod over New
Deal agencies. She did another column about the National Youth Administration, ". . . a last shot . . . but FDR says a wave has engulfed
Congress & there is no use fighting it! They voted him without debate
$2,000,000,000 for shipyards & cut T.V.A. after 3 days of debate!" A
sentence summarized the military situation: "Corregidor makes me feel
miserable inside but I'm afraid we are in for worse all summer. F.D.R.
says what happens to the Russians this summer is the hump we have to
get over. Nothing else matters as much." America's treatment of its
Negroes obsessed her: "I've seen so many people today but the only interesting ones were some Negroes working in the government who want
me to meet with them once a month & hear what they are doing. I told
them it would have to be unofficial & without publicity if I did it but I
think I'll do it. A channel to the President for good & bad things might
be useful."

She was like a mother hen about the first baby that Earl and Simone
expected: "I've lunched with Simone & taken her to choose the baby
things I wanted to give her. Since we came in I've written Maude Gray
& the verses for Earl's birthday party tonight & I've put in a call for you
& I feel happy."

Her letter to Maude in Dublin was full of family news. It also
showed the thrust of her thinking:

It was wonderful to get your letter of March 20th & I'm glad to be able to tell you that Anna is back at work & says she feels well. We had a wonderful second visit when I went out the end of March to see James & Johnnie & Anna was just back from the hospital. I was there for John & Sisty's joint birthday & it was a happy time. I saw James' 'Raiders' now they are off & a man brought me a message from James in Honolulu yesterday & took a letter back. Elliott arrived from the Africa trip with 18,000 plates 2 days ago. They photographed every single thing they were sent to get but he brought back a little African bug & has some kind of dysentery from which I hope he soon recovers. Fjr. is still getting well but at least they found out at last he had a blood infection & it is gradually clearing up. I'll find out about the taxes. I don't think both of us should have paid.

The hams are a gift & I'm so glad they reach you in good condition.

The houses at 65th St. are empty at last. I am settled here & it is a nice apartment* with a lovely view & perfectly suited to F. if he ever comes!

Earl is staying here till quarters are built at Floyd Bennett field but it takes him 1-½ hrs. each way to work so he hopes they'll soon have quarters. I'm having a party for him tonight as it is his birthday & his wife has come down. They expect a baby in July.

Tomorrow I go to H.P. for the day as F. is there for the weekend & the Norwegians are there. Fjr. & Ethel with 2 friends have gone up too & if Elliott can get thro' his reports he & Ruth will come on & go up with me for the day tomorrow.

The navy news seems encouraging today & everyone seems happier. I wish we could soon bring this to an end.

Joe Lash is now in Miami training in aviation ground work & all the young men who worked for me in O.C.D. or whom I've known in the college groups are somewhere in camp & they write such interesting letters. This generation is much more serious than the 1918 army was in regards the future. Elliott thinks nothing of the British high command in Africa & less of what they have done in sanitation & education through their years of control. He thinks from all he heard that Italy did a far better job of giving rather than taking in Eritrea. Of course don't say this but he says the Colonials all feel the same way.

The final surrender in Corregidor made us sad but it was a gallant fight. Production goes well now & the country is taking rationing without a murmur.

My love to David & a world of love to you dear.

When Ruth and Elliott arrived at her apartment for lunch the next day, all waited for Fjr., who was driving down from Hyde Park. "At 2:45 he appeared having driven down with Harry [Hopkins] & Paulette Goddard who had spent the night at H.P." She had not waited with lunch but served Fjr. sandwiches in the living room while everyone lis-

* 29 Washington Square West in Greenwich Village.

tened to Churchill's broadcast. "I had to miss some because I was on the telephone twice—therefore [although] I thought it well delivered & clever but rather apologetic & not inspiring."

Trude arrived at the Washington Square apartment, "breathless," as Eleanor wrote, and, having heard from me that I would be only twenty-two days in Miami, they dispatched a telegram to "Pvt. Joseph Lash . . . MRS R AND HER SECRETARY MRS P ARRIVE FRIDAY MORNING 555 2 ROOMS AND SITTING ROOM RESERVED PANCOAST HOTEL MUCH LOVE MRS R AND MRS P." An explanatory letter followed:

> We found ourselves, soon having made our plans, ready to wire you & I think the wire was a little crazy but the essential information was in it & I have a feeling I may call you one of these nights for it was so wonderful to hear your voice! She [Trude] was worried about publicity & I told her I was telling all the big wigs I would see the press once & then say no more. She can be my secretary & I need not give her name & she can stay out of sight. It might be better if she went alone but I don't think it really would be. . . .

They intended to take the 11 P.M. plane from Washington on Thursday, May 14, and a Secret Service car would meet them and take them to the Pancoast Hotel, which overlooked the parade ground. Her letter to me went on:

> Col. Smith is there who used to be an aide & I've written Sec. Lovett saying I wanted to be fairly free as 2 of us were going down to see all we could of a friend who was a private but he thought we ought to see the set up as it was so wonderful & if they wanted me to do so would the Secretary arrange with the C.O. tho' I did not want them to take any trouble etc. & I wanted as little publicity as possible as I wanted a rest etc.! Trude said she would tell Eliot she was going but no one else. . . .
>   I can't imagine you shorn. I loved your hair but I guess I'll still love you without it!

She had discussed the trip with Franklin, and a note informed him: "Trude Pratt & I leave 11 p.m. Thursday night & I get back Monday morning."

I was not excused from drill, but the three days seemed idyllic to all of us, and Sunday late, when Trude was out walking with me, Eleanor penned me a note to be read after they left:

> I want to forget that there is a war with all it means of sorrow & sacrifice & have this happy time go on. Perhaps however, it had to be for us all just as I think it is the thing which is probably making Trude clear in her mind & heart. You are both good to me & I am very grate-

ful to you & I love you both so very dearly but you above all always.
We three can have as good a time together as I could ever want &
there is real selfishness in my prayer for the end of the war for to me it
means being together as much as possible always.

But then came a jolt and Eleanor felt obliged to report the episode
after she returned to Washington:

I have thought of you all day on K.P. & I fear you will have it for several days. Just as we were waiting for the plane in the car last night
Col. Smith said 'Didn't you want Lash to come out with us?' Trude &
I both said you had to be back & she said she had gone over with you &
thought it wise you were on time as there seemed to be some bets on
it. Whereupon Col. Smith said 'Oh! I told the Captain to give him a
pass so he could come but I told him to be extra rough on him the
next few days. It will be better for him because the others will be looking for him to get favors after your visit.' I felt Trude stiffen & I was
tempted to say that you would be the last to ask for any special privileges or to want any favors. Then I said 'I suppose you know the Dies
Com.'s attitude?' & he said 'Oh! yes, Army Intelligence sent us an elaborate record on him!' As I thought it over afterwards I realized I had
been very selfish in this whole thing. I wanted to believe I could make
things possible for you both which might not otherwise be possible—a
terrible form of egotism!
    I know that Trude is clear in her own mind & heart. You will man-
age to be together with much less anxiety & hurt to you than if I am
along. No use my pretending that I shan't long to see you & grieve that
I can't, but it will be better for both of you & it is your joint happiness
that I want. . . .

Eleanor's letter did not surprise me. I took it for granted, I told her,
that Army Intelligence was keeping an eye on me. But it rekindled my
fears that I was an embarrassment to her. At the same time I felt that if
any effort to go to officers' candidate school succeeded it would be attributed to her influence. But I could not get myself to urge our friendship to go underground, an unhappy arrangement for all of us. The
"three days" in Miami, Trude wrote, "seem to have changed the whole
world." A last paragraph in her letter to Eleanor answered by implication the latter's fears she was doing us harm: "To be together with you
and Joe was altogether right—and I'm sure when it is all over we will
belong together."
    The two women were relieved to learn that I had suffered no reper-
cussions as a result of their visit. I wrote to them:

You must not worry about me. I was quite relieved as a matter of fact
to learn from your letter that Colonel Smith's object was merely to
show the other men that I'm not getting special favors because of your
friendship. Trude's way of putting it had made it sound worse. But in

any event little has happened so far except that one of the Sergeants, one of the toughest, let me know that they're going to be tough with me, and that I wasn't going to get away with drilling. Since I have had no desire to escape the ardors of drilling, because it *has* advantages, that hasn't worried me. Nor did the Sgt.'s efforts to trip me up on my knowledge of the General Orders. I have had no extra k.p. or guard duty. Even if I did that wouldn't worry me. I would gladly take a week's k.p. for another weekend like the last . . . certainly things were made easier for Trude and me because you were here. For one thing I doubt if I could have gotten Friday off otherwise. . . .

She was "overjoyed," Eleanor wrote to me, "to find you had not been made to really suffer because of my visit. I'm enclosing Trude's note to me & the last paragraph makes me happy. Perhaps my selfishness hasn't [been] bad & won't have any bad results this time." A note from Tommy confirmed her pleasure in the trip: "Mrs. R. told me that she had enjoyed every minute of her trip to Miami Beach," but, candid as always, Tommy went on: "I am surprised that nothing was said about either you or Trude, or Mrs. R.'s reasons for going to Miami."

I reproached myself for selfishness in allowing her to be involved, but she softly rebuked me:

Why do you ask if you were selfish? Trude asked that too. You were darlings & my happiness is in knowing you are happy not in being in your way! When the war is over let's pray you will be happy together & when you have time to spare you'll share some of it & you will find me always waiting for you with open arms. We'll always be good companions & I'll be so interested in all you accomplish. . . .

The subject came up again when she and Trude had lunch together in New York:

She spoke of how you both felt that I gave too much & you were always receiving. So I tried to make her understand what being loved & included as a close part of your lives meant to me. You can't know of course & I doubt if I ever can tell you, but if you don't let me be a nuisance but really are happy being around & come to feel a real kinship of love & reliance on each other in which we are honest, you will have given me the most precious thing in the world. Confused but perhaps you'll understand!

As the training officers had predicted on my arrival, almost three weeks to the day I was shipped out. I immediately called Trude and then Tommy, since Eleanor was away. "Darling," I wrote to Trude on the train north, "I cannot tell you how excited I have been. . . . I couldn't sleep after I spoke with you, and when I finally verified the rumor I literally danced with joy." Another paragraph said: "Thirty of us are on the way up to weather stations at different air bases—10 to Maryland, 10 to Va. and 10 to Bolling Field, D.C. I'm in the last group. . . . It will be a practical course in weather observation—lasting probably 2 months."

Eleanor welcomed my arrival in Washington: "I got in by plane to find you had talked to Tommy & I am thrilled and so happy to think of you near. I called Trude at once & gave her the news & she said 'Something happened inside us last weekend and now everything goes wonderfully.'" She set aside a room on the third floor of the White House for me to use whenever I had a pass to leave the field and had no other plans. Restrictions at Bolling Field, even on a recently drafted GI were relatively light, and a few days later I was off on a three-day pass, which I spent in New York, where Trude was, and a few days later went into Washington for dinner at the White House. "Haven't I just seen you for three days?" I wrote to Trude from Bolling Field:

Then why do I have the constant feeling that there is so much I want to talk to you about—not about ourselves—a great certainty is beginning to form within me about ourselves—but about the world and its business—chiefly its politics.

I started this letter before dinner (I'm at the White House) and was summoned to the President's study for cocktails. You and I never seem to be on time where the C-in-C is involved. He was in a jovial mood so I guess the visit of Mr. 'Brown'* has gone well. Mrs. R. says that the Pres. feels he got onto a warmer personal basis with Mr. 'Brown.' It amuses me that with the Pres. who is so coldly impersonal himself and with Mr. 'Brown' who belongs to a clan that prides itself on its ability to evaluate people & events impersonally, the object becomes one of getting onto a plane of discourse that has more warmth.

Did I ever tell you that one weekend at H.P. when Mackenzie King† was there and some Vassar girls, we got onto a discussion of postwar organization. The Pres. then talked about a monopoly of post-war military power in the hands of England and the United States. I meekly asked—what about Russia, and the Pres. dismissed it? Tonight Jane Plimpton‡ asked the Pres. anent a remark of his that we would police the aggressor nations after the war to see that they didn't rearm—who would do the policing? The Pres. remarked: ourselves, the English, the Russians, and the Chinese. Mrs. R. & I both looked at one another and smiled. Then he said, 'If we hang together,' and that he thought we would.

I would say that the President's admiration of the English has gone down and the acceptance of the Russians & Chinese up considerably in the last few months.

* Mr. "Brown" was the code name for Vyacheslav M. Molotov, Soviet Commissar of Foreign Affairs, whose fateful visit to the White House, where he had pressed for an early second front, had just been concluded.
† Canada's Prime Minister.
‡ Vassar student body head who had attended the Campobello Summer Institute.

It was a jolly dinner and I wished you were there. There were 6 of us
—Jane, a Mrs. Emmett, Margaret Suckley who runs the H.P. library,
Mrs. R. & me. The Pres. is expecting visits from the Kings of Greece &
Jugoslavia. He calls them 'Look & See' visits. They would like to come
and stay at the W.H. for the duration. But they're only allowed one
night & then are sent over to Blair House, where the cost of feeding
them is borne by the govt.!

Lots of discussion about India. The Pres. is convinced that England
will not be able to hold India but says 'England doesn't know it yet.'
He considers it impossible to deal with the Indian problem so long as
Gandhi is a key figure—but has a great respect for Nehru.

Mrs. R. said that Mr. 'Brown' came in to see her and had told Harry
that he wanted to. She liked him and felt that he was an open, warm
sort of person. They talked about women in Mr. 'Brown's' country.
Mrs. R. said she was greatly interested and had wanted to visit the
country and see for herself. Mr. 'Brown' said he would remember that.
I think Mrs. R.'s visiting the place would have electrifying effect. Mr.
'Brown' is certainly thorough.

You will be wondering what I am doing off the field this weekend.
Through some error my name was down in the book for a pass this
weekend and it was granted me. As soon as I learned I went down to
my Warrant Officer and said I didn't want the pass, that I was on duty
Sunday and wanted the pass for next weekend. He told me to go ahead
and use the pass anyway but could give me no assurance about next
weekend. I think I shall die if I can't come up next Saturday, so, darling, pray. . . .

Committed though Trude was to me, I groused to Eleanor because
Trude did not put everything aside to be with me. Eleanor began to
sense that beyond any insecurity that was rooted in Trude's hesitations
was a strong streak of jealousy in me. She dealt with it gently. James
and Romaine were flying East and, grounded by a storm in Dallas, were
delayed:

I wish I could break my afternoon & evening engagements but I know
it would spoil their 'occasions' & since I can get back by 1 a.m. I am
going. I've left a note for them & I hope James knows I long to hug
him. How horrid conflicts are. You see they arise in every relationship
even such stable ones, as with one's own children!

That James might resent her not being in Washington when he and
Romaine arrived there was a sign of her attentiveness to her children's
feelings as well as my benefit. She might have added that she was herself a model of how to handle jealousy. "Most people when supplanted
in love feel jealous," it has been noted. "What matters is how you deal
with jealousy." She had confessed in *This Is My Story** to being "jeal-

* Page 130.

ous beyond description," on her honeymoon trip with Franklin through the Italian Dolomites, when he, Eleanor being pregnant, had gone mountain climbing with a "charming" Miss Gandy, and she had passed it off with the remark, "Miss Gandy has since become one of my very good friends!" But more than thirty years later, in a letter to Hick a report that a Kitty Gandy, who had been "an old flame" of Franklin's, suggests that the mountain-climbing episode may not have been an isolated one. She had schooled herself not to show her jealousy, even to transcend it, by seeking the other person's good. "How can she?" guests, even close friends, asked as they watched her treat Missy almost as one of her children. She had triumphed over her own jealousy and turned it into a source of strength, and that triumph also enabled her to have a sixth-sense appreciation of the vulnerability of others, including myself, to that "monster."

Eleanor's intervention with Dr. Alvin Johnson, chairman of the ISS Board, ended whatever opposition there was to Trude's succeeding me as the organization's general secretary. Although the war was emptying campuses of men, the ISS had some weighty projects under way, two summer leadership institutes, one at Campobello, the other in Asheville, North Carolina, and an International Student Assembly, organized to bring together representative students from all the United Nations, as the anti-fascist alliance was beginning to be called.

A letter to Maude that Eleanor filled with the wartime activities of her sons reflected a stoical courage:

> Fjr. promised that he'd telephone you if he could from London before he joins his destroyer the 'Mayrant' which is based in Scapa Flow. He left at noon yesterday for England & Ethel & I saw him off at Bolling Field. He seems well again. Elliott is still laid up but should soon be well. Africa seems to give them all dysentery & then he had the operation for piles which was very painful & they found him very anemic. James & his 'Raiders' are on Midway Island so the last few days have been anxious. I'll be happy when we hear from the Island itself. As you say however, one cannot rebel against death, perhaps we have to learn that life was not meant to be lived in security but with adventurous courage.

In the middle of June she and Tommy moved to Hyde Park. She went up to Albany to visit Earl and Simone:

> . . . . a gray day but the hills across the river are green & very soft. I rejoice in the Essen raid but I grieved over Cologne. I cannot bear to have things I have known & enjoyed for their beauty destroyed & the people who die & suffer everywhere. It makes me miserable inside & pray for a speedy end. I read one article on whether we would be able to hold to our magnanimous attitude toward the conquered in the future. The implication seemed to be that it was a weak attitude & we

only held it in the past because we had not greatly suffered. I hope we can hold to it & that it is more than skin deep!

My presence in Washington cheered her. "It is good to have you wandering in & out," she wrote, but she worried about my relationship with Trude. "I hope you & Trude don't need to torture each other very often, time is too precious & yet I can see what happens so well." She sought to reassure me and the same note ended: "This didn't need to be written because I talked to you & loved hearing your voice but somehow I wanted to tell you how much you mattered to me & how dearly I love you." And a later note that told of seeing Trude, at a dinner for the New School for Social Research, said she had managed to stay near enough to her "on the way out to say goodnight & be cheered when she said I had been adequate. Your star is in the ascendant Joe. I think you are going to be increasingly happy with Trude & she will be also." But at other times, although she understood, she trembled for the relationship between the two:

My heart is heavy for you & yet I hope you & Trude may have some happy restful days & nights this week. I love you dearly & I think I know what you go through. First, you must never apologize for anything like calling me when you want to talk to Trude. I understand what is going on & all the inner conflict. You mustn't hate yourself, Joe. You must trust your power over Trude more & then when you think something should be done you won't fight it because of a reason which is personal & you feel weak. Your doubt of Trude is really a doubt of your own power & Joe you have more, far more than you realize over her & over me & many other people. She & I love you but that isn't the only reason. You have intellectual & moral power which we & others feel & respect. . . . I'm worried about you both & only you have the power to reach such trust in yourself that you can give security & peace to your relationship.

Her diagnosis was sound, I assured her, and I sought to do better:

I will try to do my best to make life easier for Trude, although we had some rough spots today. You are a thousand times right that it is lack of confidence in myself that causes my lack of faith in Trude, and that much of what I seek from Trude I can only get from myself. Never have I wanted anything so much as not to be licked by this situation, but to prove stronger than it and marry Trude because of the happiness and good that would flow from such a marriage. Sometimes I feel as if this were the last lap. . . .

I realized dimly then, and much more vividly later when as an author I went through Eleanor Roosevelt's papers, how much she had felt herself to be the victim of a lack of self-confidence in her approach to Franklin in the divorce crisis, and by a rare act of self-discipline had managed to triumph over her fears to become a towering figure of strength and authority. But it was not an example that was easy to follow.

I saw General C. R. Smith, one of the creators of American Airlines, a Texan friend of Eleanor's who was now head of the Air Transport Command, about my future in the Air Corps:

> He was very discouraging about my applying for Officers School. He said I should make every effort to get into forecasters' school: then there could be no suspicion that I have made my way because of influence. I'm inquiring about forecasting school, and meanwhile am not upset that the path to a 'general's commission' is closed to me. I shall try to be useful in the Army in other ways.

In many ways Eleanor showed Trude and me how much our friendship and having me at Bolling Field enriched her life. "Trude dearest," she wrote to her from the White House just before the July 4 holiday,

> Joe thought you might like this time table & I've given him one so it may facilitate your plans.
>
> I'm looking forward to having you all at the cottage next week and though I won't be able to enjoy you as much as if I didn't have Queen Wilhelmina at the 'big house.' I'll see all I can of you however & you'll come again won't you for a weekend or a few days when I am free?
>
> Perhaps next Wed. in N.Y. you & Joe & I might dine somewhere together & settle what you want me to do & when?
>
> It was good to see you dear. I like feeling you are back & accessible! Joe slept till 9 a.m. this morning & is coming back tonight for another long sleep. Much love. E.R.

For the moment, despite my tragic airs over Trude's slowness in making her decision to seek a divorce, with my apartment in New York, to which I could repair on the weekly pass that weathermen were issued, and the companionship of Eleanor Roosevelt, which gave me the feeling of being on the "commanding heights," even though a pipsqueak of a private, I had an exciting and emotion-packed existence. A note to Eleanor reflected my gaiety:

> Yesterday I learned that the weather man's symbol for clear sky was ○. So I leave a letter saying that my heart, everything is ○ between Trude and me.
>
> I'm sorry that I have to leave before you get here. It would be fun having breakfast together, but I've been moved to a new barracks, which is at a distant point from the gate, and I'm a stranger to its customs, so I had better get back by 7:30. But I shall see you tonight.
>
> I received a very nice bath robe with a hilarious note from Tommy:

> > To Pvt. Joseph Lash
> > by order of the Great White Mother
> > executed by the first asst. step-mother.

To be used in case of fire, air-raid or
hasty expulsion!

Trude is going to ask Tommy to explain the last possibility! Much
love.

My apartment in New York, to which Trude and E.R. both had
keys, had my record collection and still was used for parties: "Inciden-
tally—in the field of post-war planning—will you buy recordings of the
'White Cliffs of Dover' and 'Don't Sit Under the Old Apple Tree.'
They'll be fun to play after the war. Also did you ever get a set of the
Spanish songs for me?"

There were occasional dinners with the President and Harry Hopkins
and other famous people, and Eleanor wrote:

> Trude dear, Here is my itinerary in case you need to reach me. Also a
> letter from Lou Harris which may interest you. I showed it to Joe. He
> came in just in time for dinner, very neat & clean to sit by Joan Fon-
> taine who looked fetching in a nurse's aide uniform. I thought Joe held
> his own in a competition with Harry Hopkins who sat on her other
> side! He was asleep when I came in from Red + meeting at ten. I'll
> take him to the field in the a.m. before I take an 8 a.m. train to Aber-
> deen. I'll be back at 2:25 & hope to see him again tomorrow night &
> then I'll be off.
>
> You'll have to look after each other while I'm gone & I hope to re-
> turn to find you both rested & more secure in each other. I love you
> both very dearly, bless you dears.

I had sometimes wondered during those Bolling Field months
whether Harry Hopkins, whom Trude and I both admired, did not dislike me. I should ask him, Eleanor advised me, and I did. On the contrary, Harry replied, he approved the way I had handled myself in a
very difficult situation. He could sympathize. Before Harry had fallen ill
and moved into the White House, reactionaries had sought to embarrass his relationship to Roosevelt and the New Deal by stories of his
membership before World War I in the Socialist Party. Both he and
the President enjoyed Trude's wit and spirit. Once he drew her aside to
counsel her about loyalties in the White House. Mrs. Roosevelt, he
said, was as fierce on that subject as the President. If she for a moment
should feel that Trude was becoming a part of the President's en-
tourage, it would affect Mrs. Roosevelt's feelings about her, he warned.

Royalty was in and out that summer, both at the White House and
at Hyde Park, and though she treated its members with absolute courtesy, to her friends she admitted some impatience and even more skep-
ticism. She apologized to Hick, who stayed in a small bedroom next to
the Lincoln Room: "You are moved into my room just for Wed. night
because the King of Greece & his Chamberlain are using the Lincoln

room & my sitting room over night." She had the least patience with
Princess Martha of Norway. As she later told Trude, who wrote to me
after she and Eleanor had gone up to the top cottage on the hill behind
her own cottage at Val-Kill, where the President was having tea with his
guests:

> Martha was there and as always I was puzzled why he seems to be so
> attracted. She says nothing, just giggles and looks adoringly at him. But
> he seems to like it tremendously—and there is a growing flirtatious inti-
> macy which is of course not at all serious. Mrs. R. explained to me last
> night that there always was a Martha for relaxation and for the non-
> ending pleasure of having an admiring audience for every breath. She is
> just a bit annoyed.

Eleanor felt differently about Princess Juliana but inwardly was awed
at the prospect of having Queen Wilhelmina as her and Franklin's
guest. "Sat., the royal visit begins!" she wrote Hick. "Pray for me. I go
over Sat. p.m. to the Hudson Shore Labor School & suggested I take the
ladies whereupon FDR nearly died!" Juliana went with her to the Eu-
thenics Institute at Vassar "& seemed to like what I said & found the Institute interesting. I talked to the Queen this afternoon & evening & I
like her. She has quality when you talk to her seriously."

Harry Hopkins and Louise Macy were to be married in July. Eleanor
was devoted to little Diana Hopkins, whom she had adopted almost as
a child of her own, but with a strong feeling that Harry, after he had
moved into the White House at the President's invitation, had dropped
her, she did not view sympathetically their remaining at the White
House.

A letter to Hick hinted at her feelings:

> Have you seen that Harry Hopkins is marrying Mrs. Macy? They are to
> be married in F.D.R.'s study on the 30th & try living here at F's
> request. I think it is hard on her & Diana. Of course, I'm away so
> much that we ought to manage to get on! She is here now also Miss
> Suckley . . . after lunch at Steve's request I take H.H. & Mrs. Macy to
> meet the press.

Eleanor felt that Louise Macy fitted into the "Martha" category—
devoted, feminine, fun-loving, and frivolous. They were attributes she
did not herself possess. She knew that she never could be the admiring
female, and while she accepted the fact that men sought their Marthas
as well as their Marys, she insisted there would be only one "First
Lady" in the White House. Was it jealousy that caused her to insist
that other women accept her authority at the White House or a shrewd
assessment of the realities of power? Whatever the deal was that she
had worked out with Franklin, when she agreed to stay married, she

recognized that she would have to insist there be no encroachment on her prerogatives.

A few days later she returned to the subject of Harry's impending marriage. "I'm worried about Harry's marriage & Diana's adjustment if they live at the White House but F.D.R. & Harry seem to think it the only way out." At the end of the month she reported to Hick: "The wedding went off very well & let's pray all goes well & happily." Not long afterwards Harry and Louise decided that they preferred living in their own place and moved out of the White House.

Six weeks after I was stationed at Bolling Field I had passed my examination as a weather observer and been made a corporal. "I just addressed the envelope to 'Corporal J.L.' & it looks impressive," she teased me, but more seriously wanted to know: "Why have you returned to 'Aunt Eleanor' in your letters? Did 'ER' seem too familiar?" That might have been it, I was ashamed to confess. There was an aura about her that deterred any "hail-fellow, well-met" intimacy. Instead of calling her "Aunt Eleanor" I addressed my letters "Dearest ER." Earl felt similarly, despite her efforts to make him treat her as one of his ladies. With Earl and me she would ask for an old-fashioned, try puffing on a cigarette, do household chores, but there was always a slight distance that separated her from those who loved her.

"Incidentally, of course at any minute I may go to Albany to welcome a new baby!" she wrote to me about Earl's hopes to sire a boy. She cherished Earl's regard but was clear-eyed about what love meant to him, as her monthly letter to Maude indicated:

> . . . Earl's baby, a boy, came last Saturday & I spent Sunday with them. After a week during which I had visited the International Student Service Institutes at Asheville, North Carolina & Campobello. I was a bit weary but Earl's enthusiasm was contagious! The baby is really lovely. Simone, the girl he married is very nice but she adores him & does as he wishes. He doesn't know what it is to love unselfishly but perhaps a child or two will teach him! He's a very good naval officer & loves his work. He's at the naval air station outside N.Y. & goes on patrol every day besides his welfare & physical fitness duties. . . .

One paragraph in her letter to Maude presaged events to come and showed how much she hungered for a real job to do:

> There is a very remote chance that sometime FDR may let me go to England this summer or autumn or winter if by doing so I can serve some good purpose both there & here & of course if I go I'll go to Ireland but it is all very vague & would be short & secret till my return so don't mention.

She was even more guarded in her note to Hick: "F & I dined alone last night & I took the occasion to suggest I'd like some war work but I doubt if it bears fruit."

Her devotion to Hick remained unflagging in solicitude but diminished in intensity. As late as 1940, she had sent to Hick 213 letters and received 137. That number fell to 92 and 50 respectively in 1941. In 1942 it would be 42 and 26. Eleanor saw Hick often during the weekdays that the latter spent in Washington as executive director of the Women's Division of the Democratic National Committee. Her tiny room on the second floor of the White House was adjacent to the Lincoln Room and shared a bathroom with the latter. But her emotional life since the mid-Thirties centered on her little cottage in Long Island, where her beloved dog, Prinz, stayed. There she had one group of friends; in Washington it was another. Eleanor occupied a special niche, but there were also Gladys Tillett, the North Carolina housewife and politician who chaired the Women's Division, Representative Mary Norton, a congresswoman from Mayor Hague's Jersey City, who chaired the House Labor Committee with force and determination and in a way that labor approved, and Representative Helen Gahagan Douglas.

In 1942 a new character was introduced into Hick's letters to Eleanor: "I'm about to dine with Marion Harron," she wrote. Judge Marion Harron had been a member of the United States Tax Court since 1936. The position required outstanding legal competence, especially in a woman, as well as banking know-how. Judge Harron, who was ten years younger than Hick's approximately fifty years of age, was a good-looking woman with a partiality for mannish mannerisms. Unmarried, she lived in the Washington suburb of Chevy Chase with her mother. Hick preserved Marion's letters, although Marion destroyed hers. "These are," wrote Doris Faber of the Harron archive, "beyond any doubt love letters." Early in July 1942, Hick from Long Island wrote to Eleanor in Washington: "Marion Harron came up to go down to the country with me. We came up on the 6 o'clock train last night, arrived at 10, spent the night here and now are about ready to start out." Eleanor's mild reply suggested that Hick had been less than forthcoming about the growing relationship: "Hick dearest, it was good to get your Thursday letter, but I wish you had spent the night at my apartment!"

A month later Hick confirmed the new relationship: "Just a note while waiting for Marion to stop by for me . . ." She was going with Marion to stay with her at Chevy Chase. She intended to stay there most of the remaining summer.

Except for the drastic reduction in letters there is no indication that it bothered Eleanor to have Hick and Marion in love. She had ceased long ago to be involved in Hick's emotional life. She continued to be a loyal friend, but her chief concern was with her boys and with Trude and me: "Joe Lash may spend any night in the big Lincoln room so don't be surprised," she warned Hick.

Hyde Park meant an exchange of visits with Elinor and Henry Morgenthau, whose farm at Fishkill was less than an hour's drive away. They were friends with whom she talked candidly, and, as she wrote to me, they reciprocated:

> This evening has been interesting. Henry Morgenthau wanted to talk to F.D.R. about a new idea for preventing inflation so he & Elinor came to dine & then stayed on after FDR & Tully* went home to work. Henry then unburdened his soul about Harry Hopkins & I was troubled about some things he said. Tommy & I have talked about it but the same things worry her that worry me. I can't help wondering what you would think, perhaps I'll get a chance to ask you someday.
>
> Tomorrow a.m. at 11:30 Tommy & I are to go over & unpack barrels for F.D.R. & then some dull people come to lunch. I shall look for Trude & Vera† in the afternoon with joy.

I had other concerns. As I explained to her and Trude, although my way of life away from the post as well as on it was rigidly prescribed, there seemed to be plenty to worry about:

> The Commanding Officer of the Post has just been through the barracks, and of all the things he settled on, after I had scrubbed the floor, shaved, changed uniforms, washed a window, straightened up the lockers, etc. in a flash, was that I needed a haircut! And my name was taken for that reason, which means I'll probably have to water the lawn for a couple of days or some punishment like that. If it isn't one thing, it's another. I hope it does not cut into my days off too severely. You would have been amused at the way the fellows cheered me on when I was frantically trying to get the barracks cleaned up—and myself the same time.

But a few days later a somewhat discouraged soldier wrote to his girl, who immediately communicated the news to Eleanor, who in fact already knew it from the Washington papers that the press, which had discovered his presence at Bolling Field, had given him a bad day:

> This has been an awful day in its impact, altho I've found it quite amusing as it went along. It started with me scrubbing the latrine when one of my barracks' mates burst in with the *Times-Herald* story of my 'soft' berth. A moment later I was told to call Operator 87 in N.Y. I was sure it was you but it turned out to be the *Journal-American*. Then the Field Press Relations Dept. called to say the photographers were

---

* Grace Tully, F.D.R.'s chief secretary after Missy suffered a stroke.
† Vera Pratt was Trude's seven-year-old daughter.

clamoring for my picture and intimated I should turn them down, which I was glad to do.

And so it has gone all day. In the middle of reading the barometer I got called away to answer a call from the *World-Telegram*. The Press Office pulled me out to take my picture, deciding after having talked with me, to send out a picture themselves. So we spent two hours posing for photographs in the barracks—polishing my shoes, cleaning my rifle, outside saluting & looking grim, in the weather office plotting a map. I doubt whether they'll be used, but it was decent of the Field authorities. Also they showed me a release they were sending in which Colonel Peterson calls me one of his 'best' weather observers, & which makes clear there has been no favoritism.

Colonel Eaton, who is commanding officer for all weather men east of the Mississippi was here by chance & I talked with him. He said he thought it best if I were transferred to another field. I told him that would seem to confirm the newspaper charges & he was impressed with the argument. He told me that irrespective of whether I was sent to another station, I would still be in the country when the next exam for forecasting school was given Sept. 7 and if I passed that exam I would certainly be admitted, if not, I would be sent into foreign service as I made clear I desired.

The fellows here are all for me & plenty indignant & ready to issue statements or fight the reporters for me! And that has pleased me more than anything. . . .

Their indignation matched that of Eleanor, who wrote to me that night:

I read both pieces in the Washington papers & found nothing in to-night's World Telegram. The 2 I read seemed pretty weak, trying to make something by inference that they had no foundation for & couldn't prove. I hate to have you persecuted because they want to be disagreeable to me or to the administration. Believe it or not I'd like to help & not hinder you & then things like this happen & then I think that no matter what . . . might be said about you & Trude it could not hurt you more & I should take my bad influence out of your lives & your work. Of course I know I can't for I've given you too much of my heart & my thought but I wouldn't blame you if you decided not to bear the burden of my friendship any longer!

The newspaper flurry passed. Trude often came to Washington in connection with the approaching International Student Assembly to talk to various Allied ambassadors (including Maxim Litvinov) to whom she had letters of introduction from Under-Secretary of State Sumner Welles. I usually accompanied her, leaving her at chancellory doorsteps. I both helped and hindered her, we were often, it seemed, as she said, "clawing" at each other. "When I told you about the Assembly Committee just now," a note commented, "I thought you and I were going to talk over possibilities from the Committee. It never entered my mind that you would consider this too in the light of old unreasonable grudges. How can I work if I'm only to work with people whom you do not suspect—and whom don't you suspect?"

Eleanor tried to keep us from tearing at each other:

> I am uneasy about you because I feel that the many Assembly needs are perhaps crowding out the personal needs just now. Please try to neglect the other things a little & pass the exam with high marks & tomorrow night I'm going to do my best to see that you & Trude get a long evening together!

She urged me to ease my pressure on Trude:

> I wish you could feel so sure of your own strength that you could leave Trude rather free for a week or two until her move is over. If you can get free time together enjoy it but don't have too many fundamental discussions till Trude is settled & both of you are rested. Women are always unsettled when their homes are disrupted & not running smoothly.

She sought with the power of her own love and selflessness to help the two of us over the rough spots. She helped her two old friends Esther Lape and Elizabeth Read. The latter had been ill for several years. They had given up the house on East Eleventh Street which she once had shared, and lived in Westbrook, Connecticut, where they owned a unique piece of land that fronted on the shore:

> It was sad being with Elizabeth today. She made such a fight to live for Esther's sake & yet I wonder if we should cling to those we love where life is so full of suffering. Perhaps being needed & loved compensates for the suffering though. Who can tell?

To be needed and loved was a constant theme with her and certainly explained in part her relationship to her friends, but there was an obverse side to it—that love was unselfish and derived its strongest satisfaction from giving.

A note to Hick in mid-August showed her preoccupation with the International Student Assembly: "The ISS Assembly is giving us all plenty of work but I think it will be very interesting. Now I'm trying to get the State Dept. to expedite 3 young delegates from Russia through Teheran!" The meetings at the beginning of September lived up to all expectations. The governments of the United Nations sent delegations that represented the young people in their fighting services as well as universities. They crowded into the basement of the White House, where the President in an address noted the unusual attention given their sessions by the Axis radio and advised the delegates of the twenty-nine United Nations that "the better world . . . will be made possible only by bold vision, intelligent planning and hard work."

Despite inexperience as a parliamentarian Trude presided over the plenary sessions, with Mrs. Roosevelt and me in the audience urging her on with silent encouragement. Behind the scenes all the conflicts that bedeviled the United Nations were being fought, such as the Soviet insistence on a second front, anti-colonialism, especially self-determination for India, a demand that was championed by the large U.S. delegation, led by Louis Harris, and firmly resisted by the British delegates. However, unity was maintained and a ringing manifesto adopted.

Eleanor had personally invited Harold Laski, who then was a leader of the British Labour Party, to come to the United States to address the assembly. He was willing but had to bow out. Years later, when the Roosevelt-Churchill correspondence became available to scholars, among the documents was a message from Prime Minister to President indicating that he did not like the idea of Laski's coming to the United States. The President agreed. Midterm congressional elections were coming up and he did not think the British Socialist's presence would help Democratic prospects. The U.S. Embassy indicated to him that his presence in the United States would not be convenient. If Eleanor knew, which is unlikely, she did not tell her closest friends.

There is a report on the International Student Assembly that circulated among the top men in the FBI which it is doubtful Mrs. Roosevelt knew of or ever saw. It was supplied to the author under the Freedom of Information and Privacy Act (FOIPA) and described as coming from "Official and Confidential Files, Director's Office." The deletions were made by the FBI in supplying the document to me.

I had done considerable behind-the-scenes work at the assembly and had flunked the first exam for forecasting school. As I struggled anew to master the requisite physics and mathematics, I wondered whether I would be able to make it. "What do you mean if you do not pass the forecaster's exam in Nov.?" Eleanor fired back from Seattle. "You said you were sure you could & I'm sure you can if you work for it so please do!"

In Seattle she went with Anna to a rally built around an assembly UN team that included Ludmilla Pavlichenko, the Russian woman sniper. This wartime heroine had come to Hyde Park with a few others who had been delegates, and, misunderstanding my sudden shove of a fully dressed Trude into the pool, she had intervened protectively. Ludmilla's chief, perhaps single, theme at the United Nations rallies around the country was a second front. As Eleanor wrote to us from Seattle:

> The meeting here tonight was a great success. Anna thinks Ludmilla's speech is pretty straight propaganda. While the others speak for the United Nations, she speaks for the Soviet. I can tell you & Trude more of that when we meet. They are all hardworked & she is tired.

FEDERAL BUREAU OF INVESTIGATION

DATE December 1, 1942

MEMORANDUM FOR THE DIRECTOR

RE: MRS. ELEANOR ROOSEVELT
INTERNATIONAL STUDENT ASSEMBLY

███████████████████████ the Bureau has furnished a copy of a confidential report on
the International Student Assembly held in Washington, D. C., September 3 through
September 5, 1942. This report was made by representatives of Pax Romana (World
Secretariat of National Federations of Catholic University Students).

I wanted to bring to your attention some of the information obtained
in this report which has particualr reference to the activities of Mrs. Roosevelt
in the recent meeting of the Assembly. The information also involves Joseph Lash,
who, you will recall, is said to be very close to Mrs. Roosevelt; Molly Yard, an
executive officer of the International Students Service; and Mrs. Trude V. Pratt,
also of the International Students Service. It is recalled that the International
Students Service sponsored the International Student Assembly at which the problems
of students during the war and postwar periods were discussed. Representatives of
the various Allied Nations and students who were labeled as "anti-Fascist" from such
countries as France, Belgium and Germany were in attendance.

The report ████████████████ furnished was prepared by Pax Romana which,
it is noted, did not take part in the Assembly but merely sent observers because
of its interest in international student affairs and, from a review of the report,
because of the belief that the Assembly might be Communist influenced. Besides
dealing with the Assembly and the various discussions to a great length, the observers sent by Pax Romana furnished their conclusions relative to the Assembly.

It appears that the dominating voice at the Assembly was that of the Sovi
delegation which secured the support of Great Britain and of Mrs. Pratt. It is said
that Mrs. Roosevelt was always on hand to use her personal influence on those who
threatened to oppose openly the Great Power line. An example is cited in this respect to the effect that when the Lithuanian delegation openly denounced, in a round
table discussion, Russian aggression and atrocities in Lithuania, Molly Yard was
immediately dispatched from an inner room to summon the unruly one to the presence
of Mrs. Roosevelt. There she was induced to sacrifice her particular interests "for
the larger common good of the Assembly".

In describing Mrs. Roosevelt's position with regard to the Assembly, it
was said in the report that the Assembly was controlled by a small, unofficial,
cohesive inner circle of Mrs. Roosevelt, Mrs. Pratt, Joe Lash and Molly Yard. Mrs.

(INFORMATIVE MEMORANDUM - NOT TO BE SENT TO FILES SECTION)

Roosevelt was further described as its patron: Mrs. Pratt, its clever chairman, Joe Lash, its unofficial philosopher: and Molly Yard, its keen organizer. The observers further state they believe Mrs. Roosevelt has a sincere interest in youth and realizes the political value of the International Student Assembly both in winning the war and influencing the determination of the terms of the peace.

Concerning the association between Mrs. Roosevelt and Joe Lash, it was stated that possibly Mrs. Roosevelt is being "used" by him if Lash is still "intellectually a Communist". It was stated, however, that it could not be conclusively proven that Lash is a Communist although throughout the report it was hinted that the belief is that he was at one time at least a Communist sympathizer.

In the report, Alan Booth, General Secretary of the International Students Service of Great Britain, who was at the Assembly, is referred to constantly as a source of information, especially relative to Mrs. Roosevelt, Joe Lash, Molly Yard and Mrs. Pratt, thus implying the British know something of the association between Joseph Lash and Mrs. Roosevelt. Booth is said, in the report, not to consider Lash honest intellectually and believe him capable of concealing certain plans from Mrs. Roosevelt. Booth, while he was in Washington, stayed at the White House during the Assembly and while there could observe what he termed an unusual friendship between Mrs. Roosevelt and Joseph Lash which he further classified as "the patronizing or motherly type". It should be noted further that it is reported in the memorandum that Joseph Lash, Molly Yard and Mrs. Elliot Pratt had free access to the White House.

From the report on the entire Assembly, it appears that it was guided or maneuvered almost exclusively by Mrs. Roosevelt, Joseph Lash, who prior to that time had entered the Armed Forces, Mrs. Pratt and Molly Yard as representing, if not controling, the International Students Service in this country. It is claimed that they in turn acceded to practically every demand or suggestion of the Russian delegation and that consequently the delegates of Great Britain and China had to accede. The "credo" of the Assembly in it's first draft was written by Joseph Lash, then corrected by Mrs. Roosevelt and subsequently corrected and changed by the presiding committee which, it is said, acceded to every suggestion of the Russian delegation.

Respectfully,

D. M. Ladd

D. M. Ladd

This is nauseating E

Such was the way the International Student Assembly appeared to some.

Eleanor's fifty-eighth birthday was on October 11. She asked the President to invite me to the small birthday dinner he had for her. She wrote:

> I've been wearing your flower all afternoon & evening & enjoying it so much but especially the thought that you brought it to me. I didn't wear it last night because I felt catty remarks might be made!
>
> I long to see you both & tell you many things I learned tonight in a talk with F.D.R. Also I want to know how you felt about lunch & most important of all just about you & Trude. That is the really important thing, how our personal relationship & the essentials of decent living develop for us all. I love you dearly, & whether you like it or not I feel it in my bones that I'm going to cling very closely to you in whatever years lie before me!

The great event before her was her state visit to wartime England. She wanted to go. The visit was an outcome of her talk with Franklin in which she had asked for some war work. On such occasions usually she told friends and family she'd just as lief not go or not do anything. She made such statements sometimes because she had discovered so often that plans might be canceled. There was also the stoic's resignation to the absurdity of events. But this time there were no such footnotes to fend against disappointment. "I was leaving the 13th," she wrote to Maude Gray, "but the Queen has been ill & asked me not to arrive till the 20th . . . [she] wants me to see the Eng. women's work in addition I'm going to all our camps & hospitals."

An undated letter that she sent to me at this time, probably after I had asked for foreign service, which she said she dreaded although she understood how I felt, was filled with the unselfishness and sharingness of her love:

> Every parting has a touch of death in it but if one can achieve that sense of 'oneness' with people one loves it wards off loneliness. Nothing can ever really come between you & me. I know if experience changes you somehow I'll understand & no matter how many miles lie between us my thoughts will be with you. There is a weak ending to this book but much that is true to life. One thing stands out that love is important to the person that gives it & in the end the great healing & strengthening force.

In anticipation of her departure she prepared a series of letters for me to read while she was gone:

> It really pays to be ill, everyone is so very kind & solicitous! I did feel badly but tonight the pain is really almost all gone. I'll have one or more lamp treatments before I go to bed & be well tomorrow.
>
> I shall leave this for you to open on Nov. 1st. I can't bear to even

think that we might be saying goodbye for a long time but if you should have to go out of the country before I get back you know one thing I'm sure—that I will be waiting for your return & thinking of you every morning & every night & many other times every day. If you are moved in this country I'll come to see you as soon as I can & even in other places I'd try hard to get there sometime! I like to dream of a future in which you & Trude & the children are a part of my daily life always & together we may do many pleasant things. God grant it may come true.

The next day she penned a note for me to open on my birthday, December 2:

If you open this with Trude & me, it will be a joyous day, if not I pray for you the contentment which comes from work well done in response to the conviction that one must do it.

May all your future birthdays be celebrated with those you love near you & be happy in the knowledge that your generation is making progress. Many happy returns of the day. God bless & keep you & my devoted love to you now & always,

E.R.

The gift is someday for use in 'that' house of yours.

The next day she wrote what she thought was her final note:

Goodbye Joe dear. Bless you & take good care of yourself & Trude. Get all the happiness you can, stored up, so don't have moods. Fight them & be patient. I somehow think you'll be somewhere in this country so I can see you on my return but in any case let me know how I can help you.

Bless you. Take good care of yourself & of Trude & try to be here when I get back. I'd rather have you two meet me than anyone else in the world! I guess it would have to be at the apartment or here however!

My love dear now & always.

Air travel across the ocean did not have the scheduled certainty of later years, and two days later in New York she lamented to Hick: "Here we have sat & now we hope weather conditions are promising & we will leave tomorrow. I did all the errands which I had left undone today & signed a new will & have had a leisurely pleasant day! Cousin Susie was pathetic . . ." her letter to Hick ended.

She and Tommy were driven in a Secret Service car to a secluded entrance at the airport and boarded a flying boat for the transoceanic jump that landed them in Foynes, Ireland.

Here we are held up 24 hrs by weather & I hope we get off to Bristol tomorrow a.m. I am not supposed to be in Ireland so David & Maude who met us this a.m. in Foynes insisted that I couldn't go to the Inn & Maude & I have spent today in the Adare's house. They return tonight & I only have my plane bag but it has been wonderful seeing Maude. David has gone back to Dublin. This afternoon we took a long walk in the rain & went to look at old ruins on the Durramer estate. They date back to the early monks Maude says but her history is a bit vague so I have no date. Tommy & Mrs. (Oveta Culp) Hobby* & her lieutenant all went to the Inn & she telephoned they would go to Limerick this afternoon & I hope she enjoyed it. Ireland has charm, I think, such green grass & the little houses are quaint (& unhealthy) the carts amusing & must give one lots of exercise, & the people are pleasant & friendly.

Supposedly we will get out at 9 a.m. tomorrow weather permitting & the enemy being kind enough to send no airplanes over our route!

There seems to be food enough here but nothing but peat to burn. There is a fire in every room however which looks cheerful tho' it has little effect on the temperature!

The flight was very smooth. Both sunset & sunrise were beautiful & I had no more sense of insecurity than one has in the smaller planes over the land. The food was good & we all ate saying 'this is the last time we'll have this till we return.' If we have to go back the southern route which seems probable it will mean 2 nights but that can't be helped.

My love to Trude & you dear, I've been thinking about you & hoping the meeting was not as bad as it promised to be. No matter what happens, it isn't worth letting yourselves be made miserable by it. I hope you are concentrating both of you on your own happiness these days,

Bless you. I love you dearly
E.R.

This can't go till I reach London!

I read your letter dear, many times on the way over & thank you for all your good wishes. I hope the despair will never return dear boy & you will never be out of my mind & heart till we are all together again.

She also wrote to Hick from Ireland: "I'll be glad when Buckingham Palace lies behind me & I can go to work." But when she reached London and was met by the King and Queen and was driven to Buckingham Palace, she knew that the latter's engraved letterhead would charm her friends. She wrote to me before dinner:

I thought the paper would impress you! Tommy & I are lost in space but we have a cozy sitting room with a coal fire. I'm so full of impressions but I can't write now, however I'll dictate to Tommy tonight. We were able to leave this a.m. but only by special plane & the rain & fog are with us as usual. The evidence of bombs in Bristol & here is quite evident. The Queen showed me where they wrecked her rooms. The little Princesses were here when we arrived & are nice children & we had tea around a set table as I used to have in my girlhood. Tommy was with the ladies-in-waiting & her bedroom is a mile from mine!

* Colonel Oveta Culp Hobby, Texas publisher and head of the Women's Army Corps, WAC.

We've just done the column & I must get this ready to mail tonight. Bless you & all my love.

She wrote again on a Buckingham Palace letterhead:

Joe dearest,
I've thought of you so much today & longed for news & I think tomorrow I'll send a cable with answer prepaid so I'll know at least you haven't gone. It seems long without news, tho' every minute is packed with interest. I've dictated very full notes to Tommy every night so far & some things you will read in my column. . . .

Tommy had decided that staying with Kings is all in the day's work & being here at Chequers with the Churchills doesn't create a ripple. The Edens, Winants, the Portals (head of the R.A.F.) are here & 2 daughters Sarah & Mary. The latter understand because of their job contacts much about tomorrow & accept it as you & Trude do at home.

I've seen Elliott twice, tomorrow he spends the night with me in London & Thursday I go to see his outfit. He goes soon & not towards home.

I saw a lot of our boys at the Red + centre in London this a.m. & the world is small, one came from Poughkeepsie & one knew Jane Seaver & had been at Columbia!

I must go to bed but bless you dear, & a world of love to you & Trude. I want to know all about you both & if life is inwardly peaceful & happy for you. I wonder what happened at the I.S.S. meeting & I wish you could both be here with me. I would like to hold you both very close. I think of you so often & you are always in my heart.

Her next letter on a "1600 Pennsylvania Avenue" letterhead ("Thursday night Oct. 29th") dealt with the British equivalent of the International Student Assembly, whose organizer had been a participant in the World Youth Congress:

It was good to get your cable from New York tonight & to know that you were getting your holiday & I hope you & Trude are going to stay at Hyde Park. I am calling her in the morning as Sir Stafford & Lady Cripps dined with us tonight & assured me Betty Shields Collins had been foolish but they feel youth must be helped or the Communists will take hold. He remembers & admires you & says his boy who is a pacifist was talking of you only a few days ago. We had a pleasant time & I liked them *both*.

Today was spent visiting some of our air force—Elliott's unit among others but much of it is already gone. He was to have come up last night but could not & now may be able to come Monday tho' I shan't be surprised if he is off before that day comes.

It is hard to get at 'people' but I hope to succeed in some places somehow. We are putting in rather bad days but one sleeps well. I feel as though I'd been away for years & I find that you & Trude are in my thoughts constantly. I pray you will still be in the country at least when I get home. I don't think we can leave till the 12th at the earliest & probably not till the 14th or 15th. I'm praying we can go directly home but it may take several days. Anyway it seems to be felt that the visit is having good results here, so it is one contribution I could make. I cannot get any word of the young Russians!

I spent yesterday seeing Royalty & lunching with the ladies of the House of Commons & was so weary when we left for the play at 6 I could hardly go. The play 'Slave(?) Path' will soon be in N.Y. & I want to take you & Trude!

The blackout here is real, you never saw its like & when mixed with fog it is dreadful. We've had intermittent downpours with plain rain in between!

Joe, give Trude my love & to you my love & devotion always.

E.R.

"Westbrook Pegler took you to pieces yesterday—and Ray Clapper defended you!" Hick informed her. Clapper's column at the time of the OCD crisis had been particularly deadly.

From a palace in Badminton, Gloucestershire, where Eleanor spent the night with the formidable Queen Mother Mary, she wrote to me of the palace's beauty, filled as it was with Chinese and Japanese things and a raw temperature that drove Tommy to bed to keep warm.

Today I visited our troops—in church, at mess, in barracks, in hospital & finally at the Red Cross place run by Mrs. Theodore Roosevelt.

Canterbury was bombed yesterday, perhaps because we went there the day before. The siren has blown twice in London but no one noticed it. The blackout in the country is even worse than in London because you see no light anywhere.

They let some of our troops help with the harvest & when any of them go to families for meals they let them take some of their ration & I think it is having a good effect. The British are keen to help where they can.

I doubt now if I get off till the 15th. . . .

The unpublished diary of her trip is dated October 21 to November 17. The last letter she sent to me was dated "Nov. 5th."

Your letter of the 27th came two days ago & brought me great joy. It is good to have you & Trude happy & at peace & I hope you went to H.P. & had lots of sleep & contentment.

The young Russians arrived about 2 a.m. today & came to see me at noon. They all looked weary & send you & Trude their love & were glad to get your messages. I think I'll still be here for the conference. Betty Shields Collins & 2 other girls & 2 young men came with Lady Cripps to see me last night. They all seemed alive & interested. I cabled Trude this a.m. to get in touch with Sumner [Welles] if he had not reached her but I heard from the Ambassador later that Louise [Morley] was coming. I hope to see her. I won't be able to cable, even guardedly, about leaving so I'll tell you I fear I won't get off till the 16th or 17th but I hope to go direct & you & Trude will know as soon as I can reach a telephone after arrival!—I count on you to cable your plans if any change impends for it will be cruel to find I cannot reach you & see you soon. I miss you very much dear, but I have learned much & felt much on this trip. Everyone seems to feel that the job over here is going well & I pray it may go well at home. I'm doing a radio Sunday night from Liverpool but it has been prepared under pressure & the censor is severe so I don't know how it will go.

I've had many interesting talks but I'll tell you of those when we meet.

Cambridge yesterday was interesting. The University is not much hurt & is very beautiful. It was my introduction to Industrial billeting & a study in handling human beings. A visit to the Eagle Squadron on the way home was another & very different study. A make-up man from Hollywood is the Major of the Squadron, one of the few survivors of the original group. He looks dapper & not very strong & he is made of steel I imagine.

I.S.S. must be settled & I hope Trude cast my vote. Dr. Cohn sounds like a naughty child & don't you be too sorry for him!

The English do not like Wilkie [*sic*]. The Asst. Dean who showed him around St. Paul's said 'He's like a whirlwind. He really didn't want to see anything!' His speech was not taken seriously. The elections* do bother officials here. They wonder if it means an isolationist America again. Elliott telephoned Ruth through the White House tonight & so we talked to FDR & he seemed quite unperturbed.

Elliott, Tommy & I went shopping this p.m. (after I lunched with the Cabinet wives).† It was fun & we had tea with Muriel Martineau in her tiny home. Returned & had a talk with Ed Murrow & then we three dined alone. I think this may have to be our last evening as I'm off in the morning for the north & won't be back here till the 13th.

Tommy sends you her best. She still coughs but she bears up & I think she's been interested.

All my love Joe dear. A thousand times a day I long to have you & Trude with me. Goodnight & bless you.

E.R.

The plane that carried her back across the ocean was filled with ferry pilots and took her directly to Washington. The final note in her diary betrayed a feeling for Franklin's regard that she had long steeled herself not to expect and which clearly mattered:

We looked out & saw Secret Service men and several cars and knew that FDR had taken time off to meet us. . . . I really think Franklin was glad to see me back and I gave a detailed account of such things as

---

* The midterm congressional elections reduced the President's control, although the Democrats still had a majority.

† To Hick she wrote: "They are as dull as ours . . ."

I could tell quickly and answered his questions. Later I think he even read this diary and to my surprise he had also read my columns.

She went to see others in Washington: "Saw Arnold, Col. Stimson & Sec. Knox this a.m. & had a nice talk," she wrote to Hick. "Quite sleepy & must go tomorrow to Shangri-La*—but only for the night."

Soon after her return she caught up with the news of Trude and me. I had forwarded Eleanor's letters from England to Trude, noting "the very loving references" to the latter and reproaching myself because "she must think we are awful not having written more frequently. I guess if I would spend less time in my moods I would have more time to behave as a friend—not to speak of other things." Trude should add to my replies, which I asked her to forward: "You have a manner of stating things that's warming, informative and full of chuckles and Mrs. R. sounds lonely."

Eleanor wanted to hear about the clash in the ISS Board between the activists, who wished to promote the International Student Assembly approach, and the more traditional educators, who insisted on ISS's neutrality and non-partisanship. She favored the former and had given Trude her proxy in case there was a showdown vote. The issue had not yet been decided, she learned, nor had the relationship between Trude and me become any less tempestuous. We had days of a honeymoon-like bliss. "When we are at peace life is very good," I had written to Trude, but there were other times, as even I admitted, when "the fine times together are not illusory, but interspersed with such dreadful hours, that one *can* seriously question their reality. What I hope now is that we have arrived at an understanding where we can allow ourselves to function as normal people, and discern whether to be together is a source of fun, of strength, of peace, of love."

Trude, as Eleanor knew, responded in kind, with waves of love succeeded by gusts of self-reproach. Sometimes it seemed to me that the closer she approached to the decision to seek a divorce, the more strongly she was hit by guilt, leading her to decide to break off, as a letter to me after Eleanor's return explained:

You have always asked me to talk simply. And very simply the truth is: That I want no one else to make love to me but you, that I want to make love to no one else but you—that I am completely dependent on you in my work—and probably cannot do it without you—but that I am not willing to pay the price—that therefore I am not able to pay the price. I should like very much not to believe that this is true—but it still is. And the fault lies entirely with me. A long time ago Mrs. R.

* Later presidents called this Catoctin Mountain retreat Camp David.

said that I don't feel things as deeply as you. It struck me very much—and somehow hurt, probably because I knew she was right. I am not capable of as much love as you, of as much sympathy and compassion, and not of enough belief. Whenever we were planning for the future I was terribly uneasy somewhere—as if I allowed myself to live in a fairy tale.—You must believe me that I would have told you if it had been clear to me—and if I had known what the uneasiness meant. My conviction now that we cannot be happy together—even though there seems no other possible life—is really quite unshakeable.

At such moments Eleanor wondered whether the two would hold together. On a trip to New England after her return, she stopped off in Westbrook to see Esther and Elizabeth, and wrote to me in a note on the train that combined commiseration with my anguish with acceptance of my passion:

My thoughts have been with you ever since you left yesterday. I cannot help feeling that part of the trouble is physical weariness & the result of long emotional strain. Writing will help you but you must get sleep & rest too. Next week you will be on the night shift again which is always hard so do get a peaceful week end!

By the way, if you are in N.Y. I'll plan to celebrate the evening of Dec. 23rd with you & Trude & take the midnight to Washington. Would you like to go to the play or shall we just dine & then I'll bring over what Xmas gifts I have for you both? Tell Trude I'll give her what little things I have for your stocking as I know she will want to fill it & I'll have some things for her which I will give you!

I'm on my way now to Saybrook [Westbrook, nearby] where I'll have about three hours with Esther & Elizabeth before going on to Fall River. After the evening meeting there the Secret Service is driving me to the Statler in Boston & tomorrow morning I imagine Tom Mathers will come to breakfast! Jim Lanigan may come too. He is up there in the Navy.

I don't imagine you heard the broadcast last night, but it seemed to go well & the sponsors were pleased for they asked Betty Lindley to come & discuss a series. Mr. Pegler devoted his column more or less to me last night but I got some information yesterday which might mean a little difficulty for him, anyway we're going to find out. I'll tell you more about it.

I spoke to Trude this morning & she sounded well. A world of love.

Whatever her information about Pegler, if I ever knew it, I have forgotten. In any case, it did not end his columns on Eleanor or the Roosevelts. They would remain a part of her life whose disagreeableness only a few people were allowed to know she even noticed.

Although she had usually attributed her hectic schedule to the demands of White House protocol, now, although formal entertainments had been stopped and she had canceled paid lectures, she lamented again: "I have been so busy since I came home, I haven't had time to breathe." So she told an old friend, Mrs. Margaret Fayerweather, who lived near Albany and whom she had not gone to visit when she had dashed up there to see Earl Miller's five-month-old baby boy. "Do try to come down for a few days rest and change," she ended.

From Hyde Park the Saturday before Christmas she wrote to me that if I preferred to spend the evening of the twenty-third on which we had agreed to celebrate Christmas with Trude alone, she would understand:

> I'm sending over a few things I got to give you & Trude for Xmas, but I think they might be more useful for your party.
>
> I am so sorry you were ill & more sorry that I woke you when you need rest so badly. I've just written Trude telling her I missed seeing you but hoped you would both get some of the rest you need & feel much better.
>
> Susie will take the eggnog bowl etc. over at 4 on Wednesday & help you if you need her & then return here & wait till Trude calls her to tell her when to go & tidy up.
>
> I had a few Xmas tree trimmings left over so send them in the hope that you can use them.
>
> I feel dear that you & Trude have so little time together that you should do as you like Wednesday for dinner & not think of me. I'll be happier if I think of you two happy together so please send me word here if you decide that is what you would like to do. These are unusual times & this is a particularly difficult time for you two so I'd like you to be selfish & do what you want.
>
> I think I'll end by coming down on the 10:30 Tuesday night since FDR's train is unpredictable!
>
> Bless you darling. My love to you & I love you very much.
>
> E.R.

"This will be my Xmas letter," she wrote to Hick on the twenty-second. "I feel glad that we had a happy evening together & perhaps about once a month this winter we might spend an hour or so of an evening & read something aloud. Let's try." There was news about Madame Chiang Kai-shek and Cousin Susie and how she had "spent the evening with Earl . . . I wrote all the kids yesterday since we can't telephone but I shall miss hearing their voices, that was about all I cared about on Xmas day, the rest seems a good deal of a chore to me!"

She had been anxious about my being shipped overseas. On her return from England she had learned of my formal request for foreign service. But also I was preparing for the forecasting school exam. A note to Trude had described the situation:

> Last night I was completely absorbed in the synoptic map when Colonel Peterson, an energetic little man, came into the station. Said he had seen my letter requesting foreign service—and, as I told you, his reaction was that they hated to lose potential forecasters and he himself

would advise against my pressing the request. He said that I had just missed passing the last exam and felt I would pass the next. Then he suggested that until I go to forecasting school, or flunked the exam, I could be stationed elsewhere. I told him I preferred to remain here, but transfer is a possibility.

I had not been reassigned and I mastered the physics and mathematics sufficiently to pass the exam, as Peterson had predicted. The next session of the forecasters' school, which was in Chanute Field near Urbana, Illinois, began in late January and as the year ended I was awaiting transfer to there.

Eleanor wrote me a letter to be read on Christmas Eve:

I'm glad that they tell me I may telephone N.Y. on Xmas day so I'll call you in the morning but I want to have this with you for Xmas eve.

I know you will be lonely & I'm alone inside so much that I know it is not a happy feeling & yet you have so much understanding of Trude & have suffered so much that you seem to have won an inner peace & I hope you'll not be too sad in your own room. I like to think of you there listening to your records which are so lovely & perhaps you & I both will say a prayer tonight that you may not have to be away too far & too long. I shall pray too for years of happiness to compensate for these disturbed & confused days.

The country is very beautiful and I walked a little way alone in the woods both yesterday & today & it was good for me. Perhaps someday you & Trude & I will all be spending our holiday times here together & that might be nice for us all?

I'm reading 'Private Hargrove' & I am really entertained.

We had a successful party tonight for the soldiers. I hope tomorrow is as good. Tomorrow I'm going over after lunch to speak to the soldiers. 8 officers come to tea & 2 to dinner. I go down in the evening & Wednesday I'll see you & Trude. I hope you won't be worn out by the trip to Washington & back. Also I hope the whole family enjoyed dressing the Xmas tree!

Well, dear, I wish I could sit with you & listen to Marion [*sic*] Anderson tonight. I'd like your near presence & your hand in mine. Somehow there is reassurance in touching someone you love but Alec Woolcott [*sic*] says abiding love is only on paper so I'm glad at least I can write you! All my thoughts & prayers, my blessing & my love go to you this Xmas & may the coming year bring you greater happiness in a happier world.

Goodnight dear boy.

E.R.

"Xmas eve 1942," her next letter began, and under it she wrote, "No Xmas day":

It is late but before I go to bed 'the writingest lady' must send you a line with her new pen which I think even improves her handwriting!

I don't know if I can put in words what I want to say of gratitude &

love to you & to Trude. Last night was Xmas for me with you two whom I love & makes me hope that someday the whole season may be lived through together, happily. I've come of late years to dread, not what I do for those I love, but the mass production side & the formal impersonal things I have to do. I'm always with so many people & always so alone inside except with a very few people, so—I thank you—both—for sharing precious hours with me & giving me so much happiness. . . .

At the end of the holiday week she wrote again lines that she wanted me to read at the base:

On this New Year's eve I hope with all my heart that before another one comes around you will be back with us, free to help in the building of the better society we all hope for. I know that you are doing that now in the Army but I like you best to be your own master! May your personal life be free from problems by then & moving onward to a deep & fine understanding & a really happy life with the woman you love.

May our own friendship grow stronger & may the bonds which I feel bind me closely to you bring to you as well as to me deep contentment & security.

God bless you my dear boy, & health & happiness be yours this whole year through. This will be my nightly prayer & if thoughts can fly, mine will go to you bearing all my love, night & morning & a thousand times a day.

Devotedly
E.R.

But none of us had taken into account the intellectual and emotional horizons of military intelligence.

XX

The Altruist in Love

JANUARY 1943 for Trude and me was a month of my awaiting travel orders to take me to Chanute Field, an air force training center set in flat prairie-like fields in Illinois. Our relationship was tempestuous as always. Eleanor saw us frequently. She would become alarmed if on my day off from Bolling Field I did not check in with her or Tommy. She worried, too, about Anna and John, who had come East to discuss John's determination to leave the Seattle *Post-Intelligencer* to go into the Army. "I hope you've been too busy to notice that I've not written!" she excused herself to Hick during a visit to New York. "I've been busy, weary & no news!" The absence of news referred to Franklin's having left Washington for the Casablanca meeting with Churchill. "Anna & I have had a good day including a visit to Mme. Chiang which we all deeply appreciated."

The wife of the Generalissimo had arrived in the United States in mid-November and checked into Presbyterian Hospital in New York. Eleanor was much taken with the vibrant Chinese figure, who to her symbolized the renaissance of a great nation and, beyond that, of womanhood.

Her notes to Franklin dealt with the plans and problems of their children. They were genial, sympathetic, and cool. "Dearest Franklin, It is good to know you have safely reached 'a destination.'" Her chief item of information was that Anna and John had obtained newsprint for their newspaper. "Be careful & love from us all." She signed it "Eleanor" rather than "E.R." Her next letter was concerned with Elliott. "It was nice to get another message saying you 'were getting where you wanted to be!' " Elliott's pilot, who was in this country, had just told Ruth that Elliott was coming home briefly. Her letter to Franklin continued:

> Of course you can't see Edson here so I'm telling Ruth to tell him you would not want to be consulted but would want those in charge to do whatever was best for the service without any direction from you where it concerned your children. I hope this is right. . . .
> Much love & love to Elliott & Fjr. if you see him.
>
>   ER

Hearst was willing to have Anna continue at the Seattle *Post-Intelligencer* in John Boettiger's absence, but Eleanor had mixed feelings about the latter, a sense that the abandonment of his responsibilities at the paper, towards Anna, and the family in order to enter the service was not all that heroic.

Although busy, she had managed to prepare farewell notes for me as my departure date neared. "This is a letter in which I want to make you realize how grateful I am to 'whatever fates there be' for the past months that you have spent here. . . ." She began another long letter before she had a forwarding address for the first:

> Well, dinner & the (birthday) balls are behind me & I must go down in one minute & broadcast & then I'm coming back to write you so much that is in my heart but I haven't trusted myself to say these last few days for fear I couldn't think! (?)
> *Later* Now, my chores are done. I've talked & said thank you & laughed & been told I was gracious & the children have gone out to dance & it's midnight so soon I'll go to bed & read until I fall asleep but first oh! Joe, I'm spoiled! You & Trude have been generous of yourselves with me & I've loved feeling close to you both, especially to you, & I'm old so I haven't as much future to trust as you two have. Nevertheless I'm going to hope that the time will come again when fate will be kind & let us live near each other again & perhaps you'll like me well enough to want to come to see me often! In some ways I feel closer to you & your aspirations than I do to my own children which is something one cannot understand until one's children are grown & have become individuals so you no longer look upon them as part of yourself!
> Anna tells me Fjr. has been very inconsiderate of Ethel & she confided that as a family she liked us much better than her own family & was happier with us & if Fjr. wouldn't insult her in public she wouldn't mind his flirting with other ladies! I'm afraid he just gets bored & then he writes us both beautiful letters after he knows he's misbehaved!
> Word has come that F.D.R. has left Maine about 6 p.m. so the air journey is over safely. I'll write you anything he tells me Monday night.
> Seeing you go today & knowing that I couldn't plan on seeing you at any definite time was very hard this afternoon. I feel rebellious at

being a prisoner to this position of the President's wife but I'll work hard & the days will go by as they always have no matter how I felt inside & God grant the war may not last too long. I wish I were going to kiss you goodnight, instead of putting it on paper. I hope Trude & you are not really unhappy tonight & remember that you are going to be together soon & often. I'm so glad for you both that I.S.A.* is going to work.

That will fill in for Trude till she goes to get her divorce. I'd like to suggest that she let me find a quiet ranch for her to be on when she goes there & then I might go spend a little while with her to break the long, lonely pull. But I guess that is one of those things I'd better not offer, isn't it?

Goodnight darling, bless you & I love you dearly & miss you.

She prepared a letter to greet Franklin on his return from Casablanca:

Dearest Franklin,

Welcome home! I can't be here Sunday night as months ago I agreed to open a series of lectures at Cooper Union [New York City] but I'll be home for dinner Monday night as I don't want you to tell all the story & miss it. Anna & John, Ruth & Ethel will all welcome you here. Could we have a family birthday party Monday evening? I have to be gone for the day Tuesday but will be back Wed. a.m. Jimmy thinks, tho' his outfit has had no amphibious training yet, they will be sent off the 4th. If they could be delayed just a few days he'd try to fly back & see us but a ship is available. I suppose that won't be possible. I'm terribly sorry not to see him & I think I will now delay going west till late March because the weather will be better, since I won't see him anyway. I'm so glad Anna & John could come back to see you. Please don't speak to Congress till I get back Wed. Much love & I am so glad you are back.

E.R.

Sunday in New York before going to Cooper Union to lecture she had the presiding officer, Dr. Houston Peterson, and his wife for supper at 29 Washington Square. She wrote to me:

Here I sit at 10:45 & I feel if you could walk in or I could hear your voice on the telephone the whole world would be brighter! I like that room because wherever I sit I can look at a photograph of you & one I like. Trude came to supper in your red gown looking lovely but tired & I knew it was not an easy time. I only had sherry but we looked at each other over our glasses & drank to you while Dr. & Mrs. Peterson I hope drank to each other! I liked both of them & was sorry Trude had to go home & feed the children who were arriving from the country, as she said she would have liked to go to Cooper Union. We had a minute

* The International Student Assembly, which met in September 1942, had a council that met in New York and of which Trude was the secretary.

alone after dinner & she promised to call me tonight. Dr. Cohn is making trouble for I.S.A. but I don't see how he can hold them up. She says that she is not going to talk to him again & that to me is much to be desired. She said having you away was terribly hard & I know how she must miss you. I want to help but filling an empty heart is only possible for you to do & all I can do is help her to learn how to live with it & still get something out of life. After this when you are together you should be happy all the time!

Well, I had breakfast alone [at the White House] this morning for all the children were out late, then I read the papers & thought of you. Would you like me to send a 'Times' while you are at Chanute & did you remember to change your 'P.M.' address? Finally at 12 Anna & John appeared & we had a good time while I drank a glass of milk & ate a sandwich & at 12:30 I went to the train for the plane was 2 hrs late & I didn't dare risk waiting for it.

After I got there I arranged some little things for Earl is moving to a house at the field this week & so at my suggestion he is taking his piano & I put my long table where the piano was & will learn to use my records. At 6:45 we had supper & then we walked to Cooper Union & I talked & answered questions. The subject was 'the past ten years & a look into the future.' The place was packed & the questions were good.

I called FDR as soon as I got back & he reached Washington at 6:30 & sounded well & cheerful. He promised to repeat all he was telling the children tomorrow night for my benefit even to 'the story of a shot gun wedding which I engineered' said he! He told me to tell Mme. Chiang that he thought he had agreements which would much improve the airplane situation in China & Gen. Arnold was on his way out there. He tried to send Elliott but Gen. [Carl] Spatz said he was too valuable to him & would not let him go. I'll write you all I can remember tomorrow night.

Tommy gave me this paper at Xmas for air-mail letters but I wonder if you can read when I write on both sides?

The enclosed being a review by Paul Hagen I thought might interest you.

The streets are sloppy here but the air is soft & I hope I can fly down tomorrow.

Dr. Algernon Black comes to see me at nine & then I go to the Orthopaedic to see about my feet again & then to Mme. Chiang taking Trude. Lunch & talk at the Junior League & back to Washington. I wonder if you will send me a wire, dear, what a nuisance one can be when one longs for news of someone!

Trude hasn't called yet but I want to get this off so goodnight & bless you wherever you are & a heart full of love goes to you.

She returned to Washington, where Trude reached her with the news of my arrival at Chanute and my temporary address. Her letter that night was filled with the Casablanca meeting:

Trude wired me that you were well but cold & gave me the temporary address & I was so glad to have news of you.

We had an interesting visit to Mme. Chiang & I left Trude on the corner of 5th Ave. & 56th to go to the hair dresser when I went to the Junior League to speak at lunch. The weather was good & I flew down & we had a pleasant dinner, just Harry & Louise & the Crown Princess [Martha] & Anna & John, Ethel & Ruth. After dinner we settled down & I asked all I dared about the conference.

I gathered Mme. Chiang was much troubled by it & I told F.D.R. He insists DeGaulle is impossible & cannot muster more than 20,000 men whereas Giraud he describes as old fashioned Fr. conservative army officer, but he promises 200,000 men by spring for the liberation of France. His gun shot wedding was to get the two Frenchmen together. He told Churchill he'd produce the bride (Giraud) & Churchill must produce the groom (De Gaulle). The latter wouldn't come till Anthony Eden at FDR's suggestion said 'You go or the Br. Gov. stops paying your salary.' He left at once. I gather FDR put on all his tricks to make 'em shake hands before the cameras, & to get a signature to a document stating they wanted France freed & they would consult & collaborate to that end. FDR says 97% of political prisoners are freed only bomb throwers are still being investigated. He insists that Civil officials retained were there years before Vichy & are not fascist just African French. Peyrouton* he says arrested Laval & resigned from the Vichy cabinet when he was released & returned to the Argentine & is strongly pro-French & anti-Nazi or fascist. That these officials will be loyal to France in future, have a peaceful government with 90% Arab population & it is a military necessity to keep that population well governed & peaceful.

Stalin was invited but as Commander-in-Chief could not leave Russia. Chiang-Kai-Shek was not asked because Stalin said he could not meet him & hope to stay out of war with Japan. In any case the military problems alone were discussed & they were not China's except where they concerned getting supplies to China which she wanted. She said she wanted primarily aeroplanes.

FDR made a report to Congressional leaders this p.m. & will make one in his press conference tomorrow. He does not now intend to speak on radio.

I must go to bed, but the weather still seems good so I hope to fly tomorrow to N.Y. at 10:20 & Trude will be at the Cosmopolitan Club for lunch.

She comes down here for Thursday & Friday. Couldn't we call you or is that forbidden? Perhaps you could call me collect? Are we on the same time or are you an hour earlier?

It is good to talk with Trude about you. I miss not being able even

---

* Marcel Peyrouton had been Vichy's ambassador to Argentina. He was invited by the United States to become Governor-General of Algeria and was hated by the Gaullists.

to plan to see you here or in N.Y. Thinking about you was such a pleasant part of my life! Goodnight dear boy, bless you & take care of yourself. I love you.

Trude was at the White House when my first letter from me arrived, written to E.R. at a USO in Mattoon, Illinois. The latter was a bleak town where I and two companions from the Bolling Field weather station waited for two hours until a jeep from Chanute picked us up. Eleanor shared the letter with Trude, who had received a similar one in New York:

Dearest E.R. I never thought I would get a sense of warmth and friendliness from a U.S.O., and I guess this one seems like a godsend because this seems like such a dismal town, which one of the boys appropriately confused with Mattewan. The hostesses here are nice, one of them has beaten the three of us at ping-pong, and I turned the tables on them by feeding them those delicious candied fruits you gave me yesterday.

The train ride wasn't too bad—in fact I slept from 9:30 to 7:30 this morning—and we should be at Chanute in a few hours. We got our steak on the C. & O. last night and it was very inexpensive—the whole dinner costing $1.45.

So far it hasn't been too hard—going away—perhaps because I have the conviction that it will work out with Trude or perhaps only because I haven't yet grasped the full significance of not being where I could call the both of you at any time, & see either of you within 24 hours. I too am happy that I could spend the last eight months in Washington. If Trude and I had had any sense we would have used all the months as we did the last few weeks, and if I had not been so continuously upset because Trude & I were in trouble, I would have been a better friend to you. I can only be thankful that you are so understanding and loyal a person, that the last eight months have not taxed your patience and your love. And yet it is because of that love, as well as the peace that has come between Trude and me, that I now feel, not as if I were going into exile, but that I am moving forward on a job that has to be done, and in my own development as a person.

I have to stop now, but I will write you again when I get to Chanute.

Devotedly,
Joe

It had been a "joyous surprise" to receive it, she replied:

Mattoon is a grimy spot & both Trude & I chuckled about the desolate hostess you must try to cheer!

I am glad that peace & conviction is yours & if my love helps to lighten the burden of leaving & is a factor in your sense of development & accomplishment in this task that has to be done, I am very glad. I'm only sad myself, quite selfishly because I miss you very much, but that just has to be endured till you are back!

I did three speeches in N.Y. yesterday & the crowd at the A.F. of L. & C.I.O. & Brotherhood Auxiliaries was tremendous. About 500 women stood outside & couldn't get in. I picked Trude up afterwards, about 10:15 & we sat & talked in my room at the apartment till 11:30 when I took her home & went to the train. She had a shock about Vera but I'm so glad they have discovered it & she will be well. Poor child, she is uncomplaining!

My train was three hours late this morning & my first thought was 'What would I have done if Joe were along.' I got into the house at 10:15 & Tommy said 'Well, I've just been thinking how lucky it was Joe wasn't with you & due at the Field.' So you see how much you are in our thoughts!

I had a fairly busy day & Henry Roosevelt & the Bill Meloney's are here. Anna & John left at 5:30 & I went to the train & stayed till it pulled out for Anna seemed to want me. John has written Eisenhower asking if he could get in & serve with him & they told FDR & he is delighted. Anna can't help being a bit resentful & I understand. She'll be all right once she knows he feels he must do it but happiness is a fragile thing & she fears its shattering. I can't be delighted either. I wish pride compensated fear with me. Mr. & Mrs. Sullivan were here this morning, their 5 sons gone, I couldn't bear doing what they are being made to do & yet I think it helps them. Queer world it is!

Trude is bringing Louise & Maurice Weiting tomorrow & I have all the O.W.I. people to lunch that Louise needs to see.* At dinner we have Bill Lewis on the radio programme.

Darling you are so much in my thoughts & my heart. Goodnight. Bless you.

My letters now centered on Chanute. "Al Henry and I have retired to the latrine, he to write to his wife . . . and I to get this off to you," I wrote to Trude. "I am sitting in the classroom, which holds about 300 potential forecasters," I wrote more decorously to Eleanor. I described my schedule, noted the cold, but said that, unlike Washington, it was dry, and insisted, "I almost feel as if I am at a health resort," but to Trude I said that I would like a pair of earmuffs. "Never have I felt so certain that we will be together in the future & that it will be a happy future," I assured her.

Trude was not happy about what she saw and heard in Washington. "The good people are scared and the others triumph," she wrote to me, but what counted most at the moment for me were the sentences: "With 2 hours drill every morning you will be so strong—and with 6

---

* Louise Morley, daughter of Christopher Morley, and Maurice Weiting had been staff members of ISS. Louise went to England for the Office of War Information (OWI), where she married Peter Cochrane, once a British delegate to the International Student Assembly.

hours intellectual exercise every afternoon you will be much too bright. Did I ever tell you that I love you deeply & completely?"

Eleanor wrote the same evening:

> I've just been up & kissed Trude goodnight & put her letter where I hope it will be mailed quickly. I know she must feel lonely for you this first night here without you.
>
> Your Tuesday letter brought me dismay which Trude shared. I have written every day but one since you left so I sent a wire & I hope some day they discover your mail! Your schedule sounds healthy & strenuous & you will be a Samson when this [is] over. Trude told me sadly that you were taking the bomber course & I feel sad & anxious too & yet I understand your feeling. This facing danger is easy for oneself & never quite real but it is only too real to those who love you! . . .

The loneliness of life at Chanute, I reported, was mitigated only by "the way we are kept on the go . . . between trying to understand the stuff and memorizing it, the day zips by. I really have great difficulty with thermodynamics which is the application of mathematics and physics to meteorology." The weathermen were different from other GIs. "After noon chow we have to line up in order to march over to the lecture hall. The M.P.s pick out someone to march us over. Whenever they ask for volunteers, they get no response. In any other outfit fellows would jump at the chance to march an outfit and give commands. When they finally pick a man, he slurs his commands, and tries to be as inconspicuous as possible. The fear of being 'chicken' is a good antidote to officiousness. . . ." I complained about calisthenics and the cold. ". . . [R]eal cold—the kind which freezes the tears on your eyelashes and penetrates to your innermost parts." I had taken to wearing long johns, but when Trude threatened to get me *red* earmuffs, I put my foot down. "I would be picked up by an M.P. before I had walked 100 yards."

Calisthenics presented a more serious problem. "This morning our class was cancelled for a special meeting & we were told by the commanding officer of our squadron that he knew that 2 hours drill & calisthenics in the morning meant no time for study in the morning, but the General in charge of the Field insisted on it, and so we would have to study in the evening, but in the evening we are so tired that our minds absorb very little. If we move to Grand Rapids* we will be under the complete jurisdiction of the weather people, so conditions will be more propitious for study." Trude, E.R., and I exchanged valentines. Trude sent me a half-dozen in different handwritings. I spread them over the cot: ". . . the fellows in the barracks thinking they are all from different gals consider me now 'the great lover' . . ."

---

* Word to that effect had become more than latrine gossip.

Trude on her side wrote in detail about her travails in ISS, where some of the traditionalists on the board had brought about a divorce with the International Student Assembly and sequestered the organization's furniture, books, and the like. She would never again talk to Dr. Cohn, the leader of the older group in the ISS, she said. She was depressed because neither the A.F. of L., as expected, nor the C.I.O., because of Communist pressure on Philip Murray, would support the Norris Committee, which in 1940 had been the Norris-LaGuardia Committee of Independent Voters for Roosevelt and Wallace. She was troubled, too, as she wrote to me, about United Nations policy in North Africa. "The President is so obviously annoyed at any one who dares question the arrangements in Africa—that Mrs. R. says 'he does not feel right about [them].'"

But most of all, abetted by Eleanor, Trude was concerned with plans to go out to Urbana, which was near Chanute, to be with me for my day and a half off. "Your apt. is all dead now," she told me after she and her brother, George, had been over and finished the packing and played the Spanish records for a last time. "Do you remember me at all? . . . In 10 days I'll see you. Will you be disappointed?" She had trouble deciphering my handwriting, but "do you really believe that your letters might bore me?" . . . "But I still love you, and to know that in 2 days I'll be on a train carrying me to you—helps!" her last letter announced before taking the train for Urbana.

And always like a magical presence there was E.R. "Last week she wrote me," I wrote to Trude just before she came out, "how much she looked forward to the future when we could all be together, and she hopes she would not prove a burden! I always feel so inadequate when Mrs. R. talks like that." Eleanor wrote to me almost daily:

> I wished for you yesterday so many times! It was an interesting day but the sum total of conversations with Franklin & everything else like the Norris Com. failure gives me a sense of the magnitude of the job which we are embarked on & the weakness of the tools one must use. Trude has undoubtedly told you about the Norris Com. She may not have said that I talked to F.D.R. after he talked with Murray & Green & he said he thought it was a step in advance to get their legislative people working together & he urged them to take George Norris as their counsel. He said no formalized Com. would be accepted & he seems to accept the fact that Pressman & the Communist C.I.O. people will work with the conservatives now against any liberals.* John Lewis seems to typify this kind of support & attitude in himself!
>
> Franklin also repeated that N. Africa was not a political concern but purely a military problem. The population is 90% Arab, we must have

---

* William Green, president of the American Federation of Labor. Lee Pressman, legal adviser to Philip Murray and allied with the Communists in the C.I.O.

them orderly & friendly. Most officials have been there long before Vichy & are concerned with their jobs there & not with what goes on in France primarily. I talked about the trend here to conservatism & the alliance of certain Democrats with Republicans to defeat the administration & he said lines would be more & more clearly drawn. We might lose the next election but the Republicans would rapidly blow up. That if we went isolationist, the United Nations would really isolate *us* & we would soon be begging to be allowed to play. It all seems full of strategy & the little people will suffer as usual & I'm not happy about it! He said he had told Churchill we could not allow fascist governments to be chosen by the people anywhere, which amused me remembering how silent he was when we argued that point at dinner one night & I was saying that & some others contended that we were bound to allow complete freedom of choice.

I hope the Germans* had a good evening. Trude seemed on the whole satisfied. . . .

She was delighted to have a letter from me that was forwarded from Washington to New York. "The poems are lovely but sad." What poems they were she did not indicate, but may have been those of a friend who had just been drafted.

Later. I stopped because Trude came & then Ruth & we went to see Mme. Chiang & now I'm on the plane & this will be finished in Washington! Trude said it was wonderful to talk with you & you sounded well & wanted ear muffs but she can't find khaki ones! I could knit them but they might not fit. I'm so glad she's going out a week from this Friday to be your 'Saturday gal.' Yes dear, I'd love to see you but I'm fearful of bringing you publicity. If I ever go & see Robert Baker [son-in-law of Louis Howe] ostensibly that might work & I'll write him.—We're landing so soon!

Later. Well, they certainly are speaking up in Congress about Dies & Jerry Voorhis has at last decided he can no longer be silent which is a relief. I think Dies will get his money but if the opposition continues to grow this will be the last time. Max Lerner wrote a column on Congress in today's P.M. which I think doesn't ring true. I'm sure you will work in politics Joe dear, one way or another. That is where your interest lies & that is where your best work will be done, but we'll have to be over the kind of thing Dies stands for.

I'm glad you feel as indignant with Dr. [Alvin] Johnson as I do.

* Trude had suggested that it would interest the President to talk with a group of German refugees, most of whom were on the faculty of the New School for Social Research, and one, the theologian, Paul Tillich, was at Union Theological Seminary. The others who had come to dinner with the President & Mrs. Roosevelt and Vice-President Wallace had been Hans Staudinger, Adolf Loewe, Friedrich Pollock. Trude's comment afterwards: "The Germans were not as clear and good as last time. The White House, the Vice President *and* the President proved too much. Their manner was too professorial and in the end the President asked them to prepare school books —thus treating them as school masters which distressed Pollock especially."

Agnes told me Dorothy Paley* said many mean things about Trude &
implied certain things about my influence but since Dorothy P. refused
to pay more than a $1,000, the others are likely to feel more kindly to-
ward me! Trude says she will not serve on any committees with her & I
certainly never knew her before & see no reason for knowing her in the
future!

Tommy & I enjoyed Sat. night at Saybrook because Elizabeth
Read seemed a little better. The naval hospital wasn't too heart-rend-
ing on Sunday but I then went to see Missy & that was awful! I see no
improvement. We reached Portland, Maine about 9 p.m. Sunday night
& Mrs. Herrick met us & took us to the shipyards. They have had lots
of trouble but they have about 1,000 women at work & 3 shifts are running & at night it was a dramatic sight.

Yesterday we left for Camden [Maine] at 8 a.m. They have some
women working there even tho' they are building wooden ships. The
launching went smoothly tho' I covered myself with champagne. I was
made a member of the Penobscot Indian tribe & they sang a song of
safety for me on my 'many trails.'

I got a wire there to call James in Boston & after an hour I got
through & he is off again. Poor Romaine, she is very sad & I feel sorry
for her. Jimmy was sad too & it all seems senseless when I think of all
you young things suffer.

Tommy & I took the midnight to N.Y. & she came down by train &
I took a plane. Shortly I must go to tea at the young officers clubs.
Franklin has stayed in H.P. & won't be here till tomorrow so I have the
Morgenthaus alone to dinner. They got back from Cuba on Sunday &
Elinor still seems to think he is far from well. By the way would you
like a copy of my column daily? Tommy could make 2 & mail them.

I miss you dear, & love you & hope you find some place to work!

My protestations that Trude and I would somehow fail Mrs. R. if we
did not do "important" work, she minimized:

I like this Sandburg column because it brings out that all big things really depend on little things. Those who get decorations couldn't succeed if all down the line little people weren't true & doing their part.

I've been thinking of your remark that you & Trude had to prove
yourselves. That may be true as far as all of us have to live life day by
day true to our own ideals & all of us are in constant danger of proving
inadequate. You seem to me to have proved your ability already to
meet any standard pretty well, that is why I rely on you & trust you &
turn to you. Trude is just meeting the test & at times finds it hard, but
we are all, once we begin to try, pretty much on a level. When it
comes to recognition & public success, that is a little like winning the

* "Agnes" was Mrs. Henry Goddard Leach, and Dorothy Paley was married to
William S. Paley. Both were members of the ISS board.

decorations in war, circumstances are somewhat responsible & we only deserve credit for our preparation. You'll both win the decorations in the future I think because you've already shown you could, but if you lived very quiet & obscure lives & kept faith with your own beliefs & ideals you would seem to me just as important a person. I can see great possibilities for you to help labor in the future, in organization, in education, etc. & of course it will lead to political expression.

I have had a wire from Robert Baker* saying that the Lincoln Hotel in Urbana is best so tomorrow I will call Trude & tell her.

Elinor Morgenthau & I went to see a show of made over clothes in the Dept. of Agriculture this afternoon & I decided I had always been a stupid person in the home.

Fjr. blew in for a half hour, but he looked very tired & my rebukes were mild!

I wonder if you ever got a letter I sent from Claude Bowers† to me? I liked it & thought it might interest you, but rather think that some of those first letters may have gone astray.

[John] O'Donnell's column is poisonous isn't it?

I spent the evening with the Executive Com. of the Guild & sometimes I'll tell you my impression of the vast majority of the profession!

Joe dear, I love you very much I wish you could walk in!

She sent me an itinerary for the last two weeks in February and thought she could manage a telephone call from Columbia, Missouri. "Of course, I'll give Tommy's name." Also she was planning a speech near Chanute, but did not want to intrude on Trude's plans. "I had an interesting but very encouraging talk with Henry Morgenthau tonight. He says my fears about North African civil affairs are justified & asked me to go on prodding FDR because he feels everyone except myself will give up!" She enclosed the note that Trude had sent her along with a valentine: "I've never taken notice of Valentine's day before I knew Joe —and so this is still another day so completely connected with him. . . . It is wonderful to be able to send you a Valentine and I am very happy that you are close and I can see you and be with you."

About her impending telephone call from Columbia, Missouri, Eleanor wrote: "I feel so excited about the prospect of hearing your voice. What will I do when I actually see you!" If I were shifted to Grand Rapids, as now seemed likely, she would go there instead of to Champaign, which was near Chanute:

I feel just as you do about the State Dept. & the North African policy but I think we will see some changes. Last night Marshall Field & Louis Weiss‡ were here for dinner & we argued (of course I started &

* Son-in-law of Louis Howe.
† Prominent historian and Democrat, U. S. Ambassador to Spain and to Chile.
‡ Marshall Field III was a philanthropist, sportsman, liberal, backer of *PM* and the Chicago *Sun;* Louis Weiss was a prominent attorney.

prodded) till 9:40! F. talked convincingly but convinced no one & Mrs. Lewis Thompson* made an interesting & penetrating remark this morning. 'I think,' said she, 'that Franklin does things often from inspiration & then finds the reasons to justify them.' I wanted to add that he sometimes changed them & I think last night's talk had an effect. I liked the Yank† editorial & pray it does represent the attitude of the soldiers. F. said one most interesting thing, namely, that he looked for less trouble between us & Russia & China than between any of us & Great Britain. He had said that to me you remember but I was surprised to have him say it to others. Louis Weiss felt as disheartened as I did over the DeGaulle story.

Harry Hopkins sent for me yesterday & said he felt we should set up some United Nations machinery on postwar planning. He suggests that in all capitals the representatives meet monthly & take up questions of feeding, education, etc. I feel that what we need is more confidence in Russia & China that as a people we want to understand them & their problems & work *with* them. I asked Harry if he thought my going there now, during the war, would help here & there. He said if I thought so I should make Franklin let me go but to wait till Mme. Chiang came. She will be here next Wednesday & she is now at the Big House in H.P. I think she is going to surprise F. a good deal but she will charm him. She won't lean like Martha of Norway though! She can't be fooled either. Somehow it seems to me that she compels honesty.

Trude says your work is very hard, & having no place [to study] & no real time must be a great strain. I'm glad you drink the milk & hope someday you get enough sleep but you have a great deal to catch up on. You must fight against the melancholy Joe dear. I'm enclosing a letter that came with a valentine from Trude & I feel you can believe in her & be happy when she comes to you & feel that in spirit & in thought you are close at all times. I pray [to] St. Valentine too that he may bring us all together, but that is because I need you very much! . . .

"What about FDR's speech," she asked the next day, "did you hear it & were you convinced? We are still arguing. . . . All day I've been making arrangements for Mme. Chiang & there are many funny angles to that, which I'll write out for you some day . . ."

As she had promised, she telephoned from Columbia, where she inspected a WAAC training camp and spoke at the university, ". . . & I hope calling too early didn't mean they spread around who was calling & make it uncomfortable."

* One of the three Morgan sisters who had been children together with Franklin on the Hudson. A staunch Republican, she was also the champion of many liberal causes.

† *Yank*, sponsored by the United States Armed Forces, was a weekly written by enlisted men and was distributed on all the theaters of war.

Back in New York at the apartment, she had the leaders of the United States Student Assembly, which finally had been established by the students after the coup in ISS. "I am angrier than ever with the opposition! . . . Trude looks tired. She said at dinner she never knew how much she needed you! . . . Having George* go is hard even tho' he wants to go & she wants him to go."

She was beginning to believe she might indeed be able to go to China, and her talks with Madame Chiang spurred her hopes:

It was wonderful to get in at 7:30 this morning & find your grand letter & Dr. Frank† came to see me today & in a way what he said & what you wrote dovetailed. You are two people who must feel part of a movement. What you work for, you must believe is moving towards a better world. That is what I want to feel in belonging to a political party & I imagine socialism, if I could see it working would not disturb me. Well dear, when the war is over, we'll try to be a movement but I confess just now I think you will have to create it. Incidentally, I'm getting Harry Hopkins to see Dr. Frank.

Mme. Chiang arrived today, just FDR, the Hopkins' & Helen Gahagan with her for dinner. She is wise. She listened at dinner, on her half hour later with FDR she listened but she will talk & she has already asked FDR if I can go back with her!

I'll go wherever you are March 5th so don't worry! I called Trude today & Peter‡ was better & I shall call again tomorrow afternoon & hope all is well. Nothing must keep you two apart! I'm glad it was a nice St. Valentine's day. Trude told me about all the cards & her disguised handwriting.

I feel sad tonight because I hate our boys in N. Africa to be bombed & none of our planes able to go to their aid. They say our fields are badly placed & muddy & the planes can't get off while the Germans have concrete in Tunisia. They acknowledge their mistakes in location but the boys are paying with their lives. I get so many sad letters from mothers that I find myself weeping here all alone many an evening. I'd give almost anything if the war could end quickly & when Mr. Altschul§ said yesterday the conservative republicans were worried over Russian victories I could cheerfully have killed him! . . .

She sent me the text of Madame Chiang's speech to Congress: "Just in case you couldn't hear her & I imagine you may have been busy I

* George Wenzel, Trude's brother, was on his way to the University of Washington. A few months later he was in the armed services.
† Dr. Karl Frank (also known as Paul Hagen), leader of the German underground group called New Beginning. See page 303.
‡ Peter Pratt, Trude's son, was then not quite ten.
§ Frank Altschul was head of Lazard Frères and a prominent Republican backer of Wendell Willkie in 1940.

send this speech. She made an extemporaneous talk in the Senate which was splendid & well received. You will read my column so I won't say more. I just talked to Trude & sent you all my love. I envy her but she says you may call tomorrow night & that will be wonderful." We did call her from Urbana. "You both sounded happy but your cold also sounded very bad. . . . I can only hope that Trude was enough of a tonic to start the good germs into violent activity so you don't have to go to the hospital!"

Deftly as she used Madame Chiang's presence to promote the purposes she cared about, she still was the observer whose participation was at Franklin's sufferance and bidding. This emerged clearly in her references of a possible China trip in the survey of her private world that she regularly sent to Maude Gray.

Mme. Chiang & a niece & nephew & two trained nurses are also here for two weeks. She is a wonderful person & I marvel at her command of English. She is quick & intuitive & very clever & knows how to manage the gentlemen. I've grown very fond of her & shall be glad to go to China when FDR decides it is time to go.

I keep busy & the boys are well. . . .

She and Maude had discussed turning over the house in Tivoli, which Maude and David owned, to the ISS for one of its summer institutes. A postscript to Maude said that it would not be necessary:

I forgot to say that so many students are in the army that the International Student Service decided that no work could be done. For the present at least the Tivoli place is not wanted. Whether it will be later I can't tell.

In her talk with Harry Hopkins about postwar planning, she had coupled Russia with China, as countries whose peoples Americans had to learn to understand, and she even ventured to hope that if she were allowed to go to China she would also be able to go to Russia: "Russia is the one bright spot & even if Mr. A. tells me that each Russian victory pushes the Republican middle of the road people more to the conservatives, I'm glad the Russians progress."

She admired Madame Chiang's ability to hold her own with the men; she was struck by the exquisite beauty of the gifts that she presented and the drollery of some of the scrolls that accompanied them:

Mme. Chiang & Franklin had a wonderful press conference this morning. She is very quick & when they asked her what China needed most & she hesitated & F.D.R. said 'ammunition & war supplies & we will get them there as fast as the Lord will let us' & the next question was 'will you comment on how satisfactory the deliveries have been?' she came back with 'I will leave that to the President, & only add the Lord helps those who help themselves.' Of course the press conference roared!

She went to bed till 4 p.m. & then she arose & was given the Chi Omega Award in a fifteen-minute ceremony, but it was moving & she made a charming speech. Recalling that yesterday I had quoted to her from a letter a young man in the Army had written me saying 'that personal ambitions could never seem to him important, they must merge in a movement for the betterment of mankind' she said that was what gave her courage—The men and the women who would join in a movement so all over the world we might move forward together. You see, what you said made a deep impression on her & struck an answering spark. Great people think alike I've heard said!

She's been talking to FDR since 9:30 so I must go & rescue her & send her to bed. I'll come back then & finish.

Later 11:30. I've talked to both & finally got them to bed & F.D.R. has been given some white silk for shirts & I have the most beautiful carved ivory & I am ashamed to receive such gifts when one can give nothing to speak of in return. I have a real feeling for her though, so accepting gifts from her is not hard.

Bless you darling, goodnight & a world of love to you.

"We had a very happy time together," I wrote to E.R. after Trude left. "Some of the hours were among the happiest we have ever had. For the first time I feel as if we are on firm ground, and if I do, it is because Trude at last begins to be sure of where happiness lies for us." Trude, en route home, wrote to me from Chicago: "You know we never looked at any of the things I had brought you to see. We never even opened my brief case. There was so little time—and yet I do not remember when we had so much time, undisturbed,—without fierce strains and stresses.—My bus is leaving, there is just time to tell you that I love you now and forever." I wrote to her from Chanute: "I came back in time for calisthenics and found that the tides of everyday army life quickly closed in on me, and yesterday already is buried deep in me. . . . Was I very awful company?" She wrote in kind: "Your letter came and no letter was ever awaited more anxiously. As the hours went on being away from you became sharper and more painful and I needed something that came from you after I had seen you." The lyricism of love made poignant by separation echoed in our letters.

"Today your first letter came through," I wrote to her. "I have been so content since the last weekend, so happy in my sense of being close to you, so sure of the future, that I was a little afraid to open the letter, as if no words could live up to what I had built up in my heart. The letter was wonderful. . . . Al leaned over from his lunch to comment, 'you certainly look happy.' Everything seems possible." She had seen Eleanor. "I told Mrs. R. about our 1-½ days together in great detail—I hope I invented none. . . . And she showed me the gifts from Mme. Chiang."

"I've not got an answer from Robert Baker yet," Eleanor wrote to

Trude, "but will telephone when it comes. . . . I think I can work out a meeting in Champagne [*sic*] so I may be able to get to Joe one Saturday. Let me know if you can what weekends you go so we can spread ourselves out!"

Trude's visit had been balm for me. She planned to get her divorce in the summer, would find a new house to move into as soon as possible. We began to talk and write about a baby—black-haired and brown-eyed like the potential father: "Deborah if a girl; 'Spinoza' if a boy," the latter out of deference to the philosopher Morris Raphael Cohen, who had been my idol at City College, New York. "Now my most fervent prayers are that for a few weeks, at least, I shall be stationed in the east where I can live in that house with you & get the feel of it before going overseas. . . ." Difficult as were some of the classes in meteorology, the biggest hazard appeared to be calisthenics:

I think I told you that the forecasters 'goof off' (slip away) from calisthenics on the slightest pretext. It's not only laziness, but also a matter of finding time to study. Well, two days ago, seven fellows, as we were double-timing by an orderly room, slipped out of the Platoon and joined the line outside of the orderly room, and then when the Platoon went by, returned leisurely to the Barracks. The only hitch was that the Lieutenant in charge of calisthenics saw them slip off. It angered him to the boiling point. . . . He segregated the 300 forecasters from the other 600 fellows in our squadron who take calisthenics at 8 a.m. Then he lined us up in a huge circle on a muddy field. We knew we were in for it. Then the stupid man said, unless the 7 s.o.b.'s who slipped away stepped forward, he would work the whole gang of us. No one came forward so he started running us around in a circle and kept at it until 10 a.m. Every 20 minutes or so he would stop and ask whether the seven now were ready to come out. And with every lap we did around in the mud, the more we became partisans of the seven and the more we detested the lieutenant.

Of course the spectacle of 300 sergeants with a ringmaster in the center running our behinds off is affording all of Chanute Field great amusement. He promises us more. I hope my knee holds out. It has become a point of honor not to ask the Lieutenant anything that would seem like a favor.

I was able to write the next day:

We were victorious over the Lieutenant. Today he segregated us again, had us run a few minutes, enough, however, to cause my knee to ache badly,—and then called us to attention. Very awkwardly he announced that he knew our course was the toughest on the Field, and that in the future we would only have to do an hour's drill a day! Those of us who thought some of his uncomplimentary references, like s.o.b.'s, were meant for us, were mistaken. As for our hour's exercise, he thought it would improve our minds if we spent a good part of it running. So the 'sergeants' are all smiles today.

By the beginning of March 1943 we were again counting the days to Trude's next visit. Eleanor found a reason to come out the first week in March. Before then, however, she was sending me cough medicine that Admiral McIntire had prepared for her. The medicine received a strange welcome from my bunkmates:

> The cough medicine came. There was no White House return address and I opened the package under the curious eyes of the brood of Texans. (They were taking the course in plane maintenance.) Some ingenious person on Tommy's staff stuffed the bottle in a cardboard container that previously had held a bottle of scotch, and when the Texans saw that they let out a whoop, but when I saw the bottle which had a label on it "Dr. McIntire—for Mrs. Roosevelt," I quickly dumped the bottle into my foot locker, completely convincing the Texans that it was the right kind of cough medicine. I am afraid that when I am at class the foot locker will be raided. I should like to see the face of him who takes the first swallow.

Trude also had begun to go to class, the only one available, in advanced Russian at the Russian-American Institute, a pro-Soviet agency that regarded her presence as a form of espionage. But the Red Army was winning magnificent victories, and all three of us thought the Russian language would figure importantly in the postwar world. She wrote about E.R.'s possible trip to the Soviet Union:

> Mrs. R. told me yesterday that in all probability she will visit the land of her visitor [Madame Chiang], and that the President was quite eager to have her do it. She herself will not go unless she can also go to Russia as she does not want to create more bad feeling where too much already exists. She would however, not leave immediately, probably not before early summer. . . . She told many stories about Mme. Chiang. I think, a close human relationship is developing between them. But Mrs. R. is worried about the delicate health of Mme., says she has to rest a day after every major engagement, needs two trained nurses whom she keeps extremely busy, talks a great deal about her sister Mrs. Kung, but never mentions Mrs. Sun; I had been wondering whether she mentioned Sun only in public. I was amazed to hear that Mme. Chiang had not heard about our TVA.

But Trude's next letter reported that "Tommy does not like Mme. Chiang. Thinks she is snobbish, spoiled, undemocratic. Mrs. R. thinks that the reason might be that the two Kungs (Mme.'s niece and nephew) who are with Mme. are so difficult to get along with and impress on everyone that they are direct descendants of Confucius."

Princess Martha of Norway was back, Trude reported when Madame Chiang left Washington on a tour, "because she does not want to wait even a day to wipe out the deep impression Mme. Chiang probably made on the President. . . . [I]t is not even catty to say she behaved like an 18-year old flirt, and that it did not quite come off. Mrs. Roosevelt seems to grow in situations like that."

Fogged in at the Washington airport, Eleanor scrawled a quick note to me. She had "nearly" sent me a clipping from the *Daily Worker* "which twisted an answer I made in Missouri, but I decided you better not have anything so pernicious in your possession!" Her pen went dry so she continued in pencil:

The news is very bad. The two transports sunk are a terrible loss because it indicates the Nazi subs are more successfully active than ever. Stalin spoke out for a second front in Europe & I fear made England & the U.S.A. mad as they consider N. Africa a second front. China feels keenly that we are not getting supplies through fast enough & yet I can see the difficulty. We have to attack Japan from China & we can't till we build up an air force.

Yesterday Mme. C. laid a wreath on the unknown soldier's tomb & I found 'taps' harder than usual to bear. Somehow thinking of all the places where those bugle notes float out over the dead is not conducive to peace of mind. We went to Mt. Vernon & she liked the house & grounds, saying the fields of winter wheat reminded her of China & the house was a little like their compound. In the afternoon the cabinet came to tea & she spent an hour with FDR at night & listened to his speech.* I went to dinner, left & drove around the town in a practice blackout with one of the Commissioners, & went back to hear the speeches. I liked FDR's & it was clever to say so much in such an indirect way which could not be attacked as partisan. Gen. Vandergrift sat by me & gave no very encouraging picture of the malaria situation & seemed to feel many of the boys would have to come back to this country.

By the way I'll take a single room for you & a double room for Tommy & myself at the Lincoln Hotel for Friday & Saturday night. I hope Tommy will feel like going, if not I can change to a single room later. She wrote you longhand because the left hand still bothers her but she insists on doing the column! What time do you get up Friday night? Did you & Trude find any good place to eat or shall I order dinner to my room? What shall I bring you? I'll be in N.Y. Thursday, Friday & Sat this week so can get things better than down here. Mme. Chiang stays till Monday & Tuesday so I hope Trude may come down before she leaves & see her again. Well, I'll now read the papers & they

---

* Radio speech on Washington's birthday.

say the plane will arrive in about twenty minutes so I'll mail this & before long it may start on its way to you. I hope you can read it!

How I would love it if I were going to see you in New York! I'm quite excited at seeing Trude & hearing about you! I called her Sunday night & she said your cold was better & I hope it really is.

The same night she wrote:

I just came back from the trip to New York & have done the mail & loved finding a letter from you. I'm so glad you were happy & Trude lovely. She spent a long lunch hour with me today & I know she was completely happy, found you all she wanted, & your looks quite satisfactory as well as all the more important other things! It was good to hear about you & now don't worry about the 5th. You'll know before I have to leave on the 4th & if you are there I'll go, & if not, I wouldn't make Trude wait an extra week for anything & the 12th isn't possible anyway but the 19th is & I'll keep free till you are quite sure & come out that weekend if you are moving the 5th. I know you want to get moved because Trude told me how impossible it is at Chanute.

You'll be interested to know that Mme. Chiang has put in her Wellesley speech your idea because she was so impressed by it & she tells youth, that alone their ambitions matter little & they can accomplish little but they must be part of a movement to make a better world. She asked about you & I told her a little & someday you & Trude will go to China as part of this whole effort. . . .

A play that she saw with Elinor Morgenthau underscored her radically democratic insight. She wrote to me:

Elinor Morgenthau spent the night & we went to see 'The Patriots.' It is about Jefferson & if you despair of present-day human nature I've decided one should just review a little history! How Washington & Jefferson bore with Hamilton is extraordinary & perhaps the pen is mightier than the sword for Tom Paine seems to have been the real person who stirred the people. One must trust the people, that is the final lesson. . . .

I went to Russian Relief Hdqtrs warehouse this afternoon & was photographed giving the millionth garment to Mrs. [Edward] Carter & then to see Cousin Susie. Life is just becoming too hard for her to bear but she'll have to! Earl came in for dinner & the night & now the mail is done & I'm going to bed. Six days from now I'll be off to see you unless you are on the move! If you could be allowed to travel alone, we might have a pleasant trip together & a night in Chicago!

Trude is bringing the children to lunch tomorrow & then she is dining & we are going to the play. Sunday night she & Irene [Murray] come to Washington. I stopped in the office today & it was a nice place.—George Fischer has enlisted in the army, did you know?

Goodnight dear boy, bless you & so much love. I miss you & you are not only in my thoughts but always in my heart.

Sunday, Feb. 28th I'm enclosing Anne O'Hare McCormick's column because I thought it was so well put & raised the pertinent questions we ought to bring up. Sandburg points out the situation in Washington's day which I felt so keenly in the play the other night & Dorothy Thompson's needed to be written I think.

I got back with Tommy this a.m. & she seems better & I think will be with me if we go to you *this* week. I wrote for a room for you as well as for ourselves. If there is a meeting for bonds, we might not get through but if not, would you like us to take a bus to the field & come back with you or is that too conspicuous & shall we wait for you in our rooms ordering as good a dinner as we can?

The disorganization sounds bad at the field & the picture of all you trotting in a circle for two hours is pitiful. I'm sorry about your knee & in spite of all ailments your voice sounded good to me last night probably because I was so glad to hear it! I've had a happy three days seeing something of Trude each day but yesterday was fun from the moment I walked in & found them all waiting for lunch. The evening was light & amusing too & I hope Trude & Irene will get in tomorrow morning.

If you don't leave for Grand Rapids this week will you perhaps be moving the next week when Trude would be going out? That would be worse for I hate anything which keeps you two apart.

The hospital which I saw yesterday morning was clean & sunny but I never get over feeling rebellious that youngsters have to suffer & be maimed by war.

Rep. Starnes got into the papers as saying that he feared Russia & hoped the Germans & Russians would kill each other off. How can we blame Stalin for being suspicious? Only if we trust & believe others good intentions can they be expected to believe in ours. We can't be the only trustworthy people in the world!

Trude keeps talking about the day when a little dark head will be among the fair & I have to confess I think of that often also. I couldn't be in China if you & Trude should by chance want me round when you are married & truth to tell I don't want to go while I can still see you now & then! Of course I will go soon & get back by July if that seems the thing they want but I don't think I can go & not go also to Russia & so far FDR feels the moment for that visit hasn't come. How do you feel about it? . . .

I love you dear & hope all goes well for Friday! Good luck!

E.R.

As we walked with the little girls yesterday p.m. Trude & I looked at each other & said almost simultaneously, 'This would be perfect if Joe were here!' You are in both our minds & hearts very constantly dear boy.

She became more certain as the week progressed that she would be able to see me, and she saw Trude both in New York and Washington so that she might be able to report to me about her, for she accepted, as a fact of our relationship, that Trude was my favorite subject. She arranged also that Trude would be at the White House on her return from Chanute so that she could bring the freshest news. Her letters surged with the intense joy of her companionship with us:

Such a nice letter yesterday & then your little note this morning. Funny, I ordered enough of those pictures to give each of the children & you & Tommy one & have a few left over & I am going to ask Mme. C. to autograph when she returns in April.

The play Sat. night was light & amusing & just right for Harry Hooker & we all enjoyed it but Trude & I always miss you when we do anything together even when we are enjoying it, perhaps even more when we enjoy it. That is what it means to really establish a happy companionship. You can't have it with many people but everything you do is better if you share it with the companions you love. I know, if we have the chance, that the future holds happy hours for all of us doing all kinds of things! Trude & I had dinner alone in my sitting room last night & talked of you & longed for you. We talked of cocktails & how they only appealed as a celebration. Trude's old feeling that I ganged up with you & made it hard for her to think through for herself & I think you are right & now having reached her big decisions she is happier with me.

The kids came at 8:30 we had movies & then an hour & a half of talk & Irene did well & I felt happy about the evening. Kenneth Holland* is just back & came in. He had heard nothing about I.S.S. & is stunned & sympathetic with U.S.S.A. I think they have a good conference planned on stabilization & I have people lined up in Mr. Byrnes office & in the Treasury. Mr. Byrnes is anxious to get information into the schools because he is depressed with Congress & feels direction must come from home!

I've begun to collect things to bring to show you! Dear, you couldn't be disappointing, if I could just sit & feel you close & look at you it would mean a great deal & to talk over many things will be a joy. I look forward to saying goodnight & good morning, to having meals together, just to the little things which mean so little when you have them all the time & so much when you can't have them! I begin to feel we are to meet tho' I've been trying not to count on it too much! I'll order dinner in my room at 8:15 & try to have steak & Tommy & I will await you with open arms! We'll bring the pencils.

Has Gil Harrison† written you? If not I'm going to bring his letters along & see if you agree with my advice.

Trude has arranged for a rehearsal of the radio programme on Monday night so she'll come down Sunday evening & I can tell her all about you. I've promised to have a call in from the hotel on Friday night at 9 p.m. so we can talk to her. Somehow I feel she ought to be

* Former head of I.S.S. and member of its board.
† He had been head of the youth division of the Office of Civilian Defense along with Jane Seaver; now an enlisted man in the Army.

going but she'll go next week if you are not moving & perhaps we can have a weekend all together in Chicago the middle of April! Trude goes home early this afternoon but it has been grand having her.

I love you dear, bless you & keep your fingers crossed for Friday.

As she left for the Midwest, she was not sure that on her arrival in Urbana she might not be met with the news that the forecasters had moved to Grand Rapids. A farewell note to Trude: "I just tried to reach you on the telephone so as to say I'm off & goodbye! I hope I find Joe there! The call to you will be put in for 10 p.m. your time tomorrow Friday night as soon as I reach the hotel in Urbana. . . . It was so nice to have you here. I love you."

From Chicago she wrote to Hick: "We got in on time this morning & are at the Blackstone awaiting our breakfast; leave at 9:40 for Champaign. They have a lunch there for the war bond workers & then Robert Baker will come to tea & later Joe will turn up." Two days later, Sunday, on the train back to Chicago on a letterhead of the Lincoln Hotel in Urbana, she added: "Joe spent yesterday with us & we left early this morning. It is just about zero but clear & I hope we can fly from Chicago."

I gave her a letter for Trude:

We've just had a huge lunch (at least I did—the ladies were concerned for their 'figgers' and so confined themselves to toasted sandwiches) and I stretched out luxuriantly on the bed for a cat nap. Tommy, under Mrs. R's instructions, solicitously covered me with a shawl so that my dainty feet would not get chilled! (Imagine the problems that would confront them if they went through our barracks where the gentlemen expose more than their feet to chills in the process of snatching a nap.) Anyway I wasn't sprawled on the bed more than 10 minutes when I decided I wanted to write you and tell you how much I love you, and how much you're missed and I long for you even though this is a weekend of great fun and joy.

We've done heaps and heaps of talking—about everything, mostly about things Mrs. R. has already talked of with you. Mme. C. has of course been one of the main subjects, for Mrs. R. has developed a real feeling for her, though Tommy is more cynical. She showed me the brooch which Mme. impulsively took off (her bosom I guess) and gave to Mrs. R. and the wrist watch with the exquisite carvings. I read a delightful article that she has written for *Colliers* on the lady, although Tommy & I disagreed vehemently with one statement to the effect that Mme. is 'the greatest living woman' which brought up the old discussion with Mrs. R. concerning the degree to which her present eminence is a result of the accident of being the President's wife, and the degree to which it is a result of the use to which she placed the opportunities afforded her as First Lady. But we got exactly nowhere on the matter of the 'greatest living woman.' Said Mrs. R. with genuine questioning: 'Well, who do you consider to be greater? ! ! ! !

. . . .

We also talked about us—a lot, because it was one way of having you here. Mrs. R. made my heart leap when she said she would not want to be gone on the long trip when we were married next summer. And for the first time it seemed to me a certainty. . . .

Will you wire for rooms again? . . .

And on the train to Chicago, Eleanor wrote me a goodbye note:

I hated to see you leave & yet I'm so happy to have been with you. Separation between people who love each other, makes the reunion always like a new discovery. You forget how much you love certain movements of the hands or the glance in the person's eyes or how nice it is to sit in the same room & look at their back! I shall be so thankful when the war is over that I hope I shall always remember to treasure the gift of being with those I love.

I came across a nice paragraph just now for scribblers like myself:— 'If you do not write what you think you are deceiving people. That is a crime. If you really write what you think you make people pay attention to you uselessly. And that is a folly. He added that in this life, one could say what one thought only to one or two people.'

Perhaps one should only just write letters to those one loves! . . .

Back at the White House she sent word to me that Trude had my letter "ready for when she arrived a little after twelve last night. We talked about you & I do hope that nothing keeps her from you this coming week end. She needs you, her eyes bothered her & she doesn't look just right to me." Her worry about Trude's health went considerably further and she felt her way gingerly to telling me what was on her mind:

. . . & she [Hildur*] feels as I do that Trude should go to the doctor & have a real check-up. She looks badly. I will urge her to do this when she returns next time & I hope you will but Hildur does not want anyone to know she said anything. Now, I'm going to say something which is none of my business & please forgive me if you are angry. If by chance Trude should find a baby on the way, make her go at once & get her divorce & I don't think any agreements she may have made should interfere. She feels she must live up to certain understandings or commitments because of the children. I still think she should not go through what she has done before. She then feels guilty & untrue to you & to herself & from the health angle I think it is dangerous. Better

* Hildur Coon, a Campobello alumna, was an official of the newly established United States Student Assembly.

to devise some means of circumventing gossip & prying eyes. I know she will not want to talk to me about all this. Perhaps I should not even talk to you & perhaps there is nothing of this kind to worry her or you but somehow I felt this must be written & you must know that if in any way I could be helpful, financially or otherwise, I was to be counted on. . . .

My love to you dear, if you think I am too interfering just remember that I love you & Trude dearly & will say & do nothing to hurt you if I can help it—!

Her alarm was unnecessary. She gave Trude a letter to take with her to Urbana for me. It contained the disquieting news that Madame Chiang had discouraged publication of the article that Eleanor had written about her:

The article she prefers not to have published so it is on ice! She says she's been asked to write about me & couldn't do it & yet it would be hard to refuse if I did it.

Trude reported a more unpleasant aspect:

When I went to the apartment for tea today, Tommy was quite upset about the latest piece of information from the State Department. Harry Hopkins had apparently given orders that Mme. was to be managed by him alone while in Washington and by nobody else. Mrs. R. looked grim.

Then came another blow. The President vetoed a trip to either Russia or China:

I talked a while tonight about going to China & Russia & FDR feels I should not go for sometime. I think he hopes to meet Stalin & Chiang this spring or summer & wants to wait on that. So I think I'll go west & see all I can of you & hope that you & Trude will use the cottage for a few days alone & then let me come & see you!

The letter ended on a rare note of complaint:

Confession is good for the soul, so I'll tell you that D—is here. She has a friend & her son staying here & wants me to see innumerable guests. I would not care if she'd have them & I felt no obligation. I want to eat alone tonight & work but I have to have 7 of them for dinner while FDR has Eden, Winant & Harry.* I know I'm selfish but if I don't really like people I hate doing personal things for them! Now I've blown off & I'll try to be nice!

* Anthony Eden, British Foreign Secretary, was in Washington. Gil Winant, former Republican Governor of New Hampshire, first head of Social Security, was U. S. Ambassador to Great Britain. "Harry" was Harry Hopkins.

A strong defense of Trude against my possessiveness also carried a vigorous statement of what a "real marriage" should mean:

. . . I never get any feeling of indecision in her, just regret that he [Eliot Pratt] has to be hurt. . . . Her eyes troubled her too & if you were able to be strong & trusting I'm sure you gave her all she needed & then she would be able to reassure you. Your lack of trust is understandable after these past years but you must fight the 'fever.' You see her being trustworthy I feel, depends largely on your trust! Sounds Irish but is often true! You know nothing is ever finally won, but is always re-won by daily acts. A real marriage means continuous effort, continuous wooing & loving & understanding & forgiving. I think real friendship is the same. No real human contacts live & grow untended.

Trude made me happy by asking me to go & see the little house with her on Tuesday & she said she was going to talk it over with you, as she wanted you so much to see it & she is planning for your joint lives in it. . . .

XXI

An Object of "Special Scrutiny"

ELEANOR'S LETTERS often manifested a streak of mischievousness, especially where politicians were involved. Kindly and gracious, she had long ceased to take their prancings and posturings at face value. She met Harold Stassen, the youthful hopeful of the Republicans, and wrote to Hick: "He talks well but I can't trust him, in fact when you are with him à deux it is not quite the same person as the one who makes the speeches." The politics that counted for her were those that might ensure that the war was not being fought in vain. "Wonderful meeting of young people, 3,600 of them in Rochester, N.Y.," she reported, adding: "so there is great interest in planning for a peaceful world."

With no outward protest she deferred to F.D.R.'s decision not to let her go to Russia or China:

> F.D.R. just told me that he'd like me to go to New Zealand & Australia, 4 weeks in June. I'm glad of course as I may see James & I'll see many of our soldiers but it won't be as interesting as China or Russia!

Trude advised me: "Mrs. R. said that the President considered her trip (to China) nice but not important. She accepted his view completely." Trude painted a vivid picture of the producer John Golden's pleasure in E.R.'s company and her use of it for worthy purposes:

> We had dinner together before Mrs. R. had to go to make her big speech at the Red Cross meeting. She actually did get Martha of Nor-

way (who arrived with a retinue of five) to hold a dialogue with her, and Mme. Chiang to speak over the telephone. John Golden was in heaven. Even for him this was big. He arrived with piles of lavender and purple orchids, stuck them on Tommy's and Mrs. R.'s bosoms, and whisked them off in a big black car. His hat was at a rakish angle, chamois gloves, and his face a mixture of rascal and clown, shouting in front of "29" that everybody should see his precious load. It was very funny, Mrs. R. looked quite helpless. I stood on the sidewalk and laughed.

The next day Trude was back at "29" and Eleanor showed her documents about Allied policy in North Africa. Trude wrote: "I spent a rather terrible hour reading them. They apparently all came from the Vice President [Henry Wallace] and Mrs. R. seemed troubled because more and more often the Vice President gives her those things and never shows them to the President. She wonders why he does not feel he can." Eleanor was taking the documents to Chicago to show me when I went there the following Friday.

I've just finished the mail & a line to Trude after reading Dr. [Paul] Tillich's sermon. It seems to me labored & I like the 139th Psalm best as is. I don't have the feelings that I should have I guess in religious matters!*

I'm enclosing an itinerary so you will know where to reach me next week if any sudden changes occur in your existence.†

An old farm woman from North Carolina was brought in by Miss Doughton this p.m. to ask if I could think how the girls could be kept from marrying the soldiers to get their allotment! She's got a boy in the service & he's 27 & she's worried! Some more pictures came today of children in Europe & I went to FDR & said we must find a way to feed them. It is horrible & just can't go on.

Louis Weiss came to dine alone on the P.M. situation & I think he left happier & I was much encouraged to find that FDR said P.M. was too valuable to be given up & offered real political help.

I must tell you some of my talks with F on Spain & general politics when we meet. Sometimes I get so confused by expediencies that I would give a good deal to talk to you with your clear mind & sure political insight.

Swarthmore [College] seemed to go well last night. Do you like Nason?‡

---

* The 139th Psalm begins:
> Lord, thou hast examined me and knowest me
> Thou knowest all . . .

and ends:
> Examine me, O God, and know my thoughts
> Test me, and understand my misgivings . . .

† The whole forecasting school was waiting for orders to move to Grand Rapids, Michigan.

‡ John W. Nason, president of Swarthmore College.

She would not hear of it when I protested that I wasn't all that bright:

Your Thursday letter is here & I loved it & like to feel you enjoy conversing at the end of the day. I don't pine for brilliance. I just want what you think & feel in the ordinary course of events & the warm feeling that you write because you want to. Heaven knows, if I felt I had to write 'fine' thoughts to you I'd write very rarely. Most of the time I send off scrawls because I'm thinking about you & missing you & wanting to feel a little closer.

Trude called yesterday about the dinner here April 13th of the Friends of German Freedom at which I am going to speak & then I got her letter about the house & she fears they won't rent it to her for what she has decided she can pay. It seemed so perfect that I'm sorry but I know other places as nice can be found & now she has an ideal I'm sure she'll find the right thing.

I'm glad your aching knee is gone & the cold as well. Spring will be a help to both you & Trude & her family!

I hope you won't move next weekend but be sure to wire Thursday to the N.Y. apartment since I don't want to reach Chicago unless you are going to be there! We'll call Trude from there Saturday, won't we? I am happy at the thought of seeing you & you know I would come to Urbana if I were not fearful of embarrassing you? If you stay on I will have to come later & hope for the best! I won't bring anything to Chicago unless you write me of some special wishes but be sure to let me know if you have any.

I've just cleaned off my desk's box in which I pile so much reading material. One should go away more often for fairly long trips, it makes for order!

I find the British El Alamein battle picture won't be out for several weeks. It is a wonderful picture but I found it hard to bear.

Belle Roosevelt is here again. I find it hard to understand such complete love in the face of Kermit's curious behaviour. Sometimes I wonder if any of us ever do understand all the possibilities of understanding & devotion that can be developed.

The Red + girls came at 3:30 to be received & then the U.S.S.A. conference at 4. Churchill was on the air so I had the radio in the big dining room & we all listened & then after tea we showed 3 very good OWI films. Do they ever show you any? Everyone seems happy over the conference & I hope I can do what Molly [Yard] wants tomorrow. Hildur [Coon] & Irene [Murray] come to sleep here tonight as they have run out of space for those attending. They sound very enthusiastic.

Much, much love dear boy.

E.R.

All three, Eleanor, Trude, and I, had a vague feeling while I was at Chanute that Intelligence was keeping an eye on me. One day I had returned to my barracks after an afternoon at class, I told them, to learn from the "C.Q.," an enlisted man, that a group of Intelligence officers had arrived, shooed him off, sealed the barracks against anyone's coming in, and after a couple of hours left. I had looked at my foot locker and realized immediately that it had been searched. I had been the object of what later would be known as a "black bag" job. Perhaps Eleanor knew more than she told me, feeling that it was best for my morale not to know. In any case, I decided I had no alternative but to make the best I could out of my situation as a candidate forecaster. "I just looked up," she wrote to me from the White House on March 17, her thirty-eighth wedding anniversary, an event she did not mention, and "found my little Spanish boy right in front of your picture & he's marching so bravely, he symbolizes your spirit." She had had a "nice time with the Supreme Court" that day. She had gone there for the presentation of a sculpted head of Justice Brandeis done by Eleanor Platt. "Someday I want her to do one of you & when I die I'll give it to Trude!"

My most immediate problem during my last days at Chanute before the move to Grand Rapids was to get up to Chicago in order to spend Saturday at the Blackstone Hotel, where Eleanor and Tommy had checked in en route to Minneapolis and Seattle. Friday evening, work over, I left the field and went by bus to Chicago, arriving there after midnight. "You mustn't ever tell this to Mrs. R.," I wrote to Trude, "but I wasn't supposed to be off the field." At the last moment my weather squadron had been restricted until its members had signed the payroll. That would have meant missing the bus to Chicago. I had asked a barracks-mate to sign the payroll for me and left, a situation that turned out to be specially ironic when later I learned that Eleanor and I were being shadowed by Military Intelligence.

"I got in last night at 12:30," I wrote to Trude from the Blackstone, "and we talked for an hour and a half and then went to bed. Today we've been talking all day and Mrs. R. gave me many documents to read, all of which I found fascinating, some very, very troubling. [These were the documents about North Africa that Vice-President Wallace had given to Mrs. Roosevelt.] Then we went out for a walk and I bought some underwear. Mrs. R. insisted that I buy one garish pair to offset the monotony of G.I. clothes. Which I did. I shall don them with some apprehension before my colleagues."

Eleanor had other visitors while she was at the Blackstone. As she wrote to Hick before leaving on the midnight train for Minneapolis to speak and from where she would fly to Seattle:

We've been having wonderful weather here, sunny & windy but the view of the lake from the window is beautiful & seeing all the boys training is interesting. Louis Weiss dashed in as soon as we arrived Friday night & Joe spent twenty-four hours, & others have been in for tea & lunch but we've also done a good bit of work. Today I make my two speeches & leave at midnight. . . .

A long letter went to Franklin. It mainly concerned the liberal newspaper *PM*. Marshall Field, its publisher, and Louis Weiss, his lawyer, had realized that Eleanor was their best channel to the President. She liked *PM*. She liked them. She was tenacious.

Dearest Franklin,

Thanks for news of James & I'm glad to know all is well with you.

Louis Weiss came to see me as soon as I arrived today & said that he had your 'evidence.' [Representative John] Rankin is asking to have his bill reported or a resolution put on any tax bill, said it was aimed at Field, owner of P.M. which sought to destroy faith in Congress. Also by grape vine & a reliable source he heard that Joe Martin has said before the A.P. suit came up next month pressure would be brought on you & trading could be done, but the nature of the trade to be suggested was not disclosed. Louis Weiss thought you might like to be prepared & perhaps warn the Attorney General!

Are you having the Congressional party the 10th? If so could I ask Marshall & Louis Weiss to dine, provided they leave before any Congressman appears?

Nice weather here but we were two hours late because a wheel came off one engine! It didn't matter to us & everyone took it calmly in our car. Mr. Cotsworth of the Burlington came to the train & they take us to Minneapolis Monday night. He & Mrs. Cotsworth come in on Sunday & Joe will be here for his day off tomorrow & Tommy & I have already done lots of work. Nothing like train trips to get a lot done.

Much love—
E.R.

She also sent him, for the subject was much on her mind, a letter from "Madame de Mare," a Frenchwoman they had known quite well during World War I. Franklin liked her and he might take her advocacy of the de Gaullist resistance that Eleanor feared if it came from her might seem like nagging. Madame de Mare's strongly anti-Vichy letter might interest Franklin and it came from a woman who fervently admired him.

After I had left Eleanor wrote me:

I'm so afraid you may starve this week that I'm sending the check & $10, which is what I would have spent if you had let me buy you anything! You can consider the undies as a gift from me & I'll think of you cavorting in the flashy ones!

I can't tell you how I hated to say goodbye. I loved just sitting near you while you slept, talking with you & thinking of a happier future where I'm with you is almost the nicest part of life to me these days.

The only thing I can think of that would be nicer would be to have you home in our own surroundings for good!

I hope Trude gets out this next weekend for I know how hungry you must be for her presence & I realize how hard it is to be patient & understanding of her difficulties. I'll be so glad when the essentials are legally settled, the children in the country & Trude off to Reno even though I know the weeks there will seem endless to you but marriage will then be in sight & it will make those weeks bearable.

John Boettiger just called me from the airport. He's on his way to Washington but hopes to get back Saturday. Eisenhower sent him word via a letter from Elliott that the War Dept. must ask him so he's going on to try to get them to do so. I don't think I'll find a happy Anna & John said 'I only hope whatever I do, it is the best in the long run from the point of view of our relationship' which makes me think Anna may not yet be sure that this is the most useful thing for him to do. You & Trude won't have that to work out anyway!

I wonder how calisthenics & classes have gone today & whether you got any breakfast & how tired you are? I hope you enjoyed the day enough to make the trip worthwhile because I know it is selfish of me to let you do things just because I long to see you. Now I'm going to write Trude. I've done all the work Tommy wanted today! All my love, E.R.

Back at Chanute I wrote apologetically: "I'm sorry I was such a drowsy soul after dinner, but it was nicer drowsing in the darkness with you stroking my forehead than playing gin rummy, especially when I couldn't seem to win a game!" I had spent Monday with other weathermen loading freight cars with weather school apparatus that was to go to Grand Rapids.

The Blackstone Hotel people had given Eleanor some disquieting news. G-2 operatives had shadowed her and me and bugged her rooms.* She did not then tell me, but it made her uneasy, especially as I expected to move to Grand Rapids and had been unable to give her a mailing address there. "This is the last time I can write," she said in a final note from the Blackstone, "till I get your wire & it gives me a funny lost feeling, almost the way I feel when I only have a N.Y. or S.F.P.O. for the boys."

My next letter confirmed her fears, but it did not reach her for several days:

* The New York *Times* for November 1, 1961, reported under a Washington dateline: "A Chicago hotel room occupied by Mrs. Franklin D. Roosevelt during World War II was bugged, a former Army Intelligence agent said tonight. Listening devices picked up not only telephone conversation but also conversations in the room, according to Willis R. Adams, who is also a private investigator in the capital area." The disclosure was made on an NBC broadcast. The wiretap had been done on orders from above, Adams said, but declined to elaborate.

You will wonder why you do not hear from me, so I hope this letter reaches you before you leave Seattle. This morning at 7 a.m. all the forecasters left for Grand Rapids, but about a dozen of us were not among them. For some reason our names were not in the shipping orders. We have been told we will leave on Saturday.

It is so easy to become suspicious. Yesterday I told myself it was clerical oversight. Today I overheard the sergeant in charge of shipping say there was a 'special reason,' but I can't find anything out, and I was told to stay away from headquarters when I asked whether I could go over and make inquiries. So there is nothing to do but sit patiently and wait. . . . Up to now I have avoided a persecution complex and this really is evidence I have not succeeded as well with myself as I had thought.

I received your two Chicago letters. You were sweet to send me $10 but you spoil me. Yesterday was pay day and there was a good card game. I am ashamed to report I won $15, for if you can win $15, you can just as easily lose it, so I'm glad Trude said to me over the phone that I could play today, but I must quit when and if I lost $10 . . .

I don't know whether I should have written this to you. It will worry you unnecessarily, but I was afraid you would worry more if you didn't hear at all, and it helps me to know that you know. With much love.

Eleanor did worry for me. The information that Counterintelligence had tailed her infuriated her. Early in her White House years she had established her right not to be accompanied by Secret Service agents. It had been respected. She intended to talk to Harry Hopkins and General Marshall when she returned to Washington and insist that Army Intelligence respect her privacy. But in the meantime, she was uneasy for me: "I am beginning to be really anxious," she wrote to Trude from Anna's, "because he promised to wire me his new address & no word has come." She put a hopeful face on my silence: "I've been hoping for a wire today so this could be sent," she wrote from Seattle, "but I'll write it just because I'm thinking of you & want so much to talk with you & know what you are doing. I hope the trip hasn't been hard." The next day, she continued the same letter. "No word as yet from you & I am really worried & feel helpless for I can neither wire nor telephone." But "Saturday night," she wrote in the same letter, "I was glad to get your letter & of course worried as you were but your wire tonight is reassuring & I hope to get word tomorrow about your address. I hope the delay won't put you back in the course & I shall be glad when I get your next letter & understand what happened."

"Still no news," I wrote to Trude on April 2. "Seven of us just sit and wait. We wander from service club to PX to barracks to movies and back to the barracks to see if there's any word from the orderly room. . . . I am pretty sure we were held back because of the reason I suspected. I had taken some comfort in the fact that another boy whom I knew to be a Spanish vet had not been one of those missing from the shipping orders. At noon yesterday he too walked into the Service Club. The three of us—the ASU boy, the vet and myself cannot be a coincidence. . . . One feels so helpless, knowing neither the accusations against one, nor what is being done, or what is possible. Wanting terribly to be an accepted and hard-working part of the armed forces of the country, this sort of thing makes me turn not against the army, but against myself. Until this episode I was in my mind and feelings a forecaster, confronting the same difficulties and opportunities as my fellow forecasters. . . . Now when I arrive at Grand Rapids I will feel myself . . . a little bit of an outcast. . . . I'm certainly glad I pulled my grades up into the eighties.

"A paragraph in today's Squadron News Bulletin," I noted without comment: "Members of this command will refrain from writing letters to the President or Mrs. Roosevelt or to Congressmen and Representatives except through channels."

The next day, Saturday, there was the good news. They were "shipping out." "I was up at 5 this morning to turn in my bedding, and I sat around for a few minutes in the quietness and the shadows thrown up by the one electric bulb. All the boys were sleeping. . . . I was elated when the orders finally came through, but it was elation tempered by the knowledge that I will always be the object of special scrutiny, and it will probably bar the road to any real advancement. . . . I'd write more but I'm in charge of the nine of us going to Grand Rapids, which means I must get the tickets, records, baggage stubs, etc."

I wrote to Trude from Chicago: "I took my nine charges to Berghoff's for steaks. We had a government voucher allowing us to eat up to 75 cents worth." The hours waiting for the train to Grand Rapids I spent with the Spanish vet. "He started out as they usually do with me: 'The Administration is in a bad spot. It should have a more aggressive policy.' I had been through all this the night before with the ASU boy, so I wasn't very responsive. I was interested to watch his technique of having some fun. He searched the papers looking for a CIO dance or some left-wing affair. He finally found a CIO department store employees' dance, but I was reluctant to go, urging him to do so, however. We finally ended up seeing Casablanca."

Trude had not gone out to see me, she wrote to Eleanor, "and you have probably heard from him that the whole business of moving was bad and that he had a few worried days. But today he called from Grand Rapids and he sounded happier than he ever did from Rantoul. So perhaps it was good after all." She was going out to Grand Rapids the following weekend and we would call Eleanor from there. From the Hotel St. Francis in San Francisco, Eleanor scrawled "just a little additional line to say I was so happy to get wire just now. I was worried last night & wired Trude. Am glad setup is better & anxious to hear what your times off are." She followed that up, for in the back of her mind was her coming encounter with Harry Hopkins. "I am greatly relieved that you are safely moved," she wrote to me, "but will you tell me if anything was said which explained the delay? . . . I'm afraid I bothered you & Trude about your address but I am more suspicious than you are, someday I'll tell you why!" She had spent the day in San Francisco at military hospitals:

> I've been very busy here, hospitals, 3 of them & some heartrending things that these boys have to face. There are going to be so many boys without an arm or a leg & some who'll never walk except on crutches. Guadalcanal will haunt many a boy. This afternoon I did 2 speeches & went to 2 service men's canteens.
>
> Last evening I dined & spent the evening with Johnny & Anne & to-night they came here & we went to dine at an Armenian place. The owner & chef told me the story of his life & the history of each dish he served! I like S.F. & you & Trude & I must come here sometime to-gether! We went to see Tiny dance this evening & now I must go to bed for I have a full day here tomorrow before I take the plane at 3:30 & then we travel some 24 hrs!

A telegram went to Franklin. She would not allow him to forget about *PM*:

> PLEASE ANSWER ABOUT TWO GENTLEMEN TO DINE WITH YOU ALONE THEY CAN COME ELEVENTH STOP WILL TELEPHONE YOU TEN PM TONIGHT YOUR TIME MUCH LOVE. ELEANOR.

A note to Franklin from Seattle had shown that she was not unduly impressed with John's decision to go into the Army:

> John got back today & Monday they visit Los Angeles & break the news to Mr. Hearst. Not till then will Anna know her job in the future. I'm not very happy about them because I'm not sure John isn't doing the glamorous thing he'd enjoy instead of a hard plodding job. Well, it is his life & he must decide & Anna must decide about hers.

Trude came out to Grand Rapids and stayed at the Hotel Morton. We called Eleanor, who had returned to the White House. "Three minutes went very fast & I was sorry not to talk longer with you & not to speak to Trude. I'm enclosing a check for the call for I heard you pay & I don't want you to spend your money on me. You need it for too many other things!" She and Tommy would come out late Saturday, the seventeenth. "Why must I go over the School?" she protested, for I had suggested that she do so. The time was too short and she could do so in May. I had expressed concern lest her anger with Alvin Johnson for letting Trude down over ISS affect her support for the New School. That elicited a self-deprecatory statement about her sphere of usefulness:

> Don't worry dear, I won't let my personal feelings interfere with my doing anything I can do anywhere but I think my sphere of usefulness will be more & more circumscribed. While here, by the fact that I know only too well my interest often does more harm & [than?] good & later by the fact that I also recognize that I am wearing out a bit & will be more quickly in retirement than any of you think. FDR told me tonight after the Congressional party that the gentlemen were clamoring to go to the fronts & he thought it might be impossible to send them & in that case I would also be barred. I told him anything he decided was all right with me. I wanted to be a help & not a bother. The two gentlemen interested in papers we like to read, dined here alone tonight & the tale develops interestingly. Remind me to tell you.

She saw Harry Hopkins and General Marshall, as she would tell me later, and sent me a cryptic note that she herself described as slightly mad:

> You are going to think me crazy but until I can talk to you just try to believe I'm still sane. I've just run to earth something funny. If you have any friends who send you documents tell them to stop, a soldier should have nothing 'confidential or secret' which is not strictly personal!
>
> Your love affairs are of no interest & for once a friendship I have thought at times was harmful to you has been useful! I think you may be carefree for a time!

When I returned from the day with Trude at the Hotel Morton, there was a notice on my bunk that I had a special delivery letter awaiting me. I wrote to Eleanor:

> How we build things in our imagination. I had thought your letter was from New York telling me to be careful because of what you had learned; instead it was from San Francisco with only a casual reference to my being held back at Chanute. I told you my foot locker had been gone through a few days after I arrived here—under exactly the same circumstances as at Chanute: a group of officers came up to our floor in the Pantlind [barracks building] and chased out the enlisted men. When I returned from school things in my footlocker and barracks bag were rearranged. I don't know what they're after: whether there's a sudden fear of 'reds' in the Army, whether they've uncovered some type of organization and are trying to link me with it, whether it has to do with anti-administration politics or what. So I resolutely ignore the whole business and do as good a job here as I can.

I shall, however, not keep letters in my foot locker. I will mail you a packet each week and keep them on my person until then. I gave Trude a copy of a squadron bulletin posted at Chanute 2 days before I left, in which we were forbidden to write you or the President except through 'channels.' I'm sure it doesn't apply to personal letters but I'm curious to know why it made its appearance at this particular time.

For a few days my letters were filled with the characteristic woes of a GI forecaster, the difficulties of mastering physics, not to mention calisthenics. Also there was my regular foray to the Hotel Morton restaurant, where I ordered a steak and, ensconced behind the New York *Times*, slowly demolished it, "dining-in-state," I called it. I exchanged letters with Trude about the house we would live in, and broke from drawing synoptic charts, to write doggerel:

> To wit:
> A flower with a head of gold
> Met a weed lean and bold
> > They weren't of the same religion
> > Nor of the same race
> > They weren't a pair
> > You'd think embrace
> But the weed was staunch
> And the flower had grace
> And one around the other did lace
> And that, children, is the story of this place.

Eleanor was going to join the presidential train in Fort Worth for the President's meeting with President Avila Camacho of Mexico in Monterrey. She sent me her itinerary. "The days skipped are those I will be on the train & not reachable. . . . As you see this is rather a one-night stand proposition & I know you won't be able to write but I like you to know where I am so you can wire if you need to do so. . . . I'm glad you decided just to do a good job & think no more about any supervision. I shall be curious what they tell you about writing but in any case Trude can tell me your news! I hope your marks turn out better than you expected & I think you & Trude are safely around your worst corner!"

She wrote from the Blackstone: "Here we are back in the same rooms & I wish I were looking forward to seeing you instead of taking a train to Fort Worth. This trip has no pleasant interludes!" I should keep her informed about how things go "in every way." She underlined "every." "It is beautiful here," she wrote to Trude from Fort Worth, "& the children are lovely & my heart aches for all that Elliott is missing!" She sent Trude the call to a meeting organized by some C.O.s* to which they had invited General Hershey, head of Selective Service. The C.O.s had been "surprised that he would not allow them to hold the meeting. Can you see what the army would have said?"

An exchange of letters with Hick reflected another concern, the inclusion of women in the Administration's postwar planning: Hick had learned there were no women on the U.S. delegation to an Allied refugee conference in Bermuda. She asked Eleanor to help:

> I telephoned Sumner Welles before I left Friday. He said inclusion of women delegates was impossible as there would only be three & they were already named but they would be included as advisors. Too late for the refugee conference but he would try to include them in the food conference & in all future conferences. He had just forgotten them!

She pursued the issue on the presidential train:

> As I wrote you yesterday I spoke to Sumner before I left & as he's on the train I gave him the material on Josephine [Schain] last night. The President is agreeable to speaking in Cabinet & at press & I'll give him a memo on his return.
>
> The trip is off the record again after tomorrow but in these two days so I'll rewrite 2 columns. . . .

A letter written on the train rebuked me for not calling her collect.

> My handwriting will be worse than usual but if you can't read it, there will be nothing important lost! It was wonderful to hear your voice in Chicago & you sounded well & content. Your call did me much good but I was sorry I had talked so long when I found out you had paid for the call. Won't you ever learn to telephone me collect? It makes me feel so much more that you feel you 'belong' if you do what the boys would do! I know I treat you more like a friend & one of my own contemporaries & I feel that way but you & Trude are more to me like Anna & John. You are friends & yet you can ask anything of me & I can give you anything I wish because you are my children too. Is that too close a relationship to accept Joe Dear? It makes it easier for me to take as much as I do from you, & Trude too.
>
> . . . .
>
> I heard in Chicago that the inquiry was made about the two other boys as to whether they were with you there. The answer of course was no. Every culvert & bridge is guarded by soldiers along the route & some look as tho' sleeping in the sand was a bit dishevelling! The kids† want to play a game so I better stop since they've gone in search of a pack of cards. The ranch looked lovely yesterday & I kept thinking of all Elliott was missing. It will have to be a very good world in the future to make

---

* Conscientious objectors.
† Elliott's children were with them.

the many sacrifices worth while. I'm going to send you 'The Robe.' Perhaps you'll think it odd since one of its objects is to prove Christ's divinity but that seems to me not very important, since I believe that all of us must have something to raise us above the animal but there is in it your theory of the value of being part of a movement which transcends personal interests. It discourages me about humanity & yet you & those who think & live as you do give me the faith that some day Christ's vision may come to pass.

When she returned to Fort Worth, several of my letters greeted her. She sought to allay my jealousy of Trude and in the course of doing so hinted at some private agonies of her own:

Your letter to Washington & the one written on Monday & Tuesday both greeted me here. I am thankful the schedule is better for I couldn't bear to urge you not to write because your letters mean so much to me & yet I hated to think of your writing when you were so weary.

I am sorry about your bad telephone conversations & I realize how hard it is not to be jealous of Trude but I feel once you are married all these moods & feelings will pass & I hope you succeed in fighting them now. I'm no good person to lecture you for what you do is torture yourself, & I'm fairly good at that & used to be far worse than I am now.

You evidently never saw Helen Essary's column* & I haven't it here but I enclose one by John O'Donnell which will give you a fair idea of what she said. You see she implies that I should feel responsibility for the world therefore have a sense of guilt before the wounded. I really forget what I feel in the hospitals. I don't think I'm cruel or insensitive, but if they were men I knew or cared about as individuals I couldn't let them think I was sorry for them it seems to me they are so gallant that they call for admiration & gallantry in return. I'm completely exhausted after a hospital day & I lie awake thinking what we should do in the future for them but one goes on with daily round of life.

We got back this a.m. & the afternoon & evening in Monterrey were interesting. I like both President & Mrs. Camacho. He & FDR talked through an interpreter who had lived 9 yrs in this country, is now in the army & seemed very nice. Corpus Christi was interesting, too, a huge station with some cadets from every South American country. They gave an exhibition of dive bombing which scared me but was most skillful & interesting.

If you won't worry about my doing things for fear of its hurting me

* Helen Essary and John O'Donnell were anti-New Deal columnists, the former with the *Times-Herald*, the latter head of the Washington Bureau of the *Daily News*. Essary said: ". . . [I]t still does not become the wife of the President of the United States, the Commander in Chief of the armed forces, to look unshaken on wounded men who have been put into their misery by this country's participation in the World War . . . This war is to frightful to be spoken of in Mrs. Roosevelt's chirrupy fashion. . . ."

to be with you I probably won't worry about hurting you as a friend but when I think you & Trude worry then I worry because of drawing attention to you & I can think of a million other ways in which I might hurt you. I'm so sorry for your A.S.U. boy, you've been so wonderful about all you've gone through that you will help him but I can't help being deeply resentful for both of you.*

We leave for Phoenix by air at 6:15 & spend tomorrow in relocation camps. I just asked FDR if I could take on an American-Japanese family but he says the Secret Service wouldn't allow it. Bill has left so I'm looking for a middle-aged gardener & wife!

I love you dearly & try not to be hurt or angry with Trude. She loves you I'm sure. Bless you dear boy.

She did not know that I was no longer in Grand Rapids but on the way to a port of embarkation.

---

* An enlisted man whom I did not know had caught up with me on the street soon after my arrival in Grand Rapids, introduced himself as a former ASUer who had been in Naval Intelligence when my application for a commission was being considered. He had been the only one to defend me and as a consequence, he said, had been busted and drafted. Events were to make it impossible for me to pursue the matter further, but the more I thought about it, the more skeptical I became about this man's story and concluded he must have been a counterintelligence operative.

XXII

On Roosevelt's
Alleged "Hit List"

T HE "intelligence operation" revealed in this chapter partly explains why I decided to abridge my own standards of what does and does not belong in a historical record. I would have preferred to keep private the love letters between Trude Pratt and myself and Eleanor Roosevelt's involvement therein. But if the allegations contained in the G-2 files are to be seen correctly, they must be seen in the context of these letters.

The latter also help place Eleanor Roosevelt's relationship with Lorena Hickok in a new perspective. Eleanor Roosevelt loved deeply and lavished her affection on men as well as women with a force that was the stronger because her husband was so little able to give her the intimate companionship she craved. Her passionate nature, which hungered for affection and appreciation, mystified some. Others it confounded, especially outsiders with neat categories about sexual roles and behavior. G-2, after bugging her meetings with me and reading her letters to me, concluded that we were having an affair. Who after the travesty of such an interpretation can draw absolutist conclusions about the relationship between her and Hickok from the correspondence the latter deposited at the Roosevelt Library?

Perhaps it was my egotism or naïveté that had led me to assume that it was my radical career during the Thirties that had drawn the interest of Counterintelligence when I entered the Army. I never imagined it could, or would, go after the wife of the Commander-in-Chief and portray her, as did Colonel Boyer, head of Intelligence at Chanute, in a letter of March 3, 1943, to Colonel John Bissell (of Counterintelligence in Washington) that is reproduced here as part of a "gigantic conspiracy participated in by not only Subject and Trude Pratt but also by E.R., Henry Wallace, Henry Morgenthau, etc." Boyer made such charges even though he had the benefit, through mail covers and buggings, of reading the most private thoughts of Mrs. Roosevelt, Trude Pratt, and myself.

Under the Freedom of Information and Privacy Act (FOIPA) on January 16, 1978, I requested that an "all-reference" search of government files be made relating to me. The material engendered by this request was reviewed by government officials and some of it, not all, was released to me in October 1978. It staggered me. The counterintelligence operation disclosed a primitive mentality and a troubling identification of patriotism with what later generations have come to call a "Birchite" outlook on the world. The dislike and harassment of Eleanor Roosevelt made me tremble for current intelligence operations, since many of the men who staffed wartime intelligence graduated into the postwar investigative apparatus.

When I received the fat brown envelopes from the FOIPA Office of the U. S. Army Intelligence and Security Command and the Department of Justice, my first impulse was to file them away along with a sworn statement of the facts as I knew them and leave them to a later generation to deal with.

I was a fool to think that was possible. The story of my alleged relationship with Eleanor Roosevelt to which Westbrook Pegler used to refer during the war with a self-confidence that always puzzled me, President Roosevelt's alleged destruction of Counterintelligence, and his so-called "hit list," had been bruited about Washington among top counterintelligence operatives, especially the men around J. Edgar Hoover, for many years. One of the documents given to me was a memorandum from L. B. Nichols, a close associate of J. Edgar Hoover, to the Director, dated February 2, 1954, when Dwight D. Eisenhower was President. It began:

> The thought occurs that if the President does not know of the furor that was caused in G-2 some years ago as the result of G-2's investigation of Joe Lash and his connections with Mrs. Roosevelt, you might want to consider mentioning the incident to him. . . .

The "incident" is that recounted in the "Memorandum" of December 31, 1943,* by George Burton, another top agent of the FBI. It is entitled "Re: Dismemberment of Counterintelligence Corps, G-2." This

* See pages 492–93 for the full text.

memorandum was segregated from the FBI's main files and kept in a special file by Miss Gandy, the director's confidential secretary. There it was joined by a photostat of the G-2 file that had been maintained on me and sent to the FBI at the beginning of 1946. This system of file segregation enabled Nichols to advise Hoover, on January 18, 1951, "to tell Senator Watkins the FBI never investigated the Roosevelt-Lash incident. There is nothing from official sources on this in the FBI files." It also meant there was no investigation of the truth and accuracy of the allegations contained in the file.

The last Republican official who checked into this story of my alleged "affair" with Mrs. Roosevelt seems to have been John Dean, who asked for information that would show that the Roosevelt and Johnson administrations used the FBI for political purposes. William Sullivan, who was then one of the top FBI agents vying to succeed Hoover, was assigned to prepare a memorandum on the subject. Sullivan came up with the story of "Don Lash" (evidently the famous miler's name was on his mind). In any event John Dean, like the Eisenhower Administration earlier, did not seem to consider the story usable.

But it has remained in the files and is taken as something that approximated the truth. Thus an undated memorandum written to Hoover by another of his ambitious associates, C. D. "Duke" DeLoach, evidently in 1959, states:

> . . . Lash is Joseph Lash who, as you will recall, was extremely familiar with Eleanor Roosevelt. This is the man whom the late President Roosevelt ordered to be sent to the front within ten hours after he had been tipped off that Lash had been familiar with Mrs. Roosevelt.

These allegations are so extraordinary that I have felt it necessary to reproduce the G-2 file in its entirety as well as George Burton's FBI memorandum of December 1943. Readers can form their own judgment. Presumably the Government has withheld some material. Other documents were destroyed. The U. S. Army Intelligence and Security Command states that investigative files after 1943 were ordered burned. This 1943 cutoff date is not irrelevant. Evidently the FBI also considered it pertinent. L. B. Nichols in his memorandum to Hoover, designed to refresh his memory about the incident in the event Hoover decided to tell Eisenhower about it, thought that Roosevelt's fury at Counterintelligence might have been the reason for "the subsequent order given the Army to destroy the files on subversives."

I have omitted some documents copied by G-2 in the course of its surveillance and given to me. They consist of letters sent to me by Eleanor Roosevelt, Trude Pratt, and several friends—not to mention the Chelsea Fireproof Storage Warehouse. In the cases of Eleanor Roosevelt and Trude Pratt, the letters have been included or described in the previous chapter. In the case of the letters from friends, the summaries provided at the time by Counterintelligence officer Major Walterhouse will suffice. Also omitted is Lieutenant Ark's transcription of the bugged conversations between Trude Pratt and myself at the Urbana Lincoln Hotel, near Chanute. Their nature is amply described in Lieutenant Ark's covering letter to Chanute Intelligence.

Place: Chanute Field, Illinois
Date: March 6, 1943
File: 201 - LASH, JOSEPH P.

MEMORANDUM FOR THE OFFICER IN CHARGE:

Subject: JOSEPH P. LASH
          ASN 32326519, Sgt.
          2nd Weather Squadron
          Patterson Field, Ohio
          Att. 7th Tech. Sch. Sqdn,
From: Chanute Field, Illinois

RE: Review of Service Record
          and A.G.O. Form 20

      This officer reviewed service record and A.G.O. Form
20 of Sgt. JOSEPH P. LASH, ASN 32326519, Att. 7th Technical
School Squadron, Chanute Field, Illinois on March 6, 1943
in connection with an investigation of Subject, who is suspected of Communistic affiliations. The information obtained
follows:

1. Personal Data:
    Birth: December 2, 1909, New York, New York.
    Age: 33.
    Physical Description: Height, 5' 6 1/2"; weight 140
        lbs.; hair, black; eyes, brown; complexion,
        medium

2. Family Data:
    Father: Born in Russia
    Mother: MARY LASH, 457 West 123rd Street, New York
        City, New York, born in Russia.

3. Education:
    1931-1932: Columbia University. Received M.A. in
            English Literature.
    1927-1931: City College, New York City. Received
            AB degree.
    1923-1927   High School, New York, New York.
    1915-1923: Grammar School, New York, New York.

4. Employment:
    April 28, 1942 to present: U. S. Army.
    Previously for 6 years: Public relations man (executive
        administrative work; organizing and directing
        national and international conferences of young

(MEMO "A")

Chanute Field, Ill.
March 6, 1943
201 - LASH, JOSEPH P.

4. Employment: (continued)
          people; writing and delivering speeches, editing
          magazines and newspapers, writing articles and
          advertisements and choosing media for effective
          presentation. Organized school and summer camps
          for purpose of educating college students for more
          effective citizenship. Executive director of
          International Student Service with 18 direct
          employees and a great deal of liaison work
          between student groups and governmental and
          educational organizations. One month's intensive
          training, no combat, with Spanish Loyalist Army.
          Last employed to April 27, 1942, by International
          Student Service, 8 West 40th Street, New York
          City, New York.

5. Military History:
          January 28, 1943-present: Assigned 2nd Weather Squadron,
               Patterson Field, Ohio, attached 7th Technical
               School Squadron, Chanute Field, Illinois. Taking
               Weather Observers course. Commanding Officer,
               Captain WILLIAM E. GLASS, A.C.
          May 28, 1942-January 28, 1943: Assigned 2nd Weather
               Squadron, Patterson Field, Ohio, and detached to
               Bolling Field, D.C. Promoted to corporal on
               August 3, 1942, and to sergeant on October 3,
               1942. Took Weather Observers Course and acted
               as weather observer.
          May 4, 1942-May 28, 1942: 579th Technical School
               Squadron, Miami Schools, AAFTTC, Miami Beach,
               Florida, basic training.
          April 28, 1942-May 4, 1942: Ft. Dix, New York, Oath
               and processing.
          1927-1929: Basic ROTC (Inf.) City College, New York
               New York.

7. Addresses:
          Date not indicated: 30 West 9th Street, New York
               New York.

9. Organizations:
          Date not indicated: American Student Union for four
               years. Director of the organization.

10. Principal Amusements:
          Built radios at the age of 12. Plays handball.

                                   HARRY F. WALTERHOUSE
                                   Major, Air Corps

Place: Chanute Field, Illinois
Date: March 6, 1943
File: 201 - LASH, JOSEPH P.

MEMORANDUM FOR THE OFFICER IN CHARGE:

                             JOSEPH P. LASH
                             ASN 32326519, Sgt.
              Subject: 2nd Weather Squadron
                             Patterson Field, Ohio
                             Att. 7th Tech. Sch. Sqdn.
                             Chanute Field, Illinois

                    RE   : Report of Reliable Informant

        This officer received a report from a reliable informant
on February 15, 1943 in connection with an investigation of
Sgt. JOSEPH P. LASH, ASN 32326519, 2nd Weather Squadron,
Patterson Field, Ohio, Att. 7th Technical School Squadron,
Chanute Field, Illinois, who is suspected of Communist affilia-
tions. The report follows:

        "Our friend daily receives one, and generally two air-
mail letters. If two, both are postmarked from the same place,
New York, New York, and at the same time. These letters are
addressed in ink, and always bear air-mail stamps. From the
looks and feel of said letters, because of flexibility, texture,
and thinness of letter, I would say that they are written on a
paper such as 'onion-skin'.

        "Soldier, this date received an insured package slip
J378207.

        "Soldier also, this date, received a telegram (which as
is the custom of the telegraph office, was unsealed, and I took
the liberty of opening same and reading it.) The telegram read
as follows:

              WILL CALL YOU FROM COLUMBIA MISSOURI BETWEEN
              THIRTY-SEVEN AND FOUR.   LOVE
                                E. R.
        "The above is the original telegram...whether it was
mixed up in transit, or is in code, is to be seen. It could
have meant 'WILL CALL YOU FROM COLUMBIA MISSOURI BETWEEN FOUR
AND SEVEN-THIRTY. LOVE. E.R.

        "Soldier received a notice to call operator # 2 in
Columbia Missouri at about 6:00 PM last evening.

                    (MEMO "B")

Chanute Field, Illinois
March 6, 1943
201 - LASH, JOSEPH P.

"Soldier in question always has an array of maps and charts in front of him. Whether this pertains his class in Weather Forecasting or not, I do not know. I would say that possibly yes, but probably no...at least not as frequently as he is seen with them.

"Soldier still persists in calling for mail in person... He generally goes and secures the mail for the entire barracks at 11:00 A.M. daily.

"Any further noted variations and remarks will be forwarded."

HARRY F. WALTERHOUSE
Major, Air Corps

Memo "B"

Page 2.

Place: Chanute Field, Illinois
Date: March 6, 1943
File: 201 - LASH, JOSEPH P.

MEMORANDUM FOR THE OFFICER IN CHARGE:

JOSEPH P. LASH
ASN 32326519, Sgt.
Subject: 2nd Weather Squadron
Patterson Field, Ohio.
Att. 7th Tech. Sch. Sqdn.
Chanute Field, Illinois

RE   : Report of Reliable Informant

This officer received a report from a reliable informant on February 17, 1943 in connection with an investigation of Sgt. JOSEPH P. LASH, ASN 32326519, 2nd Weather Squadron, Patterson Field, Ohio, Att. 7th Technical School Squadron, Chanute Field, Illinois, who is suspected of Communist affiliations. The report follows:

"Soldier in question: Original station, 2nd Weather Squadron, Patterson Field, Ohio. Before arriving this station, soldier was on detached service to Bolling Field, Washington D.C. Soldier now on detached service, this station, attached 7th Tech. Sch. Sq, Barracks # 403. Soldier arrived this station 1-29-43 per SO # 33, paragraph # 71.

"Soldier is a Weather Forecasting student "B" shift 12:30 to 6:00 PM.

"Soldier's day off is Saturday.

"Number of soldier's class 43-3-B.

"Soldier did not put in for pass (100 mile) this week. To my knowledge, the only area soldier ever canvases is within the 20 mile radius as stated on regualr student pass.

"Soldier spends most of his off time in day room.

"Soldier usually tries to collect mail from mail room so that he is sure that he gets his mail. Found him doing so today.

"Soldier's service record and classification card not arrived this station as yet.

"Will forward all information pertaining this case (from

(MEMO "C")

Chanute Field, Illinois
March 6, 1943
201 - LASH, JOSEPH P.

service record and allied papers) as soon as arrival.

"Will note further actions of soldier in question."

HARRY F. WALTERHOUSE
Major, Air Corps

Memo "C: Page 2.

Place: Chanute Field, Illinois
Date: March 6, 1943
File: 201 - Lash, Joseph P.

MEMORANDUM FOR THE OFFICER IN CHARGE:

Subject: Joseph P. Lash
          ASN 32326519, Sgt.
          2nd Weather Sqdn.
          Patterson Field, O.
          Att. 7th Tech. S.S.
Re   : Chanute Field, Ill.

Review of Mail Cover

This officer reviewed results of mail cover on Sgt. JOSEPH P. LASH, ASN 32326519, 2nd Weather Squadron, Patterson Field, Ohio, Attached Seventh Technical School Squadron, Chanute Field, Illinois, on March 6, 1943, in connection with an investigation of Subject, who is suspected of Communist affiliations. The review covered the period from February 14, 1943 to March 6, 1943.

Subject received the following mail:

Date	From
2/14/43	USSA 8 West 40th St, New York, N.Y.
2/16/43	Mrs. Eleanor Roosevelt 1600 Pennsylvania Ave. Washington, D.C.
2/19/43	Chelsea Fireproof Storage Warehouse 426-438 W. 26th St. New York, N.Y.
2/19/43	World Student Service Fund 8 West 40th Street New York, N.Y.
2/22/43	Mrs. Eleanor Roosevelt 1600 Pennsylvania Ave. Washington, D. C.

(MEMO "D")

Chanute Field, Illinois
March 6, 1943
201 - Lash, Joseph P.

Date	From
2/24/43	James B. Carry C.I.O. 718 Jackson Place, NW Washington, D. C.
3/1/43	TWP 8 West Ninth St. New York, N.Y.
3/5/43	TWP 8 West Ninth St. New York, NY
3/5/43	TWP 8 West Ninth St. New York, N.Y.
3/5/43	Aaron Lash 457 West 123rd New York, N.Y.
3/6/43	Peter New York, N.Y.
3/6/43	N.Y. Telephone Co. New York, N.Y.

The letter from the USSA was dated 2/11/43 and was signed Lou. It discussed the demise of the International Student Service and its replacement by and organization of the United States Student Assembly, including some of its leaders and policies. (Exhibit I).

The first letter of Mrs. Roosevelt, dated 2/12/43, told of her plans to call Subject from Columbia, Missouri, on 2/17/43 and to meet him in Champaign, Illinois, on 3/5/43. The letter, which gossiped about important national and international figures was closed in an affectionate tone. (Exhibit II).

The letter from the Chelsea Fireproof Storage Warehouse confirmed receipt of goods stored there by Subject, while the letter received from the World Student Service Fund on 2/19/43 was a bulletin.

Mrs. Roosevelt's second letter, dated 2/18-19/43, was written in the same vein as her first. (Exhibit III).

The letter from James B. Carry, Secy.-Treas. of the C.I.O. and dated 2/22/43, showed him to be a close acquaintance of Subject. (Exhibit IV).

Chanute Field, Illinois
March 6, 1943
201 - Lash, Joseph P.

The letter from TWP (Trude), dated 2/27/43, revealed that she worked closely with Mrs. Roosevelt on youth programs. It showed that the writer had definite Leftist leanings and connections and referred to Second Front Rallies by "the party" and to an article by Laski in The Nation. A letter from George, Department of Agronomy, Washington State College, Pullman, Wash., was enclosed. (Exhibit V).

One letter from TWP, received on 3/5/43, enclosed three clippings. One was a page 1 story from the New York World Telegram of 3/3/43 and concerned the execution of two Polish Jew labor leaders by the Reds. Another was an editorial from the New York Post of 3/3/43, which rapped the present appeasement policy of the Administration with reference to France and Spain. The third was an article written by Harold J. Laski in the 2/27/43 issue of The Nation on the subject of "Platform for the Left."

The second letter received from TWP on the same day told of recent contacts of the writer with Mrs. Roosevelt, spoke of an estranged husband and her love for Subject and told of meetings and conversations of the writer with pro-Russian individuals. One part of the letter was scrawled in long hand (Exhibit VI A) and another part was typewritten (Exhibit VI B).

Peter, who wrote the letter received on 3/6/43, appeared to be the young son of Trude. He said that his mother had had drops put in her eyes and could not see and would not be able to write for a couple days. The communication from the telephone company was a bill for $4.17 for New York City telephone number Ore. 4-3977.

HARRY F. WALTERHOUSE
Major, Air Corps

Place: Chanute Field, Illinois
Date: March 6, 1943
File: 201 - LASH, JOSEPH P.

MEMORANDUM FOR THE OFFICER IN CHARGE:

                                   JOSEPH P. LASH
                          Subject: ASN 32326519, Sgt.
                                   2nd Weather Squadron
                                   Patterson Field, Ohio
                                   Att. 7th Tech Sch. Sqdn.
                                   Chanute Field, Illinois
                          RE   : Interview with a
                                   Reliable Informant

        This investigator interviewed a reliable informant
at Chanute Field, Illinois on February 16, 1943, relevant to
Subject.

        Informant disclosed that on February 15, 1943 at 6:37
P.M. in the 7th Technical School Squadron orderly room at
Chanute Field, Illinois, Subject received a person to person
telephone call that originated in Columbia, Missouri, from
Mrs. FRANKLIN DELANO ROOSEVELT.

        The conversation lasted for three minutes, ending at
6:40 P.M.

        During the conversation Subject referred to Mrs.
ROOSEVELT as "ELEANOR" and she, in return to Subject, as "Sergeant".
She inquired as to his health and to what progress he was making
in his work, especially referring to his school work at Chanute
Field.

        Mrs. ROOSEVELT referred to a girl whose name she did
not mention and remarked that "the girl had shingles."

        She inquired to Subject if he liked the President's
speech and Subject replied that it was very good.

        Subject was advised by Mrs. ROOSEVELT that she would
travel by plane from Columbia, Missouri but she did not reveal
her destination.

NOTE:

        Informant revealed that the telephone line was kept

        (MEMO "E")   Page 1

Chanute Field, Illinois
March 6, 1943
201 - LASH, JOSEPH P.

open for a period of thirty minutes and that during this period
there were seven calls trying to come through on the same line.
Each time the telephone operator in Columbia, Missouri stated
that the line was being held open for "Mrs. ROOSEVELT," or
"The First Lady."

RAYMOND W. KRAUS
Sergeant, Air Corps

Memo "E"

Page 2.

Place: Chanute Field, Illinois
Date: March 6, 1943
File: 201-LASH, JOSEPH P.

MEMORANDUM FOR THE OFFICER IN CHARGE:

JOSEPH P. LASH
ASN 32326519
Subject: 2nd Weather Squadron
Patterson Field, Ohio
Att. 7th Tech. Sch. Sqdn.
Chanute Field, Illinois

RE   : Surveillance of Subject

On Friday, March 5, 1943 at 6:00 P.M., Subject was placed under surveillance by this investigator at Chanute Field, Illinois for the purpose of ascertaining activity of Subject during the ensuing evening.

The Weather Forecasters Class at Chanute Field was dismissed at 6:35 P.M. and all men including Subject entered into marching formation in front of the brick barracks. The group marched towards Mess Hall #4 and upon reaching a point several hundred feet away from same, Subject left the formation and walked quickly to his barracks, #403, in the 7th Technical School Squadron, arriving at 6:55 P.M. Subject entered and stopped, momentarily, to scan the bulletin board afterwhich he went to his "bunk".

At 7:00 P.M. Subject left the barracks and was carrying a large brown envelope, (Approx. 10"x15") of the same type as that in which he carries his school work, and walked directly to the West Entrance gate on Chanute Field arriving there at 7:10 P.M. Subject showed his pass to the guard on duty and walked across the road where he apparently waited for a ride. (This investigator notified Lt. Ark who parked his car in the vicinity of the West gate).

Several buses passed by during the ensuing 25 minutes but did not stop because they were filled to capacity. Subject appeared nervous and concerned and walked to and fro along the road.

At. 7:37 P.M. a Rantoul, Illinois taxicab discharged a passenger at the West gate. Subject ran across the road and entered the taxi which carried Subject to the bus terminal in Rantoul.

At 7:50 P.M. Subject boarded an Urbana-Champaign, Illinois bus.

The bus arrived in Urbana, Illinois at 8:25 P.M. Subject alighted from the bus one block away from the Urbana-Lincoln Hotel and walked directly to that hotel where he entered.

(MEMO " G ")

Page 1.

Chanute Field, Illinois
March 6, 1943
201-LASH, JOSEPH P.

He walked directly to the hotel desk and spoke with the hotel
clerk. This investigator heard the hotel clerk remark to Subject that
he would have to register. Subject replied that there was a reservation
for him. The clerk stated that he would still have to register whereupon
Subject signed the blotter.

The hotel clerk then summoned a bell-hop and gave him instructions
to escort Subject to rooms 330 and 332. Subject and bell-hop entered the
hotel elevator and went to the third floor.

This investigator remained in the lobby of the hotel until 10:15 P.M.
at which time Lt. Artk issued instructions to discontinue surveillance of
Subject.

RAYMOND W. KRAUS
Sergeant.

CONFIDENTIAL

Place: Chanute Field, Illinois
Date: March 7, 1943
File: 201- LASH, JOSEPH P.

MEMORANDUM FOR THE OFFICER IN CHARGE:

Joseph P. Lash
ASN 32326519, Sgt.
Subject: 2nd Weather Squadron
Patterson Field, Ohio
Att. 7th Tech. Sch. Sqdn.
Chanute Field, Illinois

Rè   : Interview with reliable informant

This officer interviewed a reliable informant on March 5,6 and 7, 1943
in Urbana, Illinois in connection with an investigation of Subject who is suspected of Communist affiliations.

Informant stated that Mrs. Franklin D. Roosevelt had checked into the
Urbana-Lincoln Hotel, Urbana, Illinois at 11:45 A.M., March 5, 1943. She was
accompanied by her secretary, Miss Malvina Thompson, and expressed the wish that
no publicity be given to her arrival. At the time of registering for her room,
Mrs. Roosevelt stated that she expected "a young friend from Chanute Field" to
visit her and reserved room 330 for him. Mrs. Roosevelt occupied room 332.
Informant stated that the rooms had twin beds and were joined by a connecting
door.

About nine o'clock on March 5, 1943, informant stated, a soldier came
to the desk of the Urbana-Lincoln Hotel and announced that he was JOSEPH LASH,
and he understood that MRS. ROOSEVELT had a room reserved for him. He was directed to room 330.

Informant stated that MRS. ROOSEVELT had ordered dinner for three sent to
room 332 about 8:30 P.M. He also said that upon the arrival of LASH, MISS THOMP-
SON had her luggage moved into the room occupied by MRS. ROOSEVELT.

Neither MRS. ROOSEVELT nor LASH left their hotel rooms during the entire
day of March 6, 1943 except to have lunch in the Hotel dining room. Other meals
were served in their rooms, according to informant.

Mrs. Roosevelt checked out of the Hotel at 7:35 A.M., March 7, 1943 and
LASH left the hotel a few minutes before that time, according to informant. The
hotel bill for all parties occupying rooms 330 and 332 was paid by MRS. ROOSEVELT.

NOTE:
It is noted that March 6, 1943 was the regular off-duty day for LASH each
week and reference is made to the letter from MRS. ROOSEVELT (Exhibit I) in which
she stated that she would be in Champaign on March 5, 1943

(MEMO "F")

HOWARD ARK
                                        1st Lieut., A.C.

Chanute Field, Illinois
March 9, 1943
201 - Lash, Joseph P.

MEMORANDUM FOR THE OFFICER IN CHARGE:

SUBJECT: JOSEPH P. LASH
ASN 32326519, Sgt.
2nd Weather Squadron
Patterson Field, Ohio
Att. 7th Tech. Sch. Sqdn.

RE :   Results of Mail Cover

This officer reviewed results of Mail cover on Sgt.
JOSEPH P. LASH, ASN 32326519, 2nd Weather Squadron, Chanute
Field, Illinois on March 9, 1943, in connection with an inves-
tigation of Subject, who is suspected of Communistic affiliations.
The review covered the period from March 6, 1943 to March 9,
1943. Subject received the following mail:

DATE	FROM
3/8/43	Pvt. LEWIS FEUER 313th Material Sqdn Morrison Field, Fla.
3/8/43	TWP 8 W. 9th St. New York, N.Y.
3/8/43	ER Blackstone Hotel Chicago, Illinois.
3/9/43	TWP 8 W. 9th St. New York, N.Y.

The letters from Pvt. FEUER (Exhibit I) and TWP (Exhibit
II) received on March 8, 1943, gave further indication that
Subject still has an active interest in leftist movements and
individuals.

Memo_____

Page 1

Chanute Field, Illinois
March 9, 1943
201 — Lash, Joseph P.

TWP (Trude) said that she intended to visit him on
the weekend of March 14, 1943. Her letters of March 9, 1943
consisted only of the 1/23/43 and 1/30/43 copies of the
"New Statesman and Nations" a liberal English paper published
at 10 GT. Turnstile, London, England.

The letter from ER expressed her affection for Subject
and her delight in the weekend spent with him. (Exhibit III)

NOTE:

It is recommended that steps be taken to place Pvt.
FEUER under surveillance. Subject and TRUDE will be kept
under surveillance during their weekend meeting.

HARRY F. WALTERHOUSE
Major, Air Corps

Memo_____

Page 2.

Chanute Field, Illinois
March 14, 1943
201 - LASH, JOSEPH P.

MEMORANDUM FOR THE OFFICER IN CHARGE:

Subject: JOSEPH P. LASH
ASN 32326519, Sgt.
2nd Weather Squadron
Patterson Field, Ohio
Att. 7th Tech. Sch. Sq.
Chanute Field, Illinois

Re   : Results of Mail Cover

This officer reviewed results of mail cover on Sgt. JOSEPH P. LASH,
ASN 32326519, 2nd Weather Squadron, Patterson Field, Ohio, attached to 7th
Technical School Squadron, Chanute Field, Illinois, on March 14, 1943, in
connection with an investigation of Subject, who is suspected of Communistic
affiliations. The review covered the period from March 9, 1943, to March 14,
1943. Subject received the following mail:

Date	From
3-10-43	E R 1600 Pennsylvania Ave. Washington, D.C.
3-10-43	Miss Hildur Coon 204 1/2 W. 13th New York, New York
3-10-43	Molly Yard Washington, D.C.
3-11-43	Cherry Lane Laundry 65 Banow Street New York, New York
3-11-43	Lou Harris, A.S. V-7 USNR 837 John Jay USNR Midshipmen's School New York, N.Y.
3-11-43	Trude W. Pratt 8 West 9th St. New York, New York
3-11-43	E R Apartment 15-A 29 Washington Square West New York, N.Y.

Date	From
3-12-43	E R New York, N.Y.
3-12-43	Mr. & Mrs. J. Delibert 47-12 43rd Ave. L. I. C. Queens, N.Y.
3-12-43	Mary Jersey City, N.J.
3-12-43	Max Lerner 27 Sixth Avenue Brooklyn, N.Y.
3-12-43	T W P 8 West 9th Street New York. N.Y.

The letter from Cherry Lane Laundry was an advertisement. MARY of Jersey City, N.J. appeared to be a casual friend, and Mr. and Mrs. J. DELIBERT are the sister and brother-in-law of Subject, who wrote about family matters. The remainder of the letters appear as exhibits.

NOTE:

It is recommended that LOU HARRIS, V-7, USNR, 837 John Jay, USNR Midshipmen's School, New York, New York, be referred to ONI for investigation and that a background check of TRUDE W. PRATT, 8 West 9th Street, New York, New York be instituted.

HARRY F. WALTERHOUSE
Major, Air Corps

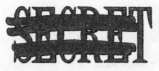

MEMORANDUM FOR THE OFFICER IN CHARGE:

                    SUBJECT: JOSEPH P. LASH
                              ASN 32326519, Sgt.
                              2nd Weather Squadron
                              Patterson Field, Ohio
                              Att. 7th Tech. Sch. Sqdn.
                              Chanute Field, Illinois

                    RE   : Surveillance of Subject

        This officer placed Subject under surveillance on
March 12, 13 and 14, 1943 at the Urbana Lincoln Hotel,
Urbana, Illinois.

        At 7:30 P.M. March 12, 1943, Subject entered room
206 in the Urbana Lincoln Hotel, Urbana, Illinois where he
was met by Mrs. TRUDE W. PRATT who had registered at the
hotel about 5:30 P.M. on the same day. A transcript of the
conversation between Subject and Mrs. PRATT during the time
they spent at the hotel on March 12, 13 and 14, 1943 is
included as Exhibit I.

        Subject and Mrs. PRATT left the hotel room about 9
o'clock on the evening of March 12, 1943. They proceeded
to the telephone booth in the lobby of the Urbana Lincoln
Hotel and placed a phone call to an unknown party. This
officer was unable to observe whether the call was completed
or not. They then had dinner in the Urbana Lincoln Hotel
dining room and walked towards the campus of the University
of Illinois. They returned to the hotel about 11 o'clock in
the evening and retired for the night in room 206. Subject
was registered in room 202 but did not occupy that room
during his stay at the Urbana Lincoln Hotel except for two
brief intervals on the evening of March 12 and March 13,
during which he disarranged the bed clothes.

        Subject and Mrs. PRATT arose about 9 o'clock on the
morning of March 13, 1943, dressed, and proceeded to the
Urbana Lincoln Hotel dining room where they had breakfast.
They returned to room 206 and engaged in conversation until
10:45 at which time they left the Urbana Lincoln Hotel and
walked about the University of Illinois campus.

        During this time this officer entered room 206 and

                        Memo _____

                                            Page 1

Chanute Field, Illinois
March 16, 1943
(201 - LASH, JOSEPH P.)

made an examination of their personal effects, luggage and
a zipper notebook which belonged to Mrs. PRATT. A typewritten
list of names of organizations was found among Mrs. PRATT's
papers, which is included as Exhibit II. There was also a
mimeographed document composed of a constitution of the
World Youth Council established by the International Youth
Conference on November 14, 1942. This document set forth
the aims, purposes and policies of the World Youth Council
and included plans for its organization. This officer
copied a letter on the dresser to Subject from Mrs. ROOSEVELT,
Exhibit III. A copy was also made of a letter from Mrs. PRATT
to Subject and contained in her notebook (Exhibit IV). This
note book contained copies of all the letters which Mrs.
PRATT had written to Subject in the past month.

This officer also inspected the pocket of the notebook which contained about a dozen letters from Subject to
Mrs. PRATT. These letters discussed Subject's life in the
barracks, his school work, and made numerous references to
organizations in which he appeared interested. References
were also made throughout these letters to Mrs. ROOSEVELT
and remarks that she had made concerning progressive movements.

Subject and Mrs. PRATT returned to the room at 2
o'clock in the afternoon, where they remained until 7 o'clock
in the evening. During this time they engaged in conversation.
At 6:30 Mrs. PRATT placed a long distance telephone call to
Mrs. ROOSEVELT at the White House, Washington, D.C.

At 7 o'clock in the evening they left the Urbana
Lincoln Hotel and did not return until 9:30. At this time
they placed a call for Mr. GEORGE WENZEL, c/o Mrs. WILSON,
105 College Avenue, Pullman, Washington. This call was not
completed. Soon after making this call Subject and Mrs. PRATT
retired.

Subject and Mrs. PRATT awakened at 6:10 on the morning
of March 14, 1943, dressed, and checked out of the Urbana
Lincoln Hotel.

Subject and Mrs. PRATT appeared to be greatly endeared
to each other and engaged in sexual intercourse a number of
times during the course of their stay at the Urbana Lincoln
Hotel. A large part of their conversation involved the health
of Mrs. PRATT's children, her marital difficulties, and purely

Chanute Field, Illinois
March 16, 1943
(201 - LASH, JOSEPH P.)

personal conversation between Mrs. PRATT and Subject involving their physical relationship with each other.

HOWARD ARK
1st Lieut., Air Corps

Memo_____

Page 3.

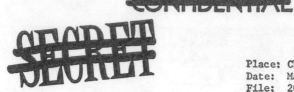

Place: Chanute Field, Illinois
Date: March 16, 1943
File: 201 – LASH, JOSEPH P.

MEMORANDUM FOR THE OFFICER IN CHARGE:

<blockquote>

Subject: JOSEPH P. LASH
ASN 32326519, Sgt.
2nd Weather Sqdn.
Patterson Field, Ohio
Att. 7th Tech. Sch. Sqdn.
Chanute Field, Illinois

Re : Results of Mail Cover

</blockquote>

This officer reviewed results of mail cover on Sgt.
JOSEPH P. LASH, ASN 32326519, 2nd Weather Squadron, Patterson Field,
Ohio, attached, 7th Technical School Squadron, Chanute Field, Illinois,
on March 16, 1943, in connection with an investigation of Subject, who
is usupected of Communistic affiliations. The review covered the period
from March 14, 1943 to March 16, 1943. Subject received the following
mail:

Date	From
3/14/43	Dr. Earl Rugg College Planing Commission Colorado State College Greeley, Colorado
3/14/43	Social Service Auxiliary Fund 416 E. 26th St. New York, N.Y.
3/15/43	E.R. 1600 Pennsylvania Avenue Washington, D.C.
3/15/43	Trude W. Pratt Chicago, Illinois
3/15/43	Chelsea Fireproof Storage Warehouse 426 – 438 W. 26th St. New York, N.Y.
3/16/43	E.R. 1600 Pennsylvania Avenue Washington, D. C.

(MEMO " ")

Chanute Field, Illinois
March 16, 1943
201 - LASH, JOSEPH P.

The letter from Dr. Rugg was a request to Subject in
his former role of Executive Secretary of the I.S.S. for some bulletins,
while the Social Service Auxiliary Fund sought a contribution. Mrs. PRATT
wrote Subject a short love note from Chicago, following a weekend with him
in Urbana, Illinois, and the Chelsea Warehouse sent Subject a bill for $4.63.

Copies were made of the two letters from E. R. and are
attached as Exhibits I and II.

NOTE:

Particular attention is invited to paragraph 3 of
Exhibit I.

HARRY F. WALTERHOUSE
Major, Air Corps

HEADQUARTERS SIXTH SERVICE COMMAND
SERVICES OF SUPPLY   PFB/LP

Office of the Director Intelligence Division
Civic Opera Building
Chicago, Illinois

March 17, 1943

IN REPLY REFER TO:
SPKOM 201 - Lash, Joseph P.
(VI/N 10-383M

Colonel John T. Bissell
Military Intelligence Service
Room 2E658
Pentagon Building
Washington, D. C.

                    RE: Joseph P. Lash, Sgt.
                          ASN 32326519
                          7th Technical School Squadron
                          Chanute Field, Illinois

Dear Colonel Bissell:

        Confirming our telephone conversation of today, I
inclose herewith one copy of each of the reports heretofore received
from Chanute Field.

        Subject was visited during the weekend of March 12-13-14
by Mrs. Trude W. Pratt, 8 West 9th Street, New York City (See Incl.
No. 4). Mrs. Pratt is the estranged wife of Elliott D. Pratt, Director
of Work Camps of the International Student Service of the United States,
1155 16th Street, N.W., Washington, D. C., Republic 3362.

        During the weekend Subject was heard to remark to Mrs.
Pratt that he wished that his commission would "come through" quickly.
Other evidence indicates that Mrs. Roosevelt is trying to secure a
commission in Military Intelligence for Subject.

        General R. E. O'Neil, Commanding Officer, Chanute Field,
is anxious to remove Subject from his Field and would cooperate in any
way to get Subject another assignment.

        Subject is a student in the Weather Forecasters' School
from which he is scheduled to graduate July 2. This School is now
located in Grand Rapids, Michigan, but Subject is on detached service
at Chanute Field. He is subject to transfer at any time to Grand
Rapids.

Colonel John T. Bissell   March 17, 1943

        So far only Intelligence personnel at Chanute Field, this
office, and yourself are advised of this case. I feel that the Asst.
Chief of Staff, G-2, Second District, AAFTTC, St. Louis, Missouri,
should be advised and I will instruct the Intelligence Officer, Chanute
Field so to advise such officer unless you advise me to the contrary
on or before Monday, March 22. The Asst. Chief of Staff, G-2, Second
District, is Lt. Colonel Fred W. Siebert, formerly Intelligence Officer
at Scott Field, Illinois, who it is believed would cooperate to the
fullest extent with this office in any handling of the case.

        As related to you during our phone conversation, it was
the first plan to arrest Subject in Champaign during the weekend of
March 13-14 on a morals charge because sexual intercourse was entered
into between Subject and Mrs. Pratt. However, the final decision was
against this. It is expected that Mrs. Pratt will return for another
visit with Subject the weekend of April 3, at which time it is believed
another opportunity will be presented to arrest Subject on a morals
charge. If the meeting of April 3 between Subject and Mrs. Pratt occurs
in Chicago as is believed likely, such arrest could be made by the
Chicago Police at the behest of this office with no complications whatever and in such a manner that there would be no publicity and that
this office would at all times be in control of the situation. Arrest
on such a morals charge would provide something concrete upon which to
base disciplinary action or a transfer of Subject by authorities in
Washington. Also, it might be thought advisable to give the arrest
sufficient publicity that E. R. would not care to intervene in the
matter.

                              Sincerely yours,

                              P. F. BOYER
                              Lt. Colonel, M.I.

5 Incls.
   #1 - Report of March 6, Review of Service Record
   #2 -   "   " March 9, Results of Mail Cover
   #3 -   "   " March 14, Results of Mail Cover
   #4 -   "   " March 16, Surveillance of Subject
   #5 -   "   " March 16, Results of Mail Cover

P. S. In reading over the above letter, I find that it is mostly filled
with comment on the illicit liaison between Subject and Trude W. Pratt.
Actually this is only a detail of the case but I have dealt with it
because it presents the most immediate chance to grapple with the Subject.

Colonel John T. Bissell   March 17, 1943

The inferences which can be drawn from the evidence of these five
enclosures are staggering. They indicate a gigantic conspiracy participated in by not only Subject and Trude Pratt but also by E. R.,
Wallace, Morgenthau, etc. Your attention is particularly invited to
the fact that Trude Pratt is the United States Representative and
Executive Secretary of the International Student Assembly, 8 West
40th Street, New York City, and is also General Secretary of the
International Student Service of the United States.

                                                    P. F. B.

The document reproduced here, as has been said, has been in the files of G-2 and the confidential files of the Director of the FBI. There it has acquired an almost gospel-like appearance of being the truth. Like the "Protocols of Zion," however, it says more about the men in G-2 and the FBI who have nursed it along than it does about the President and Mrs. Roosevelt and the former's alleged effort to dismember the Counterintelligence Corps.

In one of the FBI documents (January 18, 1951) written by special agents Ladd and Nichols, they stated: "With reference to the Mrs. Roosevelt incident we of course never investigated this. It was investigated by the CIC (CounterIntelligence Corps) prior to 1943. We do have a photostat of the G-2 file." The FBI did not, however, have the alleged tape of Mrs. Roosevelt's meeting with me at the Blackstone Hotel, although it was that tape, according to agent Burton's December 31, 1943, memorandum to Mr. Ladd that caused the President to summon Mrs. Roosevelt to the Oval Room and resulted in his order to General Arnold to have Lash on his way to a "combat post within 10 hours." "There were no recordings in the Bureau file between Mrs. Roosevelt and Lash," said Ladd and Nichols, and added, "Obviously they did have a microphone because there were recordings of conversations between Lash and Mrs. Trude W. Pratt which also reflected what transpired in the hotel room. . . ."

Mrs. Roosevelt's room was bugged. But what the recording showed, what things were said and done, that caused CIC to label them an "affair" the FBI did not know because it did not have the recording. The "Director" and his associates nevertheless considered it as true that Mrs. Roosevelt and I had been "intimate."

The letters exchanged between Mrs. Roosevelt, Trude Pratt, and me, which have been reproduced in this book show the true nature of our relationship. After I had gotten back to Chanute Field from Chicago—in other words from the reunion that had been bugged—I wrote to Eleanor: "I'm sorry I was such a drowsy soul after dinner, but it was nicer drowsing in the darkness with you stroking my forehead, than playing gin rummy. . . ." (March 1943) Was this the action, I have wondered, that led CIC to conclude that there was an affair? Who knows? CIC has not produced the tape.

It is quite possible that the CIC's investigation of the alleged misconduct of the First Lady, which it had no business to undertake without express authority from the President, and that was so mistaken in its reading of what was taking place, angered the President. After Mrs. Roosevelt had protested to Harry Hopkins and General Marshall about the bugging at the Blackstone, which the hotel people had told her about, she wrote to me: "Your love affairs are of no interest. . . . I think you may be carefree for a time!" Presumably she had learned of the Chanute colonel's readiness to arrest "Subject on a morals charge" when Trude saw me again. She would have been even more indignant, and amused, to be charged herself with what the FBI later came to call her "intimacy" with me.

What Agent Burton was told about the episode in the Oval Room does not ring true. Both Mrs. Roosevelt and the President were almost Victorian in their sense of privacy about the sexual relationship. Even after their children were grown, he never, and she rarely, and then only with Anna, spoke about the marital conflicts and problems between her and F.D.R., especially the Lucy Mercer affair. That they would have engaged in a marital "spat" in front of White House associates and CIC officials strains belief.

However, both the President and Mrs. Roosevelt would probably have considered the episode devastating proof of the CIC's incompetence and primitivism. It is believable that the President ordered measures against those responsible. But further proof of Mrs. Roosevelt's reserve in speaking about her private affairs with the President was that she was silent on the subject of the alleged "confrontation" in Franklin's office when she saw me in San Francisco just before my embarkation to the South Pacific.

Whatever sanctions the President ordered against the CIC, such as the alleged denial of a general's rank to the CIC colonel in charge, or the alleged destruction of CIC's files on subversives, they would scarcely have justified the appellation of "hit list" as is suggested by the so-called order that anybody connected with the case should be sent to the South Pacific "for action against the Japs until they were killed." F.D.R. was not a King David ordering death in battle for an inconvenient man. He was an astute and tough politician and also a God-fearing man. I cannot say I was among his friends. At best he tolerated me, as he did several others who were friends of his wife. But he genuinely liked Trude and was kind to me, as will become clear as this narrative continues.

I have tried to figure out what happened on the basis of the few things that Eleanor did tell me. All the top men who were involved in this affair—the President, Hopkins, Marshall—were preoccupied with decisions that carried the fate of nations and millions of soldiers. They would understandably be impatient with G-2 and its obsession with Eleanor Roosevelt and myself. They may well have decided that, in addition to shaking up G-2, the most expeditious way of getting rid of the Lash problem was to ship me overseas along with a group of fellow student forecasters so it would not seem that I had been singled out for this sanction.

A final comment: the dates remain puzzling. The order to leave immediately for overseas duty reached Grand Rapids on April 21. Neither the President nor Eleanor was in Washington. In fact the President had left Washington on April 13, two days after Mrs. Roosevelt had protested to Hopkins about the Blackstone bugging. When did the "confrontation" occur? When did the President summon General Arnold at 5 A.M., as the document alleges, and order him to have me out of the country and in combat within ten hours?

December 31, 1943

MEMORANDUM FOR MR. LADD

Re: DISMEMBERMENT OF COUNTERINTELLIGENCE
CORPS, G-2

It has been apparent to the writer for several months that certain powerful interests within or near the War Department have undertaken an active program aimed at the dismemberment of the Counterintelligence Corps of G-2. It is now the writer's belief that this opinion is justified because of certain information which has come to my attention and which is set out below.

Recently at a G-2 social function the writer had a long discussion with Colonel Kibler who is Officer in Charge of the Counter-Intelligence Corps. This discussion was of a very frank nature since the writer has become very friendly personally with Colonel Kibler. The Colonel stated quite frankly that the reason Counterintelligence Corps has been wrecked was that Harry Hopkins and the Secret Service has ordered it to be so wrecked. Colonel Kibler stated that through some unknown means Harry Hopkins learned that the Counterintelligence Corps was investigating Joseph Lash, former Young Communist leader who is now in the Army and that in this investigation they had run upon Mrs. Roosevelt who had come to Chicago apparently for the purpose of meeting Lash. Colonel Kibler stated that he did not know exactly how Hopkins found out about this but believed it was through some indiscretion of Colonel Furbershaw who is the Director of Intelligence, Sixth Service Command, stationed in Chicago.

Colonel John Bissell has recently been in Washington on leave and the writer spent an evening with him at his home. During the course of the evening Colonel Bissell exhibited a deep bitterness about the way he had been treated in the Army and after a period of time advised the writer of the reason why he had been so treated. He stated that he had learned that he had been recommended for a promotion to Brigadier General on several occasions and on each occasion this recommendation had been stopped in the office of Lieutenant General McNarney, Deputy Chief of Staff.

Recently while Bissell was in Washington he made some calls at the War Department and learned that he had been blackballed by the White House. He also learned that because of his record it was quite possible that at the present time, if he had not been blackballed, he would be a Major General. He also had a long discussion with Colonel Forney who succeeded Bissell as Chief, Counterintelligence Group, G-2. Forney advised Bissell that the reason he had been blackballed and the reason that he would never advance any further in the Army and would probably never be sent out of the country with troops was because he had been connected with the Joe Lash-Eleanor Roosevelt investigation in Chicago.

GCB:FIL

Forney stated to Bissell that the facts of this investigation had been disclosed to the White House through some unknown means and that shortly after Bissell left, a call was received by General Strong and Colonel Forney to proceed to the White House with the complete records of this matter at approximately 10:00 p.m. at night. When they reached the White House they were received by the President, General Watson and Harry Hopkins and were ordered to produce the entire records in this case. Colonel Forney stated to Colonel Bissell that this was extremely embarrassing in as much as the material contained a recording of the entire proceedings between Lash and Mrs. Roosevelt which had been obtained through a microphone which had been planted in the hotel room. This recording indicated quite clearly that Mrs. Roosevelt and Lash engaged in sexual intercourse during their stay in the hotel room. Forney advised Bissell that after this record was played Mrs. Roosevelt was called into the conference and was confronted with the information and this resulted in a terrific fight between the President and Mrs. Roosevelt. At approximately 5:00 a.m. the next morning the President called for General Arnold, Chief of the Army Air Corps, and upon his arrival at the conference ordered him to have Lash outside the United States and on his way to a combat post within ten hours.

After the conference was over it was learned that the President had ordered that anybody who knew anything about this case should be immediately relieved of his duties and sent to the South Pacific for action against the Japs until they were killed. Forney advised Bissell that everyone who is known to have any knowledge at all of this matter is on the permanent blacklist at the White House. Bissell stated that the only thing that kept these men from being sent to the South Pacific was that it was learned that there were too many of them to be treated in this manner. Colonel Bissell stated that the only reason that more was not done to him was that General Watson apparently came to his defense and assured the President that Bissell would not talk about this matter indiscriminately.

Respectfully,

G. C. Burton

XXIII

Shipped Overseas

FOR MILLIONS of American GIs to be shipped overseas meant loneliness, sacrifice, often danger, careers and being with families postponed. But they faced and accepted the prospect of overseas duty as part of the obligations of citizenship, for the war had to be fought. In my case it was difficult to restrain bitterness because I was sent overseas almost as a form of exile. And to Eleanor, who had looked forward to being present at a summer wedding of Joe and Trude, after the latter had her divorce and I had finished forecasting school, there was the painful conviction that it was her friendship that had brought these difficulties upon them.

On Wednesday, April 21, the day that I was ordered overseas, she was with the President at the Corpus Christi Naval Training Center. He had left Washington on April 13 on a trip that took him to war plants and training camps, and had joined up with Eleanor the day before at Monterrey for the meeting with the Camachos. I wrote to her from Grand Rapids:

Today at one o'clock ten of us were called out of class to see the Post Adjutant. He told us phoned orders had come from Washington for us to leave immediately for foreign service. We do not know in what capacity or for what purpose. We all have good grades, but not the highest grades in the class, and we cannot figure out any other common denominator.

I do not think we are going as forecasters because we still are relatively untrained, and a forecasting class has just graduated from which ten men could have been selected. It may be some type of special research.

Originally we were supposed to leave on the weekend. I called Trude immediately and she took the next train and is on the way out. But now the shipping date has been moved up and we leave tomorrow—I pray, not until I have seen Trude.

It was quite a shock. I had been banking so much on the summer and our getting married but such are the fortunes of war. I wish now more than ever I had seen you last weekend. Will you take care of Trude? I hope she will go ahead with her plans so that if I get back in the summer we can get married. And if you have a chance will you look in on my mother? I don't think I will write her until I know where I am stationed. If I write without stating where I am going, she will certainly conclude that I have been assigned the personal one-man task of bombing Tokyo.

I will not say goodbye—just my deepest love and hope that we will see one another before long, and that I have done a good job in the interim.

Two days later, April 23, Trude sent Eleanor a telegram and letter. The former she addressed to Tommy:

TRIED CALL LAST NIGHT FROM CHICAGO JOE ENROUTE TO CALIFORNIA IF POSSIBLE WILL PHONE LOS ANGELES SUNDAY AM WRITING LOS ANGELES LOVE

She wrote later that day from New York:

Dearest Mrs. R.,

This afternoon I sent a telegram from the train (in Tommy's name) only to find when I got to my list here, that you expect to be in Phoenix today and not in Tucson where I had sent my wire. So just now I wired to Deming, hoping somehow to reach you before Sunday.

The last two days were like a bad dream—and I'm still not very conscious. Wednesday afternoon Joe called, saying he and 9 others were to ship to California immediately and from there to points unknown—so I took the train 2 hours later—not knowing whether I would find Joe at Grand Rapids or not. When I got there at 11 o'cl. a.m.—yesterday (it was only yesterday) Joe expected me with his gas mask thing over his shoulder, looking very white. 10 minutes later he had to leave for Chicago—I went along—with him and the other boys—and then he and I had a little over three hours in Chicago—and at 8:15 he had to be at the station ready to leave. After several hours trying I found a space on the 11:30 out of Chicago and got back here at 8 o'cl. tonight.

About 6 o'cl. yesterday afternoon we tried to call you at Fort Worth, but Ruth said you had left,—so I do hope you will get my wire and perhaps phone or get this letter before Sunday. Joe will be at Hamilton Field near S. Francisco (he is *not* allowed to tell anyone) and if he can he will call you Sunday. He does not know when and for where they will leave. He does not know why he and 9 others were yanked out of class in the middle of the course. The orders came from Washington, that's all he knows.

I don't feel very much right now. I guess I'm still tired from trying to hold up yesterday. But we did—and I know he'll have to come back to me. Much love to you. My love to Tommy.

Somehow during the intense hours we were together Trude managed to scrawl a farewell note for me to read after we said goodbye in Chicago, of which, unfortunately, only the second page has survived:

My friend Elsa Brandstromm [had] her first when she was 44! I shall try to stay young! Live healthily, not smoke too much—exercise, write me that you aren't afraid of that. It's all so silly to write things like this —I'm just looking for comfort. It would have been so right to have a child. So now I'll pray that you may come back soon—that all you'll have to live through during the next months will be made easier by the knowledge that I am waiting for you—that your home is waiting for you . . .

T.

"Enroute to Coast," I wrote to her Friday morning:

I bought the seven fellows I'm with a drink 'from my gal,' and they send their thanks. There was a man with an accordion and soon the whole lounge was singing. We were mostly soldiers and sailors, and a few civilians. It was quite nice but a few times my heart played tricks on me—when he played 'The White Cliffs of Dover,' 'Don't Sit under the Old Apple Tree' and 'I Left My Heart.' We taught the whole car, including the accordionist, the new Air Force song 'I've Got Sixpence,' but my usual gusto when I came to the line 'no pretty little girls to deceive me,' was lacking.

I went to bed at 11:30 with a heart full of love. I didn't sleep so well because of the train's bumpiness, but when I woke up this morning my heart was still full of you and it will always be thus.

I wrote to Eleanor the same day:

By now you will have heard from Trude concerning our adventures meeting each other and the few wonderful hours we had together. We tried to reach you from Chicago, but you already had left Fort Worth. I'm banking on being able to talk with you on the phone when I get to the coast, but I've learned to take nothing for granted in the last 48 hours, and I may very well not be able to call.

I still know no more than when I wrote you on Wednesday. Perhaps we will be given some idea of our assignment when we reach the coast. Trude was grand . . .

One of my wishes has been that the three of us could be together for a little while. Now that too will have to wait. Only I do want to talk with you at least once before I go. . . . The attached letters are for my Hyde Park collection.

The next day, Saturday, the train went through Utah and Nevada. I spent much of the day reading Mark Aldanov's *The Fifth Seal*, "which I didn't like at all. It's an old man's book written about old men." I preferred Arthur Koestler on the disintegration of integrity among Russian revolutionaries:

> The Communists are stupid to have raised a row about this book, for it is a mediocre one.
>
> We are of course still completely in the dark concerning the nature of our mission, but one fact did seem to have relevance which had not occurred to us before. Four out of the ten are married men. It would seem unlikely that there would be such a large percentage of married men in a mission that was specially hazardous or for the duration . . .
>
> We are going through the Siskyous right now. They are quite impressive, and just another place I've recorded for us to see together . . . the only thing that matters is to do this job as creditably as possible and get back.

I reached San Francisco and Hamilton Field that weekend. Eleanor was in Los Angeles. She had inspected the Corona and Long Beach military hospitals when Trude reached her on the phone and told her that I was at, or about to get to, Fort Hamilton, and would try to call her when she arrived in San Francisco the next day. She immediately sent me a telegram:

> I WILL BE AT THE ST FRANCIS HOTEL SAN FRANCISCO AND DO HOPE YOU CAN COME TO SEE ME THERE TOMORROW TUESDAY AFTERNOON SHALL LOOK FORWARD TO SEEING YOU.

This time she signed it "Mrs. Franklin D. Roosevelt" instead of the usual "E.R." She suspected that the signature might galvanize officers who otherwise would be inclined to restrict me to the field. And, in fact, I was writing to Trude that, having finished my "processing," which included shots, financial arrangements, and clothing issue, "I went in to find out about passes off the field, and discovered none were to be issued which means we go out pretty fast." But before the letter was ended I had Eleanor's wire and talked with her on the phone: "Mrs. Roosevelt said she would come to the Field if I couldn't get off. The Post authorities were very decent. They knew there'd be no privacy here, so they said I could have a pass to go to Frisco tomorrow afternoon." She reserved a room for me at the St. Francis Hotel and made a reservation at Mardikian's Armenian restaurant. After we had embraced and begun talking, I learned how she had gone to Harry Hopkins and General Marshall and insisted that she was not going to be trailed by Army Counterintelligence. She had assumed, as she wrote to me, that I could feel carefree. Talking at a steady pace, as we usually did, we proceeded to Mardikian's. The two of us sent Trude a night letter:

JOE FEELING RESULTS OF SHOTS (BUT ABLE TO EAT ENORMOUS SHASLIK—
J.) PHILOSOPHICAL (E.R.) BUT AS CHEERFUL ONE CAN BE IN THE CIRCUM-
STANCES (J) WE HOPE WE SHALL ALL MEET HERE ON HIS RETURN AND
DINE AT WONDERFUL ARMENIAN PLACE. WE MISS YOU AND LOVE YOU
(SPECIAL BRAND FROM ME (J.)

Trude telegraphed Mrs. Roosevelt: "WIRE ABOUT HIS HEALTH AND
MOOD WOULD HELP MUCH LOVE."

The next morning I sent Trude a final letter on hotel letterhead. It
was a little prolix but reflected my mood and indicated how Eleanor
and I had reconciled ourselves to the way I was being shipped out:

A little while ago I woke up and as I did I felt as if you were beside me
sleeping peacefully and your face looked calm and lovely—so much so! I
think the illusion came because in the last few months I have not slept
between sheets except when you were in town. At least that is what the
teaser in me says. But I know it was really my great longing and love
for you.

It looks now as if I will be gone by Friday . . . I know now, that
even if my shipping is a political act, that I am still glad to go—that the
war against the Nazis and fascists has to be won.

I do not know anything about the Russo-Polish affair. I certainly
would not accuse the Soviet Govt. on the basis of a German com-
muniqué, but I do know that in my heart of hearts I feel the Soviet
Government is perfectly capable of executing 10,000 Poles, and accusing the Nazis of doing it, as they executed Alter & Ehrlich and called
them Nazis, as they executed thousands of their own people and be-
smirched them with the name Nazi or Jap agent . . .

As Mrs. R. said last night there are many wars going on, and they
will continue even after the war is over. They are wars that may not be
fought with tanks and planes, but they are wars nonetheless, and he es-
capes them least who is straight with his own conscience. How many
people have been driven into cynicism and despair and conservatism
because of that?

We cannot entrust our consciences to any party or power organization. But that does not mean we should lose or bury our sense of justice. That does not mean keeping clear of movements which are after
all the basis of effective political action; it does mean that once again
some of us are learning that we cannot and must not escape responsibility for our own souls.

The war against the fascists has to be won. That remains point #1
on the agenda of advancing mankind. . . .

So I go in peace, knowing that this is the dictate of duty and conscience, and knowing too that both of us will do our part, and will do
it better because we are working as comrades.

I do not know, dearest, whether I will be able to write again or at length. I want to say now that I have loved you and do love as much as it is possible for a human being to love. And I am filled with your love for me.

. . . .

And now I must stop and take a bath and see if I can rustle up a shave somewhere in this hotel. I have to be at the Field at ten a.m.

Eleanor took me to the field and afterwards wrote:

I drove back & it was hard to see the landscape. The hard part of loving is that one has to learn so often to let go of those we love, so they can do things, so they can grow, so they can return to us with an even richer, deeper love. Believe me, dear, I need you so much that you are a part of every waking hour & I waken with you & the boys in my first thoughts.

I'll see your Mother, & I'll try to make Trude love me so I can help her till you are back to make her happy. In every way I can I'll work & help Trude, when I can, to work for the things I believe you would want us to work for.

I know how you must feel but I also know, that you will do a good job & I still believe that right triumphs in the end. All that I have is yours always, my love, devotion & complete trust follow you always. My arms will be waiting to be round you again. God bless you & keep you.

I had given her the names of the other men I was with and their "next of kin"—wives, mothers, or sweethearts, and to each she wrote:

San Francisco, Calif.
April 28, 1943

My dear

Sergeant Lash who is in the same group as your young man, came into San Francisco to spend last night with us, as I happened to be here on my way back to Washington.

He asked me to write you because he knew what a shock the sudden change in plans for all of them must be, and he wanted me to tell you that all is well with them so far. They do not know when they are actually going, but they are flying, and I think I can tell you from long experience, that their first stop will be Hawaii.

I wish your young man the best of luck and a safe return to you, and may all go well with you while he is gone.

Very cordially yours,

XXIV

The Long Way Home

IN RETROSPECT, my being shipped off nine thousand miles into the "wild blue yonder"—to use the Air Corps expression—was to use Joe Heller's later phrase, "Catch 22" with a vengeance. Eleanor was told that I was on a "secret mission"; therefore, she could not be given my address. And in New Caledonia, where our little group of would-be forecasters was finally dumped, no one knew or cared about our arrival.

Eleanor, after bidding me goodbye at Hamilton Field and a quick visit with Johnny and Anne, returned to Washington. Although as yet she had no address, she promptly began a letter to me. "Joe dearest," she wrote from the White House, and dated the letter "Thursday night, April 29th":

> I watched you through the back of the car until I could see no more for the tears & I think I shall never forget how your back looked. To think it was yesterday & tonight I am here & you are I hope in Hawaii. I hope you were not as tired as I was. Somehow all my strength was gone with you & the effort to behave as usual the rest of the day was so great that I closed my eyes & leaned back in my seat in the plane at 8:30 and never moved until we were nearly in Chicago.
>
> I called Trude & she tried to be cheerful but I knew from her voice she felt as I did. I'll get to her Sat. a.m. & we'll lunch & spend most of the afternoon together. I'm trying to find out tomorrow how we can cable so we can do it Sat. noon. I'm also going to try to find out your ultimate destination & address. . . .
>
> . . . .

Your little Spanish boy is right in front of me on my desk, in front of your photograph too, & he's going to have to put lots of his spirit in me!

I'm weary tonight so goodnight dear one. I love you & miss you & shall live for the day when you are with us again.

The "Catch 22" runaround had begun. The next day she wrote to me sadly:

The War Department told me today you were on a secret mission & they could not tell me your destination for a few days & they asked me not to cable or radio till then so I fear you will be disappointed but you will know we can't do anything & we will as soon as we can. Trude will be sad when I tell her tomorrow. . . .

She went with John Golden to his play in Washington:

. . . funny, but nothing much & I couldn't be interested. That may not be the play's fault for I'm afraid my thoughts are with you & much of my heart is somewhere in your vicinity. I wish I knew where you were & what you are doing. I can say so little & yet I must write because that seems the only way of reaching out to you. I hope you don't mind, you'll know it only means I miss you & love you with all my heart.

The next day, Saturday, she saw Trude in New York:

Trude & I both cried a little this morning & we talked hard through lunch & up to 4 o'clock mostly about you & Trude & plans which must be uncertain but it is good to feel that you or rather we are thinking of possibilities. This separation has gone very deep with Trude. A light has gone out of her face & only you can bring it back, so pray God you won't be gone too long. She is being sensible though & doing as the doctor told her to do. I think we'll be very close Joe & it does help me so I hope it helps her. I miss you very much & was so glad when Trude told me she had a cable. [I had sent it en route.] It carried no date or identification but I was glad you were able to send it. Just as soon as Col. Hammond tells me it is possible we will cable you. . . .

Harry Hooker had accompanied the President on the inspection trip that included the stop in Monterrey, he took Eleanor and Trude to the theater, and after they had dropped Trude

I told him she was going out to get her divorce & wld have married you had you been here & was going to as soon as possible & he was surprisingly sympathetic & said anything he could do to help I was to let him know.

A last paragraph in this letter, which as yet had no address, dealt with the racial situation. More than within anyone else high in the

Government her strong spirit rebelled and pushed against the Jim Crow hypocrisies and institutions built into American life:

> A man, young, called Frank Taylor came to see me this p.m. after I got back from a doleful half hour with Cousin Susie. His firm is getting a 'Life & Times' of Alexander Woollcott written & they are also publishing a first novel by the Southern woman who did 'South Today.'* He says the book is fine & she shows up the economic & race situation which will be fine from a Southerner tho' I fear she will be hated even more than I am. I must read the World Telegram & go to bed. I love you dearly, dearly.

Like Eleanor, Trude was writing into the void: "Are you under palms? or in a jungle or near a beach . . . or pretty south-sea maidens . . . don't go too close!!" But the important news she had to report was that a friend, Roger Baldwin, and his wife, Evelyn Preston, had steered her to a house on West Eleventh Street in New York City that would soon be for rent. She hastened to look it over and pending Mrs. Roosevelt's reaction, decided the children and I would like it. She would send me pictures as soon as she had taken Mrs. Roosevelt to see it.

Eleanor saw Trude again on Sunday:

> Trude & all three children spent over an hour with us yesterday. Then I finally had James' two little girls alone for a half hour & then Betsy joined us for lunch & Mrs. Mortimer, Fjr. & Ethel came on here later & so lunch dragged out a bit! He brought a very interesting letter he'd been writing on the trip & then felt he couldn't mail because of the censor. He spent most of one night talking with Vincent Sheehan in N.Y.: & his conclusions on our political policy are still that it is bad. He's seen a lot of the French Navy people & says the Captain of the 'Jean Bart' frankly says he has no use for "la democracie" & prefers a king. The gunnery officer on the French destroyer which F's firing sank lost an arm & two fingers on the other hand but said he didn't mind, he liked to fight & didn't mind against whom he fought—a nice professional militarist attitude, isn't it? Fjr. said it didn't make him feel any better when he looked at him & realized he was responsible for his injuries. They are having fairly hectic trips & Fjr. is now executive officer. They should be out again soon. . . .
>
> I liked F's speech† & even tho' [John L.] Lewis announced the strike was off, still the speech was good, calm & simple. Jimmy Wechsler wrote a severe but excellent editorial on John Lewis in P.M. & it must have been hard for him to do. Mr. Baruch told me . . . of Jim Carey & thought he was a young man who would make his mark. It appears that in an argument, Jim said 'Mr. Baruch, you've taught me a great

---

* Lillian Smith.

† Fireside chat on the "Federal Seizure of the Coal Mines," May 2, 1943: "There can be no one among us—no one faction—powerful enough to interrupt the forward march of our people to victory."

deal & now I'm going to use it all against you' & the old man loved it! This Polish-Russian business is unfortunate* but I've not had a chance to talk with F. about it.

Mme. Chiang arrived this a.m. & has lost weight & looks ill. She is now talking to FDR. The Evatts (of Australia) were here & begged me to come to Australia. If I go, I'll see you, & Trude will have to be one of my secretaries! . . .

"I am still trying to find out where you are," she wrote to me on Wednesday, "as I hate to go to your Mother without definite information & Trude & I will feel better when we know where you are." She had more general news:

I am curious to see if John Lewis will now appear before the W.L.B. [War Labor Board] & if he will accept their decision. The Polish-Russian rift is off the front page but nothing has been done to heal it. . . .

The week passed and still she sought vainly to get the War Department to give her an address for me:

As the days go by & I can get no news of you I get more & more impatient. They insist it would endanger you to cable & they will let me know the minute they can but even though I thought waiting to know about the kids had taught me my lesson this seems much worse. I just want to feel, for Trude's sake as well as my own, that within twenty-four hours we've heard from each other. I got here last evening & Elinor Morgenthau came up & spent the night as she has to go to a doctor today & decide on whether to have an operation or not. . . .

At 2:30 they left & Trude & I went to see your home. It is sweet & you two can make it enchanting. We planned the rooms even including the baby which must come apparently as soon as possible. Then we went to see your mother & found her in the store. They have not been able to find a buyer yet. She was upset & found it hard to take in at first but at last she understood & I promised her if I knew anything I would let her know. She told me your sister & the baby were with her & both very well.

Trude left to take the children to the train & I came home to Mme. Chiang who arrived with a nurse & 2 secret service men!—Earl came in soon with some guests since his birthday is next Sunday & I had said he could ask people for cocktails today & at last Trude came & we had a very nice time. I am sure Mme. Chiang asked to come because she wanted to see how we lived but I think she found it pleasant. . . .

FDR thinks John Lewis intends to call a strike at the end of 2 weeks & wearily he said on the phone this morning that if people would stop fighting each other at home the war would go faster. The war news

---

* Several thousand Polish officers had been executed, presumably by the Russians, who had taken them prisoners in the partition of Poland before the Nazi invasion of Russia.

however is encouraging & the fall of Bizerte & Tunis simultaneously was good. I pray we can push on for I feel it means a speedier end.

I worry so about where you are & what you are doing & if prayers can bring you safely & speedily back to us, mine are going up very constantly. You are so needed here by the young people & by one old lady at least! . . .

Another weekend and

Still no word out of the War Dept. & Trude needs to know & yet I can do nothing. She says she wakes imagining all kinds of things & she missed you so much that she would smile at you no matter how much you wanted to quarrel with her! She & Anna found many experiences in common & I hope a friendship may grow there. It will help them both. I can help both if they will tell me their troubles, but they are nearer of an age. They feel they can understand each other better I am sure, so I hope some real relationship will develop between them. John is ready to leave from tomorrow on. . . .

We have the P.M. [Prime Minister] of G.B. [Great Britain] & the usual number arriving tomorrow & they will be here sometime Wed. for the night. Benes* is coming so the house is full to overflowing.

Dinner tonight was a funny mixture. Morris Ernst & Viola Ilma & her new husband were contrast enough but when the Robert Woods Bliss' & Mrs. William Phillips & the Adolph Millers & the Nelson Rockefellers were added it was almost too good! Trude will have told you about it so I will not elaborate. . . .

I had a bad report on the Honan famine. It is appalling reading & does not reflect great concern on the part of the central government. The V.P. came in late today very pleased with his trip but disturbed over developments in his former department. He felt great weakness there at the top & asked me to arrange for the Big Boss to see certain people which I am doing.

Finally she heard:

There was great excitement yesterday morning when Tommy gave me the enclosed message from Colonel Hammond in the Map Room. I had just come in from a long morning spent at the Naval Hospital being checked over for all the ills of old age. I called Trude in her room upstairs & we started searching my map for Noumea. It isn't so far from where James was but we couldn't decide how far from New Zealand & Australia so after we wrote you a message according to directions Trude took it down & asked the distances. I also asked if you could send a message back & what your permanent A.P.O. was. The answer came that your C.O. had been asked to allow you to radio a reply & that the temporary A.P.O. still was to be used. So we live in hope of some word soon. Just the hope has given a new sound to Trude's voice.

* Eduard Beneš, President of Czechoslovakia.

She left at 2 yesterday so as soon as I could this morning I called her to
tell her we might hope for a return message & her whole voice seemed
to come alive!

Mr. Churchill arrived at seven last night & F says it is going to be
toughest of all the conferences. I imagine command of the various undertakings brings difficult & delicate adjustments! Benes is at the W.H.
for the night also & fortunately Anna can give them tea. Dinner is a
stag affair so my absence doesn't matter. . . .

She spent hours talking with Trude and visiting possible houses that
the latter might rent after her divorce:

I feel so sorry for Anna & Trude & so many others these days that I
have no time left to think how I feel but I know since you left much
of my happiness went with you too. I miss your letters for there are
often such fundamental disagreements with the other boys that I dare
not write what I think. Only with you & Anna & Trude do I feel sure
there is no need to be discreet!

The papers are full of rumors as to the discussions now going on in
Washington but no one will know what really happens for some time.
The one encouraging thing is the news that the Germans surrender so
cheerfully [in North Africa]. They drive themselves up to the wire enclosures. I only hope it presages a similar spirit in Europe.

At last on May 15 a letter I had written from the air base at Tontouta, New Caledonia, reached her. "It was as if the whole world
changed this morning when you read Joe's letter to me," Trude immediately wrote to Eleanor. "What a nice colorful picture Joe created in
his letter—don't you think? Swimming—a tropical island—coalblack na-
tives with red hair."

My letter, written May 2, hardly suggested a "secret mission." My
group had been flown in a Navy Consolidated bomber from Hamilton
Field to the South Pacific. There we were, in effect, dumped at the
Tontouta airfield. So little were we expected that we were quartered in
open tents at a casual camp. As my first letters to Eleanor and Trude explained, no one seemed to know why we were there, and when we
finally were able to communicate with the weather detachment at Tontouta and a weapons carrier was sent to pick us up, the officers were as
mystified by our arrival as we were ourselves, and the enlisted men in
the detachment, who immediately saw us as competitors for the ratings
of staff and technical sergeant, which were strictly prorated, resented
our presence. Even the discomfort of losing our barracks bags, which
had not been on the plane when we were deposited in Tontouta and
never were retrieved—I later suspected they had been purloined by
G-2—did not diminish the pleasure of being on land again:

I am in very good health and just now am in fine spirits having had an
invigorating swim in a stream with a current so swift that no sooner

did you step in it than you were carried several yards and then had to battle your way to shore. I shaved and bathed there for the first time in three days.

The area's weather officer came out to visit us: "He was under the impression that we might be routine replacements, and thought of some beautifully isolated islands where we might be used." As it sank home that I was going to be there a long time, I sent Trude a poem:

Outpost

Become, like the crags that surround you
Indifferent to memory and pain
Shouldering in whose vast reaches
Time and the passage of storms.
Distance that reconciles these peaks
Now alone binds me to you.

To Eleanor I wrote:

Here I sit on the outside of a tent, formerly inhabited by six marines, and the sun has just come over the hills, and the cold night is rapidly receding in my memory so I feel fine.

Yesterday the Weather Officer fetched us out of the Casual Camp and now we are officially part of the 17 Weather Squadron which covers the [blanked out by censor] except for Australia. We will spend about a month here getting the hang of weather codes, plotting and analysis in the southern hemisphere and then we will be assigned to different parts of the region. Our status is that of student forecasters and we will be qualified after three months. In a way the present setup is a good one for we are getting practical knowledge that the men at Grand Rapids will have to acquire after they finish in July, and we have the feeling of doing our job that comes with overseas service. No one understands, however, why they took us out of school because we are routine replacements, and I think the Squadron would have preferred qualified men.

My first letters, apart from underlining the fact that we were "routine replacements," and scarcely the "secret mission" that the War Department insisted to Mrs. Roosevelt that I was on, spoke of New Caledonian mountains and my amazement at the coal-black "Kanakas" with their kinky, bushy coiffures, which they had dyed red, and the lithe, graceful Tonkinese whom the French colonial regime had imported to work New Caledonia's mines. Beyond such wonders there were the mosquitoes:

All of us who came over together are in a tent. We each have a canvas cot and four blankets. Until yesterday we had only two and so slept in our clothes. Each cot is encased in a rectangular netting called a

mosquito bar. Although the worst is over so far as mosquitos are concerned they are still numerous and plaguey enough to require the use
of the bars, in fact we spend off-duty hours sitting bow-legged on our
cots under our bars carrying on desultory talk, reading, writing letters.
Careful as one may be in keeping out mosquitos when we are climbing in and out of the bar, they will find their way in. . . .

Thus began the series of letters that each of us carefully numbered
and that none of us knew would stretch over a year and a half. I knew
that at my end my letters were being censored by the military, and
Eleanor and Trude wrote theirs on the assumption that they were being
opened and copied. But in mid-May there was the joy of reestablishing
communication. My first letter had reached Eleanor. The next day a
message clattered over the weather station's teletype machine:

> 160005Z CONFIDENTIAL ROUTINE GR 51
> 18 MAY '43
>
> TO COMMANDING OFFICER TONTOUTA
> FOLLOWING MESSAGE FOR TRANSMITTAL TO SGT LASH THREE TWO THREE
> TWO SIX FIVE ONE NINE BASE WEATHER STATION TONTOUTA QUOTE TO-
> GETHER ALL LOVE TRUDE SIGNED ER UNQUOTE SOLDIER SHOULD BE GIVEN
> OPPORTUNITY TO MAKE BRIEF REPLY STOP ADDRESS MESSAGE TO AGWAR
> CITE SGS COLONEL MCCARTHY STOP MESSAGE TO INCLUDE APO NUMBER
>
> COMGENSOPAC
>
> AGWAR
> SGS COLONEL MCCARTHY
> MRS. R.
>
> HEALTH O.K. LOVE APO #502, FRISCO
> JOE

Eleanor's letter to me contained more news about the talks with
Winston Churchill and Lord Beaverbrook:

At four p.m. yesterday Anna & I drove out with the cavalcade to
Shangri-La, dined & returned at midnight & on my desk I found your
first letter written Sunday, May 2d. It was so late that I didn't call
Trude but as soon as it is eight o'clock (I woke early) I will call her
though I expect she has heard too. Still it will be warming to rejoice together even over the phone! How slow the Army is here. They told me
of your whereabouts the 10th, the day we sent an army radio & tho'
they said instructions had been sent to permit an answer, none has
come & when I inquired Thursday they said you might be off on 'a job'
which might last ten days but they would let me know as soon as an
answer came!

I'll start today finding out from C.R. how & when I can get parcels
sent. I hope your barracks bags turned up for you must have lacked real
necessities. If you let me know what boys are with you & I ever establish or succeed in getting any quick news, I will always let their people
know. I kept the list I wrote to when you left.

I hope our letters have been getting through to you. I keep forgetting to number mine but since I've written at least every other day & in
any case my news has been unimportant except that it has told you
some things about Trude which she might not tell you herself. I'm
glad that you belong to the group of boys that want to take those they
love in the future & see the places they are now seeing. You & Trude
will surely be doing it some day & if you weren't wanting to share every
experience with her it would trouble me! I think she is talking & acting
with one thought in mind, 'If Joe were here, what would he say should
be done!'

Tommy has written to two ranches in a western state to get prices &
reserve space in June as we thought her name would attract no attention. Anna will join me & in June we'll spend a week there just for a
rest! George has taken his physical but when I left N.Y. Trude had
not heard his definite plans.

Now for a little general news. The P.M. is here, having come via the
Queen [*Mary?*] & brought a bigger retinue than ever. The conferences
are endless & F. says personalities of various kinds add to the difficulties
of honest differences of opinion. All the high-ups in the theatre west &
north of you are here. The Beaver also came tho' his presence is being
kept quiet. He was with us last night & fell completely for Anna &
offered to help her on her paper, long range of course, but it would be
rather experienced assistance & as he said some caustic things about her
employer [William Randolph Hearst], I couldn't help thinking he had
somewhat similar reputation along some lines himself! The 3 are constant story tellers & the P.M. has a surprising knowledge, as have so
many of his nationality of the Civil War. We followed Lee all along
the road! He is always using quotations & can quote endless poetry, to
my surprise he recited all of Barbara Fritchie!* None of them have
however the geographic knowledge, nor all around historical knowledge
& grasp of the whole picture today which our own raconteur has & he
can outtalk them all too which amused Anna & me very much.

Benes made a deep impression on Anna & also on F. He has an
agreement worked out with Uncle Joe & that is one reason for his popularity. Some postwar plans for Middle Europe which are just in the
talking stage I am not quite sure that I agree with but they will be tentative at the start I imagine & may change if circumstances indicate the
need. Benes comes to tea with me today. They seem hopeful the
Polish-Russian rift can be 'arranged' but it goes deep!

I haven't half told you how good it is to be able to have a new letter
to carry around & read at odd moments. . . .

Eleanor had an awesome psychic energy. It displayed itself most ardently in her love of others. She had to have people about her for
whom she cared and who cared for her. In 1937, when the first volume
of her autobiography, *This Is My Story*, appeared, she had four copies

---

* The poem *Barbara Frietchie*, by John Greenleaf Whittier.

bound in limp leather and she listed to whom and in what order she
wanted them sent. They were F.D.R., Anna Roosevelt Boettiger, Malvina Thompson, and Earl R. Miller. The omission of Hick from the list
was another indication that Eleanor's initial attachment to her had
eased. A similar list in 1943 would have shown another shift in the cast
of characters and their precedence. She never let a person go, but there
always had to be an "other" at the center of her emotional life.

One of the letters she wrote to me before she had an APO to which
to send it reported crisply a visit to the Naval Hospital for a routine
checkup: ". . . the ills of old age creep up on me!" She was not yet
sixty and had almost two decades ahead of her in which she would live
in what George Eliot called "deeds of daring rectitude."*

Eleanor clung to the people who enabled her to live in such a way.
Not long after I arrived in the South Pacific she wrote me that C. R.
Smith, the head of the Air Transport Command, had brought her "the
secret plans of a joint trip" with him. "It will mean stopping everywhere." Anna and Trude both had offered to go as her secretary. "Of
course they may be adamant & say only I may go. Incidentally Australia
& New Zealand officials have both asked but F is still doubtful because
of the Congressional desires to visit in large numbers on every front.!"

* From George Eliot's poem "Oh May I Join the Choir Invisible."

Index

Claes Martenszen van Rosenvelt arrived in New Amsterdam in the 1640s. By the beginning of the 18th century the Roosevelts had split into the forerunners of the Oyster Bay lines, which produced Theodore Roosevelt and his niece, Eleanor, and the Hyde Park line, which produced Franklin Delano Roosevelt.

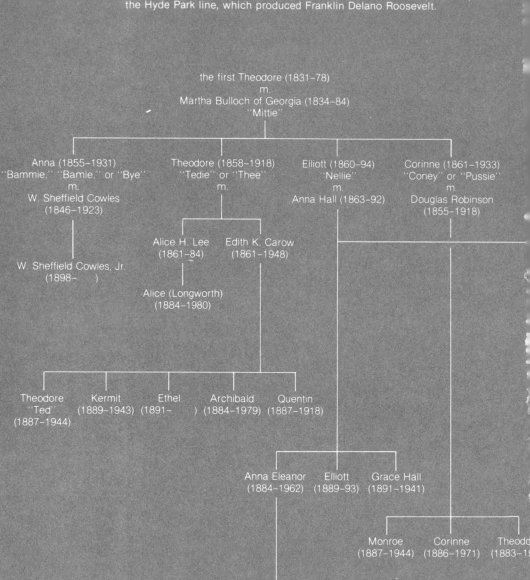